PRINCIPLES OF
DATABASE AND KNOWLEDGE – BASE SYSTEMS
VOLUME II

PRINCIPLES OF COMPUTER SCIENCE SERIES

Series Editors
Alfred V. Aho, Bell Telephone Laboratories, Murray Hill, New Jersey
Jeffrey D. Ullman, Stanford University, Stanford, California

Computer Organization
Michael Andrews
Trends in Theoretical Computer Science
Egon Börger, Editor
The Turing Omnibus
A. K. Dewdney
Formal Languages and Automata Theory
Vladimir Drobot
Advanced C: Food for the Educated Palate
Narain Gehani
C: An Advanced Introduction
Narain Gehani
C: An Advanced Introduction, ANSI C Version
Narain Gehani
C for Personal Computers: IBM PC, AT&T PC 6300, and Compatibles
Narain Gehani
An Introduction to the Theory of Computation
Eitan Gurari
Theory of Relational Databases
David Maier
An Introduction to Solid Modeling
Martti Mäntylä
Principles of Computer Design
Leonard R. Marino
UNIX: The Minimal Manual
Jim Moore
A Logical Language for Data and Knowledge Bases
Shamim Naqvi and Shalom Tsur
The Theory of Database Concurrency Control
Christos Papadimitriou
Algorithms for Graphics and Image Processing
Theo Pavlidis
Data Compression: Methods and Theory
James A. Storer
The Elements of Artificial Intelligence
Steven Tanimoto
Computational Aspects of VLSI
Jeffrey D. Ullman
Principles of Database and Knowledge-Base Systems, Volumes I and II
Jeffrey D. Ullman

OTHER BOOKS OF INTEREST

Jewels of Formal Language Theory
Arto Salomaa
Principles of Database Systems, Second Edition
Jeffrey D. Ullman
Fuzzy Sets, Natural Language Computations, and Risk Analysis
Kurt J. Schmucker
LISP: An Interactive Approach
Stuart C. Shapiro

PRINCIPLES OF
DATABASE AND KNOWLEDGE - BASE SYSTEMS

VOLUME II: The New Technologies

Jeffrey D. Ullman
STANFORD UNIVERSITY

COMPUTER SCIENCE PRESS

Library of Congress Cataloging-in-Publication Data

Ullman, Jeffrey D., 1942–
  Principles of database and knowledge-base systems.

  (Principles of computer science series, 0888-2096; 14–   )
  Includes bibliographies and indexes.
  1. Data base management. 2. Expert systems (Computer
Science) I. Title. II. Series: Principles of computer
Science series; 14, etc.
QA76.9.D3U443 1988   005.74   87-38197
ISBN 0-7167-8069-O (v. 1)
ISBN 0-7167-8162-X (v. 2)

Printed in the United States of America

Computer Science Press
1803 Research Boulevard
Rockville, MD 20850

An imprint of W. H. Freeman and Company
41 Madison Avenue, New York, NY 10010
20 Beaumont Street, Oxford OX1 2NQ, England

1 2 3 4 5 6 7 8 9 0   RRD   7 6 5 4 3 2 1 0 8 9

PREFACE

The second volume of *Principles of Database and Knowledge-Base Systems* is, to a large extent, a personal statement about what I think database system theory gives to the development of database and knowledge-base systems. Having covered the basics in the first volume, I offer the reader a vision of the ideas that will make knowledge-base systems feasible. These ideas surfaced beginning in the mid-1980's, and they form a beautiful example of how a body of theoretical notions can be translated into practice very quickly.

The reader of the first volume will note that I do not have a very ambitious definition of "knowledge." Recall that, as defined in Section 1.6 of Volume I, knowledge-base systems

1. Must deal with massive amounts of data,
2. Must do so efficiently, and
3. Must offer the user a declarative language in which to express queries of a general nature.

I have avoided grandiose notions of what knowledge and reasoning are, in favor of something one realistically could expect would have efficient algorithms for execution of queries. Thus, we have used as our declarative language a simple form of logical rules, and we continue to do so in this volume.

Synopsis of the Book

If we are to compile a declarative language, that is, a language in which we state what we want, without giving an algorithm for obtaining it, then optimization must play an important role in the system. Thus, Chapter 11, the first in this volume, covers optimization of queries in relational database systems. It is fair to say that relational query languages are the most commonly used declarative languages, and that they could not be used without well-designed query optimizers. Yet it is common in books on database systems (or in books on compilers for that matter) to ignore or minimize the subject of optimization. I hope that Chapter 11 will convince the reader there is an interesting and important body of knowledge relevant to optimization of relational query languages.

Most of the balance of the book is devoted to the technology of optimization for logic programs. Recall that logic languages can express many queries that relational query languages cannot (see Section 3.7 of Volume I). Thus, optimization of logic languages is predictably harder than optimization for relational query languages, and systems capable of optimizing logic languages are in an experimental state. Nevertheless, much has been achieved recently, and this book covers the ideas that look most promising. Chapter 12 is preparatory to this study, covering material on logic not found in Volume I, such as top-down query answering (resolution-based schemes that try to satisfy a goal). Also included is some of the specialized notation needed for further study in Chapters 13 through 16.

Chapter 13 introduces the "magic-sets" technique for processing logic. The artificial-intelligence community has long known that there are advantages both to top-down processing and to bottom-up processing (where we deduce all possible facts from the database). Very recently, a new methodology, called "magic-sets," has been developed; it lets us enjoy the advantages of both top-down and bottom-up processing, with the disadvantages of neither. This technique is rapidly finding its way into implementations of knowledge-base systems and needs to be understood by anyone working in the area. It is interesting to conjecture that resolution-based methods have had their day, and that, when fully explored, "magic sets" will prove superior for all applications, from theorem proving to query answering in knowledge-base systems.

In Chapter 14 we cover "conjunctive queries," which have an interesting and useful theory; this body of techniques is used at several points in the following chapter. Chapter 15 covers linear recursion, a restricted but very common and important special case of logic, where algorithms are known that evaluate queries even faster than the magic sets algorithm does. Then, in Chapter 16 we meet several experimental knowledge-base systems and see how the ideas of Chapters 13 through 15 are being put into practice.

The final chapter covers universal-relation systems. The universal-relation idea was developed by a number of people, the author included, in the late 1970's and early 1980's. Its intent is to provide a way of talking about databases without knowing the details of the database scheme. The canonical example is a natural-language interface to a database, where the naive user might be expected to know the attributes, that is, names for the elementary concepts of the database, but could not be expected to know the relations into which they were grouped. With this goal in mind, an extensive body of theory has been developed, concerning what connections among attributes it is reasonable for a system to infer.

At the time of the writing of this book, a few systems based on universal-relation concepts have been built, and the number is growing. In fact, a leading purveyor of relational software now offers an enhancement that allows one to treat several relations with common keys as a single universal relation. However, as we shall see in Chapter 17, this idea merely scratches the surface of what can be achieved.

Unfortunately, universal-relation systems are still quite rare in practice. Moreover, there have been a number of public attacks on the concept (see the bibliographic notes to Chapter 17), often by people who misinterpreted the concept. It takes less time to read Chapter 17 than it does to write a polemic about what is wrong with the idea, and I hope that in the future we shall see commercial systems using the universal-relation concept routinely.

Prerequisites

The reader of this volume is assumed to have familiarity with the concepts found in the first volume, although Chapters 11 and 12 begin with reviews of relevant notation and the most central concepts. Below is a list of the most important prerequisites.

Chapter 11: The relational model (Section 2.3) and relational algebra (Section 2.4); relational query languages from Chapter 4, especially QUEL from Section 4.3 and SQL from Section 4.6; physical storage and index structures, as in Sections 6.1 through 6.8.

Chapter 12: Chapter 3 (logic), especially Sections 3.1 through 3.6.

Chapter 13: Most of Chapter 12; Chapter 6, including the material on index structures and on partial-match structures (Sections 6.12 through 6.14).

Chapter 14: Relational database theory, especially Sections 7.4 and 7.11.

Chapter 15: Chapters 13 and 14; Section 2.7 on the object model; relational query languages as in Chapter 4; index and partial-match structures from Chapter 6.

Chapter 16: Chapters 11, 13, and 15; the nature of a knowledge-base system (Chapter 1); hierarchical and object-oriented models (Sections 2.6, 2.7, and 5.6); relational languages (Chapter 4, especially Section 4.3 on QUEL); Section 9.5 on lock modes.

Chapter 17: Chapter 11; QUEL from Section 4.3; most of Chapter 7 on dependency theory and normalization.

Exercises

As in the first volume, singly starred exercises require some significant thought, and the hardest exercises are doubly starred.

Bibliography and Index

The bibliography includes all works cited in this volume and/or Volume I. Likewise, the index contains entries for both volumes. Pages 1 through 587 refer to Volume I, and pages 633 through 1069 refer to Volume II.

Acknowledgements

The following people are thanked for comments that improved this manuscript:
Surajit Chaudhuri, Kwong Choy, Isabel Cruz, William Harvey, Chen-Lieh
Huang, Bill Lipa, Alberto Mendelzon, Inderpal Mumick, Jeff Naughton, Ge-
off Phipps, Raghu Ramakrishnan, Ken Ross, Shuky Sagiv, and Yumi Tsugi.

The writing of this volume was partially supported by a John Simon
Guggenheim fellowship. It was facilitated by computing equipment donated
to Stanford by IBM Corp. and AT&T Foundation.

J. D. U.
Stanford CA

TABLE OF CONTENTS

Chapter 11: Query Optimization for Database Systems   633

11.1: Basic Assumptions for Query Optimization   635

11.2: Optimization of Selections in System R   639

11.3: Computing the Cartesian Product   643

11.4: Estimating the Output Cost for Joins   647

11.5: Methods for Computing Joins   651

11.6: Optimization by Algebraic Manipulation   662

11.7: An Algorithm for Optimizing Relational Expressions   668

11.8: A Multiway Join Algorithm   673

11.9: Hypergraph Representation of Queries   676

11.10: The Quel Optimization Algorithm   679

11.11: Query Optimization in Distributed Databases   692

11.12: Acyclic Hypergraphs   698

11.13: Optimizing Transmission Cost by Semijoins   699

11.14: An Algorithm for Taking the Projection of a Join   707

11.15: The System R* Optimization Algorithm   717

Exercises   725

Bibliographic Notes   731

Chapter 12: More About Logic   734

12.1: Logic with Function Symbols   736

12.2: Evaluating Logic with Function Symbols   741

12.3: Top-Down Processing of Logic   753

12.4: Unification   760

12.5: The Relational Approach to Top-Down Logic Evaluation   766

12.6: Computing Relations During Rule/Goal Tree Expansion   776

12.7: The Rule/Goal Tree Evaluation Algorithm   783

12.8: Rule/Goal Graphs   795

12.9: Making Binding Patterns Unique   799

12.10: Reordering Subgoals   805

Exercises   817

Bibliographic Notes   822

Chapter 13: Combining Top-Down and Bottom-Up Logic Evaluation 825

13.1: The Magic-Sets Rule Rewriting Technique 825
13.2: Correctness of the Magic-Sets Algorithm 836
13.3: Efficiency of the Magic-Set Rules 841
13.4: Simplification of Magic-Set Rules 852
13.5: Passing Bindings Through Variables Only 857
13.6: Generalized Magic Sets 860
    Exercises 872
    Bibliographic Notes 875

Chapter 14: Optimization for Conjunctive Queries 877

14.1: Containment and Equivalence of Conjunctive Queries 877
14.2: Conjunctive Queries Having Arithmetic Comparisons 885
14.3: Optimization Under Weak Equivalence 892
14.4: Optimizing Unions of Conjunctive Queries 903
14.5: Containment of Conjunctive Queries in Logical Recursions 907
    Exercises 911
    Bibliographic Notes 915

Chapter 15: Optimization of Linear Recursions 917

15.1: Right-Linear Recursions 918
15.2: Left-Linear Recursions 924
15.3: Commutativity of Rules 929
15.4: Combined Left- and Right-Linear Recursions 936
15.5: A Counting Technique for Linear Rules 942
15.6: Transitive Closure 949
15.7: Closed Semirings and Generalized Transitive Closure 953
15.8: Making Nonlinear Rules Linear 963
    Exercises 974
    Bibliographic Notes 979

Chapter 16: Some Experimental Knowledge-Base Systems 982

16.1: Applications of Knowledge-Base Systems 983
16.2: The NAIL! System 987
16.3: The Language LDL 994
16.4: The LDL Query Optimizer 999
16.5: The Langauge POSTQUEL 1008
16.6: Implementation of POSTQUEL Extensions 1017
    Exercises 1021
    Bibliographic Notes 1024

Chapter 17: The Universal Relation as a User Interface   1026
17.1: The Universal Relation Concept   1026
17.2: Window Functions   1030
17.3: A Simple Window Function   1032
17.4: The Representative Instance as a Universal Relation   1033
17.5: Unique Schemes   1041
17.6: The Object Structure of Universal Relations   1044
17.7: A Window Function Using Objects   1049
17.8: Maximal Objects and Queries About Cyclic Databases   1056
    Exercises   1063
    Bibliographic Notes   1067

Bibliography   1070

Index   1115

CHAPTER 11

Query Optimization
for
Database Systems

In this chapter, we shall learn the basic techniques for query optimization. When queries are expressed in a declarative language, such as a relational query language, it is not easy for the database system to execute queries quickly. Rather, an extensive optimization phase must select, from among the many possible ways to implement a given query, one of the few efficient implementations; ideally, the best implementation must be selected.

Section 11.1 introduces the model that we use for describing and evaluating query-optimization algorithms. Section 11.2 studies an important example of an optimization algorithm that considers an exponential number of possibilities before choosing the most efficient evaluator—the System R algorithm for selection queries. The following three sections consider different ways of computing products and joins and evaluates the cost of each.

Then in Sections 11.6 and 11.7, we consider techniques for manipulating algebraic expressions to produce expressions that are more efficiently evaluated. Sections 11.8 to 11.10 are devoted to a description of the Wong-Youssefi algorithm used to optimize queries in QUEL, the language of the INGRES relational DBMS. Section 11.8 discusses an algorithm used to take the join of more than two relations, and Section 11.9 introduces a concept that is important for several different query-optimization algorithms—the representation of select-project-join queries by hypergraphs. Finally, in Section 11.10, the QUEL query optimization algorithm itself is presented.

Section 11.11 introduces the modifications to our basic model that must be made to handle distributed queries. In Section 11.12, we introduce "acyclic hypergraphs," a very interesting and important concept. In the context of distributed query optimization, the property of queries involving joins that is called "acyclicity," allows much more efficient query evaluation than is possible in the general case. Section 11.13 applies the acyclicity concept to computation of distributed joins, and the next section presents Yannakakis' algorithm, a technique for computing projections of acyclic joins that is efficient both in the distributed environment and in the uniprocessor environment. Finally, Section 11.15 discusses an algorithm used in the distributed DBMS System R* for taking distributed joins. This algorithm, like the System R algorithm discussed in Section 11.2, is one that searches an exponential number of possibilities to choose the method it prefers.

Notation for Relations

We assume the reader is familiar with the relational data model, as described in Section 2.3 of Volume I, and with relational algebra from Section 2.4. We shall mention briefly some of the notation and conventions that we use in this book to describe relations, relation schemes, and tuples.

1. Names of relations are generally capital letters, for example, R. The current value for relation R is typically denoted by the corresponding lowercase letter, for example, r. Frequently, we use the relation scheme (set of attributes) as the name of the relation; for example, ABC could be the name of a relation with attributes A, B, and C. We also treat relation names as if they were their schemes; for example, $R \cap S$ stands for the set of attributes that are common to R and S, while $r \cap s$ is the set of tuples common to the current relations for R and S. However, the context will always differentiate these two uses of intersection, so we might use $R \cap S$ to refer to the intersection of the tuples if the meaning is unambiguous.

2. Sets of attributes are often denoted by concatenation, rather than by the usual set notation. For example, ABC stands for the set of attributes $\{A, B, C\}$, and XY stands for $X \cup Y$, if X and Y are sets of attributes.

3. Tuples are named by Greek letters, for example, μ. When we want to specify the components of tuples, we write them $a_1 \cdots a_n$ or $(a_1, \ldots, a_n)$, whichever looks better in context. Either notation stands for the tuple with n components, the ith of which is a_i, for $i = 1, 2, \ldots, n$. The components of tuple μ for set of attributes X is denoted $\mu[X]$.

4. The relational algebra operators are denoted $\cup$ (union), $-$ (difference), σ (selection), π (projection), and $\times$ (Cartesian product). We also use $\bowtie$ for the natural join, $\bowtie_F$ for the join with condition F on the attributes (for example, $R \underset{\$1=\$3}{\bowtie} S$ for the equijoin that equates the first column of R to the third column of S), and $\ltimes$ for the semijoin, defined by:[1]

$$R \ltimes S = \pi_R(R \bowtie S) = R \bowtie \pi_{R \cap S}(S)$$

---

[1] Note that that R and $R \cap S$ refer to sets of attributes in the projections below.

5. Columns of relations can be represented by attribute names if we know them, or by number. We generally use $\$i$ to denote column i, although in projections, where there can be no confusion, we use i by itself. For example, $\pi_1(\sigma_{\$2=3}(R))$ asks for the first component of all those tuples of R whose second component has value 3. If several relations have the same attribute name, we can use $R.A$ to refer to attribute A belonging to relation R.

11.1 BASIC ASSUMPTIONS FOR QUERY OPTIMIZATION

Let us recall the model of computation costs we introduced in Chapter 6 (Volume I). A relation is represented in memory by a collection of records; each record corresponds to one tuple of the relation. Tuples are divided among blocks of secondary storage. Depending on the physical storage organization, the tuples of one relation may be packed into blocks used for that relation alone, or the tuples may appear in blocks that are used for tuples of several relations.

For a relation R, let T_R be the number of tuples in R, and let B_R be the number of blocks in which all the tuples of R could fit, if they were packed tightly. Note that, in general, B_R will be significantly smaller than T_R. Also, T_R/B_R is the number of tuples of R that will fit on one block.

Example 11.1: A typical storage system uses blocks of 1024 bytes. Suppose we have a relation R with 1,000,000 tuples, each 100 bytes long. Then $T_R = 1,000,000$. As ten tuples can fit on one block, R can fit in 100,000 blocks; that is, $B_R = 100,000$. □

The cost of reading or writing a relation is the number of blocks that must be read from secondary storage into main memory or written from main memory into secondary storage. We call each such operation a *block access*. The physical organization of a relation can affect greatly the cost of operations on R. For instance, if the relation R of Example 11.1 is *packed*, that is, stored in roughly as few blocks as can hold all its tuples, then we can scan all the tuples of R in B_R block accesses. On the other hand, if the tuples of R are stored on blocks, most of which contain only one tuple of R (along with tuples of other relations), then about T_R block accesses are needed to scan R, about ten times the cost of reading a packed relation.

We should understand that relations can be packed, and yet appear with a few tuples of other relations. A typical example is that discussed in Section 6.9, where we saw how, in the DBTG proposal, one relation R might be stored "via set" with another relation S. Then, each tuple of S is followed by all the tuples of R that it "owns," leading to a pattern like that of Figure 11.1, on the assumption that each tuple of S owns several tuples of R.

| tuple of S |
| tuple of R |
| tuple of R |
| tuple of R |
| tuple of S |
| tuple of R |

| tuple of R |
| tuple of R |
| tuple of R |
| tuple of S |
| tuple of R |
| tuple of R |

Figure 11.1 Packed relation R sharing blocks with another relation.

The Use of Indices

There are many structures, such as hash tables or B-trees, that are suitable as indices. Such structures let us perform selections on a relation quickly, that is, with a number of block accesses not too much greater than the number of blocks on which the desired tuples are stored. Index structures were covered in Chapter 6, so here we shall not specify any particular structure for indices. We shall only assume that whenever a relation R has an index on attribute A, then the number of block accesses to perform a selection, $\sigma_{A=c}(R)$, is roughly the number of blocks on which we find tuples of R whose value for attribute A is the constant c. In particular, we shall neglect the number of blocks we must access to examine the index itself; that number is usually comparable to, or smaller than, the number of R's blocks we must access.

Clustering and Nonclustering Indices

We can divide indices into *clustering* and *nonclustering* types, and these two types offer significantly different performance. If we have a clustering index on A, then the number of blocks holding tuples with A-value c is approximately the number of blocks on which those tuples can be packed. For example, an ISAM index used as a sparse, primary index is normally a clustering index. The tuples with $A = c$ will appear consecutively, spread over at most one more block of the main file than will hold them.[2] As long as we can expect the number of

---

[2] We shall ignore the possibility that blocks are purposely given a fraction of available space for future expansion. If such a strategy is followed, it is as if all blocks had a smaller capacity to hold tuples than we would expect by counting bytes.

tuples with $A = c$ to fill at least one block, then the number of main-file block accesses could not be more than double the theoretical minimum, and we can regard the index as "clustering."

With a nonclustering index, we must assume that the tuples of R having $A = c$ each appear on a separate block. Thus, the number of block accesses needed to find all of these tuples is about equal to the number of tuples retrieved. That is, the cost to retrieve the tuples with $A = c$ is about T_R/B_R times as great if the index is nonclustering as if it is clustering. For the relation of Example 11.1, this ratio is 10.

An example of a nonclustering index is a B-tree used as a dense index, pointing to the tuples, which are packed into the blocks of the main file. Presumably, the tuples are organized in the main file according to some primary index on an attribute other than A. For example, these tuples might be hashed into buckets according to their values in attribute B. Then we would not expect two tuples with the same A-value to appear on the same block, except by coincidence.

Image Size

There is another parameter of data that is often useful when estimating the cost of a particular operation. The *image size* of an index on attribute A of relation R, denoted $I_{R.A}$, or just I_A when R is understood, is the expected number of different A-values found in R. On the assumption that values are equally likely to occur, we can estimate the number of blocks retrieved in response to the selection $\sigma_{A=c}(R)$ by T_R/I_A if there is a nonclustering index on A, because that is the expected number of tuples retrieved. If there is a clustering index on A, we retrieve about B_R/I_A blocks, because the selected tuples are packed onto about that number of blocks.

Sources of Optimization

There are two basic kinds of optimizations found in query processors, algebraic manipulation and cost-estimation strategies. Algebraic simplification of queries is intended to improve the cost of answering the query independent of the actual data or the physical structure of the data. We shall study algebraic optimizations in the abstract in Sections 11.6 and 11.7, and in Sections 11.8 to 11.10 we consider the optimization algorithm used in the original implementation of QUEL, which is primarily algebraic. The following is an example of an important algebraic optimization: "do selections as early as possible."

Example 11.2: Suppose we have relations AB, with attributes A and B, and BC, with attributes B and C, and we wish to compute

$$\sigma_{A=d}(AB \bowtie BC) \tag{11.1}$$

Such a query will almost always be answered faster, independent of the values of relations AB and BC, and independent of the presence or absence of indices on their attributes, if we perform the selection before the join. That is, we should compute (11.1) as if it were

$$\big(\sigma_{A=d}(AB)\big) \bowtie BC \tag{11.2}$$

The reason why (11.2) is usually faster is that joins are generally much more expensive than selections. We shall, in Section 11.5, estimate the cost of particular joins performed in particular ways, but for the purposes of this example, it suffices to note that computing the join $AB \bowtie BC$ requires accessing every block on which tuples of these two relations reside at least once, perhaps more. We also must create the result of the join and store all of the blocks on which it resides. The result can be much bigger than either AB or BC, if the typical tuple of AB has a B-value that is shared by several tuples of BC.

On the average, taking the selection first will cut down the number of tuples in the first argument of the join by a factor I_A. If we pack the tuples in $\sigma_{A=d}(AB)$ tightly into blocks, then we cut down the number of blocks we must access to get the first argument of the join by at least factor I_A. We also can expect to cut down the size of the result of the join by factor I_A, which is often a more significant saving. The cost of the selection in (11.1) might be less than that in (11.2), if the result of the join is much smaller than the relation AB, that is, if the typical tuple of AB has a low probability of joining with even one tuple of BC. However, ordinarily, the cost of the selection in (11.2) will be no greater than in (11.1), and it may be much less, if the join result is larger than AB and/or if there was an index on A in AB that can be used in (11.2) but not in (11.1).

We should understand, however, that the rule "do selections as soon as possible" is no more than a sensible heuristic; there are exceptions. For example, suppose BC is empty. If the method we use for the join checks this condition immediately, then following (11.1) we immediately discover that $AB \bowtie BC$ is empty, and therefore, the value of (11.1) is the empty relation. However, following (11.2), we would perform the selection, taking some nonnegligible amount of time, and only when we proceeded to perform the join, discover that there are no tuples in the answer. $\square$

The second class of optimization strategies is those that consider issues, such as the existence of indices, to select from among alternatives the strategy that is best for the data and structure at hand. The next section covers the way System R does optimization, focusing on selections as a simple example. The System R approach is oriented toward the estimation of different strategies on the current database. Then, in Sections 11.3 to 11.5, we discuss methods for computing products and joins, and we show how to estimate the costs of the different techniques.

11.2 OPTIMIZATION OF SELECTIONS IN SYSTEM R

We shall, in this section, focus on a problem that is instructive for several reasons. First, it shows a great deal about the opportunities for optimization in even a simple kind of query. Second, it lets us sample the issues at the implementation level, and third, it is representative of the way System R does all its optimization, which is quite different from the methodology followed by many other systems (although the results are quite frequently the same).

The problem we consider is one in which we are given a query of the form[3]

$$\text{SELECT } A_1, \ldots, A_n$$
$$\text{FROM } R \qquad\qquad\qquad (11.3)$$
$$\text{WHERE } C_1 \text{ AND } C_2 \text{ AND } \cdots ;$$

Here the C_i's are conditions involving the attributes of relation R. These conditions may be composed of subconditions connected by AND, OR, NOT, IN, and so on, as for all SQL conditions. However, we assume that none of them are of the form D_1 AND D_2. It is important in this algorithm, and in many query optimization algorithms, that the conditions be broken as finely as possible into conditions connected by logical AND.

One may wonder where the implementation issues arise in queries as simple as these. First, System R takes advantage of indices whenever it can. For example, if one of the C_i's is of the form $A = c$, and there is an index on attribute A, we say that the condition C_i *matches* that index. System R will tend to favor obtaining the set of tuples with A-value c, using this index. Then these tuples can be examined for satisfaction of the other conditions, and the answer to the query is obtained.

The second source of complexity is that System R allows a great deal of flexibility in how relations are stored. We discussed several of these techniques in Section 6.11 (Volume I).

Example 11.3: We saw in Figure 6.26 how tuples of three relations,[4]

CUSTOMERS(CNAME, CADDR, BALANCE)
ORDERS(O#, DATE, CUST)
INCLUDES(O#, INAME, QUANTITY)

could be stored by System R as a nested structure

(CUSTOMERS (ORDERS (INCLUDES)*)*)*

---

[3] In this section we use the language of System R, which is SQL, for queries. The reader not familiar with SQL should review Section 4.6 in Volume I.

[4] This and other examples of the present chapter are drawn from the "Yuppie Valley Culinary Boutique" (YVCB) database, whose relations were introduced in Figure 2.8 (Section 2.3 of Volume I), and for which sample data can be found in Figure 4.2 of Section 4.2.

where each customer's tuple is followed by a sequence of tuples for each order placed by that customer, and for each such order we find an ORDERS tuple followed by tuples of the relation INCLUDES, one for each item included in that order.

Let us assume that each customer has placed several orders, and each order includes several items. Then the blocks holding this nested structure would consist primarily of INCLUDES tuples, with a few ORDERS and CUSTOMERS tuples interspersed. If that is the case, then we would regard the relation IN-CLUDES as packed, while the other two relations would not be packed. More importantly, an index on the attribute O# of INCLUDES would be a clustering index, since we expect that following the tuple for a given order number (O#), we shall find all of the INCLUDES tuples with that order number. Thus, these tuples could be retrieved in roughly as few block accesses as the minimum number of blocks needed to hold the tuples. Indices on other attributes of IN-CLUDES, and indices on all attributes of the other two relations, would be nonclustering indices. □

An Algorithm for Optimizing Simple Queries

Let us now give the details of the System R approach to optimization of queries of the form (11.3), found at the beginning of the section. Like all of System R optimization, the approach is enumerative. That is, all of the options on a preselected "menu" are enumerated; the query processor estimates the cost of using each option and takes the best choice. In more complicated situations, such as queries that involve several joins, there can be thousands of possible options, although in the simple case we cover, the number of options is usually not large. The designers of the optimizer evidently felt that time spent optimizing the typical query will be paid back in reduced time to execute the query, and most likely that is the case, especially if relations are large.

It is not feasible to enumerate all imaginable ways to implement a query, so System R, like any optimizing system, has to pick the space of strategies it will search for the best choice. The strategies considered by System R include those of the form in which we pick one of the conditions C_i, find all the tuples satisfying that condition, and then examine those tuples to see which of them satisfy the other conditions, if any. System R also considers strategies in which we begin by examining all the tuples of R and see which of them satisfy all the conditions.

Algorithm 11.1: System R Optimization Algorithm for Simple Selection Queries.

INPUT: An SQL query of the form (11.3), together with information about what indices on relation R exist, the estimated values of parameters T (the number of tuples) and B (the minimum number of blocks needed to hold R), and the estimated image sizes for indices.

OUTPUT: A way of computing the answer to this query.

METHOD: We consider the following list of methods for obtaining either R itself, or R with selection by one of the conditions applied. After selecting one method, we apply the remaining conditions to the tuples obtained.[5] For those methods that involve a choice of which index or condition to use, we must consider all possible choices. The methods are listed in approximate order of desirability, but in each case we must use the parameters T and B, possibly with estimates of image sizes as well, to judge the cost. The method with the lowest estimated cost is the output of the algorithm.

1. Get those tuples of R that satisfy a condition of the form $A = c$, where this condition matches a clustering index. If I is the image size for this index, we must read about $(1/I)$th of the tuples on the average. Since we have a clustering index, the number of block accesses required to read these tuples will be about equal to the number of blocks they would fit on if packed tightly. Thus the estimated number of block accesses for this method is B/I.

2. Use a clustering index on an attribute A, where $A \, \theta \, c$ is one of the conditions, and θ is $<$, $\leq$, $>$, or $\geq$, to obtain the subset of R that satisfies this condition. Then apply the remaining conditions to the result. Here we require about $B/2$ block accesses, since
    a) On the average we must read about half the tuples, and
    b) Because we have a clustering index, these will be packed onto about $B/2$ blocks.
    Note that the case where θ is $\neq$ is omitted here, since we can expect very limited selection to take place, and essentially all of the tuples must be retrieved. This case is covered under (5), below.

3. If there is a nonclustering index that matches a condition $A = c$, use that index to find all of the tuples with A-value c and apply the other conditions to those tuples. If I is the image size for this index, then we must retrieve about T/I tuples. They are likely to be on different blocks, since the index is nonclustering, so T/I is the estimated cost for this method.

4. If R is stored in a file by itself, we can simply read all of the tuples of R and apply the conditions to the tuples. The cost here is B, since that is the number of blocks over which R will be spread.

---

[5] As an example of a plausible option System R does not allow itself, consider the possibility that a query has more than one condition matching an index, for example WHERE A=1 AND B=17. In this case, we could do better than any of the strategies System R considers if we intersect in main memory the collections of pointers obtained by examining the indices for tuples with $A = 1$ and for tuples with $B = 17$. We would then use block accesses only to obtain those tuples that satisfy both conditions.

5. If R is not stored by itself, but it has a clustering index on any attribute, or collection of attributes, whether or not those attributes are involved in a condition of the query, use the index to obtain all the tuples of R and apply the conditions to them. The cost of this method is also B, since any clustering index guarantees that we can obtain the tuples in not many more block accesses than it takes to store them.

6. If there is a nonclustering index on attribute A, and $A\ \theta\ c$ is a condition, where θ is $<$, $\leq$, $>$, or $\geq$, use that index to get the tuples of R satisfying $A\ \theta\ c$ and apply the other conditions to the result. The cost is $T/2$, since we may expect to retrieve about half of R, and these tuples will be spread over blocks independently.

7. Use a nonclustering index of any sort to find the tuples of R and apply all of the conditions to them. The cost of this method is T.

8. If none of the above methods are available, simply scan all blocks that might contain tuples of R to retrieve them. The cost of this method is T or perhaps even more, if we cannot be sure exactly which blocks contain tuples of R. $\square$

Example 11.4: Let us consider the response of Algorithm 11.1 to the query

```
SELECT O#
FROM INCLUDES
WHERE QUANTITY >= 5 AND ITEM = 'Brie';
```

where INCLUDES is the relation mentioned in Example 11.3. Suppose that there is a clustering index for INCLUDES on O# and nonclustering indices on ITEM and QUANTITY. Suppose also that there are 1000 tuples in INCLUDES ($T = 1000$), and that ten tuples fit in one block, so $B = 100$; that is, the INCLUDES relation fits on 100 blocks. Let the image size for the ITEM index be 50; that is, we assume there are about 50 different items on order at any time. The image sizes for the other indices are irrelevant in what follows, so we do not make an assumption about them. There are no options under choice (1) of Algorithm 11.1, because the only condition that matches an index is ITEM="Brie," and ITEM does not have a clustering index. Similarly, there are no options under choice (2).

For choice (3), a nonclustering index that matches a condition, we have the ITEM index and the condition ITEM="Brie." The estimated cost of making this choice is $T/I = 1000/50 = 20$.

Choice (4), reading the INCLUDES relation from its blocks, on the assumption that the relation is stored by itself, would cost $B = 100$, if in fact INCLUDES is stored by itself. If INCLUDES is stored with the ORDERS relation, as suggested in Example 11.3, then choice (4) is not applicable. However, choice (5), the use of the clustering index on O#, has the same effect, and its estimated cost is $B = 100$.

Choice (6) is the use of a nonclustering index on an attribute involved in a condition whose comparison is neither $=$ nor $\neq$. Our opportunity here is to use the index on QUANTITY and the condition QUANTITY ≥ 5. The cost of this choice is $T/2 = 500$. Choices (7) and (8) each have cost at least $T = 1000$; they are not applicable in this example.

Thus, the least cost is achieved from the option under choice (3), where we use the ITEM index to obtain the approximately 20 tuples with ITEM="Brie" and examine each to see if the quantity is at least 5. Since each of the 20 tuples is likely to be on a different block (because the ITEM index is nonclustering), we estimate the retrieval cost at 20 block accesses. $\square$

11.3 COMPUTING THE CARTESIAN PRODUCT

A variety of strategies are available for computing the join or product of two relations, and an optimizer needs to consider which is best in a given situation. Generally, joins and products are very expensive, compared with operations on single relations, such as selections and projections, so a query optimizer must minimize the cost of joins and products whenever possible. In this section, we consider how to take a Cartesian product, and we prove that an obvious algorithm is close to optimal. In the next two sections, we show how equijoins can be computed faster than products, although not by the obvious technique of pairing all the tuples of one relation with the tuples of the other.

Before proceeding, let us introduce two additional parameters that help describe the cost of various operations.

1. Let U stand for the number of blocks needed to store the result of the computation. As the result must be written to secondary storage, U block accesses are needed to store the output. For products and joins, U often dominates the total cost.

2. Let M be the number of blocks that can fit in main memory at any one time. We shall see that a small value of M forces the same block to be read many times, thus increasing the cost of operations beyond what is needed to read the arguments and write the result.

Suppose we need to compute $R \times S$. In what follows, we shall assume that R and S are stored packed, so they can be read in B_R and B_S block accesses, respectively. If that is not the case, then it usually is efficient to read the tuples of the relations that are not packed, and make packed copies of them, which requires an additional cost T_R to read R and cost B_R to write the packed copy of R, and similarly for S.

The basic algorithm for computing the product is very simple. We execute a double loop:

for each tuple μ in R **do**
    for each tuple ν in S **do**   (11.4)
        output the tuple $\mu\nu$

We could of course, reverse the roles of R and S, using the outer loop to range over tuples in S instead.

If One Relation Fits in Main Memory

In what follows, we shall assume that $B_S \leq B_R$; the opposite case can be handled symmetrically. If $M > B_S$, that is, all of relation S fits in memory with at least one block left over, then we can read all of S, taking B_S block accesses. Then, we read each block of R, in turn, and we discard it when we read the next block of R. For each block of R, we perform the outer loop of (11.4) for each tuple of that block. The tuples ν of the inner loop are found in main memory, so no access cost is incurred. The total cost of reading input is thus $B_R + B_S$. The cost of the product is this cost, plus U, for writing the output.

We can estimate U in terms of the parameters for R and S, as follows. Let l_R be the number of bytes needed for a tuple of R, and let l_S be the same for a tuple of S. Let b be the number of bytes on a block. Notice that tuples in the result of $R \times S$, being the concatenation of tuples of R with tuples of S, will take about $l_R + l_S$ bytes. Further, there will be $T_R T_S$ tuples in the output, where T_R and T_S are the numbers of tuples in R and S, respectively. Thus, the number of blocks needed to store the output is approximately[6]

$$U = T_R T_S (l_R + l_S)/b \tag{11.5}$$

Now, notice that B_R is approximately $T_R l_R/b$, and B_S is approximately $T_S l_S/b$. Thus, we can rewrite (11.5) as

$$U = \frac{T_R T_S l_R}{b} + \frac{T_R T_S l_S}{b}$$

and then as

$$U = B_R T_S + T_R B_S \tag{11.6}$$

When we add (11.6) to the cost of reading input, which was found to be $B_R + B_S$, we find that the output cost dominates, and the total cost is almost the same as (11.6); it is

---

[6] This and other approximations we use in this section need not be exact because of information bits associated with records within blocks, space for a fraction of a record, which must remain unused within each block, and several other factors. The reader should consult Section 6.1 (Volume I) for details of how records (or the tuples they represent) are stored within blocks.

$$B_R(T_S + 1) + B_S(T_R + 1) \tag{11.7}$$

to be precise.

Example 11.5: Suppose R consists of 5000 tuples packed into 500 blocks and S is 1000 tuples on 100 blocks. Also, let $M = 101$. Then we can read all of S into memory, and still have one block left over to read the blocks of R sequentially. The total cost in block accesses of computing this product is given by the formula (11.7); it is

$$500 \times 1001 + 100 \times 5001 = 1{,}000{,}600$$

This figure makes sense, because there are five million tuples in the answer. Each is the concatenation of a tuple of R and a tuple of S, and tuples from each of these relations evidently take one-tenth of a block each. Thus, output tuples can be packed five-to-a-block, accounting for one million block accesses to store the answer. □

Products of Relations that Cannot Fit in Main Memory

When neither relation will fit in main memory, we must shuffle some blocks in and out of memory several times. Let us assume $B_S \leq B_R$, but now, assume $M \leq B_S$. It turns out that, as we shall prove, almost optimal performance can be obtained by dividing S into *segments* of $M - 1$ blocks each. We read a segment of S, and in the remaining block of main memory, we read each block of R, in turn, producing the product of each tuple in the segment with each tuple in the block of R. We repeat this process for each segment, until the entire product is taken. Formally, the algorithm is given in Figure 11.2.

```
for each segment S of relation S do
    for each tuple ν in segment S do
        for each block B of relation R do
            for each tuple μ of block B do
                output tuple μν
```

Figure 11.2 Algorithm for product of large relations.

The program of Figure 11.2 reads each block of S once, and reads each block of R once per segment. As the number of segments of S is approximately $B_S/(M - 1)$, the cost of the input for Figure 11.2 is roughly

$$B_R\left(\frac{B_S}{M - 1}\right) + B_S \tag{11.8}$$

When we include the output cost, given by (11.6), the total cost of Figure 11.2 is found to be

$$B_R(T_S + \frac{B_S}{M-1}) + B_S(T_R + 1) \tag{11.9}$$

Note that (11.9) generalizes (11.7) by replacing the term $T_S + 1$ by

$$T_S + B_S/(M-1)$$

In each formula, this term is seen to be T_S plus the number of segments of S.

Example 11.6: Suppose all is as in Example 11.5, but M is now 11. Then S must be divided into $B_S/(M-1) = 100/10 = 10$ segments. The cost of computing the product is given by (11.9); it is

$$500 \times (1000 + \frac{100}{10}) + 100 \times 5001 = 1{,}005{,}100$$

When we compare this figure with that of Example 11.5, we see that output cost continues to dominate, even though the input cost has increased by a factor of $51/6$. We shall see in Section 11.5, however, that input cost is more significant when we take joins. There, the output is generally much smaller than for the product, yet if we are not careful, the input cost for the join can be as great as for the product. $\square$

A Lower Bound on Input Cost

Evidently, the output cost, as given by (11.6), cannot be bettered, since we assume every tuple of the output must be written. However, how do we know that the input cost, (11.8), is the best we can do? In fact, we can make small improvements on (11.8), which we leave as an exercise. However, we cannot make major improvements, as the following theorem shows. The significance of Theorem 11.1 is not only for products, where output cost usually dominates anyway. It applies to any operation, such as a join, if we act as if it were a product, that is, if each tuple of one relation must "meet" each tuple of the other relation in main memory.[7]

Theorem 11.1: If we perform a product of relations R and S in a memory that can hold M blocks, then the number of block accesses we must make to read R and S is at least $B_R B_S/(M-1)$.

Proof: Consider any pair of tuples, μ from R and ν from S. At some time, the blocks holding these tuples must both be in main memory, or we cannot generate the output tuple $\mu\nu$. Let us *credit* the output tuple $\mu\nu$ to whichever of these blocks was read into main memory second. Now consider any block $\mathcal{B}$ from R being read into main memory. The amount of credit it can receive because of this reading event (exclusive of credits it might receive if it is read

---

[7] The join need not be performed this way, as we shall see in Section 11.5, and Theorem 11.1 motivates our search for better ways to compute the join.

again) is no greater than the number of tuples on $\mathcal{B}$, times the number of tuples of S then present in main memory. This number is no greater than

$$(M - 1)(T_S/B_S)(T_R/B_R) \tag{11.10}$$

that is, the number of other blocks in main memory, times the number of tuples of S on one block times the number of tuples of R on $\mathcal{B}$. Similarly, reading a block of S can generate a credit no greater than (11.10).

In order to compute the product, the amount of credit generated must be at least as great as the number of tuples in the output, that is, $T_R T_S$. Let A be the number of block accesses used for input while computing $R \times S$. Thus, $T_R T_S$ is equal to or less than A times expression (11.10), from which we obtain

$$A \geq B_R B_S/(M - 1)$$

as was to be proved. $\square$

Note that the upper bound on input cost, given by (11.8), and the lower bound, given by Theorem 11.1, differ only in the additive term B_S. The reader is invited to consider how this small gap can be narrowed; both the upper and lower bounds can be improved.

11.4 ESTIMATING THE OUTPUT COST FOR JOINS

In this and the next section, we consider algorithms for computing the natural join of two relations. If we are interested in an equijoin, we use the same techniques; we must only pretend that the attributes of one relation are renamed, so the computation is a natural join.[8] If we wish to perform a θ-join, where θ is not $=$, we are generally unable to do better than the product algorithm of Figure 11.2, although we save in output size if many tuples of the product do not meet the join condition.

A Statistical Model of Relations

When we take the join of two relations $AB(A, B)$ and $BC(B, C)$, a critical issue is how large the result will be. For instance, we observed in Example 11.2 that the question of whether to take a selection before a join can depend on the size of the result of the join. The size of the result, in turn, depends on how many tuples of BC a given tuple ab of relation AB will join with; that is, for a given B-value b, how many tuples of BC can we expect to have this B-value?

No general answer can be given to this question, of course. However, let us propose a reasonable model for "typical" relations and see what the model tells us. First, we shall assume that each attribute of each relation has an

---

[8] There is a small difference, in that the natural join deletes one copy of each pair of join attributes, while the equijoin retains both copies. When estimating sizes of the resulting tuples, we shall assume both copies are there, for convenience. Thus, our estimates will be slightly high for natural joins.

associated finite domain, the set of values that are "likely" to appear there. This domain can be taken to be the set of "active" elements from a potentially infinite domain. For example, the attribute CNAME of relation CUSTOMERS of the YVCB database may be assumed, at the time we take a join, to have as domain the set of present customers of the YVCB.

We assume that the set of potential tuples of a given relation R is the Cartesian product of the domains of all its attributes. If R has T tuples, and this product has n tuples, then we assume the current value of R is a randomly chosen set of T of the n possible tuples. Thus, each potential tuple has probability T/n of being chosen.

Finally, we assume that when we take the natural join of two relations R and S, attributes of the same name in R and S "mean" the same thing, and therefore select their values from the same domain. This assumption is probably the most tenuous, especially if the natural join is a renamed equijoin, whose equated attributes really have nothing to do with one another, for example, "find the YVCB customers whose balance equals the quantity of some item ordered by some customer." However, if the join attribute or attributes truly refer to the same notion, then it is likely that our assumptions are realistic. Moreover, as we shall see, equality of domains is not needed. We only need the containment of one domain in the other. An example will suggest what we might expect.

Example 11.7: Let us reconsider the YVCB relations CUSTOMERS, ORDERS, and INCLUDES from Example 11.3. The attribute $O\#$ from ORDERS and INCLUDES evidently means the same in both relations. Thus, we expect that any order number appearing in one relation appears in the other. An order number appearing only in ORDERS would be an order for nothing, which may not be erroneous data, but is not typical by any means. An order number appearing only in INCLUDES makes no sense and is probably erroneous.

A less obvious situation concerns the equijoin

$$CUSTOMERS \underset{CNAME=CUST}{\bowtie} ORDERS \qquad (11.11)$$

Evidently, CNAME in CUSTOMERS refers to the same domain as CUST in ORDERS. Since CNAME is the key for CUSTOMERS, we expect every current customer to appear in the domain of CNAME. Perhaps all, or most, of the customers have placed orders at any given time, so the domains of CUST and CNAME will be almost identical. However, it is also possible that only a small fraction of the customers have placed orders at any time, so the domain of CUST is much smaller than the domain of CNAME.

Fortunately, under our assumptions, it does not matter which is the case; the estimated size of the join (11.11) does not depend on what fraction of the customers actually placed orders. The intuitive reason is that each ORDERS tuple will have a value for CUST that is equally likely to appear in the CNAME attribute of any given CUSTOMERS tuple; in the example at hand, where CNAME is the key for CUSTOMERS, each CUST value appears in exactly one CUSTOMERS tuple. Thus, the size of the join will be the same as the size of the ORDERS relation, regardless of what fraction of customers have placed orders.[9] □

Implication of the Model Concerning the Output Size of Joins

We can generalize the observation of Example 11.7 regarding (11.11) by considering the natural join $AB \bowtie BC$, where there is an inclusion dependency on the B attributes; specifically, every B-value in the AB relation also appears in the B attribute of at least one tuple of BC, but not necessarily vice versa. Define D_A, D_B, and D_C to be the domains of A in AB, B in BC, and C in BC respectively. Also, use E_B for the domain of B in AB; note $E_B \subseteq D_B$. Use I_A, I_B, and I_C for the image sizes of the attributes, that is, the sizes of D_A, D_B, and D_C, respectively. Use J_B for the size of E_B. As usual, let T_{AB} be the number of tuples in AB and T_{BC} be the number of tuples in BC.

To calculate the size of $AB \bowtie BC$, consider an arbitrary tuple abc in $D_A \times D_B \times D_C$. The number of such tuples is $I_A I_B I_C$. We need only calculate the probability that abc is in the join. For abc to be in the join, ab must be in AB, and bc must be in BC. What is the probability that a random tuple bc is in BC? By our assumptions, that probability is $T_{BC}/(I_B I_C)$, the number of tuples in BC divided by the number of tuples in the product of domains $D_B \times D_C$.

Now, we must find the probability that ab is in AB. If b is a value that is in D_B but not in E_B, then the probability is zero. That case occurs fraction

$$(I_B - J_B)/I_B$$

of the time. However, fraction J_B/I_B of the time, b will be in E_B. Then the probability that ab is in AB is T_{AB} divided by the product of the sizes of the domains for A and B in relation AB, that is, $I_A J_B$. Thus, the probability that a random tuple ab chosen from $D_A \times D_B$ is in AB is

$$(\frac{I_B - J_B}{I_B}) \times 0 + (\frac{J_B}{I_B}) \times (\frac{T_{AB}}{I_A J_B}) \tag{11.12}$$

Notice that (11.12) does not depend on J_B; it reduces to $T_{AB}/(I_A I_B)$ independent of J_B. That observation is the formalization of the intuitive comment in Example 11.7 that the size of the join (11.11) does not depend on how many customers actually place orders at one time.

---

[9] More generally, if the average CUST value appeared in the CNAME component of k CUSTOMERS tuples, then the expected output size would be k times the size of ORDERS, independent of the fraction of CNAME values that were also CUST values.

When we multiply the probability that ab is in AB by the probability that bc is in BC, which we calculated earlier to be $T_{BC}/(I_B I_C)$, we get the probability that abc is in the join $AB \bowtie BC$; it is

$$\frac{T_{AB}T_{BC}}{I_A I_B^2 I_C}$$

Finally, we must multiply this probability by the number of possible tuples, which is $I_A I_B I_C$, to get the estimated size of $AB \bowtie BC$, or $T_{AB}T_{BC}/I_B$. That is, the output size is the product of the sizes of the two relations divided by the image size of the common attribute. This calculation can be generalized to the following theorem.

Theorem 11.2: Let $R(A_1, \ldots, A_j, B_1, \ldots, B_k)$ and $S(B_1, \ldots, B_k, C_1, \ldots, C_m)$ be two relations, and suppose that for each $i = 1, 2, \ldots, k$, either the domain of B_i in R is a subset of the domain of B_i in S, or vice versa. Assume that each tuple in the product of the domains of all the attributes of R is equally likely to be in R, and similarly for S. Then the expected size of $R \bowtie S$ is

$$\frac{T_R T_S}{I_{B_1} I_{B_2} \cdots I_{B_k}} \qquad (11.13)$$

where I_{B_i} is the size of the domain of B_i in R or S, whichever is a superset of the other.

Proof: We leave the proof, which generalizes the previous analysis, as an exercise. □

We can now estimate the expected number of blocks taken by the output of a join. Let I be the denominator of (11.13), that is, the product of the domain size for each attribute shared by R and S. Then $1/I$th of the tuples of the product $R \times S$ will appear in the join, so the output size is (11.6) divided by I, or

$$(B_R T_S + T_R B_S)/I \qquad (11.14)$$

However, recall that if we are taking a natural join, rather than an equijoin, duplicate copies of the join attributes are deleted from all tuples. Thus, the estimate (11.14) will be slightly high, because tuples are not as long in the output of a natural join as they are in a product or equijoin. We shall, however, ignore this difference and take (11.14) to be the output size estimate for any equijoin or natural join. .

Example 11.8: Consider the relations R and S of Example 11.5, and imagine that R is $R(A, B, C)$, while S is $S(B, C, D)$. Suppose that the inclusion dependencies $R.B \subseteq S.B$ and $S.C \subseteq R.C$ hold.[10] Finally, suppose I_B, the domain size for B in S, is 50, and I_C, the domain size for C in R, is 40. All other

---

[10] Recall the convention that $R.B$ stands for the attribute B belonging to relation R.

●

parameters of R and S are as given in Example 11.5. Then the size of the join $R \bowtie S$ is given by (11.14):

$$U = \frac{B_R T_S + B_S T_R}{I_B I_C} = \frac{500 \times 1000 + 100 \times 5000}{40 \times 50} = 500$$

This conclusion, that only one in 2000 pairs of tuples from R and S join successfully, is a reasonable one under our model of relations. A pair of tuples has 1 chance in 50 of agreeing on B and 1 chance in 40 of agreeing on C. However, we must be very careful if B and C are not independent. As an extreme example, suppose there were a functional dependency $B \to C$ that holds in both R and S.[11] Then, two tuples that agree on B are certain to agree on C, and the probability that two tuples from R and S join is $1/50$, not $1/2000$. Put another way, we would expect a join of size 20,000 blocks, rather than the 500 blocks we estimated earlier.

We can bring this situation within our model if we realize that B and C can be treated as a single attribute, say E. The inclusion dependency $R.B \subseteq S.B$, together with the assertion that functional dependency $B \to C$ holds in the combination of R and S, implies that $R.E \subseteq S.E$. The domain size of E in S is evidently 50, because each of the 50 values in the domain of B is associated with only one C-value.[12] Thus, we may regard the join $R \bowtie S$ as $AE \bowtie ED$, and calculate the output size as 1,000,000 divided by I_E, or 20,000. $\square$

11.5 METHODS FOR COMPUTING JOINS

We shall now consider several methods for computing joins, and we shall evaluate their estimated cost based on the model of the previous section. The methods considered include the obvious, selection-on-a-product approach, a technique called sort-join, where both relations are sorted on their join attributes, and methods that take advantage of various types of indices.

The formulas for expected running time of these algorithms are frequently complicated. Thus, at the end of the section, we summarize the formulas and list the dominant term or terms for each method.

Computing the Join by Selection on a Product

The obvious way to compute $R \bowtie S$ is to compute the product $R \times S$, using Figure 11.2 (as before, we assume that S is the smaller relation). However, instead of emitting every tuple $\mu\nu$, where μ is in R and ν is in S, emit only those tuples that agree on the common attributes of R and S. The cost of

---

[11] That is, two tuples that agree in B must agree in C, whether the tuples come from R, from S, or one from each.

[12] The fact that several B-values can appear with one C-value does not affect the domain size of E.

this method is the input cost, given by (11.8), plus the output cost, given by (11.14).

Example 11.9: Suppose we have the join of Example 11.8, with

$$I = I_B I_C = 2000$$

and $M = 101$, as in Example 11.5. Then the value of (11.8) is

$$500 \times (100/100) + 100 = 600$$

The value of U, as we saw in Example 11.8, is 500, so the total cost is 1100. If $M = 11$, as in Example 11.6, U doesn't change, but the input cost rises to

$$500 \times (100/10) + 100 = 5100$$

Thus, with only eleven available blocks of main memory, the join cost is 5600. Notice that in both cases, the input cost is significant, unlike Examples 11.5 and 11.6, where the operation was the Cartesian product, and output cost dominated input cost. □

The reader may check the following formula for the sum of (11.8) and (11.14), which is the total cost of taking a join by the selection-on-a-product method.

$$B_R(\frac{T_S}{I} + \frac{B_S}{M-1}) + B_S(\frac{T_R}{I} + 1) \qquad (11.15)$$

Sort-Join

Theorem 11.1 tells us we cannot do significantly better than (11.15) if we join in such a way that each block of one relation meets each block of the other relation in main memory. However, there are several ways we can preprocess the relations (or take advantage of existing indices) to avoid such unselective mixing of the two relations. We consider one of these, *sort-join*, now.

In what follows, we shall assume that our two relations to be joined are $R(A, B)$ and $S(B, C)$. The idea generalizes easily to the case where there are several attributes in common and/or several attributes belonging to one of the relations alone. We begin by sorting R on its attribute B and S on its attribute B. We then set up cursors that scan the tuples of R and S, lowest B-values first, as suggested in Figure 11.3.

Suppose we are scanning tuples ab_1 from R and b_2c from S. If one of b_1 and b_2 is smaller than the other, we move one cursor down, past the smaller one, and we leave the other cursor fixed. In this case, we can show it is not possible that the smaller matches any B-values from the other relation. If $b_1 = b_2$, then we find all the following tuples of R and S with this same B-value. We pair each of these tuples from R with each of these tuples from S, and emit the resulting tuples (deleting one copy of the common B-value). Then, we move the cursors

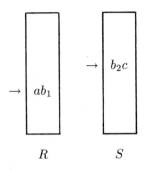

Figure 11.3 Scanning two sorted relations.

$$
\begin{array}{cc}
a_1b_1 & b_1c_1 \\
a_2b_1 & b_1c_2 \\
a_3b_2 & b_3c_3 \\
a_4b_3 & \\
\end{array}
$$

$$R \qquad\qquad S$$

Figure 11.4 Sample relations presented as sorted lists.

of the two relations just below the last of the tuples with this B-value.

Example 11.10: Suppose R and S consist of the lists of tuples in Figure 11.4. Both relations already have been sorted by B-value. We begin with our cursors at a_1b_1 for R and b_1c_1 for S. Since the B-values agree, we find all the tuples of R with this B-value, that is, $\{a_1b_1,\ a_2b_1\}$, and all the tuples of S with this B-value, namely, $\{b_1c_1,\ b_1c_2\}$. Note that the desired tuples must be in consecutive positions, following the cursors of their respective relations. When we take the product and omit one copy of b_1 from each tuple, we get four tuples, $\{a_1b_1c_1,\ a_1b_1c_2,\ a_2b_1c_1,\ a_2b_1c_2\}$, that belong in $R \bowtie S$.

We now advance the cursor of R to a_3b_2 and the cursor of S to b_3c_3. Since b_2, presumably, is less than b_3 in the sorted order, we know that there are no tuples of S with B-value b_2; if there were, they would have preceded b_3. Thus, we advance the cursor of R to a_4b_3 and leave the cursor of S fixed.

Now, we have both cursors at B-value b_3, and in each case, the tuples scanned are the only tuples of their relations with that B-value. Thus, we simply pair these tuples, generating the fifth and last tuple in the join $R \bowtie S$, which is $a_4b_3c_3$. At this point, both cursors are moved past the ends of their relations. In general, scanning might end when one cursor reaches the end of its relation, while the other still has tuples to scan. $\square$

Multiway Merge-Sort

Since relations are not ordinarily stored sorted, we must calculate the cost of sorting a relation. There are, of course, many ways to sort files. Under our cost model, where block accesses are counted, a method called *multiway merge-sort* is an excellent approach. The reader interested in the details of this algorithm can consult Aho, Hopcroft, and Ullman [1983]. Here, we shall only sketch the idea and give the analysis of its cost.

Multiway merge-sort operates by constructing *runs*, which are sequences of blocks that contain a sorted list of tuples from the given relation R. In a series of passes, R is partitioned into a set of progressively longer runs, until at last, there is only one run, and it is the entire relation R. We shall assume that there are M blocks of main memory available for holding blocks of R. Some additional blocks of memory are needed for calculation, such as finding the smallest of a set of M values, and for storing output, but we assume these blocks are reserved and not counted among the M blocks available for storing blocks of the relation to be sorted.

In the first pass, we read the blocks of R into main memory, M at a time, and sort the tuples within groups of M blocks, using any appropriate internal (main-memory) sorting algorithm, such as Quicksort (see Knuth [1973] or Aho, Hopcroft, and Ullman [1983]). Note that we do not charge anything for main-memory calculations, and in fact, the sorting of the M blocks probably takes much less time than reading these blocks from secondary storage. As a result, R is now partitioned into B_R/M runs of M blocks each.

In the pth pass, $p > 1$, we start with runs of M^{p-1} blocks each, and we group them into groups of M runs each; that is, each group consists of M^p blocks. The last group may have fewer than M runs, and therefore, its length will be less than M^p blocks. We then merge each group by the process suggested in Figure 11.5.

To perform the merge, we keep a cursor to each of the M runs in a group, as suggested in Figure 11.5. Initially, each cursor is at the beginning of the run, at the smallest element. Repeatedly, we select the smallest element from among those pointed to by the M cursors, and the cursor whose element won is advanced to the next element of that run. The selected element is appended to the current output block.

We need keep only one block from each run in main memory. When the cursor for that run moves past the block in main memory, we replace it in memory by the next block of the same run. Similarly, we need to keep only one output block in main memory (space for this block is not counted among the M blocks available for input). When one block is filled, it is moved to secondary storage, and the output block in main memory can be filled with the next tuples in sorted order.

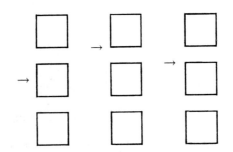

Figure 11.5 Multiway merge for $M = 3$ and $p = 2$.

After $\lceil \log_M B_R \rceil$ passes, the runs produced are of length at least B_R. Thus, the entire relation R consists of one run; that is, it is sorted.

Analysis of Sort-Join

Now let us estimate the cost of performing a sort-join on relations R and S. The final join process, suggested by Figure 11.3, has input cost $B_R + B_S$, since we need only to read each block of the sorted relations once, as we move the cursors through the relations. The output cost is estimated by (11.14), of course.

We must now estimate the cost of sorting the relations. One pass of the multiway merge-sort reads each block of the relation once, since it reads each run once. It also writes new blocks that together hold the relation, packed. Thus, each pass uses $2B$ block accesses, if the relation requires B blocks to store packed. As the number of passes is $\log_M B$,[13] the cost of performing multiway merge-sort on a relation of B blocks is $2B \log_M B$. Thus, the entire cost of sort-join is

$$2B_R \log_M B_R + 2B_S \log_M B_S + B_R + B_S + (B_R T_S + T_R B_S)/I \quad (11.16)$$

The first two terms are the cost of sorting the two relations, the next two are the cost of scanning the sorted relations for matching pairs of tuples, and the last term is the output cost.

Formula (11.16) is valid as long as there is no value b of the join attribute(s) for which the number of tuples from the two relations that share value b exceeds the number that can fit in main memory. If that were the case, then the scan of the relations suggested by Figure 11.3 could not proceed without rereading some of the blocks with value b.

Example 11.11: Let us consider the sample relations of Example 11.9, with $I = 2000$ and $M = 101$. As $B_R = 500$, $\log_M B_R$ is 2. Since $B_S = 100$, we have $\log_M B_S = 1$. Recall that $T_R = 5000$ and $T_S = 1000$. Thus, (11.16) is

---

[13] We shall omit the ceiling function from logarithms that represent numbers of passes. The reader should remember that the next higher integer number of passes is meant.

$$2 \times 500 \times 2 + 2 \times 100 \times 1 + 500 + 100 + (1,000,000/2000) = 3300$$

This figure compares poorly with the estimate 1100 for the straightforward join given in Example 11.9.

However, consider the case $M = 11$. Then $\log_M B_R = 3$ and $\log_M B_S = 2$. Our cost estimate is thus

$$2 \times 500 \times 3 + 2 \times 100 \times 2 + 500 + 100 + (1,000,000/2000) = 4500$$

This figure is less than the estimate of 5600 for the straightforward join.

In general, as the size of the relations B_R and B_S get large, with M held constant, and $B_R \geq B_S$ assumed as always, the input cost of selection-on-a-product join will grow as $B_R B_S / M$. However, the input cost of sort-join will grow as $B_R \log_M B_R$, which is significantly less. $\square$

Joins Using an Index

Let us again consider the join $R(A, B) \bowtie S(B, C)$, but now, suppose that S has a clustering index on B. Let us also assume that R is packed. Then we can take the join by reading each block of R, and for each tuple of R, use the index to find the matching tuples of S. That is, we do

> **for** each block $\mathcal{B}$ of R **do**
>   **for** each tuple ab on block $\mathcal{B}$ **do**   (11.17)
>   join ab with each tuple in $\sigma_{B=b}(S)$

Let I be the image size of B in S, and assume that the inclusion dependency $R.B \subseteq S.B$ holds; that is, every B-value appearing in R appears in S. Then the inner loop of (11.17) is done T_R times, and at each iteration, we have to retrieve, via the clustering index, about B_S/I blocks. In the outer loop, we read each block of R once, costing an additional B_R block accesses. Thus, the input cost of (11.17) is

$$B_R + \frac{T_R B_S}{I} \tag{11.18}$$

The total cost, the sum of (11.14) and (11.18), is

$$B_R \left(1 + \frac{T_S}{I}\right) + \frac{2 T_R B_S}{I} \tag{11.19}$$

We must be careful to interpret (11.18), and formulas following from it, because we have made the tacit assumption $I \leq B_S$. If not, then B_S/I is not an accurate estimate of the number of blocks retrieved in the body of (11.17), as that number cannot be less than one. If $I \geq B_S$, then we retrieve about one block of S for each tuple of R, and (11.18) must be replaced by $B_R + T_R$. A formula that generalizes (11.19) for the case where I can be greater than or less than B_S is

$$B_R\left(1 + \frac{T_S}{I}\right) + \frac{T_R B_S}{I} + T_R \times \max\left(1, \frac{B_S}{I}\right) \tag{11.20}$$

Some Other Cases of Indexed Joins

We can derive several similar formulas for related situations. If relation R is not stored packed, then we may have to access T_R blocks, rather than B_R blocks, to read R. In this case, the input cost would be $T_R(1 + B_S/I)$, instead of (11.18); the output cost does not change, of course. If R is packed, but the index of S on B is nonclustering, then each iteration of the inner loop of (11.17) must retrieve about T_S/I blocks, and the input cost would be $B_R + T_R T_S/I$. If the index is nonclustering and R is not packed, then the input cost is $T_R(1 + T_S/I)$.[14] Finally, we could derive similar formulas, with R and S interchanged, if there is an index of R on B that we can use.

In all of the above, we have assumed that $R.B \subseteq S.B$. If the inclusion dependency goes the other way, then (11.18) will still be a good estimate of the input cost, assuming that the image size of $S.B$ is no larger than B_S, but we have to interpret I as $I_{R.B}$, rather than $I_{S.B}$, even though the index is still on S. The appropriate formula for the case $S.B \subseteq R.B$, allowing both $I_{S.B} \leq B_S$ and $I_{S.B} \geq B_S$, is

$$B_R\left(1 + \frac{T_S}{J}\right) + \frac{T_R}{J}\left(B_S + \max(B_S, I)\right) \tag{11.21}$$

where $J = I_{R.B}$ and $I = I_{S.B}$.

Example 11.12: Let us take up our running example, with $B_R = 500$, $T_R = 5000$, $B_S = 100$, and $T_S = 1000$. Suppose that $R.B \subseteq S.B$, and $I = I_{S.B} = 50$. Finally, we assume that there is a clustering index on B in S. As $I \leq B_S$, we may apply (11.19), whose value is

$$500\left(1 + \frac{1000}{50}\right) + \frac{2 \times 5000 \times 100}{50} = 30,500$$

Suppose all is the same, but now $S.B \subseteq R.B$ and $J = I_{R.B} = 200$. Then we may apply (11.21) to obtain the cost

$$500\left(1 + \frac{1000}{200}\right) + \frac{5000}{200}\left(100 + \max(100, 50)\right) = 8000$$

As another case, suppose again that $S.B \subseteq R.B$, and $J = I_{R.B} = 200$. However, suppose the index on $S.B$ is nonclustering. Then the input cost rises to

---

[14] Note that $I \leq T_S$ certainly holds, so we do not have to make allowance for the possibility that T_S/I is an underestimate of the number of blocks retrieved.

$$B_R + T_R T_S / J = 500 + (5000 \times 1000)/200 = 25,500$$

while the output cost, as given by (11.14) with J in place of I there, remains the same, at 5,000. Thus, the total cost rises from 8000 to 30,500. $\square$

Joins Using Two Indices

We can do even better if there is an index on B in both relations. Suppose first that both indices are clustering. We can find the set of B-values by examining one of the indices. We may as well use the index with the smaller image size; assume that is the index on B of S, and let I be $I_{S.B}$. As we access the index on B in S, we shall encounter all I values of B in turn. We thus shall not charge for finding this set of values. Note that it is unnecessary to find the set of B-values in R, because those absent from S will not appear in the result of the join anyway.

Once we have the set of B-values, we can run through them, retrieving the relevant tuples from R and S. Formally

> **for** each B-value b **do**
>   join the tuples of $\sigma_{B=b}(R)$ with $\sigma_{B=b}(S)$ (11.22)

Analysis of Two-Index Join

Let us estimate the cost of (11.22), assuming $S.B \subseteq R.B$. The body of (11.22) is performed I times. The average number of blocks of R retrieved in one iteration is at most $\max(1, B_R/J)$, where J is $I_{R.B}$; it could be less if many values in the domain of B in S were not in the domain of B in R. The number of blocks of S retrieved is about $\max(1, B_S/I)$. Thus, the input cost for this join method is at most

$$I \times \left(\max(1, \frac{B_R}{J}) + \max(1, \frac{B_S}{I}) \right)$$

When we calculate the output cost by (11.14), we must remember that the image size is the larger of the two image sizes of the join attribute. Thus, I in (11.14) is J here, and the total cost of the double-index join is

$$I \max\left(1, \frac{B_R}{J}\right) + \max(I, B_S) + \frac{B_R T_S + T_R B_S}{J}   (11.23)$$

We leave as an exercise the modifications to (11.23) necessary when the indices are not both clustering.

Example 11.13: Let us consider the join of Example 11.12 with clustering indices on B in both R and S. Assume that $I = 50$ and $J = 200$. Then the value of (11.23) is

$$50 \times \max\left(1, \frac{500}{200}\right) + \max(50, 100) + \frac{500 \times 1000 + 100 \times 5000}{200} = 5225$$

Notice that the output cost, 5000, is almost the entire cost in this example. □

Creating a Clustering Index

Since there appears to be considerable advantage to joining with a clustering index on each join attribute, let us consider how fast we could create such an index if it did not exist. Suppose we have a relation $R(A, B)$, and let I be the image size for B, the attribute on which we shall create the clustering index. What we shall actually do is create a hash table with about I buckets, and in each bucket, we place copies of all the tuples of R whose B-value hashes to that bucket. On average, there will be one B-value per bucket.

Suppose we can only afford to use M blocks of main memory to hold the contents of the buckets as we form them. As in the analysis of sort-join, we do not count among these M blocks certain other main-memory requirements, such as the space to store the program and a single block for reading input. We shall create the I-bucket hash table in several passes, which are analogous to the passes we used in multiway merge-sort.

Select a hash function that hashes tuples into I buckets numbered 0 to $I - 1$. We cannot partition R into all I buckets at once, if $I > M$, because we would spend too many block accesses swapping blocks for the buckets in and out of main memory, as tuples of R were hashed to random buckets. However, we can divide R into M "superbuckets," each representing I/M of the buckets. We keep one block for each superbucket in memory, and when it is full, we move it to secondary memory and start a new block for that superbucket. On the first pass, we shall use superbucket 0 to represent buckets 0 through $(I/M) - 1$, superbucket 1 to represent buckets I/M through $(2I/M) - 1$, and so on. We read each block of R, hash each tuple of the block, and if a tuple belongs in bucket i, we place it in superbucket $\lfloor iM/I \rfloor$.

In general, the pth pass, $p > 1$, starts with superbuckets that each represent I/M^{p-1} buckets and ends with more, smaller superbuckets, each representing I/M^p buckets. During the pass, we work on one superbucket at a time, partitioning the buckets it represents into M groups of buckets; each group corresponds to one of the new superbuckets. We read each superbucket once in a pass, and we keep M blocks representing the M smaller superbuckets, writing out a block when it is full. After $\log_M I$ passes, the new superbuckets represent single buckets, and we are done.

Analysis of Join by Index Creation

The number of block accesses used by this index-creation technique is computed as follows. Each pass reads and writes about B_R blocks, as all of the superbuckets into which R is partitioned are read, and the new superbuckets, with a finer partition, are written. Thus, the cost of the $\log_M I$ passes is

$$2B_R \log_M I \tag{11.24}$$

Formula (11.24) will be an underestimate if $I > B_R$. For then, the final pass or passes will divide R into more buckets than are needed to store R packed; therefore, those passes will use more than $2B_R$ block accesses. An upper bound on the cost, without assuming $I \geq B_R$ is

$$2 \max(I, B_R) \log_M I \tag{11.25}$$

We leave a more accurate formula as an exercise.

Suppose we want to take the join $R(A, B) \bowtie S(B, C)$, but there are no indices on B for either relation. Then we can use the technique above to create these indices, paying an extra amount indicated by (11.25) for each. Assume that $I_{R.B}$ is denoted J and $I_{S.B}$ is I. Also assume the inclusion dependency $R.B \subseteq S.B$, with the consequent $J \geq I$. Then the cost of this method is (11.23) plus the cost of creating indices for R and S. The latter costs are given by (11.25), with the appropriate substitutions of variables. The formula for total cost is

$$(I + 2J \log_M J) \times \max\left(1, \frac{B_R}{J}\right) + \max(I, B_S)(1 + 2 \log_M I) +$$
$$\frac{B_R T_S + T_R B_S}{J} \tag{11.26}$$

Example 11.14: Let us reconsider the data of Example 11.13. With $M = 101$, we have $\log_M J = 2$ and $\log_M I = 1$. Thus, the value of (11.26) is

$$(50 + 2 \times 200 \times 2)\left(\max(1, \frac{500}{200})\right) + \left(\max(50, 100)\right)(1 + 2 \times 1) +$$
$$\frac{500 \times 1000 + 5000 \times 100}{200} = 7425$$

With $M = 11$, we get $\log_M J = 3$ and $\log_M I = 2$; the cost increases to 8625. $\square$

Summary and Comparisons

In Figure 11.6 is a table of the principal join methods considered in this section. In addition to the explicitly listed assumptions, we make the global assumptions and conventions that follow.

1. The model of random relations that was given in Section 11.4 applies.
2. Relations are stored packed.
3. The join is $R(A, B) \bowtie S(B, C)$. R and S have T_R and T_S tuples, respectively, and fit on B_R and B_S blocks, respectively.

Method	Assumptions	Cost	Dominant Terms
Selection-on-a-product	$R.B \subseteq S.B$ or $S.B \subseteq R.B$	(11.15)	$B_R B_S / M$
Sort-join	$R.B \subseteq S.B$ $B_R/J + B_S/I \le M$	(11.16)	$B_R \log B_R,\ B_S \log B_S,$ $B_R T_S/I,\ B_S T_R/I$
Clustering index on $S.B$	$R.B \subseteq S.B$	(11.20)	$B_R T_S/I,\ B_S T_R/I,\ T_R$
Clustering index on $S.B$	$S.B \subseteq R.B$	(11.21)	$B_R,\ B_R T_S/J,$ $B_S T_R/J,\ T_R I/J$
Two-index join	$S.B \subseteq R.B$ $B_R/J + B_S/I \le M$	(11.23)	$I,\ B_R T_S/J,\ B_S T_R/J$
Two-index join with index creation	$S.B \subseteq R.B$ $B_R/J + B_S/I \le M$	(11.26)	$J \log_M J,\ B_R \log_M J,$ $B_S \log_M I,\ B_R T_S/J,$ $B_S T_R/J$

Figure 11.6 Comparison of join methods.

4. I is $I_{S.B}$, the image size of B in S, and J is $I_{R.B}$, the image size of B in R.
5. M is approximately the size of main memory, excluding space needed to hold the program, and in some cases, one input or output buffer.

We also know that $I \le T_S$ and $J \le T_R$. Further, if inclusion dependency $S.B \subseteq R.B$ is assumed, then we know $I \le J$, and if the opposite inclusion is assumed, then $I \ge J$. We use these inequalities to eliminate certain terms of formulas that are therefore smaller than another term of the same formula.

The second column in Figure 11.6 gives special assumptions that are needed to make the cost formulas, given by equation number in the third column, valid. However, we can distinguish two types of assumptions. The inclusion dependencies between the domains of B in R and S are needed to make the estimates of output size valid. If the inclusion dependencies do not hold, then the outputs will, on the average, be smaller, so the cost formulas are upper bounds on the true costs. The second type of assumption states that the size of main memory must be large enough to hold all the tuples of R and S that share a common B-value, that is, $B_R/J + B_S/I \le M$. If that relationship does not hold, then certain operations, which we assumed can take place in main memory, actually require additional block accesses to shuffle blocks in and out of main memory, as we did in the product algorithm of Figure 11.2. Thus, if these conditions are violated, the cost given in column 3 will be a low estimate.

The last column of Figure 11.6 lists the dominant terms. In finding the dominant terms from each formula, we assumed that B_R, B_S, T_R, T_S, I, and J grow in proportion, but M remains constant. The formulas were expanded, and any term that was asymptotically no larger than another was eliminated, leaving the "dominant terms." Of course, depending on the values of the parameters, any one of the dominant terms for a formula could prove largest.

The dominant terms tell us which methods will be best as the relations get large, but the size of main memory remains fixed. In particular, the only dominant term that is quadratic in the size of the relations is $B_R B_S / M$ from selection-on-a-product join. Other terms either grow as the product of the relation size and the logarithm of that size, for example, $B_R \log_M J$ from the join with index creation, or linearly with the size of relations, for example, $B_R T_S / I$. Note that we assume I, the image size of $R.B$, grows in proportion to B_R, the number of blocks taken by relation R.

Thus, for large relations, we expect selection-on-a-product join to perform worst, although it can be quite efficient for small relations, because of its simplicity.[15] The joins that use an index perform best, but they are not an option if those indices do not exist. Then, either sort-join or index-creation join are viable alternatives. The particular values of the parameters determine which is best in a given situation.

11.6 OPTIMIZATION BY ALGEBRAIC MANIPULATION

So far, in this chapter, we have compared strategies for performing basic relational operations: selection, product, and join. Now, let us look at the complete problem of turning a query, written in some relational query language, into a sequence of relational algebra steps that, together, form an efficient algorithm for answering the query.

The first thing a query processor does is turn the query into an internal form that resembles relational algebra. For example, the QUEL query processor,[16] whose optimization algorithm will be discussed in the Section 11.10, begins by assuming a Cartesian product of relations $R_1 \times R_2 \times \cdots \times R_k$, if the applicable range statements are of the form

        range of t_i is R_i

for $i = 1, 2, \ldots, k$. Then the where-clause of the QUEL query is replaced by a selection, and the components mentioned in the retrieve-clause are obtained by

---

[15] We must be careful about our model when we talk about selection-on-a-product. The reason is that we don't count computation performed in main memory. That is probably valid when we, say, read a few blocks and then sort them; the sorting time is less than the time to read from secondary storage. However, selection-on-a-product join repeatedly reads one block of R, and then compares its tuples with all the tuples on $M - 1$ blocks of S. This main-memory computation can be a significant cost if M is large.

[16] See Section 4.3 of Volume I.

a projection. In fact, the basic query forms of Query-by-Example and SQL are also replaced by similar algebraic expressions, a projection on a selection on a product.[17]

Equivalence of Expressions

Before we can "optimize" expressions we must understand clearly when two expressions of relational algebra (hereafter referred to as *relational expressions*) are equivalent. First, let us recall that there are two definitions of relations in use (see Section 2.3), and they have somewhat different mathematical properties. The first viewpoint is that a relation is a set of k-tuples for a fixed k, and two relations are equal if and only if they are the same sets of tuples. The second viewpoint is that a relation is a set of mappings from a set of attribute names to values. Two relations are deemed equal if they are the same set of mappings. A relation in the first sense can be converted to a relation in the second sense by providing attribute names for the columns. We can convert from the second definition of relation to the first by picking a fixed order for the attributes.

We shall here use only the second definition, that a relation is a set of mappings from attributes to values. The justification is that existing query languages all allow, and generally require, names for columns in a relation. More importantly, in any application of which we are aware, the order in which the columns of a table are printed is not significant, as long as each column is labeled by the proper attribute name. Where possible, we adopt names for attributes of each relation computed by a relational expression, from the names of attributes for the expression's arguments. We also require that names be provided for the result of a union or set difference.

A relational expression whose operands are relations $R_1, R_2, \ldots, R_k$ defines a function whose domain is k-tuples of relations $(r_1, r_2, \ldots, r_k)$, each r_i being a relation of the arity appropriate to R_i. The value of the function is the relation that results when we substitute each r_i for R_i and then evaluate the expression. Two expressions E_1 and E_2 are *equivalent*, written $E_1 \equiv E_2$, if they represent the same mappings; that is, when we substitute the same relations for identical names in the two expressions, we get the same result. With this definition of equivalence, we can list some useful algebraic transformations.

Laws Involving Joins and Cartesian Products

In Theorem 2.2 (Section 2.4 of Volume I), we proved that natural join was commutative and associative. Similar algebraic laws hold for θ-joins and products, and we state these here.

---

[17] See Sections 4.4 and 4.6, respectively.

1. *Commutative laws for joins and products.* If E_1 and E_2 are relational expressions, and F is a condition on the attributes of E_1 and E_2, then

$$E_1 \underset{F}{\bowtie} E_2 \equiv E_2 \underset{F}{\bowtie} E_1$$

$$E_1 \bowtie E_2 \equiv E_2 \bowtie E_1$$

$$E_1 \times E_2 \equiv E_2 \times E_1$$

2. *Associative laws for joins and products.* If E_1, E_2, and E_3 are relational expressions, and F_1 and F_2 are conditions, then

$$(E_1 \underset{F_1}{\bowtie} E_2) \underset{F_2}{\bowtie} E_3 \equiv E_1 \underset{F_1}{\bowtie} (E_2 \underset{F_2}{\bowtie} E_3)$$

$$(E_1 \bowtie E_2) \bowtie E_3 \equiv E_1 \bowtie (E_2 \bowtie E_3)$$

$$(E_1 \times E_2) \times E_3 \equiv E_1 \times (E_2 \times E_3)$$

The reader may be surprised by some of these laws; for example, we asserted in Section 2.4 that the product was *not* commutative. The difference is that here we are using the set-of-mappings definition of relations, while in Section 2.4 we used the set-of-lists definition. For example, let us see why $E_1 \times E_2 \equiv E_2 \times E_1$ holds in the present model. First, note that we distinguish attributes from two different relations, even if those attributes have the same name. Thus, let R and S be the relations that are the values of E_1 and E_2, respectively. Then attribute A of R is called $R.A$ in the product of E_1 and E_2, while attribute A of S is called $S.A$. We can abbreviate either $R.A$ or $S.A$ by A, if A is an attribute of only one of R and S.

Let ρ be a tuple in $E_1 \times E_2$. Then there is a tuple μ in R and a tuple ν in S, such that for all attributes A of R, $\rho[R.A] = \mu[A]$, and for all attributes A of S, $\rho[S.A] = \nu[A]$. Now consider the product $E_2 \times E_1$, which must also contain a tuple τ formed from μ and ν. Evidently, $\tau[R.A] = \mu[A]$ and $\tau[S.A] = \nu[A]$ for all attributes A of R and S, respectively. Thus, τ is ρ. Since ρ is an arbitrary tuple, it follows that $E_1 \times E_2 \subseteq E_2 \times E_1$. The opposite inclusion is no less trivial, so we conclude that $E_1 \times E_2$ and $E_2 \times E_1$ are the same relation.

Laws Involving Selections and Projections

The cascade of several projections can be combined into one. We express this fact by

3. *Cascade of projections.*

$$\pi_{A_1,\ldots,A_n} \left(\pi_{B_1,\ldots,B_m}(E) \right) \equiv \pi_{A_1,\ldots,A_n}(E)$$

Note that the attribute names $A_1, \ldots, A_n$ must be among the B_i's for the cascade to make sense.

Similarly, the cascade of selections can be combined into one selection that checks for all conditions at once. The following equivalence allows us to combine or break up arbitrary sequences of selections.

4. *Cascade of selections.*

$$\sigma_{F_1}\big(\sigma_{F_2}(E)\big) \equiv \sigma_{F_1 \wedge F_2}(E)$$

Since $F_1 \wedge F_2 = F_2 \wedge F_1$, it follows immediately that selections can be commuted, that is,

$$\sigma_{F_1}\big(\sigma_{F_2}(E)\big) \equiv \sigma_{F_2}\big(\sigma_{F_1}(E)\big)$$

5. *Commuting selections and projections.* If condition F involves only attributes $A_1, \ldots, A_n$, then

$$\pi_{A_1,\ldots,A_n}\big(\sigma_F(E)\big) \equiv \sigma_F\big(\pi_{A_1,\ldots,A_n}(E)\big)$$

More generally, if condition F also involves attributes $B_1, \ldots, B_m$ that are not among $A_1, \ldots, A_n$, then

$$\pi_{A_1,\ldots,A_n}\big(\sigma_F(E)\big) \equiv \pi_{A_1,\ldots,A_n}\Big(\sigma_F\big(\pi_{A_1,\ldots,A_n,B_1,\ldots,B_m}(E)\big)\Big)$$

In the above equivalence, it may appear that the extra projection on the right, $\pi_{A_1,\ldots,A_n,B_1,\ldots,B_m}$, is redundant. However, that is a quirk of notation. A projection throws away attributes, as well as preserving some. In particular, if the relation for E has an attribute C that is not among the A's or B's, then on the right C is projected out before the selection, while on the left it is projected out after the selection.

6. *Commuting selection with Cartesian product.* If all the attributes mentioned in F are attributes of E_1, then

$$\sigma_F(E_1 \times E_2) \equiv \sigma_F(E_1) \times E_2$$

As a useful corollary, if F is of the form $F_1 \wedge F_2$, where F_1 involves only attributes of E_1, and F_2 involves only attributes of E_2, we can use rules (1), (4), and (6) to obtain

$$\sigma_F(E_1 \times E_2) \equiv \sigma_{F_1}(E_1) \times \sigma_{F_2}(E_2)$$

Moreover, if F_1 involves only attributes of E_1, but F_2 involves attributes of both E_1 and E_2, we can still assert

$$\sigma_F(E_1 \times E_2) \equiv \sigma_{F_2}\big(\sigma_{F_1}(E_1) \times E_2\big)$$

thereby pushing part of the selection ahead of the product.

7. *Commuting selection with a union.* If we have an expression $E = E_1 \cup E_2$, we may assume the attributes of E_1 and E_2 have the same names as those of E, or at least, that there is a given correspondence that associates each

attribute of E with a unique attribute of E_1 and a unique attribute of E_2. Thus we may write

$$\sigma_F(E_1 \cup E_2) \equiv \sigma_F(E_1) \cup \sigma_F(E_2)$$

If the attribute names for E_1 and/or E_2 actually differ from those of E, then the formulas F on the right must be modified to use the appropriate names.

8. *Commuting selection with a set difference.*

$$\sigma_F(E_1 - E_2) \equiv \sigma_F(E_1) - \sigma_F(E_2)$$

As in (7), if the attribute names of E_1 and E_2 differ, we must replace the attributes in F on the right by the corresponding names for E_1. Note also that the selection $\sigma_F(E_2)$ on the right is not necessary; we could replace it by E_2 if we wished. However, it is usually at least as efficient to perform the selection as it is to obtain the value of the expression E_2, and in many cases, $\sigma_F(E_2)$ is easier to compute than E_2, because the former is a smaller set than the latter.

We shall not state all the laws for pushing a selection ahead of a join, since a join can always be expressed as a Cartesian product followed by a selection, and, in the case of the natural join, a projection. The rules for passing a selection ahead of a join thus follow from rules (4), (5), and (6). The rules for moving a projection ahead of a Cartesian product or union are similar to rules (6) and (7). Note that there is no general way to move a projection ahead of a set difference. However, there is one useful rule that applies to a natural join and takes advantage of the implied equalities among attributes used in the definition of the natural join; we state it here, and leave its generalization to equijoins as an exercise.

9. *Commuting selection with natural join—special case.* If F is a condition that involves only attributes shared by both E_1 and E_2, then

$$\sigma_F(E_1 \bowtie E_2) \equiv \sigma_F(E_1) \bowtie \sigma_F(E_2)$$

Observe that we are not making ourselves extra work by pushing the selection down both branches of the expression tree. The selection reduces the size of the relations for both E_1 and E_2, thus saving work in both branches.

10. *Commuting a projection with a Cartesian product.* Let E_1 and E_2 be two relational expressions. Let $A_1, \ldots, A_n$ be a list of attributes, of which $B_1, \ldots, B_m$ are attributes of E_1, and the remaining attributes, $C_1, \ldots, C_k$, are from E_2. Then

$$\pi_{A_1, \ldots, A_n}(E_1 \times E_2) \equiv \pi_{B_1, \ldots, B_m}(E_1) \times \pi_{C_1, \ldots, C_k}(E_2)$$

11. *Commuting a projection with a union.*

$$\pi_{A_1,\ldots,A_n}(E_1 \cup E_2) \equiv \pi_{A_1,\ldots,A_n}(E_1) \cup \pi_{A_1,\ldots,A_n}(E_2)$$

As in rule (7), if the names of attributes for E_1 and/or E_2 differ from those in $E_1 \cup E_2$, we must replace $A_1, \ldots, A_n$ on the right by the appropriate names.

Principles for Algebraic Manipulation

Now that we have a list of useful equivalences, we can formulate the rules regarding the preferred direction in which to apply them. There is no algorithm that is guaranteed to produce the optimal expression equivalent to a given one, but the following principles are generally useful.

1. *Perform selections as early as possible.* This transformation on queries, more than any other, is responsible for saving orders of magnitude in execution time, since it tends to make the intermediate results of multistep evaluations small. Thus, in rules (6)–(9), we prefer to replace expressions on the left with their equivalents on the right.

2. *Combine certain selections with a prior Cartesian product to make a join.* As we have seen, a join, especially an equijoin, can be considerably cheaper than a Cartesian product of the same relations. When the result of Cartesian product $R \times S$ is the argument of a selection, and that selection involves comparisons between attributes of R and S, the product is really a join. Note that a comparison involving no attribute of R or no attribute of S can be moved ahead of the product and be applied to S or R, respectively, which is even better than converting the product to a join.

3. *Combine sequences of unary operations.* A cascade of unary operations— selection and projection—can be combined by applying them in a group as we scan each tuple. Similarly, we can combine these unary operations with a prior binary operation, if we apply the unary operations to each tuple in the result of the binary operation as we construct it.

4. *Look for common subexpressions in an expression.* If the result of a common subexpression (an expression appearing more than once) is not a large relation, and it can be read from secondary memory in much less time than it takes to compute it, then it is advantageous to precompute the common subexpression once. Subexpressions involving a join that cannot be modified by moving a selection inside it generally fall in this category. Common subexpressions will appear frequently when queries are expressed in terms of views, since we must substitute the same expression for each occurrence of the view. If several queries are part of one compiled program, then we also have the opportunity of looking for common subexpressions among all of the queries at once.

11.7 AN ALGORITHM FOR OPTIMIZING RELATIONAL EXPRESSIONS

We can apply the laws of Section 11.6 to "optimize" relational expressions. The resulting "optimized" expressions obey the principles set down in that section, although they are in no sense guaranteed to be optimal over all equivalent expressions. We shall attempt to move selections and projections as far down the parse tree of the expression as we can, although we want a cascade of these operations to be organized into one selection followed by one projection. We also group selections and projections with the preceding binary operation—union, product, join, or difference—where possible.

Some special cases occur when a binary operation has operands that are selections and/or projections applied to leaves of the tree. We must consider carefully how the binary operation is to be done, and in some cases we wish to incorporate the selection or projection into the binary operation. For example, if the binary operation is union, we can incorporate selections and projections below it in the tree with no loss of efficiency, as we must copy the operands anyway to form the union. However, if the binary operation is Cartesian product, with no following selection to make it an equijoin, we would prefer to do selection and projection first, leaving the result in a temporary relation, as the size of the operand relations greatly influences the time it takes to execute a full Cartesian product.

The output of our algorithm is a *program*, consisting of the following kinds of steps.

1. The application of a single selection or projection,
2. The application of a selection followed by a projection, or
3. The application of a Cartesian product, union, or set difference to two operands, perhaps preceded by selections and/or projections applied to one or both operands, and possibly followed by these operations.

We assume steps (1) and (2) are implemented by a pass through the operand relation, creating a temporary relation. Steps of type (3) are implemented by applying selection and/or projection to each tuple of operand relations, if appropriate, each time the operand tuple is accessed, and applying the following selection and/or projection, if appropriate, to each tuple generated as part of the resulting relation. The result goes into a temporary relation.

Algorithm 11.2: Optimization of Relational Expressions.

INPUT: An expression of relational algebra.

OUTPUT: A program for evaluating that expression.

METHOD: Perform each of the following steps, in order.

1. Use rule (4) to separate each selection $\sigma_{F_1 \wedge \cdots \wedge F_n}(E)$ into the cascade

   $$\sigma_{F_1}(\cdots(\sigma_{F_n}(E))\cdots)$$

2. For each selection, use rules (4) through (9) to move the selection as far down the tree as possible.

3. For each projection, use rules (3), (10), (11), and the generalized rule (5) to move the projection as far down the tree as possible. Note that rule (3) causes some projections to disappear, while the generalized rule (5) splits a projection into two projections, one of which can be migrated down the tree if possible. Also, eliminate a projection if it projects an expression onto all its attributes.

4. Use rules (3)–(5) to combine cascades of selections and projections into a single selection, a single projection, or a selection followed by a projection. Note that this alteration may violate the heuristic "do projection as early as possible," but a moment's reflection will serve to convince one that it is more efficient to do all selections, then all projections, in one pass over a relation than it is to alternate selections and projections in several passes.

5. Partition the interior nodes of the resulting tree into *groups*, as follows. Every interior node representing a binary operator ×, ∪, or − is in a group along with any of its immediate ancestors that are labeled by a unary operator (σ or π). Also include in the group any chain of descendants labeled by unary operators and terminating at a leaf, except in the case that the binary operator is a Cartesian product and is not followed by a selection that combines with this product to form an equijoin.

6. Produce a program consisting of a step to evaluate each group in any order such that no group is evaluated prior to its descendant groups. □

Example 11.15: Let us consider a library database consisting of the following relations.

        BOOKS(TITLE, AUTHOR, PNAME, LC#)
        PUBLISHERS(PNAME, PADDR, PCITY)
        BORROWERS(NAME, ADDR, CITY, CARD#)
        LOANS(CARD#, LC#, DATE)

The attributes used above that are not self-explanatory are

PNAME	=	publisher's name
LC#	=	Library of Congress number
PADDR	=	street address of a publisher
PCITY	=	city in which a publisher is located
CARD#	=	library card number
DATE	=	date on which a book was borrowed

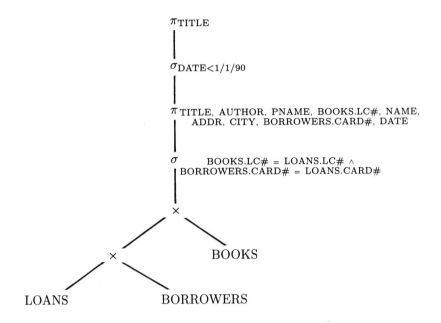

Figure 11.7 Parse tree of expression.

Suppose there is a view $XLOANS$ that contains additional information about books borrowed. $XLOANS$ is the natural join of $BOOKS$, $BORROWERS$, and $LOANS$, and it might, for example, be defined as

$$\pi_S\big(\sigma_F(LOANS \times BORROWERS \times BOOKS)\big)$$

where selection condition F is

BORROWERS.CARD# = LOANS.CARD#
$\wedge$ BOOKS.LC# = LOANS.LC#

while S is the list of attributes in the view

TITLE, AUTHOR, PNAME, LC#, NAME,
ADDR, CITY, CARD#, DATE

We might wish to list the books that were borrowed before some date, say 1/1/90, by posing the query

$$\pi_{\text{TITLE}}\big(\sigma_{\text{DATE}<1/1/90}(XLOANS)\big)$$

After substituting for $XLOANS$, the expression above has the parse tree shown in Figure 11.7.

The first step of the optimization is to split the selection F into two, with conditions BOOKS.LC# = LOANS.LC# and

BORROWERS.CARD# = LOANS.CARD#

respectively. Then we move each of the three selections as far down the tree as possible. The selection $\sigma_{\text{DATE}<1/1/90}$ moves below the projection and the two selections by rules (4) and (5). This selection then applies to the product $(LOANS \times BORROWERS) \times BOOKS$. Since DATE is the only attribute mentioned by the selection, and DATE is an attribute only of $LOANS$, we can replace

$$\sigma_{\text{DATE}<1/1/90}\big((LOANS \times BORROWERS) \times BOOKS\big)$$

by

$$\big(\sigma_{\text{DATE}<1/1/90}(LOANS \times BORROWERS)\big) \times BOOKS$$

then by

$$\Big(\big(\sigma_{\text{DATE}<1/1/90}(LOANS)\big) \times BORROWERS\Big) \times BOOKS$$

We have now moved this selection as far down the tree as possible. The selection with condition BOOKS.LC# = LOANS.LC# cannot be moved below either Cartesian product, since it involves an attribute of $BOOKS$ and an attribute not belonging to $BOOKS$.[18] However, the selection on

BORROWERS.CARD# = LOANS.CARD#

can be moved down to apply to the product

$$\sigma_{\text{DATE}<1/1/90}(LOANS) \times BORROWERS$$

Note that LOANS.CARD# is the name of an attribute of

$$\sigma_{\text{DATE}<1/1/90}(LOANS)$$

since it is an attribute of $LOANS$, and the result of a selection takes its attributes to be the same as those of the expression to which the selection is applied.

Next, we can combine the two projections into one, π_{TITLE}, by rule (3). The resulting tree is shown in Figure 11.8. Then by the extended rule (5) we can replace π_{TITLE} and $\sigma_{\text{BOOKS.LC\#}\,=\,\text{LOANS.LC\#}}$ by the cascade

π_{TITLE}
$\sigma_{\text{BOOKS.LC\#}\,=\,\text{LOANS.LC\#}}$
$\pi_{\text{TITLE, BOOKS.LC\#, LOANS.LC\#}}$

We apply rule (10) to replace the last of these projections by

---

[18] We could use the commutative and associative laws of products on the product $LOANS \times BORROWERS \times BOOKS$, and then move this selection down one level, but then we could not move the selection on BORROWERS.CARD# = LOANS.CARD# down.

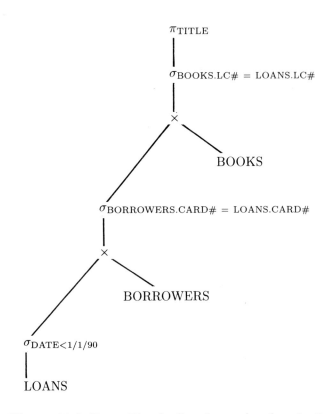

πTITLE

σBOOKS.LC# = LOANS.LC#

×

BOOKS

σBORROWERS.CARD# = LOANS.CARD#

×

BORROWERS

σDATE<1/1/90

LOANS

Figure 11.8 Tree with selections lowered and projections combined.

πTITLE, BOOKS.LC#

applied to *BOOKS*, and πLOANS.LC# applied to the left operand of the higher Cartesian product in Figure 11.8.

The latter projection interacts with the selection below it, by the extended rule (5), to produce the cascade

πLOANS.LC#
σBORROWERS.CARD# = LOANS.CARD#
πLOANS.LC#, BORROWERS.CARD#, LOANS.CARD#

The last of these projections passes through the Cartesian product by rule (10) and passes partially through the selection σDATE<1/1/90 by the extended rule (5). We then discover that in the expression

πLOANS.LC#, LOANS.CARD#, DATE

the projection is superfluous, since all attributes of *LOANS* are mentioned. We

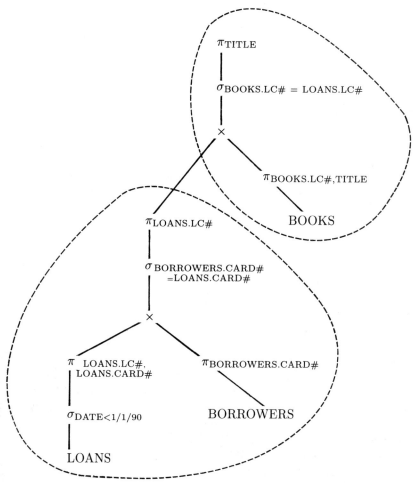

Figure 11.9 Final tree with grouping of operators.

therefore eliminate this projection. The final tree is shown in Figure 11.9. In that figure we have indicated groups of operators by dashed lines. Each of the Cartesian products is effectively an equijoin, when combined with the selection above. Obviously a program executing Figure 11.9 will perform the lower group of operations before the upper. $\square$

11.8 A MULTIWAY JOIN ALGORITHM

We now begin the study of the optimization algorithm used to process QUEL queries,[19] often called the Wong-Youssefi algorithm. In addition to using the

---

[19] QUEL is the language of the INGRES DBMS, and is described in Section 4.3.

idea that selections and projections should be performed as early as possible, the QUEL processor uses three other ideas that we have not yet encountered.

1. A heuristic for ordering the joins and products involved in a query.
2. Conversion of a join into a semijoin followed by a join.
3. A particular method for taking certain joins that involve three or more relations.

We shall begin by discussing the third of these points, in this section; the following section gives the complete algorithm.

Methods for Taking a Three-Way Join

Suppose we wish to take the natural join $Q(A, B) \bowtie R(B, C) \bowtie S(C, D)$. By the commutative and associative laws, we can join in any order we wish. The worst thing we could do is to start by taking $Q \bowtie S$, since this join is really a Cartesian product. Better is to take the join $Q \bowtie R$, and then join the result with S. Starting with $R \bowtie S$ is an equally good way, on the average, because of the symmetry of the situation. However, there is an approach, described below, that involves taking both joins at once, and this method is frequently better than any sequence of two joins.

To make the comparison simple, let us assume that all three relations, Q, R, and S, are of identical size; they each have T_0 tuples and can be stored packed in B_0 blocks. We also assume that the image size of each attribute in each relation is I_0, and we assume $I_0 \leq B_0$, so the simple formula (11.19) in Section 11.5 can be applied to determine costs. Finally, among the many possible assumptions we could make about indices, let us assume that there are clustering indices on B in Q and on C in S, and no others.

If we use the indexed-join method to join Q with R, then we incur cost

$$B_0 + 3B_0T_0/I_0$$

by (11.19). The output size for this join is $2B_0T_0/I_0$, by (11.14), and the number of tuples in the relation $Q \bowtie R$ is T_0^2/I_0. When we apply (11.19) again, this time to the join of the already computed relation $Q \bowtie R$ with relation S, we get a cost for this join of $2B_0T_0/I_0 + 4B_0T_0^2/I_0^2$. When we add the cost of the first join, we get a total cost for computing $(Q \bowtie R) \bowtie S$ of

$$B_0 + \frac{5B_0T_0}{I_0} + \frac{4B_0T_0^2}{I_0^2}$$

However, the above formula counts the writing of the intermediate relation $Q \bowtie R$ onto secondary storage, and then reading the same relation back into main memory. The total cost of the writing and reading is $4B_0T_0/I_0$. We can instead take the first join, $Q \bowtie R$, and the second join, $(Q \bowtie R) \bowtie S$, in an interleaved fashion, keeping tuples generated by the first join in main memory, and using them, as soon as possible, as input to the second join.[20] Hence, the true cost is the formula above, minus $4B_0T_0/I_0$, or

$$B_0 + \frac{B_0T_0}{I_0} + \frac{4B_0T_0^2}{I_0^2} \tag{11.27}$$

Had we joined $R \bowtie S$ first, we would have found the cost to be exactly the same.

However, there is a better way to compute the triple join $Q \bowtie R \bowtie S$. Run through all the tuples of R, and let bc be a typical tuple. Find all of the tuples ab in Q and all of the tuples cd in S, and produce all tuples of the form $abcd$ for the result. Formally

> **for** each tuple bc **in** R **do**
>   emit all the tuples in $\sigma_{B=b}(Q) \bowtie \{bc\} \bowtie \sigma_{C=c}(S)$ (11.28)

To understand the natural join in (11.28), we should realize that $\{bc\}$ is a relation over attributes BC, while the selections on Q and S produce relations over AB and CD, respectively.

The cost of (11.28), under the same assumptions as above, is easy to compute. We must, however, assume that the join in the body of (11.28) can be taken in main memory; that is, $2B_0/I_0 \leq M$. Under that additional constraint, we can use the clustering indices on $Q.B$ and $S.C$ to perform the selections $\sigma_{B=b}(Q)$ and $\sigma_{C=c}(S)$ in time B_0/I_0 each, and doing so we retrieve two groups of T_0/I_0 tuples each. The tuples emitted in the body of (11.28) thus number, on the average, T_0^2/I_0^2, and they therefore occupy $3B_0T_0/I_0^2$ blocks.[21] Thus, the output cost for the body of (11.28) is $3B_0T_0/I_0^2$, to which we must add the input cost, $2B_0/I_0$. Finally, we multiply by T_0, the number of times the loop is iterated, and we add B_0 for the cost of reading R, to get the cost of program (11.28), which is

$$B_0 + \frac{2B_0T_0}{I_0} + \frac{3B_0T_0^2}{I_0^2} \tag{11.29}$$

Depending on the ratio T_0/I_0, which of course cannot be less than 1, the value of (11.27) ranges from the same value as (11.29) [if $T_0 = I_0$] to 4/3 the value of (11.29) [if T_0 is much greater than I_0].

Thus we see the desirability of implementing a natural join of three rela-

---

[20] Not every join method allows this piping of arguments from one to the other, but the particular method we chose looks at each tuple of $Q \bowtie R$ only once, and the order of these tuples doesn't matter; thus, the technique works here.

[21] It would appear that tuples in the three-way natural join are only twice as long as tuples from the three relations, so $2B_0T_0/I_0^2$ blocks should serve. However, recall that, for uniformity, we have assumed throughout this chapter that joins preserve all components, as an equijoin would, rather than deleting redundant components as in a natural join. In particular, (11.27) is computed under that assumption.

tions, two of which have sets of attributes that do not overlap, by *decomposing* the relation that overlaps the other two, that is, by running through the tuples of the latter relation.

Decomposition Join

We can generalize the above simple example and generalize the join algorithm suggested by (11.28). Suppose we wish to compute $R \bowtie S_1 \bowtie \cdots \bowtie S_n$, where

1. S_i and S_j do not share an attribute, if $i \neq j$, and
2. R shares attributes with all of the S_i's.

R here corresponds to $R(B, C)$ in the above example, while the S_i's here are $Q(A, B)$ and $S(C, D)$ in the example.

```
for each tuple μ in R do begin
    for i := 1 to n do
        compute Tᵢ = Sᵢ ⋉ {μ};
        /* Tᵢ is those tuples of Sᵢ that agree with μ
           on the attributes Sᵢ shares with R */
    emit {μ} ⋈ T₁ ⋈ ⋯ ⋈ Tₙ
end
```

Figure 11.10 Decomposition join.

We can compute this expression by the *decomposition join* algorithm shown in Figure 11.10. The cost of decomposition join is a complex function of the set of available indices and the size parameters of the relations involved, as is its comparison with other approaches to computing the same expression. However, the example above is typical and suggests that decomposition join should be viewed favorably.

11.9 HYPERGRAPH REPRESENTATION OF QUERIES

When we present the query optimization used in QUEL, we shall use an entirely different notation from that found in the original description of the algorithm. We adopt the "hypergraph" notation to represent queries and use the semijoin as a fundamental operation, tools that, as we shall see, figure in several other query optimization algorithms as well. In this section, we shall introduce the hypergraph notation for queries.

Consider a query of the form

$$\sigma_{F_1 \wedge \cdots \wedge F_n}(R_1 \times \cdots \times R_k) \tag{11.30}$$

Each F_i may be an arbitrarily complex condition, but we assume it is not the logical AND of two or more conditions. The R_i's are not necessarily distinct relations. We construct for expression (11.30) a *hypergraph*, which is a graph whose "edges" are sets with any number of nodes; we call such an "edge" a *hyperedge*. This hypergraph, called the *connection hypergraph*, has a node for each attribute of each of the R_i's. If R_i and R_j each have attribute A, even if R_i and R_j are the same relation, we create different nodes for attributes $R_i.A$ and $R_j.A$.

However, if one of the F_j's is of the form $A = B$, where A and B are attributes, then we merge the nodes for A and B. Mergers are "transitive"; if among the F_j's are $A = B$ and $B = C$, then all of A, B, and C have their nodes merged into one.

The hyperedges of the connection hypergraph are formed from the F_j's and the R_i's, as follows.

1. For each R_i there is a hyperedge consisting of all the nodes for the attributes of R_i. We call these *relation hyperedges*, and we represent them by solid circles, or other closed shapes, enclosing all the nodes of the hyperedge.

2. For each F_j that is not of the form $A = B$, for variables A and B, nor of the form $A = a$, for constant a and variable A,[22] create a hyperedge containing all of the attributes mentioned in F_j. Such hyperedges are called *condition hyperedges*, and they are represented by dashed curves.

Note that the occurrence of two hyperedges consisting of the same set of nodes is possible, although two R_i's in a formula like (11.30) that are the same relation will have their attributes differently named and will not be identical in the hypergraph. However, we could have two conditions on the same sets of attributes, or a condition on the set of attributes of a single relation. In these cases, we shall have to name each of the hyperedges, so they are distinguished.

```
range of t is BOOKS
range of s is PUBLISHERS
range of u is BORROWERS
range of v is LOANS
retrieve(u.NAME)
    where t.LC# = v.LC#
          and u.CARD# = v.CARD#
          and t.PNAME = s.PNAME
          and u.CITY = s.PCITY
```

Figure 11.11 A QUEL program.

---

[22] When we say "of the form $A = a$," we include conditions where the constant appears first, as in $a = A$.

Example 11.16: Let us reconsider the relations of Example 11.15, and suppose we have the QUEL program of Figure 11.11. That is, print all persons who have borrowed a book published in the city in which they live. In algebra, this query is expressed by the Cartesian product

$$BOOKS \times PUBLISHERS \times BORROWERS \times LOANS$$

to which we apply the selection indicated in the where-clause and then project onto BORROWERS.NAME. The connection hypergraph for this query is shown in Figure 11.12.[23]

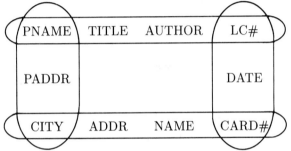

Figure 11.12 The connection hypergraph for the query of Figure 11.11.

To see how Figure 11.12 is obtained, notice that the first three conditions of the where-clause of Figure 11.11 equate attributes with the same name from different relations. For example, the first condition equates $BOOKS.LC\#$ with $LOANS.LC\#$. We therefore merge the nodes for these attributes, and we have chosen to call the merged node $LC\#$. The second and third conditions are treated similarly. In the fourth condition, we equate attributes with different names, $CITY$ and $PCITY$, and we have chosen to use the former name for the merged node. □

Example 11.17: Let us consider a more complex, abstract example of the connection hypergraph construction. Consider the Cartesian product

$$AB \times CDE \times FG$$

where relation names are relation schemes; for example, the first relation, AB, has attributes A and B. Let the selection condition

$$A = C \wedge (B < C \vee B < D) \wedge G < E \wedge F = f \wedge B = b \qquad (11.31)$$

be applied to this product. The corresponding connection hypergraph is shown in Figure 11.13.

---

[23] Strictly speaking, we have not yet discussed how the projection represented by the retrieve-clause of Figure 11.11 is to be represented. Temporarily, assume that the retrieval calls for all attributes.

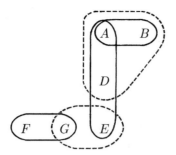

Figure 11.13 Connection hypergraph for selection (11.31).

The first condition in (11.31) tells us we must equate the nodes for attributes A and C; we have chosen A as the name of the merged node. The
second condition, $B < C \vee B < D$, is an example of a complex condition that
cannot be broken further into the AND of conditions. It is represented in Figure
11.13 by the dashed hyperedge containing A, B, and D. Note that A substitutes for C in this hyperedge, because we merged the nodes A and C, and we
called the resulting node A. The third condition of (11.31) is represented by the
hyperedge $\{E, G\}$. The last two conditions of (11.31), which equate variables
to constants, are not reflected in Figure 11.13. We shall see how such constants
are accounted for in the query-optimization process next. $\square$

11.10 THE QUEL OPTIMIZATION ALGORITHM

We shall now describe the Wong-Youssefi algorithm, introducing each of the
important notions in turn. We begin by describing how the algorithm is driven
by a process of reducing hypergraphs, where hyperedges are eliminated one-by-
one. We describe the way hyperedges are chosen for elimination, and we explain
how projections are incorporated into the queries represented by hypergraphs.
Finally, we state the algorithm formally, summarizing all of these ideas.

Notation

The QUEL optimization algorithm reduces the connection hypergraph by eliminating edges. At all times, we associate a relation $R(E)$ with each remaining
relation hyperedge E, and we associate a condition $C(E)$ with each condition
hyperedge E. The relation $R(E)$ may have its value changed from time to time,
although $C(E)$ never changes. We use $R_0(E)$ to denote the database relation
represented by the relation hyperedge E, initially; $R_0(E)$ also never changes.

We also use a relation-valued variable RESULT$(\mathcal{G})$ for each hypergraph $\mathcal{G}$
that we construct during the reduction process. The value of RESULT$(\mathcal{G})$ is
assigned once, and that value is intended to be the natural join of the relations
$R(E)$ for all the relation hyperedges E of $\mathcal{G}$, followed by the selection for the
conditions of the condition hyperedges of $\mathcal{G}$. While the value of $R(E)$ may

change, we use, in the above join, the value of $R(E)$ that existed at the time hypergraph $\mathcal{G}$ was created by the reduction process.

Initialization

Initially, $R(E)$, for relation hyperedge E, is formed by applying to $R_0(E)$ any selections for conditions of the form $A = a$, where a is a constant and A is an attribute of the represented relation. That is, initially, $R(E) = \sigma_F\big(R_0(E)\big)$, where F is the conjunction of all conditions in the query that equate an attribute of $R_0(E)$ to a constant.[24] The condition hyperedges initially, and forever, correspond to the selection conditions they represent.

Example 11.18: In Figure 11.12, the four relation hyperedges each correspond to their complete relations, BOOKS, for example, because there are no selection conditions that equate an attribute to a constant in the query of Figure 11.11.

In Figure 11.13, we have the following correspondences between hyperedges and relations.

1. Hyperedge $\{F, G\}$ represents FG; that is, $R_0(\{F, G\}) = FG$. Because of the selection condition $F = f$ in (11.31), we have $R(\{F, G\}) = \sigma_{F=f}(FG)$.
2. $R(\{A, D, E\})$ is the full relation CDE.
3. $R(\{A, B\}) = \sigma_{B=b}(AB)$.
4. Condition hyperedge $\{G, E\}$ represents condition $G < E$ from (11.31). That is, $C(\{G, E\}) = $ "$G < E$."
5. $C(\{A, B, D\}) = $ "$B < C \vee B < D$." $\square$

Reducing the Connection Hypergraph

We proceed to eliminate hyperedges from a connection hypergraph $\mathcal{G}$, one at a time, and as we do, we form the program $\text{PROG}(\mathcal{G})$ that will compute $\text{RESULT}(\mathcal{G})$. There is a basis case, where $\mathcal{G}$ consists of a single relation hyperedge E. Then, $\text{RESULT}(\mathcal{G})$ will be regarded as a synonym for $R(E)$, and $\text{PROG}(\mathcal{G})$ is empty. It turns out that there will never be a case where a reduced connection hypergraph consists of a single condition hyperedge and nothing else.

For each elimination, we add one or more steps to the program being formed, so that the relation for the old hypergraph can be computed from the relation for the new. The key to the Wong-Youssefi algorithm is the order in which hyperedge eliminations are performed; we discuss hyperedge ordering later in this section. The rules for performing the reductions are

---

[24] Conventionally, F is identically true if there are no such conditions. Also, the reader should understand that if two of the R_i's in the product of (11.30) are the same database relation, then the selection conditions F will specify which copy of that relation is meant, and it is only to the hyperedge corresponding to that copy that we apply the condition.

1. If a hypergraph $\mathcal{G}$ is the union of two or more disjoint hypergraphs, $\mathcal{H}_1, \ldots, \mathcal{H}_k$, then it is easy to see that

    $$\text{RESULT}(\mathcal{G}) = \text{RESULT}(\mathcal{H}_1) \times \cdots \times \text{RESULT}(\mathcal{H}_k)$$

    Thus, the program for $\mathcal{G}$ is

    $$\text{PROG}(\mathcal{H}_1); \ \text{PROG}(\mathcal{H}_2); \ \cdots \ ; \ \text{PROG}(\mathcal{H}_k);$$
    $$\text{RESULT}(\mathcal{G}) \ := \qquad\qquad\qquad\qquad\qquad (11.32)$$
    $$\text{RESULT}(\mathcal{H}_1) \times \text{RESULT}(\mathcal{H}_2) \times \cdots \times \text{RESULT}(\mathcal{H}_k)$$

2. If we eliminate from hypergraph $\mathcal{G}$ a condition hyperedge E, and the resulting hypergraph is $\mathcal{H}$, then $\text{PROG}(\mathcal{G})$ is

    $$\text{PROG}(\mathcal{H});$$
    $$\text{RESULT}(\mathcal{G}) \ := \ \sigma_{C(E)}\big(\text{RESULT}(\mathcal{H})\big) \qquad\qquad (11.33)$$

    It should be clear that $\text{RESULT}(\mathcal{G})$ is computed correctly by (11.33), if $\text{RESULT}(\mathcal{H})$ is correct.

3. Suppose we eliminate from hypergraph $\mathcal{G}$ a relation hyperedge E, and further suppose the resulting hypergraph consists of connected components $\mathcal{H}_1, \ldots, \mathcal{H}_k$; $k = 1$ is, of course, a possibility. Then $\text{PROG}(\mathcal{G})$ is

    > **for** each relation hyperedge F that intersects E **do**
    > $\quad R(F) \ := \ R(F) \ltimes R(E);$
    > $\text{PROG}(\mathcal{H}_1); \ \text{PROG}(\mathcal{H}_2); \ \cdots \ ; \ \text{PROG}(\mathcal{H}_k); \qquad (11.34)$
    > $\text{RESULT}(\mathcal{G}) \ := \ R(E) \bowtie \text{RESULT}(\mathcal{H}_1) \bowtie \cdots \bowtie \text{RESULT}(\mathcal{H}_k)$

    To see why (11.34) computes the desired relation for $\mathcal{G}$, note that replacing $R(F)$ by the semijoin $R(F) \ltimes R(E)$ cannot change the resulting relation, because a "dangling" tuple in $R(F)$ that does not join with any tuple in $R(E)$ surely could not participate in the join of the relations for all the relation hyperedges.

Finally, if $\mathcal{G}$ is the complete hypergraph for the query, then the program that answers the query is $\text{PROG}(\mathcal{G})$, preceded by any selections for conditions in the query that equate an attribute to a constant.

Example 11.19: Let us consider the connection hypergraph $\mathcal{H}$ of Figure 11.13, whose initial relations and conditions were given in Example 11.18. We have not yet discussed the order in which reductions are to be applied, so for the moment, let us simply pick an order in which to eliminate the hyperedges. First, we shall eliminate the condition hyperedge $\{G, E\}$, which leaves two disjoint components. One, which we shall call $\mathcal{H}_2$, has only hyperedge $\{F, G\}$, and the other is $\mathcal{H}_3 = \{\{A, D, E\}, \{A, B, D\}, \{A, B\}\}$. Let $\mathcal{H}_1$ be the union of $\mathcal{H}_2$ and $\mathcal{H}_3$; that is, $\mathcal{H}_1$ is $\mathcal{H}$ minus the condition hyperedge $\{G, E\}$. By (11.33), we must follow the program for $\mathcal{H}_1$ by the step

(1) $R(\{F, G\})$:= $\sigma_{F=f}(FG)$;
(2) $R(\{A, B\})$:= $\sigma_{B=b}(AB)$;
(3) $R(\{A, D, E\})$:= $CDE(A, D, E) \ltimes R(\{A, B\})$;
(4) RESULT($\mathcal{H}_4$) := $R(\{A, D, E\}) \bowtie R(\{A, B\})$;
(5) RESULT($\mathcal{H}_3$) := $\sigma_{B<C \vee B<D}\big(\text{RESULT}(\mathcal{H}_4)\big)$;
(6) RESULT($\mathcal{H}_1$) := $R(\{F, G\}) \times \text{RESULT}(\mathcal{H}_3)$;
(7) RESULT($\mathcal{H}$) := $\sigma_{G<E}\big(\text{RESULT}(\mathcal{H}_1)\big)$

Figure 11.14 Program for Figure 11.13.

$$\text{RESULT}(\mathcal{H}) \;:=\; \sigma_{G<E}\big(\text{RESULT}(\mathcal{H}_1)\big)$$

and by (11.32), the program for $\mathcal{H}_1$ is the programs for $\mathcal{H}_2$ and $\mathcal{H}_3$, followed by the step

$$\text{RESULT}(\mathcal{H}_1) \;:=\; \text{RESULT}(\mathcal{H}_2) \times \text{RESULT}(\mathcal{H}_3)$$

For $\mathcal{H}_2$, the base case applies, so RESULT($\mathcal{H}_2$) is just a synonym for $R(\{F, G\})$. Now, we must construct the program for $\mathcal{H}_3$. It turns out that the next hyperedge to eliminate is $\{A, B, D\}$, which leaves

$$\mathcal{H}_4 = \{\{A, D, E\},\; \{A, B\}\}$$

We use (11.34) to eliminate the hyperedge $\{A, B\}$. Since the resulting hypergraph is a single relation hyperedge, $\{A, D, E\}$, the computation of RESULT($\mathcal{H}_4$) is

$$R(\{A, D, E\}) \;:=\; R(\{A, D, E\}) \ltimes R(\{A, B\});$$
$$\text{RESULT}(\mathcal{H}_4) \;:=\; R(\{A, D, E\}) \bowtie R(\{A, B\});$$

These steps are followed by

$$\text{RESULT}(\mathcal{H}_3) \;:=\; \sigma_{B<C \vee B<D}\big(\text{RESULT}(\mathcal{H}_4)\big)$$

Finally, to get the program for the original query, we precede these steps by

$$R(\{F, G\}) \;:=\; \sigma_{F=f}(FG);$$
$$R(\{A, B\}) \;:=\; \sigma_{B=b}(AB);$$

As there are no selections of the form $A = a$ that apply to relation CDE, there is no initial assignment for hyperedge $\{A, D, E\}$. Thus, initially, $R(\{A, D, E\})$ is the relation CDE, but with attributes named A, D, and E. The complete program is shown in Figure 11.14.

This program does its selections as early as possible, so it is similar to what we would obtain from Algorithm 11.2, discussed in Section 11.7. However, there are two differences. First, line (3), the semijoin step, is not necessary, since on line (4), the result of line (3) is joined with the same relation, $R(\{A, B\})$, that was used in the semijoin on line (3). However, the semijoin on line (3) could make the join run faster, depending on the particular relations involved; the actual QUEL algorithm combines steps (3) and (4) anyway. The other difference is that Algorithm 11.2 combines the selection at line (7) with the product at line (6), to make a join. There is some advantage to doing so when the selection condition is not an equality, but when the selection is an equality, the savings are usually substantial. The QUEL algorithm also combines selections with a previous product or join, as in lines (4) and (5) and in lines (6) and (7). □

Small Relations

The QUEL optimization algorithm takes advantage of the typical query form, in which a selection greatly restricts the size of one relation. We may regard the result of that selection as "small." If the small relation needs to be joined with another relation, then it is likely that the result will be small as well, on the assumption that each tuple of one relation joins with only a few tuples of the other relation. The "smallness" of relations thus propagates. Sometimes, there are no selections of the form $A = a$ to begin with, so the QUEL algorithm starts by applying semijoins to reduce the size of one or more relations. Such reduced relations are also regarded as "small."

```
range of c is CUSTOMERS
range of o is ORDERS
range of i is INCLUDES
retrieve (c.CNAME, c.CADDR)
    where c.CNAME = o.CUST
        and o.O# = i.O#
        and i.INAME = "Brie"
```

Figure 11.15 Find the customers who ordered Brie.

Formally, we shall say a relation is *small* under the following conditions.

1. A relation is small if it is the result of the application of a selection of the form $A = a$ to any relation.

2. A relation R is small after its value has been computed by a semijoin $R \ltimes S$.

Note that there are other situations in which it makes sense to consider a relation "small," for example, if it is formed by selection and/or projection of a small relation, but such extensions of the idea do not figure into the QUEL optimization algorithm.

Example 11.20: Let us consider the three YVCB relations *CUSTOMERS*, *ORDERS*, and *INCLUDES*, last mentioned in Example 11.3 of Section 11.2. A typical query, "Find the names and addresses of all the customers who ordered Brie," is shown in Figure 11.15, and its hypergraph is shown in Figure 11.16. There, we use CNAME for the attribute of that name in *CUSTOMERS* and for the attribute CUST of *ORDERS*, to which CNAME is equated by the where-clause in Figure 11.15. O# is used for the attribute with that name in both *ORDERS* and *INCLUDES*, since these attributes are likewise equated in Figure 11.15.

for CUSTOMERS   for ORDERS   for INCLUDES

Figure 11.16 Hypergraph for query of Figure 11.15.

The only selection that equates an attribute to a constant applies to the *INCLUDES* relation, where tuples are selected for INAME = "Brie." Thus, initially, only the hyperedge for *INCLUDES* is small. As we shall see, the Wong-Youssefi algorithm favors eliminating a hyperedge with a small relation. Thus, the next step in evaluating the query of Figure 11.15 would be to apply (11.34) with E being the hyperedge for *INCLUDES*. Rule (11.34) applies a semijoin to the hyperedge $\{CNAME, DATE, O\#\}$ for *ORDERS*, so the relation for that hyperedge becomes small. Next, (11.34) is applied to the hyperedge for *ORDERS*, which results in a semijoin applied to *CUSTOMERS*; therefore, that relation becomes small. The resulting program is shown in Figure 11.17.[25] We name hyperedges by their associated relation; we refer to the entire hypergraph as $\mathcal{G}$, and the two hyperedges on the left as $\mathcal{H}$.

In Figure 11.17, we have not accounted for the projection implied by the retrieve-clause of Figure 11.15; we take that matter up next. Notice, however, that Figure 11.17 is likely to be an efficient way to implement the query, since we can expect only a small fraction of the *INCLUDES* tuples will be for Brie, only a small fraction of the orders will include Brie, and a minority of the customers will order Brie at any one time. Thus, the selection and semijoins cut down the sizes of their relations significantly, and the relations we call "small"

---

[25] The Wong-Youssefi algorithm combines the third and fourth statements here, to avoid a semijoin immediately followed by a join of the same relations, just as steps (3) and (4) of Figure 11.14 are combined.

$$R(INCLUDES) := \sigma_{\text{INAME=``Brie''}}(INCLUDES);$$
$$R(ORDERS) := ORDERS \ltimes R(INCLUDES);$$
$$R(CUSTOMERS) := CUSTOMERS \ltimes R(ORDERS);$$
$$\text{RESULT}(\mathcal{H}) := R(CUSTOMERS) \bowtie R(ORDERS);$$
$$\text{RESULT}(\mathcal{G}) := \text{RESULT}(\mathcal{H}) \bowtie R(INCLUDES);$$

Figure 11.17 Program for query of Figure 11.15.

really are significantly smaller than the relations from which they were derived.
□

Handling Projections

When the query does not call for a relation over all of the attributes in the hypergraph, we must modify our rules for hyperedge elimination so that at each step we deal with only those attributes that the constructed program will later need. Thus, we "push projections as far down the tree as possible." The key to doing so easily is the notion of a *distinguished node*. Intuitively, distinguished nodes of a hypergraph $\mathcal{G}$ are those that must be attributes of RESULT($\mathcal{G}$). The rules for when a node is distinguished are

1. If $\mathcal{G}$ is the initial hypergraph for a query, then node N is distinguished if and only if N represents an attribute mentioned in the retrieve-clause; that is, N is an attribute of the output relation.
2. If we form $\mathcal{H}$ by eliminating a hyperedge E from $\mathcal{G}$, then a node N is distinguished in $\mathcal{H}$ if and only if either N is distinguished in $\mathcal{G}$, or if N is in E (and is a node of $\mathcal{H}$, of course).
3. If $\mathcal{G}$ is the union of disjoint hypergraphs $\mathcal{H}_1, \ldots, \mathcal{H}_k$, then a node N is distinguished in $\mathcal{G}$ if and only if it is distinguished in whichever of the $\mathcal{H}_i$'s contains N.

Example 11.21: Let us reconsider the hypergraph $\mathcal{G}$ of Figure 11.16. According to the query of Figure 11.15, the only distinguished nodes of $\mathcal{G}$ are CNAME and CADDR, because these are mentioned in the retrieve-clause. When we eliminate hyperedge $INCLUDES$ to form $\mathcal{H}$, we make O# distinguished in $\mathcal{H}$, because it is in both $\mathcal{H}$ and in the eliminated hyperedge. CNAME and CADDR, being present in $\mathcal{H}$, are also distinguished nodes of that hypergraph. Finally, when we eliminate hyperedge $ORDERS$ from $\mathcal{H}$, we make CNAME distinguished in the remaining hypergraph (the hyperedge $CUSTOMERS$ alone), because CNAME was present in the eliminated hyperedge. However, CNAME would be distinguished anyway, because it is distinguished in $\mathcal{H}$. CADDR is also distinguished in the final hypergraph, which consists of only the hyperedge $CUSTOMERS$. □

To be sure the program we construct for a hypergraph projects out nondistinguished nodes as soon as possible, we shall design a procedure $EVAL$ that takes as arguments a hypergraph $\mathcal{G}$ and a set of distinguished nodes $\mathcal{D}$, and emits a program that computes $\text{RESULT}(\mathcal{G})$, projected onto the nodes of $\mathcal{D}$. There are three cases, analogous to the program fragments of (11.32), (11.33), and (11.34). In describing the calculation of distinguished nodes in these cases, it is useful to adopt the notation $\text{NODES}(\mathcal{G})$ for the set of nodes of hypergraph $\mathcal{G}$.

1. If $\mathcal{G}$ is the union of at least two disjoint hypergraphs $\mathcal{H}_1, \ldots, \mathcal{H}_k$, then $EVAL(\mathcal{G}, \mathcal{D})$ executes the steps of Figure 11.18(a). The appropriate sets of distinguished nodes for the $\mathcal{H}_i$'s are computed, $EVAL$ is called recursively on each to emit the appropriate program steps, and finally, the product step from (11.32) is emitted.

2. If from $\mathcal{G}$ we eliminate relation hyperedge E to form one or more disjoint, connected hypergraphs $\mathcal{H}_1, \ldots, \mathcal{H}_k$, then $EVAL(\mathcal{G}, \mathcal{D})$ executes the steps of Figure 11.18(b). These steps generate a program analogous to (11.34), with a final projection onto $\mathcal{D}$.

3. If $\mathcal{H}$ is formed from $\mathcal{G}$ by eliminating a condition hyperedge E, then $EVAL(\mathcal{G}, \mathcal{D})$ executes the steps of Figure 11.18(c). The recursive call to $EVAL(\mathcal{H}, \mathcal{E})$ emits $\text{PROG}(\mathcal{H})$, and the final step emits a statement that both performs the selection of (11.33) and projects the result onto $\mathcal{D}$.

All of these techniques are summarized in the following algorithm, which also explains how the hyperedges are ordered for removal.

Algorithm 11.3: QUEL Query Optimization Algorithm (Wong-Youssefi Algorithm).

INPUT: A project-select-product query, with the selection condition decomposed into conjuncts, as

$$\pi_\alpha\big(\sigma_{F_1 \wedge \cdots \wedge F_n}(R_1 \times \cdots \times R_k)\big)$$

OUTPUT: A program for computing the input expression.

METHOD: First, let us note that the actual algorithm does not generate a program, but rather executes the steps of the program we generate. It is hoped that by speaking in terms of constructing a program, we shall make the algorithm more understandable.

In what follows, we use the notation developed earlier in this section. In particular, for each relation hyperedge E, there is a program variable $R(E)$, and for each hypergraph $\mathcal{H}$ there is a program variable $\text{RESULT}(\mathcal{H})$.[26] We

---

[26] Sometimes, $R(E)$ or $\text{RESULT}(\mathcal{H})$ will stand for other variables that denote the intended relation. For example, $R(E)$ may stand for the relation named $R_0(E)$ at the beginning of the program, and $\text{RESULT}(\mathcal{H})$ may stand for $R(E)$, if $\mathcal{H}$ is only hyperedge E.

```
for i := 1 to k do begin
    𝓔ᵢ := 𝒟 ∩ NODES(ℋᵢ);
    EVAL(ℋᵢ, 𝓔ᵢ)
end;
emit "RESULT(𝒢) := RESULT(ℋ₁) × ⋯ × RESULT(ℋₖ)"
```

(a) Case of disjoint hypergraphs.

```
for each relation hyperedge F that intersects E do
    emit "R(F) := R(F) ⋈ R(E)";
for i := 1 to k do begin
    𝓔ᵢ := (𝒟 ∪ E) ∩ NODES(ℋᵢ);
    EVAL(ℋᵢ, 𝓔ᵢ)
end;
emit "RESULT(𝒢) :=
    π_𝒟(R(E) ⋈ RESULT(ℋ₁) ⋈ ⋯ ⋈ RESULT(ℋₖ))"
```

(b) Eliminating a relation hyperedge E.

```
𝓔 := (𝒟 ∪ E) ∩ NODES(ℋ);
EVAL(ℋ, 𝓔);
emit "RESULT(𝒢) := π_𝒟(σ_{C(E)}(RESULT(ℋ)))"
```

(c) Eliminating a condition hyperedge E.

Figure 11.18 The procedure $EVAL(\mathcal{G}, \mathcal{D})$.

describe the algorithm in three phases: initialization, hypergraph reduction, and a cleanup phase that compacts statements of the program in certain situations.

Phase I: *Initialization.* From the given expression, ignoring the projection, construct the connection hypergraph $\mathcal{G}_0$, according to the method of Section 11.9. Let $\mathcal{D}_0$ be the set of distinguished attributes for $\mathcal{G}_0$, that is, the set of attributes mentioned in the projection list α. For each relation hyperedge E in $\mathcal{G}_0$, if there are one or more selection conditions, say $F_{i_1}, \ldots, F_{i_m}$, that are of the form $A = a$, where A is an attribute of $R_0(E)$, and a is a constant, generate the program statement

$$R(E) := \sigma_{F_{i_1} \wedge \cdots \wedge F_{i_m}}(R_0(E))$$

Any such E now corresponds to a "small" relation, where "small" must be taken in the technical sense defined earlier in the section.

Other edges, those to which no selection of the form $A = a$ applies to their relation, are not initially small. $R(E)$ refers to the relation $R_0(E)$ in that case.

Phase II: *Hypergraph Reduction.* We apply the recursive procedure

$$EVAL(\mathcal{G}, \mathcal{D})$$

which we define below, to the hypergraph $\mathcal{G}_0$ and set of distinguished nodes $\mathcal{D}_0$, created in the initialization. In general, $EVAL(\mathcal{G}, \mathcal{D})$ returns RESULT($\mathcal{G}$), the name of the relation into which the program generated by $EVAL$ will compute the relation defined by $\mathcal{G}$ and $\mathcal{D}$. As we proceed, the hypergraph that is the first argument of $EVAL$ must indicate which are the edges E such that $R(E)$ is a small relation. We assume that such information is attached to hyperedges, although we do not represent it explicitly.

$EVAL$ is a recursive procedure, whose basis is a hypergraph that consists of one relation hyperedge E. Its action in that case is to generate no program steps, and to return as its result the relation name $R(E)$.[27]

The recursive portion of procedure $EVAL$ has three stages. First, we decide which of cases (a) to (c) of Figure 11.18 applies to $\mathcal{G}$. Then, in cases (b) and (c), we select the proper hyperedge to eliminate from $\mathcal{G}$. Finally, we do the steps indicated by the appropriate case in Figure 11.18. The details of the stages are

1. If $\mathcal{G}$ consists of two or more disjoint hypergraphs, then Case (a) applies. Stage 2 is absent, and in Stage 3 we execute the steps of Figure 11.18(a). Otherwise, $\mathcal{G}$ is a connected hypergraph. If $\mathcal{G}$ has at least one relation hyperedge that

   i)   Intersects at least one other relation hyperedge, but

   ii) Does not intersect any condition hyperedge,

   then in Stage 2, we chose to eliminate one of these relation hyperedges. If $\mathcal{G}$ is connected, but there are no relation hyperedges satisfying (i) and (ii), then in Stage 2 we shall eliminate a condition hyperedge. The only uncovered case is that $\mathcal{G}$ consists of exactly one relation hyperedge E. If so $EVAL$ returns $R(E)$ as the relation RESULT($\mathcal{G}$), as was mentioned above, concerning the basis.

2a. As mentioned in (1), if $\mathcal{G}$ consists of two or more disjoint hypergraphs, then Stage 2 is vacuous; we do not select a hyperedge for elimination.

2b. Here, there is at least one hyperedge that meets conditions (i) and (ii) mentioned in Stage 1, and we must choose one to eliminate. We proceed to remove from consideration some of the candidate hyperedges. The rules we follow, in order, are

---

[27] Note that we do not project single relations onto their distinguished attributes, relying on the algorithm to do the projection at a more convenient time, later. There is one exception, which must be treated as a special case. If $\mathcal{G}_0$ consists only of one hyperedge, then we must do the projection immediately.

$i)$ If any of the candidate hyperedges currently represent small relations, then remove from consideration all of the candidate hyperedges that are *not* small.

$ii)$ If any of the remaining candidate hyperedges will, when deleted from $\mathcal{G}$, disconnect $\mathcal{G}$ into two or more disjoint hypergraphs, then remove from consideration all hyperedges that *do not* disconnect $\mathcal{G}$.

$iii)$ If more than one candidate still remains, pick one arbitrarily.

Preference (i) enforces the heuristic that we should take advantage of small relations to reduce the size of other relations represented by the hypergraph. Preference (ii) reflects our desire to apply the efficient multiway join of Section 11.8, rather than successive two-relation joins.

2c.   Here, we found in Stage 1 that it is necessary to eliminate a condition hyperedge. If there are several candidates, consider the hypergraphs $\mathcal{H}_E$ that result if we delete candidate edge E from $\mathcal{G}$. If for any E, $\mathcal{H}_E$ allows an application of preference (i) from Stage 2(b), that is, a small relation's hyperedge may be eliminated from $\mathcal{H}_E$, then chose one such E arbitrarily. If none allow preference (i), but some allow preference (ii), then choose one of these. Otherwise, choose any condition hyperedge for elimination.

3.   In Stage 3, we apply to $\mathcal{G}$ whichever of cases (a)–(c) was chosen in Stage 1. In the last two cases, the edge E is the one selected in Stage 2. However, there are two exceptions in case (b). First, should some $\mathcal{H}_i$ consist of a single relation hyperedge F, then we omit the semijoin step,

$$R(F) := R(F) \ltimes R(E)$$

The reader should note that when we do perform the semijoin step in case (b), the relation $R(F)$ becomes a "small" relation. The second exception is that if $\mathcal{H}_i$ has no distinguished nodes, we omit it from the join in case (b).

Phase III. *Final Code Fixup.* If there is a statement of the form $R := Exp$, where Exp is any expression, and later a statement $T := \theta(R)$, where θ is a selection or projection, and R is not assigned between these two statements, then delete the second, and replace the first by $T := \theta(Exp)$.[28] [29] $\square$

We shall now give a series of examples that illustrate various aspects of Algorithm 11.3.

---

[28] The actual algorithm checks for this situation during its execution, but we find it easier to explain what is going on by deferring these details to a final "peephole optimization" phase at the end.

[29] Note that we never assign a relation name more than once, except in the case of a selection during initialization followed later by a semijoin, in Case 2(b). Since semijoin is not a unary operation, it cannot be θ. We conclude that R is not used, except in the computation of T, and therefore, eliminating the first statement cannot change what the program computes.

Example 11.22: Let us consider the hypergraph of Figure 11.13, which we introduced in Example 11.17 (Section 11.9). We shall assume that its query calls for a relation over all of the attributes, so all nodes are distinguished. The reader should review Figure 11.14, which is a program that solves this query, although it is not exactly the program generated by Algorithm 11.3.

In the initialization phase, we select for $F = f$ and $B = b$ on the relations FG and AB, respectively. Thus, we generate lines (1) and (2) of Figure 11.14. The hyperedges FG and AB initially represent small relations; ADE does not.

When we enter Phase II, we find in Stage 1 that we must eliminate a condition hyperedge, because all of the relation hyperedges intersect condition hyperedges. Then, in Stage 2(c), we consider the two candidates, $\{G, E\}$ and $\{A, B, D\}$. We find that the elimination of either allows the elimination of a relation hyperedge with a small relation, in the reduced hypergraph. We pick $\{G, E\}$ to eliminate, arbitrarily; this move exposes the small relation $\{F, G\}$.

We now have disjoint hypergraphs, as was discussed in Example 11.19. One of these is a single hyperedge, $\{F, G\}$, so the base case of $EVAL$ applies. The relation returned by $EVAL$ in Case (a) of Figure 11.18 (the case for disjoint hypergraphs) is $R(\{F, G\})$.

The other hypergraph, which we called $\mathcal{H}_3$ in Example 11.17, is

$$\mathcal{H}_3 = \{\{A, B\}, \{A, B, D\}, \{A, D, E\}\}$$

In Stage 1 we again find we must eliminate a condition hyperedge, and the only choice is $\{A, B, D\}$. When we do so, we have the hypergraph that was called $\mathcal{H}_4$ in Example 11.17, consisting of only the relation hyperedges $\{A, B\}$ and $\{A, D, E\}$. Only the former is small, so we choose to eliminate it in Stage 2(c). The code generated by Figure 11.18(b) is line (4) of Figure 11.14. Note that the semijoin step in Figure 11.18(b) is skipped (that is, line (3) of Figure 11.14 is not generated here), because $\mathcal{H}_4$ with $\{A, B\}$ deleted is only a single hyperedge, $\{A, D, E\}$, and the special case of Stage 2(b) applies. Also, when we call $EVAL$ on the remaining hypergraph $\{A, D, E\}$, the basis of $EVAL$ applies, and relation $R_0(\{A, D, E\}) = CDE(A, D, E)$ is returned.

Now, we complete the recursive call to $EVAL$ on the hypergraph $\mathcal{H}_3$, by applying the selection of line (5) in Figure 11.14; this step comes from Figure 11.18(c). Next, we finish the call to $EVAL$ on the pair of disjoint hypergraphs, $\mathcal{H}_3$ and $\{F, G\}$, which results in line (6) of Figure 11.14, due to the rule of Figure 11.18(a). Finally, we complete the call to $EVAL$ on the original hypergraph, yielding line (7) of Figure 11.14, from the rule of Figure 11.18(c).

Now, we enter Phase III. We find that lines (6) and (7) are an instance of the second rule, so we may apply the selection to RESULT$(\mathcal{H}_1)$ and make the product a $<$-join. We also combine the selection of step (5) with the join of step (4). The resulting code is shown in Figure 11.19. $\square$

$$R(\{F, G\}) \ := \ \sigma_{F=f}(FG);$$
$$R(\{A, B\}) \ := \ \sigma_{B=b}(AB);$$
$$\text{RESULT}(\mathcal{H}_3) \ := \ \sigma_{B<C \vee B<D}\big(CDE(A, D, E) \bowtie R(\{A, B\})\big)$$
$$\text{RESULT}(\mathcal{H}) \ := \ R(\{F, G\}) \underset{G<E}{\bowtie} \text{RESULT}(\mathcal{H}_3);$$

Figure 11.19 Final program for Figure 11.13.

Example 11.23: Let us reconsider the query of Figure 11.15, whose hypergraph $\mathcal{G}$ was given in Figure 11.16. As in Examples 11.20 and 11.21, we shall refer to the hyperedges of $\mathcal{G}$ by the relations, $CUSTOMERS$, $ORDERS$, and $INCLUDES$, to which they correspond.

We note that the selection for INAME = "Brie" in the query makes the relation $INCLUDES$ small in $\mathcal{G}$, and also accounts for the initial selection step

$$R(INCLUDES) \ := \ \sigma_{\text{INAME}=\text{"Brie"}}(INCLUDES)$$

The retrieve-clause makes nodes $CNAME$ and $CADDR$ distinguished in $\mathcal{G}$, as discussed in Example 11.21.

Thus, in Phase II we first eliminate the hyperedge $INCLUDES$, to form the hypergraph $\mathcal{H} = \{CUSTOMERS, \ ORDERS\}$. The reason is that we favor small relations in Stage 2(b). The distinguished nodes for $\mathcal{H}$ are $CADDR$, $CNAME$, and $O\#$, as was discussed in Example 11.21. The step

$$R(ORDERS) \ := \ ORDERS \ltimes R(INCLUDES)$$

is generated according to Figure 11.18(b), and as a result, $R(ORDERS)$ is considered small in $\mathcal{H}$.

Now, we favor elimination of the small relation $ORDERS$ from $\mathcal{H}$, resulting in the hypergraph $\mathcal{H}_1$ with only hyperedge $CUSTOMERS$ and distinguished nodes $CNAME$ and $CADDR$. In this case, the relation RESULT($\mathcal{H}_1$) is $CUSTOMERS$, and we use the special case of Figure 11.18(b), where the semijoin is omitted, to produce only the step

$$\text{RESULT}(\mathcal{H}) \ := \ $$
$$\pi_{\text{CNAME, CADDR, }O\#}\big(CUSTOMERS \bowtie R(ORDERS)\big)$$

In general, we would complete $EVAL$ on $\mathcal{G}$ by generating the statement

$$\text{RESULT}(\mathcal{G}) \ := \ \pi_{\text{CNAME, CADDR}}\big(\text{RESULT}(\mathcal{H}) \bowtie R(INCLUDES)\big)$$

However, one the the exceptions in Stage 3 applies, and $R(INCLUDES)$ is omitted from the join because it has no distinguished nodes.[30]

---

[30] Note that $O\#$ is distinguished only in $\mathcal{H}$.

The program generated by Phase II is shown in Figure 11.20. It is similar to Figure 11.17, but includes the steps needed to project out the nondistinguished attributes. In Phase III, the projections in the last two steps of Figure 11.20 are combined into a single projection. $\square$

$$R(INCLUDES) := \sigma_{\text{INAME="Brie"}}(INCLUDES);$$
$$R(ORDERS) := ORDERS \ltimes R(INCLUDES);$$
$$\text{RESULT}(\mathcal{H}) :=$$
$$\pi_{\text{CNAME, CADDR, O\#}}(CUSTOMERS \bowtie R(ORDERS));$$
$$\text{RESULT}(\mathcal{G}) := \pi_{\text{CNAME, CADDR}}(\text{RESULT}(\mathcal{H}))$$

Figure 11.20 Application of Algorithm 11.3 to query of Figure 11.15.

Example 11.24: Suppose we eliminate the condition INAME = "Brie" in Figure 11.15. Then $\mathcal{G}$ has no small relations, so in Stage 2(b) we pick the one hyperedge, $ORDERS$, that disconnects $\mathcal{G}$. The recursive calls to $EVAL$ are on single hyperedges, $CUSTOMERS$ and $INCLUDES$, so the entire program consists of the step

$$\text{RESULT}(\mathcal{G}) :=$$
$$\pi_{\text{CNAME, CADDR}}(CUSTOMERS \bowtie ORDERS \bowtie INCLUDES)$$

This triple join is taken by the multiway join method of Section 11.8, which is applicable because $CUSTOMERS$ and $INCLUDES$ do not have attributes in common (if they did, then $ORDERS$ would not have disconnected $\mathcal{G}$). $\square$

11.11 QUERY OPTIMIZATION IN DISTRIBUTED DATABASES

In the following sections, we shall discuss some query optimization algorithms that are suitable for a distributed environment, such as that covered in Chapter 10 (Volume I). The principal distinction between distributed and nondistributed query processing is that when the database and its processors are distributed, it is usually very expensive to move data from one site to another. Thus, the cost measure we seek to optimize is less a function of processing time than of the amount of data transmitted.

Fragments

We shall begin by discussing the way relations can be broken into "fragments," which are then distributed to various nodes of the distributed database. We take the viewpoint that there are *logical* relations in the database that do not really exist, but that are composed of fragments, principally by the union and natural join operators. Queries and updates are made by the user on the logical relations. There are also *physical* relations that actually exist in the database, and these are fragments of the logical relations. The distinction between "logical" and "physical" data here is akin to the view/conceptual distinction introduced in Section 1.2 (Volume I), rather than to the conceptual/physical distinction, even though we shall often refer to the actual data as "physical."

Any relation may be composed of *fragments*. We consider two methods of composing relations.

1. A relation R may be the natural join of several fragments,

   $$R = R_1 \bowtie \cdots \bowtie R_n$$

   If we view R as a table, the R_i's each represent a set of columns of the table, so we call them *vertical fragments* of R.

2. A relation R may be the union of several fragments, $R = R_1 \cup \cdots \cup R_n$. Here, the table for R has been divided by rows, so we call the R_i's *horizontal fragments*. We do not necessarily assume that the R_i's are disjoint.

Each logical relation of the distributed database is assumed to be composed of fragments (there could be only one), and each fragment might exist at a different node. Moreover, some fragments might themselves be logical relations, built from fragments, and so on.

Example 11.25: The database of a bank is likely to be distributed, since it is natural that each branch would maintain the data that pertained to its own accounts and loans. The benefit in doing so is that customers banking at their usual branch could make transactions without necessarily communicating over a link. So doing may save a small amount of time, but more importantly, it limits the amount of traffic sent over the relatively low-capacity links.

ACCOUNTS(BRANCH, A#, BALANCE)
LOANS(BRANCH, L#, AMOUNT)
HOLDS(A#, CNAME)
OWES(L#, CNAME)
CUSTOMERS(CNAME, ADDRESS)

Figure 11.21 Relations of a bank's database.

Suppose we have the logical relations shown in Figure 11.21. We shall assume that the $ACCOUNTS$ and $LOANS$ relations are broken into horizontal fragments, one for each branch, and that in particular, a tuple μ with $\mu[BRANCH] = b$, that is, an account at branch b, is stored in fragment $ACCOUNTS_b$, which is located in the node at branch b. Similarly, the $LOANS$

relation is composed of horizontal fragments $LOANS_b$ for each branch b, with loans by branch b physically located at b.

The $HOLDS$ and $OWES$ relations are similarly fragmented horizontally into relations $HOLDS_b$ and $OWES_b$ for the accounts and loans made by each branch. The $CUSTOMERS$ relation might be horizontally fragmented as well, perhaps with the tuple for a customer duplicated if he had accounts or loans at more than one branch, so that address data would be available at any branch likely to need such data. However, for the sake of an example, we shall assume that the $CUSTOMERS$ relation is not fragmented at all, but is kept as a physical relation at the main branch.

In the above, all fragments are horizontal fragments. However, any time we wish to have a view that is the join of two or more physical relations, we have a vertical decomposition. For example, we might like a view that was the natural join of $HOLDS$ and $CUSTOMERS$, so addresses would appear with accounts as if in one relation. Then $HOLDS$ and $CUSTOMERS$ would be vertical fragments of this view. These vertical fragments would be distributed over several nodes, since we have assumed that $CUSTOMERS$ is kept at the main branch, while $HOLDS$ is itself distributed among all of the branches. Example 11.26 will give another motivation for vertical fragmentation; such fragmentation helps when we try to optimize certain queries. □

Queries Involving Fragments

Let us assume that the user "sees" the logical relations and performs queries on the logical relations only. We shall begin from the point we were at in Section 11.6, where we have an algebraic expression representing a query, and we wish to use algebraic manipulation to convert the query into one that could be executed faster. Here, a query is expressed in terms of the logical relations, and the logical relations are expressed in terms of their fragments, using the operations of union and natural join.

In this manner, we construct an expression whose operands are the physical relations. We can apply the transformations of Section 11.6, chiefly the pushing of selections as far down the expression tree as possible. The order and exact method of implementing the operators of the transformed tree still require careful consideration, and we shall examine the issues in the next sections.

Guard Conditions

Associated with a horizontal fragment we often find a *guard* condition that must be satisfied by every tuple in the fragment. For example, the fragment $ACCOUNT_b$ in the banking database of Example 11.25 has the guard $BRANCH = b$. That is, we know the value of the branch in the fragment at branch b is b itself. We shall henceforth assume that each logical and physical relation has a guard; it could be the always-true condition, which is tantamount to no guard at all.

In general, if a fragment R has guard g, then we can replace any use of R in an expression by $\sigma_g(R)$, without changing the result of the expression. When we pass other selections down the tree, we may find that a selection applied to R conflicts with g. If so, we can eliminate R from the expression entirely.

Example 11.26: Consider the banking database from Example 11.25. Suppose there are three branches, which we shall designate 1, 2, and 3. The query of concern is to print all of the customers who hold an account at branch 1 with a balance greater than $1000.

Interestingly, if we use the fragmentation scheme described in Example 11.25, we shall not do very well, because we shall not be able to express the fact that the fragments of *HOLDS* at branches 2 and 3 contain no tuples for accounts at branch 1. The reason is that BRANCH is not an attribute of *HOLDS*, and we therefore cannot express the desired condition with a guard condition. Thus, we might wish to redesign the fragmentation scheme to enable this condition to be expressed.

In our new design, we shall use a logical relation

R(BRANCH, A#, BALANCE, CNAME)

R is fragmented horizontally into R_1, R_2, and R_3, with the tuples in R_b having value b in the BRANCH component. Further, each R_b is fragmented vertically into A_b, with attributes BRANCH, A#, and BALANCE, and H_b with attributes A# and CNAME. These fragments substitute for *ACCOUNTS* and *HOLDS*, respectively, in the scheme of Example 11.25.

We shall put the guard $BRANCH = b$ on R_b. Thus, in place of R_1 we use $\sigma_{\text{BRANCH}=1}(R_1)$, and so on. In terms of physical fragments, we use

$\sigma_{\text{BRANCH}=1}(A_1 \bowtie H_1)$

for R_1, and of course, we use $R_1 \cup R_2 \cup R_3$ for R in the query

$\sigma_{\text{BRANCH}=1 \wedge \text{BALANCE}>1000}(R)$

The expression tree for this query, in terms of the physical fragments, is shown in Figure 11.22.

The upper selection, $\sigma_{\text{BRANCH}=1}$, can be pushed down past the union in Figure 11.22. As selections should be, it is pushed down every subtree to which it applies. The attribute BRANCH is, naturally, present in all three terms of the union, so the selection is pushed down to each child of the union node in Figure 11.22. On meeting $\sigma_{\text{BRANCH}=2}$ and $\sigma_{\text{BRANCH}=3}$ in the second and third subtrees, it combines to get a vacuous condition like $\sigma_{\text{BRANCH}=1 \wedge \text{BRANCH}=2}$.[31]

---

[31] Testing for conditions that are never true is hardly trivial in general. However, in

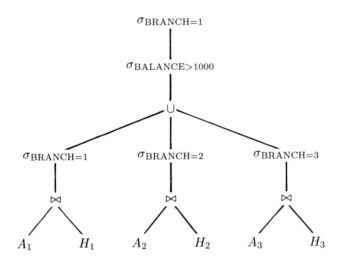

Figure 11.22 Initial algebraic expression.

We can therefore excise the second and third subtrees, whereupon the union is left with only one term and can be eliminated.

When we pass the top selection down to the first subtree, it combines with an identical selection to form one instance of the selection $\sigma_{\text{BRANCH}=1}$. Since the latter condition is the guard for $A_1 \bowtie H_1$, it is optional, and we can choose to delete it after it has interacted with all other selections. We shall therefore assume that the selection $\sigma_{\text{BRANCH}=1}$ is no longer present. The selection $\sigma_{\text{BALANCE}>1000}$ is pushed down to the relation A_1 only, since $BALANCE$ is not an attribute of H_1. The final tree is shown in Figure 11.23.

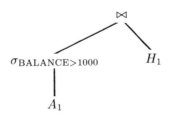

Figure 11.23 Final expression.

practice, noticing terms of the form $X = a \wedge X = b$, where $a \neq b$, or more generally, $X \ \theta_1 \ a \wedge X \ \theta_2 \ b$, where both conditions cannot be true simultaneously, is probably sufficient.

In general, we still must consider the order of operations, the use of indices, and many other optimization issues on trees like Figure 11.23. In this case, however, all of the physical relations that remain are at one node, that of branch 1, and the optimization may proceed as for nondistributed queries. $\Box$

Updates to Logical Relations

Let us now briefly consider how updates to logical relations are performed. To insert a tuple μ into logical relation R, we must insert into some fragments of R. We shall define the algorithm recursively, so the insertion of μ results in insertions into one or more fragments of R. If these fragments are physical relations, the meaning of insertion is obvious. If they are logical relations, apply the insertion algorithm recursively.

If $R = R_1 \bowtie \cdots \bowtie R_n$, then insert $\mu[R_i]$ into R_i for each i. If

$$R = R_1 \cup \cdots \cup R_n$$

find one i such that the guard for R_i is satisfied by μ, and insert μ into R_i. If no such i exists, the insertion is impossible. If we have a choice of i's, we would prefer to insert into a local fragment, that is, one at the same node as the insertion request, to save time sending messages.

Deletion of tuple μ from R presents more of a problem. If R is composed of horizontal fragments, then we simply delete μ from each of those fragments in which it is present. However, if R is fragmented vertically, we do not know what to do. If we simply delete $\mu[R_i]$ from R_i for each i, we shall accidentally delete from R all tuples ν such that $\nu[R_i] = \mu[R_i]$ for some i.

The solution used in System R* is to create for each tuple inserted into logical relation R a unique *tuple identifier*. In effect, the relation scheme for R is given another attribute TID that functionally determines all of the other attributes. Furthermore, every vertical fragment of R must include TID in its scheme. Thus, when inserting a tuple μ into R, the system invents a unique tuple identifier value for μ, and inserts the projections of μ, with the TID value included, into all of the fragments of R.

Now suppose we wish to delete a tuple μ from R. We find for each R_i the set S_i of tuples $ab_1b_2 \cdots b_k$ in R_i, such that a is the TID component, and

$$b_1 \cdots b_k = \mu[R_i]$$

Having obtained the set S_i for each R_i, we take the natural join

$$S_1 \bowtie \cdots \bowtie S_n$$

The result will be zero or more tuples of the form $a\mu$, where a is a tuple identifier, and μ is the tuple we are trying to delete. We now know the tuple identifier or identifiers (if μ appeared more than once in R) for μ, and we can delete $a\mu[R_i]$ from R_i, $i = 1, 2, \ldots, n$, for each such a.

11.12 ACYCLIC HYPERGRAPHS

In several of the algorithms to be discussed, there is a restriction on hypergraphs, called "acyclicity," that plays an important role. It appears that queries whose hypergraphs are "acyclic" have a number of optimization algorithms that are simpler and more efficient than is possible in the general case. In this section we shall define the concept and give some examples; subsequent sections will give the applications.

There are many equivalent definitions for the notion of "acyclic" hypergraph, in the sense relevant to database systems.[32] The definition we use here is probably the simplest; it is the generalization of the idea that in a tree (which is the only kind of connected, ordinary graph that is acyclic), we can remove leaves, one at a time, until there is nothing left.

GYO Reduction

Let E and F be two hyperedges, and suppose that the attributes in $E - F$ are *unique to* E; that is, they appear in no hyperedge but E. Then we call E an *ear*, and we term the removal of E from the hypergraph in question *ear removal*. We sometimes say "E is removed in favor of F" in this situation. As a special case, if a hyperedge intersects no other hyperedge, then that hyperedge is an ear, and we can remove that hyperedge by "ear removal."

The *GYO-reduction* of a hypergraph[33] is obtained by applying ear removal until no more removals are possible. A hypergraph is *acyclic* if its GYO-reduction is the empty hypergraph; otherwise, it is *cyclic*.

Different sequences of ear removals will lead to the same irreducible hypergraph, so the GYO-reduction of a hypergraph is unique. In proof, note that a potential removal will still be possible if another removal is chosen. For example, suppose E_1 could be removed in favor of E_2. If we do an ear removal of a hyperedge other than E_2, we can still remove E_1. The hard case is when we first remove E_2 in favor of some E_3. We need to show $E_1 - E_3 \subseteq E_1 - E_2$, so E_1 is still an ear and can be removed in favor of E_3. Suppose not. Then there is some node N in $E_1 - E_3$ that is not in $E_1 - E_2$. Thus, N is in E_1 and E_2, but not in E_3. It follows that $E_2 - E_3$ has a node, N, that is not unique to E_2, contradicting the assumption that E_2 was an ear that could be removed in favor of E_3. We have thus proved

---

[32] None of these definitions, incidentally, is equivalent to the one generally used by graph theorists.

[33] The term "GYO-reduction" is an acronym for the people who introduced the concept. Graham [1979] is the first known work to study this process in the context of hypergraphs for queries, while Yu and Ozsoyoglu [1979] studied the same process from a slightly different point of view. Interestingly, equivalent ideas were used in statistics from the early 1970's; see the bibliographic notes.

Theorem 11.3: The GYO-reduction of a hypergraph is unique, independent of the sequence of ear removals chosen. □

Example 11.27: The hypergraph of Figure 11.12 (Section 11.9) is cyclic, and in fact, no ear removals are possible. Let us name the hyperedges by the relations from which they came; $PUBLISHERS$ is on the left, $BOOKS$ on top, $LOANS$ on the right, and $BORROWERS$ at the bottom. We cannot eliminate $BOOKS$ in favor of $PUBLISHERS$, for example, because

$$BOOKS - PUBLISHERS$$

includes attribute LC#, which is also an attribute of $LOANS$. Similarly, we cannot eliminate $BOOKS$ in favor of $LOANS$, because $BOOKS - LOANS$ includes attribute PNAME of $PUBLISHERS$.

A similar argument applies to each of the four hyperedges in Figure 11.12. Thus, that hypergraph is its own GYO-reduction. Since the GYO-reduction is not empty, the hypergraph is cyclic. □

Example 11.28: Consider the hypergraph of Figure 11.13, also from Section 11.9. $\{F, G\}$ is an ear, because $\{F, G\} - \{G, E\} = \{F\}$, and F is unique to hyperedge $\{F, G\}$. In the hypergraph with $\{F, G\}$ removed, $\{G, E\}$ is an ear and can be removed in favor of $\{A, D, E\}$.

Since $\{A, B\} - \{A, B, D\} = \emptyset$, we may remove $\{A, B\}$. Now, either of $\{A, B, D\}$ and $\{A, D, E\}$ may be removed in favor of the other, leaving only a single hyperedge. A lone hyperedge may always be removed; that fact is the special case in the definition of ear removal. Thus, we have reduced Figure 11.13 to the empty hypergraph, and we conclude that it is acyclic. □

Example 11.29: Consider the strange hypergraph of Figure 11.24(a). This hypergraph appears to have a cycle, consisting of $\{A, B, C\}$, $\{C, D, E\}$, and $\{A, E, F\}$. In fact, if the hypergraph consisted of only these three hyperedges, it would indeed be cyclic, as the reader may check.

However, with the hyperedge $\{A, C, E\}$ included, we find that $\{A, B, C\}$ is an ear, because $\{A, B, C\} - \{A, C, E\} = \{B\}$, and B appears only in $\{A, B, C\}$. Similarly, $\{C, D, E\}$ and $\{A, E, F\}$ are ears, and their removal leaves only the hyperedge $\{A, C, E\}$, which can be removed as can any lone hyperedge. Thus, Figure 11.24(a) is acyclic.

Figure 11.24(b) helps explain the "paradox," since it redraws the same hypergraph in a more tree-like form, with $\{A, C, E\}$ at the center. However, we should be aware of a subtlety brought out by this example; unlike ordinary graphs, it is possible for an acyclic hypergraph to have a subgraph that is cyclic. □

11.13 OPTIMIZING TRANSMISSION COST BY SEMIJOINS

We saw in Section 11.10 how the Wong-Youssefi algorithm frequently reduces

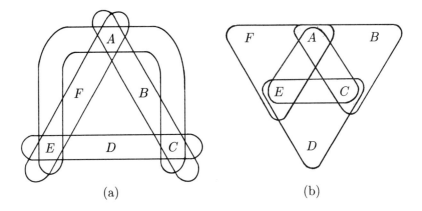

(a)   (b)

Figure 11.24 An acyclic hypergraph.

the size of a relation by applying the semijoin. However, in the uniprocessor environment for which that algorithm was designed, it generally doesn't matter whether or not we apply semijoins in simple situations, such as a hypergraph consisting of only two hyperedges, R and S. We specified Algorithm 11.3 to avoid the semijoin in this case; that is, we simply compute $R \bowtie S$ and take the projection onto the distinguished nodes.

However, in a distributed environment where transmission cost must be minimized, it is often more efficient to take the semijoin. That is, we should compute the value of $R \bowtie S$ by computing $(R \ltimes S) \bowtie S$ or $(S \ltimes R) \bowtie R$. Suppose that R and S are relations or fragments found at different sites, consisting of T_R and T_S tuples, respectively. Also assume that the cost of transmitting n tuples is $c_0 + n$, in appropriate units; c_0 is a fixed overhead cost charged to each transmission, and n represents the incremental cost of transmitting the n tuples.

If we transmit T_R to the site of S and take the join there, the cost is $c_0 + T_R$, and if we instead transmit S to the site of R, we pay $c_0 + T_S$. Thus, the transmission cost of taking the join in one of the obvious ways is

$$c_0 + \min(T_R, T_S)$$

Another approach is to project one relation, say S, onto the common attributes, $R \cap S$, and ship it to the site of the other relation, R. There, we use the natural join to filter out from R all those tuples that are "dangling," that is, they agree with no tuple of S. That is, we compute $R \ltimes S$ at the site of R. Then we ship $R \ltimes S$ to the site of S, and join it with S. Since

$$(R \ltimes S) \bowtie S = R \bowtie S$$

(because only dangling tuples are removed from R by the semijoin), we have computed $R \bowtie S$ at the site of S. In summary, the five steps taken are

1. Compute $\pi_{R \cap S}(S)$ at the site of S.[34]
2. Ship $\pi_{R \cap S}(S)$ to the site of R.
3. Compute $R \ltimes S$ at the site of R, using the fact that

$$R \ltimes S = R \bowtie \pi_{R \cap S}(S)$$

4. Ship $R \ltimes S$ to the site of S.
5. Compute $R \bowtie S$ at the site of S, using the fact that

$$R \bowtie S = (R \ltimes S) \bowtie S$$

There is a symmetric strategy, with R and S interchanged, of course.

The transmission cost of the above method is incurred at steps (2) and (4); as for the straightforward method, let us ignore the cost of calculation done locally. Let T'_S be the number of tuples in $\pi_{R \cap S}(S)$ and T'_R the number of tuples in $\pi_{R \cap S}(R)$.[35] Let T''_R be the number of tuples in $R \ltimes S$, and T''_S the number of tuples in $S \ltimes R$. Then the cost of step (2) above is $c_0 + T'_S$ and the cost of step (4) is $c_0 + T''_R$. When we consider the possibility of using the strategy with R and S interchanged, we conclude that the minimum transmission cost for the semijoin-based strategy is $2c_0 + \min(T'_S + T''_R,\ T'_R + T''_S)$. Thus, the semijoin strategy is more efficient than the straightforward method if

$$c_0 + \min(T'_S + T''_R,\ T'_R + T''_S) < \min(T_R, T_S) \qquad (11.35)$$

The conditions that help make (11.35) true are

1. The transmission overhead, c_0, is not great compared with the incremental cost of shipping a small number of tuples.
2. R and S are roughly the same size.
3. T'_S and T''_S are significantly less than T_S, and similarly for R. That is, each relation has many tuples that agree on the common attributes of R and S, and there are many dangling tuples.

Thus, there are times when the semijoin approach to the join of two relations is advantageous, and times when it is not. However, when more than two relations need to be joined, the opportunities for dangling tuples grow. The reason is that a tuple μ from one relation must find tuples from all of the other relations that agree on common attributes in all possible ways, if μ is to participate in a tuple of the result, that is, if μ is not a dangling tuple of the join.

---

[34] Recall that $R \cap S$ in the projection operation refers to the schemes of relations R and S, not to the current values of those relations.

[35] The tuples in the projections are, presumably, shorter than the tuples of R and S, but we shall, conservatively, assume they are the same length in the cost calculations to follow.

Thus, the more relations we join, the more opportunities there are to find and eliminate dangling tuples.

Semijoin Programs

We shall study the effects of different sequences of semijoins on a collection of relations $R_1, \ldots, R_k$ whose natural join we wish to compute. We write a semijoin step as $R_i := R_i \ltimes R_j$. However, the intention is not that the original relation R_i's value is changed, but that a temporary relation receives the new value.[36] A *semijoin program* is a sequence of semijoin steps.

Example 11.30: Consider the relations of Figure 11.25, and suppose that we wish to calculate the natural join $AB \bowtie BC \bowtie CD$. If the three relations are at different sites, we we may wish to execute some semijoin program, to reduce the number of tuples in the relations before shipping two of them to the site of the third.

A	B		B	C		C	D
1	2		1	2		1	2
2	4		2	4		2	4
3	6		3	6		3	6
4	8		4	8		4	8

Figure 11.25 Three relations to be joined.

For example, we could execute the program

$$
\begin{aligned}
AB &:= AB \ltimes BC \\
BC &:= BC \ltimes CD \qquad\qquad\qquad (11.36) \\
CD &:= CD \ltimes BC
\end{aligned}
$$

The first step eliminates tuples $(3, 6)$ and $(4, 8)$ from AB, and the second step does the same to BC. The third step eliminates $(1, 2)$ and $(3, 6)$ from CD. If we then take the join of the three relations, we find that the only tuple in the join $ABCD$ is $(1, 2, 4, 8)$. That is, tuple $(2, 4)$ is still dangling in both AB and BC, and tuple $(2, 4)$ continues to dangle in CD. Thus, the program (11.36) is somehow inadequate; it eliminated some, but not all, of the dangling tuples. □

---

[36] In Algorithm 11.3 we used temporary names like $R(E)$ for the current value of the relation corresponding to hyperedge E. The reader should suppose that here we likewise invent a new name to hold the result of each semijoin step.

Full Reducers

When we take the join $R_1 \bowtie \cdots \bowtie R_k$, the ideal condition is that there are no dangling tuples in any of the R_i's, for then, every tuple we ship between sites is essential. We call R_i *reduced* (with respect to the relations $R_1, \ldots, R_k$) if it has no dangling tuples; that is, $R_i = \pi_{R_i}(R_1 \bowtie \cdots \bowtie R_k)$. A semijoin program is called a *full reducer* for $R_1, \ldots, R_k$ if after executing that program, each R_i is reduced, independent of the initial values of the relations.

Example 11.31: We saw that (11.36) is not a full reducer. A full reducer for the relations of Figure 11.25 is

$$
\begin{aligned}
BC &:= BC \ltimes AB \\
CD &:= CD \ltimes BC \\
BC &:= BC \ltimes CD \\
AB &:= AB \ltimes BC
\end{aligned}
$$

We shall show in Theorem 11.4 that this program reduces AB, BC, and CD independent of the initial values of these relations, as is required for a program to be a full reducer. However, the reader can observe that it has the desired effect on the particular relations of Figure 11.25. The first step changes BC to $\{(2,4), (4,8)\}$, and the second then changes CD to have only the tuple $(4,8)$. At the third step, BC is further reduced to have only the tuple $(2,4)$, and finally, AB is reduced to the one tuple that agrees with it on B, which is $(1,2)$. Thus, the three relations have each been reduced to the one tuple that participates in the three-way join to yield the tuple $(1,2,4,8)$. $\square$

Unfortunately, not every set of relations has a full reducer, as the next example shows.

Example 11.32: Let our relations be AB, BC, and AC, and for some n, suppose the current values of these relations are $AB = \{a_1 b_1, a_2 b_2, \ldots, a_n b_n\}$, $BC = \{b_1 c_1, b_2 c_2, \ldots, b_n c_n\}$, and $AC = \{a_2 c_1, a_3 c_2, \ldots, a_{n+1} c_n\}$. A moment's reflection tells us that the join of these three relations is empty. However, it is also easy to show by induction on i, that after i steps of any semijoin program, no tuple will be deleted from any of the three relations unless it has a value with subscript i or less, or a subscript $n - i + 1$ or more. For example, $a_3 c_2$ could not be deleted until the second step. In fact, it takes six steps to delete that tuple from AC; the shortest such program is shown in Figure 11.26.

The conclusion we draw is that no one semijoin program can reduce even one of the relations AB, BC, and AC independently of their values. In proof, any such program would have some number of steps, say k. Then letting $n = 2k + 2$ above, we conclude that after k steps, the tuple $a_{k+1} b_{k+1}$ remains in AB, so the program did not reduce AB. Similarly, the tuples $b_{k+1} c_{k+1}$ and $a_{k+2} c_{k+1}$ say the same things about BC and AC.

If we change the tuple $a_{n+1} c_n$ to $a_1 c_n$ in relation AC, we see an even more

$$AB := AB \ltimes AC$$
$$BC := BC \ltimes AB$$
$$AC := AC \ltimes BC$$
$$AB := AB \ltimes AC$$
$$BC := BC \ltimes AB$$
$$AC := AC \ltimes BC$$

Figure 11.26 Semijoin program to eliminate tuple $a_3 c_2$ from relation AC.

serious phenomenon. The join $AB \bowtie BC \bowtie AC$ is still empty, but now, no semijoin step can change any of the three relations. The reason is that the set of values in the columns for the two occurrences of attribute A (in AB and AC) have the same set of values, $\{a_1, \ldots, a_n\}$, and a similar statement holds for B and C. Thus, not only is there no one semijoin program that reduces the relations independent of their initial values, but now there is no semijoin program at all that works for this initial database. $\square$

It turns out that the acyclicity property, introduced in the previous section, determines whether a join has a full reducer. We construct the hypergraph for the join as if it were a query, using the construction of Section 11.9. If the hypergraph is acyclic, then a full reducer exists, and it can be constructed by the method described in the theorem below. If the hypergraph is cyclic, then no full reducer exists.

Theorem 11.4: A join expression has a full reducer if and only if its hypergraph is acyclic.

Proof: The "only if" portion, showing that cyclic hypergraphs do not have full reducers, is left as a rather difficult exercise generalizing Example 11.32. Note that the hypergraph for that example, $\{\{A, B\}, \{B, C\}, \{A, C\}\}$, is cyclic.

However, the "if" part of the theorem is implied by the following algorithm for constructing a full reducer. The algorithm is defined inductively, starting with "joins" of a single relation R, for which the empty program suffices, and proceeding to progressively larger sets of relations that have an acyclic hypergraph.

Suppose we have an acyclic hypergraph $\mathcal{G}$ of more than one edge. Then by definition, it has an ear, say the hyperedge for relation S. As S is an ear, there must be some edge T such that each node in S is either unique to S or is in T. The remaining hypergraph $\mathcal{H}$, formed from $\mathcal{G}$ by removing hyperedge S and all nodes unique to S, must also be acyclic. By the inductive hypothesis, $\mathcal{H}$ has a full reducer. We precede the steps of the full reducer for $\mathcal{H}$ by $T := T \ltimes S$, and then follow it with the step $S := S \ltimes T$.

We claim that the resulting program is a full reducer for $\mathcal{G}$. Suppose there were a dangling tuple remaining in one of the relations. S cannot have a dangling tuple, since after the final step, every tuple μ in S agrees with some tuple ν of T, and, by the inductive hypothesis, ν, like any tuple of T, joins with tuples from all of the relations in $\mathcal{H}$; that is, ν is not dangling in $\mathcal{H}$. Since S shares no common attributes with any relation but T, μ must also join with ν and its "companions" from the other relations.

We must also show that each relation R other than S has no dangling tuples. It did not have any tuples that were dangling in $\mathcal{H}$, by the inductive hypothesis, but could it have a dangling tuple in $\mathcal{G}$? We claim not, because the first step of the program for $\mathcal{G}$, $T := T \ltimes S$, guaranteed that every tuple ν in T joins with some tuple of S. Thus, a collection of tuples, one from each of the relations of $\mathcal{H}$, can be extended to join with some tuple in S; that is, we can extend joins over $\mathcal{H}$ to become joins over $\mathcal{G}$. The final step, $S := S \ltimes T$, eliminates from S only tuples that do not join with any tuples in the final relation T, so we can still extend all joins over $\mathcal{H}$ to joins over $\mathcal{G}$. $\Box$

Example 11.33: The semijoin program from Example 11.31 is created by the algorithm of Theorem 11.4. We first remove the ear $\{A, B\}$, generate the step $BC := BC \ltimes AB$, and apply the algorithm to the hypergraph

$$\mathcal{H} = \{\{B, C\}, \{C, D\}\}$$

We chose $\{B, C\}$ as the ear, generated the step $CD := CD \ltimes BC$, and applied the algorithm to the remaining hypergraph, consisting of the hyperedge $\{C, D\}$ alone. That is the basis case, and we do nothing.

Now, we complete the call on the hypergraph $\mathcal{H}$, by generating

$$BC := BC \ltimes CD.$$

Last, we complete the application of the algorithm to the entire hypergraph with the step $AB := AB \ltimes BC$. $\Box$

Finding the Reduction of a Single Relation

Often a query does not require the reduction of all the relations involved in a join, but only one particular relation. If the hypergraph of the joined relations is cyclic, we still cannot find a finite semijoin program guaranteed to reduce that relation. However, if the hypergraph is acyclic, we can use the first half of the full reducer constructed in Theorem 11.4.

Suppose we want the reduction of relation R. We shall show that it is always possible to find an order of ear removals for an acyclic hypergraph that makes any designated R the last to be eliminated. Thus, when we apply the recursive program-construction algorithm of Theorem 11.4, we end the recursion with a call on the hypergraph consisting of R alone, and from that point on, we do not assign a new value to R. Thus, we may discontinue the semijoin program at that point, producing only the first half of the steps of the full reducer.

The next example illustrates the technique. It also points out how, if the site requesting the answer to the query is also the site of R, we can avoid taking any joins at all; the sequence of semijoins provides the answer. If we need the answer at another site, we are probably best off computing the result at the site of R, and then shipping the answer to the requesting site.

Example 11.34: Let us reconsider the query of Figure 11.15 (Section 11.10), whose hypergraph is shown in Figure 11.16; that query asks us to find the customers who ordered Brie. Suppose that the three relations, $CUSTOMERS$, $ORDERS$, and $INCLUDES$, are located at different sites, and it is sufficient to compute the answer at the site of $CUSTOMERS$. The query applies a selection for INAME = "Brie" to the $INCLUDES$ relation, so we really want the join of the relations $CUSTOMERS$ and $ORDERS$ with a new relation $I = \sigma_{\text{INAME}=\text{"Brie"}}(INCLUDES)$. When we have reduced $CUSTOMERS$, we can produce the answer, which is the CNAME and CADDR columns of this reduced relation. That calculation can be done locally, so the transmission cost of the query is the cost of the semijoin program only.

We thus wish to GYO-reduce the hypergraph of Figure 11.16 in such a way that $CUSTOMERS$ is eliminated last. As I is an ear initially, we choose that hyperedge (the hyperedge corresponding to $INCLUDES$ in Figure 11.16) to eliminate first. Then, $ORDERS$ becomes an ear, and we can eliminate that hyperedge next. Finally, we must choose $CUSTOMERS$. The semijoin program generated to this point, which is all that we need, is

$$ORDERS \ := \ ORDERS \ltimes I$$
$$CUSTOMERS \ := \ CUSTOMERS \ltimes ORDERS$$

Now, suppose that the query of Figure 11.15 asked for the dates of orders for Brie, rather than for the names and addresses of customers ordering Brie. That is, the retrieve statement in Figure 11.15 is replaced by

```
retrieve (o.DATE)
```

Then we would eliminate the ears corresponding to hyperedges $CUSTOMERS$ and I first, leaving $ORDERS$ for last, and the semijoin program would be

$$ORDERS \ := \ ORDERS \ltimes CUSTOMERS$$
$$ORDERS \ := \ ORDERS \ltimes I \qquad\qquad (11.37)$$

It would be equally proper to perform the steps in the reverse order, of course.

One might wonder whether the first step of (11.37) is really needed. That is, does not the query ask only for the dates of orders for Brie, and should we not be able to answer that without considering the addresses or balances of customers placing those orders? As written, (11.37) only produces the dates of orders for Brie that are placed by customers appearing in the $CUSTOMERS$ relation. Without the first step, "dangling" orders would also be printed. It is not clear which approach is better or more natural. We take up the subject in Section 14.3, when we talk about algorithms for optimizing under "weak equivalence" of queries, where the effects of dangling tuples are neglected, and more efficient evaluation algorithms sometimes result. □

The phenomenon we saw in Example 11.34 was not an accident. It is always possible to defer elimination of one designated hyperedge until the last. The next theorem proves this fact.

Theorem 11.5: In any acyclic hypergraph, given any particular hyperedge E, we can find a sequence of ear removals that makes the hypergraph empty and removes E at the last step.

Proof: The proof is an induction on the number of hyperedges in a hypergraph $\mathcal{G}$. The basis, one hyperedge, is trivial. Suppose the result true for hypergraphs of fewer than n hyperedges, and let $\mathcal{G}$ have exactly n hyperedges. If there is a hyperedge, other than E, that is an ear of $\mathcal{G}$, remove it, and apply the inductive hypothesis to the remaining hypergraph to prove that E may be eliminated last.

The hard case is if E is the only ear of $\mathcal{G}$. We shall, in effect, show that cannot be the case if $\mathcal{G}$ is acyclic and has more than one hyperedge. Suppose E is the only ear, and let F be the one other hyperedge of $\mathcal{G}$ that has nodes in common with E. Let $\mathcal{H}$ be the hypergraph that results when E is eliminated from $\mathcal{G}$. By the inductive hypothesis, $\mathcal{H}$ has a sequence of ear removals that removes F last. If $\mathcal{H}$ consists of only F, then in $\mathcal{G}$, F was an ear, contradicting the assumption that E was the only ear of $\mathcal{G}$.

Thus, $\mathcal{H}$ has at least two hyperedges, and there is some other hyperedge $G \neq F$ of $\mathcal{H}$ that is an ear in $\mathcal{H}$. G cannot share nodes with E, or else E was not an ear of $\mathcal{G}$. Thus, G is also an ear of $\mathcal{G}$, contradicting the assumption that E was $\mathcal{G}$'s only ear. □

11.14 AN ALGORITHM FOR TAKING THE PROJECTION OF A JOIN

In this section we shall study a semijoin-based algorithm for computing the projection of a natural join, that is, for evaluating an expression of the form

$$\pi_{A_1,\ldots,A_n}(R_1 \bowtie \cdots \bowtie R_k) \tag{11.38}$$

where the A_i's are attributes found among the R_j's. The problem is a generalization of the question addressed at the end of the previous section (reducing a single relation), where $A_1, \ldots, A_n$ were attributes of a single relation. It includes, as a special case, the problem of computing the join itself, since the list $A_1, \ldots, A_n$ can be all of the attributes found among all of the relations. Our problem also includes queries involving equijoins, rather than natural joins, since, by an argument mentioned previously, we can always rename attributes so it appears that what we are computing is a natural join. Finally, we include queries involving selections, provided each condition involves attributes of only one relation; in that case, we can apply the selections to the relations before taking the join.

When we compute the join of relations, it is possible that the answer has many more tuples than the arguments have. In fact, the output can be exponentially bigger than the input, even if no join taken is a Cartesian product, as the next example shows.

Example 11.35: Consider the natural join

$$A_1 A_2 \bowtie A_2 A_3 \bowtie \cdots \bowtie A_{k-1} A_k \qquad (11.39)$$

and let the relation for each of the schemes $A_i A_{i+1}$, $i = 1, 2, \ldots, k - 1$, be the relation of Figure 11.27. This relation pairs each of the odd integers 1 and 3 with each of the even integers 2 and 4, in all possible ways.

A_i	A_{i+1}
1	2
1	4
2	1
2	3
3	2
3	4
4	1
4	3

Figure 11.27 "Odd-even" relation.

It is easy to see that the tuples in the output of (11.39) are all those of the forms

$$oeoe \cdots \text{ (length } k)$$
$$eoeo \cdots \text{ (length } k)$$

where o stands for an odd number, 1 or 3, and e stands for an even number, 2 or 4. There are thus 2^{k+1} tuples in the output. However, the input consists of k relations with eight tuples each, so its size is $O(k)$. Thus, the upper bound on output size for joins, as a function of input size, is at least exponential. We leave it as an exercise for the reader to show that the output size can grow no faster than exponentially in the input size for any join. □

From Example 11.35, we should not expect the number of tuples shipped in a distributed calculation of (11.38) to be bounded, in general, by any small function of the input size; neither should we expect the total amount of work performed in a single-site evaluation of the query to be bounded in that sense.

Restricting our attention to acyclic hypergraphs doesn't help, because the expression (11.39) has an acyclic hypergraph. However, we might hope that the transmission cost and/or total computational work could be bound by a low-degree polynomial in the sum of the input and the output size. That is, in fact, the case for joins whose hypergraph is acyclic, but not for general hypergraphs.

Let us begin with an example that illustrates the problem for cyclic hypergraphs. Then, we show that the full reducer semijoin program gives an almost-linear cost, as a function of input plus output size, for the case where no projection is present. Finally, we give an algorithm for handling an arbitrary projection on a join, whose hypergraph is acyclic, with a quadratic cost as a function of input-plus-output size. In each of these algorithms, "cost" refers either to the transmission cost or to the number of steps taken by a uniprocessor at a single site; the differences are slight.

Example 11.36: Consider the cyclic natural join

$$A_1A_2 \bowtie A_2A_3 \bowtie \cdots \bowtie A_{k-1}A_k \bowtie A_kA_1 \tag{11.40}$$

where k is odd. Suppose that the current value for every relation scheme A_iA_{i+1} and A_kA_1 is the "odd-even" relation given in Figure 11.27. We may make the following observations.

1. The input size is $O(k)$.

2. The output size is zero. That is, the tuples in the join of all but the last term of (11.40) are of the form $oeoe\cdots o$ or of the form $eoeo\cdots e$, when regarded as tuples over the scheme $A_1A_2\cdots A_k$; that is, they begin and end with a value of the same parity, because k is odd. When we join $A_1A_2 \bowtie \cdots \bowtie A_{k-1}A_k$ with the last term, A_kA_1, we see that tuples in the latter relation, which are of the form oe or eo, cannot join with any tuples that have either oo or ee for attributes A_1 and A_k. Thus, the join (11.40) is empty.

3. No semijoin involving two of the relations that are input to (11.40) can affect either relation. The reason is that both attributes of both relations have exactly the same set of values, $\{1, 2, 3, 4\}$.

4. Any join of m of the relations from (11.40), $2 \le m < k$, has at least 2^{m+2} tuples. This observation is an easy induction on m. We must note that until m reaches k, any such join is the Cartesian product of *chains* of the form $A_jA_{j+1} \bowtie A_{j+1}A_{j+2} \bowtie \cdots \bowtie A_{l-1}A_l$. The number of tuples in such a join of $l - j$ relations is 2^{l-j+2}, as was observed in Example 11.35. It follows that the number of tuples in the product of chains, comprised of m relations in all, is at least 2^{m+2}.

5. If we compute (11.40) by semijoins of input relations, followed by joins, then the last join must be between two relations, at least one of which is

the join of $(k + 1)/2$ or more of the input relations. Thus, by (3) and (4), the size of this relation is at least $2^{(k+5)/2}$, which is exponential in the sum of the input and output sizes.

Of course, the claim that some intermediate result must be exponential in size, as a function of the sum of input and output sizes, assumed that the only operations we are allowed are semijoins of input relations and joins. There are other algorithms that might do better on the particular data of this example, although it is doubtful they could do better on all expressions of the form (11.38), and on all databases. For example, an algorithm could check for exactly the situation above, where the expression is of the form (11.40) and each of the relations are the one in Figure 11.27. This algorithm could deduce the answer was $\emptyset$ without computing any joins.

However, that algorithm would be useless on other problems. It appears that no algorithm can, in general, evaluate all expressions of the form (11.38), including those with cyclic hypergraphs, in less than exponential time in the worst case. The reason is that one can show a polynomial-time (as a function of input-plus-output size) algorithm for that problem would imply $\mathcal{P} = \mathcal{NP}$. A proof is left as an exercise. $\square$

The Cost of the Full Reducer

The full reducer for a connected, acyclic hypergraph $\mathcal{G}$ with k hyperedges is easily seen to perform $2k - 2$ semijoins. Moreover, for each hyperedge E, except the last to be eliminated, we transmit a projection of E once, to the site of that hyperedge F, in favor of which E is removed. This transmission occurs when we perform the step $F := F \ltimes E$. Later, we send back to the site of E a subset of what we sent to F, when we perform the step $E := E \ltimes F$. There are no other transmission steps, but those accounted for in this manner. Thus, the total transmission cost does not exceed twice the sum of the sizes of the k relations.[37] That is, for any connected, acyclic hypergraph $\mathcal{G}$, the transmission cost of the full reducer program grows linearly in the input size. In fact, we can make the stronger claim that the total number of tuples transmitted is no more than twice the input size, independently of k and independently of the particular acyclic hypergraph $\mathcal{G}$.

Now, let us consider the amount of local computation performed. The chart of Figure 11.6 (Section 11.5) shows that there are ways to take a join, and therefore a semijoin, in time that grows at most as $n \log n$, where n is the total number of tuples in the relations being joined ($n = T_R + T_S$, in the notation of Figure 11.6). If the right indices are present, $O(n)$ time suffices. During the execution of the full reducer, no relation grows bigger than its initial value, and

---

[37] We should also include $(2k - 2)c_0$, where c_0 is the overhead of transmission, but c_0 is a constant, and we may regard k as a constant as well, if the hypergraph $\mathcal{G}$ is fixed.

we presume that most shrink. Thus, if I is the total input size, $O(kI \log I)$ is an upper bound on the amount of computation performed by the full reducer.

If we fix our attention on one hypergraph $\mathcal{G}$, then k is a constant and can be ignored. Thus, the work is just slightly more than linear in the input size. However, if we allow $\mathcal{G}$ and k to vary, then we cannot bound the work independently of k, as we did for transmission cost.

Having computed the full reduction, we can ship all of the reduced relations to one site to take their joins. As relations have not grown, the transmission cost for this step is no more than I.

We must then compute the join of all k relations, $R_1, \ldots, R_k$, locally. We can bound this step in terms of the output size U, although not in terms of the input size I. We compute the join in the reverse order to that in which we performed ear reduction. That is, suppose $S_1, \ldots, S_k$ is the permutation of $R_1, \ldots, R_k$ such that S_1 was the first ear removed, S_2 the second, and so on, as we reduced the hypergraph of $R_1, \ldots, R_k$. Then we join the S_i's in reverse order, starting with S_k. When we join S_i to $S_{i+1} \bowtie \cdots \bowtie S_k$, we cannot decrease the size of the relation, because every tuple of S_i joins with at least one tuple of $S_{i+1} \bowtie \cdots \bowtie S_k$; the last semijoin step that assigned a new value to S_i guarantees that S_i has no dangling tuples with respect to $\{S_{i+1}, \ldots, S_k\}$.

As a consequence, no intermediate join can have more tuples than the output relation. Recall that is not the case for cyclic joins (which cannot be fully reduced, in general), as Example 11.36 showed. We must take $k-1$ joins, each of relations no larger than U, the output size.[38] From the analysis summarized in Figure 11.6, $O(U \log U)$ time suffices for each. Thus, the total amount of work to compute the join of k distributed relations, whose hypergraph is acyclic, is bounded by $O\big(k(I \log I + U \log U)\big)$. The transmission cost alone is $O(I)$, independent of k, as long as the hypergraph is acyclic.

Computing a Projection of an Acyclic Join

Now, let us consider the case where we have a project-join expression of the form (11.38), and the hypergraph for the join expression is acyclic. As we want only a projection of the join of all the relations, the output size could be much smaller than the join of the relations, so the analysis above, dependent as it was on the value of U, might not apply. It turns out that we cannot bound the total cost so closely in this more general case, but we can still bound the cost by a polynomial in I and U.

It is helpful to view the algorithm for evaluating (11.38) as building a "parse tree" of an acyclic hypergraph. In the parse tree, the nodes correspond to the hyperedges, and E is a child of F if we eliminate E by ear removal, in

---

[38] We counted only the number of tuples, not their length, but the output tuples are as long as any tuples in intermediate relations, anyway.

favor of F.

Example 11.37: The hypergraph of Figure 11.28(a) has the parse tree of Figure 11.28(b). For example, we can remove both $\{A, B, C\}$ and $\{B, F\}$ in favor of $\{B, C, D\}$, remove $\{D, E, G\}$ in favor of $\{C, D, E\}$, and then remove $\{B, C, D\}$ in favor of $\{C, D, E\}$. The latter hyperedge is removed last, as a special case of ear removal, so it appears at the root. Note that there are other parse trees for the same hypergraph. In fact, Theorem 11.5 implies that we may make whichever hyperedge we wish be the root. □

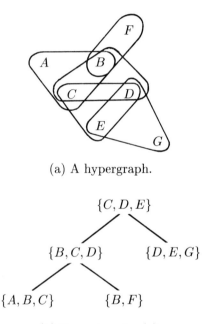

(a) A hypergraph.

$$\{C, D, E\}$$

$$\{B, C, D\} \qquad \{D, E, G\}$$

$$\{A, B, C\} \qquad \{B, F\}$$

(b) Parse tree for (a).

Figure 11.28 Constructing the parse tree for a hypergraph.

Algorithm 11.4: Computation of a Project-Join Expression with an Acyclic Hypergraph (Yannakakis' Algorithm).

INPUT: We are given an expression $\pi_X(R_1 \bowtie \cdots \bowtie R_k)$, where the hypergraph $\mathcal{G}$, whose edges are the relation schemes for $R_1, \ldots, R_k$, is acyclic. We are also given relations r_i for R_i, $i = 1, 2, \ldots, k$.

OUTPUT: The value of the input expression applied to the given relations.

METHOD: Perform the following steps.

1. Reduce all of the relations by executing the full reducer semijoin program for $\mathcal{G}$ on the given relations.

2. Construct a parse tree P for $\mathcal{G}$.

3. Visit each node of P, other than the root, in some bottom-up order; that is, visit each node after having visited all its children. Suppose we visit the node of P corresponding to hyperedge R, and its parent in P is S. Then in the GYO-reduction of $\mathcal{G}$ we eliminated R in favor of S. Replace the current relation for S by

    $$\pi_{S \cup (X \cap R)}(R \bowtie S)$$

    X is the set of *distinguished attributes* of $\mathcal{G}$, that is, the attributes onto which the final projection is made. Also, note that in the subscript, R, X, and S are sets of attributes, while in the join, R and S refer to the current relations R and S, as per our usual conventions.

4. Project the relation at the root of P onto the set of attributes X. This step can, and should, be performed at the time we join the last child of the root with the root, during step (3).

The crux of the algorithm is step (3), where the relation for S is joined with the relations at each of its children, in turn. Each time we perform a join, we project out those attributes that are not in the scheme of S and are not distinguished. It is easy to see that after joining S with the relations at all its children, while following a bottom-up order on the whole tree, the value of the relation at node S will be the join of the initial relations for S and for all of its descendants, projected onto the union of the attributes of S and whatever attributes in X appear among the descendants of S. $\square$

Example 11.38: Suppose that in the hypergraph of Figure 11.28, nodes A and G are distinguished. That is, the expression we wish to compute is

$$\pi_{AG}(ABC \bowtie BF \bowtie BCD \bowtie CDE \bowtie DEG)$$

In Figure 11.29 are initial, fully reduced relations corresponding to the five relation schemes of Figure 11.28(b). Had the given relations not been reduced, we would have reduced them in step (1) of Algorithm 11.4.

Let us visit the relation ABC first and join it with its parent, BCD. The scheme of the parent becomes $ABCD$, since A is distinguished, and the other three attributes were part of the scheme at the parent originally. The relation for the parent becomes $\{a_1b_1c_1d_1,\ a_1b_1c_1d_2,\ a_2b_1c_1d_1,\ a_2b_1c_1d_2\}$, the natural join of ABC and BCD.

Next, let us visit BF. We must join this relation with the relation $ABCD$ at its parent, and then project out F, since F is not distinguished, and is not an attribute of the parent. Since the relations are reduced, we can predict that this join will have no effect on the parent relation. In general, we can skip the

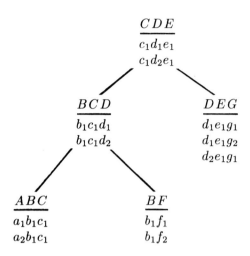

Figure 11.29 Initial relations.

join, with its parent, of any relation that has no distinguished attributes. The relations and schemes are now as shown in Figure 11.30.

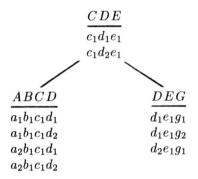

Figure 11.30 Relations and schemes after visiting ABC and BF.

Now, let us visit $ABCD$ in Figure 11.30. We join it with its parent, CDE, and then project out the attribute B, because that attribute is neither distinguished nor present in the scheme of the parent. The resulting relation for the root is shown in Figure 11.31(a). Finally, we visit DEG and join this relation with its parent, which now has scheme $ACDE$. Since G is distinguished, no projection is necessary, and the scheme at the root becomes $ACDEG$. The value of that relation is shown in Figure 11.30(b).

$ACDE$	$ACDEG$	AG
$a_1c_1d_1e_1$	$a_1c_1d_1e_1g_1$	a_1g_1
$a_1c_1d_2e_1$	$a_1c_1d_1e_1g_2$	a_1g_2
$a_2c_1d_1e_1$	$a_1c_1d_2e_1g_1$	a_2g_1
$a_2c_1d_2e_1$	$a_2c_1d_1e_1g_1$	a_2g_2
	$a_2c_1d_1e_1g_2$	
	$a_2c_1d_2e_1g_1$	
(a)	(b)	(c)

Figure 11.31 Final relations computed.

Finally, at step (4) of Algorithm 11.4 we project the root relation, Figure 11.31(b), onto the distinguished attributes, A and G, to get the answer, which is shown in Figure 11.31(c). In practice, this projection would be performed as we computed the relation of Figure 11.31(b). $\square$

We shall show that the work done by Algorithm 11.4 is essentially quadratic in the sum of the input size I and the output size U. The following lemma is needed to bound the size of the intermediate relations during step (3) of Algorithm 11.4.

Lemma 11.1: At no time during the execution of step (3) of Algorithm 11.4 does any relation get larger than $2IU$, where I and U are the input and output sizes, respectively.

Proof: We begin by observing that at all times, the relation at the node for S has a value that is

$$\pi_{S \cup Y}(S \bowtie S_1 \bowtie \cdots \bowtie S_m) \qquad (11.41)$$

where

1. $S_1, \ldots, S_m$ are those relations that are descendants (not necessarily proper) of one of the children C of S such that C has already been visited (and therefore, all descendants of C have been visited).

2. Y is the set of distinguished attributes found among the S_i's that are not attributes of S. Note that Y and S are disjoint sets of attributes, and $Y \subseteq X$.

The proof is an easy induction on the number of nodes visited, and we leave this part for the reader.

Let T stand for $S \bowtie S_1 \bowtie \cdots \bowtie S_m$, so (11.41) is $\pi_{S \cup Y}(T)$. Observe that

$$\pi_{S \cup Y}(T) \subseteq \pi_S(T) \times \pi_Y(T) \qquad (11.42)$$

To see why (11.42) holds, recall that S and Y are disjoint. If μ is a tuple in

$\pi_{S \cup Y}(T)$, then $\mu[S]$ is in $\pi_S(T)$ and $\mu[Y]$ is in $\pi_Y(T)$. Thus, μ is in

$$\pi_S(T) \times \pi_Y(T)$$

Now, we use the fact that the relations to which step (3) applies are reduced. First, we note that $\pi_S(T) = S$, since S is one of the relations in the join T, and S has no dangling tuples. Thus, the size of $\pi_S(T)$ is no greater than I, since surely S is no larger than the entire input.

Second, we note that $\pi_Y(T)$ can be no larger than U. The proof consists of two observations

1. $\pi_Y(T) = \pi_Y(R_1 \bowtie \cdots \bowtie R_k)$. The reason is that, because the relations are reduced, every tuple in T extends to at least one tuple over all of the attributes, when all of the relations $R_1, \ldots, R_k$ are joined.

2. $Y \subseteq X$, so $\pi_Y(R_1 \bowtie \cdots \bowtie R_k)$ can be no larger than $\pi_X(R_1 \bowtie \cdots \bowtie R_k)$.

But $\pi_X(R_1 \bowtie \cdots \bowtie R_k)$ is the output, so (1) and (2) imply that the size of $\pi_Y(T)$ is no greater than U. We may now invoke (11.42) to argue that $\pi_{S \cup Y}(T)$ has size no greater than $2IU$. In detail, let t_1 be the number of tuples in $\pi_S(T)$ and t_2 be the number of tuples in $\pi_Y(T)$. Let l_1 be the length of a tuple in $\pi_S(T)$ and l_2 be the length of a tuple in $\pi_Y(T)$. Then $l_1 t_1 \leq I$, and $l_2 t_2 \leq U$. Now $\pi_{S \cup Y}(T)$ has at most $t_1 t_2$ tuples, by (11.42), and their length is $l_1 + l_2$. Thus, its size is at most $(l_1 + l_2)t_1 t_2$. Finally, observe that $l_1 + l_2 \leq 2l_1 l_2$.[39] Thus, the size of $\pi_{S \cup Y}(T)$ is no more than $2l_1 l_2 t_1 t_2 = 2IU$. $\square$

Theorem 11.6: For a fixed query of the form (11.38), Algorithm 11.4 requires communication cost and running time that are polynomial in the size, I, of its input relations, the size, U, of its output relations, and the number, k, of relations in the join of (11.38).

Proof: Step (1), applying the full-reducer semijoin program, requires $O(I)$ communication and $O\big(k(I \log I + U \log U)\big)$ total computation time, as we have seen. Step (2), construction of a parse tree, is implicit in the discovery of the full reducer. To find the full reducer or the parse tree takes time at most the product of the number of hyperedges times the number of nodes in the hypergraph constructed from (11.38). On the assumption that there are no empty relations in the input, the size of the hypergraph cannot exceed I, and if there are empty relations, that fact can be discovered in $O(k)$ time and the empty relation produced as the output immediately, without performing steps (3) and (4) of Algorithm 11.4. We conclude that $O(kI)$ time suffices to find the full reducer for step (1) and to find the parse tree in step (2), in all but the trivial case where there is an empty relation. Thus, we can neglect the cost of step (2), since the estimate we use for step (1) is higher, both in transmission

---

[39] Of course, usually, $l_1 + l_2$ is much less than $l_1 l_2$. However, because of the possibility that $l_1 = l_2 = 1$, we need the factor 2 so the claim holds generally.

cost [there is none in step (2)] and in computation cost.

For step (3), we must transmit $k - 1$ relations; none are larger than $2IU$, by Lemma 11.1. Thus, the total transmission cost is $O(kIU)$. This amount dominates the transmission cost of step (1), and can be taken to be, within a constant factor, the transmission cost of the entire algorithm. For the computation cost, we take $k - 1$ joins, whose input and output relations are all bounded by size $2IU$. Thus, a method such as sort-join offers running time $O(IU \log(IU))$ per join, for a total cost of $O(kIU \log(IU))$.

Finally, the projection of step (4) requires no communication and takes time $O(IU)$. We conclude that step (3) dominates both the transmission cost and the total computation time, so the algorithm as a whole has transmission cost $O(kIU)$ and running time $O(kIU \log(IU))$. $\square$

11.15 THE SYSTEM R* OPTIMIZATION ALGORITHM

System R* is the experimental extension of System R to the distributed environment. Like its parent, it performs optimization in an exhaustive way, confident that the cost of considering many strategies will pay off in lower execution costs for queries.

The optimization algorithm applies to an algebraic query of the kind discussed in Section 11.11, where the expression to be optimized represents the query applied to logical relations, which in turn are expressed in terms of physical relations. The operators assumed to appear in the query are the usual select, project, natural join, and union, plus a new operator CHOICE, which represents the ability of the system to choose any of the identical, replicated copies of a given relation. That is, if relations R_1, R_2, and R_3 are copies of one relation, at different nodes, and S_1 and S_2 are also copies of another relation, then we might express the join of these two relations as

$$CHOICE(R_1, R_2, R_3) \bowtie CHOICE(S_1, S_2)$$

We could, for example, save transmission cost by picking copies of R and S that were at the same node and joining them there.

One modification we shall make to expression trees is to combine nodes having the same associative and commutative binary operator into a single node, provided the nodes being combined form a tree, with no intervening nodes labeled by other operators. The three binary operators, union, natural join, and choice, are all associative and commutative, so this rule applies to each of them. A tree of nodes labeled by just one of these binary operators we shall call a *cluster*. All the nodes of a cluster will be replaced by a single node, and the children of the nodes in the cluster become children of the new node. The parent of the new node is the same as the parent of the one node in the cluster that is an ancestor of all the nodes in the cluster. The result of these operations we call a *compacted tree*.

Example 11.39: The expression tree in Figure 11.32(a) is replaced by the tree in Figure 11.32(b). We have combined the two nodes labeled ∪, since they form a cluster, and the three nodes labeled ⋈ also happen to be arranged in a tree; thus they are a cluster and are replaced by a single node. □

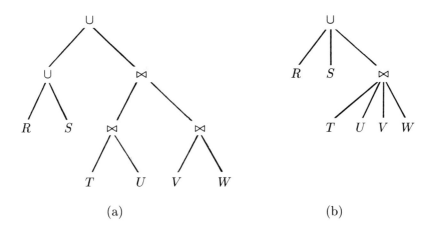

(a)   (b)

Figure 11.32 Replacement of clusters by single nodes.

Let us now enumerate the strategies for evaluation that System R* considers. We shall assume that each relation is at a single site. If a relation is replicated, then we shall give the replicas different names, and apply the *CHOICE* operator to the collection of replicas. We assume also that the query asks for a specific expression to be computed at a specific site of the network; the expression is represented as a compacted tree. The algorithm below considers all ways to evaluate the nodes of the compacted tree, taking into account

1. The various orders in which an operator like union or join of many relations can be performed as a sequence of binary steps,
2. The various sites at which each node of the tree could have its result computed, and
3. Several different ways that the join could be computed.

The Cost Function

When the algorithm considers each of the options listed above, it must evaluate the cost of these methods. The actual cost function used in System R* is quite complex; it takes account of the computation cost at a site as well as the transmission cost. We have had the flavor of the sort of analysis that is used at a single site in Section 11.2, so we shall, for simplicity, take a less detailed cost function that only accounts for the transmission cost. That is, as in Section 11.11, we shall assume that the cost of sending a message is, in appropriate units, equal to the number of tuples sent, plus a constant c_0.

Join Methods

The options for taking a union of two relations are fairly clear. We can ship one relation to the site of the other or ship them both to a third site. The costs of these three approaches are obvious, given the cost function above. The options given a $CHOICE$ operator are also clear; the cost is zero for any site at which one of the relations in the choice resides, and otherwise the cost equals the cost of shipping one of the replicas to the desired site. Which replica is shipped doesn't matter, since the costs are the same, under our model.

However, with the join of two relations R and S, the set of options is not so well defined. The algorithm to be described has five options that can always be used, and two others that can be used when R and S are both at the same site. These options are the following.

1. Ship R to the site of S and compute the join there. The cost is c_0 plus the size of R.

2. Ship S to the site of R and compute the join there. The cost is c_0 plus the size of S.

3. Ship R and S to a third site and compute the join there. The cost is $2c_0$ plus the sum of the sizes of R and S.

4. Perform a semijoin $S \ltimes R$, before obtaining the relevant tuples of S and moving them to the site of R. That is, compute $\pi_{R \cap S}(R)$ at the site of R, ship these tuples to the site of S, and there compute $S \ltimes R$. Ship the result to the site of R. The cost of this method is estimated to be $2c_0 + T_R(1 + T_S/I)$, where T_R and T_S are the number of tuples in R and S, and I is the "image size," that is, the size of the projection of S onto $R \cap S$. That is, at most T_R tuples are shipped from the site of R to the site of S, and therefore $T_R T_S/I$ is an upper bound on the average number of tuples shipped back to the site of R.[40] We could estimate the cost more closely by considering the size of $\pi_{R \cap S}(R)$, but this method will only make sense when R is very small anyway.

5. There is another method similar to (4), in which the roles of R and S are reversed.

We call strategies (1)–(3) *fetches*. Strategies (4) and (5) are referred to as *lookups*.

If R and S are at the same site, there are several other strategies we shall consider.

---

[40] T_S is another upper bound, but this method is, in practice, only used when $T_R < I$.

6. Compute the join at the site of the two relations and leave it there. Since we charge only for transmission in our simple model, the cost of this action is zero.

7. Compute the join at the site of the two relations and ship the result to another site. The cost is the cost of shipping the result relation. Note that we could also use strategy (3), shipping the unjoined relations to a new site and joining them there. Which is preferable depends on how the size of the join compares with the sum of the sizes of R and S.

The Algorithm for Selecting an Evaluation Strategy

We can now present our simplified version of the System R* algorithm for query evaluation.

Algorithm 11.5: Selecting a Processing Strategy for a Distributed Query.

INPUT: A query in the form of a compacted tree, with operators select, project, join, union, and choice, sites for all of the argument relations, guard conditions for these relations, and a site at which the result must appear.

OUTPUT: A preferred order of application of the operators and sites at which the results of these operations should appear.

METHOD: The first stage of the algorithm is to generate all of the possible evaluation sequences, representing them as ordinary expression trees, with binary operators. We begin by pushing selections and projections as far down the tree as possible, using Algorithm 11.2. When we encounter a $CHOICE$ operator, we push the selection or projection to each child of a node labeled $CHOICE$. We also use the technique of Section 11.11 to eliminate subtrees whose guard conditions conflict with a selection and to eliminate redundant guard conditions as in Example 11.26.

We then proceed up the tree, beginning at the leaves. On visiting a node, we generate for that node a set of expression trees, each of which must be considered when finding the least cost application order.

Basis: The basis, a leaf node labeled R, yields a set consisting of the one expression, R.

Inductive Step: Let n be a node of the compacted tree. Suppose the children of n, say $c_1, \ldots, c_k$, have each been processed, so we have for each child c_i a set $\mathcal{S}_i$ of expressions.

Case 1: If the operator at n is selection or projection, then $k = 1$, and we form the set of expressions for n by applying the same operator as is at n to the root of each expression tree in $\mathcal{S}_1$.

Case 2: If the operator is $CHOICE$, the set of expressions for n is the union of the $\mathcal{S}_i$'s for $i = 1, 2, \ldots, k$.

Case 3: If the operator at n is $\cup$, we consider all unordered binary trees with k leaves. For example, Figure 11.33(a) shows the three unordered trees with three leaves designated a, b, and c. Since the children of each node are unordered, the first of these could as well have been exhibited as any of the trees in Figure 11.33(b), where we have shown the two different orders of a and b, and the two different orders of c and the parent of a and b, in all possible combinations.

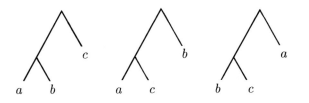

(a) The three unordered binary trees with three leaves.

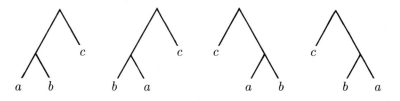

(b) The four ordered trees that are represented by one unordered tree.

Figure 11.33 Illustration of unordered trees.

It is sufficient to consider only unordered trees; the way we group operands of a union may make a difference in the efficiency, but there can be no difference whether we compute $E_1 \cup E_2$ or $E_2 \cup E_1$. A similar remark holds for the join operator, to be discussed next. We complete construction of the expressions for node n by taking each of the unordered trees, with interior nodes labeled $\cup$, and placing at the leaf for c_i any of the expression trees in $\mathcal{S}_i$, making the replacements for the leaves in all possible ways.

Case 4: If the label of n is $\bowtie$, we proceed exactly as for a union, except that $\bowtie$ labels the interior nodes of the unordered tree.

Now we must do the second stage of the algorithm, the computation of the best evaluation strategy for each of the expression trees constructed for the root by the first phase. We now have binary trees, and again we work on each tree from the leaves up. At each node, we must compute the cost of evaluating the expression whose root is at that node, with the result left at each of the possible sites. Remember that the exact cost of operations depends not only on the formula for charging for messages shipped, which we take to be c_0 plus the message length, but also on our estimate of the size of relations computed by the subexpressions. We shall assume that such an estimate is available, and later, we shall give an example of one possible way of making the estimate.

Basis: At a leaf node labeled R, the cost of evaluation at the site of R is zero, and the cost of evaluation at any other site is equal to the cost of shipping R, that is, c_0 plus the number of tuples in R.

Inductive Step: Consider an interior node n. If the label of n is a selection or projection, then that operation can be performed at the same site that the expression rooted at the child of n was computed. Thus, the least cost to compute n at site α equals the cost of computing the child of n at α.

Suppose the label of n is $\cup$. To find the least cost of computing n at site α, we find the minimum over all sites β and γ, of the cost of computing the children of n at β and γ, plus (if $\beta \neq \alpha$) the cost of shipping the first child's result, plus (if $\gamma \neq \alpha$) the cost of shipping the result of the second child.

If the label of n is $\bowtie$, we consider, for each site α, the cost of computing the children of n at some sites β and γ, and using any of the join methods (1)–(7) described prior to Algorithm 11.5 that apply. The least cost method is chosen to evaluate n, of course.

Having computed the cost of evaluating each of the expressions in our set at each of the sites, we find that expression with the lowest cost of evaluation for the desired output site. We must also consider the cost of computing the result at another site and shipping the result to the desired site. Having found the least cost expression, we must find the evaluation method used at each node. The proper evaluation method for a node is the one that assigned the least cost to that node. We can either recompute costs for the winning tree, to see which method is best at each node, or as we evaluate all of the possible trees, we can label each node with the proper method to use. $\square$

Example 11.40: We shall give a simple illustration of the calculations involved in Algorithm 11.5. First, we must settle on a way of estimating the sizes of the results of operations, in particular, the join. We shall assume we know for each relation R and each subset X of the attributes in R's relation scheme, an image size, that is, the expected number of tuples in $\pi_X(R)$. As a special case, we know the expected number of tuples in R itself, since we may let $X = R$.

Suppose R and S are two relations to be joined, and let T_R and T_S be our estimates of the numbers of tuples in these relations. Let the image sizes for the set of attributes $R \cap S$ be I_R and I_S for R and S, respectively. A plausible estimate of the size of $R \bowtie S$ begins by considering the smaller of I_R and I_S; say it is I_R. Then we shall suppose that each member of $\pi_{R\cap S}(R)$ is present in the larger set $\pi_{R\cap S}(S)$. In fact, we shall assume that each tuple in R joins with an average number of tuples from S, that is T_S/I_S tuples. Thus, the size of

$R \bowtie S$ is estimated to be $T_R T_S / I_S$, or more generally, considering that either image size could be smaller,

$$\frac{T_R T_S}{max(I_R, I_S)}$$

Note that this formula agrees with (11.13) in Theorem 11.2, as long as we make the simplifying assumption that either all common attributes A of R and S satisfy the inclusion dependency $R.A \subseteq S.A$, or they all satisfy $S.A \subseteq R.A$.

Suppose that our expression requires us to take the join of three relations $P(A, B)$, $Q(B, C)$, and $R(C, D)$, which are located at three different sites α, β, and γ, respectively. As in Figure 11.33, there are three unordered trees with leaves labeled P, Q, and R, corresponding to the fact that we could take the join of any two of the three relations first. Let us assume the following constants for the problem.

1. $T_P = 10$, $T_Q = 1000$, and $T_R = 100$.
2. The image size I_{PB}, the estimated size of $\pi_B(P)$, is 10.
3. The image size I_{QB} is 20.
4. $I_{QC} = 500$.
5. $I_{RC} = 25$.
6. $c_0 = 10$.

Let us first consider joining P and Q first, and then joining the result with R. If we wish to compute the result at site α, we have two choices. We could fetch Q to α, at a cost of $c_0 + T_Q = 10 + 1000 = 1010$. Alternatively, we could examine each of the ten tuples of P and lookup the matching tuples of Q for each of them. The cost of this operation is

$$2c_0 + T_P(1 + T_Q/I_{QB}) = 20 + 10(1 + 50) = 530$$

Thus, the cost of computing $P \bowtie Q$ at site α is $min(1010, 600) = 600$.

If we wished to evaluate $P \bowtie Q$ at β instead, then there would be the two symmetric strategies, where we do a fetch or a lookup of P. The costs of these operations are, respectively, $c_0 + T_P = 20$ and $2c_0 + T_Q(1 + T_P/I_{PB}) = 2020$. We therefore prefer the fetch operation in this case, with a cost of 20.

Finally, we must evaluate the cost of computing $P \bowtie Q$ at γ. Here we must ship both relations to γ at a cost of $2c_0 + T_P + T_Q = 1030$. It is worth noting that we could do better by shipping P to β, computing the join there, and shipping the result to γ. However, there is no need to consider this approach now, since when we compute the cost of the complete expression, we shall discover that it is cheaper to evaluate $P \bowtie Q$ at β even if we want the result of that join at γ. On the other hand, if $P \bowtie Q$ were the final expression, and we wanted the result at γ, Algorithm 11.5 would tell us it is cheaper to compute the result at β and ship.

Now we must consider the cost of evaluating the entire expression,

$$(P \bowtie Q) \bowtie R$$

at each of the three sites. To begin, we must obtain our estimate of the size of $P \bowtie Q$. By the formula explained above, this size is

$$T_{PQ} = T_P T_Q / max(I_{PB}, I_{QB}) = 10 \times 1000/20 = 500$$

We can also estimate an image size for I_{PQC}, the projection of $P \bowtie Q$ onto C. Each of the 500 C-values appearing in Q is present in T_Q/I_{QC} tuples, that is, two tuples. As the ratio of I_{PB} to I_{QB} is $1/2$, and we assume every B-value in P is also present in Q, it follows that half the tuples in Q will have a matching B-value in P, and will appear in the join. Thus, of the two tuples with C-value c, the probability is $3/4$ that at least one of them will appear in the join. Thus the image size I_{PQC} will be approximately $\frac{3}{4}I_{QC} = 375$.

Finally, we shall need an estimate for the size of the join of all three relations. By our estimating rule, this number is

$$T_{PQR} = T_{PQ} T_R / max(I_{PQC}, I_{RC}) = 500 \times 100/375 = 133$$

Now we must consider for each of the three sites, the best way to compute $(P \bowtie Q) \bowtie R$ at that site. The choices include which site should $P \bowtie Q$ be computed at, and which of the methods (1)–(7) should be used to join $P \bowtie Q$ with R. The options are summarized in Figure 11.34.

Site of Result	Site of $P \bowtie Q$	Strategy	Cost of Joining R with $P \bowtie Q$		Cost of $P \bowtie Q$		Total Cost
α	α	Fetch R	$c_0 + T_R = 110$		530	=	640
		Lookup R	$2c_0 + T_{PQ}(1 + T_R/I_{RC}) = 2520$		530	=	3050
	β	Fetch PQ, R	$2c_0 + T_{PQ} + T_R = 620$		20	=	640
	γ	Fetch $PQ \bowtie R$	$c_0 + T_{PQR} = 143$		1030	=	1173
		Fetch PQ, R	$2c_0 + T_{PQ} + T_R = 620$		1030	=	1650
β	α	Fetch PQ, R	$2c_0 + T_{PQ} + T_R = 620$		530	=	1150
	β	Fetch R	$c_0 + T_R = 110$		20	=	130
		Lookup R	$2c_0 + T_{PQ}(1 + T_R/I_{RC}) = 2520$		20	=	2540
	γ	Fetch $PQ \bowtie R$	$c_0 + T_{PQR} = 143$		1030	=	1173
		Fetch PQ, R	$2c_0 + T_{PQ} + T_R = 620$		1030	=	1650
γ	α	Fetch PQ	$c_0 + T_{PQ} = 510$		530	=	1040
		Lookup PQ	$2c_0 + T_R(1 + T_{PQ}/I_{PQC}) = 253$		530	=	783
	β	Fetch PQ	$c_0 + T_{PQ} = 510$		20	=	530
		Lookup PQ	$2c_0 + T_R(1 + T_{PQ}/I_{PQC}) = 253$		20	=	273
	γ	None needed	0		1030	=	1030

Figure 11.34 Strategies for evaluating the join of three relations.

From Figure 11.34 it is clear that if we want the result at site β, we must compute $P \bowtie Q$ at β (by fetching P to β), then fetching R to β, with a total cost of 130. It seems that if we want the result at α, we have two choices with the same cost, 640. For example, we could compute $P \bowtie Q$ at β (by fetching P), then fetch that result and R to α. However, we must, according to Algorithm 11.5, also consider computing the result at another site and shipping the result to α, against the cost of 640 given by Figure 11.34. In this case, computing the result at β, then shipping it with a cost of $c_0 + T_{PQR} = 143$, has a total cost of 273, which is less than the 640 given by Figure 11.34 for computation at α. Similarly, an alternative optimal strategy for computing the result at γ is to compute at β and ship, with a cost of 273, which is identical to the value given in Figure 11.34.

We are not yet done; we must consider the other two unordered trees, which involve joining P with R first, or Q with R first. The former case is not really a join but a Cartesian product, and we shall rule it out of consideration because of the size of the intermediate result, even though we said we would not consider that cost. The latter strategy, joining Q and R first, will not prove superior to what we have already, since our first step must ship a minimum of 100 tuples, that being the smaller of T_Q and T_R. $\square$

EXERCISES

11.1: Suppose a relation $ABCD$ has a clustering index on A and nonclustering indices on the other attributes; the four indices have image sizes of 50, 10, 20, and 100, respectively. The number of tuples in the relation is 10,000, and the relation would fit on 500 blocks. Find all of the ways to evaluate the query according to Algorithm 11.1.

$$\pi_A \left(\sigma_{A=0 \wedge B=1 \wedge C>2 \wedge D=3}(ABCD) \right)$$

Which method is the least costly?

11.2: Some of the data structures of Chapter 6 (Volume I) provide clustering indices, and some provide nonclustering indices. Indicate which of these structures yield clustering indices, which yield nonclustering indices, and which do not yield indices at all in the sense required for the System R optimization algorithm of Section 11.2. You may make reasonable assumptions about the uniformity of the data with which each structure is presented.

a) A hash table, with records stored in the buckets.

b) A hash table with records stored in a heap and pointed to by the buckets.

c) A B-tree, with records stored in the leaves.

d) A k-d-tree.

e) A B-tree whose leaves point to linked lists of records with a fixed key value (for example, as in a multilist structure).

11.3: Suppose we have relations R, with 1,000,000 tuples, and S, with 100,000 tuples. Also, assume 20 of R's records fit on one block, and 100 of S's records fit on one block.

    a)   What is the output cost of computing $R \times S$?

    b)   What is the input cost of $R \times S$ if $M = 100$, that is, if there are 100 blocks of main memory?

    c)   Repeat (b) if $M = 1000$.

** 11.4: Find the exact number of block accesses needed to take the product of relations, as a function of their sizes and the number of blocks of main memory. A simpler problem is to find improvements in both the upper bound $B_R B_S / (M - 1) + \min(B_R, B_S)$ implied by (11.8) in Section 11.3 and the lower bound of $B_R B_S / (M - 1)$ given by Theorem 11.1.

11.5: Suppose the relations R and S of Exercise 11.3 are $R(A, B)$ and $S(B, C)$, and let the image size for B be 500. For the join $R \bowtie S$, estimate

    a)   The output size.

    b)   The cost of selection-on-a-product join.

    c)   The cost of sort-join.

    d)   The cost of index-join, assuming a clustering index on $S.B$.

    e)   The cost of index-join, assuming a clustering index on $R.B$.

    f)   The cost of index-join, assuming a nonclustering index on $S.B$.

    g)   The cost of index-join, assuming a nonclustering index on $R.B$.

    h)   The cost of two-index join, assuming clustering indices on both $S.B$ and $R.B$.

  * i)   The cost of two-index join, assuming nonclustering indices on both $S.B$ and $R.B$.

    j)   The cost of creating clustering indices on $S.B$ and $R.B$, assuming $M = 100$.

11.6: Suppose the relations R and S of Exercise 11.3 are $R(A, B, C)$ and $S(B, C, D)$. Let the inclusion dependencies $R.B \subseteq S.B$ and $S.C \subseteq R.C$ hold, with image sizes for $R.B$, $S.B$, $R.C$, and $S.C$ of 100, 200, 50, and 10, respectively. For the join $R \bowtie S$, estimate

    a)   The output size.

    b)   The cost of sort-join.

* 11.7: In the situation described in Exercise 11.6, how would one take advantage of a clustering index on $S.B$, and no other indices, to perform a join efficiently. Generalize your approach to relations $R(A, B, C)$ and $S(B, C, D)$ of any size, with arbitrary image sizes.

* 11.8: Prove Theorem 11.2, that, under the model of Section 11.4, the estimated output size for a join is the product of the sizes of the relations, divided by the product of the domain sizes for the common attributes.

11.9: Suppose we take the join $R(A, B) \underset{R.B\theta S.B}{\bowtie} S(B,C)$. Estimate the output size, as a function of the relation sizes,

a)   If θ is $<$.

b)   If θ is $\neq$.

* 11.10: Modify the estimated cost (11.16) for sort-join if M, the number of blocks of main memory is sufficiently small that the expected number of tuples with a given value for the common attribute exceeds the number that can fit in main memory. Assume the relations joined are $R(A, B)$ and $S(B,C)$, and that I is the image size for B in both relations.

* 11.11: Justify formula (11.21) in Section 11.5.

* 11.12: Modify formula (11.23) in Section 11.5 for the case that the indices are nonclustering.

* 11.13: Modify formula (11.25) in Section 11.5 to account for the possibility that $I > B_R$.

* 11.14: Do any of the join methods in Figure 11.6 dominate another of the methods when

a) M is fixed?

b) M grows in proportion to the other parameters?

11.15: Redo the table of Figure 11.6 for the case that the join is really a semijoin; that is, estimate the cost of $R(A, B) \ltimes S(B)$.

11.16: Many of the join methods of Figure 11.6 can save time if we combine input and output operations for temporary relations (that is, we avoid writing out and then immediately reading back in the same relation). Revise each of the formulas, where possible, to save these input/output steps.

11.17: Verify each of the identities in Section 11.6.

11.18: Generalize rule (9) in Section 11.6 (pushing selections both ways through a join) to certain expressions with a product rather than a join. For example, consider what should be done to $\sigma_{B=0}(\sigma_{B=C}(AB \times CD))$.

11.19: Show that the equation

$$\pi_S(E_1 - E_2) \equiv \pi_S(E_1) - \pi_S(E_2)$$

is not valid in general.

11.20: The *Beer Drinkers' Database* consists of relations

> FREQUENTS(DRINKER,BAR)
> SERVES(BAR,BEER)
> LIKES(DRINKER,BEER)

Write relational algebra expressions for the following queries and optimize them according to Algorithm 11.2.

a)   Find the drinkers that frequent a bar that serves a beer that they like.

b)   Find the drinkers that drink at the same bar with a drinker who likes "Potgold" beer.

c)   Find the drinkers that drink at the same bar with a drinker who likes a brand of beer that the bar serves and Charles Chugamug likes.

11.21: Use Algorithm 11.3 (the Wong-Youssefi algorithm) to optimize the queries of Exercise 11.20.

* 11.22: Redo the analysis of Section 11.8 regarding the three-way join

$$Q(A, B) \bowtie R(B, C) \bowtie S(C, D)$$

assuming

a)   There is a clustering index on $R.C$, as well as the clustering indices on $Q.B$ and $S.C$ assumed in Section 11.8.

b)   There are only nonclustering indices on $Q.B$ and $S.C$.

c)   There are no indices at all.

d)   There are clustering indices on $Q.B$ and $S.C$, Q is ten times as big as R, and R is ten times as big as S.

11.23: Construct the connection hypergraph for the query $\sigma_F(R)$, where R is the join

$$AB \bowtie BCD \bowtie BEF \bowtie FGH \bowtie GI \bowtie HJ$$

and F is the condition $D < E \wedge A = 0 \wedge I = 1$.

11.24: Find the GYO-reduction of your hypergraph from Exercise 11.23. Is your hypergraph cyclic or acyclic?

11.25: Apply the Wong-Youssefi algorithm to the query of Exercise 11.23.

* 11.26: Show that if hypergraphs are restricted to have hyperedges of size 2 (that is, they are ordinary graphs), then the only acyclic hypergraphs, according to the definition given in Section 11.11 (GYO-reduction of the hypergraph is empty) are the forests.

** 11.27: A set of relations $R_1, \ldots, R_n$ is said to be *locally consistent* if for all i and j, $\pi_{R_i}(R_i \bowtie R_j) = R_i$, or put another way, no R_i has any dangling tuples with respect to the join of R_i with any one of the other relations R_j. We say $R_1, \ldots, R_n$ is *globally consistent* if for all i, $\pi_{R_i}(R_1 \bowtie \cdots \bowtie R_n) = R_i$; that is, no R_i has any dangling tuples with respect to the join of all the relations.[41]

---

[41] "Globally consistent" is another common term for what we called "fully reduced" in Section 11.13.

a) Show that if the hypergraph of $R_1, \ldots, R_n$ is acyclic, then these relations are locally consistent if and only if they are globally consistent. Since it is obvious that global consistency always implies local consistency, what is really asked for is a proof that if $R_1, \ldots, R_n$ is acyclic and locally consistent, then it is globally consistent.

b) Show the converse of (a), that is, if $R_1, \ldots, R_n$ is cyclic, then there are values we can assign to the relations that are locally consistent, but not globally consistent.

11.28: Express the following queries about the bank database of Example 11.26, in terms of the fragments given by that example.

a) Print the customers that (possibly jointly) hold account number 123.

b) Print the customers that have accounts at branch 1 and some other branch.

11.29: Optimize the queries of Exercise 11.28 by algebraic manipulation.

11.30: Suppose the beer drinkers' database of Exercise 11.20 is distributed in such a way that at every brewery, there is a fragment of the $SELLS$ relation for only the beers brewed by that brewery. Also, every bar has a fragment of the $FREQUENTS$ relation with the tuples mentioning that bar. The $LIKES$ relation is at a central site.

a) What are the guard conditions for each fragment?

b) Express and optimize the queries of Exercise 11.20 in terms of this distributed database.

11.31: What is the effect on the fragments of Example 11.26 of inserting the fact that customer Jones has account number 123 at the Main St. branch, with a balance of $100?

11.32: Show the claim of Example 11.32 (Section 11.13) regarding the length of the shortest semijoin sequence needed to remove certain tuples from the particular relations discussed there.

11.33: Show the "only if" part of Theorem 11.4—that no cyclic hypergraph has a full reducer.

11.34: In Example 11.31 we gave a full reducer of four steps for the join

$$AB \bowtie BC \bowtie CD$$

a) Show that there is no full reducer with fewer than four steps.

b) Find all of the four-step full reducers.

11.35: Consider the query

$$\pi_{A,E,J,K}(AB \bowtie BCD \bowtie DE \bowtie BFG \bowtie FHI \bowtie IK \bowtie HJ)$$

a) Construct the hypergraph for the join and show that it is acyclic.

b) Find a parse tree for the hypergraph in which BFG is the root.

c) Construct the full reducer for this join, using the ear-reduction sequence that corresponds to your parse tree from (b).

d) Give the sequence of steps performed by Algorithm 11.4 (Yannakakis' algorithm) after the full reducer sequence of steps from (c).

* 11.36: In Example 11.35 we showed that a join could have output size that is exponential in the input size. Let us assume that the size of a relation is the number of tuples in the relation times the number of attributes in the relation; that is, the size is the total number of components of all the tuples in the relation. The input size for a join is the sum of the sizes of all the relations involved in the join.

a) Show that there is a polynomial $p(n)$ such that no join with an input size of n has output size greater than $2^{p(n)}$.

b) Show that the join of m relations of size m can have an output size as great as m^{m+1}.

* 11.37: In Example 11.36 we made the claim, listed as item (4) in that example, that any join of m relations in the join of line (11.40) of Example 11.36 has at least 2^{m+2} tuples. Provide a formal proof of this claim.

** 11.38: We also claimed in Example 11.36 that a polynomial-time algorithm (as a function of the sum of the input and output sizes) to evaluate an arbitrary projection of a join would imply $\mathcal{P} = \mathcal{NP}$. Show that to be the case by proving the following stronger result. It is $\mathcal{NP}$-complete to test whether the join of a given set of relations over given relation schemes is empty.[42]

* 11.39: Show that in step (3) of Algorithm 11.4, if R has no distinguished attributes, then we need not take the join of R with its parent at all; we can just prune R from the parse tree.

** 11.40: Let us consider how many hyperedges an acyclic hypergraph of n nodes can have. We assume that no two hyperedges may be identical, and we add some additional constraints in each part below. In each case, find the maximum number of hyperedges there can be in an acyclic hypergraph meeting the constraints.

a) All hyperedges are of size 2.

b) All hyperedges are of size 3.

c) Hyperedges can be of any size.

d) Hyperedges can be of any size, but no hyperedge can be a subset of another.

---

[42] Notice that cyclic joins are essential to the proof. If we restrict ourselves to acyclic joins, there is a polynomial-time test (reduce the relations and check if they are empty).

* 11.41: Complete the proof of Lemma 11.1 (Section 11.14) by showing the induction claimed at the beginning of that lemma, concerning the sequence of values that each relation S in the parse tree assumes during Yannakakis' algorithm.

11.42: Repeat Example 11.40 (Section 11.15) with the parameters $T_P = T_Q = T_R = 1000$, $I_{PB} = 100$, $I_{QB} = 20$, $I_{QC} = 200$, and $I_{RC} = 50$.

* 11.43: In Figure 11.33 (Section 11.15) we showed the three unordered binary trees with three leaves and the four ordered trees corresponding to each of them.

   a) How many unordered binary trees with four leaves are there?
   b) How many ordered trees correspond to each?

BIBLIOGRAPHIC NOTES

The earliest papers on query optimization for expressions of relational algebra include Hall [1976], Minker [1978], Pecherer [1975], and Smith and Chang [1975]. The heart of these algorithms is moving selections as far down the tree as possible, although a variety of other useful manipulations are suggested. This strategy of optimization by doing selections first is attributed to Palermo [1974].

System R Optimization

Algorithm 11.1 for optimizing selections in System R is found in Astrahan et al. [1976] and Griffiths et al. [1979]. More on the System R query optimizer can be found there and in Chamberlin et al. [1981a]. Astrahan, Schkolnick, and Kim [1980] discusses performance evaluation of the System R optimizer.

Join Algorithms

Algorithms for taking the join can be found in Gotlieb [1975], Kim [1981], Ibaraki and Kameda [1984], Valduriez [1987], and Valduriez and Boral [1987]. In addition, Shapiro [1986] discusses algorithms for taking joins in a large "main" memory, without need for secondary storage.

Optimization in Distributed Systems

Algorithm 11.5 is from Selinger and Adiba [1980]. More on the System R* distributed query optimizer can be found in Daniels et al. [1982] and Mackert and Lohman [1986].

   Apers, Hevner, and Yao [1983] is another useful reference on distributed query optimization. Several of the papers mentioned under the next heading are also relevant to distributed query optimization.

   The first systematic study of fragmentation is Dayal and Bernstein [1978, 1982], while Ceri and Pelagatti [1980] and Adiba [1980] developed an algebra of *multirelations* (lists of relations), of which we only scratched the surface in

Section 11.11. The guard condition technique is from Maier and Ullman [1983b].

Select-Project-Join Queries

Several of the more complex algorithms discussed in this chapter are designed to deal with special cases of queries involving joins or products, to which a selection and/or projection is applied. Algorithm 11.3 is from Wong and Youssefi [1976]. This algorithm was extended by Chakravarthy and Minker [1986] to handle several expressions (with common subexpressions) at once. Algorithm 11.4, for taking the projection of an acyclic join, is from Yannakakis [1981].

The concept of the full-reducer semijoin sequence is from Bernstein and Goodman [1981a], while Bernstein and Chiu [1981] was an earlier attempt at applying semijoins to distributed queries in which joined relations shared only one attribute. Gouda and Dayal [1981] study optimal semijoin sequences. Chiu [1981] considered optimal sequences of semijoins for *chain queries*, where the relations of the join are ordered in such a way that each intersects only the one before and the one after.

Yao [1979] is an examination of optimization algorithms for select-project-join queries. Smith [1985], Smith and Genesereth [1985], and Swami and Gupta [1988] consider heuristics for ordering joins.

Acyclic Database Schemes

The notion of an acyclic database scheme, as presented here, is from Fagin, Mendelzon, and Ullman [1982]. An equivalent, but rather different definition ("tree queries"), was given in Bernstein and N. Goodman [1981a], who also showed that this class, and only this class, of joins has full reducers. Malvestuto [1986] pointed out that the same concept has played a role in statistics since L. Goodman [1970] and Haberman [1970].

The GYO test for acyclicity was discovered independently by Graham [1979] and Yu and Ozsoyoglu [1979]. Tarjan and Yannakakis [1984] give a linear time test for acyclicity.

A variety of equivalent definitions for acyclic schemes have been given, including Beeri, Fagin, Maier, and Ullman [1983], Goodman and Shmueli [1982, 1983], and D'Atri and Moscarini [1986]. Fagin [1983] identifies four different notions of acyclicity and compares their properties. Following this paper, our notion of acyclicity is often referred to as "alpha-acyclicity."

One can also generalize acyclicity to schemes with dependencies; the most normal way is through the equivalent definition "local consistency equals global consistency" discussed in Exercise 11.27. Laver, Mendelzon, and Graham [1983] gave an acyclicity test for schemes with functional dependencies. Sacca, Manfredi, and Mecchia [1984] gave a characterization of such schemes assuming infinite relations were allowed, and Sagiv and Shmueli [1986] did the same on the (normal) assumption that relations are finite.

Transformation-Based Optimizers

There are several projects attempting to build general-purpose, modular database system components. The optimizer module for such systems involves pattern matching on expression trees and tree transformations and/or rewriting.

These systems include GENESIS (Batory [1988], Batory, Leung, and Wise [1988]) at the University of Texas; EXODUS (Carey et al. [1986], Graefe and DeWitt [1987]) at the University of Wisconsin; and Starburst (Schwarz et al. [1986], Freytag [1987], Lohman [1988], Lee, Freytag, and Lohman [1988], and Haas et al. [1988]) at IBM-Almaden.

Other Optimization Topics

Algorithms for execution of joins and other operations on multiprocessors have been studied by Goodman [1981], Bitton, Boral, DeWitt, and Wilkinson [1983], Ullman [1984], and DeWitt and Gerber [1985]. The key idea is that hashing tuples of relations to be joined, to buckets whose addresses depend on the values in the common attributes only, allows a large number of processors to be brought to bear on a single join.

The following three papers cover additional optimization issues not discussed in this chapter. Sacco and Schkolnick [1986] discusses optimization of buffer utilization (allocation of main memory to blocks) as we shuffle blocks in and out of secondary storage during a query. Schkolnick and Tiberio [1985] considers optimization of update operations. Sellis [1986] discusses optimization involving several queries at once.

Jarke and Koch [1984] surveys query optimization. Gray and Putzolo [1987] is a short paper offering some important principles for optimization.

CHAPTER 12

More
About
Logic

We shall now resume the study of logical rules as a way to express knowledge, which we began in Chapter 3 (Volume I). We begin by examining Horn-clause rules with function symbols in Section 12.1, and in Section 12.2 we discuss the natural least-fixed-point semantics for such rules. There, we extend the "bottom-up" approaches of Chapter 3, called "naive" and "semi-naive" evaluation, to allow function symbols in rules. In Section 12.3 we consider "top-down" evaluation of logical rules, with and without function symbols, and the advantages and disadvantages of this approach, compared with "bottom-up," evaluation, are explored. The technique defined here for top-down processing is the method used by Prolog, and it is sometimes referred to as "SLD-resolution" or "LUSH-resolution." Section 12.4 gives an algorithm for unification, an essential step in top-down processing of logic.

Subsequent sections lay the groundwork for Chapters 13 to 15, which cover optimization of queries that are expressed as logical rules. Sections 12.5 to 12.7 are a discussion of what is, in a sense, a "straw-man" algorithm for evaluating logical queries in a top-down fashion; it may be regarded as a relation-oriented version of SLD-resolution. We introduce some important concepts for further study of efficient algorithms: sideways information passing and top-down passing of binding relations. However, the primary reason for studying this algorithm is so we can understand what the more efficient algorithms of Chapter 13 are doing, and see why they are no less efficient and no less general than the simple top-down, relation-based algorithm.

In Section 12.8 we introduce a useful tool for describing the interactions among rules, the "rule/goal graph." Section 12.9 shows how to use the rule/goal graph to determine the binding pattern (set of bound arguments) of each predicate as we process the rules top-down. We also introduce in Section 12.9 two constructions that are very important for the "magic sets" algorithms of Chapter 13: making binding patterns unique and "rectifying subgoals." The last section explains how to use the rule/goal graph to select a good order for the subgoals of the various rules.

Notation for Logic

The following conventions were followed in Volume I, when we discussed logic, and we adopt them here.

1. A logical rule is written

    $$H \text{ :- } G_1 \text{ \& } \cdots \text{ \& } G_k.$$

    H is called the *head*, and $G_1, \ldots, G_k$ are the *subgoals*. The subgoals together are called the *body*. The head and each of the subgoals are *atomic formulas*, whose form is $p(t_1, \ldots, t_n)$, where p is a *predicate symbol*, and the t's are arguments. In Volume I, arguments could be only variables or constants, while here we shall allow more general expressions, to be defined in Section 12.1. The meaning of the rule is "if $G_1, \ldots, G_k$ are true, then H is true."

2. Certain subgoals have predicates that are given a conventional interpretation, that of an arithmetic comparison operator, for example, $X < Y$. These subgoals and their predicates are called *built-in*. Other subgoals have uninterpreted symbols as predicates. These predicates represent finite relations; we call them *ordinary* subgoals and predicates.

3. Predicate symbols are denoted by character strings beginning with a lowercase letter, for example, p or foo. Variables are denoted by character strings beginning with a capital letter.

4. Certain predicates are defined by the rules; that is, they appear as the head of one or more rules. these are called IDB (*intensional database*) predicates. Other predicates are not defined by rules, but by a stored relation, and these are called EDB (*extensional database*) predicates. An EDB predicate can only appear in subgoals; an IDB predicate can appear in both heads and subgoals.

5. Corresponding to each ordinary predicate is a relation—an "EDB relation" for an EDB predicate and an "IDB relation" for an IDB predicate. Whether p is an EDB or an IDB predicate, the value of the corresponding relation P is a collection of tuples. However, if p is an IDB predicate, then P is not stored, but is constructed as needed from the rules. A tuple of relation P can be denoted by any of the notations used for tuples in general, for example, μ, abc, or (a, b, c). We also use the notation $p(a, b, c)$, that is, the predicate name with arguments corresponding to the components of the tuple. We may say "$p(a, b, c)$ is true" to mean that abc is in the relation P. Finally, when there is no confusion, we may refer to the relation for p

as p itself.

6. A rule is *safe* if every variable that appears in the head also appears in the body, in a nonnegated, ordinary subgoal. Safety was introduced in Chapter 3 as a way to guarantee that finite EDB relations implied that the IDB relations were also finite. As we shall see, safety is not sufficient to guarantee finite IDB relations when there are function symbols in the logic. We shall continue to assume that rules are safe unless stated otherwise, however.

12.1 LOGIC WITH FUNCTION SYMBOLS

In Volume I we restricted ourselves to logic in the datalog style, where the arguments of predicates are only variables or constants. That is perfectly reasonable when we model relational query languages, which can be viewed as notations for nonrecursive datalog. There are, however, some situations described more easily by the use of arguments that are *terms* built from variables, constants, and *function symbols*. Terms may be defined recursively by

1. A variable is a term.
2. A constant is a term.
3. If f is a function symbol, and $T_1, \ldots, T_k$ are terms, then $f(T_1, \ldots, T_k)$ is a term.

In full first-order logic, the arguments of predicates may be arbitrary terms, rather than constants or variables only. We shall continue to use the Prolog style of rules, that is, Horn clauses, with possibly negated subgoals in the body.[1] Tuples of EDB relations will be permitted to have components that are arbitrary terms, rather than being restricted to be simple constants, as heretofore.

Unless we state otherwise, we assume that terms in EDB relations do not have variables, but there are some interesting applications where these terms do have variables. Terms without variables are called *ground terms*. A predicate whose arguments are ground terms is a *ground atom*. We may view a ground atom as a tuple of a relation, but the components of these tuples are not necessarily elementary values (for example, integers or character strings); they can be terms with nontrivial structure.

Example 12.1: One simple use of function symbols is to incorporate into relations some of the structure that is possible in the hierarchical model. Thus, we might store an EDB relation *emps* with the scheme

$$emps\Big(name(F, L),\ addr\big(street(N, S), city(C, T, Z)\big)\Big) \tag{12.1}$$

---

[1] Of course, a "Horn clause" with a negated subgoal is not, technically, a Horn clause at all. However, as we saw in Section 3.6, under certain circumstances, such rules may be used sensibly.

Here, *emps* is a predicate symbol with a binary relation. The first argument is a term consisting of the binary function symbol *name* applied to arguments F and L, representing the first and last name of the employee. Note that the variables F and L will, in each tuple of the relation, be replaced by two appropriate constants.

The second component is the binary function symbol *addr* applied to two arguments that are themselves nontrivial terms. The first is function symbol *street* applied to variables N and S, standing for number and street name, respectively, while the second is function symbol *city* applied to variables C, T, and Z, standing for city name, state name, and zip code. A possible tuple of the *emps* relation is

$$emps\Big(name(arnold, avarice),\ addr\big(street(23, lois\_lane),$$
$$city(yuppie\_valley, calif, 94720))\big)\Big)$$

While we suggested that (12.1) was the "scheme" for the relation *emps*, in fact, we gain power from the use of function symbols if we permit many different "schemes" and apply appropriate function symbols to help interpret the data. For example, if an employee lives in an apartment, then instead of a term $street(N, S)$ in the first component of *addr*, we wish to have a term $apt\big(A, street(N, S)\big)$, where A is the apartment number. Thus, if Esther Eggplant lives in an apartment building next door to Arnold Avarice, we could have the *emps* "tuple"

$$emps\Big(name(esther, eggplant),\ addr\big(apt(3d, street(21, lois\_lane)),$$
$$city(yuppie\_valley, calif, 94720))\big)\Big)$$

Suppose we wish to print addresses in the customary format: the employee's name on line 1, the apartment number if there is one on the next line, the street address on the next line, and the city, state, and zip on the last line. Thus, the third line will contain the street if the first component of the address has an apartment number, that is, if the function symbol is *apt*. If the function symbol is *street*, then the third line contains the information in the second component of *addr*. We can express these observations as rules with function symbols. The following rules define a predicate *print3*, which we might think of as the set of third lines of the addresses of all the employees.

```
print3(N,S)  :- emps(X,addr(apt(Y,street(N,S)),Z)).
print3(C,T,Z) :- emps(U,addr(street(V,W),city(C,T,Z))).
```

Notice how the structure provided by the function symbols not only allows us to deduce the meaning of different fields in a tuple, but also it allows us to ignore the structure of parts of tuples in which we are not interested. For example, Z in the first rule stands for whatever is in the *city* field of the *addr* portion of the tuple.

The reader should not be overly concerned by the fact that the two rules for *print3* use different numbers of arguments. Formally, the relation for *print3* is assumed to have one particular arity, and it would not make sense to place in that relation tuples of different arities. However, what is intended in this example is that all the components of a *print3* tuple are printed in the order of appearance (and actually, we should have added necessary spaces and a comma after the city); there is no IDB relation for *print3* constructed. To be formally correct, we could wrap the arguments of *print3* in a function symbol, since function symbols can be used with different numbers of arguments. That is, we could write the heads of the rules for *print3* as $print3(line(N, S))$ and $print3(line(C, T, Z))$. $\square$

In Example 12.1, function symbols were, in effect, used to create named record structures, and to define alternative structures for the fields of records. That capability is often a convenience, although in principle it can be dispensed with. For example, we could have defined an ordinary ("flat") relation with format

$$emps(F, L, A, N, S, C, T, Z)$$

where the A (apartment) component is null for those who do not dwell in an apartment.

When rules are recursive, however, the use of function symbols allows us to create an infinite set of potential values that may appear in relations, as the next example shows. Notice that datalog rules are not powerful enough to create values that did not already exist in the EDB relations or in the rules themselves.

Example 12.2: Addition can be defined recursively as follows. Suppose we have a predicate symbol $int(X)$ that is intended to be true if X is a (nonnegative) integer and a predicate $sum(X, Y, Z)$ that is to be true if and only if the sum of X and Y is Z. Suppose also that we have the function symbol *succ* with the intention that $succ(X)$ is the integer $X + 1$. Finally, we have the constant 0, with its obvious meaning. Then the term $succ(0)$ is our way of saying "1," $succ(succ(0))$ is "2," and so on; the integers other than 0 do not exist in any other form. Then the rules we desire are shown in Figure 12.1.

That is, the first two rules in Figure 12.1 define 0, $succ(0)$, $succ(succ(0))$, and so on, to be integers. The third rule says that the sum of any integer and 0 is that integer, and the last says that $X + (Y + 1) = Z + 1$, if $X + Y = Z$; put another way, $X + (Y + 1) = (X + Y) + 1$. These rules are sufficient to generate all and only the true addition facts.

For example, $int(0)$ follows from rule (1). Then, from rule (3), $sum(0, 0, 0)$

```
(1)  int(0).
(2)  int(succ(X))  :- int(X).

(3)  sum(X,0,X)  :- int(X).
(4)  sum(X,succ(Y),succ(Z))  :- sum(X,Y,Z).
```

Figure 12.1 Rules for defining addition.

is true. Applying rule (4) to this fact we have $sum\big(0, succ(0), succ(0)\big)$, that is, $sum(0, 1, 1)$. From rule (2), we infer $int\big(succ(0)\big)$, that is, $int(1)$. Then rule (3) gives us $sum(1, 0, 1)$ and (4) gives us $sum(1, 1, 2)$. In these facts we have used 1 to stand for $succ(0)$ and 2 to stand for $succ(1) = succ\big(succ(0)\big)$. Note that both int and sum have infinite relations, even though the rules of this example are safe. $\square$

Let us observe that although the syntax for function symbols and predicate symbols is the same (strings beginning with a lowercase letter), there is no confusion between these two types of symbols. Function symbols take domain values as arguments and return domain values. Predicate symbols take domain values as arguments but return truth values (true or false). Thus, in Example 12.2, *succ* takes one integer as an argument and returns an integer, while *sum* takes three integer arguments; it returns true if the third is the sum of the first and second, and it returns false otherwise. In Example 12.1 we can see a function symbol like *name* as taking two domain elements, character strings in this case, and returning an "object" of type "record of two character strings."

In our next example, we see how function symbols can be used both to create an infinity of potential new objects and to give clues that let us decipher the structure of the object. It is a very trivial example of a reasoning system about a world with five states. It allows us to describe the true facts about transitions from state to state, thus letting us to plan how to get from one state to another. In a realistic situation, there might be millions of states, and the power of a knowledge-base system would be needed to deduce the necessary facts efficiently.

Example 12.3: Let us consider a simple "blocks world" with three blocks, A, B, and C, which may be placed in piles only if the piles are in decreasing size order. Block A is larger than B, which is larger than C. The five possible states of the system, a through e, are shown in Figure 12.2.

The legal moves of the system are expressed by an EDB relation $GO(S, T)$ that is intended to be true if and only if state S can become state T by one "move." Here, a move shifts the position of one block, removing it from the block or the floor on which it rests and placing it either on the floor or on a larger block that is itself uncovered. For the states of Figure 12.2, the relation

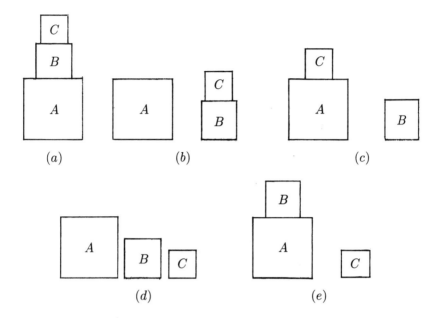

Figure 12.2 Blocks-world states.

GO consists of the ten tuples that, written as ground atoms, are

$$go(a,e) \quad go(b,c) \quad go(b,d) \quad go(c,b) \quad go(c,d)$$
$$go(d,b) \quad go(d,c) \quad go(d,e) \quad go(e,a) \quad go(e,d)$$

Let us use a binary function symbol g, and let $g(S,T)$ be a term representing the possibility that state S can be transformed into state T by one or more moves. We define the unary predicate *true* with the intention that $true(X)$ holds exactly when term X represents a statement about state transitions that is true. For example, we would naturally have the rule

(1) `true(g(S,T)) :- go(S,T).`

Here, *go* is presumed to be the EDB predicate that corresponds to the EDB relation *GO*.

   We also need a rule that defines what "goes to by one or more moves" means, that is,

(2) `true(g(S,T)) :- true(g(S,U)) & true(g(U,T)).`

   Next, we may wish to talk about "accessible" states. Suppose we are given a unary EDB relation $ACC(S)$ of states S that are initially accessible. For example, *ACC* may contain only the one state in which we initially find the blocks world. We may then use unary function symbol $a(S)$ to represent the possibility that state S is accessible after some number of moves. The rules for when an accessibility condition is true are

```
(3) true(a(S)) :- acc(S).
(4) true(a(S)) :- true(a(T)) & true(g(T,S)).
```

In rules (1) through (4), the use of function symbols is not essential; we could remove the "true" everywhere it appears, treating a and g as if they were predicates rather than function symbols, and the rules would say essentially the same thing. However, there are other things we can say with the approach taken here that are considerably more natural when we use function symbols. For example, we may wish to use terms that express conditions more complicated than "goes" or "accessible." We could, for example, use binary function symbols *or* and *and* to represent the logical OR and AND of two conditions. We could then include in our "knowledge base" rules defining AND and OR

```
(5) true(or(X,Y)) :- true(X).
(6) true(or(X,Y)) :- true(Y).
(7) true(and(X,Y)) :- true(X) & true(Y).
```

Notice that these rules do not depend on the structure of the terms X and Y; they could be "goes" facts, "accessible" facts, or the conjunction or disjunction of several facts. Also notice that rules (5) and (6) are not safe, since they each have a variable that appears in the head but not the body. There are two approaches to fixing this problem.

1. Write another predicate *possible*(X) that says X is a term that might be true, i.e., all its constants come from the EDB relations GO and ACC. We can use *possible* to restrict the range of the variable that otherwise would not appear in the body. For example, (5) could be rewritten

   ```
   true(or(X,Y)) :- true(X) & possible(Y).
   ```

2. We could accept the unsafe rules. That prevents us from applying a rule to infer all of the true facts, since from a fact like $true\bigl(g(a,e)\bigr)$ follow an infinity of facts with different values of Y in rule (5). However, it would not prevent us from answering questions about particular facts, like "is $or\bigl(g(a,b),\ g(c,d)\bigr)$ true?"

The exercises examine both of these possibilities. □

12.2 EVALUATING LOGIC WITH FUNCTION SYMBOLS

In this section, we shall generalize the techniques for evaluating rules without function symbols that were introduced in Sections 3.3 and 3.4 of Volume I. The reader who is not familiar with these methods and concepts is advised to reread those sections before proceeding.

In Chapter 3 we offered Algorithm 3.3, called "naive evaluation," for computing the least fixed point of a collection of rules with no negated subgoals. The idea is to start by assuming the IDB relations are all empty, then repeatedly to compute new values for the IDB predicates, by applying the rules to the EDB relations and the current values of the IDB relations. When the rules are datalog, this process eventually converges to a finite relation, which is the "meaning" of the rules, as we saw in Section 3.3. When there are function symbols, we can show that a least fixed point exists, but it may be infinite, in which case no finite number of repetitions of the loop of naive evaluation suffices to reach the least fixed point.

We also gave, in Chapter 3, a more efficient algorithm, called "semi-naive evaluation," Algorithm 3.4. Naive evaluation, once it discovers a fact, rediscovers it on subsequent passes. Semi-naive evaluation avoids discovering the same fact in the same way twice, by insisting that each time we apply a rule, at least one of the subgoals uses a fact that was just discovered on the previous round. We shall describe these algorithms in more detail later in the section.

To begin, we shall offer some informal examples of the operation that we called EVAL$(p, R_1, \ldots, R_n)$ in Chapter 3. This operation takes relations $R_1, \ldots, R_n$ for the subgoals of all the rules for predicate p and produces the relation for p that we get by "applying" the rules to the relations. That is, we look for substitutions for the rules' variables that make each subgoal a tuple of the corresponding relation. The set of successful substitutions for the variables is called the "relation for the rule"; its attributes are the variables appearing in the rule. We then take each tuple in the relation for the rule, evaluate the head with that substitution, and take the resulting ground atom to be a tuple of the relation for p.

Example 12.4: Let us return to Example 12.2, where we discussed a logical definition of addition facts. This example is particularly simple, since there are no function symbols in the subgoals. Thus, EVAL operates almost as in Chapter 3, but when we find a successful substitution for the variables, and we make the substitution into the head, we get nontrivial terms as arguments.

Let us first apply naive evaluation to only rules (1) and (2) of Example 12.2, defining a unary relation *int*. Note there is no EDB for the rules of this example.

We initialize the IDB relation for *int* to $\emptyset$. Then, on pass 1 of Algorithm 3.3, rule (2) yields nothing, because $int(X)$ has no tuples. However, rule (1) produces the tuple 0 for relation *int*.

On pass 2, the first rule produces only 0 again, but the second rule now has a value, 0, for X, and so produces the tuple $succ(0)$ for *int*. Note that this tuple has one component, and that component is a term with function symbol *succ*.

On the third pass, X can also take on the value $succ(0)$; technically, the relation for rule (2) is a relation over attribute X, namely $\{0, succ(0)\}$. This new value for X yields the new tuple $succ(succ(0))$ for *int*. In general, the *i*th pass produces one new tuple, $succ^{i-1}(0)$, for *int*.[2] As a result, the value of the relation *int* in the least fixed point is the set of nonnegative integers $\{0, 1, 2, \ldots\}$, with integer i represented by term $succ^i(0)$. Thus, the rules of Example 12.2 define *int* to be an infinite relation, and an infinite number of iterations of the loop of naive or semi-naive evaluation is necessary to "attain" this solution.

A similar process occurs when we follow rules (3) and (4) to compute the relation *sum*. On the first pass, the subgoals in the bodies of both rules have empty relations, so no *sum* tuples are produced. On pass 2, *int* contains 0, so rule (3) produces tuple $(0, 0, 0)$ for *sum*.

On pass three, *int* also contains $succ(0)$, so rule (3) produces

$$\big(succ(0), 0, succ(0)\big)$$

Also, *sum* contains $(0, 0, 0)$, so rule (4) yields $\big(0, succ(0), succ(0)\big)$. In general, the reader can check that the addition fact

$$sum\big(succ^i(0), succ^j(0), succ^{i+j}(0)\big)$$

is added on pass $i + j + 2$, using rule (3) if $j = 0$ and rule (4) if $j > 0$. No other tuples are added to *sum*. Thus, *sum* also is an infinite relation in the least fixed point, requiring an infinite number of passes to attain. $\square$

In a sense, infinite relations like *int* and *sum* of Example 12.4 are not computable at all, since we never reach the least fixed point of their defining rules, no matter how long we run naive evaluation. On the other hand, the noncomputability of the relations does not contradict the fact that they are well defined by the process of taking the least fixed point, and in the next section we shall see how we can use rules defining infinite relations to get some answers in finite time. In particular, we can often answer the question whether a particular tuple is in such a relation, even if we can never construct the complete relation.

Example 12.5: Now, let us reconsider Example 12.3. To begin, suppose only rules (1) and (2) are available. Recall these rules are

(1) `true(g(S,T)) :- go(S,T).`
(2) `true(g(S,T)) :- true(g(S,U)) & true(g(U,T)).`

On the first pass, relation *true* is empty, so rule (2) yields nothing. EDB relation GO consists of the ten tuples given in Example 12.3. Thus, on pass 1 the relation for rule (1) is $GO(S, T)$. From each of the ten tuples in this relation we construct a term $g(S, T)$, and this term becomes the lone component in a

---

[2] $f^j(X)$ stands for the application of function symbol f j times, that is $f(f(\cdots(f(X))\cdots))$ [j times].

one-component tuple of the unary relation for *true*. Thus, after pass 1, the relation for *true* contains $g(a, e)$, $g(e, d)$, and eight other tuples, each with a single component.[3]

Subsequent passes yield no new tuples by rule (1), but now rule (2) begins to yield new tuples for *true*. To see how, let us first evaluate the relation for rule (2), given that the relation for *true* is the ten tuples of one component each, shown in Figure 12.3. Recall that the relation for this rule will have attributes S, T, and U, corresponding to the three variables appearing in the body of the rule. Each tuple must have values s, t, and u for these variables, such that both of the subgoals $true\big(g(S, U)\big)$ and $true\big(g(U, T)\big)$ become tuples of the relation for *true* when we substitute s for S, t for T, and u for U.

$$g(a, e) \qquad g(b, c) \qquad g(b, d) \qquad g(c, b) \qquad g(c, d)$$
$$g(d, b) \qquad g(d, c) \qquad g(d, e) \qquad g(e, a) \qquad g(e, d)$$

Figure 12.3 Initial relation for predicate *true*.

To see what values s, t, and u might be, we match each subgoal with each tuple of the relation *true*, which gives us values for those variables appearing in that subgoal, S and U for the first subgoal and U and T for the second. Then, we take the natural join of the sets of tuples for each subgoal.[4] In our particular example, we must match the subgoal $true\big(g(S, U)\big)$ against each of the ten tuples in the relation *true* of Figure 12.3. For example, comparing the lone component $g(S, U)$ with the first tuple, $g(a, e)$, we see that a match is possible, and the value of S becomes a, while U becomes e. In fact, for each of the ten tuples in *true*, the match succeeds, and we get the relation

$$\{ae, \ bc, \ bd, \ cb, \ cd, \ db, \ dc, \ de, \ ea, \ ed\} \tag{12.2}$$

which we shall call $Q_1(S, U)$, for the first subgoal of rule (2). For the second subgoal, $true\big(g(U, T)\big)$, we also construct a relation, which we may call $Q_2(U, T)$. The value of Q_2 is easily seen to be the same as Q_1, that is (12.2). However, while Q_1 is a relation over attributes S and U, in that order, Q_2 is over U and T, in that order.

---

[3] Do not get confused between function symbols and predicate symbols. In this context, g is a function symbol, while *true* is the predicate symbol; $g(a, e)$ is a single component of a tuple for *true*, while a and e are not components of a tuple, but rather arguments of the function symbol g.

[4] This join corresponds to Step (3) of Algorithm 3.1, where we joined relations called the Q_i's constructed by relational algebra from each of the subgoals. The difference is that here, the relations for each subgoal cannot necessarily be constructed by relational algebra from the relation for the predicate of that subgoal, as the Q_i's were constructed from the R_i's in Algorithm 3.1. Rather, we need to apply a more powerful operation, called "term matching," to be discussed shortly, on the tuples.

We now take the join $R = Q_1 \bowtie Q_2$ to get the relation for rule (2). R contains 22 tuples, each with components for attributes S, U, and T, respectively. Some of these tuples are aea [from ae and ea] bcd [from bc and cd], bde, and edc. For each tuple, we construct the one-component tuple $g(S, T)$ that the head of rule (2) says belongs in the relation for $true$. For example, the four tuples of R mentioned above yield the following tuples for $true$: $g(a, a)$, $g(b, d)$, $g(b, e)$, and $g(e, c)$. Of these, only the second was already known to be in $true$.

The iterative computation of $true$ using only rules (1) and (2) will eventually converge, because unlike Example 12.4, we do not build up progressively larger terms; here all terms for the lone component of relation $true$ are of the form $g(x, y)$, where x and y are values appearing in the EDB relation GO (these values are a through e in our example data). If GO is finite, as it must be, then $true$ cannot be given an infinite number of different tuples.

On the other hand, if we used rules (5) through (7) of Example 12.3, then we could build up an infinity of different tuples in $true$. For example, suppose we applied rule (7):

```
true(and(X,Y)) :- true(X) & true(Y).
```

On pass 2, when $true$ has the ten tuples of Figure 12.3, any one of them could match X and any could match Y. Thus, the relation for the first subgoal, $true(X)$, has the ten values for X: $\{g(a, e), g(b, c), \ldots\}$ and the relation for the second subgoal has the same relation, but the attribute is Y. That is, X and Y, being variables, can each match any term.

The relation for rule (7) thus consists of the 100 tuples over attributes X and Y, the Cartesian product of the relation of Figure 12.3 with itself. When we substitute for X and Y in the head of rule (7), we get 100 tuples for $true$, of which $and\big(g(a, e), g(b, c)\big)$ is an example. These tuples are available at the next pass to match X and Y in rule (7) to build still bigger terms, like

$$and\Big(and\big(g(a, e), g(b, c)\big), \ and\big(g(b, d), g(c, b)\big)\Big)$$

and so on.

The rules (5) and (6) present a bigger problem since they are not safe rules. We need to solve the problem by one of the ways suggested in Example 12.3: rewriting the rules to be safe, or not trying to use them in a naive-evaluation algorithm, where we compute all the head values that come from substitutions of ground terms for the variables of the body. □

Term Matching

As we saw from the above examples, the operation we called "term matching" plays a fundamental role in the generalization of naive or semi-naive evaluation. That is, we are given a subgoal, which is an atomic formula normally containing variables, and we try to match it with a ground atom, that is, with a tuple of the relation for the predicate that appears in the subgoal. When we match an arbitrary atomic formula with a ground atom, we substitute for each of the variables of the first formula to make it identical to the second. The following algorithm tests whether such a substitution exists, and finds it if so.

Algorithm 12.1: Term Matching.

INPUT: An atomic formula F with variables $X_1, \ldots, X_n$ ($n \geq 0$) and a ground atom G.

OUTPUT: If it exists, the unique substitution τ on the variables $X_1, \ldots, X_n$ such that when, for all i, we substitute $\tau(X_i)$ for each occurrence of X_i in F, the result is G. If there is no such τ, we indicate failure.

METHOD: Initially, $\tau(X_i)$ is undefined for all i. We then apply the recursive procedure *match* shown in Figure 12.4 to F and G. If the call $match(F, G)$ succeeds (returns `true`), then $\tau(X_i)$ will be defined for all i, and this substitution is the term matching that is produced as output. If the call fails (returns `false`), then no term matching exists.

The idea behind the procedure $match(A, B)$ is that if A is a single variable, we must have $\tau(A) = B$, no matter what term B is. If $\tau(A)$ has not yet been defined, we define it to be B, and should we later try to define $\tau(A)$ to be something else, then we fail. If A is a term or the entire atomic formula, then we consider each of the arguments of A, and compare them with the corresponding arguments of B, by a recursive call to *match*. If the numbers of arguments in A and B are different, or if their outermost operators (often called the *principal functors*) of A and B are different, then we fail. Otherwise, we succeed only if all the recursive calls succeed, and we fail if one or more fail. □

Example 12.6: Let us match atomic formula $p\big(f(X, Y),\ g(X)\big)$ against ground atom

$$p\Big(f\big(h(a), b\big),\ g\big(h(a)\big)\Big)$$

The principal functors of both are p, and they each have two arguments, so we must match argument $f(X, Y)$ against $f\big(h(a), b\big)$ and $g(X)$ against $g\big(h(a)\big)$.

For the first pair, we again find that the principal functors, f, agree, and that the number of arguments is two in each case. Thus, we recursively match X against $h(a)$ and Y against b. These matches succeed, giving us $\tau(X) = h(a)$ and $\tau(Y) = b$. Then we consider the second pair, where the principal functors are both g, and each has one argument, X and $h(a)$, respectively. Now, since $\tau(X)$ is defined, we must verify that $\tau(X)$ is identical to the expression against which X is being matched. It is, in this case, so we have checked all subexpressions, and the match succeeds.

A simple example where the match fails is $p(X, X)$ against $p(a, b)$. The first

```
procedure match(A,B): boolean;
/* A is an expression; B is an expression without
    variables.  It returns true if it finds a
    match and false if not.  */
if A is a single variable then
    if τ(A) is undefined then begin
        τ(A) := B; return(true); end
    else /* τ(A) is defined */ if τ(A) = B then return(true)
    else /* τ(A) is defined and is not equal to B */
        return(false)
else begin /* A is not a single variable */
    let A = θ(T₁,...,Tₖ);
    /* here, θ could be a predicate or function symbol */
    if B is not of the form θ(S₁,...,Sₖ) then
        return(false);
    for i := 1 to k do match(Tᵢ, Sᵢ);
    if any of the calls to match returns false then
        return(false)
    else return(true)
end
```

Figure 12.4 Term matching algorithm.

call to *match* spawns calls $match(X, a)$ and $match(X, b)$. The first succeeds, but sets $\tau(X) = a$. Then, the second call checks that $\tau(X) = b$, finds it does not, and fails, causing the entire algorithm to fail. □

Term matching is the heart of two operations needed in the generalized naive and semi-naive evaluation algorithms that work for rules with function symbols. The operations, called ATOV (arguments-to-variables) and VTOA (variables-to-arguments), can be thought of as generalized relational algebra operations. We describe these operations, and then give the generalized evaluation algorithms.

Converting from Arguments to Variables

The relation for a rule body is constructed from relations for the subgoals of the body. Each relation for a subgoal has attributes corresponding to the arguments of the predicate for that subgoal. Our first task is to convert the relations for the subgoals to relations over the variables mentioned in that subgoal, using the operation ATOV. The relations for the subgoals, converted to the viewpoint of variables, can then be joined to find the relation for the body of the rule. This relation, in turn, is converted to a relation for the head, by translating from the viewpoint of variables to the viewpoint of arguments; the VTOA operation, to be described shortly, is used.

The argument-to-variable conversion algorithm for a single subgoal is outlined in Figure 12.5. It converts a relation P, whose attributes correspond to the arguments of a predicate p, into a relation $Q = \text{ATOV}(G,P)$, whose attributes correspond to the variables appearing in the subgoal G; G must be a subgoal with predicate p. To do so, we term-match each tuple of P with the atomic formula G, and each time we match successfully, we create a tuple of Q from the term matching τ. Notice how ATOV can be thought of as a generalized selection or projection, since, like these operations of relational algebra, they process tuples one at a time, to convert one relation to another.

```
let P be the relation for a subgoal p(t₁,...,tₖ);
let X₁,...,Xₙ be the variables appearing in this subgoal;
let Q, the output relation, have scheme X₁ ··· Xₙ and
  be empty initially;
for each tuple (s₁,...,sₖ) in P do
    if there is a term matching τ for subgoal p(t₁,...,tₖ)
        and tuple p(s₁,...,sₖ) then
          add to Q the tuple (τ(X₁),...,τ(Xₙ))
end
```

Figure 12.5 Converting from arguments to variables.

Q_1	Q_2
$h(c)$	$g\big(f(a), a\big)$
$h\big(h(d)\big)$	$g\Big(f\big(f(a)\big), f(a)\Big)$

(a) Relation for q.

R_1	R_2
c	b
$h(d)$	$g(b, c)$

(b) Relation for r.

Figure 12.6 Relations for subgoals.

Example 12.7: Consider the following rule:

$$p\big(f(X),\ g(X,Y)\big) :- q\Big(h(Z),\ g\big(f(X),X\big)\Big)\ \&\ r(Z,Y). \tag{12.3}$$

Let the relation for the first subgoal consist of the two tuples shown in Figure 12.6(a), and let the relation for the second subgoal, $r(Z,Y)$, be that of Figure 12.6(b).[5] If we term-match the first subgoal of (12.3) with the first tuple of Figure 12.6(a), we get the term matching $\tau_1(X) = a$ and $\tau_1(Z) = c$. When we do the same for the second tuple of Figure 12.6(a), we get the matching $\tau_2(X) = f(a)$ and $\tau_2(Z) = h(d)$. Thus the output of the algorithm of Figure 12.5, when applied to Figure 12.6(a) and the first subgoal of (12.3), is

X	Z
a	c
$f(a)$	$h(d)$

We now term-match the second subgoal of (12.3), $r(Z,Y)$, with the two tuples of Figure 12.6(b). The result of the algorithm of Figure 12.5 on these two tuples is the relation

Y	Z
b	c
$g(b,c)$	$h(d)$

We can take the natural join of the two relations above, to get the relation for the body of (12.3), which is given in Figure 12.7. Notice that in this simple example of a join, each tuple from one relation joins with exactly one tuple of the other relation. Also, each tuple of the relations for the subgoals matches the subgoals, and thus yield tuples over the variables of those subgoals. In typical cases, tuples in the relations for the subgoals may not term-match with the subgoals themselves; it is also typical that the join has dangling tuples and has tuples that join with several tuples of another relation. □

X	Y	Z
a	b	c
$f(a)$	$g(b,c)$	$h(d)$

Figure 12.7 Example relation for the body of (12.3).

---

[5] We shall adopt the convention of using P_i for the attribute name of the ith argument of predicate p, and similarly for other predicate names.

Converting from Variables to Arguments

Given a relation $R(X_1, \ldots, X_n)$ for the body of a safe rule, we can construct the relation S for the head by the algorithm of Figure 12.8. In brief, we look at each tuple μ of the relation R for the body, and substitute for each variable X that appears in the head the value of the component of μ that corresponds to attribute X. The tuple that results when we substitute for all variables of the head H, according to the tuple μ, is a tuple of the relation $S = \text{VTOA}(H, R)$.

```
for each tuple μ of relation R do begin
    for each variable X appearing in head H do
        replace all occurrences of variable
            X in H by μ[X];
    let the resulting head predicate be p(t₁,...,tₘ);
    add the tuple (t₁,...,tₘ) to S
end
```

Figure 12.8 Constructing a relation for the head from that of the body.

Example 12.8: Suppose that the relation for the body of (12.3) is the one in Figure 12.7. The scheme of that relation is XYZ, since the attributes correspond to the variables in (12.3). There are two tuples in the relation; in the first, all three components are simple constants, while in the second, all three happen to be nontrivial terms, consisting of function symbols and constants.

When we substitute the first tuple, (a, b, c), for (X, Y, Z) in the head of (12.3), the head becomes $p\big(f(a),\ g(a, b)\big)$. The arguments of this atom become the first and second components of a tuple in the relation for the head. When we make a similar substitution for the second tuple, we get a second tuple for the head relation, which thus is the relation shown in Figure 12.9. $\square$

P_1	P_2
$f(a)$	$g(b, c)$
$f\big(f(a)\big)$	$g\big(f(a),\ g(b, c)\big)$

Figure 12.9 Resulting relation for the head of (12.3).

We shall summarize the above operations in the following algorithm, which computes the relation for a rule head from the relations for the subgoals. In addition to combining the ATOV and VTOA operations, we must include a join of the converted relations for the ordinary subgoals (those not defined by an arithmetic comparison such as $>$), and we must perform a selection for all the built-in (arithmetic comparison) subgoals.

Algorithm 12.2: Construction of the Relation for a Rule Head from Relations for its Subgoals.

INPUT: Relations $R_1, \ldots, R_k$ for subgoals $G_1, \ldots, G_k$ of a given safe rule r.

OUTPUT: The relation for the head of rule r.

METHOD: Let $X_1, \ldots, X_m$ be the entire list of variables appearing among $G_1, \ldots, G_k$.

1. For each ordinary subgoal G_i, use the algorithm of Figure 12.5 to convert relation R_i, which is a relation over the arguments of the predicate of G_i, into a relation $Q_i = \text{ATOV}(G_i, R_i)$ over the variables that appear in G_i.

2. Compute the join $Q = Q_1 \bowtie \cdots \bowtie Q_k$ (omit Q_i if G_i is built-in).

3. Apply to Q a selection for each of the built-in subgoals of r, if any. Note that, because rules are assumed safe, it must be that built-in subgoals can be expressed in terms of the attributes of Q. The result is the relation for the body of r.

4. Use the algorithm of Figure 12.8 to compute the relation for the head of r from the relation for the body of r.

In practice, steps (2) to (4) will be combined, so that we never compute the relation over all the attributes of the rule. Rather, as we compute the partial results $Q_1 \bowtie \cdots \bowtie Q_i$, for $i = 2, 3, \ldots, k$, we project out unnecessary attributes and perform selections as soon as possible. An attribute (which is a variable of r) is only necessary if it appears either in the head of r, or in a later subgoal, G_j, for some $j > i$. The matter is discussed in more detail in Section 12.6. □

Naive Evaluation

Algorithm 12.2 forms the heart of a naive-evaluation algorithm that generalizes Algorithm 3.3. We state that algorithm formally here.

Algorithm 12.3: Naive Evaluation.

INPUT: A collection of safe rules, possibly involving function symbols, and relation $R_1, \ldots, R_k$ for the EDB predicates mentioned in the bodies of these rules.

OUTPUT: If it is finite, the least fixed point of the rules, with respect to the given EDB relations. If that least fixed point is infinite, we produce an infinite sequence of approximations that approaches the least fixed point as a limit; that is, each tuple that is in an IDB relation of the least fixed point appears in some finite approximation, and in all approximations thereafter.

METHOD: We begin assuming the relation P for each IDB predicate p is empty. Suppose that at some time, we have approximations $P_1, \ldots, P_m$ for the IDB predicates $p_1, \ldots, p_m$. We obtain the next approximation for p_i by computing

$$P_i' = \text{EVAL}(p_i, R_1, \ldots, R_k, P_1, \ldots, P_m)$$

as follows.

1. For each rule for p_i, apply Algorithm 12.2, using the appropriate relation among $R_1, \ldots, R_k$ and $P_1, \ldots, P_m$ for each ordinary subgoal of that rule.

2. Take the union, over all rules for p_i, of the relations constructed in (1). The result is P_i'.

We then compare the P_i''s with the P_i's. Since EVAL is a monotone operation (see Section 3.4), even with its extended meaning used in this section, we know that $P_i \subseteq P_i'$ for all i. If $P_i' = P_i$ for all i, then we have converged to the least fixed point, and we may halt. If some P_i is a proper subset of P_i', then we must replace the P's by their corresponding P''s, and repeat the process, just described, obtaining new approximations for the IDB relations. Note that, when there are function symbols in the rules, it is possible that we never reach a round where the P's and the P''s are equal; in that case, this "algorithm" runs forever, producing progressively larger approximations to the infinite least fixed point. □

Semi-Naive Evaluation

Corresponding to Algorithm 12.3 there is a more efficient variant, just as Algorithm 3.4 corresponds to Algorithm 3.3 in Chapter 3. We shall review the essence here, which is to "differentiate" the rules. That is, for each IDB predicate p we have another IDB predicate Δp, representing the change to p in one round. That is, the relation for Δp_i is intended to be the difference $P_i' - P_i$ in Algorithm 12.3.

We can differentiate a rule in a manner reminiscent of the product rule of differential calculus. That is, we replace a rule

$$H \text{ :- } G_1 \text{ \& } \cdots \text{ \& } G_n.$$

having one or more IDB subgoals (subgoals with an IDB predicate), by one rule for each IDB subgoal. If G_i is an IDB subgoal, then we have rule

$$\Delta H \text{ :- } G_1 \text{ \& } \cdots \text{ \& } G_{i-1} \text{ \& } \Delta G_i \text{ \& } G_{i+1} \text{ \& } \cdots \text{ \& } G_n.$$

Example 12.9: Consider rule (7) of Example 12.3:

```
true(and(X,Y)) :- true(X) & true(Y).
```

Both subgoals are IDB subgoals, so we have two rules

```
Δtrue(and(X,Y)) :- Δtrue(X) & true(Y).
Δtrue(and(X,Y)) :- true(X) & Δtrue(Y).
```

Together, they define the predicate $\Delta true$ in terms of itself and the predicate $true$. $\square$

The intuitive idea behind semi-naive evaluation is that on each round, we want Δp to have exactly the tuples that were discovered for p on the previous round of naive evaluation. A "new" tuple for p, that is, one not discovered on a previous round, must use at least one tuple that was not discovered before the previous round. Thus, each new tuple for p on one round of naive evaluation will be produced by one of the differentiated rules for p; it might be produced by more than one, if it uses more than one new tuple. Note also that a "new" tuple might not really be new, since it may have been produced by another rule for p previously. The technique is summarized in the next algorithm.

Algorithm 12.4: Semi-Naive Evaluation.

INPUT: A collection of safe rules, possibly involving function symbols, and relation $R_1, \ldots, R_k$ for the EDB predicates mentioned in the bodies of these rules.

OUTPUT: If it is finite, the least fixed point of the rules, with respect to the given EDB relations. Otherwise, we produce an infinite sequence of approximations, as in Algorithm 12.3.

METHOD: We begin by constructing the differentiated rules for all the IDB predicates, as described above. The algorithm consists of a loop, possibly infinite, in which we produce successive approximations to the IDB relations. We initialize the relation P for each IDB predicate p to be empty, and we initialize the relation ΔP for Δp by applying the EVAL procedure of Algorithm 12.3, but only to those rules for p that have no IDB subgoals (others would produce no contribution anyway). We then execute the following steps in a loop.

1. If all the ΔP's are empty, then break the loop. Here, we have converged to the least fixed point, which will be the relation P for each IDB predicate p.

2. Otherwise, replace each IDB relation P by $P \cup \Delta P$.

3. For each IDB predicate p, compute a new differential relation $\Delta P'$ by applying Algorithm 12.2 to each of the differentiated rules for p, using the EDB relations $R_1, \ldots, R_k$, the current relations $P_1, \ldots, P_m$ for the IDB predicates, and the differential relations $\Delta P_1, \ldots, \Delta P_m$ as needed, and taking the union over all the differentiated rules for p.

4. For each IDB relation p, compute $\Delta P = \Delta P' - P$, and go to step (1). $\square$

12.3 TOP-DOWN PROCESSING OF LOGIC

We have defined the meaning of logical rules to be a least fixed point, computed by starting with only the facts of the EDB and repeatedly applying rules from right to left, that is, from body to head. This type of computation is often called *bottom-up*, because we implicitly construct trees that describe the proof of an IDB tuple from the leaves up, working toward the root. That tree has a node for each tuple used, and the children of the node for tuple μ are the tuples from the relations for each of the subgoals that were used to construct μ by applying some rule.[6]

Example 12.10: Let us consider the rules of Example 12.3. Figure 12.10 shows a proof tree for the fact $true\big(g(a,d)\big)$. This fact was constructed by rule (2) from the facts $true\big(g(a,e)\big)$ and $true\big(g(e,d)\big)$; these were taken from the relations for the first and second subgoals of rule (2), respectively. In turn, they were each placed in that relation by rule (1), since $go(a,e)$ and $go(e,d)$ are given EDB facts. Notice that the order in which these tuples are placed in their respective relations by Algorithm 12.3 is bottom-up according to the tree of Figure 12.10. That is, the leaves $go(a,e)$ and $go(e,d)$ are in their EDB relations initially. Then, the atoms on the second level of the tree, $true\big(g(a,e)\big)$ and $true\big(g(e,d)\big)$, are inferred on pass 1, while the root is inferred on the second pass. □

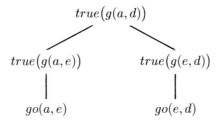

Figure 12.10 Proof tree.

Bottom-up processing of logic is sometimes called *forward-chaining*. The explanation for this locution is that rules are sometimes regarded as having a "natural" direction in which they should be applied, that is, from body to head, or from antecedent to consequent: "if such-and-such is true, then this is also true." Reasoning in this way is thought of as "forward" reasoning.

---

[6] Technically, the proof tree might be a DAG (directed, acyclic graph), since a tuple could be used in several places. Alternatively, we can allow a tuple μ to appear at several different nodes, and repeat parts of a proof if necessary. If we do so, then the proof tree may be assumed to be a true tree.

Reasoning from Goals

There is another mode of reasoning, called *top-down* or *backward-chaining*, in which we start with the goal we would like to prove, and we consider ways in which we might succeed in proving the goal. Those familiar with Prolog are aware that language uses top-down reasoning with an order of processing goals and their subgoals determined by the order in which rules are listed in the Prolog program. The following is an example that happens to mimic Prolog's algorithm of search, but an understanding of Prolog is not needed to follow the example.

Example 12.11: Suppose we are given the rules of Example 12.3 and the goal $true\big(g(a,d)\big)$ to prove. One way to do so is to apply rule (1) of Example 12.3,

(1) `true(g(S,T)) :- go(S,T).`

in such a way that the head becomes the desired goal. To deduce what tuple would have to be in the relation for rule (1), we term-match the head $true\big(g(S,T)\big)$ against the goal, $true\big(g(a,d)\big)$, finding $S = a$ and $T = d$. Thus, to apply rule (1) in such a way that tuple $true\big(g(a,d)\big)$ is generated, we need a tuple (a,d) in the relation for rule (1); recall that relation has two components, corresponding to variables S and T, in that order. The only way we could get $S = a$ and $T = d$ is if the subgoal $go(a,d)$ were a tuple of the relation GO. But GO is an EDB relation, and we suppose it consists of the ten tuples listed in Example 12.3. These tuples do not include (a,d), so rule (1) does not help us achieve the goal $true\big(g(a,d)\big)$.

Now, let us consider using rule (2) of Example 12.3,

(2) `true(g(S,T)) :- true(g(S,U)) & true(g(U,T)).`

to prove our initial goal, $true\big(g(a,d)\big)$. The head of rule (2) is the same as the head of rule (1), so we again match $S = a$ and $T = d$. If we make these substitutions in the body of rule (2) we get subgoals $true\big(g(a,U)\big)$ and $true\big(g(U,d)\big)$.

We work on each of these in turn, first trying rule (1), then (2). When we match the head of rule (1) against $true\big(g(a,U)\big)$, we find something we have not seen before: both formulas have variables. The goal is really asking for some value of U for which $true\big(g(a,U)\big)$ can be proved. In this case, the way to match is obvious; S in the head of rule (1) matches a, and T matches U.[7] If we substitute a for S and U for T, the body of rule (1) becomes $go(a,U)$. Since go is an EDB predicate, we can only satisfy the goal by finding a value of U such that (a,U) is a tuple of GO. In this case, there is exactly one value that U can take, namely, e, although in general there could be zero, one, or many

---

[7] In general, the process of matching two terms with variables so they become the same is called "unification." It is a complex process in the worst case, and we shall give an algorithm for unification in the next section.

such values.

The binding of U to value e, which occurred when we considered the first subgoal of rule (2), affects the second subgoal, which was $true\bigl(g(U,d)\bigr)$ but now becomes $true\bigl(g(e,d)\bigr)$. We attempt to satisfy it too, first by rule (1). That task is easy, since the body of rule (1) becomes $go(e,d)$, and (e,d) is a tuple of the EDB relation GO. We have now satisfied all subgoals of rule (2), and the original goal has been proved. Its proof is the tree of Figure 12.10. $\square$

Backtracking

In Example 12.11, we proceeded fairly directly from goal to proof. The only detour we took was that our initial attempt to prove the goal $true\bigl(g(a,d)\bigr)$ by rule (1) failed. However, there are many other places we could have failed. For example, if $go(e,d)$ were not an EDB fact, then the subgoal $true\bigl(g(e,d)\bigr)$ would fail. We would have to backtrack to the first subgoal of rule (2) and try to find another value of U besides e.

Since there are no more tuples of the form (a,U) in GO, we would try to achieve goal $true\bigl(g(a,U)\bigr)$ by applying rule (2). Before doing so, we should understand that the use of U in the goal and in rule (2) are not the same. Rather, U in rule (2) is a "local variable," with the same name, perhaps, as a variable of the goal, but not thereby identical to it. Thus, to avoid confusion, we should rewrite rule (2) for its application to subgoal $true\bigl(g(a,U)\bigr)$ with a new variable in place of U, for example,

```
true(g(S,T)) :- true(g(S,V)) & true(g(V,T)).
```

When we match (technically we "unify") the head of this rule with the goal $true\bigl(g(a,U)\bigr)$ we find $S = a$ and $T = U$. We are thus sent to achieve goal $true\bigl(g(a,V)\bigr)$, which is really no different from the goal $true\bigl(g(a,U)\bigr)$ that we were trying to achieve.

This exploration illustrates the point that top-down search, with backtracking to try alternative rules when one fails, can easily lead to a loop. In fact, loops can occur when performing a top-down search, even when the rules are datalog, and therefore a bottom-up solution will always converge. For example, the rules for transitive closure of a graph

```
path(X,Y) :- edge(X,Y).
path(X,Y) :- path(X,Z) & path(Z,Y).
```

are really no different from rules (1) and (2) of Example 12.3. When we start with a goal like $path(a,b)$, where for no value of W is (a,W) a tuple of the EDB relation for $edge$, we go into the same sort of loop as we described above, generating goals $path(a,Z)$, $path(a,Z_1)$, $path(a,Z_2)\cdots$. In fact, the same thing would happen, by a more complex process, even if $edge(a,W)$ were true for some value of W, as long as there is no path from a to b in the graph.

We shall not discuss in detail the backtracking algorithm used by Prolog to search for ways to achieve a goal. Rather we shall give one more example where backtracking is used so top-down processing of rules can obtain complete relations, rather than single tuples that match a given goal. Beginning in Section 12.5, we shall discuss more efficient ways to process complete relations in a top-down manner.

Example 12.12: Suppose we wished to take the natural join

$$R(A, B) \bowtie S(B, C)$$

of two EDB relations R and S. We could use a rule like

```
j(A,B,C) :- r(A,B) & s(B,C).
```

and apply it to a goal $j(X, Y, Z)$. However, what happens during a Prolog-like, top-down search is that each tuple (a, b) in R is tried in turn, until one with a value of b that matched some tuple (b, c) in S is found. At that point, the goal is satisfied, with $X = a$, $Y = b$, and $Z = c$.

That is not exactly what the join means; it asks for *all* pairs of matching tuples from R and S. If we processed the above rule bottom-up, say by Algorithm 3.2, we would indeed get all pairs of matching tuples. We can fix the problem by introducing a subgoal $fail$, as is used in Prolog,[8] to force backtracking to occur repeatedly. That is, we write

```
j(A,B,C) :- r(A,B) & s(B,C) & fail.
```

The effect of this rule with goal $j(X, Y, Z)$, processed top-down, is that we begin by taking the first tuple of R, say (a_1, b_1), and looking for tuples of S that match b_1. When we find one, say (b_1, c_1), we proceed to the third subgoal, $fail$, which causes us to backtrack to the second subgoal, $s(B, C)$, again.[9] On backtracking, we look for another tuple matching b_1, say (b_1, c_2), in S. We fail again when we reach the $fail$ subgoal, and eventually on backtracking to the subgoal $s(B, C)$ we shall find in S no more tuples with first component b_1.

At that point, we fail back to the first subgoal, which finds another tuple in R, say (a_2, b_2). Now the same process repeats, eventually finding all the tuples of S with first component b_2. We then fail back to the first subgoal, obtain the third tuple of R, and so on.

Eventually, we find no more tuples of R. At that point, the entire rule has failed, but before doing so, it has generated all of the tuples in the join of R and S. If we had inserted an action such as print before the $fail$, then the entire

---

[8] When $fail$ appears as a goal in a Prolog program, it is treated as a subgoal that had failed to match anything.

[9] In a real Prolog program, there would presumably be some sort of action that used the tuple, appearing to the left of the $fail$. For example, we might print the tuple that was found.

join would have been printed. $\square$

Comparison of Top-Down and Bottom-Up Methods

We presume that the object of any algorithm for "processing" logic is to produce the relation, or relevant portion of a relation, that is needed to answer some query. Examples of queries that ask for parts of relations are

$$sum\left(succ^{47}(0), succ^{92}(0), W\right) \tag{12.4}$$

that is, what is the sum of $47 + 92$, using the representation of addition given in Example 12.2, and

$$true\left(or\left(g(a,b), g(a,c)\right)\right)$$

referring to Example 12.3; this query asks whether it is true that either state a can become state b or that state a can become state c, or both.

For query (12.4), the bottom-up approach would start to compute the entire int and sum relations. Recall from Example 12.4, that after 141 passes, the fact that $47 + 92 = 139$ would be established, so the value $W = succ^{139}(0)$ would be found. In this case, the value of W is unique, but in general, there would be no way to tell that we did not need to proceed with additional passes to find other values of W. Further, if we are given a query with no solution, then the bottom-up method would surely run forever looking for the first solution.

In contrast, the top-down method would consider rule (4) in Example 12.2, which is

(4) `sum(X,succ(Y),succ(Z)) :- sum(X,Y,Z).`

and try to match (really "unify") its head with the goal

$$sum(succ^{47}(0), succ^{92}(0), W)$$

This unification succeeds, with $X = succ^{47}(0)$, $Y = succ^{91}(0)$, and $W = succ(Z)$. Thus, the subgoal in the body of rule (4) becomes

$$sum(succ^{47}(0), succ^{91}(0), Z)$$

We then unify the head of rule (4) with this subgoal, after replacing Z in the rule by Z_1 to avoid a conflict of variables. This unification yields $X = succ^{47}(0)$, $Y = succ^{90}(0)$, and $Z = succ(Z_1)$, leading to subgoal $sum(succ^{47}(0), succ^{90}(0), Z_1)$.

After 90 more iterations, we reach subgoal $sum(succ^{47}(0), 0, Z_{91})$, and we have established the relationships among local variables introduced along the way, as follows:

$$W = succ(Z), \ Z = succ(Z_1), \ Z_1 = succ(Z_2), \dots, Z_{90} = succ(Z_{91}).$$

Now, with the middle argument of sum equal to 0, rule(3) of Example 12.2,

   (3) `sum(X,0,X) :- int(X)`

which has heretofore been unable to match any subgoal (because *succ* and 0 are different nonvariables), suddenly unifies, setting up subgoal $int(succ^{47}(0))$. That subgoal leads to 47 applications of rule (2) and 1 application of rule (1) of Example 12.2, to establish the truth of $int(succ^{47}(0))$. We shall omit the details.

   The unification of $sum(succ^{47}(0), 0, Z_{91})$ with the head of rule (3) also has the effect of establishing the substitution $Z_{91} = succ^{47}(0)$. That value propagates, telling us $Z_{90} = succ^{48}(0)$, and so on, until finally we find $W = succ^{139}(0)$. Thus, we have our answer to the addition problem; $47+92 = 139$. In finding this answer, the top-down method has focussed on exactly the subgoals we needed to establish the answer. The amount of time spent deriving the answer is thus proportional to the numerical value of the answer.

   In contrast, the bottom-up method, at the least, would establish all of the facts it could establish in 141 passes, which includes all of the facts

$$sum(succ^i(0), succ^j(0), succ^{i+j}(0))$$

where $i+j \leq 139$ This work is proportional to the square of the numerical value of the answer we obtain, and therefore proportional to the square of the time spent by the top-down method. Further, the bottom-up method uses space proportional to the number of facts it derives, while top-down uses space only proportional to the longest stack of subgoals it creates, which could be much less than the number of facts.

   On the other hand, we should not conclude that the top-down method is generally superior to the bottom-up method. We noted earlier that on rules like rules (1) and (2) of Example 12.3, top-down processing can get stuck in a loop, while the bottom-up method will plod along and eventually get the answer.

   There is another way that bottom-up can beat top-down, even when both get the answer eventually. Recall from Example 12.12 our discussion of how a join could be taken top-down. If we extend that idea to join three relations, $R \bowtie S \bowtie T$, each having n tuples, then the top-down procedure will take $O(n^3)$ time to explore all n^3 lists of three tuples, one from each relation. That is, suppose we write the rules for the join as

   `j₁(A,B,C,D) :- r(A,B) & j₂(B,C,D).`
   `j₂(B,C,D) :- s(B,C) & t(C,D).`

Then the top-down method will, for each tuple in R, compute the entire join j_2 anew.[10]

   However, if we compute $R \bowtie S \bowtie T$ bottom-up, we take much less time,

---

[10] That would be true even if we substituted for j_1 in the first rule to make a single rule with three subgoals, r, s, and t.

unless the join is really a Cartesian product and the output is as large as $\Omega(n^3)$. If we recall Section 11.5, we see that the join of two relations of size n can be computed in time $O(n \log n)$ plus the time to write the output. For example, if the image sizes for attributes B and C are each n, then the join $S \bowtie T$ has size $O(n)$, and so does the join of all three relations. Thus, the entire join can be computed in $O(n \log n)$ time bottom-up.

A third disadvantage of top-down methods is that they require unification. In contrast, we can evaluate logical rules bottom-up using the simpler operation of term-matching, as we saw in Section 12.2.

We shall see in Chapter 13 that top-down is never better than bottom-up, when the best techniques are used in each case. In particular, the "magic-sets" rule-rewriting technique converts any set of rules into ones that can be evaluated as fast by semi-naive evaluation as the original rules were evaluated top-down. Moreover, there are many cases where the transformed rules are much more efficiently evaluatable than were the old rules.

12.4 UNIFICATION

The essential step when processing logical rules top-down is *unification*, the operation whereby we take two atomic formulas, each with variables, and find a substitution for each variable, so the two formulas become identical. Such a substitution is called a *unifier*. Unlike term matching, in unification, the expressions we substitute for variables will often themselves involve variables. Thus, any expressions could be substituted for these variables and the resulting formulas would still be identical. As a consequence, there may be more than one unifier for a pair of formulas.

We shall give an algorithm that produces the *most general unifier* (MGU) of two formulas. That substitution has the property that it is a unifier, and any other unifier can be constructed from the MGU by substitution for its variables. Thus, the MGU is the "simplest" substitution that makes the two formulas identical.[11]

In the algorithm that follows, we tacitly assume that the first atomic formula is a goal, and the second the head of a rule that we hope unifies with the goal, and therefore might help to deduce the goal. This viewpoint has two consequences.

1. Since the variables of the rule are "local," we shall assume that there are no variables in common between the two formulas.

2. If we have a choice of substituting a variable of the first formula for a variable of the second or vice versa, we substitute for the variable of the second. This choice makes it more transparent when variables of a goal

---

[11] Technically, the MGU is only unique up to renaming of variables, but we shall speak of "the" MGU, since the particular variables used are not significant.

carry forward to their subgoals, but it is not essential for top-down processing.

Algorithm 12.5: Computing the Most General Unifier.

INPUT: Atomic formulas F and G with disjoint sets of variables.

OUTPUT: The most general unifier of F and G or an indication that none exists.

METHOD: There are two phases. In the first, we determine which subexpressions of the formulas F and G must become identical in the MGU. In the second phase, we determine whether an MGU exists. We check for an immediate contradiction, where two identical subexpressions have different nonvariable symbols that must be equated, and if we find such a pair, we conclude that there is no MGU. We then attempt to construct the MGU, which must exist in principle, but may be infinite. If this attempt to construct the MGU fails, then we conclude that it is infinite, and therefore not usable. In that case, we say that "no MGU exists."

Phase I: *Finding equivalent subexpressions.* The first step is to build a tree for each of F and G, representing their structure as expressions in the obvious way. That is, we define the tree for term or atomic formula T recursively, as follows.

1. If T is a variable or a constant, then the tree for T is a single node labeled T.
2. If T is of the form $\theta(T_1, \ldots, T_k)$, where θ is a predicate or function symbol,[12] and $T_1, \ldots, T_k$ are terms, then the tree for T has a root labeled θ and has children that are the roots of the trees for $T_1, \ldots, T_k$, in that order, from the left.

Now, having built the trees for F and G, we attempt to group their nodes into equivalence classes, represented by the equivalence relation $\equiv$. If we are unsuccessful in completing the construction of $\equiv$ by the rules below, then no unifier exists. Intuitively, $n \equiv m$ if and only if, in any unifier the expressions represented by the subtrees with roots n and m must be made identical. The rules defining $\equiv$ are

a) If r_F and r_G are the roots of the two trees, then $r_F \equiv r_G$. This rule follows from the definition of unification; we require that the two atomic formulas become the same.

b) If $n \equiv m$, then nodes n and m must have the same number of children; if not there is no unifier for F and G. If they have children $c_1, \ldots, c_k$ and $d_1, \ldots, d_k$, respectively, then $c_i \equiv d_i$ for all i. The motivation for this rule is that in order for the expressions of n and m to be made identical, they must have the same number of subexpressions, and corresponding

---

[12] We must consider operators that are both function symbols and predicates, even though it is only at the outermost level that predicates appear.

subexpressions must be made identical.

c) If n and m are labeled by the same variable, then $n \equiv m$. The reason is that we may choose only one substitution for a variable X, so every node labeled X must become the same expression under any unifier.

d) $n \equiv n$ for any node n; if $n \equiv m$, then $m \equiv n$, and if $n \equiv m$ and $m \equiv p$, then $n \equiv p$. These rules reflect the basic properties of the notion "becomes the same thing." For example, if n "becomes the same thing" as m, then m "becomes the same thing" as n. Thus, $\equiv$ is an equivalence relation; that is, $\equiv$ partitions the nodes into disjoint sets such that nodes in the same set "become the same thing" while nodes not in the same set need not "become the same thing."

Phase II: *Testing for, and constructing the MGU.* Having grouped the nodes into equivalence classes by repeatedly applying (a) through (d) until no more nodes can be grouped together, we consider each equivalence class in turn. First, if any class has two nodes that are labeled by two different symbols, neither of which is a variable, then there is no unifier. The reason is that no substitution for variables can make two subexpressions be identical, if their roots are different symbols and neither is a variable.

Assuming a unifier is still possible, we try to find an order to treat the equivalence classes and find for each class a representative expression. We use τ for the MGU, and initially, we let τ be undefined for each variable. The following rules define τ for some of the variables; if there is an MGU, then they will eventually define all of the variables. The first rule serves as a basis and the second can be applied repeatedly.

1. If a class contains only nodes labeled by variables, pick one, preferring a variable from the first expression if there is one. Let the selected variable be X. Then for each variable Y labeling a node in the class, set $\tau(Y) = X$. Note $\tau(X) = X$ as a consequence.

2. Suppose a class contains one or more nodes labeled by variables and also at least one node labeled by a constant, function symbol, or predicate. Suppose also, that one of the latter nodes represents an expression E in which all variables, if any, have had τ defined for them.[13] Let $\tau(E)$ be the result of substituting $\tau(X)$ for all occurrences of X in E, for each variable X. Then for every variable Y labeling a node in this class, let $\tau(Y) = \tau(E)$.

If the above steps succeed in defining $\tau(X)$ for all variables X, then τ is the MGU; otherwise, there is no MGU; that is, the given atomic formulas are not unifiable. $\square$

---

[13] An important part of the proof of correctness for this algorithm is showing that it does not matter which of two expressions in the same equivalence class we choose.

Several examples where unifiers do or do not exist should make the steps of Algorithm 12.5 clearer.

Example 12.13: First, we consider a fairly complicated case where the MGU does exist. The two atomic formulas are

$$p\Big(f\big(X, g(X)\big),\ g\big(g(Y)\big)\Big)$$

and

$$p\Big(f\big(g(U), V\big),\ g(V)\Big)$$

The trees representing these expressions are shown in Figure 12.11, and the nodes are numbered 1 through 15 for reference.

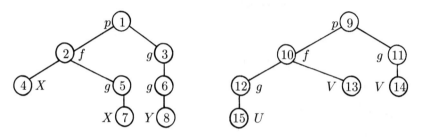

Figure 12.11 Expression trees for atomic formulas of Example 12.13.

We now group the nodes into equivalence classes. Rule (a) says $1 \equiv 9$, because these are the roots of the two formulas. Rule (c) says $4 \equiv 7$ because both are labeled with variable X, and $13 \equiv 14$ because both are labeled V. Rule (b) tells us that the corresponding children of 1 and 9 are equivalent; that is, $2 \equiv 10$ and $3 \equiv 11$. Likewise, corresponding children of the equivalent pair 2 and 10 are equivalent, so $4 \equiv 12$ and $5 \equiv 13$.

Now, we can use rule (d) to infer that 4, 7, and 12 all belong in one equivalence class, that is, each is equivalent to the other two. The reason is that $4 \equiv 7$ and $4 \equiv 12$ have both been found. Similarly, $13 \equiv 14$ and $5 \equiv 13$ tell us that 5, 13, and 14 are all equivalent.

Since $3 \equiv 11$, rule (b) says that their children are also equivalent; that is, $6 \equiv 14$. Thus, by (d), 6 is also equivalent to 5 and 14.

Now, since $5 \equiv 6$, rule (b) says that their children are equivalent, so $7 \equiv 8$. Thus, 8 joins the class of 4, 7, and 12, and the equivalence classes are

$$
\begin{array}{lll}
4 \equiv 7 \equiv 8 \equiv 12 & 1 \equiv 9 & 2 \equiv 10 \\
5 \equiv 6 \equiv 13 \equiv 14 & 3 \equiv 11 & 15
\end{array}
$$

Now, no more equivalent pairs can be found by rules (a) to (d), so we are done with this phase. A straightforward check shows that no equivalence class contains two distinct nonvariable symbols. For example, the nodes of the class $\{5, 6, 13, 14\}$ are all labeled with g or V, and of these, only g is a nonvariable.

Now, we try to define the substitution τ. The class containing 15 alone has only variables, so we pick one, the lone choice being U, and we define $\tau(U) = U$. Next, we can consider the class $4 \equiv 7 \equiv 8 \equiv 12$. All of the nodes but 12 are labeled by variables X or Y, and node 12 represents expression $g(U)$, whose only variable has had τ defined. We therefore set $\tau(X)$ and $\tau(Y)$ to

$$\tau\big(g(U)\big) = g\big(\tau(U)\big) = g(U)$$

Next consider the class $5 \equiv 6 \equiv 13 \equiv 14$. Two of the nodes, 13 and 14, are labeled V, while the other two represent expressions $g(X)$ and $g(Y)$. Both of these expressions have τ defined for their variables, and whichever we choose we get $\tau(V) = g\big(g(U)\big)$, since $\tau(X) = \tau(Y) = g(U)$. We have now defined the MGU τ completely by

$$\begin{aligned} \tau(U) &= U & \tau(X) &= g(U) \\ \tau(Y) &= g(U) & \tau(V) &= g\big(g(U)\big) \end{aligned}$$

We get the atomic formula

$$p\bigg(f\Big(g(U), g\big(g(U)\big)\Big),\ g\Big(g\big(g(U)\big)\Big)\bigg)$$

when we make this substitution in either of the given atomic formulas. $\square$

Example 12.14: Now let us consider a pair of formulas that do not have a unifier. Consider $p(X, X)$ and $p\big(f(Y), g(Z)\big)$. Their trees are shown in Figure 12.12, and the equivalence classes we obtain by applying rules (a) to (d) of Algorithm 12.5 are

$$7 \qquad 8 \qquad 1 \equiv 4 \qquad 2 \equiv 3 \equiv 5 \equiv 6$$

Since $5 \equiv 6$, but 5 and 6 have different function symbols as labels, there is no way to construct a unifier. Intuitively, these expressions cannot be unified because there is no way X can become "f of something" and also "g of something" at the same time. It should be clearly understood that only variables are subject to substitution, so we cannot substitute for f or g. $\square$

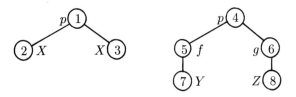

Figure 12.12 Expression trees for nonunifiable formulas.

Example 12.15: Finally, let us consider a very subtle case, where the equivalence classes do not have two nodes labeled by different nonvariables, yet we cannot find a unifier because there is no variable with which we can start to construct the substitution. The reason is that for each variable, the equivalence class containing the nodes labeled by that variable also contains a node corresponding to an expression that involves another variable. Thus, we never define τ for any variable by rule (1) in Phase II of Algorithm 12.5.

Our two formulas are $p(X, f(X))$ and $p(f(Y), Y)$. Their trees are shown in Figure 12.13, and their equivalence classes are

$$1 \equiv 5 \qquad 2 \equiv 4 \equiv 6 \qquad 3 \equiv 7 \equiv 8$$

The class for X, which contains nodes 2, 4, and 6, cannot be used to define $\tau(X)$ until the expression of node 6, that is $f(Y)$, is defined, which means $\tau(Y)$ must be defined before $\tau(X)$. Similarly, consideration of the class $3 \equiv 7 \equiv 8$ tells us that $\tau(X)$ must be defined before $\tau(Y)$, so that the expression of node 3 may be defined. Since rules (1) and (2) do not succeed in defining τ for all variables, there is no unifier for these two expressions.

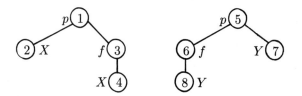

Figure 12.13 Expression trees for formulas with infinite MGU.

In a sense, these formulas do have an MGU, but it is not finite. If we think of $\tau(X)$ and $\tau(Y)$ both being the infinite "term" $f(f(\cdots(f(X))\cdots))$, then both formulas become

$$p\big(f(f(\cdots(f(X))\cdots)),\ f(f(\cdots(f(X))\cdots))\big)$$

However, such a unifier is not very useful when we are trying to do top-down exploration of goals, so we do not consider infinite terms to be acceptable in unifiers. □

We shall now sketch the reasons Algorithm 12.5 works. Many of the steps are left for the reader to work out or to consult one of several references on the subject.

Theorem 12.1: Algorithm 12.5 correctly computes the most general unifier of its given atomic formulas if it exists.

Proof: First, an easy induction on the number of times rules (a) to (d) are applied shows that when two nodes are made equivalent, their expressions are necessarily the same under any unifying substitution. This part is left for the reader. It has two consequences.

1. The unifier produced by the algorithm is the most general unifier.
2. If the algorithm says there is no unifier, because two equivalent nodes have different numbers of children or different, nonvariable labels, then there really is no unifier.

We next turn our attention to the proof that the substitution τ, if it is produced, does make the two expressions identical. The crux of the proof is showing that when there are two or more nodes in an equivalence class that are not labeled by variables, then τ makes both of their expressions the same, and therefore, it did not matter which one we chose to be $\tau(Y)$ for each variable Y labeling a node in the class. Let $n \equiv m$ be two such nodes. Then the labels of n and m are the same and the number of children each has is the same, or else Algorithm 12.5 would have declared that no unifier exists. Further, the pairs of corresponding children must be equivalent, by rule (b). Thus, we may prove by induction on the sum of the heights of the two nodes n and m that the substitution τ makes their expressions the same. $\square$

12.5 THE RELATIONAL APPROACH TO TOP-DOWN LOGIC EVALUATION

In Section 12.3 we considered Prolog's tuple-at-a-time approach to top-down query evaluation. We shall now consider a variation on this approach where backtracking is replaced by the "simultaneous" exploration of alternative rules for each goal. This section is an informal introduction to the technique. In the two following sections, the algorithms are stated formally and justified. The reader should not expect to grasp all the details immediately, but should follow the extended example of this section to get the flavor of the concepts involved.

We shall continue to treat subgoals of a single rule in order, from the left; in Section 12.10, we shall discuss how one might pick an appropriate order for the subgoals. When we assume "simultaneous" consideration of different rules, we are not supposing parallel implementation, but rather that computation time be shared among the various rules for a goal. In contrast, the Prolog style of evaluation does not work on the second rule until all exploration from the first rule has been completed.

Rule/Goal Trees

When exploring goals, their rules, and their subgoals, think of each consideration of a goal or rule as an "event." We may build a tree of events, called a *rule/goal tree*, in which each event is represented by a node. Associated with each node is a description of the goal or rule, with variables named according to a convention given below. The rule/goal tree for a given goal, G_0, is constructed as follows.

1. The root is a goal node for G_0.

2. Suppose node n is a goal node for goal G, and let G have predicate p. Then for each rule r for p, unify the head of r with G. If the unification is successful, create a node for a modified version of rule r that is a child of node n. Specifically, we perform the following steps to obtain the modified rule r.

   a) First, rename variables of r, if necessary, so r has no variables in common with G.

   b) When we perform the unification of the head of r with G, prefer to substitute for variables appearing in the head of r, whenever possible.

   c) When we substitute for a variable X appearing in the head of r, we must make that substitution for all occurrences of X, not only in the head of r, but throughout r.

   d) All variables Y of r that do not appear in the head are "local" to r. We identify these variables for this particular activation record for r by subscripting them with the number of ancestors of this activation record that are rule nodes, including the present node.[14]

3. The children of a rule node are goal nodes corresponding to each of the subgoals in the body of the rule. At these goal nodes, as in the rule, the substitution of 2(c) has been made.

Example 12.16: Consider the following rules for defining ancestors in terms of an EDB relation par, where $par(C, P)$ means that P is a parent of C.

$$r_1: \quad \text{anc(X,Y)} \;\text{:- par(X,Y).}$$
$$r_2: \quad \text{anc(X,Y)} \;\text{:- par(X,Z) \& anc(Z,Y).}$$

In words, r_2 says that Y is an ancestor of X if there is some individual Z such that Z is a parent of X and Y is an ancestor of Z.

Suppose the relation P for predicate par is as shown in Figure 12.14; edges represent pairs (x, y) in P, with the child below, and the parent above. Let us begin with the goal $anc(j, W)$, that is, find all of j's ancestors; this goal becomes the root of the rule/goal tree, the upper levels of which are shown in Figure 12.15.

We begin by creating children of the root for each of the rules r_1 and r_2. For r_1, we unify the head, $anc(X, Y)$ with the goal $anc(j, W)$, and we find that

---

[14] As we shall see, goal nodes appear at odd-numbered levels, starting at the root, which is level 1, and rule nodes appear at even levels. Thus, the proper subscript is one-half the level number.

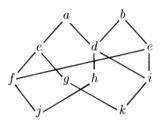

Figure 12.14 The relation P for predicate *par*.

$X \equiv j$ and $Y \equiv W$.[15] In the MGU we must use the constant j in place of the variable X, but we can use either variable W or Y. Since we wish to eliminate the variables of the head, we use W, so the MGU turns the head of r_1 into $anc(j, W)$, which happens to be the same as the goal. The same substitution of j for X and W for Y is made throughout rule r_1, so the instance of that rule at the first child of the root is

```
anc(j,W) :- par(j,W).
```

When we consider r_2, we have the same head, $anc(X, Y)$ as for r_1, so we perform the same unification of the goal with the head, resulting in the same substitution of j for X and W for Y. We apply this substitution to the entire second rule, and we create local variable Z_1 in place of Z; the subscript 1 is selected because we are at the first level of rule nodes. Thus, for the second child of the root we have instance

```
anc(j,W) :- par(j,Z₁) & anc(Z₁,W).
```

of rule r_2.

Now we consider the first child of the root, the child corresponding to rule r_1. This node has a child for each subgoal in the body of r_1. As there is only one subgoal, there is only one child, a goal node for $par(j, W)$. As *par* is an EDB predicate, and therefore has no rules, this goal node is a leaf.

Now, consider the second child of the root, the one corresponding to r_2. It has two goal node children, the first for subgoal $par(j, Z_1)$ and the second for $anc(Z_1, W)$. The first of these, having an EDB predicate, is a leaf. The second, $anc(Z_1, W)$, has rule-node children for rules r_1 and r_2. We unify the heads of the two rules, which, recall, are both $anc(X, Y)$, with the subgoal $anc(Z_1, W)$. When we unify the heads of r_1 and r_2 with this subgoal, the instances of the two rules at the rule-node children of goal node $anc(Z_1, W)$ become

---

[15] We shall say that two terms are equivalent in a unification when we really mean that the nodes labeled with these terms are equivalent.

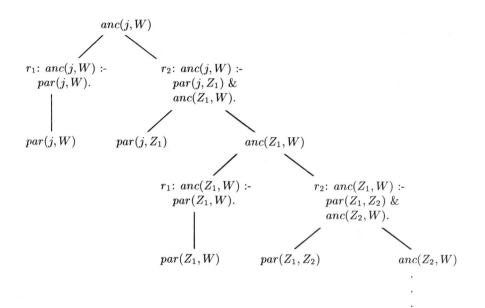

Figure 12.15 Rule/goal tree for goal $anc(j, W)$.

```
anc(Z₁,W)  :- par(Z₁,W).
anc(Z₁,W)  :- par(Z₁,Z₂) & anc(Z₂,W).
```

Note that the local variable Z becomes Z_2 in the second rule, because it is introduced at the second level of rule nodes.

Figure 12.15 shows the expansion of the rule/goal tree to the depth we have taken it, plus an additional level of goal nodes. The process we have followed repeats indefinitely, with each ancestor goal node having children for the two rules. The first rule terminates in a *par* leaf, but the second rule spawns a *par* leaf and another *anc* goal node. □

In principle, a tree such as Figure 12.15 involves an infinite number of goals. We can list them all here:

1. $anc(j, W)$.
2. $anc(Z_i, W)$ for $i = 1, 2, \dots$.
3. $par(j, W)$.
4. $par(j, Z_1)$.
5. $par(Z_i, W)$ for $i = 1, 2, \dots$.
6. $par(Z_i, Z_{i+1})$ for $i = 1, 2, \dots$.

Note that if we think of j as Z_0, then (1), (3), and (4) become special cases of (2), (5), and (6), respectively.

As we mentioned, it is our intent to work on all rules for the same goal "in parallel," while we work on only one subgoal of each rule at a time, in left-to-right order. The notion of "in parallel," or "simultaneous" computation can be interpreted as breadth-first construction of the rule/goal tree. That is, we work on all nodes at one level and create their children, before working on any node at the next lower level. In practice, we shall not be concerned with the exact order in which we visit nodes in the rule/goal tree. Rather, we shall simply make sure that any node whose entire subtree can complete, will in fact complete eventually.

Propagation of Bindings and Answers

As we build the rule/goal tree, we construct certain relations at each node.

1. At each goal node n, we have a *binding relation* M.[16] The goal at n will have zero or more arguments that are "bound," in the sense that all variables appearing in that argument are given bound values, either from a constant, like j in Figure 12.15 being passed from above, or by a finite set of tuples being passed "sideways," because they appear in a previous subgoal, as in Example 12.12 (Section 12.3). The tuples of M represent bindings for these bound arguments.

2. At each rule node there are *supplementary relations* S_0, $S_1, \ldots$, with S_i corresponding to the point in the rule body with i subgoals to the left. The supplementary relations represent the bindings of those variables that have either been bound by the binding relation for the goal node's parent (applied to the rule's head) or that have appeared in a previous subgoal of the rule. Again, Example 12.12 illustrates the process of binding variables that we mimic with the supplementary relations.

3. Both rule and goal nodes have *answer* or *result* relations. In the case of a goal node, this relation is the set of tuples that match the goal and are provable from the rules, while for a rule node, this relation has those tuples that match the head of the rule and are provable by a sequence of rule applications, ending with the rule at that node. The result relation for the root goal node is the answer to the query.

Example 12.17: Let us consider the computation on the tree of Figure 12.15. Suppose we work for a while on the left child of the root. To compute the relation for that rule node, we must find the relation for the goal node $par(j, W)$. Since *par* is an EDB predicate, we need only term-match the goal $par(j, W)$ to the tuples in the relation P; that is, we find those tuples with first (child)

---

[16] The M stands for "magic set," as discussed in Chapter 13.

component j, and for each such tuple, the second component becomes a value for W. Thus, the relation for the goal node $par(j, W)$ is $\sigma_{\$1=j}(P) = \{jf,\ jh\}$, according to the data for P given in Figure 12.14. Note that the result relation is over all arguments of par, even though we know the first argument must be j.

It seems that we can simply pass these two tuples up to the rule node that is the left child of the root, and then to the root itself, to demonstrate that jf and jh are tuples that match the root goal, $anc(j, W)$. However, we should not be deceived by this simple example, where there are no function symbols and where variables have convenient names, into thinking that the process of passing tuples up from goals to rules and from rules to goals, is so simple in general. Rather, the translation we have to perform is suggested by the following steps, which are similar to the bottom-up rule-evaluation process of Algorithm 12.3.

1. Convert the relation $\{jf,\ jh\}$ for $par(j, W)$ into a relation over (some of) the variables that appear in the instance of rule r_1,

    ```
    anc(j,W) :- par(j,W).
    ```
    (12.5)

    which appears at the left child of the root in Figure 12.15. We term-match subgoal $par(j, W)$ with each tuple of the relation $\{jf,\ jh\}$, which we should think of as $\{par(j, f),\ par(j, h)\}$, obtaining values f and h for W. That is, we compute $\text{ATOV}\big(par(j, W),\ \{jf, jh\}\big)$, producing the relation $\{f, h\}$, whose lone attribute is W.

2. Take the natural join of the relation for each subgoal of (12.5). Since there is only one subgoal, the join is trivial in this case, and we get the relation $\{f, h\}$ for the body of (12.5). The relation scheme is still W, of course.

3. Compute the relation for the head, $anc(j, W)$, of (12.5). We do so by applying VTOA to the relation for the body of (12.5) and the head of (12.5), that is, $\text{VTOA}\big(anc(j, W),\ \{f, h\}\big)$. Thus, the head of (12.5) is given the relation, $\{jf,\ jh\}$.

4. Now, the relation for the head of (12.5) is passed to its parent, the root node in this case, intact. Thus, jf and jh are answers to the query; that is, f and h are ancestors of j.

Let us now consider the right child of the root, a rule node for the instance of rule r_2

```
anc(j,W) :- par(j,Z₁) & anc(Z₁,W).
```
(12.6)

We begin by working on the first subgoal, $par(j, Z_1)$. Since this goal has an EDB predicate, we can again solve it by lookup, and we find the familiar relation $\{jf,\ jh\}$ for this subgoal. These tuples are passed up to the right child of the root, where they establish, by a calculation similar to the one for the left child of the root, that the relation for subgoal $par(j, Z_1)$ is $\{f, h\}$, but here it has scheme Z_1.

We now perform "sideways information passing," to establish that for the subgoal $anc(Z_1, W)$, Z_1 can only have the values f and h. In a sense, the first argument of $anc(Z_1, W)$ has become bound to the unary relation $\{f, h\}$, much as the first argument of $par(j, W)$ was bound to j. The difference is that in the latter case, the binding was established by unification, as we created the rule/goal tree; in the former, the binding is to a set of constants (or more generally, a set of tuples), and the binding is established by sideways information passing through the supplementary relations, after we have explored part of the tree.

With this binding for Z_1, we can explore the tree from $anc(Z_1, W)$, and a fortuitous sequence of events leads us to terminate our exploration of the theoretically infinite tree. We find, by a process similar to that followed so far, that when we get to the goal node $anc(Z_2, W)$, we have established the binding $\{c, d, e\}$ for Z_2; note those are exactly the grandparents of j in Figure 12.12, just as the binding for Z_1 is the parents of j. Then, when we explore to the goal node $anc(Z_3, W)$ (not shown explicitly in Figure 12.15), we find that Z_3 is bound to the great grandparents of j, that is, $\{a, b\}$. Lastly, when we reach goal node $anc(Z_4, W)$, Z_4 is bound to $\emptyset$.

At this point, we know there is no reason to explore further, since the relation for $anc(Z_4, W)$ must be empty, no matter how far we explore. Notice how the sideways information passing has established that there are no tuples for the relation of subgoal $anc(Z_4, W)$ that could yield answers to the original query. In effect, we have used a sequence of semijoins to discover that one subgoal in the rule/goal tree is empty, and, therefore, that the tree below this subgoal need not be explored. This occurrence was not altogether an accident. We only need to know that the par relation is finite and has no cycles, both of which are the case for Figure 12.14, and we are guaranteed that after a finite number of levels, some Z_i will get the binding $\emptyset$.

Thus, we can calculate after a finite amount of time that the relation for goal node $anc(Z_1, W)$ is

$$\{fc, \ fe, \ hd, \ fa, \ fb, \ ha, \ hb\} \tag{12.7}$$

This relation is translated into an identical relation with scheme $Z_1 W$ for the subgoal $anc(Z_1, W)$ in the instance (12.6) of r_2, and that relation is joined with relation $\{f, h\}$, which has scheme Z_1, for subgoal $par(j, Z_1)$ in (12.6). The result is a relation with scheme $Z_1 W$ for the body of r_2 at the right child of the root; it is identical to relation (12.7), and its scheme is $Z_1 W$.

Finally, we construct the relation for the head, $anc(j, W)$, of instance (12.6) of r_2, by pairing the constant j with the second (W) components of the tuples in (12.7).[17] These tuples,

$$\{jc,\ je,\ ja,\ jb,\ jd\}$$

together with the tuples jf and jh found earlier, form the complete relation for the root of Figure 12.15. $\square$

Why the Method Works

It is not hard to show that, when we follow the above algorithm, every tuple implied to be in the answer relation for a subgoal is a fact that follows logically from the database and the rules. The converse is much harder to prove; it says that every fact F of the form $p(t_1, \ldots, t_k)$, for predicate p and ground terms $t_1, \ldots, t_k$, such that $p(t_1, \ldots, t_k)$ unifies with a given subgoal, will actually be generated in the result relation for that subgoal after consideration of some number of levels, depending on F, of the rule/goal tree. Intuitively, construction of the most general unifier places the least restriction on rule heads needed to guarantee that the rule will produce all of the facts that both

1. Follow from the rule, and
2. Imply the goal with which the head is unified.

We also need the observation that sideways information passing only restricts the possible values of variables by eliminating tuples that will not join with relations for the other subgoals anyway.

We shall not attempt to prove the completeness of the approach described in this section, that is, if a fact matches a goal, then it will be derived after a finite number of steps. Papers showing the completeness of top-down, or "resolution" methods of proving theorems are mentioned in the bibliographic notes.

If we accept as proven that the rule/goal tree expansion method uncovers all proofs of facts that are instances of the given query, then this algorithm is equivalent to bottom-up evaluation of rules, as long as rules are of a form where the least fixed point and the set of provable facts are the same. That class of rules includes Horn clauses, even those with function symbols, although when there are function symbols, neither the top-down nor bottom-up approaches is guaranteed to converge after a finite time, since there could be an infinite number of facts matching the query. When there are negated subgoals, even stratified ones, we cannot expect the set of provable facts to be equivalent to the "perfect" model, which was the one given in Section 3.6 (Volume I) as the meaning of stratified logic programs.

---

[17] In practice, we would not instantiate the full relation for the body, but would try to perform projections as early as possible. For example, since the hypergraph for the subgoals of the body of r_2 is acyclic, we could use Algorithm 11.5 to construct the relation for the head directly.

There is a problem with the rule/goal tree expansion method of query evaluation, a problem with which we shall deal in Chapter 13. The method may be forced to explore an infinite tree, even though the answer to the query is finite. Especially, when the rules are datalog rules, that is, there are no function symbols, we know that there are only finitely many possible answers, since every answer must be constructed from constants appearing in the rules and constants in the finite database.

Example 12.18: The ancestor rules of Examples 12.16 and 12.17 are datalog rules. However, if the *par* relation is cyclic,[18] then we must explore the entire, infinite rule/goal tree that is suggested by Figure 12.15. Of course, after some point, we shall never generate any more new facts to match the goal at the root, but the simple algorithm we describe now lacks a mechanism for discovering that we have the complete answer; that capability will be added in Chapter 13, when we combine top-down and bottom-up methods in the "magic-sets" technique. □

Comparing Rule/Goal Tree Expansion with Backtracking

It is worth noting that, unlike rule/goal tree expansion, the tuple-at-a-time backtracking scheme of Section 12.3 is not guaranteed to find a proof, even if one exists. Sometimes, backtracking gets into an infinite loop when following the first rule it tries for a goal, and thus never gets to consider other rules for the same goal. If the untried rules lead to proofs of facts matching that goal, the top-down backtracking technique will fail to discover them. Of course, to make the comparison fair, we must assume that the backtracking algorithm is looking for all facts that match the query, not just for the first one. Thus, we implicitly fail after finding each successful match, as discussed in Example 12.12, for instance.

Example 12.19: If we reverse the order of the ancestor rules of Example 12.16, so they appear as

```
anc(X,Y) :- par(X,Z) & anc(Z,Y).
anc(X,Y) :- par(X,Y).
```

then the first rule will send Prolog into a loop if the *par* relation has cycles. For example, if $par(1,2)$ and $par(2,1)$ are both true, then a query like $anc(1,W)$ sends us into a loop, where we repeatedly generate subgoals $anc(1,W)$ and $anc(2,W)$, alternately, as the reader may check.

Moreover, if we reverse the order of the subgoals in the recursive rule, or

---

[18] One might question whether it makes sense to consider a cyclic parenthood relationship. However, if we interpret *par* simply as arcs in a directed graph, then ancestry corresponds to paths in that graph, as was discussed in an example from Section 12.3. Surely, cyclic directed graphs are very common.

use two *anc* subgoals (analogous to the use of two *path* subgoals in Section 12.3), we do not change the least fixed point of the rules, but we create even more severe problems. The rules

```
anc(X,Y) :- anc(X,Z) & par(Z,Y).
anc(X,Y) :- par(X,Y).
```

send Prolog into an infinite loop on any ancestor query, regardless of the EDB relation *par*.

One might suppose that situations in which the top-down backtracking approach fails to explore the whole rule/goal tree could be avoided if we ordered the rules properly. For example, a Prolog programmer quickly learns to list the basis rules before the recursive rules, thereby avoiding problems such as those above. However, we can easily find ourselves in a situation where two rules for a predicate each lead both to some finitely provable facts and to an infinite loop from which the backtracking scheme never recovers. Rule/goal tree expansion will follow both infinite paths, but will also, after a finite time, prove all of the provable facts that match the query.

```
p(X) :- q(X).
p(X) :- r(X).
q(X) :- a(X).
q(X) :- c(X,Y) & q(Y).
r(X) :- b(X).
r(X) :- c(X,Y) & r(Y).
```

Figure 12.16 Example where backtracking cannot reach all provable facts.

Figure 12.16 gives an abstract example of this situation. Suppose a, b, and c are EDB relations, consisting of the facts $a(3)$, $b(4)$, $c(1,2)$ and $c(2,1)$, and our query is $p(W)$, that is, find all of the p facts. If we start with the first rule for p in Figure 12.16, we shall immediately discover that $p(3)$ is true, thanks to the rule $q(X)$:- $a(X)$. However, before we finish exploring from goal $q(X)$, we must try the second rule for q, which leads to an infinite loop, where we repeatedly explore the goal $q(X)$, with X bound to $\{1,2\}$. Thus, we never uncover the fact $p(4)$.

Similarly, suppose we start with the rule $p(X)$:- $r(X)$ for p. Then we shall uncover only $p(4)$, before the recursive rule for r sends us into an infinite loop.

In contrast, if we construct and explore the rule/goal tree, we shall quickly discover both $p(3)$ and $p(4)$, after expanding the root goal for four levels, that is, after reaching the third level of goals. We also follow both infinite paths, one where goal $q(X)$ repeats, and the other where $r(X)$ repeats. □

12.6 COMPUTING RELATIONS DURING RULE/GOAL TREE EXPANSION

Now we shall take a closer look at the general algorithms for computing the relations associated with the nodes of a rule/goal tree. First, let us review and formalize the kinds of relations we compute.

1. At each goal node there is an answer (or result) relation, whose components correspond to the arguments of the goal.

2. At each rule node there is an answer (result) relation whose components correspond to arguments of the rule head.

3. At each goal node there is a binding relation, whose components correspond to those arguments of the goal that are bound. The same arguments are also bound in the head of every rule-node child of this goal node. We say that variables appearing in one of these bound arguments of a rule head are "bound by the head" of that rule.

4. At each rule node for a rule with k subgoals, there are supplementary relations $S_0, \ldots, S_k$. The arguments of a supplementary relation correspond to (some of the) variables of its rule instance. In particular, S_i has arguments corresponding to those variables that are both bound and relevant after considering the first i subgoals. Recall that variables are bound either by appearing in a bound argument of the head or by appearing in one of the first i subgoals; variables are *relevant* if they appear either in the head or in the $(i + 1)$st or a subsequent subgoal.

The reader should understand clearly that bindings are tuples, with one or more components. Roughly, a tuple μ binding certain arguments or variables means that during the backtracking algorithm of Section 12.3, these arguments or variables are *simultaneously* given the values found in the components of μ. In the simple example of the previous section, we saw only one argument or variable bound at a time.

Each of the relations in (1) through (4) is computed from the values of one or more other relations. As we shall see in the next section, it requires a delicately chosen sequence of operations to make sure that each tuple belonging in a relation at some node of the rule/goal tree is placed there eventually. However, in this section, we shall simply study the matter of how tuples should, in principle, be placed in these relations. These calculations are summarized in the following paragraphs.

Sideways Information Passing

Let us consider a rule node with rule instance $H \text{ :- } G_1 \text{ \& } \cdots \text{ \& } G_k$. For $i = 1, \ldots, k$, we compute S_i from S_{i-1} and the relation for subgoal G_i. That is, let the result relation for the child of this rule node corresponding to subgoal G_i

be R_i, and let $Q_i = \text{ATOV}(G_i, R_i)$. Then S_i is computed by joining $S_{i-1} \bowtie Q_i$ and then projecting out any irrelevant variables.

Example 12.20: Consider the rule

$$p(f(X),Y) \; :- \; q_1(X,U,V) \; \& \; q_2(g(U,W),f(U)) \; \& \; q_3(W,X,Y). \quad (12.8)$$

Suppose we are given a relation $S_0(X)$ that provides a set of values for variable X. The remaining three supplementary relations are computed by

$$S_1(X,U) :- \pi_{XU}\big(S_0(X) \bowtie Q_1(X,U,V)\big).$$
$$S_2(X,W) :- \pi_{XW}\big(S_1(X,U) \bowtie Q_2(U,W)\big).$$
$$S_3(X,Y) :- \pi_{XY}\big(S_2(X,W) \bowtie Q_3(W,X,Y)\big).$$

Where Q_i is the relation for the ith subgoal, translated from the point of view of arguments of q_i to the point of view of variables, as described above.

For example, X and U are attributes of S_1, because they are both bound and relevant. In particular, X is bound because it is bound by the head (it is an attribute of S_0) as well as Q_1, while it is relevant because it is used later on, both in subgoal q_3 and in the head. U is bound in Q_1, and it appears subsequently in q_2. V is not an attribute of S_1 because, although it is bound by Q_1, it appears neither in q_2, q_3, nor the head. $\square$

An equivalent way to express the operation of sideways information passing is with a rule that combines the argument-to-variable conversion with the natural join. That is, let $sup_i(X_1, \ldots, X_n)$ and $sup_{i-1}(Y_1, \ldots, Y_m)$ be predicates corresponding to the two supplementary relations S_i and S_{i-1}, and let $p(t_1, \ldots, t_l)$ be the ith subgoal. Then we can write

$$sup_i(X_1, \ldots, X_n) :- sup_{i-1}(Y_1, \ldots, Y_m) \; \& \; p(t_1, \ldots, t_l). \quad (12.9)$$

If we let the relation R_i be the relation for the p subgoal in (12.9), then tuples for the body of (12.9) are formed by finding assignments τ for the variables of the body that

1. Form tuples in S_{i-1}, when restricted to $Y_1, \ldots, Y_m$, and

2. Make $\tau\big(p(t_1, \ldots, t_l)\big)$ a tuple of R_i.

But condition (2) is the same as saying that τ, restricted to the variables appearing in $p(t_1, \ldots, t_l)$, is a tuple of $Q_i = \text{ATOV}\big(p(t_1, \ldots, t_l), R_i\big)$. Thus, the join of S_i and Q_i is accomplished by the logical AND of the subgoals in (12.9), and the projection onto the relevant variables is accomplished by the fact that irrelevant variables will not appear among the X's.

For instance, the rules corresponding to the sideways information passing of Example 12.20 can be written

```
sup₁(X,U) :- sup₀(X) & q₁(X,U,V).
sup₂(X,W) :- sup₁(X,U) & q₂(g(U,W),f(U)).
sup₃(X,Y) :- sup₂(X,W) & q₃(W,X,Y).
```

Passing Bindings from Rules to Goals

Suppose we have a rule node corresponding to rule instance H :- G_1 & $\cdots$ & G_k. We can pass bindings from supplementary relation S_{i-1} to the goal-node child corresponding to G_i as follows.

1. First, we must determine which arguments of G_i are bound. An argument is bound if and only if all variables appearing therein are bound, that is, all variables of that argument are attributes of S_{i-1}.

2. Let G_i' be the predicate of G_i with all and only the arguments of G_i that are bound according to S_{i-1}.

3. Compute $M = \text{VTOA}(G_i', S_{i-1})$.

Example 12.21: Let us consider rule (12.8) from Example 12.20. S_0 binds only variable X, and that is enough to bind the first argument of the first subgoal, $q_1(X, U, V)$. Thus, the binding relation for the first goal-node child of the rule node for (12.8) has one argument and is obtained by computing $\text{VTOA}\big(q_1(X), S_0(X)\big)$. Note that $q_1(X)$ is the first subgoal of (12.8) restricted to the bound argument.

Now consider the second subgoal, $q_2\big(g(U, W),\ f(U)\big)$. S_1 has arguments X and U, which are enough to bind the second argument, but not the first. Note that the first argument, $g(U, W)$ is not bound, even though it is "partially bound," because one of its two variables is bound. Thus, the binding for the second goal-node child is

$$\text{VTOA}\Big(q_2\big(f(U)\big), S_1(X, U)\Big)$$

That is, we take each tuple μ in S_1, let $t = \mu[U]$, and make $f(t)$ a one-component tuple in the binding relation for the second goal-node child.

Finally, the third subgoal, $q_3(W, X, Y)$, has its first two arguments bound by $S_2(X, W)$. The binding relation for this subgoal,

$$\text{VTOA}\big(q_3(W, X), S_2(X, W)\big)$$

is a copy of S_2 with the order of columns reversed. $\square$

The operation of passing bindings from supplementary relations to binding relations can also be expressed as a rule. That is, suppose $S_{i-1}(X_1, \ldots, X_n)$ is the $(i-1)$st supplementary relation, and the ith subgoal is $p(t_1, \ldots, t_m)$. Let arguments $i_1, \ldots, i_k$ of this subgoal be bound by S_{i-1}. Then m, the predicate corresponding to the binding relation for the ith subgoal, is

$$m(t_{i_1}, \ldots, t_{i_k}) \colon\!- sup_{i-1}(X_1, \ldots, X_n).$$

We leave the correctness of this rule as an exercise.

Passing Bindings from Goals to Rules

Now, suppose we have a goal node for goal G, with binding relation M. Further, suppose this goal node has a rule-node child for rule instance $H \colon\!- G_1 \& \cdots \& G_k$, where head H unifies with G. The bindings for arguments of G also bind the same arguments of H. In turn, these arguments bind whatever variables appear in them, and the bindings for the variables become tuples of the zeroth supplementary relation for this rule node. That is, $S_0 = \text{ATOV}(H', M)$, where H' is H restricted to the arguments that are bound by M.

Example 12.22: Suppose there is a goal node for predicate p, whose binding relation M binds the first argument only. One child of this goal node corresponds to the rule (12.8), with head $p(f(X), Y)$. The binding for the first argument of p binds variable X, but not Y, so S_0 at this node has scheme X; its value is $\text{ATOV}(f(X), M)$. That is, we look at each tuple of M and take its lone component. If that component is of the form $f(t)$ for any term t, then t becomes the lone component of a tuple of S_0. A tuple of M that is not of the form $f(t)$ yields nothing for S_0. $\square$

This operation too can be expressed as a rule, the correctness of which is left as an exercise. Let $p(t_1, \ldots, t_n)$ be our goal node, and $p(s_1, \ldots, s_n)$ the head of the rule node. If the binding relation M binds arguments $i_1, \ldots, i_k$, and $X_1, \ldots, X_m$ are the variables found in these arguments of the head, that is, among $s_{i_1}, \ldots, s_{i_k}$, then the rule for computing S_0 at this rule node is

$$sup_0(X_1, \ldots, X_m) \colon\!- m(s_{i_1}, \ldots, s_{i_k}).$$

Passing Answers from Rules to Goals

When a rule node produces its answer relation, it contributes those answers to its goal-node parent.[19] As we discussed above, a rule node for a rule with k subgoals computes supplementary relation S_k, which binds all of the variables that are relevant after the kth subgoal, that is, exactly those variables that appear in the head. We need only to convert S_k from the point of view of variables to the arguments point of view, applied to the head H. That is, the answer relation for this rule node is $\text{VTOA}(H, S_k)$.

---

[19] Note that answer relations from goal nodes contribute to their rule-node parents by combination with the previous supplementary relation, to form the next supplementary relation, as described when we covered "sideways information passing." Thus, we need not say anything more about this, the second operator needed as we pass answers up to the root.

For example, rule (12.8) has a final supplementary relation $S_3(X, Y)$, and a head $p(f(X), Y)$. The result relation is thus

$$\text{VTOA}\Big(p(f(X), Y),\ S_3(X, Y)\Big).$$

That is, we take each tuple of S_3 and put function symbol f around the first component, leaving the second component intact.

We can express this operation as well in rule form

$$H :\text{-}\ sup_k(X_1, \ldots, X_n).$$

if $X_1, \ldots, X_n$ are the variables of the kth supplementary relation, and H is the head of the rule. We can even dispense with the final supplementary set altogether, and go directly from S_{k-1} to H with

$$H :\text{-}\ sup_{k-1}(Y_1, \ldots, Y_m)\ \&\ G_k.$$

Here, $Y_1, \ldots, Y_m$ are the variables of the $(k-1)$st supplementary relation, and G_k is the kth subgoal of the rule.

Finally, let us note that the result relation for a rule node is one of several relations that make up the result relation for its goal-node parent. In order to produce the result for the goal node, we must take the union of the results for each rule-node child of that goal node.

The reader may observe from the example of the previous section that it is not always clear when a complete result has been produced, and therefore, we may have difficulty producing result relations at either goal or rule nodes. In fact, without result relations at goal nodes, we cannot do sideways information passing, and therefore we cannot even develop binding sets for second and subsequent subgoals. In the next section, we shall see that all of the calculations that we implied were done on complete relations are, in fact, done incrementally in almost all cases. Thus, the calculations of this section really are performed, but not necessarily on complete relations at once.

Improvements in the Passing of Bindings

We saw in Example 12.21 that it is possible, when there are function symbols, for an argument to be "partially bound." Since we regard an argument as bound only when all variables appearing in that argument are bound, we may lose some binding information, as the following example shows.

Example 12.23: Suppose G_i is subgoal $q_2(g(U, W),\ f(U))$, and H is rule head $q_2(g(A, B),\ C)$ for some rule r, whose body is not important. Also assume that S_1, the prior supplementary relation at some rule node n, binds W, but not U (unlike Example 12.20, where we assumed U was bound). Then neither argument of G_i is bound by S_1, since U appears in both. Thus, G_i' is $q_2()$, that is, a zero-argument predicate. When we set $M = \text{VTOA}(G_i', S_1)$, we find none of the variables are bound in M, so that relation consists of the empty tuple alone. Thus, in the rule-node child corresponding to r, the zeroth supplementary relation will also have no attributes; that is, no variables are bound by the head of rule r.

However, it seems intuitive that variable B is bound in the head of this instance of rule r. That is, if we unify G_i with H, B and W are identified, and the values of W, which we can obtain from S_1 at the rule node n, become values of B at the rule node for r that is a grandchild of n. That is, we skip over goal nodes, jumping directly from a rule node to its descendants two levels below. By doing so, we can sometimes avoid losing bindings due to partially bound arguments that look completely unbound at the intermediate goal nodes. □

We can formalize the process used in Example 12.23. Suppose we have a subgoal G_i of some rule, and H is a rule head that unifies with G_i. We can pass bindings from the supplementary relation S_{i-1} in the rule node n where G_i is located, to S_0 for the grandchild of n corresponding to the rule r with head H, as follows.

1. Assume that r is rewritten so H and G_i share no variables. Unify G_i with H, and let the MGU be τ.

2. Identify bound variables of both H and G_i as follows.

   a) A variable of G_i bound by S_{i-1} is bound.
   b) For any variable X, if X appears in $\tau(Y)$ for some bound variable Y, then X is also bound.
   c) For any variable X, if all variables of $\tau(X)$ are bound, then X is bound.

   Rules (a) to (c) are applied repeatedly, until no more bound variables can be found.

3. Construct S, the zeroth supplementary relation for rule instance $\tau(r)$. Its attributes are all the variables of H that are found in step (2) to be bound. For each tuple μ in S_{i-1} at rule node n, we construct a tuple ν of S, by mimicking the inferences of (2b) and (2c) above. That is,

   b) If X appears in $\tau(Y)$ for some bound variable Y (whose value t we may assume has already been found), then strip away symbols, if necessary, from t to obtain the value of X; the operation is essentially ATOV. If no value of X is thus defined, and X is a variable of H, then ν does not exist. If X is a variable of G_i, it is possible that ν exists, but it may not derive any of its components from X.
   c) If $\tau(X)$ consists only of variables whose values have been determined, construct the value for X by substitution; the operation is essentially VTOA.

If we are successful in constructing from μ a value for every component of ν (i.e., for every variable that is an attribute of S), then we add ν to S. If any component of ν is undefined, then μ makes no contribution to S.

Example 12.24: Let us consider a subtle example based on Example 12.13. Let the subgoal G_i be

$$p\Big(f\big(X, g(X)\big), \; g\big(g(Y)\big)\Big)$$

and let the head H be

$$p\Big(f\big(g(U), V\big), \; g(V)\Big)$$

Recall from Example 12.13 that the MGU is

$$\begin{array}{ll} \tau(U) = U & \tau(X) = g(U) \\ \tau(Y) = g(U) & \tau(V) = g\big(g(U)\big) \end{array}$$

Suppose that Y is an attribute of S_{i-1}, but X is not. Thus, by rule (2a), Y is bound. Since U appears in $\tau(Y)$, we conclude by (2b) that U is bound. It then follows by (2c) that V and X are also bound.

Hence, both variables appearing in the head are bound, and the scheme for S is UV. We construct S from S_{i-1} as follows. Let μ be any tuple in S_{i-1}, and let $t = \mu[Y]$. If t is of the form $g(s)$, then s is the value of U, and $g\big(g(s)\big)$, or $g(t)$, is the value of V. Thus, $\big(s, g(t)\big)$ is a tuple of S. If t is not of the form $g(s)$, then μ does not yield a tuple for S. $\square$

Despite the fact that skipping from rule nodes to their grandchildren, when passing bindings down the rule/goal tree, can sometimes produce more bound variables, we shall use the technique first described, of going through the intermediate goal nodes. One reason is that for datalog, it is easy to see that arguments cannot be partially bound unless they are completely bound, because arguments can only be constants or single variables. Even in nondatalog cases, there is no guarantee that there will be partially-bound arguments, or that anything can be gained by treating them specially. The most compelling reason will only appear when we consider the magic-sets rule-rewriting technique in Chapter 13. There, we shall see that there is a significant savings in the number of rules needed by going through the intermediate goals. However, should there be the need to do so, either the rule/goal tree algorithm to be described formally in the next section, or the magic-sets technique can be modified to do more precise passing of bindings, as we have described here.

Improving Sideways Information Passing

Another modification to the basic algorithm that sometimes can improve performance is to revise the way bindings are passed sideways. That is, we assumed bindings were passed through supplementary relations, one for each position in the rule body, and each supplementary relation had as attributes exactly the bound and relevant variables at that position. However, we can sometimes save work, as the next example shows, by using another pattern of information passing.[20]

Example 12.25: Consider the rule

$$p(X,Y) :- q_1(X,Z) \& q_2(X,W) \& q_3(Z,Y) \& q_4(W,Y). \tag{12.10}$$

Suppose that at some rule node for (12.10), the goal-node parent binds the first argument of p, but not the second. Then S_0 has attribute X, S_1 has attributes X and Z, and most importantly, S_2 has attributes X, Z, and W. For convenience, let S_0 have n different values, and suppose the relations for q_1 and q_2 each have m values of the second argument associated with each value of the first argument. Thus, S_2 has nm^2 tuples.

However, suppose we compute the result relation for (12.10) by taking

$$\pi_{XY}\big(S_0(X) \bowtie Q_1(X,Z) \bowtie Q_3(Z,Y)\big)$$

and intersecting it with

$$\pi_{XY}\big(S_0(X) \bowtie Q_2(X,W) \bowtie Q_4(W,Y)\big)$$

where Q_i is the relation for q_i, $1 \le i \le 4$. The first step in each case, joining $S_0 \bowtie Q_1$ and $S_0 \bowtie Q_2$, produces a relation of size nm, by our assumption. If W and Z have large domain sizes, we may suppose that joining with Q_3 and Q_4, respectively, does not increase the size of the relations involved. If that is the case, then our alternative method of evaluating the result relation never produces any relation as large as S_2. The alternative method is therefore more efficient by about a factor of m. The intuitive reason for this improvement is that in (12.10), the roles played by variables W and Z are independent, yet their values are paired in S_2, effectively taking a useless Cartesian product. $\Box$

We should be aware of the opportunity sometimes afforded by varying the sideways information passing strategy. However, we shall, in the future, assume that only the "standard" method of passing information sideways is used; that is, we compute each of the supplementary relations in turn.

12.7 THE RULE/GOAL TREE EVALUATION ALGORITHM

We are now ready to put the informal algorithm of Section 12.5 together with the techniques of Section 12.6, to form the complete rule/goal tree expansion and evaluation algorithm. We shall begin with the basic algorithm, which does

---

[20] We do not take advantage of the option to reorder subgoals. Rather, in this example, we still pass bindings from left to right only, but we do so in a manner other than the construction of supplementary relations.

a preorder traversal, that is, a depth-first search, of the rule/goal tree, assuming all branches will terminate in a finite time; termination might occur because the predicates encountered are not recursive, or because we eventually find empty sets of bindings, as we did in Example 12.17. We then discuss how to modify the algorithm so it is queue-based, that is, it performs breadth-first search of the rule/goal tree, as was implicit in Section 12.5.

Initial Bindings

For uniformity, we shall treat constants in the query somewhat differently from the way we dealt with constant j in Examples 12.16 and 12.17. Here, we shall assume that all arguments of the query are variables, but we may supply a relation to the root of the rule/goal tree, providing bindings for certain arguments of the root goal.

For example, instead of starting the rule/goal tree of Figure 12.15 with the root goal $anc(j, W)$, we shall use the goal $anc(Z_0, W)$ as the query. We then provide that goal the unary binding relation $\{j\}$, whose attribute corresponds to the first argument of anc. Note how the choice of Z_0 in place of j fits in with the pattern of variables used in Figure 12.15.

The Basic Algorithm

We shall now present the simple form of the rule/goal tree expansion and evaluation algorithm for which we have been preparing. As many of the details were given already, we shall allude to several algorithms and techniques from the previous sections.

Algorithm 12.6: Rule/Goal Tree Expansion and Evaluation.

INPUT: A collection of safe rules, a database, a goal G_0 that is the query, and a relation M_0 that binds zero or more of the arguments of G_0.

OUTPUT: The relation of tuples that satisfy the query G_0, according to the given database. However, if the rules and database do not guarantee convergence (for example, because the rules are recursive), then this "algorithm" may in fact run forever, and will not produce an answer.

METHOD: The heart of the algorithm is a pair of recursive routines

1. $expandGoal(M, G, R)$ takes goal G, binding relation M for zero or more of G's arguments, and returns result relation R, over all the arguments of G. Result R is the set of tuples that can be inferred from the given rules and database, match goal G, and agree with some one tuple of M on all arguments in the scheme of M.

2. $expandRule(S_0, r, R)$ takes rule instance r and zeroth supplementary set S_0, which binds zero or more variables of r, and produces result relation R, whose attributes correspond to the arguments of the head of r. The value

of R is the set of tuples that match the head of r, are inferred from the database and rules, and agree with some one tuple of S_0 in all variables for which S_0 has an attribute.

These routines are exhibited in Figure 12.17. Some additional details are as follows.

1. For procedure *expandGoal* of Figure 12.17(a):

   a) Line (1) lets us terminate searches that are guaranteed not to return any tuples. This step is essential if the search of some recursive rule/goal trees, as in the example of Section 12.5, are to converge.
   b) Line (6) requires a unification, as described in Section 12.4.
   c) Line (7) passes bindings from goals to rules, as in Section 12.6.

2. For the procedure *expandRule* of Figure 12.17(b):

   a) Line (3) passes bindings from rules to goals, also as described in Section 12.6.
   b) Line (5) translates a relation that represents an answer from the argument viewpoint to the viewpoint of variables.
   c) Line (6) performs sideways information passing, as described in Section 12.6.
   d) In line (7), the set S_k will be a relation over exactly those variables that appear in the head H, as discussed in Section 12.6.

The algorithm itself consists of a call to $expandGoal(M_0, G_0, R_0)$, followed by the printing of the answer, the relation returned as R_0. $\square$

Example 12.26: Let us redo the example of Section 12.5 according to Algorithm 12.6. We make the modification that the query goal is now $anc(Z_0, W)$, with the binding $\{j\}$ for Z_0. Figure 12.15, with this modification, is repeated as Figure 12.18.

To begin, we call $expandGoal\big(M_0,\ anc(Z_0, W),\ R_0\big)$, where $M_0 = \{j\}$; R_0 is the name of the relation that we shall compute. This call results in two more calls, $expandRule(S_0^1,\ r_1^1,\ R^1)$ and $expandRule(S_0^2,\ r_2^2,\ R^2)$, where S_0^1 and S_0^2 are each relations with scheme Z_0 and value $\{j\}$, constructed according to line (7) of $expandGoal$.[21] Rule instances r_1^1 and r_2^2 correspond to the children of the root in Figure 12.15 (with Z_0 in place of j), and are

r_1^1: anc(Z_0,W) :- par(Z_0,W).
r_2^2: anc(Z_0,W) :- par(Z_0,Z_1) & anc(Z_1,W).

Now let us follow the first of these calls to *expandRule*. At line (3) we get the binding relation $M^3 = \{j\}$ with scheme PAR_1, the first argument of *par*, for the subgoal $par(Z_0, W)$. That results in a call to

---

[21] We shall assign parameter names for each call by using a new number for each call and superscripting all of its variables by this number.

procedure $expandGoal(M, G, R)$;
begin

(1)   **if** $M = \emptyset$ **then begin** R := $\emptyset$; **return end**;
(2)   **if** G is a goal with an EDB predicate **then begin**
(3) R := $M \bowtie P$; **return end** /* P is the relation
             for the predicate of G. Note this operation
             is a selection on the database relation P */
         /* here, G has an IDB predicate */
(4) R := $\emptyset$ /* we accumulate relations for each of G's
           rule heads in R */
(5)   **for** each rule r whose head H unifies with G **do begin**
(6)   let τ be the MGU of H and G;
(7)   compute $S_0 = \text{ATOV}(H', M)$; /* H' is $\tau(H)$ restricted
             to arguments that are attributes of M */
(8) $expandRule(S_0, \tau(r), R_r)$;
(9) R := $R \cup R_r$
       end
end

(a) Procedure to expand goal nodes.

procedure $expandRule(S_0, r, R)$;
begin

(1)   let $r = H$:- G_1 & ... & G_k;
(2)   **for** i := 1 **to** k **do begin**
         /* compute bindings for ith subgoal */
(3) M_i := $\text{VTOA}(G_i', S_{i-1})$; /* G_i' is G_i restricted to arg-
             uments whose variables are attributes of S_{i-1} */
(4) $expandGoal(M_i, G_i, R_i)$;
         /* convert R_i to the viewpoint of variables and use
             it to compute the next supplementary relation */
(5) Q_i := $\text{ATOV}(G_i, R_i)$;
(6) S_i := $\pi_T(S_{i-1} \bowtie Q_i)$; /* T is the set of variables
             that appear in the scheme of S_{i-1} or Q_i, and also
             appear in one of $H, G_{i+1}, \ldots, G_k$ */
       end;
(7) R := $\text{VTOA}(H, S_k)$
end

(b) Procedure to expand rule nodes.

Figure 12.17 Recursive procedures of Algorithm 12.6.

$$expandGoal\big(M^3,\ par(Z_0, W),\ R^3\big)$$

which at line (3) of $expandGoal$ returns with $R^3 = \{jf,\ jh\}$, according to the relation for par given in Figure 12.14 of Section 12.5.

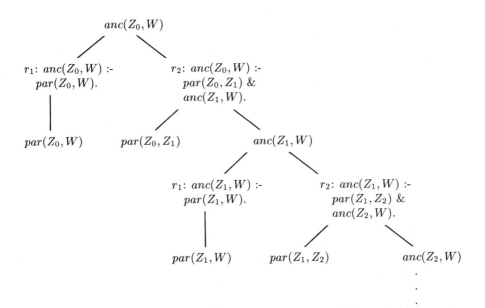

Figure 12.18 Rule/goal tree for goal $anc(Z_0, W)$.

The first call to $expandRule$ is complete, so we may consider the second call, the one for rule instance r_2^2. Here, for the first subgoal, $par(Z_0, Z_1)$, we again compute at line (3) binding set $M^4 = \{j\}$, and proceed as for r_1^1 with a call

$$expandGoal\big(M^4,\ par(Z_0, Z_1),\ R^4\big)$$

that returns $R^4 = \{jf,\ jh\}$. At line (5) of $expandRule$, we convert R^4 to Q^4, a relation with scheme $Z_0 Z_1$ and value $\{jf,\ jh\}$. Then at line (6) we compute the next supplementary relation

$$S_1^2(Z_0, Z_1) = \pi_{Z_0 Z_1}\big(S_0^2(Z_0) \bowtie Q^4(Z_0, Z_1)\big) = \{jf,\ jh\}$$

Recall that S_0^2 has scheme Z_0 and value $\{j\}$ in the above computation. S_1^2 has both variables Z_0 and Z_1 in its scheme, because Z_0 is found in the head, and Z_1 is found in a subsequent subgoal of r_2^2. Thus, the projection has no effect in this case.

We now return to the loop of line (2) in the execution of *expandRule* for rule instance r_2^2, and we consider the second (and last) subgoal, $anc(Z_1, W)$. At line (3) we compute binding relation $M^5 = \{f, h\}$, whose lone attribute corresponds to the first argument of *anc*. We are lead at step (4) to a call

$$expandGoal(M^5, \; anc(Z_1, W), \; R^5)$$

If we formalize the discussion of Example 12.17 (Section 12.5), in terms of Algorithm 12.6, we discover that eventually, this call terminates and returns

$$R^5 = \{fc, \; fe, \; hd, \; fa, \; fb, \; ha, \; hb\}$$

The key observation is that after several levels of recursive calls, we reach the "top" of the genealogy in Figure 12.14, resulting in a call

$$expandGoal(\emptyset, \; anc(Z_4, W), \; R)$$

Line (1) of *expandGoal* intercepts this situation and terminates the recursion, correctly returning $R = \emptyset$.

Now, let us revisit the call of *expandRule* for r_2^2. At line (5), we compute Q^5; it is the same relation as R^5, but its scheme is $Z_1 W$. At line (6) we compute

$$S_2^2(Z_0, W) = \pi_{Z_0 W}\left(S_1^2(Z_0, Z_1) \bowtie Q^5(Z_1, W)\right) = \{jc, \; je, \; ja, \; jb, \; jd\}$$

Recall $S_1^2 = \{jf, \; jh\}$, and its scheme is $Z_0 Z_1$, while Q^5 is the relation given above as R^5, but with scheme $Z_1 W$.

Finally, the loop of lines (2) through (6) terminates, and we compute the returned relation R^2; it is the same as S_2^2 above, but its components correspond to the two arguments of predicate *anc*.

Now, we have completed both calls made by the original call,

$$expandGoal(\{j\}, \; anc(Z_0, W), \; R_0)$$

and at line (9) we have been accumulating the relations returned by the two calls to *expandRule*. Thus, we may set

$$R_0 = \{jf, \; jh, \; jc, \; je, \; ja, \; jb, \; jd\}$$

which is the answer to the query. $\square$

A Queue-Based Version of Rule/Goal Tree Expansion

Algorithm 12.6 terminates only in those situations where the backtracking, top-down scheme of Section 12.3 terminates. In a sense, we cannot do better without reordering the subgoals of some rules, because Algorithm 12.6 terminates whenever the rule/goal tree can be made finite by excising nodes to which an empty set of bindings is passed. In another sense, we can improve on Algorithm 12.6 if we adopt the breadth-first, or queue-based order of node exploration, suggested in Section 12.5. If we do, and if the answer is finite, we shall converge eventually to the correct answer, even though it is difficult to tell we have converged.[22]

We shall sketch the necessary modifications to Algorithm 12.6, so that the top-down tree expansion algorithm will converge to the query's answer, just as the bottom-up method does. The reader should remember from Section 12.2 that, when function symbols are involved, it is possible that the answer is infinite, and therefore, convergence does not occur at any finite time. Nevertheless, we can show that the limits of what the bottom-up and the queue-based top-down algorithms produce are the same. That is, a fact inferred by one method is eventually inferred by the other.

Algorithm 12.6, with its mutually recursive procedures *expandGoal* and *expandRule*, is easily seen to visit nodes of the rule/goal tree in a depth-first order; that is, it makes a preorder traversal of the fully expanded tree. Instead of stacking activations of the two procedures, as one normally does, we could put the calls on a queue. So doing has the effect of executing the calls corresponding to the nodes of the rule/goal tree level-by-level, that is, in a breadth-first search of the tree.

If we visit nodes in this order, we are not prepared to provide bindings in some cases. For example, suppose we have a rule instance r with subgoals G_1 and G_2. When we visit the rule node for r, we put the goal nodes for G_1 and G_2 at the end of the queue. The binding relation for G_1 will be available now, provided S_0, the zeroth supplementary relation for r, is available. However, the binding relation for G_2 is not available, and will not be available until we have completely explored the tree rooted at G_1, which may never happen, since that tree may be infinite. Thus, we shall expand G_2, when it reaches the head of the queue, with the binding relation that is obtained from whatever tuples we know are in S_1, perhaps none. At intervals, new bindings for G_2 may be discovered and passed down the tree as far as the tree has grown.

Propagation of New Information

As we expand the tree level-by-level, we sometimes discover new facts. All such facts have an origin that is a goal node with an EDB predicate, for which we look up the database and produce the answer relation for that goal. The discovery of tuples in the answer relation for one node can have a rippling effect, as follows.

1. Answer tuples for a goal node G_i can join with a supplementary set S_{i-1} at the parent rule node to produce new tuples in the next supplementary relation, S_i, at that rule node.

---

[22] In comparison, bottom-up logic evaluation, as discussed in Section 12.2, makes it easy for us to tell when convergence has occurred; we simply check that at one round, nothing is added to any predicate.

2. Additional tuples in a supplementary relation S_i can
    a) Produce new binding tuples for the goal node of subgoal G_{i+1}.
    b) Produce new answer tuples for the rule node, if S_i is the last supplementary relation; that is, there are only i subgoals.
    c) Produce new tuples for the next supplementary relation S_{i+1}, by combining with tuples already found for subgoal G_{i+1}.

3. New binding tuples for a goal node can produce
    a) New tuples for the zeroth supplementary relations of its rule-node children.
    b) New answer tuples, if the goal has an EDB predicate.

4. New answers for a rule node can produce new answers for its goal-node parent.

Each addition of tuples to the answer relation belonging to some goal node in the portion of the tree already constructed can thus spawn events in which tuples are added to one or more other relations, usually at different nodes. It turns out that this spawning of new tuples cannot go on indefinitely if the rule/goal tree remains fixed; the next lemma proves this contention.

Lemma 12.1: If we have a finite portion of the rule/goal tree constructed, and some new tuples for the answer relation of some goal node are discovered, the propagation rules described above result in only a finite number of operations in which new tuples are inserted into some answer relation, supplementary relation, or binding relation.

Proof: New answer tuples can propagate upwards, resulting in new answers for its rule and goal ancestors. At each rule ancestor, the supplementary relations $S_i, S_{i+1}, \ldots$ can receive new tuples if G_i is the subgoal of the rule receiving new answers. In fact, it is essential that supplementary relations be augmented all of the way to the right end of the rule, if the rule node is to obtain new answers. Figure 12.19 suggests this process.

However, the augmented supplementary relations can spawn new bindings down the tree. Bindings are passed downward further, from binding relations for goals, to supplementary relations for rules. We must observe that any such bindings are at nodes to the right of the original goal node (G in Figure 12.19). It is possible for these additional tuples in binding relations to "turn around" and produce new answer tuples in two situations.

1. Bindings are passed to an EDB goal, and answers are produced by database lookup.
2. Bindings that are passed to the zeroth supplementary relation for a rule propagate all of the way to the end of the rule using tuples already found as answers for the various subgoals of the rule. Thus, we produce new answers for that rule node and for the goal node above it.

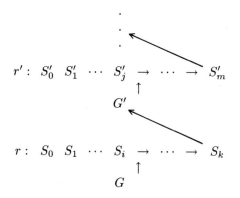

Figure 12.19 Passing answers up and to the right.

It may not be obvious that (2) can ever occur; we give an example after this proof is completed.

As mentioned, any goal node receiving new answer tuples must lie to the right of the goal node whose additional answer tuples started this propagation. Let us regard such goal nodes as new sources of answer tuples, unrelated to the propagation of the original answer tuples. Thus, each source's propagation must die out after a finite number of steps, perhaps to be replaced by new "sources" to the right of the old source. Since the rule/goal tree is fixed, new sources of answer tuples cannot be created forever. Thus, there is a limit on the number of changes induced by an initial discovery of new answers, including all propagation from secondary sources. □

Example 12.27: Figure 12.20 shows a hypothetical rule node and its current supplementary relations. We also show the goal nodes for the subgoals $q(X, Z)$ and $t(Y)$, along with their current binding relations (indicated by the downward arrow) and their current answer relations, going upward.[23]

Suppose that we propagate the additional binding tuple ab to S_0. The existence of ae in the answer relation for q tells us abe must be added to S_1. Then, the existence of tuple b in the answer relation for t gives us abe in S_2, and this tuple is also an answer tuple for the rule node. □

Example 12.28: Now let us have an example of the entire process of generating the rule/goal tree and propagating new tuples. We shall reconsider the rule/goal tree discussed in Example 12.26 and shown in Figure 12.18. We begin as in Example 12.26, with the call to $expandGoal\big(M_0,\ anc(Z_0, W),\ R_0\big)$, and $M_0 = \{j\}$. That call places on the queue two more expansion actions,

---

[23] We use variables as attributes rather than arguments; in this simple datalog example, there is no difference.

X Y
a d
c b

S_0

X Y Z
a d e
c b f

S_1

X Y Z
c b f

S_2

$$p(X, Y, Z) \quad :- \quad q(X, Z) \quad \& \quad t(Y)$$

$$\downarrow \quad q \quad \uparrow \qquad \downarrow \quad t \quad \uparrow$$

Q_1		X Z	T_1		Y
a		a e	b		b
c		c f	d		

Figure 12.20 Example where bindings yield answers immediately.

$expandRule\big(S_0^1,\ r_1^1,\ R^1\big)$ and $expandRule\big(S_0^2,\ r_2^2,\ R^2\big)$, where $S_0^1 = S_0^2 = \{j\}$. These are executed in turn, and they spawn three more actions for the queue, corresponding to the third level of Figure 12.15,

$$expandGoal\big(M^3,\ par(Z_0, W),\ R^3\big)$$
$$expandGoal\big(M^4,\ par(Z_0, Z_1),\ R^4\big)$$
$$expandGoal\big(M^5,\ anc(Z_1, W),\ R^5\big)$$

Here, $M^3 = M^4 = \{j\}$, but unlike Example 12.26, the initial value of M^5 is $\emptyset$. The reason is that we have not yet had time to process the goal $par(Z_0, Z_1)$, and thereby develop values for Z_1 to pass sideways.

When we process the goal node $par(Z_0, W)$, we generate the answer tuples $\{jf,\ jh\}$ for R^3, and these tuples must be allowed to join with the zeroth supplementary set for the rule node above, that is S_0^1, so tuples may be added to the next supplementary relation, S_1^1. We add jf and jh to S_1^1. Since this supplementary relation is the last for its rule node, we use it to generate answers for the rule node, which puts jf and jh in R^1. That, in turn, puts these tuples in the answer relation R_0.

Now, consider the next goal node on the queue, $par(Z_0, Z_1)$. We similarly generate answer tuples $\{jf,\ jh\}$, and these join with the zeroth supplementary relation, S_0^2, at the rule node above, to yield the same two tuples for S_1^2. This, supplementary relation, not being the last for its node, does not propagate answers upward, but it does propagate bindings downward to goal node $anc(Z_1, W)$. Thus, M^5 is set equal to $\{f,\ h\}$. The balance of the simulation is omitted; the ideas are similar. $\square$

In summary, we have described a variant of Algorithm 12.6, which we shall call *queue-based rule/goal tree expansion* (QRGT). In QRGT, expansion of nodes occurs level-by-level, and at each stage, propagation of new tuples for binding relations, supplementary relations, and answer relations is possible. These relations thus converge to their correct value; in some cases, for example, if the rules are datalog rules, then convergence will occur after a finite time. Otherwise, the values of the relations approach, but never reach, their correct values, in the sense that every tuple belonging to a relation will eventually be added to the relation, although there is no finite time at which all necessary tuples are in all of the relations.

Equivalence of Bottom-Up and Top-Down Computations

When we compare the top-down QRGT algorithm with bottom-up computation, that is, with naive or semi-naive evaluation, we find an important similarity: tuples are eventually generated by QRGT if and only if they match the root goal and they are generated bottom up. Since the bottom-up computation is likely to generate as well many tuples that neither match the root goal, nor match any other goal needed to infer tuples for the root goal, it appears that QRGT provides considerably more "focus" than bottom-up. That is, top-down is better at avoiding the inference of irrelevant tuples. There is a compensating factor that convergence is easier to detect when computing bottom-up. However, in the next chapter we shall see that the advantages of both methods can be combined into one general technique. For the moment, let us sketch the proof that top-down and bottom-up query evaluations yield the same answer.

Theorem 12.2: The QRGT variant of Algorithm 12.6 eventually produces a tuple (ground atom) $\mu = p(t_1, \ldots, t_k)$ in response to query goal G with binding relation M_0, if and only if μ

1. Is inferred bottom-up from the same logical rules,
2. Agrees with some tuple of M_0 on the attributes of M_0, and
3. Term-matches G.

Proof: The "only if" portion is easy. An induction on the number of steps of QRGT tells us that only tuples matching their goals and binding relations are ever generated. A similar induction shows that all tuples produced for answers are correctly inferred from the rules and would therefore be generated bottom-up.

Now consider the "if" part, that is, if μ is generated bottom up from the database and rules, matches some goal G, and agrees with some tuple of the binding relation for G, then μ is eventually added to the answer relation for G, during QRGT. The proof is an induction on the number of steps required to infer μ bottom-up. The basis, zero steps, only occurs if G's predicate is an

EDB predicate. Then μ is placed in the answer relation by lines (2) and (3) of *expandGoal*, or by a propagation action of type (3b) if the goal node for G was "expanded" before the binding tuple that matches μ was propagated to G.

For the induction, suppose μ is inferred bottom-up by a use of rule

$$r: H :\text{-} G_1 \& \cdots \& G_m$$

Then G, H, and μ all have the same predicate symbol.[24] Moreover, the head H becomes μ when some substitution ρ is applied to this rule; that is, $\rho(H) = \mu$. Since we are given that G term-matches μ, it must also be the case that $\mu = \phi(G)$ for some substitution ϕ. Now, let τ be the MGU of G and H. By Theorem 12.1, since ϕ and ρ, applied to G and H, respectively, make G and H identical, these two substitutions must be obtainable by substitutions on $\tau(G)$ [which equals $\tau(H)$]. That is, $\rho = \rho'\tau$ and $\phi = \phi'\tau$.

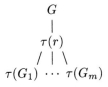

Figure 12.21 Part of a rule/goal tree.

Let ν_i, $i = 1, 2, \ldots, m$, be the tuples that are used to infer μ bottom-up using rule r; that is $\nu_i = \rho(G_i)$. In the rule/goal tree, the goal node for G has a child for the rule instance $\tau(r)$, which has children for each of the goals $\tau(G_1), \ldots, \tau(G_m)$, as suggested in Figure 12.21. Since $\rho = \rho'\tau$, each ν_i term-matches $\tau(G_i)$; that is, $\nu_i = \rho'\big(\tau(G_i)\big)$.

We know that each ν_i is inferred bottom-up using fewer steps than are used for μ; thus the inductive hypothesis applies to the ν_i's. Now it is simple to show, for $i = 1, 2, \ldots, m$ in turn, that

1. A tuple matching ν_i is eventually placed by the top-down algorithm in the binding relation for goal node $\tau(G_i)$.
2. Hence, by the inductive hypothesis, each ν_i is eventually placed in the answer relation for $\tau(G_i)$.

Thus, we can infer that μ is placed in the answer relation for $\tau(r)$, and therefore in the answer relation for G. When we let G be the root goal, we have the theorem. $\square$

---

[24] Recall that we may write tuples as ground atoms with the appropriate predicate symbol.

12.8 RULE/GOAL GRAPHS

We shall now introduce the "rule/goal graph" representation for a collection of Horn clauses, which will have several uses subsequently. In the next section, we use it to perform the following useful transformation on rules. In certain query-evaluation algorithms to be discussed later, it is useful to assume that no predicate p will ever appear in a goal, during a top-down expansion, with two different binding patterns. The rule/goal graph helps us transform rules so that condition holds. In Section 12.10, we show how the rule/goal graph helps us to find good orderings for the subgoals in a collection of rules.

Adornments

Whenever, during rule/goal tree expansion, we create a goal node, say

$$p(t_1, \ldots, t_k)$$

that goal node is given a binding relation for some subset of p's arguments. We can indicate which arguments are bound and which are not by an *adornment*, or *binding pattern*, that is, by a string of b's and f's of length k, if p has k arguments. If the ith symbol of the adornment is b, then the ith argument of p is bound; that is, the binding relation for the goal node includes an attribute for the ith argument. If the ith symbol of the adornment is f, then the ith argument of p is free; that is, there is no attribute for the ith argument in the binding relation for the subgoal.

A goal that is an instance of predicate p with a binding relation represented by the adornment α is denoted p^α. For example, in Figure 12.18 (Section 12.7), each of the subgoals with predicate *anc* has the first argument bound and the second argument free. Thus, each of the *anc* goal nodes can be represented by the adorned predicate anc^{bf}.

Rule Adornments

We also need to indicate the bound/free status of variables in a rule. As we process subgoals from left to right during rule/goal tree expansion, variables that were free become bound. The algorithm to decide when a variable becomes bound in a rule

$$r: H :\text{-} G_1 \& \cdots \& G_k$$

is simple, and follows from the sideways information passing algorithm described in Section 12.6.

1. A variable appearing in a bound argument of the rule head is bound before processing any subgoals.
2. A variable is bound after processing subgoal G_i if it was bound before processing G_i or if it appears anywhere in G_i.

An adornment for a rule indicates which variables are bound at a point and which are free. The notation we use for a *rule adornment* is a superscript of the form $[X_1, \ldots, X_m \mid Y_1, \ldots, Y_n]$, where the X's are bound and the Y's are free. The adornment for rule r, prior to consideration of any subgoals, is attached as a superscript to r_0, while the adornment that applies after the consideration of the ith subgoal is a superscript of r_i.[25]

Example 12.29: Consider the recursive ancestor rule, which we have called r_2.

$$r_2: \quad \texttt{anc(X,Y)} \ \texttt{:- par(X,Z) \& anc(Z,Y)}$$

Suppose that *anc* is called with a binding for the first argument. Then in the rule before consideration of any subgoals, only X is bound, and we represent this fact by the adorned rule $r_{2.0}^{[X \mid Y,Z]}$.

The first subgoal, $par(X, Z)$, provides a binding for Z, so the situation after consideration of the first subgoal is represented by $r_{2.1}^{[X,Z \mid Y]}$. There is no need to represent the situation after the last subgoal is considered; all the variables will be bound by then, assuming the rule is safe. $\square$

Constructing a Rule/Goal Graph

We can represent the patterns of binding that occur in a rule/goal tree by a finite structure called a *rule/goal graph*. Suppose we are given a set of Horn-clause rules and a query goal. If p is the predicate of the query, and α is the adornment that has b whenever the query specifies a value for the corresponding argument and has f whenever no value is specified, then we begin construction of the rule/goal graph for this query with the node p^α. We then consider each node in the rule/goal graph and expand it according to the following rules. As we expand, we add *goal nodes*, which are adorned predicates, and *rule nodes* which are nodes representing a rule and some number of the subgoals for that rule. Using the notation described above, we have r_0, with an adornment, to represent rule r before considering any subgoals, and r_i, with an adornment, to represent rule r after considering its first i subgoals.

1. A goal node with an EDB predicate has no successors.

2. A goal node that is an IDB predicate p with an adornment α has successors corresponding to all of the rules with head predicate p. If r is such a rule, then p^α has successor

$$r_0^{[X_1, \ldots, X_n \mid Y_1, \ldots, Y_m]}$$

---

[25] Often, we call the rules $r_1, \ldots, r_l$; in that case, we attach the adornments for rule i to $r_{i.j}$, $j = 0, 1, \ldots, l - 1$.

where $X_1, \ldots, X_n$ are all of the variables that appear in an argument of r's head that is bound according to adornment α, and $Y_1, \ldots, Y_m$ are the other variables of r.

3.   Consider a rule node $r_i^{[X_1, \ldots, X_n | Y_1, \ldots, Y_m]}$, $i \geq 0$, and suppose $q(t_1, \ldots, t_k)$ is the $i + 1$st subgoal of r.

   a)   One successor of this rule node is a goal node q^β; β is the adornment that makes the jth argument of q bound if all variables appearing in t_j are among the bound variables of the rule so far (i.e., among $X_1, \ldots, X_n$). β makes the jth argument free otherwise.

   b)   If $i+1$ is less than the number of subgoals in rule r [that is, $q(t_1, \ldots, t_k)$ is not the last subgoal of r], then node

$$r_i^{[X_1, \ldots, X_n | Y_1, \ldots, Y_m]}$$

has a second successor, the node

$$r_{i+1}^{[X_1, \ldots, X_n, U_1, \ldots, U_j | V_1, \ldots, V_l]}$$

where $U_1, \ldots, U_j$ are those variables among $Y_1, \ldots, Y_m$ that appear in $q(t_1, \ldots, t_k)$, and $V_1, \ldots, V_l$ are the remaining variables of the Y's.

Example 12.30: Let us consider the following two rules that define "cousins at the same generation," that is, individuals in a genealogy that have some common ancestor the same number of generations away from each. As a special case, each person in the database is defined to be his own "cousin at the same generation"; siblings are also "cousins." We assume that *person* is a unary EDB relation containing the set of individuals mentioned in the database, and $par(C, P)$ is another EDB relation whose tuples (c, p) mean that p is a parent of c.

```
r₁:  sg(X,X) :- person(X).
r₂:  sg(X,Y) :- par(X,Xp) & par(Y,Yp) & sg(Xp,Yp).
```

The first rule says that every person is at the same generation as himself, and the second says that X and Y are at the same generation if they have parents Xp and Yp, respectively, such that Xp and Yp are at the same generation.

Let us suppose that the query is of the form sg^{bf}, that is, given an individual (or a set of individuals), find all facts $sg(a, b)$ such that a is in the given set of individuals. Figure 12.22 shows the rule/goal graph that is created by starting with this query and following the given order of subgoals in r_2.

The children of the root correspond to the two rules for sg. In each case, the binding on the first argument of sg provides a binding for variable X and no other. For rule r_1, the binding on X makes the one and only argument of the lone subgoal $person(X)$ bound, as indicated by the goal node $person^b$, the child of $r_{1.0}^{[X|]}$. Note that the latter node may be interpreted as saying "rule r_1 before

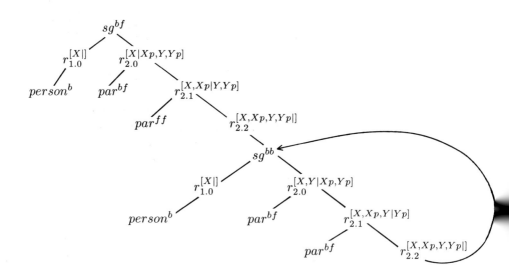

Figure 12.22 Rule/goal graph for same-generation rules.

consideration of any subgoals, has variable X bound and no free variables."

The other child of the root,

$$r_{2.0}^{[X|Xp,Y,Yp]}$$

has child par^{bf}, representing the first subgoal of r_2. The adornment is bf, because the binding on X provides a binding for the first argument of $par(X, Xp)$, but not for the second. It also has child

$$r_{2.1}^{[X,Xp|Y,Yp]}$$

indicating that, after the first subgoal, Xp, as well as X, is bound.

The latter node has child par^{ff}; the adornment indicates that bindings for X and Xp do not provide bindings for either argument of the second subgoal, $par(Y, Yp)$. It also has child

$$r_{2.2}^{[X,Xp,Y,Yp|]}$$

which indicates that after processing the first two subgoals of r_2, we have bindings for all of the variables. Thus, this node has child sg^{bb}, which represents the third and last subgoal of r_2; by the time we reach this subgoal, both its arguments are bound.

We now have a second node for predicate sg, this time with adornment bb. It is expanded in much the same way that the first node, sg^{bf} was. The adornments of the rule node are different, but by the time we get to the third subgoal, we have sg^{bb} again. Thus, we need add no more nodes, and the construction of the rule/goal graph is complete.

Note, however, that we could have merged the two occurrences of $person^b$ and the three occurrences of par^{bf}. We could also merge the two nodes for $r_{2.2}$. We shall not make such mergers here or elsewhere. Rather, we prefer to show each occurrence of an EDB subgoal separately, and we prefer to expand separately each rule node.[26] □

It turns out that the order of subgoals in r_2 is not likely to be the best we could have chosen. The reason is that, when starting with sg^{bf}, we are forced to evaluate par^{ff}, that is, to include the entire par relation in a join to evaluate r_2. Intuitively, we would like to avoid evaluation of subgoals that do not have at least one bound argument whenever possible, since typically, binding even one argument will cut down significantly on the number of tuples. It happens that for the same-generation example, we can avoid examining the full par relation if we move the sg subgoal into the middle of the body; that is, we rewrite the rules as

r_1:   sg(X,X) :- person(X).
r_3:   sg(X,Y) :- par(X,Xp) & sg(Xp,Yp) & par(Y,Yp).

The rule/goal graph for these rules and query sg^{bf} is shown in Figure 12.23.

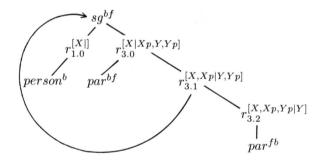

Figure 12.23 Improved rule/goal graph after reordering subgoals.

12.9 MAKING BINDING PATTERNS UNIQUE

From a rule/goal graph, we can determine the binding patterns with which each predicate is called. With that information, we can "split" predicates, so

---

[26] The motivation for doing so is additional clarity. Repeating EDB goals tends to avoid long arcs, and expanding each rule occurrence independently helps us visualize the sideways information passing without following long arcs.

each IDB predicate has a unique binding pattern associated. The technique is simple.

1. For each adornment α of an IDB predicate p, such that p^α appears in the rule/goal graph, create a new predicate p_α.

2. For each of p's rules, say r, make a copy r_α of the rule with p_α as the head predicate.

3. Examine the rule-node child r_0 of the goal node p^α. Extending to the right of a node r_0 will be a chain of nodes called $r_1, \ldots, r_k$, where k is the number of subgoals of r. These will have a collection of goal-node children, corresponding to the subgoals of r.

    a) If q^β is such a goal node, and q is an EDB or built-in predicate, leave the corresponding subgoal in r_α the same as it is in r.

    b) If q is an IDB predicate, then change the predicate in the corresponding subgoal of r_α to q_β.

Example 12.31: Consider the "same-generation" rules of Example 12.30 and the rule/goal graph of Figure 12.22. The IDB predicate sg has two goal nodes, with adornments bf and bb. We thus create two predicates, sg_bf and sg_bb. The first rule, r_1, has only the EDB subgoal $person$, so the two copies of r_1 are the same, except for the head predicate.

The rule r_2 has an EDB subgoal, $sg(Xp, Yp)$, and whether the head predicate is sg_bf or sg_bb, the adornment for this subgoal is found, in Figure 12.22, to be bb. Thus, the bodies of the two versions of r_2, which we call r_2_bf and r_2_bb, both have subgoal $sg\_bb(Xp, Yp)$. The new set of predicates and rules is shown in Figure 12.24. $\square$

```
r₁_bf:   sg_bf(X,X)  :- person(X).
r₂_bf:   sg_bf(X,Y)  :- par(X,Xp) & par(Y,Yp) & sg_bb(Xp,Yp)

r₁_bb:   sg_bb(X,X)  :- person(X).
r₂_bb:   sg_bb(X,Y)  :- par(X,Xp) & par(Y,Yp) & sg_bb(Xp,Yp)
```

Figure 12.24 Split rules for same-generation.

It happens that, should we build the rule/goal tree with root goal sg_bf and a binding for the first argument, then the adornments tell us the binding patterns of the goal nodes. That is, all occurrences of a goal node with predicate sg_bf (there is only one — the root) have binding pattern bf, and all occurrences of sg_bb have both arguments bound. In general, all nodes with predicate p_α in a rule/goal tree will have at least the bindings indicated by α, but in some situations, there can be other bindings. The next example illustrates the point.

Example 12.32: Consider the rules

r_1:   p(X,Y) :- s(X,Y).
r_2:   p(X,Y) :- q(X,W) & p(Y,Y).

and let the query goal be p^{ff}, that is, a query asking for the entire p relation. The rule/goal graph starting with goal node p^{ff} is shown in Figure 12.25.

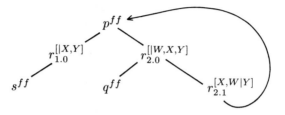

Figure 12.25 Rule/goal graph for rules of Example 12.32.

One would expect from Figure 12.25 that all calls to p are with both arguments free. However, if we expand the rule/goal tree with root goal $p(X,Y)$, and neither argument bound, we get the first five levels shown in Figure 12.26. The first occurrence of r_2 has subgoal $p(Y,Y)$, and neither argument of p has been bound, either by an occurrence of Y in a bound argument of the head or by its presence in a previous subgoal. That is what the rule/goal graph of Figure 12.25 predicts. However, by the time we get to the instance of r_2 in the lower right corner of Figure 12.26, we notice that when subgoal $p(Y,Y)$ is reached, the value of Y is bound because of its presence in the previous subgoal $q(Y,W_2)$. Thus, p^{bb} appears to be the proper binding for this subgoal, a fact that is at variance with the rule/goal graph in Figure 12.25. □

Rectifying Subgoals

It is not hard to see that the source of the problem in Example 12.32 is the fact that the two arguments of subgoal $p(Y,Y)$ are the same variable. That leads to "aliasing" between X and Y in the head of r_2, and a binding for X implicitly is a binding for Y as well. The solution, at least for datalog rules, is to eliminate duplicate occurrences of variables in IDB subgoals and to eliminate constants appearing in subgoals. That is, we must "rectify" subgoals, just as we rectified heads in Section 3.3 (Volume I).[27] Note that rectifying heads is not sufficient, as the heads in Example 12.32 are rectified.

We shall say that a subgoal is *rectified* if each of its arguments is a distinct variable. The property of rectified subgoals that we shall exploit is that the

---

[27] A rule was considered *rectified* in Section 3.3 if the arguments of its head were distinct variables.

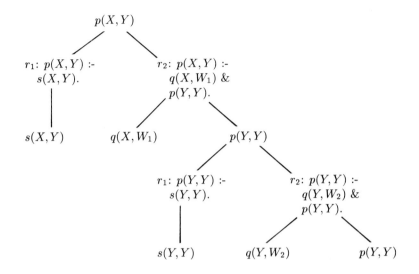

Figure 12.26 Rule/goal tree for goal $p(X, Y)$.

unification of a rule head with a rectified subgoal is trivial and results in a rule instance identical to the original rule. This property, in turn, will guarantee that the binding patterns in the rule/goal tree match those predicted by the rule/goal graph. The next algorithm shows how to rectify subgoals. It is guaranteed only to work for datalog, although it can succeed on some nondatalog examples.

Algorithm 12.7: Making Binding Patterns Unique.

INPUT: A set of datalog rules and a query goal.

OUTPUT: A revised set of rules such that in the rule/goal tree expansion of the query goal, each predicate occurs in goal nodes with only one binding pattern. If the given rules are safe, so are the revised rules.

METHOD: We begin by rectifying the subgoals. Consider some subgoal that has one or more occurrences of duplicate arguments and/or constant arguments, say $p(X_1, \ldots, X_k)$; some of the X's could be constants. Let $Y_1, \ldots, Y_m$ be all of the variables appearing among the X's; presumably, $m < k$.

1. Create a new predicate $p'(Y_1, \ldots, Y_m)$, and substitute it for the subgoal $p(X_1, \ldots, X_k)$. For example, we would substitute $p'(U, V)$ for the subgoal $p(U, U, V, a)$.

2. Consider each rule r with head $p(Z_1, \ldots, Z_k)$; assume that variables of r have been renamed, if necessary, so none are identical to any of the variables among the X's. Unify $p(Z_1, \ldots, Z_k)$ with $p(X_1, \ldots, X_k)$, substituting X's for Z's wherever possible, and let the resulting MGU be τ. Create a corresponding rule for predicate p' by substituting $\tau(Z_i)$ for each occurrence of a variable Z_i in the body of r, $i = 1, 2, \ldots, k$. Let the head of the new rule be $p'\big(\tau(Y_1), \ldots, \tau(Y_m)\big)$.[28] We claim that the resulting rule is safe if r is safe. It is left as an exercise to show that $\tau(Y_j)$, which is $\tau(X_i)$ for some i (because $Y_j = X_i$), must be equal to $\tau(Z_i)$. If Z_i is a constant, then so is $\tau(Y_j)$, so there could be no violation of safety. If Z_i is a variable, then it appears in the body of r because r is safe.

If there are other occurrences of predicate p that have the same pattern of equalities among its arguments, and the same constants, if any, then we can substitute p' for p in these subgoals, provided we make an appropriate selection of variables for these subgoals, analogous to $Y_1, \ldots, Y_m$ in (1) above.

This process of replacing predicates of subgoals and creating rules for the new predicates can be repeated many times. In fact, applications of the transformation can create new opportunities for its application in the new rules. However, all new predicates have fewer arguments than the predicate from which they were created, so the process cannot got on forever. Thus, at some point, we have a set of rules, none of whose subgoals have repeated variables.

The final step is to construct the rule/goal graph for these rules and the original query goal. Then split predicates to make the bindings for each predicate be unique, as described at the beginning of this section. Let the query goal have predicate p and binding pattern α; that is, α has b in exactly those positions that correspond to arguments in which the query provides a constant value. Then revise the query to have predicate p_α and the same arguments. The result is an equivalent collection of rules and query, in whose rule/goal tree no predicate will appear with two different binding patterns. $\square$

r_1:   p(X,Y) :- s(X,Y).
r_2:   p(X,Y) :- q(X,W) & p$_1$(Y).

r_3:   p$_1$(Y) :- s(Y,Y).
r_4:   p$_1$(Y) :- q(Y,W) & p$_1$(Y).

Figure 12.27 Rules with rectified subgoals.

---

[28] Note that this transformation still makes sense if the subgoal $p(X_1, \ldots, X_k)$ in question is a subgoal of r, although renaming of variables would then take place.

Example 12.33: Consider the rules of Example 12.32. There is only one occurrence of duplicate variables, subgoal $p(Y,Y)$ in r_2. We thus create new predicate p_1, and modify r_2 to be

$$r_2: \quad \texttt{p(X,Y)} \texttt{ :- } \texttt{q(X,W)} \texttt{ \& } \texttt{p}_1\texttt{(Y)}.$$

We also create new versions of r_1 and r_2 for predicate p_1. That is, we must unify the heads of r_1 and r_2 with the offending subgoal, $p(Y,Y)$. Before doing so, we rename the variable Y in r_1 and r_2; let us think of it as U. Then both rules have head $p(X,U)$, and the unifications each equate X, Y, and U. We pick Y as the representative for all; that is, $\tau(X) = \tau(Y) = \tau(U) = Y$; the resulting rules are shown in Figure 12.27. The rule/goal graph for these rules is in Figure 12.28. □

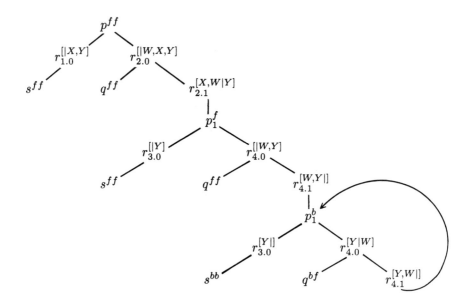

Figure 12.28 Rule/goal graph for rules of Figure 12.27.

Theorem 12.3: Suppose we build the rule/goal tree for the given query and for the rules constructed by Algorithm 12.7. Then each predicate p_α of those rules appears in goal nodes only with the binding pattern (set of bound arguments) α.

Proof: We shall show by induction on the depth of an occurrence of a goal node with predicate p_α, that α is the binding pattern for this goal node; that is, the bound arguments correspond exactly to the b's in α. The basis is the root node of the rule/goal tree, and Algorithm 12.7 selects the predicate for the revised query so that the binding pattern is correct.

For the induction, we first note that since subgoals are rectified, all unifications are trivial, so every rule node in the tree corresponds to a rule instance that is identical to the original rule, except perhaps for renaming of variables, which is of no significance. Thus, for each rule node in the rule/goal tree, the sideways information passing binds exactly the same variables after each subgoal that are bound in the expansion of that rule in the rule/goal graph. It follows that if, say, a goal node p_α is given the binding pattern α, then each goal node two levels below, say q_β, will be given the binding pattern β. Further details are left as an exercise. $\square$

12.10 REORDERING SUBGOALS

When we construct the rule/goal graph, we have the option to reorder the subgoals of a rule as we expand the corresponding rule nodes. If we follow Algorithm 12.7 and create a new predicate p_α for each adornment α of each original predicate p, then we can order the subgoals of the rules for p_α as we wish, independently of the order of the corresponding subgoals in any other variant of p. In fact, even if we do not split p, we can compute the rule/goal graph in such a way that different subgoal orders are used for different instances of the same rule. Our justification is that the least fixed-point semantics of rules, as defined in Sections 3.4 and 12.2, does not depend on the order in which we list the subgoals.

The problem of ordering subgoals in a rule is similar to the problem of ordering the join of many relations, which we discussed in Chapter 11. However, when we evaluate rules, we ordinarily do not have available relations for all the subgoals initially. Rather, through the process of sideways information passing, we develop bindings for some of the subgoals, and only then do we attempt to instantiate the relevant portion of the relation for that subgoal. To do otherwise might force us to compute the entire relation for some IDB predicates, when all we wanted was a small fraction of that relation.

Further, it is possible that some subgoals can only be evaluated with certain binding patterns. Some examples of this phenomenon are the following.

1. Built-in predicates usually require some bindings. For example, the subgoal $X = Y$ cannot be "evaluated" unless at least one of X and Y is bound. If, say, X is bound to the set of values $\{a_1, \ldots, a_n\}$, then we can use the finite relation $\{(a_1, a_1), \ldots, (a_n, a_n)\}$ for subgoal $X = Y$. If neither X nor Y is bound, then there is an infinite set of pairs that makes the subgoal true.

2. Similarly, subgoal $X < Y$ cannot be "evaluated" unless both X and Y are bound; otherwise an infinite set of pairs satisfies this subgoal.

3. We may wish to declare that EDB relations cannot be evaluated unless
    there is at least one bound attribute on which that EDB relation has an
    index. For if there is no such attribute, then we must examine the entire
    relation, even if there are some bound arguments whose corresponding
    attributes do not have indices.

4. An IDB predicate whose rules involve function symbols may be evaluable
    if certain arguments are bound, but not if they are free; the next example
    illustrates the point.

Example 12.34: Suppose we have a database of "good" elements, that is, a
unary relation *good*. Let us construct lists by using the binary function symbol
cons. That is, $cons(H, T)$ represents the list with head element H and tail
(remaining elements) T. We shall also use the constant *nil* to represent the
empty list. Then we can define "good lists" by the rules

r_1: goodList(nil).
r_2: goodList(cons(H,T)) :- good(H) & goodList(T).

That is, the empty list is good, and a list is good if the first element H is good,
and the balance of the list, represented by the tail T in r_2, is a good list.

For example, the list a, b, c would be represented by the term

$$cons\Big(a, cons\big(b, cons(c, nil)\big)\Big) \tag{12.11}$$

Assume a, b, and c are each in the relation for *good*. Then rule r_2 tells us that
a, b, c is a good list if b, c is a good list. Further, b, c is good if list c is a good
list. Finally, r_2 says that c is a good list if the empty list is good, and r_1 affirms
that the empty list is good.

If we ask a query of the form $goodList^b$, say a query with argument (12.11),
then we can answer the query. For instance, we can deduce, by rule/goal tree
expansion, that (12.11) is a good list, provided a, b, and c are good. However,
if we pose the query $goodList(X)$, that is, find all the good lists, we have an
instance of the adorned goal $goodList^f$. The result of this query is infinite
whenever EDB relation *good* is nonempty. Thus, we cannot expect rule/goal
tree expansion, or any other query evaluation algorithm, to return an answer.
The conclusion is that, while we can allow a subgoal with binding pattern
$goodList^b$, we cannot allow one with pattern $goodList^f$. □

The Feasibility Problem for Rule/Goal Graphs

One can develop a number of heuristics for picking an order for subgoals, and
we shall return to this topic shortly. However, to begin, let us pose the question
of ordering subgoals as one of feasibility. That is, suppose we are told which
adornments for EDB predicates are permissible and which are not. Can we build
a rule/goal graph for a given query and given rules, that uses only permissible

adornments on the EDB goals?[29]

Example 12.35: Let us consider a slightly more complex version of the "same-generation" rules

$$r_1: \quad \texttt{sg(X,X) :- person(X).}$$
$$r_2: \quad \texttt{sg(X,Y) :- par}_1\texttt{(X,Xp) \& par}_2\texttt{(Y,Yp) \& sg(Yp,Xp).}$$

The difference between these rules and the ones studied previously is that here we have reversed the order of the arguments in the sg subgoal. Since sg is evidently symmetric in its two arguments, it doesn't matter whether we say $sg(Yp, Xp)$, as we have done here, or $sg(Xp, Yp)$, as we did previously. However, the new order of arguments does affect the binding patterns for the sg predicate, and it will illustrate the advantage of ordering subgoals differently for different adornments.

In our new version of the rules, we also show subscripts 1 and 2 for the par subgoals. That notation does not imply we are using two different relations for parenthood. Rather, we shall carry along the subscripts to indicate which par subgoal corresponds to various par goal nodes in rule/goal graphs that we develop.

Suppose first that we use the subgoals in the order written. Then, starting with the sg^{bf} query goal, we develop the rule/goal graph shown in Figure 12.29. For example, the instance of r_2 for the sg^{bf} goal gets a binding for X from the head, binds Xp when it reaches par_1, then calls par_2^{ff}, since neither argument Y nor Yp of par_2 is bound at that point. Finally, sg^{bb} is called, since both arguments Yp and Xp are bound when we reach the third subgoal. The expansion of sg^{bb} is similar to the expansion of sg^{bf}, and we omit it.

Now consider the rule/goal graph of Figure 12.30. Here, we again start from query goal sg^{bf}, but we reorder subgoals judiciously, preferring subgoals with the most bound arguments. Then we avoid ever having to evaluate par^{ff}; that is, we never have to access the entire relation for par. That could well be a significant saving, since with indices on both attributes, the EDB relation par can, normally, be accessed far more efficiently with either argument bound to a finite set, than with both arguments free.

Thus, in the instance of r_2 for the goal sg^{bf}, we first work on par_1^{bf}, which provides a binding for Xp. Since we prefer subgoals with bound arguments, we next choose $sg(Yp, Xp)$, whose adornment is fb, as Xp is now bound and Yp is not. Last, we work on par_2^{fb}. The instance of r_2 for the sg^{fb} goal is treated symmetrically. We first work on par_2^{bf}, since we have only a binding for Y.

---

[29] More generally, we could build the rule/goal graph for one or more mutually recursive IDB predicates and imagine that all other predicates appearing in subgoals are EDB subgoals. In reality, these subgoals could have "lower-level" IDB predicates, whose possible adornments have already been determined. We shall examine a system using this generalization in Section 16.2.

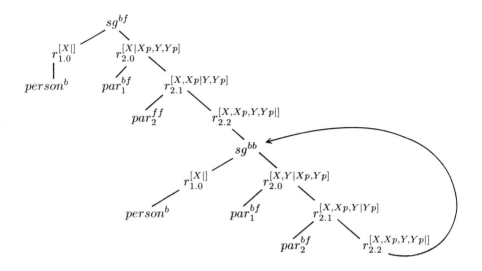

Figure 12.29 Rule/goal graph with no subgoal reordering.

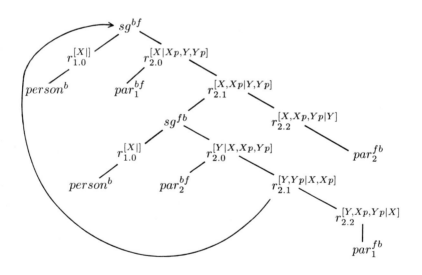

Figure 12.30 Rule/goal graph with judicious ordering of subgoals.

Then we work on sg^{bf}, and last on par_1^{fb}. Note that the adornments for the two instances of r_2 are similar, but the order of subgoals is different for the two rules, and neither order matches the natural order in which the subgoals were written. $\square$

The Bound-is-Easier Assumption

Intuitively, replacing a free argument of a predicate by a bound argument cannot make the predicate harder to evaluate. There is good reason to believe this principle, and we give its justification in the next paragraph. However, since we cannot prove it for any possible model of computation, we shall refer to it as an assumption, the *bound-is-easier assumption*. The motivation for making this assumption is that it simplifies subgoal ordering significantly. It allows us, once we find a feasible choice for the next subgoal, to "cast that choice in concrete," never having to backtrack to find another feasible choice.

Formally, define the relation $\leq$ on adornments by saying $\alpha \leq \beta$ if β has b in every position where α has b. For example, $ffb \leq fbb$, and $fbf \leq fbf$. However, $bfff \leq fbbb$ is false, because of the first positions of the two adornments. Now, suppose $\alpha \leq \beta$. If we have an algorithm to evaluate p^{α}, then surely we can evaluate p^{β}; just evaluate the relation for p^{α} with the given bindings for those arguments that are bound in α. Then, if β has additional bound arguments, apply a selection to the relation for p^{α} to get the relation for p^{β}. However, the converse is not true; we might be able to evaluate p^{β} but not p^{α}. Example 12.34 covered a simple case where $\alpha = f$ and $\beta = b$.

Thus, we shall adopt the bound-is-easier assumption; that is, we shall assume that whenever we can evaluate p^{α}, we can also evaluate all adorned goals p^{β}, where $\alpha \leq \beta$. That assumption has two useful consequences. First, when listing the adornments for which we can evaluate a predicate, we need to list only those adornments that are minimally bound.

Example 12.36: Suppose EDB relation *par* has indices on both arguments, and it is required that some bound argument have an index, if we are to evaluate an EDB subgoal. We need only state that par^{bf} and par^{fb} are permissible. It then follows that par^{bb} is also permissible. However, par^{ff} would not be permissible. $\square$

Second, the bound-is-easier assumption allows us to select an ordering for subgoals of a rule in a greedy way. Suppose we have a set of bound variables for the head of rule r, and we know that some subgoal p^{α}, where α is the appropriate adornment given the variables bound by the head, is permissible. Then we cannot err if we assume that p^{α} is the first subgoal for r.

More precisely, suppose that after picking p^{α} as the first subgoal, we discover that no order for the remaining subgoals gives us permissible adornments for all subgoals. However, suppose that had we chosen some other subgoal, q^{β}, first, then a successful order L for all subgoals can be found. In L, the subgoal p appears somewhere. Delete it and place p^α at the front of L to make a new ordering M. We claim that M has no impermissible subgoals. Suppose in M that s^γ is impermissible. Then in L, the corresponding adornment is s^δ. We can see that $\delta \leq \gamma$. The reason is that p^α, at the beginning of M, binds any variable that the corresponding subgoal did in the middle of L. Thus, whether s precedes or follows p in L, every variable that was bound when we reach subgoal s in L will be bound when we reach it in M. Since p^α is known to be permissible, and since s^γ must be permissible because s^δ is, we conclude that M has only permissible subgoals. Therefore, our assumption that no ordering could succeed if it began with p^α is false.

The above observations are generalized in the following lemma. However, before proceeding, let us observe that the notion of permissible adornments can apply to IDB, as well as EDB, subgoals. That is, we specify permissibility for EDB subgoals, but, as a consequence, some adornments for IDB predicates become permissible, in the sense that they can appear in a rule/goal graph, and others are not permissible, meaning that there is no rule/goal graph in which they can appear. In the following lemma, all subgoals, whether IDB or EDB, are assumed to have their set of permissible adornments known.

Lemma 12.2: Under the bound-is-easier assumption, suppose we have a rule with subgoals $G_1, \ldots, G_n$, and suppose that, based on particular bindings of the head, we have determined that the first k subgoals could be $G_{i_1}, \ldots, G_{i_k}$; that is, each of these subgoals has a permissible adornment in the order shown. Suppose also that G_j, one of the remaining subgoals, is permissible with the bindings for variables implied by the head and the k previously selected subgoals. Then we may assume without loss of generality that G_j is the next subgoal. More precisely, if there is any feasible order for the subgoals at all, then there is one that begins $G_{i_1}, \ldots, G_{i_k}, G_j$.

Proof: The proof is a simple generalization of the argument given above, and we leave it as an exercise. $\Box$

Example 12.37: To make the point more concrete, consider the rule

```
p(X,Y) :- q(X,Z) & s(Z,W) & t(W,Y).
```

Suppose that adorned goals q^{bf}, q^{fb}, s^{ff}, t^{fb}, and of course, their "more bound" versions, are permissible; note that t^{bf} is not permissible. Let us be given the goal p^{bf}, so we start with a binding for variable X. Our heuristic, that we prefer subgoals with as many bound arguments as possible, suggests that we should pick $q(X, Z)$ to be first. Since q^{bf} is permissible, that is an acceptable choice.

We now have a binding for Z as well as X, and we may next tackle s^{bf}, another permissible subgoal. However, for the third subgoal, we can only chose

$t(W, Y)$. Y is not yet bound, and t^{bf} is not a permissible adornment. Thus, we have "lost"; it is not possible to find a feasible ordering for the subgoals.

However, the fault does not lie with our choice of $q(X, Z)$ as the first subgoal. We could have chosen $s(Z, W)$ first, since s^{ff} is permissible. However, then, only $q(X, Z)$ could go second, and when we are left with $t(W, Y)$, we have the same set of bound variables as before—all but Y. Since no adornment for $t(W, Y)$ is permissible unless Y is bound, we still fail, and indeed there is no feasible subgoal order for this rule. $\Box$

An Algorithm for Feasibility of Rule/Goal Graphs

Suppose we have an algorithm **A** that takes the following information.

1. A rule $H :- G_1 \& \cdots \& G_n$.
2. An adornment for the head predicate of the rule.
3. Information telling which adornments are permissible for the predicates of all the subgoals of the rule.

Further, suppose Algorithm **A** finds, if it exists, a *feasible* order for the subgoals, that is, an order in which the adornment of each subgoal is

a) Permissible, and
b) Correct, given the bindings for the head and the bindings of variables implied by the previous subgoals in the selected order.

Then we can find a rule/goal graph for a given query goal by the following algorithm.

Algorithm 12.8: Feasibility Test for Rule/Goal Graphs.

INPUT: We are given a collection of rules, an adorned query goal p^α, a list of the permissible adornments for the EDB goals, and an algorithm **A**, as described above, for finding feasible orders of subgoals. We make the bound-is-easier assumption, so the list of permissible EDB goals implicitly includes all their more bound versions; that is, if q^β is on the list, then q^γ is implicitly on the list whenever $\beta \le \gamma$, even if we do not say so explicitly.

OUTPUT: A rule/goal graph for p^α, if one exists, or an indication that there is none.

METHOD: We maintain a set F of *forbidden* adorned goals. Initially, F consists of those adorned EDB goals that are not among the given permissible adorned EDB goals; no IDB goal is initially in F. Intuitively, we are going to make the optimistic assumption that all IDB predicates are permissible with any adornment, until the algorithm **A** tells us otherwise, by failing to find a feasible ordering for one of the rules for that adorned IDB predicate.

We also maintain a set I of *interesting* adorned IDB goals. Initially, only p^α is in I. Later, we place an adorned goal in I if it appears in the ordering selected by **A** for one of the rules of an adorned IDB goal already in I. We remove q^β from I and place it in F if we find that there is no feasible ordering for one or more of the rules for q.[30]

```
for each adorned goal q^β in I do
    for each rule r for predicate q do begin
        use algorithm A to find a feasible ordering for
            the subgoals of r, given that β is the adornment
            for the head of r and that F is the set of
            impermissible adorned goals;
        if an ordering is found then
            add to I the adorned predicate for each IDB
                subgoal in the selected order
        else begin
            delete q^β from I;
            insert q^β into F
                /* by implication, q^γ is also put
                in F for all γ ≤ β */
        end
end
```

Figure 12.31 One pass of Algorithm 12.8.

The heart of the algorithm is shown in Figure 12.31. There, we take our current knowledge about what adorned goals are not permissible, as represented by F, and our current knowledge about what adorned IDB goals we have to handle, as represented by I, and check that there is a feasible order for every rule for every interesting adorned goal. Those adorned goals found not to have a subgoal order for some rule are discovered to be forbidden, and are therefore moved from I to F. Further, we may, while ordering subgoals of one rule, find an adornment for one of its IDB predicates that we have not seen before. If so, we must add this adorned goal to the set I.

The complete algorithm consists of the initialization described above, and an iteration, in which we perform the steps of Figure 12.31 until one of two things happens.

1.   We remove p^α from I and place it in F.

2.   On one pass, we do not change I.

---

[30] We could attempt to remove adorned goals from I if we find them no longer "interesting," but this nuance will not be considered here.

In case (1), we have demonstrated that there are no orders for the subgoals of the rules for p and the rules for any other predicates appearing in I, that make all the subgoals of all these rules have permissible adornments, according to the given information for the EDB predicates. Thus, there is no rule/goal graph containing p^α.

In case (2), we know that each adorned goal in I has, for each of its rules, an ordering of its subgoals giving each subgoal an adornment that

a) Is in I if it is an IDB subgoal, and
b) Is not in F if it is an EDB subgoal.

Thus, we can construct a rule/goal graph containing p^α as follows. For each adorned goal q^β in I, we have a goal node, and the children of this node are the rule nodes for q, with subscript 0 and their proper superscripts representing bound variables. Descending in a chain to the right from each of these rule nodes $r_0^{[L_0|M_0]}$ are nodes $r_i^{[L_i|M_i]}$, for $i = 1, 2, \ldots, k-1$, if rule r has k subgoals. Here, L_i and M_i are intended to represent appropriate lists of variables.

Each of the nodes $r_i^{[L_i|M_i]}$, for $i = 0, 1, \ldots, k-1$, also has a goal-node child. That child has the predicate of the ith subgoal of r in the selected order, and has the appropriate adornment. By (a) above, if the subgoal is an IDB subgoal, then this adorned goal is also in the constructed rule/goal graph. By (b), if the subgoal is EDB, then it has a permissible adornment, and we may add a goal node for this adorned EDB predicate. Thus, every node in the constructed rule/goal graph has the requisite children also in the rule/goal graph, and all EDB goal nodes are permissible. We have therefore constructed a feasible rule/goal graph containing the query goal.[31] □

Example 12.38: Let us reconsider the "twisted" same-generation rules of Example 12.35. Suppose the query corresponds to adorned goal sg^{bf}, and the algorithm **A** orders subgoals heuristically, by choosing at each step that unchosen subgoal that

1. Has a permissible binding pattern,
2. Has as many bound arguments as any unchosen subgoal satisfying (1), and
3. Appears to the left of any other unchosen subgoal satisfying (1) and (2).

Also, assume that par^{ff} and $person^f$ are impermissible adornments, but any other adornment for par and $person$ is permissible.

Initially, $I = \{sg^{bf}\}$ and $F = \{par^{ff}, person^f\}$. For sg^{bf}, algorithm **A** picks the only possible order for rule r_1; since $person^b$ is not in F, **A** succeeds on r_1. For r_2, **A** picks the order par_1^{bf}, sg^{fb}, par_2^{fb}. The IDB adorned subgoal

---

[31] In some cases, where adorned goals become interesting in one pass, and later become uninteresting because there is no longer any way to reach them from the query goal, we shall be able to trim parts of the constructed rule/goal graph and still have a feasible rule/goal graph for the query.

sg^{fb} is added to I, so on the next pass, **A** must find orders for the subgoals of the two rules with both adornments for the heads, bf and fb. Since no more adorned goals were added to F, the treatment of sg^{bf} is the same. For sg^{fb}, rule r_1 again has the only possible order, and for r_2, **A** picks the order par_2^{bf}, sg^{bf}, par_1^{fb}. Now, no more adorned IDB goals must be added to I, and we have succeeded in finding orders for all the rules for all the members of I, without using any adorned goal in F. The resulting rule/goal graph was exhibited in Figure 12.30. $\Box$

Example 12.39: To see some of the nuances of Algorithm 12.8, consider the nonrecursive rules

$$r_1: \quad \texttt{p(X,Y)} \quad \texttt{:- q(X,Z) \& r(Z,Y).}$$
$$r_2: \quad \texttt{q(X,Z)} \quad \texttt{:- s(X) \& t(Z).}$$

Let the only forbidden adorned EDB goal be t^f; all adornments for EDB predicates r and s are permissible. Start with query goal p^{bf}, and suppose that the ordering algorithm is **A** from Example 12.38. Initially, $I = \{p^{bf}\}$ and $F = \{t^f\}$. We thus apply **A** to order r_1, obtaining the list of subgoals q^{bf}, r^{bf}. We then add adorned IDB goal q^{bf} to I.

On the next pass, we treat p^{bf} the same. However, **A** finds no order for the subgoals of r_2, with adornment bf for the head, since t^f is forbidden, and there is no way to bind the argument Z of subgoal $t(Z)$, if Z is not bound by the head of r_2. Thus, we move q^{bf} to F, leaving $I = \{p^{bf}\}$ and $F = \{t^f, q^{bf}\}$.

On the third pass, we again tackle r_1 with head binding pattern bf. However, now q^{bf} is forbidden, so algorithm **A** can only select the order r^{ff}, q^{bb}, which is feasible, since neither adorned goal is in F. Thus, q^{bb} is added to I.

Now, on the fourth pass, p^{bf} is handled the same way as on the third pass, but we must also consider r_2 with head binding pattern bb. Now **A** produces the order of subgoals s^b, t^b, which is feasible. On this pass, we add no adorned IDB goal to I, and we found feasible orders for all the rules of all the adorned goals in I. Thus, we terminate successfully. The resulting rule/goal graph is shown in Figure 12.32. $\Box$

Theorem 12.4: Algorithm 12.8 correctly determines if there is a feasible rule/goal graph including the given query goal.

Proof: In the description of the algorithm, we showed how to construct a feasible rule/goal graph when the algorithm terminates with success. We must consider the converse: why can there be no rule/goal graph containing the query goal if the algorithm places the query goal in F? On the assumption that algorithm **A** is correct, that is, it finds a feasible ordering if one exists, we can show by induction on the number of adorned goals placed in F that each adorned goal q^β in F can appear in no rule/goal graph. Intuitively, the reason is that we can put q^β in F only when there exists a rule for q such that

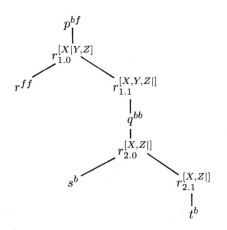

Figure 12.32 Rule/goal graph for Example 12.39.

every order of the subgoals for that rule must use a subgoal with an adornment already in F. The easy inductive proof is left as an exercise. Thus, when the query goal is placed in F, it too can appear in no rule/goal graph, and the theorem is proved. $\square$

Theorem 12.5: Suppose that algorithm **A** has running time $T(m)$ on a rule of length m. Then on rules of total length n, whose IDB predicates have arity no greater than k, the running time of Algorithm 12.8 is $O\big(n^{2k+3}T(n)\big)$.

Proof: If the rules are of total length n, there can be no more than n IDB predicates. As these predicates have arity at most k, there can be no more than n^k adornments for each, or a total of n^{k+1} adorned goals. On each round of Algorithm 12.8, we must either terminate, move an adorned goal from I to F, or add to I a new adorned goal, one that has never before been in I. Thus, there can be no more than $2n^{k+1}$ rounds. On each round, the principal cost is finding an ordering for each rule for each adorned goal in I. There are at most n^{k+1} members of I, at most n rules for each, and at most $T(n)$ time is taken ordering any one rule with a given binding pattern for the head. Thus, each round takes time at most $n^{k+2}T(n)$, and the theorem follows when we multiply this quantity by the maximum number of rounds. $\square$

Heuristic Ordering Algorithms

Using the bound-is-easier assumption, there are reasonable choices for the algorithm **A** that are at most quadratic in n, the length of the rule; that is, $T(n)$ in Theorem 12.5 can be $O(n^2)$. For example, we could use the heuristic suggested in Example 12.38, of favoring subgoals with the most bound arguments, provided that the binding pattern makes the subgoal permissible, and breaking ties in favor of the leftmost subgoal. This heuristic **A** is shown in detail in Figure 12.33.

```
(1)   V := all variables bound by the head;
(2)   mark all subgoals "unchosen";
(3)   for i := 1 to m do begin
(4)       b := -1;
(5)       for each unchosen subgoal G do begin
(6)           find the bound arguments of G, given that V is
                  the set of bound variables;
(7)           if there are c > b bound arguments of G and with
                  this binding pattern G is permissible then begin
(8)               b := c;
(9)               H := G
              end;
(10)          if b ≠ -1 then begin
(11)              mark H "chosen";
(12)              add to V all variables appearing in H
              end
(13)          else fail
          end
      end
```

Figure 12.33 Subgoal ordering heuristic.

We suppose that the algorithm of Figure 12.33 is called with a rule with m subgoals and a given binding pattern for its head. We are also given a set of forbidden adorned goals, referred to in line (7). Several local variables are used.

1. V is a set of variables, those that are bound, either because they are bound in the head [V is initialized in line (1)], or because they appear in a chosen subgoal [line (12)].

2. In the loop of lines (5) through (9), we select an unchosen subgoal with the largest number of bound arguments. Variable b is used to record the greatest number of bound arguments seen so far; it is initialized to -1 at line (4) so that some choice will always be made; that is, the test of line (7) will eventually succeed if there are any permissible, unchosen subgoals. Variable H is used to record the current candidate for the subgoal with the most bound arguments. Variable c is the number of bound arguments for the subgoal under consideration.

After considering all subgoals, if there are any feasible, unchosen subgoals, we make H chosen and adjust V to include the variables of H at lines (11) and (12). However, if b remains at -1, that is, we could find no choice of next subgoal, then we fail at line (13) and terminate the algorithm of Figure 12.33. The outer loop of lines (3) through (13) selects a subgoal to be the ith in the order, for each $i = 1, 2, \ldots, m$, in turn. If all selections can be made, then the order in which the subgoals are selected; that is, they appear as H in line (11), is the desired order. If any selection fails, then there is no feasible ordering, according to Lemma 12.2.

If we analyze the running time of Figure 12.33, we get the following corollary to Theorem 12.5.

Corollary 12.1: If we use the heuristic **A** of Figure 12.33, then the running time of Algorithm 12.8 on rules of total length n, having predicates of maximum arity k, is $O(n^{2k+5})$.

Proof: We have only to note that $T(n)$ is $O(n^2)$ in Theorem 12.5, if this heuristic is used. That is, the inner loop of lines (5) through (9) scans the subgoals, taking time proportional to the length of the rule, provided we use an appropriate data structure, such as a hash table, for V, so we can look up variables quickly and see if they are bound. Thus, the time taken by the inner loop is $O(n)$. It follows that the body of the outer loop of lines (3) through (13) also takes $O(n)$ time. Since the body is executed $m \leq n$ times, we conclude that $T(n)$ is $O(n^2)$. $\square$

In particular, if there is a bound on the arity of predicates, then Corollary 12.1 says that Algorithm 12.8 with this heuristic takes polynomial time. If k is not bounded, then the running time is exponential.

EXERCISES

12.1: We could represent persons as terms as

$$person\bigl(N,\ mother(M),\ father(F)\bigr)$$

where N is replaced by the name of the person, M is replaced by a term representing the person who is the mother of the person N or by the constant unk (unknown), and F is likewise a term representing the father of the person, or unk. Note that M and F, if they are not unk, are terms with principal functor $person$, so persons are represented by arbitrarily large terms, representing their ancestry as far back as it is known. Suppose that the database consists of a single EDB relation PERSONS, whose tuples are unary and consist of a $person$ term as described above. Write rules to express the following relations.

a) The set of pairs (X, Y) such that X is a child of Y.

b)   The set of pairs (X, Y) such that Y is the grandmother of X.

* c) The set of pairs (X, Y) such that Y is an ancestor of X.

12.2: Write the rules for lines 1, 2, and 4 of addresses, as in Example 12.1.

12.3: In Example 12.3 we pointed out that rules (5) and (6), expressing the meaning of logical OR, were not safe. One solution to the problem is to write rules for a predicate *possible*, such that *possible*(T) is true whenever T is a term whose arguments are constants found in the EDB relations GO and/or ACC; presumably the function symbols of T are those used in any rules we have for the predicate *true*, for instance, g, a, *and*, and *or* in Example 12.3. Write the rules that define the predicate *possible*.

12.4: Another approach to the nonsafety problem is to consider the bindings provided by the query. Give an algorithm that takes a collection of rules and a binding pattern (adornment) for some predicate and determines whether the set of tuples that are inferred from a finite database *and match a query with the given binding pattern* is finite.

12.5: We can generalize the "blocks world" problem of Example 12.3 to a world with an arbitrary number of "blocks" as follows. Suppose we have an EDB predicate *smaller*(B, C) that says block B is smaller than block C; assume for convenience that *smaller* is transitively closed. We have a function symbol $on(B, P)$ that says block B is on top of pile of blocks P. P can be the constant symbol *table*, so $on(a, table)$ represents block a alone, and $on\big(b, on(a, table)\big)$ represents b on top of a. We also have the function symbol $list(P, L)$, where P is a pile of blocks on the table, and L is either a list of piles of blocks on the table (formed with the function symbol *list*), or the constant symbol *nil*. Write rules for the following predicates.

a)   *pile*(P) meaning that P is a legal pile of zero or more blocks on the table; that is, each block b is either on the table or on a pile whose top block is larger than b.

b)   *disjoint*(P, Q) meaning that P and Q are disjoint piles of blocks on the table. *Hint*: Remember that piles must be sorted in size order.

c)   *state*(L) meaning that all the piles in the list L are mutually disjoint.

d)   *move*(L, M) meaning that state (list of disjoint piles) L can become state M by one or more legal moves, where a move consists of taking a block from the top of one pile and moving it to the top of another pile, while maintaining legality; that is, the top block of the receiving pile must be larger than the block moved.

12.6: Verify that in Example 12.4, the tuple

$$sum\big(succ^i(0), succ^j(0), succ^{i+j}(0)\big)$$

is added to the relation for *sum* at round $i + j + 2$ of naive or semi-naive evaluation.

* 12.7: A possible improvement to naive or semi-naive evaluation is to use the new value of an IDB relation as soon as it is computed, rather than waiting for the next round to use it. Suppose we evaluate the rules of Exercises 12.2 and 12.4 (Figure 12.1) so that the new relation for *int* is computed before the relation for *sum*. Then, on what round will the *sum* fact of the previous exercise be added to the relation for *sum*? What if we compute *sum* before *int* in each round?

12.8: We wish to match the ground atom

$$f\Big(h\big(g(a,b)\big),\ g\big(b,h(c)\big)\Big)$$

against each of the following atoms.

a) $f(X,Y)$.

b) $f\Big(h(X),\ g\big(b,h(X)\big)\Big)$.

c) $f\Big(h\big(g(X,Y)\big),\ g(Y,Z)\Big)$.

d) $f\big(g(X),\ h(Y)\big)$.

For each, tell whether a matching exists and give the substitution, if so.

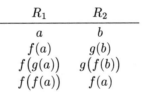

Figure 12.34 The relation R.

12.9: Suppose we have the relation R whose value is the four tuples shown in Figure 12.34. Perform the following translations.

a) $Q(X,Y) = \text{ATOV}\Big(p\big(f(X),g(Y)\big),\ R\Big)$.

b) $Q(X,Y) = \text{ATOV}\Big(p\big(f(X),X\big),\ R\Big)$.

c) $P = \text{VTOA}\Big(p\big(h(X,Y),g(X)\big),\ R(X,Y)\Big)$.

2.10: Suppose we have the parent-ancestor rules of Example 12.16, and the relation for *par* is a single chain,

$$\{(i, i + 1) \mid 0 \le i < n\}$$

Describe the behavior of the following algorithms on this data, assuming the query $anc(0, X)$, that is, find the ancestors of individual 0.

   a)   Prolog's SLD resolution, as described in Section 12.3.
   b)   The basic rule/goal tree expansion algorithm (Algorithm 12.6).
 * c)   The queue-based version of Algorithm 12.6 (QRGT).

2.11: Unify each of the atoms (a) through (d) of Exercise 12.8 with the atom $f(h(U), U)$. Give the MGU if it exists.

2.12: Repeat Exercise 12.11 with the atom $f(U, g(V, U))$.

2.13: In Section 12.6 we gave rules that express certain operations: (i) passing bindings from (supplementary relations for) rules to subgoals; (ii) passing bindings from goals to (the zeroth supplementary relations of) rules; (iii) passing answers from rules to goals. Show that the rule constructions given in Section 12.6 to express these operations are each correct.

2.14: We also gave in Section 12.6 a method for passing bindings from rules to the zeroth supplementary relations of their grandchildren in the rule/goal tree directly, that is, not going through binding relations for the intermediate goal nodes. Prove that for datalog rules, the bindings obtained are the same as for the ordinary method, where we do go through goal nodes.

2.15: Example 12.25 illustrated the point that our technique of passing bindings linearly from left to right need not be as good as some ad-hoc *sideways information passing strategy* (SIPS). Show that for the rule of Example 12.25, reordering the subgoals and then using the standard SIPS cannot result in performance better than that of the SIPS used in that example, although the standard SIPS can approximately equal the ad-hoc SIPS if the order of subgoals is selected properly.

2.16: Find an example where an ad-hoc SIPS is significantly better than the standard SIPS, regardless of what order is chosen for the subgoals.

2.17: Modify the QRGT algorithm of Section 12.7 to pass bindings directly from rule/nodes to rule nodes, as discussed at the end of Section 12.6.

2.18: Modify the rule/goal graph construction of Section 12.8 to use passing of bindings from rule nodes to rule nodes, directly.

2.19: Construct the rule/goal graph for the *goodList* rules of Example 12.34, for the adorned goals

   a) $goodList^b$.
   b) $goodList^f$.

Use the heuristic of Example 12.38 to order subgoals. That is, favor sub-goals with the most bound arguments, and favor subgoals to the left in the initial ordering to break ties. This exercise may be done either (i) in an ad-hoc manner, or (ii) by Algorithm 12.8.

12.20: Construct the rule/goal graph for the following rules

r_1: p(X,Y) :- q(X,Y).
r_2: p(X,Y) :- p(X,Z) & p(Z,W) & p(Y,W).

and the query goal p^{bf}. Use the heuristic of Example 12.38 to order sub-goals, and use either (i) an ad-hoc construction or (ii) Algorithm 12.8.

12.21: Rewrite the rules of Exercise 12.20 so that binding patterns are unique in any rule/goal tree expansion starting with query goal p^{bf} and using the subgoal-ordering heuristic of Example 12.38.

12.22: Rectify the following rules.

p(X,Y) :- q(X,X,Z,Y) & q(X,Z,W,a).
q(A,B,C,D) :- p(A,B) & p(C,D).
q(A,B,C,D) :- q_0(A,B,C,D).

* 12.23: Prove that whether you rectify subgoals first and then split predicates to make binding patterns unique or you first split predicates and then rectify subgoals, you get the same result. *Note:* You must assume that there is no reordering of subgoals when you construct a rule/goal graph in the predicate-splitting process. Also, whenever you rewrite rules, you preserve the order of subgoals.

12.24: Prove that Algorithm 12.7 (making binding patterns unique) preserves safety; that is, if the given rules are safe, so are the constructed rules.

12.25: Complete the proof of Theorem 12.3 by showing that goal nodes for pred-icate p_α in the rule/goal tree always have the binding pattern α.

12.26: Complete the proof of Lemma 12.2. That is, show that a greedy heuristic succeeds in finding an order for subgoals whenever one exists, given the bound-is-easier assumption.

12.27: Complete the proof of Theorem 12.4. That is, show that any adorned goal placed in F cannot appear in a feasible rule/goal graph.

2.28: Sometimes, Algorithm 12.8 can leave an adorned goal q^β in I, even though in the rule/goal graph it constructs for the query goal, the node for q^β is not reachable from the node for the query goal. Give an example of this phenomenon.

2.29: Consider the rules of Exercise 12.22, as written. What adornments for the IDB predicates p and q are permissible if the permissible adornments for the EDB predicate q_0 are

  a)   Any adornment?
  b)   All but $ffff$?
  c)   Only those adornments with at least two b's?

2.30: Sometimes we can express a query involving function symbols with rules
      that have rectified subgoals; the *goodList* rules of Example 12.34 are one
      instance. Find an example of a query that cannot be expressed with recti-
      fied subgoals, and prove your claim.

2.31: We used the set of "interesting" adorned goals, I, in Algorithm 12.8 in
      order to give us a "top-down" algorithm, where we avoided ever having
      to examine the rules for an adorned goal unless there was some reason to
      believe that we needed to do so. Suppose we simplified Algorithm 12.8 by
      assuming every adorned IDB goal was interesting. What effect would that
      change have on the worst-case running time of the algorithm?

BIBLIOGRAPHIC NOTES

A number of relevant references appeared in the bibliographic notes of Chapter
3 (Volume I), and some of these will be mentioned briefly here. Three general
references are Lloyd [1984] on logic programming, and the surveys Gallaire,
Minker, and Nicolas [1984] and Minker [1987] on applications of logic to database systems.

Naive and Semi-Naive Evaluation

As mentioned in Chapter 3, the fundamentals of bottom-up (least-fixed-point,
or "naive" evaluation) are found in Van Emden and Kowalski [1976], Apt and
Van Emden [1982], and Chandra and Harel [1982].

    Semi-naive evaluation is a fundamental idea, which keeps reappearing, as
in Bayer [1985], Bancilhon [1986], Balbin and Ramamohanarao [1986], and
Gonzalez-Rubio, Rohmer, and Bradier [1987]. Sacca and Zaniolo [1988] extend the idea to handle rules with "stratified negation" (see Section 3.6 or the
references below).

Top-Down Evaluation

The fundamental paper is Robinson [1965] on resolution theorem proving.
Kowalski and Kuehner [1971] and Hill [1974] examined restricted cases of resolution, leading to the SLD-resolution (top-down, backtracking) strategy used
in Prolog. A survey of these developments is in Kowalski [1988]. Also see the
texts by Tanimoto [1987] and Genesereth and Nilsson [1988] for discussions of
resolution theorem proving.

    Convergence of top-down evaluation is considered in Afrati et al. [1986]
and Ullman and Van Gelder [1988]. The matter of different SIPS (sideways

information passing strategies) was examined by Van Gelder [1986b] and Beeri and Ramakrishnan [1987]; the term "SIPS" is from the latter.

The issue of "top-down safety," that is, safety of rules when we can take advantage of certain bindings at the head, as mentioned in Exercise 12.4, was explored by Zaniolo [1986], Ramakrishnan, Bancilhon, and Silberschatz [1987], and Kifer, Ramakrishnan, and Silberschatz [1988]. There are a number of safety-related references in Chapter 3.

Rule/Goal Graphs

The rule/goal graph is from Ullman [1985]. There are a number of other forms of graphs that carry less information, but have found use in logic processing, such as "connection graphs" (Kowalski [1975], Sickel [1976]). Mendelzon [1985] and Debray and Warren [1986] offer other approaches to the discovery of binding patterns.

Morris [1988] gives an algorithm for constructing rule/goal graphs when reordering of subgoals is permitted and there are forbidden adornments; it is essentially Algorithm 12.8, although the simplified presentation given here, and the analysis of its running time in Theorem 12.5, are by M. Y. Vardi. Ullman and Vardi [1988] show that the feasibility of rule/goal graphs requires exponential time in general (but note it can be done in polynomial time assuming a bound on the arity of predicates, per Corollary 12.1).

Prolog and Databases

There are a large number of projects designed to apply Prolog's logic processing algorithm to database queries. These include Warren [1981], Bocca [1986], Kellog, O'Hare, and Travis [1986], Moffat and Gray [1986], Sciore and Warren [1986], Ceri, Gottlob, and Wiederhold [1987], Ioannidis, Chen, Friedman, and Tsangaris [1988], and Napheys and Herkimer [1988]. Also see the references in Chapter 16 to the NU-Prolog system.

Expressiveness of Languages

There has been a considerable body of work on logic languages that are more expressive than the Horn-clause logic discussed in this chapter. Chandra [1988] is a survey of the general subject. Chapter 3 contains references and comments; some of the references are repeated here.

One of the central issues in extended languages is how one deals with negation. Ginsberg [1988] is a volume of papers in the field. The first feasible approach, "stratified negation," was covered in Section 3.6. The key references are Apt, Blair, and Walker [1985] and Van Gelder [1986].

More recently, treatments of negation that are more powerful (able to express more queries) have been considered. One, "inflationary semantics," applies the rules in a fixed-point calculation, but does not throw out any tuple from an IDB relation, even if newly discovered negative facts remove the justification for inferring the positive fact. This idea is from Kolaitis and Papadimitriou [1988]. Its power was explored in Kolaitis [1987] and Abiteboul and Vianu [1988].

Other recent approaches to the problem include Ross, Van Gelder, and Schlimpf [1988], Van Gelder [1988], Shepherdson [1988], and Imielinski and Naqvi [1988].

Another important enhancement of logic languages is the ability to deal with set-valued variables. This direction has been explored by Beeri, Naqvi, Ramakrishnan, Shmueli, and Tsur [1987], Kuper [1987, 1988], and Shmueli and Naqvi [1987]. Also see the references to the LDL system in Chapter 16.

In Hull and Su [1988] and Paredaens and Van Gucht [1988], logics for "complex objects," an even more general expansion of the types of variables, is explored.

CHAPTER 13

Combining Top-Down
and
Bottom-Up
Logic Evaluation

We now explain the "magic sets" technique for rewriting logical rules so bottom-up evaluation offers all the advantages associated with top-down as well as bottom-up evaluation. In this approach, rules and a query are used to construct new rules that answer the query, although they are generally not equivalent to the original rules. Section 13.1 gives the algorithm for rewriting rules, and the proof of its correctness is found in Section 13.2. Section 13.3 shows that for datalog, the rewritten rules are guaranteed to be as efficient, when semi-naive evaluation is applied, as the original rules are when the top-down algorithm of Sections 12.5 through 12.7 (called QRGT) is used.

In Section 13.4, we see how to simplify the magic-sets rules by eliminating some predicates, and Section 13.5 briefly discusses the modifications that are needed to avoid losing bindings, as was illustrated in Example 12.23; the cost of doing so is an increased number of rules. Then, in Section 13.6 we introduce the generalized magic-sets rule-rewriting technique, which offers the benefits of both top-down and bottom-up processing for arbitrary logic programs (magic sets only makes that guarantee for datalog). However, the generalized method requires that we work with relations whose tuples may not be ground atoms, but could involve variables. The disadvantage of doing so is that joins of tuples become, in effect, unifications.

13.1 THE MAGIC-SETS RULE REWRITING TECHNIQUE

Recall our discussion of the ancestor rules

r_1:   anc(X,Y) :- par(X,Y).
r_2:   anc(X,Y) :- par(X,Z) & anc(Z,Y).

beginning with Example 12.16 (Section 12.5). We observed that answering the query $anc(j, W)$, where j is a particular individual, could be performed rather efficiently top-down. That is, we could build and explore a rule/goal tree, considering only individuals who are ancestors of j. In comparison, the bottom-up algorithms, Algorithms 12.3 and 12.4, would construct the entire *anc* relation. If most of the individuals mentioned in the *par* relation are not ancestors of j, the bottom-up approach must take much more time than the top-down approach. However, there are a number of reasons why bottom-up calculation is preferable to top-down.

1.   If we are not careful how we do top-down calculation, we can get trapped in infinite loops and never find the answer. That would be the case if we followed the simple preorder traversal approach of Algorithm 12.6 (Section 12.7) on a *par* relation that had cycles.

2.   If we follow the QRGT version of Algorithm 12.6 discussed at the end of Section 12.7, we do not get trapped by cycles, but detecting termination, even for datalog rules, is not easy.[1]

3.   Even when convergence of rule/goal tree expansion is assured, we can be led to expand the same subgoal many times in the tree, thus repeating significant amounts of work.

4.   The bottom-up algorithms can make use of efficient techniques for taking joins of massive relations. (Recall that join is the central step in the operation EVAL, which, in turn, is the heart of semi-naive evaluation; see Section 12.2.) In comparison, the top-down approach tends to deal with many small relations, each associated with one of the nodes of the rule/goal tree. If we use QRGT, where the tree is explored breadth-first, we do not even have these relations as wholes; rather we construct them little by little, in a relatively unpredictable manner.

5.   Top-down algorithms require unification, but bottom-up algorithms only need term-matching, a simpler operation.

Fortunately, there is a way to get the advantages of both top-down and bottom-up methods. We rewrite a given set of rules and a query goal in such a way that the new set of rules produces the answer to the query. Moreover, if we apply the semi-naive evaluation method to the new rules, then each step we perform can be mapped into at least one step of QRGT, applied to the original rules. Thus, the bottom-up evaluation of the new rules is no more expensive than the top-down evaluation of the old rules. Detection of convergence is easy for the bottom-up algorithm, when the rules are datalog. If there are function

---

[1] Recall that safe datalog rules are guaranteed to produce a finite answer from a finite database; thus, their evaluation surely terminates. However, knowing that an evaluation converges eventually, and detecting when convergence occurs, are quite different matters.

symbols, convergence after a finite number of rounds is not guaranteed, but if we do converge, we know it immediately, because we reach a round in which no more facts are added to any IDB relation.

The Unique Binding Property

The algorithm for modification of the rules is closely related to the way we organized the evaluation of rule/goal trees in Algorithm 12.6. The key idea is that we do not even consider whether a fact $p(\mu)$ is true, for IDB predicate p and tuple μ, unless we have established that such a fact would be "interesting," in the sense that μ matches a tuple of the binding relation for one of p's goal nodes.

In order for the notion of a "binding pattern" for a predicate to make sense, we require our rules to have the *unique binding property* with respect to a given adorned goal. A logic program (set of rules) has the unique binding property if, when we construct the rule/goal graph starting with that adorned goal and respecting the order of the subgoals of rules as written, no IDB predicate appears with two different adornments. We can always obtain rules with the unique binding property, if we construct the rule/goal graph and split each IDB predicate into different predicates for the different adornments, as suggested by Algorithm 12.7.

Magic Predicates

Assuming the unique binding property, we create for each IDB predicate p a *magic predicate*, which we shall call m_p. The arguments of the magic predicate for p correspond to those arguments that the unique binding pattern for p makes bound. For example, if p's binding pattern is $bfbf$, then m_p is a binary relation whose tuples are bindings for the first and third arguments of p.

The intent of m_p is that $m\_p(\nu)$ should be true if and only if, in the rule/goal tree, ν is a binding passed to some goal node with predicate p. That is not exactly right, because in the rule/goal tree there may be binding sets that cover more arguments than the supposedly "unique" binding pattern for p; Example 12.32 illustrated this point. Any such additional bindings are ignored in the magic predicates, which cannot lead to incorrect behavior, but may make the evaluation of the resulting rules less efficient than they could be.

Supplementary Predicates

We also use predicates that represent the supplementary relations, which were used for sideways information passing in Chapter 12. If r is a rule with k subgoals, we shall use predicates $sup_{r.i}$ for $i = 0, 1, \ldots, k - 1$. The arguments of $sup_{r.i}$ are variables of rule r, and they correspond to the arguments of the ith supplementary relation for rule r, as defined in Section 12.6. That is, they are all those variables of r that are either

1. Bound in the head (according to the unique binding pattern for the head), or

2. Appear in one of the first i subgoals of r and also appear in a later subgoal or in the head.

Note that we do not use the last supplementary relations, as we did in Algorithm 12.6, preferring to go directly from the last subgoal to the head. The difference is not essential; we could have cut out a step in Algorithm 12.6, at the cost of making it slightly more complicated.

As we usually refer to rules as $r_1, \ldots, r_n$, we shall adopt the following convention. If an enumeration of the rules is understood, then $sup_{j.i}$ will stand for the ith supplementary predicate for rule r_j; that is, $sup_{r_j.i}$ and $sup_{j.i}$ will be treated as synonyms. We trust that the ambiguity, which is technically present in this convention, will not cause difficulty in practice.

The Basic Magic-Sets Transformation

We shall now give a mechanical way to convert a given set of rules and a query into a new set of rules, with a predicate whose relation is the answer to the query. We shall give some examples and show that the new set of rules mimics rule/goal tree expansion. Thus, the new rules can be shown both correct, because they produce the same answer as rule/goal tree expansion, and relatively efficient, because they perform no more work than the latter algorithm. In Section 13.4, we shall discuss some modifications to the technique that simplify the rules and preserve the efficiency with which bottom-up evaluation can be performed.

Algorithm 13.1: Magic-Sets Rule Transformation.

INPUT: A collection of rules and a query goal $q(s_1, \ldots, s_n)$. We assume that the rules have the unique-binding property with respect to this query goal.

OUTPUT: A new set of rules such that the relation for q is the answer to the query.

METHOD: We begin by creating the following new predicates.

$i)$ *Magic predicates for the IDB predicates.* For each IDB predicate p, m_p is the magic predicate for p. The arguments of m_p are the bound arguments of p; recall that the binding pattern for each IDB predicate is assumed unique.

$ii)$ *Supplementary predicates.* For each rule r_j, with k subgoals, create supplementary predicates $sup_{j.i}$, for $i = 0, 1, \ldots, k - 1$.

We now create rules for each of these new predicates, and we create new rules for the original IDB predicates.

1. *Rules for the magic predicates.* Let p be an IDB predicate, and consider each of the subgoals of the given rules that has predicate p. Suppose p appears in the ith subgoal of rule r_j, and this subgoal is $p(t_1, \ldots, t_n)$. Let the arguments for the $(i-1)$st supplementary relation be the variables $U_1, \ldots, U_l$. Finally, let the list of arguments of p that are bound in the binding pattern for p be $i_1, \ldots, i_m$. Then we create the rule

$$m\_p(t_{i_1}, \ldots, t_{i_m}) :\text{-} sup_{j.i-1}(U_1, \ldots, U_l).$$

For example, suppose the subgoal in question is $p(f(X), Y)$, and the arguments of the $(i-1)$st supplementary predicate for rule r_j are X, U, and V. Then the first argument of p is bound, and the second is free. Thus, m_p has only one argument, and one of the rules for m_p will be

```
m_p(f(X))  :- sup_{j.i-1}(X,U,V).
```

Notice that rules of this type implement the variable-to-argument translation VTOA discussed in Section 12.2.

2. *Rules for the zeroth supplementary predicates.* Let rule r_j have head $p(t_1, \ldots, t_n)$, and suppose that $i_1, \ldots, i_m$ are the bound arguments of p. Further, let $X_1, \ldots, X_l$ be the variables that are bound by the head of r_j, that is, the variables appearing among $t_{i_1}, \ldots, t_{i_m}$. Then the one rule defining $sup_{j.0}$ is

$$sup_{j.0}(X_1, \ldots, X_l) :\text{-} m\_p(t_{i_1}, \ldots, t_{i_m}).$$

For example, let r_j have head $p(f(X,Y), Z)$, and suppose that only the first argument of p is bound. Then the zeroth supplementary relation for r_j has arguments corresponding to variables X and Y, and its rule is

```
sup_{j.0}(X,Y)  :- m_p(f(X,Y)).
```

Note that this rule implements the argument-to-variable conversion ATOV mentioned in Section 12.2.

3. *Rules for the other supplementary predicates.* For each rule r_j, having k subgoals, and for each $i = 1, 2, \ldots, k-1$, we create a single rule for $sup_{j.i}$. Let the variables of r_j that are attributes of the $(i-1)$st supplementary relation for r_j be $U_1, \ldots, U_l$, and let the variables that are attributes of the ith supplementary relation for r_j be $V_1, \ldots, V_m$. Finally, let $p(t_1, \ldots, t_n)$ be the ith subgoal of r_j. Then we have the rule

$$sup_{j.i}(V_1, \ldots, V_m) :\text{-} sup_{j.i-1}(U_1, \ldots, U_l) \ \& \ p(t_1, \ldots, t_n).$$

Note that the V's will always appear either among the U's or among the arguments of p, so the above rule is safe. For example, suppose that the ith subgoal is $p(f(X), Y)$, the variables bound by $sup_{j.i-1}$ are W, X, and Z, while those bound by $sup_{j.i}$ are W, Y, and Z. (Apparently, X is not needed past the ith subgoal, but Y is.) Then the rule for $sup_{j.i}$ is

$$\text{sup}_{j.i}(\text{W,Y,Z}) \; \text{:- } \; \text{sup}_{j.i-1}(\text{W,X,Z}) \; \& \; \text{p(f(X),Y)}.$$

4.   *Rules for the IDB predicates.* Let p be an IDB predicate, and let r_j be one of the rules for p. Finally, suppose r_j has $k \geq 1$ subgoals. Then we obtain tuples for the predicate p from the $(k-1)$st supplementary predicate and the last subgoal. That is, if $U_1, \ldots, U_l$ are the variables that are attributes of the $(k-1)$st supplementary relation for r_j, $h(t_1, \ldots, t_n)$ is the head of r_j, and the kth subgoal of r_j is $p(v_1, \ldots, v_m)$, then we have rule

$$h(t_1, \ldots, t_n) :\!\text{- } sup_{j.k-1}(U_1, \ldots, U_l) \; \& \; p(v_1, \ldots, v_m).$$

For example, suppose r_j looks like

$$\text{h(f(X),Y)} \; \text{:- } \; \cdots \; \& \; \text{p(Z,g(W,Y))}.$$

where there are k subgoals in all, and the variables appearing in the $(k-1)$st supplementary relation are W, X, and Y. Then one of the rules for IDB predicate h is

$$\text{h(f(X),Y)} \; \text{:- } \; \text{sup}_{j.k-1}(\text{W,X,Y}) \; \& \; \text{p(Z,g(W,Y))}.$$

Note that these rules combine two steps of the QRGT algorithm, since we do not use a predicate corresponding to the kth supplementary relations; rather we go directly to the head from the $(k-1)$st supplementary relation. There is an exception to rule (4) when there are zero subgoals in a rule. In that case, there is no "$(k-1)$st supplementary relation," and we construct the head from $sup_{j.0}$ alone; that is, the rule is

$$h(t_1, \ldots, t_n) :\!\text{- } sup_{j.0}(U_1, \ldots, U_l).$$

where $U_1, \ldots, U_l$ are the arguments of the zeroth supplementary predicate for rule r_j.

5.   *The initialization rule.* Let the query goal be $q(s_1, \ldots, s_n)$, and suppose that $i_1, \ldots, i_m$ are the bound arguments of the query; that is, $s_{i_1}, \ldots, s_{i_m}$ are ground terms. Then we have the rule

$$m\_q(s_{i_1}, \ldots, s_{i_m}).$$

Intuitively, this rule says we are interested in tuples of q that match the constants of the query. $\square$

In examples, we shall refer to the rules of the five types listed above as *Groups* I through V, respectively. Note that only the Group V rule depends on the query. The other rules depend on the binding pattern of the query, although not on the particular constants involved. The rules generated by Algorithm 13.1 often will be referred to as *magic-set rules* or *magic rules*.

Example 13.1: Let us consider the original "same-generation" rules,

r_1:   `sg(X,X) :- person(X).`
r_2:   `sg(X,Y) :- par(X,Xp) & sg(Xp,Yp) & par(Y,Yp).`

as in Example 12.30 (Section 12.8), with the query $sg(a, W)$; that is, we are interested in finding the cousins of individual a. Note we have reordered subgoals to get the preferred rule/goal graph of Figure 12.23.

The rules of the five groups are shown in Figure 13.1. For example, rule (1) appears because the second subgoal of r_2 is an sg subgoal. At that point in the rule, only X and Xp are bound, so only the first argument of sg is bound. In fact, bf is the unique adornment associated with sg in these rules, so we know the magic predicate for sg will have only one argument. In rule (1), the argument of m_sg is a copy of the first argument of subgoal sg in r_2, and the arguments of $sup_{2.1}$ are the bound variables after the first subgoal of r_2.

Group I

(1)   `m_sg(Xp) :- sup`$_{2.1}$`(X,Xp).`

Group II

(2)   `sup`$_{1.0}$`(X) :- m_sg(X).`
(3)   `sup`$_{2.0}$`(X) :- m_sg(X).`

Group III

(4)   `sup`$_{2.1}$`(X,Xp) :- sup`$_{2.0}$`(X) & par(X,Xp).`
(5)   `sup`$_{2.2}$`(X,Yp) :- sup`$_{2.1}$`(X,Xp) & sg(Xp,Yp).`

Group IV

(6)   `sg(X,X) :- sup`$_{1.0}$`(X) & person(X).`
(7)   `sg(X,Y) :- sup`$_{2.2}$`(X,Yp) & par(Y,Yp).`

Group V

(8)   `m_sg(a).`

Figure 13.1 Magic-sets transformation of same-generation rules.

We can show the following facts for each tuple added to one of the IDB relations in Figure 13.1, by induction on the number of rounds of bottom-up evaluation.

1. The relations m_sg, $sup_{1.0}$, and $sup_{2.0}$ each represent the set of (not necessarily proper) ancestors of individual a.

2. Supplementary relation $sup_{2.1}$ is that subset of the EDB relation par such that the first argument is an ancestor of a,

3. Supplementary relation $sup_{2.2}$ is the set of pairs (X, Yp), such that X is an ancestor of a and Yp is a cousin of X, but Yp is one generation older than X.

4. The only tuples added to sg itself are those pairs (X, Y) that are cousins at the same generation, and X is an ancestor of a.

Thus, the modified rules avoid inferring any sg facts that do not, at least, have the potential to help derive facts of the form $sg(a, b)$ for some b. In comparison, the original rules derive facts $sg(c, d)$, where c is not an ancestor of a. Such a fact could not be used in a proof of any fact of the form $sg(a, b)$, and thus are provably unnecessary if our goal is to answer the query $sg(a, W)$. □

Note that the rules of Figure 13.1 can be simplified. For example, we can substitute m_sg for both $sup_{1.0}$ and $sup_{2.0}$. We shall take up these simplifications in Section 13.4.

Example 13.2: Now, let us consider an example with function symbols, based on the "good list" rules of Example 12.34,

r_1: `gl(nil).`
r_2: `gl(cons(H,T)) :- g(H) & gl(T).`

Here, we use g for $good$ and gl for $goodList$, to make the rules more concise. The query goal is $gl(l_0)$, where l_0 is a given list; it doesn't matter which. A suitable rule/goal graph for these rules is shown in Figure 13.2.

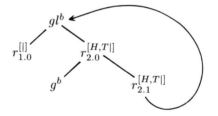

Figure 13.2 Rule/goal graph for rules of Example 13.2.

The rules generated by Algorithm 13.1 are shown in Figure 13.3. One subtlety we have not previously encountered is seen in rule (2), where the predicate $sup_{1.0}$ has no arguments.[2] In effect, $sup_{1.0}()$ denotes either `true`

---

[2] In this case, it has no arguments because rule r_1 has no variables. In other situations, the rule could have variables, but none of them are bound by the head; again the magic predicate would have zero arguments.

Group I

(1) $m\_gl(T)$:- $sup_{2.1}(H,T)$.

Group II

(2) $sup_{1.0}()$:- $m\_gl(nil)$.
(3) $sup_{2.0}(H,T)$:- $m\_gl(cons(H,T))$.

Group III

(4) $sup_{2.1}(H,T)$:- $sup_{2.0}(H,T)$ & $g(H)$.

Group IV

(5) $gl(nil)$:- $sup_{1.0}()$.
(6) $gl(cons(H,T))$:- $sup_{2.1}(H,T)$ & $gl(T)$.

Group V

(7) $m\_gl(l_0)$.

Figure 13.3 Magic-sets transformation for "good list" rules.

or `false`, and rule (2) says that its value is `true` if *nil* is in the relation m_gl, and `false` otherwise.[3] Also note that rule (5) is an example of the exception for Group IV, a rule with zero subgoals, where we obtain the head from the zeroth supplementary relation.

We can show the following by induction on the number of rounds of naive evaluation applied to the rules of Figure 13.3.

1.   Relation m_gl consists of those suffixes of l_0 that are preceded only by good elements; in particular, *nil* is in m_gl if and only if all elements of l_0 are good.

2.   Relation $sup_{2.0}$ has tuple (H, T) if and only if the list $cons(H, T)$ is a suffix of l_0 and is preceded only by good elements, while $sup_{2.1}$ is the subset of $sup_{2.0}$ defined by the additional condition that H also be good.

3.   Relation gl is empty if l_0 does not consist exclusively of good elements. If all elements of l_0 are good, then gl consists of all the suffixes of l_0. $\square$

Example 13.3: Our next example uses rules with two recursive subgoals in one body. It also illustrates an important point about how to model arithmetic.

---

[3] Technically, we must think of "true" as meaning a relation with zero attributes, containing only the empty tuple, and of "false" as a relation with no attributes and no tuples. If we do so, then the evaluation algorithms for rules that we have been using generalize properly.

The rules in question are

r_1:   p(X,Y,D) :- a(X,Y,D).
r_2:   p(X,Y,D) :- p(X,Z,E) & p(Z,Y,F) & D=E+F.

The intent is that a is an EDB predicate, and $a(X, Y, D)$ means that there is an arc from node X to node Y, of length D. The IDB predicate $p(X, Y, D)$ similarly means that there is a path of length D from X to Y.

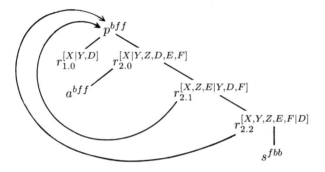

Figure 13.4 Rule/goal graph for path-length rules.

The third subgoal of r_2, $D = E + F$, is not of a type we have seen before, since we never incorporated arithmetic operators, like addition, into our notation for rules. However, we may think of it as an EDB subgoal $s(D, E, F)$, with the permissible binding patterns fbb and bbb only. The "EDB" relation s consists of the infinite set of triples such that the first element is the sum of the second and third. As with built-in predicates like $<$, we can only "join" the relation for s with relations for other subgoals after a finite set of values for the second and third arguments has been found, that is, after E and F are bound.[4] Thus, the rules may be written

r_1:   p(X,Y,D) :- a(X,Y,D).
r_2:   p(X,Y,D) :- p(X,Z,E) & p(Z,Y,F) & s(D,E,F).

Let us suppose that the query goal is p^{bff}, that is, find all the nodes reachable from a given node x_0, and find the length of each path to each node. A rule/goal graph for these rules and query is shown in Figure 13.4. It is not the only possible rule/goal graph, since we could have switched the order of the two p subgoals in r_2. However, the s subgoal can only be third, since only then

---

[4] In principle, we could allow any two of D, E, and F to be bound; for example, we could compute E as $D - F$ if values for D and F were given. If we are willing to do the implied subtraction, then we could allow any binding pattern for s that had no more than one f.

can E and F be bound, as required if the adornment of s is to be permissible. This rule/goal graph is clearly the preferred choice, as it avoids occurrences of a^{fff}.

Group I

(1)   m_p(X) :- sup$_{2.0}$(X).
(2)   m_p(Z) :- sup$_{2.1}$(X,Z,E).

Group II

(3)   sup$_{1.0}$(X) :- m_p(X).
(4)   sup$_{2.0}$(X) :- m_p(X).

Group III

(5)   sup$_{2.1}$(X,Z,E) :- sup$_{2.0}$(X) & p(X,Z,E).
(6)   sup$_{2.2}$(X,Y,E,F) :- sup$_{2.1}$(X,Z,E) & p(Z,Y,F).

Group IV

(7)   p(X,Y,D) :- sup$_{1.0}$(X) & a(X,Y,D).
(8)   p(X,Y,D) :- sup$_{2.2}$(X,Y,E,F) & s(D,E,F).

Group V

(9)   m_p(x_0).

Figure 13.5 Magic-sets transformation for paths rules.

The reader should be alert to the fact that, even though the above rules are datalog, that is, there are no function symbols, we expect that the answer will be infinite if the arcs have cycles. The reason is that s, although treated as an EDB relation, is really infinite. When there are cycles, the bottom-up evaluation of the rules could have r_2 applied an infinite number of times. At each round, the relation for p is finite, yet there are new length values generated at each round, and the rules never converge.[5] Nevertheless, we can apply the magic-sets transformation to the above rules and get the logic program shown in Figure 13.5. If a is a finite relation representing an acyclic graph, then these rules will converge bottom-up, as will the set of rules $\{r_1, r_2\}$, but if a has cycles, we expect neither set of rules to converge. □

---

[5] In a sense, the addition operation plays the role of a function symbol, so the rules for path length behave as though they were not datalog.

13.2 CORRECTNESS OF THE MAGIC-SETS ALGORITHM

We need to show that the magic-sets transformation is "correct," in the sense that the new rules produce the same answer to the query as the old. The relationship between what the old rules and the new rules compute is somewhat subtle. Suppose that the query involves IDB predicate p, with bindings for some of its arguments. Then the transformed rules will produce a relation for p that is generally a proper subset of what the original rules produce for p. Fortunately, nothing that is lost will match the query goal, which guarantees that the answer to the query, before and after transformation, is the same. One part, that nothing is inferred by the new rules that was not inferred by the old, is isolated in the following lemma.

Lemma 13.1: Let p be an IDB predicate that appears in the input rules ("original rules") of Algorithm 13.1. If, in the transformed rules produced by that algorithm (the "new rules"), the fact $p(t_1, \ldots, t_n)$ can be deduced, then the same fact is deduced by the original rules.

Proof: In the proof of this lemma, we may ignore the magic predicates m_q. We shall prove that for each supplementary predicate $sup_{r.i}(X_1, \ldots, X_m)$, for an original rule r, each tuple μ in the relation for $sup_{r.i}$ agrees, on common attributes, with tuples of the relations for the first i subgoals of r. More formally, μ satisfies the following condition:

1. Let the variables $X_{j_1}, \ldots, X_{j_l}$ be the subset of $X_1, \ldots, X_m$ that appear among the first i subgoals of r; that is, they are all the arguments of $sup_{r.i}$, except those that appear in the head but in none of the first i subgoals.

2. Let μ' be μ projected onto $X_{j_1}, \ldots, X_{j_l}$.

3. Then μ' is in $\pi_{j_1, \ldots, j_l}(Q_1 \bowtie \cdots \bowtie Q_i)$. Here, Q_j is the relation obtained by

   i) Computing the relation for the jth subgoal of rule r, according to the original rules, and then

   ii) Translating from arguments to variables, with the ATOV operator of Section 12.2.

We prove this claim, along with the claim of the lemma: tuples added to the relation for any IDB predicate p in the derived rules are also added to the relation for p in the original rules. The proof is by induction on the rounds of the bottom-up computation algorithm (Algorithm 12.3), applied to the new rules. Before beginning the induction, note that the inductive hypothesis holds vacuously for the zeroth supplementary predicates, because that hypothesis speaks of projection of the relations for those predicates onto the variables found among the first zero predicates of a rule.

Basis: For round 1 of bottom-up evaluation, the claim holds vacuously, because only Groups II, III, and IV can yield tuples discussed in the hypothesis. Group

II rules assign tuples to zeroth supplementary relations, and we observed that there is nothing to prove about such tuples. Groups III and IV have supplementary predicates in their bodies, and in round 1, those predicates have empty relations.

Induction: Again Group II rules can be ignored. The Group III rules generate tuples for a supplementary predicate $sup_{r.i}$, and each such rule has two subgoals:

1. $sup_{r.i-1}$, whose arguments are those variables that are attributes of the $(i-1)$st supplementary relation for r.
2. The ith subgoal of r, say $p(t_1, \ldots, t_k)$, with its arguments as written in rule r.

Let μ be a tuple added to the relation for $sup_{r.i}$ at some round. Then we know that:

a) μ agrees, in their common attributes, with some tuple ρ that was added to $sup_{r.i-1}$ before the current round.

b) μ agrees, in their common attributes, with a certain tuple ν; ν comes from some tuple ν', by the argument-to-variable conversion process discussed in Section 12.2. Furthermore, ν' is placed in the relation for p, according to the new rules, prior to the current round.

We know, by (a) and the inductive hypothesis, that ρ is a projection of a tuple in $Q_1 \bowtie \cdots \bowtie Q_{i-1}$. Also by the inductive hypothesis, ν' is in the relation for p, according to the original rules. Hence, ν is in Q_i. By (b), μ agrees, in common attributes, with ν. Thus, μ is a projection, onto the appropriate set of variables, of a tuple in $Q_1 \bowtie \cdots \bowtie Q_i$; that tuple is the join of ρ and μ. This observation proves part of the inductive hypothesis.

The remaining part of the inductive hypothesis concerns the Group IV rules; these rules produce tuples for the head predicate of a rule r in terms of the last subgoal and the last supplementary predicate for that rule. Using the same argument as for the Group III rules, we conclude that each tuple μ that satisfies the body of the Group IV rule for original rule r, is a projection of the join of the Q_j's for all the subgoals of r. It follows that μ can be extended to a substitution that makes the body of r true. Therefore when we substitute $\mu[X]$ for each variable X in the head predicate of r, we get a tuple that is placed in the relation for that predicate, when the bottom-up Algorithm 12.3 is applied to the original rules. Thus, the entire inductive hypothesis is proved, and with it the lemma. $\square$

We now know that every answer to the query returned by the new rules is also returned by the original rules. Next, we must show the opposite: that every answer returned by the original rules is also returned by the new rules. In the following lemma, we relate what happens when we perform rule/goal tree expansion on the original rules to what happens when we perform bottom-up evaluation on the transformed rules.

A subtlety of which we must be aware is that, in the rule/goal tree, a goal node with predicate p can have more bound arguments than are indicated by the supposedly unique binding pattern of p. That would not be the case if the original rules are datalog and have been processed by Algorithm 12.7 to make the bindings unique. However, in general, it is possible for some goal nodes in a rule/goal tree to have "extra" bound arguments; fortunately it is not possible that fewer arguments are bound than are expected by the binding pattern for the predicate. Also, in a way to be made precise in the next lemma, the arguments of the supplementary relations of a rule node are at least sufficient to cover all the variables of the rule that the rule/goal graph says should be bound.

Lemma 13.2: Suppose a set of "original" rules that satisfy the unique binding property are transformed by Algorithm 13.1 into "new" rules. Suppose we run queue-based rule/goal tree expansion (QRGT) on the original rules and Algorithm 12.3 (bottom-up evaluation) on the new rules. Then

a)   If at some goal node for IDB predicate p, tuple μ is in the binding relation for that node, then there is some μ' in the relation for m_p, where μ' is the projection of μ onto the arguments of p that are bound according to the unique binding pattern for p.

b)   If tuple μ is returned as an answer at some goal node with IDB predicate p, then μ is in the relation for p when we evaluate the new rules.

c)   Suppose that at some rule node for rule r, say one where the substituted instance of r is $\tau(r)$, tuple μ is in the ith supplementary relation. Let the attributes (variables) of the ith supplementary relation for $\tau(r)$ be $U_1, \ldots, U_n$. Let $X_1, \ldots, X_m$ be the variables of r [not $\tau(r)$] that are bound after i subgoals of r; that is, the X's are the attributes of $sup_{r.i}$ in the new rules. Then the tuple

$$\mu' = \Big(\mu\big(\tau(X_1)\big), \ldots, \mu\big(\tau(X_m)\big)\Big)$$

is in the relation for $sup_{r.i}$.[6]

Proof: We shall prove all three claims simultaneously, by induction on the number of steps taken by the QRGT algorithm. Before proceeding, let us note that by an easy induction on the number of steps of rule/goal tree expansion, we can infer that every goal node with some predicate p has a binding pattern that

---

[6]   The expression for μ' takes advantage of the fact that tuple μ is really a mapping from attributes $U_1, \ldots, U_n$ to values. We have used only expressions like $\mu[U_i]$ for the value of μ in the component for the attribute U_i, but μ, like any mapping, extends naturally to terms like $\tau(X_1)$, or even to literals and rules, provided μ has components for all the variables (attributes) mentioned in the expression to which μ is applied.

binds at least all the variables that are bound in the unique binding pattern for p.

Basis: Zero steps of rule/goal tree expansion. The only tuple given initially, is that in the binding relation for the root. The Group V rule guarantees that this tuple will be in the magic set for the query predicate, proving (a). Parts (b) and (c) hold vacuously in the basis, since no tuples fit the description before any steps of tree expansion are carried out.

Induction: There are three parts, corresponding to claims (a), (b), and (c) in the statement of the lemma.

(a) Suppose μ is added to the binding relation for some goal node. Then this goal node has a rule-node parent, corresponding to some substituted instance of a rule r, say $\tau(r)$. Let the goal in question be the $(i+1)$st subgoal of $\tau(r)$, and let that subgoal be $p(t_1, \ldots, t_k)$ in r. Thus, in $\tau(r)$ the $(i+1)$st subgoal appears as $p(\tau(t_1), \ldots, \tau(t_k))$.

Tuple μ must be derived from some tuple ν that was previously added to the ith supplementary relation S_i at the rule node for $\tau(r)$; μ is obtained from ν by the variable-to-argument conversion operator VTOA. That is, we apply the mapping ν to each of the arguments $\tau(t_{i_1}), \ldots, \tau(t_{i_l})$ of the $(i+1)$st subgoal, where $i_1, \ldots, i_l$ are the bound arguments of p. Thus, we may write

$$\mu = \left(\nu\big(\tau(t_{i_1})\big), \ldots, \nu\big(\tau(t_{i_l})\big) \right) \qquad (13.1)$$

Now, let $X_1, \ldots, X_m$ be the variables of r that are bound and relevant just before the $(i+1)$st subgoal; that is, the X's are the attributes of $sup_{r.i}$. The inductive hypothesis applies to ν, so by part (c) in the statement of the lemma, we conclude that

$$\nu' = \left(\nu\big(\tau(X_1)\big), \ldots, \nu\big(\tau(X_m)\big) \right) \qquad (13.2)$$

is in the relation for $sup_{r.i}$. [Note that ν and ν' here are μ and μ' in the statement of (c).]

It is important to observe that (13.2) makes sense; in particular, $\nu\big(\tau(X_j)\big)$ is defined for $j = 1, 2, \ldots, m$. The reason is that the only way X_j can become bound is if it appears in a bound argument of the head or in one of the first i subgoals of r. As we mentioned at the beginning of the proof, any argument of the head predicate p that is bound in the unique binding pattern for p will also be bound in the rule node for $\tau(r)$; other arguments might be bound as well. Thus, any variable that appears in $\tau(X_j)$ will be bound before the $(i+1)$st subgoal in $\tau(r)$ as well as in r. Finally, if X_j appears in r after the ith subgoal, then any variable appearing in $\tau(X_j)$ will appear in $\tau(r)$ after the ith subgoal; that is, if X_j is relevant, so is any variable in $\tau(X_j)$. We conclude that $\tau(X_j)$ cannot involve any variables but the U's mentioned in clause (c) of the lemma, which are the bound and relevant variables after the ith subgoal.

Finally, the Group I rule defining m_p is

$$m\_p(t_{i_1}, \ldots, t_{i_l}) \text{ :- } sup_{r.i}(X_1, \ldots, X_m).$$

When we substitute ν' from (13.2) in the body of this rule, we deduce that μ, as given by (13.1), is in the relation for m_p. That is, ν' turns each X_j into $\nu(\tau(X_j))$, so it turns the head of the Group I rule into (13.1). Thus, part (a) of the inductive hypothesis is proved.

(b) There must be some rule r for p and a rule node N, with rule instance $\tau(r)$, at which tuple μ is produced, and that is a child of the goal node in question. Let r have k subgoals, and let the $(k-1)$st supplementary relation at N be $S_{k-1}(U_1, \ldots, U_m)$. Finally, let the kth subgoal of r be $p(t_1, \ldots, t_j)$, and let the head of r be $h(s_1, \ldots, s_l)$. Thus, in the substituted instance, these atoms are $p(\tau(t_1), \ldots, \tau(t_j))$ and $h(\tau(s_1), \ldots, \tau(s_l))$, respectively.

If μ is produced in the relation for h at N, there must be some tuple ρ, over the variables (attributes) $U_1, \ldots, U_m$, and whatever additional variables appear in the kth subgoal, such that

1. $\rho[U_1, \ldots, U_m]$ is a tuple of supplementary relation S_{k-1},
2. ρ agrees with the argument-to-variable conversion of some tuple ν that is in the relation for subgoal $p(\tau(t_1), \ldots, \tau(t_j))$, and
3. μ is obtained from ρ by evaluating the head predicate; that is,

$$\mu = \Big(\rho(\tau(s_1)), \ldots, \rho(\tau(s_l)) \Big)$$

Condition (2) is equivalent to the statement that

$$\nu = \Big(\rho(\tau(t_1)), \ldots, \rho(\tau(t_j)) \Big)$$

if we extend tuple ρ, as usual, to be a mapping on terms involving the variables that are attributes of ρ.

Now, we may apply the inductive hypothesis to the tuples known to be in S_{k-1} and to tuples returned by the goal node for the kth subgoal. By part (c) of the inductive hypothesis,

$$\Big(\rho(\tau(X_1)), \ldots, \rho(\tau(X_n)) \Big)$$

is in the relation for $sup_{r.k-1}$, where $X_1, \ldots, X_n$ are the arguments for $sup_{r.k-1}$. By (b) of the inductive hypothesis and (2) above, ν is in the relation for p, if p is an IDB predicate. If p is an EDB predicate, then ν is in its relation because that relation is the same at all goal nodes for p in the rule/goal tree and is equal to the database relation for p.

In the new rules, the rule for h that is derived from r is

$$h(s_1, \ldots, s_l) \text{ :- } sup_{r.k-1}(X_1, \ldots, X_n) \ \& \ p(t_1, \ldots, t_j).$$

This rule's body is satisfied if we substitute $\rho(\tau(X))$ for each variable X that is among $X_1, \ldots, X_n$, or that appears in $p(t_1, \ldots, t_j)$. But when we make this substitution, the head becomes $h(\mu)$, proving that μ is in the relation for predicate h.

(c) This part uses the same ideas as the first two parts, and we leave the proof as an exercise. $\square$

We can now put the previous two lemmas together and prove the correctness of the magic sets algorithm.

Theorem 13.1: The answer produced by the rules constructed in Algorithm 13.1 is correct.

Proof: Lemma 13.1 showed that every answer produced bottom-up by the new rules is also produced bottom-up by the original rules. Theorem 12.2 tells us the answers produced by QRGT and the bottom-up approach are the same. Then, Lemma 13.2(b) implies that every answer returned by the rule/goal tree expansion of the original rules is returned by the new rules, evaluated bottom-up. $\square$

13.3 EFFICIENCY OF THE MAGIC-SET RULES

We want to show that the efficiency of bottom-up execution of the new rules compares favorably with other ways to obtain the answer to the query. It is not realistic to expect that the transformed rules are as efficient as any method whatsoever on any query. However, at least for datalog rules, we can show that they are no less efficient than the QRGT algorithm applied to the original rules. Since the latter algorithm simulates SLD-resolution (when the latter converges), and SLD-resolution is, by reason of its use in Prolog, the most successful known approach to answering general queries expressed in logic, the implication is that magic-sets is likely to be the method of choice, in general, for datalog rules. In fact, magic sets frequently improves upon SLD resolution or QRGT for non-datalog programs as well. As we shall see in Section 13.6, a generalization of magic sets, where relations can have nonground tuples, completely dominates the top-down approaches.

Semi-Naive Evaluation

To begin, note that we should evaluate these rules, like any rules, by the "semi-naive" evaluation method, Algorithm 12.4, rather than by the "naive" Algorithm 12.3. In the previous section, we compared QRGT to the naive algorithm. However, since Algorithms 12.3 and 12.4 produce the same answer, we could just have well shown that QRGT produces the same result as semi-naive evaluation.

A Cost Model

Let us assume that all relations R are stored in such a way that, given a tuple μ over a subset of the attributes of R, we can find all tuples in R that agree with μ, in time proportional to the number of matching tuples. If there is no matching tuple, we shall assume the lookup cost is one time unit.

This assumption is not too unrealistic if we create the appropriate indices on relations. If the relations correspond to predicates of rules constructed by Algorithm 13.1, and we evaluate these rules by semi-naive evaluation, then the only times we look up a tuple are

1. When we insert it into a relation, and we wish to check that it does not already appear there.
2. When a tuple appears in Δp for some predicate p, and we wish to compare it with the tuples of the (full) relation for some other predicate q.

Case (1) implies that we need an index on the set of all attributes; for example, we could use a hash table whose hash function maps entire tuples to buckets.[7]

Case (2) occurs in a limited number of situations. First, note that none of the rules generated by Algorithm 13.1 have more than two subgoals, so (2) is general enough. In the Group III and IV rules, a supplementary predicate appears along with either an IDB subgoal or an EDB subgoal; each supplementary predicate appears exactly once among these rules. If it appears with an IDB subgoal, the relation for the supplementary predicate needs one index, on that set of its attributes that, as variables, appear in the other subgoal. If the second subgoal is EDB, then it never changes, so the supplementary relation needs no index. Similarly, the relation for the other subgoal needs an index on its bound arguments. If the rules have the unique-binding property, then each IDB relation needs only one index, no matter how many times it appears as a subgoal. EDB relations may need more, since their predicates can appear with several different binding patterns.

When we talk about the QRGT algorithm, we may make corresponding assumptions about indices. However, note that in QRGT the relations correspond to individual tree nodes, rather than to predicates. We shall count the same unit time to do lookups on relations in a QRGT expansion, as in a bottom-up evaluation of the predicates generated by Algorithm 13.1.

Events

When we perform semi-naive evaluation on the rules produced by Algorithm 13.1, there are two kinds of *events* that together account for the running time of the algorithm.

---

[7] See Chapter 6 of Volume I for a description of storage structures for relations.

(A) A new tuple for some predicate p is discovered; that is, the tuple is inserted into the relations for p and Δp.

(B) We identify a pair of matching tuples from the relations for Δp and q or p and Δq, where p and q are the predicates of the two subgoals of some rule in Groups III or IV.

As we shall argue below, all running time for the semi-naive evaluation algorithm can be charged to events, and all events are charged $O(1)$ time under our cost model. Thus, running time can be estimated, to within a constant factor, by counting events.

We must show that all running time is accurately accounted for. Consider first an event of type A, where we insert a tuple μ into the relation for predicate p. To this event we charge the cost of initiating a search for matching tuples in each rule body where predicate p appears. Recall that we must charge a time unit for the lookup, even if we fail to find any matches. Each match found is charged to its own type B event. If p appears as the lone subgoal of a Group I or II rule r, then we charge the type A event insertion-of-μ-into-p the cost of creating another tuple ν and checking whether it is already in the relation for the head of rule r, provided ν is already in that relation (and thus there is no insertion of ν to charge as a separate type A event). The number of rule bodies with predicate p is a constant, depending only on the rules and not on the size of the database. Thus, the cost of a type A event is $O(1)$ under our cost model.

To an event of type B we charge the cost of inserting the tuple for the head predicate that is produced by the matching pair, in the case that this tuple already exists in the head predicate (in which case there is no type A event to charge for the insertion). We also charge unit time for consideration of the pair itself. Thus, the cost of a type B event is $O(1)$.

When we perform QRGT, we similarly can partition the work into events of types A and B. Type A events are those in which a tuple is added to

1. A binding relation at a goal node with an IDB predicate,
2. The result relation of a goal node with an IDB predicate, or
3. A supplementary relation at a rule node.

We do not count as an event the addition of a tuple to the result relation for a rule node; that tuple is immediately added to the result of the goal-node parent, and the cost can be charged to the latter type A event.[8]

Type B events are those where tuples in supplementary relation S_i at some rule node are matched with tuples in the result relation for the $(i+1)$st goal-node child of N.

Not all the costs of QRGT are accounted for by the above scheme; for

---

[8] In an efficient implementation, we would not even create result relations for the rule nodes, but rather accumulate their tuples at the goal node above.

example, we ignore the creation of the tree itself. Also, we do not count the passing of bindings to EDB relations as events in QRGT. However, the number of events is a lower bound on the cost of QRGT, which is all that we shall need in what follows.

Subgoal-Rectified Datalog

We can show that semi-naive evaluation of the rules transformed by Algorithm 13.1 executes no more events than does QRGT, in one very significant case. Recall rules are said to be subgoal-rectified if all subgoals have lists of distinct variables for their arguments; of course, different subgoals may use the same variable. The output of Algorithm 12.7 is subgoal-rectified, so we know that every set of datalog rules can be put in this form.

The importance of the subgoal-rectified property is that in QRGT, every instance of rule r may be taken to be r itself; that is, all unifications are trivial. The following lemma is the heart of the proof that the transformed rules are evaluated bottom-up at least as efficiently as QRGT evaluates them. We must later show that Algorithm 12.7, the step that makes the rules subgoal-rectified and gives them the unique-binding property, does not slow down QRGT. If the transformation of Algorithm 12.7 produced rules that could not be evaluated efficiently by any means, then our comparison would be suspect.

Lemma 13.3: Suppose we are given a set of "original" rules that are subgoal-rectified and have the unique-binding property, and that Algorithm 13.1 produces from these, and from a certain query goal, a set of "new" rules. Then for each event E of type A or B that occurs when we evaluate the new rules by semi-naive evaluation, we can identify a corresponding event F at some node of the QRGT expansion of the query goal according to the original rules, as follows.

a) If E is the insertion of a tuple μ into the relation for some IDB predicate p, then F is an insertion of μ into the relation returned by some goal node with predicate p.

b) If E is the insertion of μ into a magic predicate m_p, then F is an insertion of μ into the binding relation for some goal node with predicate p.

c) If E is the insertion of tuple μ into a supplementary predicate $sup_{r.i}$, then F is the insertion of μ into the ith supplementary relation at some rule node for r.

d) If E pairs a tuple μ in the relation for some $sup_{r.i}$ with a matching tuple ν in the relation for the $(i + 1)$st subgoal of r, then F is the pairing of μ, in the ith supplementary relation at some rule node N for r, with ν in the result relation for the $(i + 1)$st goal-node child of N. This case covers matching in the bodies of rules of Groups III and IV.

Proof: The proof is an induction on the order in which events occur during semi-naive evaluation. In one round, all of the type B events, which pair tuples in the bodies of the rules, occur before all of the type A events, which construct new tuples from the bodies and insert them into the relations for the heads of rules. We shall not give the entire induction, most of which is straightforward. Rather, we concentrate on the most difficult situation, where we have a type B event in which tuples from the body of a Group III or IV rule are paired. We show that a corresponding type B event occurs during QRGT. Then we prove that the resulting type A event, where a tuple is added to the next supplementary relation (by a Group III rule) or to an IDB predicate (by a Group IV rule), also corresponds to an event during QRGT.

Thus, suppose we have a rule body

$$sup_{r.i}(X_1, \ldots, X_m) \ \& \ p(Y_1, \ldots, Y_k). \tag{13.3}$$

where the Y's are distinct variables, but there may be some overlap between the X's and the Y's. Let the type B event consist of the pairing of μ in the relation for $sup_{r.i}$ with a matching tuple ν from the relation for p. Presumably, at least one of μ and ν was added to its relation on the previous round, and the other was added on a prior round as well (unless p is an EDB predicate); thus, the inductive hypothesis applies to each, although it is vacuous for an EDB predicate.

By the inductive hypothesis, there is some rule node N in the rule/goal tree such that the ith supplementary relation, $S_i(X_1, \ldots, X_m)$, at N contains μ. Note that we may assume, by the subgoal-rectified property, that the instance of r at N is r itself. Thus, the attributes of the supplementary relations at N are the same variables as the corresponding arguments of the predicates $sup_{r.j}$, for each j. Also, the bound arguments of the IDB subgoals of N are the same as the unique binding pattern for the predicates of those subgoals.

If p is an IDB subgoal, we need to show that ν agrees with some tuple ρ in the binding relation for the $(i + 1)$st subgoal, $p(Y_1, \ldots, Y_k)$, of r at node N. For then we know, by Theorem 12.2, that ν will be placed eventually in the relation returned by the $(i+1)$st goal-node child of N, which we shall call node M. To that end, let $Z_1, \ldots, Z_n$ be the variables found among $X_1, \ldots, X_m$ and also found among $Y_1, \ldots, Y_k$. Then there is a Group I rule

$$m\_p(Z_1, \ldots, Z_n) :\!- sup_{r.i}(X_1, \ldots, X_m).$$

Since μ satisfies the body, the projection of μ onto $Z_1, \ldots, Z_n$, which we shall call ρ, satisfies the head.

By the same reasoning, ρ is placed in the binding relation for M. Thus, by Theorem 12.2, ν eventually enters the relation returned at M, and a type B event, in which μ is paired with matching tuple ν at node N, occurs.

If p is an EDB subgoal, there is nothing to prove. That is, ν is always in the relation for p. We have thus shown that each type B event during semi-naive evaluation corresponds to a type B event during QRGT.

Now suppose that (13.3) is the body of a Group III rule, so the head is $sup_{r.i+1}(U_1, \ldots, U_l)$, where the U's are all found among the X's or the Y's. Then the tuple ψ, which has components for each of the U's, and agrees with both μ and ν on common attributes, is added to the relation for $sup_{r.i+1}$. By the same reasoning, ψ is added to the $(i+1)$st supplementary relation at N as well. In terms of the inductive hypothesis, whenever we find a type A event, in which a tuple ψ is added to the relation for a supplementary predicate, such as $sup_{r.i+1}$, we can identify a pair of matching tuples μ and ν that led to that event, and by the argument just pursued, μ and ν are also paired at some rule node N, during QRGT expansion. Thus, the matching type A event for ψ occurs at N as well.

A similar argument shows that if (13.3) is a Group IV rule, the type A event in which a tuple is added to some IDB predicate during semi-naive evaluation, is mimicked, during QRGT expansion, by an insertion of the same tuple into the result relation at some rule node N, and then into the result relation for its goal-node parent. The remaining inductive cases are left for the reader. $\square$

Note that QRGT does some extra steps not reflected in the magic-sets rules. For example, QRGT constructs final supplementary relations for rules and then computes result relations from these, rather than going directly to the head from the previous supplementary relation, as magic sets does. QRGT computes binding relations for EDB subgoals, while magic sets avoids this step, performing lookups directly from the supplementary relations, when the joins implicit in rules of Groups III and IV are executed. None of these differences are essential. We explained QRGT as we did for simplicity, but we could have added the "improvements" found in Algorithm 13.1 to QRGT as well.

Theorem 13.2: Suppose we are given "original" rules, that are subgoal-rectified datalog, and that satisfy the unique-binding property. Let these rules be transformed into "new" rules by Algorithm 13.1. Then the running time of semi-naive evaluation on the new rules is at most proportional to the running time of QRGT on the original rules.

Proof: It suffices to observe that two events during semi-naive evaluation are never associated, by Lemma 13.3, with the same event during QRGT expansion. The reason is that each event of type A involves a unique tuple and a particular predicate; each type B event involves a unique pair of tuples and a particular pair of predicates. $\square$

While Theorem 13.2 only implies that semi-naive evaluation of the new rules cannot be more than a constant factor slower than QRGT expansion of the original rules, in fact the smaller constant of proportionality probably goes with the semi-naive evaluation. The latter algorithm can take advantage of economies of scale due to the fact that it deals with a few large relations rather than many small ones. Moreover, in many cases, the number of events during QRGT will far exceed the number during semi-naive evaluation, since QRGT may repeat the same work at many different nodes.

There is, however, another concern. Suppose we start with a datalog program P_1 and apply Algorithm 12.7 to develop an equivalent datalog program P_2 that is subgoal-rectified and has the unique-binding property. We then use Algorithm 13.1 to transform P_2 and a query goal into a "magic" program P_3. Theorem 13.2 tells us that P_3 compares favorably with P_2; but does P_3 therefore compare well with P_1? The answer is "yes," as the following corollary to Theorem 13.2 explains.

Corollary 13.1: The running time of semi-naive evaluation on datalog program P_3, above, is at most proportional to the running time of QRGT on P_1.

Proof: Consider QRGT expansion, from the same query goal, applied to P_1 and P_2. We need to show that the sequences of events during the two expansions take, to within a constant factor, the same amount of time.

The first transformation of Algorithm 12.7 reduces the number of arguments of subgoals, say by replacing a subgoal $p(X, X)$ by $p'(X)$, for some new predicate p'. This transformation changes the names of the predicates that appear in corresponding steps of P_1 and P_2. It also changes the rules used, since the rules for p' are the rules for p with the two arguments of the head identified and merged. However, it is a simple induction on the number of steps performed by QRGT, that the behaviors of P_1 and P_2 are essentially the same. The only difference is that in the expansion of P_1 we may find a relation with tuples that have two components identical, or set equal to a constant, while in P_2, only one copy of the identical columns appears, and the constant column will not appear at all.

The second transformation of Algorithm 12.7 simply renames predicates to guarantee unique bindings; it has no effect on the running time.[9] Thus, P_2 is no slower than P_1. □

Limitations of the Magic-Sets Transformation

There are some logic programs and query goals, not covered by Theorem 13.2, for which Algorithm 13.1 transforms the rules into a set that are as efficient, or more so, than the originals. For instance, the "goodList" rules of Example 13.2 are not subgoal-rectified datalog, yet the conclusion of Theorem 13.2 holds for these rules as well. However, there are datalog programs without the subgoal-rectified property, for which semi-naive evaluation of the "magic" rules (not

---

[9] Note that Algorithm 12.7 does no reordering of subgoals. If we were able to reorder subgoals while constructing P_2, then P_2 could run faster or slower than P_1. However, reordering of subgoals presumably improves the speed on the average.

preceded by the rectification algorithm) is much slower than QRGT on the original rules. There are also examples of non-datalog rules where, during QRGT, the binding pattern of every goal node for an IDB predicate p is the same, and equals the binding pattern of p in the rule/goal graph, yet again, semi-naive evaluation of the "magic" rules is less efficient than QRGT on the original rules. We illustrate these points in the next two examples.

Example 13.4: Consider the rules

r_1:   p(X,Y,W) :- a(X,Y,W).
r_2:   p(X,Y,W) :- b(W,Y,Z) & p(X,X,Z).

These rules are similar to the rules of Example 12.32, and their rule/goal graph, respecting the given order of subgoals, is shown in Figure 13.6. Note that ffb is the unique binding pattern for p, if we start with a query of that binding pattern.

Let us suppose that the EDB consists of the two tuples $\{(1,2,3), (3,4,5)\}$ in the relation for b, and a large number of tuples of the form $(m,n,5)$, where m and n are not both 4, in the relation for a. Further, let the query goal be $p(X,Y,1)$. Figure 13.7 shows the rule/goal tree expanded out as far as it goes with this query goal. For convenience, we have replaced variables that are bound to singletons by those singletons. For example, the goal node $p(X,X,3)$ is really $p(X,X,Z_1)$, with Z_1 bound to $\{3\}$.

Evidently, each of the a goal nodes in Figure 13.7 fails to find any matches in the EDB relation for a. That is, goals $a(X,Y,1)$ and $a(X,X,3)$ match nothing, because the last component is 5 in all tuples for a, and $a(4,4,5)$ matches nothing because we ruled out the possibility that the first two components of an a-tuple are both 4. More importantly, the subgoal $b(5,4,Z_3)$ in the lower-right corner finds no matches in the EDB relation for b. Thus, $\emptyset$ is passed sideways as the binding for Z_3, whereupon the subgoal $p(4,4,Z_3)$, shown as $p(4,4,\emptyset)$, is known to return the empty set, and the rule/goal tree exploration ceases.

Now, let us consider the magic rules constructed by Algorithm 13.1, which are shown in Figure 13.8. With the same EDB, the relations for predicates m_p, $sup_{1.0}$ and $sup_{2.0}$ each contain the unary tuples 1, 3, and 5; to see why, start with rule (7) and apply rules (3), (4), and (1), in round-robin fashion. Then, by rule (5), all the tuples in the relation for a are added to the relation for p. Since the number of tuples for a of the form $(m,n,5)$ can be as large as we like, we see that the time to evaluate the magic rules is arbitrarily greater than the time to evaluate the original rules by the QRGT algorithm. $\square$

Example 13.5: The next example bears substantial resemblance to Example 13.4, but here we exploit function symbols to cause the rule/goal tree to terminate with no answer tuples discovered, while the magic rules produce many irrelevant tuples. The significant property that these rules have, but the rules of Example 13.4 do not, is that here, the binding pattern at each IDB goal node

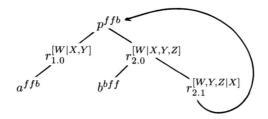

Figure 13.6 Rule/goal graph for rules of Example 13.4.

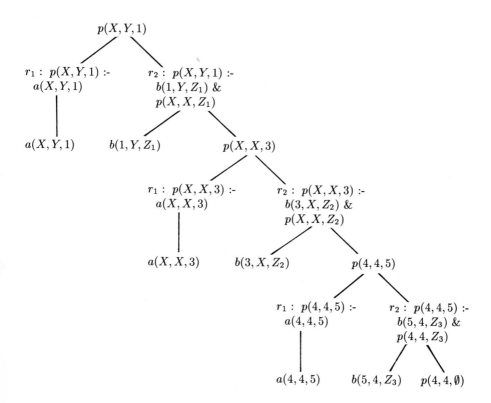

Figure 13.7 Rule/goal tree for rules of Example 13.4.

in the rule/goal tree is the same, p^{bf} in particular. (Note that in Example 13.4 we saw the binding pattern bbb, as well as ffb.) The rules are

r_1: p(X,Y) :- a(X,Y).
r_2: p(X,Y) :- b(X,Z) & p(Z,f(Y)).

Group I

(1) $m\_p(Z)$:- $\sup_{2.1}(W,Y,Z)$.

Group II

(2) $\sup_{1.0}(W)$:- $m\_p(W)$.
(3) $\sup_{2.0}(W)$:- $m\_p(W)$.

Group III

(4) $\sup_{2.1}(W,Y,Z)$:- $\sup_{2.0}(W)$ & $b(W,Y,Z)$.

Group IV

(5) $p(X,Y,W)$:- $\sup_{1.0}(W)$ & $a(X,Y,W)$.
(6) $p(X,Y,W)$:- $\sup_{2.1}(W,Y,Z)$ & $p(X,X,Z)$.

Group V

(7) $m\_p(1)$.

Figure 13.8 Magic rules for Example 13.4.

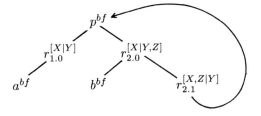

Figure 13.9 Rule/goal graph for rules of Example 13.5.

and their rule/goal graph is shown in Figure 13.9.

Let us suppose that the EDB relation for b is $\{(1,2)\}$, while the relation for a consists of many tuples of the form $(2,n)$. Here, we assume n is an integer; in particular, n does not match any term of the form $f(X)$ for any X. The rule/goal tree for query goal $p(1,Y)$ is shown in Figure 13.10. As in Figure 13.7, we show goals with arguments bound to singletons as if that argument were the element of the singleton set, and we show the argument bound to the empty set as $\emptyset$. The rule/goal tree terminates as shown, because the goal $b(2,Z_2)$ returns the empty set for Z_2, which tells us that the goal $p(Z_2, f(f(Y)))$ cannot produce any tuples. Note especially that goal node $a\big(2, f(Y)\big)$ does not match any of the tuples $(2,n)$ in the relation for a, because no constant n can match

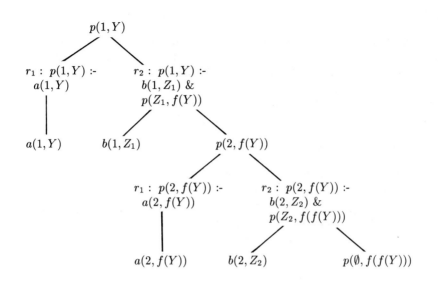

Figure 13.10 Rule/goal tree for rules of Example 13.5.

Group I

(1)   m_p(Z) :- sup$_{2.1}$(X,Z).

Group II

(2)   sup$_{1.0}$(X) :- m_p(X).
(3)   sup$_{2.0}$(X) :- m_p(X).

Group III

(4)   sup$_{2.1}$(X,Z) :- sup$_{2.0}$(X) & b(X,Z).

Group IV

(5)   p(X,Y) :- sup$_{1.0}$(X) & a(X,Y).
(6)   p(X,Y) :- sup$_{2.1}$(X,Z) & p(Z,f(Y)).

Group V

(7)   m_p(1).

Figure 13.11 Magic rules for Example 13.5.

a term of the form $f(Y)$.

However, as in the previous example, the magic rules produce many tuples for the relation p; all the a-tuples become p-tuples eventually. The magic rules are shown in Figure 13.11, and the reader can check that the unary tuples 1 and 2 are placed in the relations for m_p, $sup_{1.0}$ and $sup_{2.0}$, resulting in all the tuples of the EDB relation for a, which are of the form $(2, n)$, being placed in the relation for p during semi-naive evaluation. $\square$

13.4 SIMPLIFICATION OF MAGIC-SET RULES

We can eliminate any IDB predicate p that does not appear as a subgoal of one of its own rules by the steps shown in Figure 13.12. Informally, we substitute, for each subgoal with predicate p, the body of each of the rules for p, after unifying the rule head with the subgoal.

```
for each occurrence of p in a subgoal G of some
    rule s do begin
      for each rule r with head predicate p do begin
          rename the variables of r so r shares
            no variable with s;
          let τ be the most general unifier of the
            head of r and the subgoal G;
          create a new rule s_r by taking τ(s) and replacing
            the subgoal τ(G) by the body of τ(r)
      end;
      delete rule s;
    end;
    delete the rules with p at the head
```

Figure 13.12 Elimination of predicate p.

Example 13.6: Suppose p has two rules

    r_1: p(f(X),Y) :- t(X,Y).
    r_2: p(X,a) :- u(X) & v(X).

Also suppose for simplicity that there is only one use of p, that in the rule

    r_3: q(X,Y) :- p(X,Z) & s(Z,Y).

We begin by rewriting r_1 and r_2 so they share no variables with r_3; they become

    r_1: p(f(U),V) :- t(U,V).
    r_2: p(U,a) :- u(U) & v(U).

Now, we unify the head of r_1 with the subgoal $p(X, Z)$, which gives us the MGU $\tau(X) = f(U)$, $\tau(Z) = \tau(V) = V$, and $\tau(U) = U$. For Y, which is not involved in the unification, we must assume $\tau(Y) = Y$. Then r_3 becomes

```
τ(r₃):   q(f(U),Y)  :-  p(f(U),V) & s(V,Y).
```

and $\tau(r_1)$ is

```
p(f(U),V)  :-  t(U,V).
```

When we substitute the body of $\tau(r_1)$ for the subgoal $p\big(f(U), V\big)$ in $\tau(r_3)$, we get the new rule

```
r₄:   q(f(U),Y)  :-  t(U,V) & s(V,Y).
```

One might wonder whether r_4 is less general than r_3, since r_4 only applies if the first argument of q is of the form $f(U)$ for some U, while r_3 has no such restriction. Indeed, r_4 is less general. However, r_4 reflects the condition that must hold if r_3 is applied to some goal, and then r_1 is applied to the p subgoal of r_3. For q-goals that do not match the head of r_4, the only way to expand them by QRGT (using the original rules) is for r_3 to be followed by r_2, a case that we consider next.

When we unify the head of r_2 with the p-subgoal of r_3, we get the MGU $\rho(X) = \rho(U) = U$, and $\rho(Z) = a$. We may extend ρ to Y by taking $\rho(Y) = Y$. Then, substituting the body of $\rho(r_2)$ for the p-subgoal in $\rho(r_3)$, we get

```
r₅:   q(U,Y)  :-  u(U) & v(U) & s(a,Y).
```

Finally, we discard r_1, r_2, and r_3, leaving the equivalent pair of rules, r_4 and r_5. $\square$

Theorem 13.3: The transformation of Figure 13.12 does not change the relation computed for any of the predicates that remain after transformation.

Proof: We shall leave the details of this proof as an exercise. The key idea is to look at the rule/goal trees produced for some query, using both the old rules and the new. We may transform the rule/goal tree for the old rules into one using the new rules, as follows. In the tree for the old rules, each time we have a goal node N with predicate p, we combine N's rule-node children with N's rule-node parent; that is, we combine two levels of rule nodes into one, making the appropriate substitution indicated by the algorithm in Figure 13.12.[10] The effect is that in the revised tree, rules from the new set have replaced the corresponding rules from the old set, as suggested in Figure 13.13. If we make this change everywhere a goal node with predicate p appears, we shall create a tree using the new rules, which produces the same relation at each of its nodes as was produced at the corresponding node of the old tree. $\square$

---

[10] Note that p is assumed not to appear as a subgoal in its own rules.

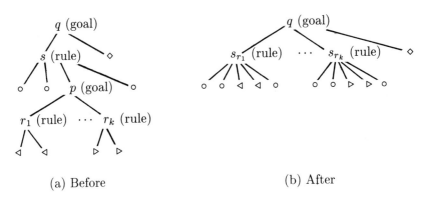

(a) Before   (b) After

Figure 13.13 Transformation to eliminate predicate p.

Predicate Elimination Applied to the Magic-Set Rules

Ordinarily, the transformation of Figure 13.12 causes extra work; there is an increase in the number of rules, and the rules get longer. However, in two situations it makes sense to eliminate a predicate p. As before, we assume that p does not appear as a subgoal of its own rules. It is then advantageous to eliminate p whenever

1. p has only one rule, and p appears in only one subgoal, or
2. p has only one rule, and its body has only one subgoal; p may appear as a subgoal any number of times.

Let us consider when these conditions apply to the predicates and rules generated by the magic-sets algorithm. First, each zeroth supplementary predicate has only one rule, in Group II, and its body has length one. Thus, case (1) always applies to a zeroth supplementary predicate, and we can eliminate them by substituting the appropriate magic predicate for the zeroth supplementary predicate in a rule of Group III or IV.

The other supplementary predicates also have only one rule, but these rules, in Group III, have bodies of length two. Thus, only (2) could apply. If the jth subgoal of rule r_i is an IDB subgoal with predicate p, then there will be two uses of $sup_{i.j-1}$: once in a rule of Group I for the magic predicate m_p, and the other in Group III or IV, when $sup_{i.j-1}$ is used to compute either $sup_{i.j}$ or the head of r_i. If the jth subgoal is EDB, then the use of $sup_{i.j-1}$ in Group I is missing. Thus, we can eliminate each supplementary predicate that corresponds to a point just before an EDB subgoal.

There are often other opportunities to apply (1) or (2). For example, a magic predicate may have only one rule (don't forget to count the Group V rule, however). All rules for magic predicates in Group I have bodies consisting of a single subgoal with a supplementary predicate, so (2) applies if the magic predicate has a single rule.

Example 13.7: Let us consider the magic rules of Figure 13.1 (Section 13.1) for the same-generation rules. These rules are repeated in Figure 13.14, for convenience.

(1)   m_sg(Xp) :- sup$_{2.1}$(X,Xp).
(2)   sup$_{1.0}$(X) :- m_sg(X).
(3)   sup$_{2.0}$(X) :- m_sg(X).
(4)   sup$_{2.1}$(X,Xp) :- sup$_{2.0}$(X) & par(X,Xp).
(5)   sup$_{2.2}$(X,Yp) :- sup$_{2.1}$(X,Xp) & sg(Xp,Yp).
(6)   sg(X,X) :- sup$_{1.0}$(X) & person(X).
(7)   sg(X,Y) :- sup$_{2.2}$(X,Yp) & par(Y,Yp).
(8)   m_sg(a).

Figure 13.14 Magic-sets transformation of same-generation rules.

We begin by eliminating the zeroth supplementary predicates, which are defined by rules (2) and (3). We substitute $m\_sg(X)$ for $sup_{1.0}(X)$ and $sup_{2.0}(X)$ in rules (4) and (6), so the latter become

(4)   sup$_{2.1}$(X,Xp) :- m_sg(X) & par(X,Xp).
(6)   sg(X,X) :- m_sg(X) & person(X).

Rules (2) and (3) can then be eliminated.

Notice that in Figure 13.14, all occurrences of a predicate have exactly the same arguments, so it appears as if no renaming of variables, as required in the algorithm of Figure 13.12, has been done when we constructed the new rules (4) and (6). However, strictly speaking, the new rules (4) and (6) were derived by following the algorithm of Figure 13.12 exactly.

We may eliminate the predicate $sup_{2.2}$, which is defined by rule (5), if we substitute the body of (5) in rule (7). The remaining five rules are shown in Figure 13.15. Note that further applications of the algorithm of Figure 13.12 are legal, but would make the program slower. For example, we could eliminate $sup_{2.1}$ if we substituted the body of rule (4) in rules (1) and the rewritten (7). However, we would now interrogate the EDB relation for par twice for each value of X that appears in the magic predicate $m\_sg(X)$. □

Example 13.8: A similar sequence of transformations applies to the "good list" rules of Example 13.2 (See Figure 13.3). The resulting set of five rules is shown in Figure 13.16.

We may also perform a similar sequence of steps on the "paths" rules of Example 13.3. However, we should note that rules (1) and (6) define the predi-

```
(8)     m_sg(a).
(1)     m_sg(Xp) :- sup_{2.1}(X,Xp).

(4)     sup_{2.1}(X,Xp) :- m_sg(X) & par(X,Xp).

(6)     sg(X,X) :- m_sg(X) & person(X).
(7)     sg(X,Y) :- sup_{2.1}(X,Xp) & sg(Xp,Yp) & par(Y,Yp).
```

Figure 13.15 Improved magic rules for same-generation.

```
(7)     m_gl($l_0$).
(1)     m_gl(T) :- sup_{2.1}(H,T).

(4)     sup_{2.1}(H,T) :- m_gl(cons(H,T)) & g(H).

(5)     gl(nil) :- m_gl(nil).
(6)     gl(cons(H,T)) :- sup_{2.1}(H,T) & gl(T).
```

Figure 13.16 Simplified "good list" rules.

cates m_p and $sup_{2.0}$ to be identical. When we eliminate $sup_{2.0}$ by substituting the body of rule (6) into rule (1), the latter rule becomes

```
    m_p(X) :- m_p(X).
```

Such a rule evidently serves no purpose, and we may eliminate it. The final set of rules is shown in Figure 13.17. □

```
(9)     m_p($x_0$).
(2)     m_p(Z) :- sup_{2.1}(X,Z,E).

(5)     sup_{2.1}(X,Z,E) :- m_p(X) & p(X,Z,E).

(7)     p(X,Y,D) :- m_p(X) & a(X,Y,D).
(8)     p(X,Y,D) :- sup_{2.1}(X,Z,E) & p(Z,Y,F) & s(D,E,F).
```

Figure 13.17 Simplified "paths" rules.

Direct Generation of the Simplified Rules

The following useful observation can be made about the transformations discussed above. Suppose we have a rule r with subgoals $G_1, \ldots, G_n$. Let $G_{i+1}, \ldots, G_j$ be EDB subgoals; G_i may be either an EDB or an IDB subgoal. Then it is possible to rewrite the rules to eliminate the supplementary predicates $sup_{r.i}, \ldots, sup_{r.j-1}$ and develop the rule

$$A \text{ :- } B \text{ \& } G_i \text{ \& } \cdots \text{ \& } G_j. \tag{13.4}$$

where A is either

1. An atomic formula with predicate $sup_{r.j}$, if $j < n$, or
2. The head of rule r, if $j = n$.

B is an atomic formula with either predicate $sup_{r.i-1}$, or with a magic predicate that has been substituted for that supplementary predicate. We leave the proof of this observation as an exercise.

Should we make this transformation, it is important that the rule (13.4) be evaluated from left-to-right. The reason is that we want to look up only a restricted subset of the EDB predicates' relations, for the subgoals $G_{i+1}, \ldots, G_j$. That restriction must be obtained for G_k from the join of the relations for B and $G_i, \ldots, G_{k-1}$.

Normally, we prefer to generate as few rules as possible. If that is the case, we should group subgoals as in (13.4) whenever we can. That is, G_i should only be the first subgoal, G_1, or an IDB subgoal in (13.4). As a result, all EDB subgoals get grouped either with the first IDB subgoal to their left, or with the first subgoal, if that subgoal has an EDB predicate.

13.5 PASSING BINDINGS THROUGH VARIABLES ONLY

Recall from our discussion in Section 12.6, especially Example 12.23, that when there are function symbols, we can lose information by converting supplementary predicates to magic predicates and then back to zeroth supplementary predicates of other rules. The motivation for doing so anyway is that fewer rules are generated if we follow Algorithm 13.1, than if we avoid using the magic predicates. Let us briefly discuss the modifications to Algorithm 13.1 that are needed if we go directly between supplementary predicates, rather than using the magic predicates.

First, we must revise the notion of a rule/goal graph to avoid the IDB goal nodes altogether. If a rule r's ith subgoal has an IDB predicate p, then the rule node r_{i-1} has successor r_i as usual, but also has a successor s_0 for each rule s whose head predicate is p. Successor s_0 has whatever bound variables can be deduced by binding the variables that r_{i-1} says are bound, unifying the ith subgoal of r with the head of s, and making bound for s_0 any variable that unifies with a term all of whose variables are bound by r_{i-1}. The details were covered in Section 12.6.

There is one exception to the avoidance of goal nodes for the IDB predicates. If p is the query predicate, then we need a goal node p^α, where α is the appropriate adornment. This adornment determines the bound variables for the rule nodes s_0 that are added to the rule/goal graph initially; here, s ranges over all rules with head predicate p. Nodes representing other sets of bound variables, for these or other rules, are added to the rule/goal graph on demand, as in the usual construction described in Section 12.8.

Now, when we generate the magic rules, we define $sup_{s.0}$ directly in terms of $sup_{r.i-1}$. The necessary rule is constructed thusly. After renaming variables of s, if necessary, unify the ith subgoal of r, say $p(t_1, \ldots, t_k)$, with the head of rule s, say $p(u_1, \ldots, u_k)$, and let τ be the MGU. Then determine the bound variables for the head as described at the end of Section 12.6. That is, we know

1. The variables $X_1, \ldots, X_n$ that are bound by (are arguments of) $sup_{r.i-1}$ are bound.
2. If $\tau(Y)$ contains X, and Y is bound, then X is bound.
3. If all variables appearing in $\tau(X)$ are bound, then X is bound.

Let $Y_1, \ldots, Y_m$ be the variables of the head of s that are determined to be bound if we apply this process until all bound variables are found. Then we generate the rule

$$sup_{s.0}\big(\tau(Y_1), \ldots, \tau(Y_m)\big) \text{ :- } sup_{r.i-1}\big(\tau(X_1), \ldots \tau(X_n)\big).$$

Finally, we must replace the Group V rule that initializes the magic set for the query predicate, since this magic predicate will no longer be present. If the query predicate is p, we term-match the head of each rule r for p with the query. Thus, we obtain a tuple μ of bindings for the variables that are arguments of $sup_{r.0}$, and we generate the bodyless rule

$$\text{sup}_{r.0}(\mu).$$

for each rule r.

Example 13.9: Let us reconsider the same-generation rules of Example 13.1, with the query goal sg^{bf}. As these are datalog rules, the passing of bindings is no different from what was discovered in Example 12.30 (Section 12.8). However, the rule/goal graph, shown in Figure 13.18, differs from the "standard" rule/goal graph, which was given in Figure 12.23, in that the successors of rule node $r_{2.1}$ are now rule nodes $r_{1.0}$ and $r_{2.0}$, instead of the goal node sg^{bf}; $r_{2.2}$ remains a successor of $r_{2.1}$.

When we generate the magic-set rules the Group I rules are eliminated. The Group II rules define the zeroth supplementary predicates in terms of other supplementary predicates, rather than magic predicates. Groups III and IV are unchanged, and Group V now has one basis rule for each of the sg rules. These rules are shown in Figure 13.19. □

Example 13.10: Now, let us consider part of a more complicated example based on Example 12.24. Let the ith subgoal of rule r be

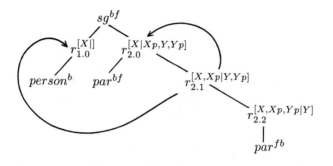

Figure 13.18 New form of rule/goal graph.

Group II

(1) $\mathrm{sup}_{1.0}(X)$:- $\mathrm{sup}_{2.1}(X,Xp)$.
(2) $\mathrm{sup}_{2.0}(X)$:- $\mathrm{sup}_{2.1}(X,Xp)$.

Group III

(3) $\mathrm{sup}_{2.1}(X,Xp)$:- $\mathrm{sup}_{2.0}(X)$ & $\mathrm{par}(X,Xp)$.
(4) $\mathrm{sup}_{2.2}(X,Yp)$:- $\mathrm{sup}_{2.1}(X,Xp)$ & $\mathrm{sg}(Xp,Yp)$.

Group IV

(5) $\mathrm{sg}(X,X)$:- $\mathrm{sup}_{1.0}(X)$ & $\mathrm{person}(X)$.
(6) $\mathrm{sg}(X,Y)$:- $\mathrm{sup}_{2.2}(X,Yp)$ & $\mathrm{par}(Y,Yp)$.

Group V

(7) $\mathrm{sup}_{1.0}(a)$.
(8) $\mathrm{sup}_{2.0}(a)$.

Figure 13.19 Magic-set rules with bindings passed from rules to rules.

$$p\Big(f\big(X,g(X)\big),\ g\big(g(Y)\big)\Big)$$

and let the head of rule s be

$$p\Big(f\big(g(U),V\big),\ g(V)\Big)$$

As in Example 12.24, let us suppose that Y is an argument of $sup_{r.i-1}$, and X is not. In the MGU, from Examples 12.13 and 12.24, we have $\tau(X) = \tau(Y) = g(U)$, $\tau(U) = U$, and $\tau(V) = g\big(g(U)\big)$. Thus, the rule defining the bindings of

U and V in terms of the binding for Y is

$$\text{sup}_{s.0}(\text{U},\text{g}(\text{g}(\text{U}))) \ :- \ \text{sup}_{r.i-1}(\text{g}(\text{U})). \tag{13.5}$$

Note that even though V is not mentioned in (13.5), it receives a value, which is given by the second argument of $sup_{s.0}$. Intuitively, (13.5) says that for each value assumed by Y, if it is not of the form $g(t)$, then unification of the head of s with the ith subgoal of r yields no tuple for the head. If Y is $g(t)$ for some ground term t, then U becomes t, and V becomes $g\big(g(t)\big)$. $\square$

Let us again observe that this modification to Algorithm 13.1 offers the advantage that it may, with rules that have function symbols, provide some additional bound arguments beyond what Algorithm 13.1 itself can provide. The disadvantage is that the modified method can produce approximately the square of the number of rules produced by Algorithm 13.1 itself. That is, for each subgoal, say the ith subgoal of rule r, Algorithm 13.1 produces one Group I rule that defines the magic predicate for p (the predicate of r's ith subgoal) in terms of $sup_{r.i-1}$. That algorithm also produces one rule of Group II for each of p's original rules; those rules define the zeroth supplementary predicates of the rules for p in terms of m_p. Thus, the total number of Group I and II rules equals the number of IDB subgoals plus the number of rules.

In comparison, if we go directly from each supplementary predicate, such as $sup_{r.i-1}$ in Example 13.10, to each of the zeroth supplementary predicates for the rules of p, then the number of rules we generate is the sum, over all the IDB subgoals in all the rules, of the number of rules that the predicate for that subgoal has. In the extreme but common case, where there is one IDB predicate p with n rules, and the average rule has one IDB subgoal, then Algorithm 13.1 generates n Group I rules for m_p and n Group II rules. In comparison, the modified algorithm generates n rules for each IDB subgoal, or n^2 rules.

13.6 GENERALIZED MAGIC SETS

When rules are not subgoal-rectified datalog, we saw in Examples 13.4 and 13.5 (Section 13.3) that the magic-sets rules may not be efficiently evaluatable bottom-up. If we examine these examples, we see two problems. In Example 13.4, we saw that computing the bindings for the third argument of p did not tell the full story. The top-down exploration of Figure 13.7 shows how it is possible to deduce more than a binding for the third argument. The rightmost grandchild of the root, the goal node $p(X, X, 3)$, tells us not only a binding for the third argument; it also tells us that the first two arguments are equal, although we do not know either. When we follow the rightmost path in the tree for two more levels, we come to goal node $p(4, 4, 5)$, and here we see that the equality between arguments deduced two levels earlier has led to actual binding of the first and second arguments.

The weakness of the magic-sets technique is that, while it records bindings for bound arguments, it doesn't record other useful relationships, such as the equality of two arguments. Example 13.5 illustrates another important relationship not represented by magic sets—the structure of terms as arguments. That is, the rightmost grandchild of the root in Figure 13.10 has a subgoal $p(2, f(Y))$, which, while it doesn't bind the second argument, imparts to it a special structure. That structure, which is also ignored by magic sets, is important when we reach the leaf $a(2, f(Y))$, because it enables us to rule out all of the tuples in the EDB relation for a that have a second component not of the form $f(Y)$.

Suppose we regard the magic predicate m_p as having arguments corresponding to all of the arguments of p. We can then let the tuples in m_p correspond to a goal node in the rule/goal tree, together with one possible binding found in the binding set for that goal node. Tuples of this nature carry all the information that the goal nodes and binding relations carry during QRGT execution. The only problem is that these "tuples" are of a kind we have never seen before; they may have variables appearing as components or parts of components.

Example 13.11: Consider the predicate p of Example 13.4. The magic predicate m_p, like p, has three arguments. The query, $p(X, Y, 1)$, yields the tuple $(X, Y, 1)$ for the relation corresponding to m_p. Recall that in the magic rules of Figure 13.8, m_p has only one component, corresponding to the third component of p, and the initial tuple in m_p is just 1. In practice, there is little difference between a tuple of constants and the same tuple padded out in other attributes with distinct variables. However, the bindings for other p-nodes in the rule/goal tree of Figure 13.7 provide tuples that are not related so simply to the tuples that are placed in m_p by the magic rules of Figure 13.8.

When we pass bindings for Z_1 sideways at the second level of goal nodes, we get only the binding $Z_1 = 3$ for the goal node $p(X, X, Z_1)$. That yields the tuple $(X, X, 3)$ for the relation of m_p, which is not the same as the tuple 3 found by the rules of Figure 13.8, because the dual occurrence of X tells us more than that the third component is 3. Note also that if the EDB predicate b bound Z_1 to a set of several values, rather than to the singleton $\{3\}$, there would be a tuple (X, X, i) in m_p for each value i provided for Z_1.

Finally, at the third level of goal nodes, we pass the binding $Z_2 = 5$ to the goal node $p(X, X, Z_2)$, which yields the tuple $(4, 4, 5)$ for m_p. Lower levels of the rule/goal tree pass the empty set of bindings to the p-subgoals, so there are no more tuples for m_p. Thus,

$$m\_p = \{(X, Y, 1), (X, X, 3), (4, 4, 5)\}$$

should be the complete relation for m_p. $\square$

We also need to modify our notion of a supplementary predicate, so their relations can carry information other than bound values for variables. Since the magic predicates now have components for all arguments of the head, we need to consider all variables appearing in the head as "bound," even though the "binding" may be to another variable appearing in a tuple of the magic predicate's relation. The extra information carried by the supplementary relations is the same as the information carried by a particular rule instance in the rule/goal tree. These modifications to the magic and supplementary predicates, together with the modifications to the rules described below, will be called the *generalized magic-sets* construction.

Example 13.12: For the rules of Example 13.4,

$$r_1: \quad \text{p(X,Y,W)} \ :- \ \text{a(X,Y,W)}.$$
$$r_2: \quad \text{p(X,Y,W)} \ :- \ \text{b(W,Y,Z)} \ \& \ \text{p(X,X,Z)}.$$

If we follow Algorithm 13.1, with query p^{ffb}, the predicate $sup_{2.1}$ has only arguments W, Y, and Z in the rules of Figure 13.8, and these provide a binding for only the third argument of p. In the generalized magic-sets technique, we include X among the attributes of $sup_{2.1}$, simply because X appears in the head of r_2. $\square$

Modification of the Magic-Set Rules

To construct the generalized magic-set rules, we make the following modifications to Algorithm 13.1. First, as mentioned, the magic predicate m_p now has arguments identical to those of IDB predicate p itself. The supplementary predicate $sup_{r.i}$ has arguments corresponding to all variables that appear in the head of rule r and all variables that appear in any of the first $i-1$ subgoals of r and also appear in any of the ith and subsequent subgoals. The changes to the rules themselves are listed by group.

1. Group I rules define the magic predicates. If rule r_j has an IDB subgoal $p(t_1, \ldots, t_n)$ appearing as the ith subgoal, and $X_1, \ldots, X_m$ are the variables that are arguments of $sup_{j.i-1}$, then there is a Group I rule

    $$m\_p(t_1, \ldots, t_n) :- sup_{j.i-1}(X_1, \ldots, X_m).$$

    Note that this rule differs from the rule given by Algorithm 13.1 in that the head is an exact copy of the subgoal, rather than the subgoal restricted to the bound arguments.

2. Group II rules define the zeroth supplementary predicates. If rule r_j has head $p(t_1, \ldots, t_n)$, and $X_1, \ldots, X_m$ are the variables appearing in the head, then there is the Group II rule

    $$sup_{j.0}(X_1, \ldots, X_m) :- m\_p(t_1, \ldots, t_n).$$

Again, the difference is that Algorithm 13.1 restricts this rule to bound arguments and variables, while here we include all arguments and variables.

3. There is no change to the Group III rules, except that the supplementary predicates may have additional arguments, as indicated above.

4. Likewise, the Group IV rules are changed only by augmenting the set of arguments of the supplementary predicate appearing in the rule.

5. The Group V rule is changed to include all of the arguments in the query, whether free or bound. That is, if the query is $p(t_1, \ldots, t_n)$, then the Group V rule is

$$m\_p(t_1, \ldots, t_n).$$

Note that this rule is not safe, if there are any variables in the query. However, the generalized magic-sets technique deals quite easily with unsafe rules; we simply put variables in tuples. In this case, we put the tuple $(t_1, \ldots, t_n)$ in the relation for m_p. In situations where the rules defining the answer are unsafe, we shall find nonground tuples in the answer relations.

Example 13.13: Let us consider the rules of Example 13.4,

r_1: p(X,Y,W) :- a(X,Y,W).
r_2: p(X,Y,W) :- b(W,Y,Z) & p(X,X,Z).

with the query $p(X, Y, 1)$. The generalized magic-set rules are shown in Figure 13.20. These rules should be compared with Figure 13.8. Notice, for example, that X has been added as an argument of $sup_{2.1}$. The predicate m_p now has three arguments, and in rule (1), the arguments of m_p are a copy of the arguments of the p-subgoal in r_2. □

Example 13.14: Now consider the rules from Example 13.5,

r_1: p(X,Y) :- a(X,Y).
r_2: p(X,Y) :- b(X,Z) & p(Z,f(Y)).

with query $p(1, Y)$. The rules constructed by the generalized magic-set algorithm are shown in Figure 13.21. These should be compared with the rules of Figure 13.11. □

Evaluating the Generalized Magic-Set Rules

When we apply one of the bottom-up algorithms, naive or semi-naive evaluation, to the generalized magic rules, we must be prepared to deal with variables and nontrivial terms in tuples. The easy part is computing relations for the head of a rule from the relation for the body. Recall the relation for the body is a relation over all variables in the rule; it is constructed for ground tuples by Algorithm 12.2. We may perform the same VTOA construction to evaluate the relation

Group I

(1)   m_p(X,X,Z) :- sup$_{2.1}$(W,X,Y,Z).

Group II

(2)   sup$_{1.0}$(X,Y,W) :- m_p(X,Y,W).
(3)   sup$_{2.0}$(X,Y,W) :- m_p(X,Y,W).

Group III

(4)   sup$_{2.1}$(W,X,Y,Z) :- sup$_{2.0}$(X,Y,W) & b(W,Y,Z).

Group IV

(5)   p(X,Y,W) :- sup$_{1.0}$(X,Y,W) & a(X,Y,W).
(6)   p(X,Y,W) :- sup$_{2.1}$(W,X,Y,Z) & p(X,X,Z).

Group V

(7)   m_p(X,Y,1).

Figure 13.20 Generalized magic rules for Example 13.13.

for the head that we did in Section 12.2 (bottom-up evaluation), realizing that variables in tuples of the body's relation are treated like constants when we perform VTOA. In fact, we can even allow rules to be unsafe. If a variable X appears in the head, but nowhere else, we simply leave it as a variable when constructing the relation for the head.

Example 13.15: Suppose the head of our rule is $p(X, f(Y))$, and the relation for the body of this rule is

X	Y	Z
a	B	c
$g(A)$	A	d

Note that here, and elsewhere in this section, we adopt the convention that variables of rules are represented by letters near the end of the alphabet, while variables in tuples are represented by letters near the beginning of the alphabet.

For the first tuple, (a, B, c), we substitute a for X and B for Y to obtain the tuple $(a, f(B))$ for the head relation. For the second tuple, we substitute $g(A)$ for X and A for Y, yielding the head tuple $(g(A), f(A))$. $\square$

The more difficult part is constructing the relation for the body of a rule by "joining" tuples that have variables. We shall explain the algorithm for the case of two subgoals; the generalization will then be obvious. Suppose the subgoals

Group I

(1)   m_p(Z,f(Y)) :- sup$_{2.1}$(X,Y,Z).

Group II

(2)   sup$_{1.0}$(X,Y) :- m_p(X,Y).
(3)   sup$_{2.0}$(X,Y) :- m_p(X,Y).

Group III

(4)   sup$_{2.1}$(X,Y,Z) :- sup$_{2.0}$(X,Y) & b(X,Z).

Group IV

(5)   p(X,Y) :- sup$_{1.0}$(X,Y) & a(X,Y).
(6)   p(X,Y) :- sup$_{2.1}$(X,Y,Z) & p(Z,f(Y)).

Group V

(7)   m_p(1,Y).

Figure 13.21 Generalized magic rules for Example 13.14.

are $p(t_1,\ldots,t_n)$ and $q(s_1,\ldots,s_m)$, and suppose the relations for p and q have tuples $(u_1,\ldots,u_n)$ and $(v_1,\ldots,v_m)$, respectively. The situation is suggested by Figure 13.22. We may assume that the variables of tuple $(u_1,\ldots,u_n)$ do not appear in $(v_1,\ldots,v_m)$ or in either subgoal, and similarly for the other tuple. That is, the only sharing of variables occurs between the two subgoals.

Subgoals $p(t_1,\ldots,t_n)$ & $q(s_1,\ldots,s_m)$
Tuples $(u_1,\ldots,u_n)$ $(v_1,\ldots,v_m)$

Figure 13.22 Subgoals and tuples.

Intuitively, a tuple with variables represents all ground tuples that could be created by substituting ground terms for the variables. However, not all ground tuples so created necessarily will match the corresponding subgoal. To tell which ground tuples will match, we unify the tuple μ with the subgoal, because the MGU τ thus created represents the minimal constraints necessary to assure that a substitution for the tuple $\tau(\mu)$ will match the subgoal.

However, it is not sufficient that the tuples are unified with their corresponding subgoals, because the subgoals generally share variables, and we must be sure that the substitution for a variable X, as we unify both tuples with their corresponding tuples, is consistent. Therefore, we must unify both subgoals with a pair of their corresponding tuples simultaneously. That is, we choose a "dummy" predicate name d, and create atom

$$d(t_1, \ldots, t_n, s_1, \ldots, s_m)$$

from the subgoals of Figure 13.22 and atom

$$d(u_1, \ldots, u_n, v_1, \ldots, v_m)$$

from the tuples of Figure 13.22. We then unify these atoms. If the unification is unsuccessful, then this pair of tuples yields nothing for the relation of the body. If there is an MGU τ, then the tuple $(\tau(X_1), \ldots, \tau(X_k))$ is added to the relation for the body, where $X_1, \ldots, X_k$ are all of the variables appearing in either subgoal.

The relation for the rule body is the set of all tuples so constructed, as we pair the tuples from the relation for one subgoal with the tuples in the relation for the other subgoal, in all possible ways. The resulting relation is called the *unification join* of the relations for the subgoals.

Example 13.16: Let us follow the bottom-up evaluation of the magic rules generated in Example 13.13. First, note that we can simplify the rules as we did in Section 13.4; the resulting rules are shown in Figure 13.23.

(7)   `m_p(X,Y,1).`

(1)   `m_p(X,X,Z) :- sup`$_{2.1}$`(W,X,Y,Z).`

(4)   `sup`$_{2.1}$`(W,X,Y,Z) :- m_p(X,Y,W) & b(W,Y,Z).`

(5)   `p(X,Y,W) :- m_p(X,Y,W) & a(X,Y,W).`

(6)   `p(X,Y,W) :- sup`$_{2.1}$`(W,X,Y,Z) & p(X,X,Z).`

Figure 13.23 Simplified magic rules for Example 13.16.

Figure 13.24 shows the EDB relations A and B for predicates a and b, respectively, that we assumed in Example 13.4. That is, B contains two particular tuples, and A consists of a large number of tuples, each with third component 5 and first two components not both equal to 4.

Let us simulate bottom-up evaluation, computing relations M for predicate m_p, P for p, and S for $sup_{2.1}$. On the first round, only rule (7) generates any tuples. Note that the body of rule (7) is empty, so the relation for its body should be regarded as consisting of the empty tuple. That tuple can be padded with components for the variables X and Y, which appear only in the head of this unsafe rule. The lone tuple in the relation for the body is thus

$$\frac{X \quad Y}{A \quad B}$$

Note that we follow the convention of using letters at the beginning of the alphabet for variables in tuples. The particular names used in tuples do not matter; we could have used X and Y, of course.

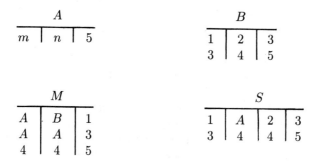

Figure 13.24 Relations used in Example 13.16.

When we translate the tuple (A, B) to the head relation, we get the tuple $(A, B, 1)$ for the relation M, as indicated in Figure 13.24. On the next round, we can use this tuple in rule (4), along with the tuples of the relation B, to create tuples for the relation of the body of rule (4); these tuples have arguments corresponding to variables $WXYZ$.

Let us begin by matching the tuple $(A, B, 1)$ from M with the tuple $(1, 2, 3)$ from B. The dummy atom constructed from the subgoals of rule (4) is

$$d(X, Y, W, W, Y, Z) \tag{13.6}$$

Note that we simply copy the arguments of the two subgoals of rule (4), in the order of appearance. The dummy atom for the tuples is

$$d(A, B, 1, 1, 2, 3)$$

The MGU τ for this atom and (13.6) exists and is

$$\tau(W) = 1 \qquad \tau(X) = \tau(A) = A$$
$$\tau(Y) = \tau(B) = 2 \qquad \tau(Z) = 3$$

Thus, the resulting tuple for the body relation is

$$\frac{W \quad X \quad Y \quad Z}{1 \quad A \quad 2 \quad 3}$$

and this tuple is also a tuple of the head, $sup_{2.1}$, of rule (4), as indicated by the relation S in Figure 13.24.

We now must match tuple $(A, B, 1)$ against the other tuple in the relation for predicate b, which is $(3, 4, 5)$. That is, we must unify (13.6) with the atom

$$d(A, B, 1, 3, 4, 5)$$

Evidently, W cannot match both 1 and 3, so no tuple for the rule is created.

Now we can use the tuple $(1, A, 2, 3)$ for $sup_{2.1}$ in rule (1) to create the tuple $(A, A, 3)$ for m_p. That, in turn, is used in rule (4) to match with the tuple $(3, 4, 5)$ from relation B. We must unify atom (13.6) with the atom

$$d(A, A, 3, 3, 4, 5)$$

and we find that the MGU τ is $\tau(X) = \tau(Y) = \tau(A) = 4$, $\tau(W) = 3$, and $\tau(Z) = 5$. The resulting tuple for $sup_{2.1}$ is $(3, 4, 4, 5)$, and this tuple yields $(4, 4, 5)$ for m_p, by rule (1).

We claim that there are no more tuples deduced. None of the three tuples in M match any of the tuples in relation a. The first two, $(A, B, 1)$ and $(A, A, 3)$, do not match any, because all tuples in relation a have third component 5. The last tuple, $(4, 4, 5)$, cannot match because this tuple was explicitly ruled out of a. Thus, rule (5) yields nothing. Rule (6) cannot yield any tuples as long as P remains empty. Finally, there are no undiscovered matches between the tuples of M and the tuples of relation B, as the reader may check. We conclude that the relation P, and therefore the answer to the query, is empty. $\square$

Example 13.17: A similar sequence of events happens when we execute the rules of Example 13.14 bottom-up. We show the rules in Figure 13.25 with the simplifications of Section 13.4 applied.

```
(7)     m_p(1,Y).
(1)     m_p(Z,f(Y))  :- sup2.1(X,Y,Z).

(4)     sup2.1(X,Y,Z)  :- m_p(X,Y) & b(X,Z).

(5)     p(X,Y)  :- m_p(X,Y) & a(X,Y).
(6)     p(X,Y)  :- sup2.1(X,Y,Z) & p(Z,f(Y)).
```

Figure 13.25 Simplified magic rules for Example 13.17.

Suppose we have the EDB relations of Example 13.14, where the relation for b has only the tuple $(1, 2)$, and the relation for a consists of tuples of the form $(2, n)$, for various values of constant n, none of which are of the form $f(Y)$ for any Y. Let M be the relation for m_p and S the relation for $sup_{2.1}$. Then on round (1) of bottom-up evaluation, we place the tuple $(1, A)$ in M by rule (7). On the second round, we add $(1, A, 2)$ to S by rule (4), and on the third round we add $(2, f(A))$ to M, by rule (1). At that point, none of the rules yield any more tuples, so we conclude that the answer to the query is empty. Notice particularly that in rule (5), neither $(1, A)$ nor $\big(2, f(A)\big)$ unifies with any tuple from a. $\square$

Subsumption

When adding tuples with variables to relations, we must be careful to recognize that two distinct tuples may actually be the same. For instance, in Example 13.16, we added the tuple $(A, A, 3)$ to relation M. If we later tried to add the tuple $(B, B, 3)$ to M, we must realize that these are really the same tuple, with different variable names, and not add the latter tuple. More importantly, if we add the tuple $(B, C, 3)$ to M, we must delete the tuple $(A, A, 3)$, because the former is more general than the latter. That is, $(A, A, 3)$ in M says we are interested in tuples for predicate p where the third component is 3 and the first two components are equal; $(B, C, 3)$ says we are interested in p-tuples with a third component of 3 and any first and second components. Hence, $(A, A, 3)$ will not result in any p-tuples beyond what $(B, C, 3)$ produces, and we may delete $(A, A, 3)$ from M without changing what the rules compute.

We say tuple μ *subsumes* tuple ν if there is some substitution for the variables of μ that turns it into ν. If μ and ν each subsume the other, then they are *equivalent*. Any tuple that is subsumed by another tuple in the same relation may be removed from that relation, and either of two equivalent tuples in the same relation may be removed without changing what the relation represents. That is, if μ is subsumed by ν, then any substitution of ground terms for the variables of μ can be mimicked by a substitution on ν.

Testing for subsumption is easy. To test whether μ subsumes ν, treat each of the variables of ν as a distinct constant, and see whether μ term-matches the resulting tuple. For example, $(B, C, 3)$ subsumes $(A, A, 3)$, because of the substitution $\tau(B) = \tau(C) = A$. However, there is no substitution for A that makes $(A, A, 3)$ become $(B, C, 3)$, so the former does not subsume the latter.

Use of subsumption to eliminate tuples is often essential for efficiency, or even for convergence of the query evaluation. The next example illustrates the point.

Example 13.18: Consider the rules

```
p(X)  :- p(f(X)).
p(X)  :- a(X).
```

Note that, as long as the EDB relation for a is finite, the relation for p will be finite; it consists of all the tuples in a plus those that can be obtained by stripping away the unary function symbol f one or more times. For example, if a has the one-component tuple $f\big(f(1)\big)$, then p has the three tuples $\{1,\ f(1),\ f\big(f(1)\big)\}$.

If we apply the generalized magic-sets algorithm to these rules, with the query $p(X)$, that is, find all p facts, and then simplify according to Section

```
(1)      m_p(X).
(2)      m_p(f(X)) :- m_p(X).
(3)      p(X) :- m_p(X) & p(f(X)).
(4)      p(X) :- m_p(X) & a(X).
```

Figure 13.26 Simplified rules for Example 13.18.

3.4, we get the four rules shown in Figure 13.26. Suppose we do not use subsumption. Rule (1) tells us tuple A, that is, a single component consisting of a variable, is in M, the relation for m_p. Then rule (2) tells us $f(A)$, $f\big(f(A)\big)$, and so on, are in M, and the computation never stops.

However, note that $f(A)$ is subsumed by A, and so is each of the tuples we try to place in M, since A is the most general possible one-component tuple. Thus, we should not add any of these tuples to M; the correct value of M is $\{A\}$, that is, a single tuple, whose lone component is a variable. If we do, then rule (4) simply tells us that anything in a is in p, and rule (3) lets us strip f's off tuples in p to get new tuples in p. This process terminates after a finite time if we start with a finite number of tuples, each with a finite number of f's, as the EDB relation for a. $\square$

Analysis of the Generalized Magic-Set Algorithm

We contend that the rules constructed by the generalized magic-set algorithm are evaluated by semi-naive evaluation in time no worse than proportional to the time taken by QRGT on the original rules. However, to make this claim, we need an assumption that is open to question: as for Theorem 13.2, we must suppose that we can find the tuples in a given relation that match given values in some of their components, in constant time. For the basic magic-sets algorithm, Algorithm 13.1, that assumption was fairly realistic, as "match" meant to have identical constants, and index structures are known to provide close to constant-time performance. However, for the generalized magic-sets algorithm, "match" means "unify," and there is no reason to believe that we can select the tuples that unify with a given tuple quickly. There are certain data structures for "partial-match retrieval" (see Sections 6.12 through 6.14 of Volume I) that can help, and they have even been implemented and shown to offer reasonably good performance for the problem of finding unifying tuples.[11] If we are willing to ignore this retrieval problem, then we can claim the following theorem.

Theorem 13.4: The generalized magic-set rules, executed by semi-naive eval-

---

[11] See the references to the NU-Prolog system in Chapter 16.

uation with subsumption, never take time that is more than proportional to the time taken by QRGT applied to the original rules.

Proof: We shall only outline the proof, which parallels the proof of Lemma 13.3 and Theorem 13.2. We must again identify "events," which are the insertion of a tuple into a relation or the matching of tuples from the two subgoals in the body of a Group III or IV rule. For each tuple μ added to a magic predicate, say m_p, there is a goal node N for predicate p in the rule/goal tree during QRGT and a binding tuple passed down to N, such that μ is the result of substituting those bindings for the appropriate arguments in the instance of p at node N. Similar claims are made for the tuples for the supplementary predicates and the answer tuples. Then, an induction like that of Lemma 13.3 proves that every event during the bottom-up evaluation of the magic rules is mirrored by at least one event during QRGT. $\square$

While Theorem 13.5 only claims that the magic rules are not worse (by more than a constant factor) than the original rules executed top-down, we should be aware that the generalized magic rules can be much better than the rules from which they came. For instance, the rules of Example 13.18, when transformed by the generalized magic-sets algorithm into the rules of Figure 13.26, execute as efficiently as one could imagine possible for the problem they solve, However, the original rules (or even the transformed rules of Figure 13.26) will go into an infinite loop, where the infinite sequence of goals

$$p(X),\ p\big(f(X)\big),\ p\Big(f\big(f(X)\big)\Big),\dots$$

is generated, if we execute either QRGT or Prolog on these rules.

Comparison of Methods

It appears that the development of database applications for logic processing, where all solutions, rather than a single solution, is wanted, has caused rapid evolution in the way we think about processing logic. The situation may be analogous to that in parsing, where top-down methods, such as recursive descent, were for a long time thought the preferred way to parse, but more recently it has come to be realized that bottom-up parsing, for example, LR-parsing, offers everything that top-down offers, both in terms of language recognition and in terms of translation.[12] In logic processing, it appears that top-down or resolution-based methods are likewise dominated by bottom-up methods, as concepts like magic-sets become fully known and explored.

At the least, the basic magic-set algorithm is usually the method of choice for datalog, and for some nondatalog examples. However, there are some special classes of rules where magic-sets are beaten by other bottom-up methods; these

---

[12] See Aho, Sethi, and Ullman [1986] for a discussion of these issues.

techniques are discussed in Chapter 15. It appears likely that for many, if not all, realistic examples, the generalized magic-sets technique will allow us to find the appropriate data structures so that unification joins, where we find pairs of tuples in two relations that unify with each other, can be taken efficiently. As an important special case, if the given rules are subgoal-rectified datalog, then the tuples in the relations computed by the generalized algorithm are just the tuples of the basic algorithm, padded out with distinct variables in the extra components. In that case, it is easy to show that the unification joins are really ordinary joins, and the usual index data structures provide adequate support, as was discussed in Section 13.3.

EXERCISES

13.1: Transform the rules

```
path(X,Y) :- red(X,Y).
path(X,Y) :- path(X,U) & blue(U,V) & path(V,Y).
```

assuming a query of the form $path^{bf}$, and using

a)   Algorithm 13.1 (the basic magic-sets algorithm).

b)   The modified technique of Section 13.5, where magic predicates are omitted.

c)   The generalized magic-sets technique of Section 13.6.

If we think of *red* and *blue* as representing red and blue arcs in a graph, then *path* represents paths of alternating red and blue arcs, beginning and ending with a red arc.

13.2: Repeat Exercise 13.1 on the rules of Figure 13.27 with the query goal $expression^b$. These rules represent the construction of arithmetic expressions with operators + and ×, and parentheses to control order of evaluation.

```
expression(plus(E,T))) :-
        expression(E) & term(T).
expression(E) :- term(E).

term(times(T,F)) :- term(T) & factor(F).
term(T) :- factor(T).

factor(parens(E)) :- expression(E).
factor(F) :- identifier(F).
```

Figure 13.27 Rules for arithmetic expressions.

13.3: Repeat Exercise 13.2 with the query *expression*^{f}. What happens when you try to evaluate the magic rules bottom-up?

13.4: Repeat Exercise 13.1 with the rules of Example 12.2 (Figure 12.1) and the query *sum*^{bbf}.

13.5: It is possible to write the "same-generation" rules as

```
sg(X,X).
sg(X,Y) :- par(X,Xp) & sg(Xp,Yp) & par(Y,Yp).
```

Here, the first rule is evidently unsafe. Repeat Exercise 13.1 on these rules, with the query *sg*^{bf}. Does the unsafety of the given rules create problems when we evaluate the magic rules bottom-up?

13.6: Simplify the rules you generated for each of parts (a) to (c) in (*i*) Exercise 13.1, (*ii*) Exercise 13.2, (*iii*) Exercise 13.3, (*iv*) Exercise 13.4, (*v*) Exercise 13.5.

∗ 13.7: Prove the claim of Example 13.1 about what m_sg, $sup_{2.1}$, $sup_{2.2}$ and sg represent.

∗ 13.8: Prove the claim of Example 13.2 about what m_gl, $sup_{2.0}$, $sup_{2.1}$, and gl represent.

∗∗ 13.9: For the paths rules of Example 13.3, determine what each of the predicates in the magic rules of Figure 13.5 represent and prove your conclusion.

∗ 13.10: Suppose we construct a rule/goal tree for rules that have the unique binding property with respect to a given query goal. Show that in the rule/goal tree, every goal node has at least the bound arguments that are indicated for its predicate by the unique binding for that predicate.

13.11: Suppose we have an "EDB" predicate $equals(A, B, C, D)$ that is true whenever $A = B$ and $C = D$. What adornments for *equals* should be permissible if we want to pretend the relation for *equals* is finite (as for predicate s in Example 13.3)?

13.12: Prove part (c) of Lemma 13.2.

13.13: Complete the proof of Lemma 13.3.

13.14: Simulate semi-naive evaluation on the magic rules of

a)   Example 13.4.
b)   Example 13.5.

In each case, show that a large number of tuples are placed in the relation for p, even though none of these answer the query.

3.15: Complete the proof of Theorem 13.3.

3.16: Prove that the simplification rule given at the end of Section 13.4 always works. That is, we can eliminate the ith supplementary predicate for a rule if $i = 0$ or if $i > 0$ and the $(i + 1)$st subgoal is EDB.

3.17: Show that if Algorithm 13.1 is applied to safe rules, then the resulting magic rules are safe.

3.18: Define a tuple with variables to be *dull* if each component is either a ground term or a variable that appears nowhere else in the tuple. Thus, (a, A, b, B) is dull, but (a, A, b, A) and $(a, A, b, f(B))$ are not. Define GROUND(μ) to be the components of tuple μ with ground terms. For example, GROUND($aAbB$) = ab. If R is a relation that is *homogeneous*, in the sense that the components with ground terms in each tuple of R are the same, then let GROUND(R) be the union of GROUND(μ) for each tuple μ in R. Suppose that we use the unification join of Section 13.6 to compute the relation R for the body of a rule with subgoals G_1 and G_2, whose relations are R_1 and R_2, respectively. Let R_1 and R_2 be homogeneous, and let G_1' and G_2' be G_1 and G_2 restricted to components where R_1 and R_2, respectively, have ground terms. Finally, assume all tuples of R_1 and R_2 are dull. Prove the relationship

$$\text{GROUND}(R)=$$
$$\text{ATOV}\big(G_1', \text{GROUND}(R_1)\big) \bowtie \text{ATOV}\big(G_2', \text{GROUND}(R_2)\big)$$

Less formally, for dull tuples, the unification join gives us what we would get if we threw away all nonground components, evaluated the body as if they were ordinary tuples (tuples with no variables), and then padded the resulting tuples with variables that appear only once, to add components for those variables of the rule that appear only in unbound components of R_1 and R_2.

3.19: Suppose we perform the basic magic-sets construction (Algorithm 13.1) on a datalog program with the subgoal-rectified and unique-binding properties, and that the resulting logic program is $\mathcal{P}_1$. Also, we perform the generalized magic-sets construction of Section 13.6 on the same datalog rules to produce the logic program $\mathcal{P}_2$.

   a) Show that the relations defined by $\mathcal{P}_2$ will have only dull tuples.[13]

   b) Show that for each predicate q appearing in $\mathcal{P}_1$ and $\mathcal{P}_2$ (note the sets of predicates are the same), if Q is the relation for q produced by $\mathcal{P}_2$, then the relation for q produced by $\mathcal{P}_1$ is GROUND(Q).

3.20: Complete Example 13.17 by showing that no more tuples can be added to the relations for p, m_p, or $sup_{2.1}$.

---

[13] The terms "dull" and GROUND used in parts (a) and (b) are defined in Exercise 13.18.

13.21: Suppose we have the rules of Example 13.18,

```
p(X) :- p(f(X)).
p(X) :- a(X).
```

with a finite EDB relation for a?

a) What happens if naive or semi-naive evaluation (without subsumption) is performed on these rules?

b) What happens if QRGT is performed on these rules with a query goal p^f?

c) What happens when naive or semi-naive evaluation is performed on the corresponding magic rules of Figure 13.26, again assuming no subsumption?

d) What happens when QRGT is performed on the rules of Figure 13.26 with the query p^f?

13.22: In Figure 13.28 are five tuples with variables in some components. Which of these are subsumed by others?

	X	Y	Z
$i)$	a	$f(B)$	$f(C)$
$ii)$	A	$f(B)$	C
$iii)$	a	B	C
$iv)$	$f(A)$	$f(B)$	c
$v)$	A	$f(A)$	c

Figure 13.28 Tuples containing variables.

13.23: Compute $\text{VTOA}\big(p(W, X, Y), R\big)$, where R is the relation of Figure 13.28.

13.24: Write an algorithm to take the unification join of k relations for any $k \geq 2$.

BIBLIOGRAPHIC NOTES

The "magic sets" technique of rule rewriting was expressed for linear rules by Bancilhon, Maier, Sagiv, and Ullman [1986]. Independently, Rohmer, Lescoeur, and Kerisit [1986] described a method similar to Algorithm 13.1. Algorithm 13.1 itself is from Beeri and Ramakrishnan [1987], where it is called "generalized, supplementary magic sets." The simplified rules described at the end of Section 13.4, where supplementary predicates are used only for IDB predicates, is based on the "minimagic" algorithm of Sacca and Zaniolo [1987a].

The generalized magic-sets construction of Section 13.6 was first published by Ramakrishnan [1988]. It was also discovered independently by Seki [1988].

Theorem 13.2, showing bottom-up dominates top-down for datalog, is from Ullman [1988].

Stratified Logic

When a logic program has stratified negation, the straightforward magic-sets construction sometimes leads to nonstratified rules. Algorithms for dealing with this problem have been considered by Balbin, Port, and Ramamohanarao [1987], Port, Balbin, Meenakshi, and Ramamohanarao [1988], Kemp and Topor [1988], Seki and Itoh [1988], and Balbin, Meenakshi, and Ramamohanarao [1988].

Memoing

There is a long list of seemingly unrelated papers that, in essence, express the same idea, often called "memoing." The concept is to reduce the work of bottom-up computation by remembering when a query has been asked (i.e., remembering the goal nodes of the rule/goal tree) and setting up a network of producers and consumers, where answers to one query are passed to other queries that may be able to use those answers in inferences.

McKay and Shapiro [1981] was an early implementation of this idea. Pereira and Warren [1983] propose "Earley deduction," a technique for memoing patterned after the parsing algorithm due to Earley [1970]; the technique was further explored by Porter [1986].

The following papers examine this idea in its various guises: Lozinskii [1985], Kifer and Lozinskii [1985], Dietrich and Warren [1985], Neiman [1986], Tamaki and Sato [1986], Van Gelder [1986b], Dietrich [1987], and Vielle [1987, 1988]. It appears that all these techniques are subsumed by the generalized magic-sets method mentioned earlier.

Bancilhon and Ramakrishnan [1986] survey and compare many of these papers, as well as the magic-set papers discussed above.

Other Optimization Techniques

There are a number of interesting approaches that should be mentioned, but are not related to the material found in other chapters. Gangopadhyay [1987] explores rule-rewriting schemes that are independent of the binding pattern of the query. Ioannidis and Wong [1987a] investigate local improvements to expressions for queries by the technique known as "simulated annealing."

The MRS system of Genesereth [1983] allows programmer control of evaluation techniques, with different methods used for different predicates. Treitel and Genesereth [1987] and Treitel and Smith [1988] explore the combination of top-down and bottom-up techniques, with the appropriate technique applied to each predicate.

CHAPTER 14

Optimization
for
Conjunctive Queries

In this chapter we focus on optimization of single rules, which are often called *conjunctive queries*, because a rule is the conjunction (logical AND) of its subgoals. In Chapter 11 we saw some heuristics for evaluating the join of several relations, which is very much like evaluating the body of a rule. Each of these techniques assumed that the join of all the relations, or some projection of that join, was what we really wanted. However, there are certain situations where it is advantageous to eliminate subgoals wherever possible.

In Section 14.1 we begin the development of methods to eliminate subgoals from a rule, and we find that there is an exact algorithm to do so; that is, the algorithm eliminates all subgoals that can be eliminated without changing the answer to the query. The next section extends the techniques to rules that have built-in (arithmetic comparison) subgoals. In Section 14.3, we investigate optimization under "weak equivalence," where we assume that all relations mentioned in the subgoals are projections of a single relation; that is, there are no dangling tuples. This form of optimization is generally appropriate for optimizing expressions of relational algebra or its equivalents, such as relational calculus. Section 14.4 extends the ideas to minimize unions of conjunctive queries, and Section 14.5 shows how to test containment of one conjunctive query in the infinite union of conjunctive queries that correspond to a recursive logical rule.

14.1 CONTAINMENT AND EQUIVALENCE OF CONJUNCTIVE QUERIES

Before proceeding to the technical development, let us consider two examples that illustrate why we need to know when the result of one conjunctive query is contained in, or is equal to, what another conjunctive query produces. These examples also illustrate two reasons why we might be faced with conjunctive queries that allow us to eliminate some of their subgoals without changing what the query produces:

1.   Conjunctive queries produced by expanding recursive rules, and
2.   Conjunctive queries defined on a database view.

Example 14.1: Let us investigate the following pair of rules, which define "funny paths." The significance of "funny paths" should not be overestimated; we merely propose these rules to illustrate a technique.

r_1:   fp(X,Y) :- e(X,Y).
r_2:   fp(X,Y) :- e(Y,X) & fp(X,Z).

Informally, rule r_1 says that any edge is a funny path, and r_2 says that there is a funny path from X to Y if there is an edge from Y to X and there is a funny path from X to someplace.

Logic programs with a single basis rule and a single linear-recursive rule can be analyzed by repeatedly substituting both rules for the recursive subgoal, using essentially the algorithm of Figure 13.12.[1] However, after substituting for the recursive subgoal, we do not delete its rules. Moreover, as the recursive predicate appears in the body of one of its subgoals, that predicate does not disappear.

When we make the substitution, we shall rename the local variables of the rule whose body is being substituted, so there is no confusion regarding variables that happen to have the same name but are in truth different variables. The convention we shall use is that the ith time we perform this substitution, we subscript all the variables of the rule with i.

For the case at hand, rule r_1, which represents zero applications of the recursive rule, contributes the "expanded" rule

a_0:   fp(X,Y) :- e(X,Y).

We shall enumerate the "answer" rules a_i, where i is the number of uses of the recursive rule r_2 followed by one use of the basis rule r_1. We shall also enumerate rules b_i representing i substitutions of r_2 into itself, without a use of r_1.

Suppose we now substitute r_1 and r_2 for the recursive subgoal $p(X, Z)$ in r_2. We rewrite the rules by subscripting all variables by 1, that is,

r_1:   fp(X$_1$,Y$_1$) :- e(X$_1$,Y$_1$).
r_2:   fp(X$_1$,Y$_1$) :- e(Y$_1$,X$_1$) & fp(X$_1$,Z$_1$).

To make the substitution, we must unify the subgoal $fp(X, Z)$ with the heads of the two rules, both of which are $fp(X_1, Y_1)$. We therefore substitute X for

---

[1] In fact, more general sets of rules, including those with nonlinear rules, can also be expanded this way. See Exercise 14.20.

X_1 and Z for Y_1. The result is the two rules

```
a₁:  fp(X,Y) :- e(Y,X) & e(X,Z).
b₁:  fp(X,Y) :- e(Y,X) & e(Z,X) & fp(X,Z₁).
```

To continue the sequence, we substitute r_1 and r_2 into b_1. This time, the rules look like

```
r₁:  fp(X₂,Y₂) :- e(X₂,Y₂).
r₂:  fp(X₂,Y₂) :- e(Y₂,X₂) & fp(X₂,Z₂).
```

and unification of their heads with the recursive subgoal of b_1, which is $fp(X, Z_1)$, requires replacing X_2 by X and Y_2 by Z_1. We thus get the expanded rules

```
a₂:  fp(X,Y) :- e(Y,X) & e(Z,X) & e(X,Z₁).
b₂:  fp(X,Y) :- e(Y,X) & e(Z,X) & e(Z₁,X) & fp(X,Z₂).
```

If we carry out the substitution repeatedly, we observe the following simple pattern. Rule a_i, for $i \geq 3$ is

```
aᵢ:  fp(X,Y) :- e(Y,X) & e(Z,X) &
         e(Z₁,X) & e(Z₂,X) & ⋯ & e(Z_{i-2},X) & e(X,Z_{i-1}).
```

while b_i is

```
bᵢ:  fp(X,Y) :- e(Y,X) & e(Z,X) &
         e(Z₁,X) & e(Z₂,X) & ⋯ & e(Z_{i-1},X) & fp(X,Zᵢ).
```

Let us consider the English interpretation of a_2: there is a funny path from X to Y if

1. There is an edge from Y to X, and
2. There exists Z such that there is an edge from Z to X, and
3. There exists Z_1 such that there is an edge from X to Z_1.

Condition (1) implies condition (2); that is, if for some value of Y, $e(Y, X)$ is true, then we can pick that value of Y as the value of Z, to make $e(Z, X)$ true. It follows that conditions (1) and (3) are equivalent to a_2; that is, a_2 can be simplified to

```
a₂:  fp(X,Y) :- e(Y,X) & e(X,Z₁).
```

Now, notice that a_2 is really the same as a_1; the only difference is that a_2 has local variable Z_1 where a_1 has Z. More generally, in a_i, for $i \geq 3$, whatever value of Y makes $e(Y, X)$ true also serves to make $e(Z, X)$, $e(Z_1, X)$, $e(Z_2, X)$, and so on, true. Thus, a_i is equivalent to

```
aᵢ:  fp(X,Y) :- e(Y,X) & e(X,Z_{i-1}).
```

Again, this rule is a_1 with Z renamed.

We conclude that every a_i, for $i > 1$, produces the same set of "funny paths" as a_1. It is easy to check that a_i produces exactly the same set of tuples as are produced along the path of the rule/goal tree in which r_2 is applied i times and then r_1 is applied once. As all root-to-leaf paths in the rule/goal tree starting from root $fp(X,Y)$ are of this form for some i, the answer to the query $fp(X,Y)$ is the union of the a_i's. But, as we just observed, a_i, for $i > 1$, contributes nothing beyond what a_1 contributes. Thus, the recursion with which we started is really equivalent to the two nonrecursive rules

```
fp(X,Y) :- e(X,Y).
fp(X,Y) :- e(Y,X) & e(X,Z).
```

Thus, by discovering redundant conjuncts in the rules that were formed by expanding a linear recursion, we were able to simplify the recursion to an extent not attainable by the means discussed in Chapter 13. □

Example 14.2: Now, let us consider an optimization of a different sort. Suppose that we have in our database an employee-department relation ED and a department-manager relation DM. Suppose also that we have declared a view $EDM = ED \bowtie DM$, and we expect that queries will be stated in terms of this view. We might ask the query "for what department does Sam Sloth work?" In terms of the view EDM, that query is

$$\pi_D\big(\sigma_{E=\text{'sloth'}}(EDM)\big)$$

or, expanding the definition of EDM,

$$\pi_D\big(\sigma_{E=\text{'sloth'}}(ED \bowtie DM)\big) \tag{14.1}$$

Intuitively, it seems that we do not need the DM term in the join; that is, (14.1) should be equivalent to

$$\pi_D\big(\sigma_{E=\text{'sloth'}}(ED)\big) \tag{14.2}$$

However, (14.1) and (14.2) do not produce the same answer when there is a dangling tuple for Sam Sloth in the ED relation. That is, suppose ED contains the tuple (Sloth, Toy), but DM contains no tuple for the Toy Department. Then (14.2) produces the answer "Toy," while (14.1) does not.

This example also illustrates a question regarding the elimination of conjuncts, since the two relational algebra expressions (14.1) and (14.2) could as well have been expressed as conjunctive queries,

```
answer(D) :- ed(sloth,D) & dm(D,M).
```

and

```
answer(D) :- ed(sloth,D).
```

respectively. There is a sense in which the subgoal $dm(D, M)$ is redundant, and we shall take up the matter again, when we consider "weak equivalence" in Section 14.3. □

Definitions of Equivalence and Containment

In order to decide whether a conjunct can be eliminated, we need to tell whether one conjunctive query is contained in another, in the sense that every answer returned by the first is returned by the second. We then can test equivalence of conjunctive queries by testing containment in both directions. Finally, we can test whether a conjunct can be eliminated from the body of a conjunctive query, by testing whether the query is equivalent to itself with the conjunct in question removed. We shall first develop the theory assuming that the subgoals are all "ordinary" subgoals, with predicates that represent EDB relations. In the next section, we extend the theory to include "built-in" subgoals, with predicates that are arithmetic comparison operators.

Let Q_1 and Q_2 be two conjunctive queries. We say that $Q_1 \subseteq Q_2$ (Q_1 *is contained in* Q_2) if for every EDB, the relation for the head predicate of Q_1 is a subset of the relation for the head predicate of Q_2. We say $Q_1 \equiv Q_2$ (Q_1 *is equivalent to*) Q_2 if for every EDB, the relations for the head predicates of Q_1 and Q_2 are the same. Note that $Q_1 \equiv Q_2$ if and only if $Q_1 \subseteq Q_2$ and $Q_2 \subseteq Q_1$. Also, it is important to understand that containment and equivalence of conjunctive queries refer to what happens for arbitrary values of the extensional database; it is not sufficient to examine a single database to conclude containment or equivalence. For instance, we concluded in Example 14.1 that $a_1 \equiv a_2$, where a_1 and a_2 are the conjunctive queries

a_1: `fp(X,Y) :- e(Y,X) & e(X,Z).`
a_2: `fp(X,Y) :- e(Y,X) & e(Z,X) & e(X,Z`$_1$`).`

because, as we argued, these rules produce the same relations for their heads, no matter what relation for predicate e we assume.

The key to the test for containment is the "symbol mapping," a concept that was introduced in Section 7.11. The purpose there was to compare dependencies, an issue that is related closely to the question of containment of conjunctive queries; we leave an exploration of this relationship to the exercises. Here, a symbol mapping h substitutes for the variables appearing in a conjunctive query, and we allow the value of $h(X)$ to be an arbitrary term. The symbol mapping extends naturally to apply to terms and atoms, if we let h be the identity on all constants, function symbols, and predicate symbols.

Let Q_1 and Q_2 be two conjunctive queries:

Q_1: $I :- J_1 \& \cdots \& J_l.$
Q_2: $H :- G_1 \& \cdots \& G_k.$

A symbol mapping h is said to be a *containment mapping* if h turns Q_2 into Q_1; that is, $h(H) = I$, and for each $i = 1, 2, \ldots, k$, there is some j such that $h(G_i) = J_j$. Note there is no requirement that each J_j be the target of some G_i, so $h(Q_2)$ could look like Q_1 with some subgoals missing.

The following theorem relates containment mappings and containments of conjunctive queries. Its proof technique is an important one — showing that if a simple test fails then we can use the conjunctive query itself to provide a counterexample to the containment. We saw a similar idea in Algorithm 7.2 (Volume I), where we tested a join for losslessness, and we shall see several examples in this chapter as well.

Theorem 14.1: Let Q_1 and Q_2 be as above. Then $Q_1 \subseteq Q_2$ if and only if there is a containment mapping from Q_2 to Q_1.[2]

Proof: *If*: Suppose such a containment mapping h exists, and consider a particular EDB. A tuple μ is in the relation for the head of Q_1, for this EDB, if and only if there is some substitution τ for the variables of Q_1 that makes each subgoal of Q_1 an EDB fact, that is, the tuple formed from the arguments of that subgoal is in the EDB relation for that subgoal's predicate.

In Q_2, let us substitute $\tau\big(h(X)\big)$ for each variable X.[3] We know that $h(H) = I$, so $\tau\big(h(H)\big) = \tau(I)$, which is μ with the head predicate attached. Moreover, we know that $h(G_i) = J_j$ for some j, so $\tau\big(h(G_i)\big) = \tau(J_j)$, which we know is an EDB fact. Thus, the substitution τh applied to Q_2 produces μ in the relation for the head. Since μ is an arbitrary tuple produced by Q_1 from the given EDB, we know that Q_2 produces a superset (not necessarily proper) of what Q_1 produces from this EDB. Further, as the EDB is arbitrary, we may conclude that $Q_1 \subseteq Q_2$.

Only If: Suppose now that $Q_1 \subseteq Q_2$. Construct a particular EDB as follows. Think of each variable of Q_1 as if it were a constant, different from the constant associated with any other variable or with the constants that appear in Q_1 itself. Let τ be defined so that $\tau(X)$ is the constant associated with X, for each variable X, and τ is the identity on other symbols.[4] Then let the EDB consist of exactly the facts $\tau(J_1), \ldots, \tau(J_l)$. That is, if J_j is the subgoal $p(t_1, \ldots, t_n)$, then $\big(\tau(t_1), \ldots, \tau(t_n)\big)$ is a tuple of the relation for p. Evidently, if we apply Q_1 to this database, we obtain at least the fact $\tau(I)$.

Since $Q_1 \subseteq Q_2$, we know we obtain $\tau(I)$ when we apply Q_2 to the same database. That is, there is some substitution ρ for the variables of Q_2, such that $\rho(G_i)$ becomes a fact of this EDB for each i, and $\rho(H) = \tau(I)$. Equivalently, $\rho(G_i)$ is $\tau(J_j)$ for some j. It follows that $\tau^{-1}\rho$ is the desired containment map-

---

[2] The reader should observe that containment mappings go from the larger, or more general, rule to the smaller, or more restrictive, one.

[3] Note that τ and h are the same kind of object—mappings from variables to terms. We have used τ and some other Greek letters for general mappings of this type, but we continue to use h and sometimes g for containment mappings, to emphasize the special role these mappings play.

[4] In a sense, the substitution of constants for variables is a "red herring"; we could just as well leave the variable symbols intact and simply regard them as constants. However, we shall use τ to make explicit when we think of variables as constants.

ping h. Note that τ^{-1} makes sense because τ is a one-to-one correspondence; τ^{-1} simply replaces each constant by the corresponding variable, recreating the subgoals of Q_1. □

Example 14.3: Consider again the conjunctive queries from Example 14.1:

a_1:   fp(X,Y) :- e(Y,X) & e(X,Z).
a_2:   fp(X,Y) :- e(Y,X) & e(Z,X) & e(X,Z_1).

From a_2 to a_1 we may use the containment mapping $h(X) = X$, $h(Y) = h(Z) = Y$, and $h(Z_1) = Z$. Then $h(a_2)$ is exactly a_1, showing $a_1 \subseteq a_2$.

Conversely, consider the containment mapping g from a_1 to a_2 defined by $g(X) = X$, $g(Y) = Y$, and $g(Z) = Z_1$. Then $g(a_1)$ is a_2 with the middle subgoal, $e(Z, X)$, missing. We therefore conclude that $a_2 \subseteq a_1$. Since the containment runs in both directions, we conclude that $a_1 \equiv a_2$, which we also argued informally in Example 14.1. □

Example 14.4: For an example of noncontainment, consider the conjunctive queries

Q_1:   p(X,Y) :- q(X,f(Z)) & q(f(Z),Y).
Q_2:   p(X,Y) :- q(X,Z) & q(Z,Y).

We immediately see that $Q_1 \subseteq Q_2$; the containment mapping defined by $h(X) = X$, $h(Y) = Y$, and $h(Z) = f(Z)$, from Q_2 to Q_1, suffices by Theorem 14.1.[5]

However, exploration fails to discover a containment mapping from Q_1 to Q_2. The reason why is not hard to see. In Q_2, substitute 0, 1, and 2 for X, Y, and Z, respectively. Then the two subgoals of Q_2 become the facts $q(0, 2)$ and $q(2, 1)$, or equivalently, the EDB relation for q consists of the tuples $\{02, 21\}$. For this EDB, Q_2 produces the fact $p(0, 1)$, that is, the tuple 01. However, when we apply Q_1 to this EDB, we note that $f(Z)$ cannot match any of the constants 0, 1, or 2, so the answer produced by Q_1 on this EDB is $\emptyset$. Thus, it is not true that on every EDB, the relation produced by Q_2 is a subset of what Q_1 produces. We therefore conclude that $Q_2 \subseteq Q_1$ and $Q_1 \equiv Q_2$ are false. □

Minimization of Conjunctive Queries

Given a conjunctive query Q, we might wish to find a *minimal equivalent* conjunctive query Q', that is a conjunctive query equivalent to Q, having as few subgoals as any equivalent to Q. Our first thought might be that we could find Q' by eliminating redundant subgoals of Q. In principle, we also have to consider the possibility that minimal equivalents for Q are not related to Q in any simple way, such as by deleting subgoals. However, it turns out that our first thought is correct, as the following corollary to Theorem 14.1 shows.

---

[5] Note that $h(Z)$ is defined to be the term $f(Z)$, not "the value of f applied to Z."

Corollary 14.1: If Q is any conjunctive query, then there is a minimal equivalent query Q' formed from Q by deletion of zero or more subgoals of Q.

Proof: Let Q_m be any minimal equivalent for Q. By Theorem 14.1 there are containment mappings h from Q to Q_m and g from Q_m to Q. Let new conjunctive query Q' be formed from the head of Q and a body consisting of those subgoals of Q that are the image of some subgoal of Q_m according to mapping g. We claim that $Q' \equiv Q$. The identity containment mapping shows $Q \subseteq Q'$,[6] while the containment mapping composed of h followed by g is a containment mapping from Q to Q' that shows $Q' \subseteq Q$.

Evidently, Q' meets the requirement that its subgoals are a subset of those of Q. It also meets the requirement that it is an equivalent for Q that has a minimum number of subgoals. In proof, note that g maps each subgoal of Q_m to one subgoal of Q', and therefore, Q' cannot have more subgoals that Q_m. As Q_m has a minimum number of subgoals, so does Q', and in fact, it must be that Q_m and Q' have the same number of subgoals. $\square$

Example 14.5: Observe the conjunctive queries a_i, for $i \geq 2$, in Example 14.1. For each i, we can apply the containment mapping that sends X and Y to themselves, sends Z, $Z_1, \ldots, Z_{i-2}$ to Y, and sends Z_{i-1} to itself. This containment mapping demonstrates that in a_i, only the first and last subgoals are needed; the others are redundant. $\square$

Incidentally, we can actually prove something stronger than Corollary 14.1. All minimal equivalents Q_m are formed from Q by deletion of subgoals, reordering of subgoals, and renaming of variables. Since reordering and renaming are "trivial" operations, there is a strong sense in which the minimal equivalent for Q is unique. We leave a proof of this claim as an exercise.

Efficiency of Minimization for Conjunctive Queries

Theorem 14.1 does not tell us how to find a minimal equivalent to a conjunctive query. Suppose we want to test whether conjunctive query

$$Q_1: I :\text{-} J_1 \ \& \ \cdots \ \& \ J_l.$$

is contained in

$$Q_2: H :\text{-} G_1 \ \& \ \cdots \ \& \ G_k.$$

A straightforward approach is to consider all assignments from the G's into the J's; there are l^k such assignments. We can test each assignment A, to see if there is a symbol mapping h that explains A. That is, if $A(i) = j$, then we treat the variables of J_j as if they were constants, and term-match G_i

---

[6] In general, a conjunctive query is contained in the query formed by any subset of its subgoals. Intuitively, each subgoal eliminated loosens the conditions expressed by the body of the rule.

against J_j. Such a term matching, if possible, provides a value of $h(X)$, for each variable X that appears in G_i. If we perform the matching for all i, and we get no conflicting definitions of $h(X)$ for any X, then the h so constructed is a containment mapping that shows $Q_1 \subseteq Q_2$. If we try all such assignments A, and find that none is explainable by a symbol mapping, then Q_1 is not contained in Q_2, because no containment mapping exists.

The same idea applies to minimization of conjunctive queries. We need to consider assignments A from the subgoals of some conjunctive query Q into Q's own subgoals. Try first the assignments that send all subgoals to one, then all to two, and so on, until we succeed in finding a symbol mapping that justifies the assignment A. At that point, the subgoals in the range of A form the body of a minimal equivalent query.

These algorithms can take time that is exponential in the size of the input, that is, the length of the conjunctive query or queries. One may wonder if there isn't some much more efficient way to answer questions of containment or minimization. Unfortunately, the problem is $\mathcal{NP}$-complete, so it is unlikely that a significantly faster algorithm for the general case can be found. There are polynomial-time algorithms for minimization and containment in some common special cases; see the bibliographic notes.

14.2 CONJUNCTIVE QUERIES HAVING ARITHMETIC COMPARISONS

In the previous section, we assumed that all subgoals of conjunctive queries had EDB predicates, and we showed that the condition under which $Q_1 \subseteq Q_2$ is the existence of a containment mapping from Q_2 to Q_1. From more basic principles, we would expect that $Q_1 \subseteq Q_2$ holds exactly when the body of Q_1 logically implies the body of Q_2 (assuming the heads are the same), and the import of Theorem 14.1 is that it shows such implication can only occur when each subgoal of Q_2 is implied by some one subgoal of Q_1. That is, the containment mapping from Q_2 to Q_1 means that each subgoal of Q_2 is a generalization of a subgoal of Q_1. When we have subgoals with built-in predicates, it is again sufficient that these predicates appearing in Q_1 logically imply those in Q_2.

We therefore need an algorithm for testing implications involving arithmetic inequalities. The reader should see an analogy between what we do now and the way we handled functional dependencies in Section 7.3 (Volume I). There, we gave a collection of axioms ("Armstrong's axioms"), and we showed that they were sound (only inferred true statements) and complete (were able to infer every true statement). Then, we gave an algorithm to determine the effect of applying the axioms to a given set of dependencies, knowing that the resulting set of dependencies were all those that were true for the given relation.

For functional dependencies, the notion of "truth" is well defined, since we have a clear definition of what it means for a functional dependency to hold in a relation. Here, to pin our algorithm on a notion of "truth," we shall assume that values for variables are chosen from the integers. However, any infinite, totally ordered set, such as the rationals or reals, would serve as a model of the axioms as well.

Axioms for Inequalities

We shall assume that we are given a collection of inequalities of the form $X < Y$, $X \leq Y$, or $X \neq Y$, where X and Y are variables whose values range over the integers. Note we do not permit equalities $X = Y$. The reason is that, if $X = Y$ is a subgoal of some conjunctive query, we may rewrite the rule by substituting X for Y. We also eliminate the possibility that $X \leq Y$ and $Y \leq X$, where X and Y are different variables. The reason for making this assumption is that should these two inequalities hold, then $X = Y$ holds, and we can replace Y by X, thereby simplifying the conjunctive query.

The axioms we shall use for inequalities are

A1: $X \leq X$.
A2: $X < Y$ implies $X \leq Y$.
A3: $X < Y$ implies $X \neq Y$.
A4: $X \leq Y$ and $X \neq Y$ imply $X < Y$.
A5: $X \neq Y$ implies $Y \neq X$.
A6: $X < Y$ and $Y < Z$ imply $X < Z$.
A7: $X \leq Y$ and $Y \leq Z$ imply $X \leq Z$.
A8: $X \leq Z$, $Z \leq Y$, $X \leq W$, $W \leq Y$, and $W \neq Z$ imply $X \neq Y$.

The first five are elementary properties of $<$, $\leq$, and $\neq$. A6 and A7 are transitivity laws for $<$ and $\leq$. A8 looks somewhat mysterious; it says that if there are two values, W and Z, that both lie between two other values X and Y, and it is known that W and Z are different, then X must be strictly smaller than Y.

Soundness of the Axioms

For Armstrong's axioms, the relevant models were relations. Here, the relevant models are assignments of integers to the variables. To show the axioms sound, we must show that they each hold in each model. A1 to A7 are well-known properties of integers. A8 requires a little thought. Suppose some assignment of integers to the variables W, X, Y, and Z makes W and Z each lie between X and Y, and makes $W \neq Z$. The fact that $X \leq W \leq Y$ already tells us that $X \leq Y$; but could X in fact equal Y? If $X \leq W \leq Y$ and $X = Y$, then $W = X$. Likewise, we can conclude $Z = X$. It follows from the properties of integers (really properties of equality) that $W = Z$. But we assumed $W \neq Z$, which is a contradiction.

We have thus proved that the axioms A1 to A8 are sound, if the models are assignments of integers to variables.

Completeness of the Axioms

As for Armstrong's axioms, the hard part is showing our axioms are complete. We shall follow the plan used in Section 7.3. Starting with a given set of inequalities S, we may compute S^+, the set of inequalities that follow logically, using our axioms A1 to A8. We prove that for any inequality $X\theta Y$ not in S^+, there is some assignment of variables to integers that makes everything in S^+ true, but violates $X\theta Y$.

Lemma 14.1: Let S be a set of inequalities involving a finite set of variables V, such that we cannot derive from S, using A1 through A8, an inequality of the form $X < X$, or a pair of inequalities $X \leq Y$ and $Y \leq X$, for X and Y distinct variables. Then every inequality $X\theta Y$ not in S^+ has some assignment of integers to the variables of V that makes everything in S^+ true but $X\theta Y$ false.

Proof: The inequality can be of three types.

Case 1: θ is $\leq$. We need to construct an assignment that satisfies S^+ but makes $Y > X$. Let A be the set of variables A such that $X \leq A$ is in S^+, and let B be those variables B for which $B \leq Y$ is in S^+. Let $C = V - A - B$. The relationships among these three sets of variables are suggested by Figure 14.1. Note that for typical elements A in A, B in B, and C in C, it is possible that $B \leq C$ and/or $C \leq A$, but not $C \leq B$ (else by A7, C would be in B), or $A \leq C$ (then, C would be in A). Also, it is not possible that there is an element in the intersection of A and B, for then $X \leq Y$ would be in S^+, contrary to our assumption. Since C was defined to be disjoint from A and B, we conclude that all three sets are disjoint.

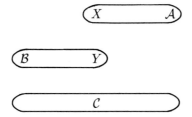

Figure 14.1 Partition of V into three sets.

Now, we topologically sort each of A, B, and C with respect to the order $\leq$; that is, we find an order for the variables of A, such that if $A_1 \leq A_2$ is in S^+, then A_1 precedes A_2 in the order, and likewise for elements of B and C. The assumption that we cannot derive both $A_1 \leq A_2$ and $A_2 \leq A_1$, if A_1 and A_2 are distinct, assures us that these topological orders can be found. Note that Y will come last in the order for $\mathcal{B}$, and X will come first in the order for $\mathcal{A}$.

Now we order all of the variables in $\mathcal{V}$, as follows.

1.   The elements of $\mathcal{B}$, in order.
2.   The elements of $\mathcal{C}$, in order.
3.   The elements of $\mathcal{A}$, in order.

Finally, we assign distinct integers $1, 2, \ldots$ to the variables in this order.

In this assignment, X is given a larger value than Y, so $X \leq Y$ does not hold. Now, we must show that every inequality in S^+ holds in this assignment. Since no variables are assigned the same integer, all $\neq$ inequalities hold.

Consider $U \leq V$ in S^+. If U and V are the same variable, surely $U \leq V$ holds. If U and V are in the same block ($\mathcal{A}$, $\mathcal{B}$, or $\mathcal{C}$) of the partition, then $U \leq V$ holds, because the topological order of each block respects the inequality. If U is in $\mathcal{B}$, and V is in $\mathcal{A}$ or $\mathcal{C}$, then the inequality holds because everything in $\mathcal{B}$ precedes everything in the other blocks. Similarly, if U is in $\mathcal{C}$ and V is in $\mathcal{A}$, there is no problem. We are left with the possibility that U is in $\mathcal{A}$ and V in $\mathcal{B}$ or $\mathcal{C}$, or that U is in $\mathcal{C}$, and V is in $\mathcal{B}$. However, if U is in $\mathcal{A}$, and $U \leq V$ is in S^+, then V would be in $\mathcal{A}$, by axiom A7. Thus, V could not be in $\mathcal{B}$ or $\mathcal{C}$. Similarly, if V is in $\mathcal{B}$, then it is not possible that $U \leq V$ and U is in $\mathcal{C}$, because U would have to be in $\mathcal{B}$, by A7.

Finally, we must consider inequality $U < V$ in S^+. As we can rule out the possibility that U and V are the same variable, the argument given for the inequality $U \leq V$ applies to $U < V$, and we conclude that $U < V$ is satisfied by the constructed assignment. Hence, the assignment satisfies S^+ but not $X \leq Y$.

Case 2: θ is $\neq$. We shall leave some of the details for this case to the reader. We begin by observing that it is not possible to have both a variable Z such that $X \leq Z$ and $Z \leq Y$ are in S^+ and also a variable W such that $Y \leq W$ and $W \leq X$ are in S^+, because then we would have both $X \leq Y$ and $Y \leq X$, which we have ruled out in our assumptions. We shall assume without loss of generality that there is no such W.

Let $\mathcal{D}$ be X, Y, and the set of Z such that $X \leq Z \leq Y$ in S^+. Define $\mathcal{A}$ to be those variables A such that $D \leq A$ is in S^+, for some D in $\mathcal{D}$, but A is not itself in $\mathcal{D}$. Similarly, $\mathcal{B}$ is the set of B not in $\mathcal{D}$, such that $B \leq D$ for some D in $\mathcal{D}$. $\mathcal{C}$ is the set of variables that remain. The arrangement is suggested by Figure 14.2.

Topologically sort each of these sets of variables, and combine the orders in the sequence $\mathcal{B}$, $\mathcal{C}$, $\mathcal{D}$, and $\mathcal{A}$. Assign distinct integers to the variables in this order, but give all the members of $\mathcal{D}$ the same integer. Surely $X \neq Y$ is not satisfied by this assignment. However, one can argue as in Case 1, that all inequalities in S^+ are satisfied. The argument is left for an exercise, but for

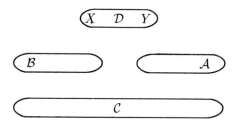

Figure 14.2 Partition of V for Case 2.

one useful detail, note that A8 is needed here to guarantee that we cannot have $U \neq V$ in S^+, for any U and V in $\mathcal{D}$.

Case 3: θ is <. If $X \leq Y$ is not in S^+, then use the construction of Case 1; the resulting assignment satisfies S^+ but not $X < Y$. If $X \neq Y$ is not in S^+, use the construction of Case 2; the resulting assignment satisfies S^+ but not $X < Y$. If both $X \leq Y$ and $X \neq Y$ are in S^+, then $X < Y$ is in S^+ by A4, contrary to the assumption for Case 3. $\square$

Containment of Conjunctive Queries with Built-in Subgoals

In Theorem 14.1, we saw that when there were no arithmetic comparison (built-in) subgoals, the existence of a containment mapping from Q_2 to Q_1 was both necessary and sufficient for $Q_1 \subseteq Q_2$ to hold. When there are built-in subgoals and ordinary subgoals, a containment mapping for the ordinary subgoals is still necessary, as long as the built-in subgoals of Q_1 are not contradictory. (If the comparisons in Q_1 cannot be satisfied, then Q_1 produces the empty set, and $Q_1 \subseteq Q_2$ holds independent of the ordinary subgoals.) A containment mapping on the ordinary subgoals, coupled with the condition that the built-in subgoals of Q_2 imply the built-in subgoals of Q_1, is sufficient to show $Q_1 \subseteq Q_2$. However, as we shall show after proving the sufficiency, it is not necessary; there can be interactions among the ordinary and built-in subgoals that allow $Q_1 \subseteq Q_2$ to hold even though the built-in subgoals of Q_1 do not imply those of Q_2.

Theorem 14.2: Let Q_1 and Q_2 be two conjunctive queries:

$$Q_1: I :\text{-} J_1 \& \cdots \& J_l \& K_1 \& \cdots K_n.$$
$$Q_2: H :\text{-} G_1 \& \cdots \& G_k \& F_1 \& \cdots F_m.$$

Where the J's and G's are ordinary subgoals and the K's and F's are built-in subgoals. Let the following conditions hold:

1. There is a containment mapping h from the variables of Q_2 to the variables of Q_1 such that every ordinary subgoal of Q_2 is turned into an ordinary subgoal of Q_1.
2. For each $i = 1, 2, \ldots, m$, $h(F_i)$ is implied by the built-in subgoals of Q_1.

3. $h(H) = I$.

Then $Q_1 \subseteq Q_2$.

Proof: The argument is very close to that of the "if" portion of Theorem 14.1. Suppose μ is a tuple in the relation for the head of Q_1. Then there is an assignment τ of integers to the variables of Q_1 that makes the J's and K's true and makes the head I become μ. Then assign each variable of Q_2 the integer $\tau\big(h(X)\big)$. We know that $\tau\big(h(G_i)\big)$ is $\tau(J_j)$ for some j, and therefore $\tau\big(h(G_i)\big)$ is an EDB fact under this substitution. We also know that $\tau\big(h(F_i)\big)$ is implied by the $\tau(K_j)$'s, and therefore $\tau\big(h(F_i)\big)$ is a true arithmetic relationship. Thus, the substitution τh makes the body of Q_2 true. Finally, we know that $\tau\big(h(H)\big) = \tau(I) = \mu$. We have thus shown that whatever Q_1 produces from an EDB will also be produced by Q_2; that is, $Q_1 \subseteq Q_2$. $\square$

Example 14.6: Consider the conjunctive queries

$$Q_1: \quad \text{p(X,Y)} \text{ :- } \text{q(X,Y,Z)} \text{ \& } \text{X<Z}.$$
$$Q_2: \quad \text{p(X,Y)} \text{ :- } \text{q(X,W,Z)} \text{ \& } \text{q(X,Y,U)} \text{ \& } \text{X}\neq\text{U} \text{ \& } \text{X}\leq\text{Z}.$$

Let the containment mapping h be defined by $h(X) = X$, $h(Y) = h(W) = Y$, and $h(Z) = h(U) = Z$. Then $h\big(q(X,W,Z)\big)$ and $h\big(q(X,Y,U)\big)$ are both $q(X,Y,Z)$, so condition (1) of Theorem 14.2 is satisfied. Also, $h(X \neq U)$ is $X \neq Z$, and $h(X \leq Z)$ is $X \leq Z$. Both $X \neq Z$ and $X \leq Z$ are implied by $X < Z$, the built-in subgoal of Q_1. Thus, condition (2) is satisfied. Finally, $h\big(p(X,Y)\big)$ is $p(X,Y)$, so (3) is satisfied; we conclude that $Q_1 \subseteq Q_2$. $\square$

Unfortunately, the conditions of Theorem 14.2 are not necessary for a containment to hold between two conjunctive queries. It is true that condition (1) is necessary; that is, there must be a containment mapping between the ordinary subgoals if there is to be containment (an exception occurs if there are contradictory built-in subgoals); the proof is essentially that of the "only if" portion of Theorem 14.1. However, there can be interactions between the ordinary and built-in subgoals that make condition (2) unnecessary, as the next example shows.

Example 14.7: Consider the conjunctive queries

$$Q_1: \quad \text{p(X,Y)} \text{ :- } \text{q(X,Y)} \text{ \& } \text{r(U,V)} \text{ \& } \text{r(V,U)}.$$
$$Q_2: \quad \text{p(X,Y)} \text{ :- } \text{q(X,Y)} \text{ \& } \text{r(U,V)} \text{ \& } \text{U}\leq\text{V}.$$

Intuitively, Q_1 makes p be either a copy of q or empty; it is a copy of q whenever the relation for r has both some tuple and its reverse. Q_2 makes p be a copy of q if r has some tuple whose first component does not exceed its second component, and makes p empty otherwise.

Surely condition (2) of Theorem 14.2 does not hold, because there are no built-in subgoals of Q_1 to imply $h(U \leq V)$. However, if we think about the meaning of the rules, we see that whenever we have both ab and ba in the relation for r, we must have either $a \leq b$ or $b \leq a$. If $a \leq b$, pick $U = a$ and $V = b$, to satisfy the last two subgoals of Q_2; if $b \leq a$, pick $U = b$ and $V = a$. Thus, whenever Q_1 returns the relation for q as an answer, Q_2 does too, from which it follows that $Q_1 \subseteq Q_2$. □

Minimization of Conjunctive Queries with Built-in Subgoals

Optimization of conjunctive queries becomes considerably more difficult when we have built-in subgoals. We can still use the technique outlined in the previous section; try deleting a subset of the subgoals of a conjunctive query Q, to form a new conjunctive query Q'. Then, see if there is a containment mapping h that satisfies the conditions of Theorem 14.2. The possible substitutions for each variable of Q can be limited by considering all possible assignments from the subgoals of Q to the chosen subset.

Unfortunately, the condition of Theorem 14.2 is only sufficient to show the containment $Q' \subseteq Q$ (and therefore equivalence, since $Q \subseteq Q'$ is obvious). There is no guarantee that the chosen subset of the subgoals is as small as possible; there may be a smaller set of subgoals that is not a subset of those of Q, yet is equivalent to Q, as the next example shows.

Example 14.8: Consider

$$Q: \quad \text{p(X,Y)} \quad :\text{-} \quad \text{q(X,Y)} \ \& \ \text{X} \neq \text{Y} \ \& \ \text{X} \leq \text{Y}.$$

It is easy to show that Q is not equivalent to the query formed from any subset of its subgoals. However,

$$\text{p(X,Y)} \quad :\text{-} \quad \text{q(X,Y)} \ \& \ \text{X} < \text{Y}.$$

is an equivalent conjunctive query with fewer subgoals. □

Another simplification that doesn't work in general would be to minimize the ordinary subgoals and the built-in subgoals independently. However, the next example shows that is not possible.

Example 14.9: Let Q be defined by

$$Q: \quad \text{p(X,Y)} \quad :\text{-} \quad \text{q(X,Y)} \ \& \ \text{q(X,Z)} \ \& \ \text{Y} < \text{Z}.$$

If the built-in subgoal were not present, we could eliminate the middle subgoal, $q(X, Z)$. However, the containment mapping h that allows the deletion of $q(X, Z)$, which is $h(X) = X$ and $h(Y) = h(Z) = Y$, also maps $Y < Z$ into $Y < Y$, which is surely false. Thus, $h(Q)$ is not equivalent to Q.

Put another way, Q calls for those tuples ab in the relation for q such that there is some other tuple ac in the relation for q such that $b < c$. If we eliminate $q(X, Z)$ from Q, then the query calls for those ab in the relation for q such that there is some integer c, not necessarily appearing in the EDB, such that $b < c$. Since the latter condition is always true, Q with the middle subgoal deleted simply produces the relation for q as an answer. □

Efficiency of Testing Implication of Arithmetic Inequalities

In order to apply the test of Theorem 14.2, we need to tell whether one set of inequalities T follows from another, S. We compute S^+, by applying the axioms A1 to A8 until they no longer generate any new inequalities. Then, we check whether T is a subset of S^+.

It is left for an exercise to show that the following algorithm computes S^+ and takes $O(n^3)$ time when there are n inequalities in S.

1. Convert each $<$ relationship, say $X < Y$, into $X \leq Y$ and $X \neq Y$.
2. Compute the transitive closure of the $\leq$ relationships.
3. Apply axiom A8 to infer additional $\neq$ relationships.
4. Reconstruct the $<$ relationships using axiom A4; that is, $X < Y$ if $X \leq Y$ and $X \neq Y$ are now known.

Note that after step (1) there are still $O(n)$ inequalities to work with, and the number of variables cannot be more than $2n$. The time-consuming parts are steps (2) and (3). Step (2) can be done in $O(n^2)$ time by performing a depth-first search, from each variable, of the graph whose nodes are the variables and whose arcs are the $\leq$ relationships (see Aho, Hopcroft, and Ullman [1983]).

Step (3) can be done in $O(n^3)$ time. For each pair X and Y, we find all those Z such that $X \leq Z \leq Y$, in $O(n)$ time, just by enumerating the Z's and checking whether $X \leq Z$ and $Z \leq Y$ are both known. Then, we must check if any two such Z's are related by $\neq$. That also takes $O(n)$ time, but the algorithm requires a little thought. The trick is to realize that it is sufficient to check the $O(n)$ original $\neq$ pairs, that is, those given in S and those added in step (1). It is not necessary to check the new $\neq$ pairs added in step (3); a proof is left to the reader. The total time for step (3) is $O(n)$ times the square of the number of variables, which is bounded above by n^2. Thus, $O(n^3)$ time suffices for step (3).

14.3 OPTIMIZATION UNDER WEAK EQUIVALENCE

Let us recall Example 14.2 in Section 14.1, where we compared two algebraic expressions of the form[7]

$$\pi_D\big(\sigma_{E=a}(ED \bowtie DM)\big)$$
$$\pi_D\big(\sigma_{E=a}(ED)\big)$$

and observed that they are formally inequivalent, but only because of the possibility that there are dangling tuples, in the ED relation, that do not match any tuple in the DM relation. It is easy to check that, on the assumption of no dangling tuples, the two expressions are equivalent; both produce the departments of employee a.

---

[7] We use constant symbol a here, instead of the name "sloth" in Example 14.2.

One way to formalize the notion of "no dangling tuples" is to postulate the existence of a "universal" relation over all the attributes, E, D, and M in this case, and to suppose that the actual relations are projections of the universal relation onto the appropriate set of attributes. If we call the universal relation EDM, then we can rewrite the above two expressions as

$$\pi_D\Big(\sigma_{E=a}\big(\pi_{ED}(EDM) \bowtie \pi_{DM}(EDM)\big)\Big)$$
$$\pi_D\Big(\sigma_{E=a}\big(\pi_{ED}(EDM)\big)\Big)$$

It turns out that these expressions are equivalent in the sense discussed in Section 14.1, where dangling tuples are allowed. Note, however, that EDM is the only EDB relation, and there can be no dangling tuples when there is but one relation. We could, for example, write these expressions as conjunctive queries over an EDB relation $u(E, D, M)$; they are

```
answer(X)  :-  u(a,X,Y) & u(W,X,Z).                    (14.3)
answer(X)  :-  u(a,X,Y).                                (14.4)
```

We shall see shortly why (14.3) and (14.4) are equivalent to the given expressions of relational algebra. The equivalence of (14.3) and (14.4) is easy to show, using the test of Theorem 14.1.

Tableaux

When we assume a set of attributes and a single relation over all attributes, there is a notation, called a *tableau*, that is somewhat simpler to work with than are conjunctive queries. A tableau is a two-dimensional array, whose columns correspond to the attributes. We may head the columns by the attribute names, or we may omit the attributes, if they are understood.

The first row, called the *summary*, gives the arguments of the result of the query, that is, the arguments of the head of the equivalent conjunctive query. For each attribute A that corresponds to an argument of the result, there is a variable or constant in the column for A. Other columns are blank in the summary. Variables that appear in the summary are called *distinguished variables*; other variables are *nondistinguished*. Horizontal lines are drawn above and below the summary for clarity.

The remaining rows, just called *rows*, represent the subgoals of the conjunctive query. The subgoal $u(Y_1, \ldots, Y_n)$ is represented by the row $Y_1 \cdots Y_n$, assuming that the arguments of the "universal" predicate u correspond, in order, to the columns of the tableau. However, we use the convention that a blank in a row represents a variable that appears nowhere else, not even in other positions holding a blank.[8]

---

[8] This is the same convention that Query-by-Example (Section 4.4 of Volume I) uses to

E	D	M
	X	
a	X	Y
W	X	Z

(a) Tableau for (14.3)

E	D	M
	X	
a	X	Y

(b) Tableau for (14.4)

Figure 14.3 Two tableaux.

Example 14.10: The tableaux corresponding to the queries (14.3) and (14.4) are shown in Figure 14.3. In each case, the attributes correspond to Employees, Departments, and Managers. We could have replaced W, Y, and Z by blanks, since they appear only once; we could not replace a by a blank, because it is a constant, not a variable. □

The meaning of a tableau is the same as that of a conjunctive query formed as follows.

1.   The head consists of some predicate p with arguments equal to the non-blank entries of the summary, in order.

2.   The body consists of one subgoal for each row. The predicate of each subgoal is u, standing for the "universal" relation. The arguments of the subgoal for a row are the entries of that row, in order. However, a blank entry must be replaced by a variable that appears nowhere else.

Notice how the meanings of the tableaux in Figure 14.3 correspond to the conjunctive queries they were intended to represent.

An obviously equivalent, and frequently useful, way to look at tableaux, is that they define mappings, from a relation U for predicate u, to a relation over the attributes with nonblank entries in the summary. The mapping for a tableau T produces the set of tuples μ such that some substitution for the symbols in the tableau makes each row become a tuple of U and makes the nonblank entries of the summary become μ. Note that we must substitute for the blanks in the rows, but since they represent unique variables, any substitution whatsoever is acceptable. On the other hand, the substitution for a variable that appears several times in the rows must be chosen carefully, so all of the

---

avoid having to fill out skeletons with irrelevant variables. In fact, the general similarity between a tableau and a Query-by-Example skeleton should be noted.

rows simultaneously become tuples of U.

Constructing Tableaux

There is a straightforward way of constructing tableaux for a wide variety of relational algebra expressions, although not for all expressions. The operations we can handle are:

1. Selections that equate a variable to a constant or to another variable.[9]

2. Projections.

3. Natural joins. As a special case of the natural join, we can handle intersections of two relations over the same set of attributes. We can also handle equijoins if the attributes of the relations involved are renamed so the equated attributes have the same name, and no others do. Even Cartesian products can be handled if the attributes are renamed to be disjoint; all of these operations become special cases of a natural join.

Algorithm 14.1: Construction of a Tableau for a Select-Project-Join Expression.

INPUT: An algebraic expression involving relation variables as arguments, and equality-selections, projections, and natural joins as operators.

OUTPUT: A tableau equivalent to the expression, on the assumption of no dangling tuples; that is, all relations are projections of a single universal relation.

METHOD: We construct a tableau for each subexpression of the given algebraic expression, working up the tree from the leaves.

Basis: The basis is a leaf, that is, a relation variable $R(A_1, \ldots, A_n)$. The tableau we create has a summary and a single row. Both have distinguished variables in the columns for each of the A_i's and blanks elsewhere.

Induction: We consider three cases, depending on the type of the outermost operator.

Case 1: Suppose we have a subexpression $\pi_{A_1,\ldots,A_n}(E)$, and we have constructed the tableau T for E. To reflect the projection, we delete from the summary of T all the symbols in columns not among the A_i's, replacing them by blanks. The deleted variables still appear in the rows, but they are now nondistinguished variables.

---

[9] We can handle more general selections if we simply attach conditions to the tableaux. However, then we are limited to the theory of Section 14.2, where we have only a sufficient condition for eliminating subgoals in the presence of arithmetic inequalities.

Case 2: Suppose instead that we have subexpression $\sigma_F(E)$. If the condition F is $A = B$, then identify the distinguished variables in the summary of T for the columns A and B.[10] If the condition F is $A = c$, where c is a constant, we replace all occurrences of the distinguished variable for A by the constant c.

Case 3: The third case is that of an expression $E_1 \bowtie E_2$. Let T_1 and T_2 be the tableaux constructed for E_1 and E_2, respectively. Assume, without loss of generality, that if both T_1 and T_2 have distinguished variables in the summary column for attribute A, then those variables are the same, but that otherwise, T_1 and T_2 have no variables in common, either in the summary or the rows. If necessary, rename the variables of T_2 to make this condition true. The tableau T we construct for $E_1 \bowtie E_2$ has as rows, all the rows of T_1 and all the rows of T_2. The summary of T is constructed as follows.

1. If both T_1 and T_2 have blanks in a particular column of their summaries, so does T.

2. If one of T_1 and T_2 has a blank in a particular column of its summary, T has what the other of T_1 and T_2 has in that summary column.

3. If both T_1 and T_2 have variables in a given column of the summary, then these variables must be the same. T also has that variable in the given summary column.

4. If one of T_1 and T_2 has a variable X in a column of its summary, and the other has a constant a in the corresponding summary column, then substitute a for X wherever X appears in T, T_1, and/or T_2, and place a in the corresponding column of T's summary.

5. If T_1 and T_2 have different constants in the same column of their summaries, then the join $E_1 \bowtie E_2$ is empty. Modify T to have an empty summary, which we shall conventionally take to denote a tableau that maps every EDB to the empty relation.

A brief rule for remembering (1) to (5) above is that variables take precedence over blanks and constants take precedence over variables.

The rows of T are the rows of T_1 plus those of T_2. Any substitutions of constants for variables required by rule (4) above are made before the rules of T are constructed. $\square$

Example 14.11: Consider the expression of relational algebra

$$\pi_D\big(\sigma_{E=a}(ED \bowtie DM)\big)$$

The attributes for the tableaux will be E, D, and M, in that order. We begin with a tableau for the relation variable ED, whose attributes are E and D.

---

[10] By *identifying* two symbols we mean to replace one by the other or replace both by a third symbol. Each occurrence of the symbols must be replaced by this common symbol, not just the occurrences in the summary. It is irrelevant what symbol we choose as the common symbol, as long as it is not one of the other symbols of the tableau.

This tableau can be written as in Figure 14.4(a). Here, we use variables X and Y for the columns of both the summary and the lone row. Similarly, the tableau for DM is shown in Figure 14.4(b).

E	D	M
X	Y	
X	Y	

(a) Tableau for ED

E	D	M
	U	V
	U	V

(b) Tableau for DM

Figure 14.4 Tableaux for base case.

Working up the tree, we need a tableau for the expression $ED \bowtie DM$. This tableau is formed from the two tableaux in Figure 14.4 by identifying the symbols Y and U in the summary column for D, since D is a common attribute of the two operands of the join. Let us replace U by Y. No other changes of symbols are necessary, and the resulting tableau is shown in Figure 14.5(a). Notice how the two summaries of the tableaux of Figure 14.4 have been merged in Figure 14.5(a), and the rows of Figure 14.4 each appears in Figure 14.5(a), after replacing U by Y.

Next, we apply the selection $\sigma_{E=a}$ to the tableau of Figure 14.5(a). To do so, we replace distinguished variable X, which appears in the summary column for E, by the constant a to which it is equated. The result is shown in Figure 14.5(b).

Finally, we apply the projection π_D to Figure 14.5(b). The entries in the summary, other than the middle column, are replaced by blanks, resulting in the tableau of Figure 14.5(c). Note that V has become a nondistinguished variable. Also, observe that the tableau of Figure 14.5(c) is identical to that of Figure 14.3(a); with variables renamed. $\square$

Theorem 14.3: On the assumption that there are no dangling tuples, that is, each operand relation R represents the projection of a "universal" relation U onto the attributes of R, Algorithm 14.1 constructs, from an expression E, a tableau T whose mapping is the same as the mapping defined by E.

E	D	M
X	Y	V
X	Y	
	Y	V

(a) Tableau for $ED \bowtie DM$

E	D	M
a	Y	V
a	Y	
	Y	V

(b) Tableau for $\sigma_{E=a}(ED \bowtie DM)$

E	D	M
	Y	
a	Y	
	Y	V

(c) Tableau for $\pi_D\big(\sigma_{E=a}(ED \bowtie DM)\big)$

Figure 14.5 Tableaux constructed by join, selection, and projection.

Proof: This result is a simple induction on the number of operators in E. We shall prove the basis and the case of a join, leaving the remainder as an exercise. For the basis, an expression consisting of a relation $R(A_1, \ldots, A_n)$, the tableau evidently produces, from a universal relation U, those tuples $a_1 \cdots a_n$ such that there is some one tuple μ of U that has a_i in the component for A_i, for $i = 1, 2, \ldots, n$. But that is exactly the condition under which μ is in the relation R, since we assumed that R is $\pi_{A_1, \ldots, A_n}(U)$.

Now consider the case that $E = E_1 \bowtie E_2$, and the mappings of E_1 and E_2 are defined by the tableaux T_1 and T_2, respectively. Then the tableau T constructed for E, given a universal relation U, produces those tuples μ that are the summary of T under some substitution for the variables of T that makes all rows of T be tuples of U. Because of the way the summary of T is constructed, there must be tuples μ_1 and μ_2, over the attributes whose columns are nonblank in the summaries of T_1 and T_2, respectively, such that μ_1 and μ_2 agree with μ on their common attributes.

Since there is an assignment to all of the variables of T that produces μ, surely the same assignment to the variables of T_1 produces μ_1 and that assignment to the variables of T_2 produces μ_2. Thus, μ_1 is in E_1 and μ_2 is in E_2, by the inductive hypothesis. It follows that μ is in the relation for E, so T produces only tuples in E.

Conversely, suppose μ is in the relation for E. Then there must be tuples μ_1 and μ_2 that agree with μ in their common attributes, in the relations for E_1 and E_2, respectively. By the inductive hypothesis, there are assignments to the variables of T_1 and T_2, respectively, that make their summaries become μ_1 and μ_2. Since we renamed variables so the only variables shared by T_1 and T_2 are in the common columns of their summaries, the two assignments agree on all variables, including the common ones; they agree on common variables because μ_1 and μ_2 agree where they share an attribute. Thus, the common assignment to variables of T produces μ, showing that what E produces, T produces.

The remaining parts of the induction, where E is formed by selection or projection from a smaller expression, are left to the reader. $\square$

Weak Containment and Equivalence of Tableaux

We say that tableau T_1 is *weakly contained* in tableau T_2, written $T_1 \subseteq_w T_2$, if given any universal relation, the relation produced by T_1 is a subset of that produced by T_2. We say T_1 and T_2 are *weakly equivalent*, written $T_1 \equiv_w T_2$, if for any universal relation, the relations produced by T_1 and T_2 are the same.

The test for weak containment and equivalence is essentially that of Theorem 14.1. Recall that a tableau can be viewed as a conjunctive query if we replace each row by a subgoal with predicate u and treat all blanks as if they were variables appearing nowhere else. Thus, the following result is a simple corollary of Theorem 14.1.

Corollary 14.2: Let T_1 and T_2 be tableaux. Then $T_1 \subseteq_w T_2$ if and only if after replacing all blanks of T_1 by distinct variables, there is a symbol mapping from the variables of T_2 that turns the summary of T_2 into the summary of T_1 and turns each row of T_2 into a row of T_1.[11] $\square$

Note that a containment mapping does not have to be defined on the blanks of T_2. Whatever mapping on the rows we obtain, the variable represented by a blank can have its containment mapping defined appropriately.

Of course, $T_1 \equiv_w T_2$ if and only if mappings of the type described in Corollary 14.2 exist in both directions. Thus, Corollary 14.2 gives us a weak equivalence test too.

Example 14.12: Let T_1 be the tableau of Figure 14.3(a) and T_2 that of Figure 14.3(b). The identity mapping is a containment mapping from T_2 to T_1, so $T_1 \subseteq_w T_2$. From T_1 to T_2 we have the containment mapping h defined by $h(W) = a$, $h(X) = X$, and $h(Y) = h(Z) = Y$. Then the summary of T_2, which consists only of an X in the middle column, is turned into the summary of T_1, which is the same. Also, both rows aXY and WXZ of T_2 are turned into the row aXY of T_1. Thus, $T_2 \subseteq_w T_1$, and $T_1 \equiv_w T_2$. $\square$

---

[11] Such a symbol mapping will be called a containment mapping, as for conjunctive queries.

Minimization of Tableaux

We can also minimize the rows of a tableau just as we minimized the number of subgoals in a conjunctive query. We have the following additional corollary of Theorem 14.1 whose proof is left as an easy exercise.

Corollary 14.3: Given any tableau T, we can find a weakly equivalent tableau T' with the smallest possible number of rows by finding a containment mapping on the variables of T that is the identity mapping on the distinguished variables (so the summary is unchanged), and maps all of the rows of T into a smallest possible subset of the rows of T. T' is the summary of T with the rows that are the target of one or more rows according to this containment mapping. $\square$

Example 14.13: Consider the tableau T_1 of Figure 14.3(a). The containment mapping h defined in Example 14.12 is the identity on distinguished variable X and maps both rows into the first row, aXY. Since T_1 cannot be equivalent to a tableau with fewer than one row, we conclude that T_1 with its second row eliminated, which is T_2 of Figure 14.3(b), is a minimal, weakly equivalent tableau for T_1. $\square$

Writing Conjunctive Queries as Tableaux

It is possible to translate a conjunctive query into a tableau, by assigning a distinct column to each argument of each predicate symbol appearing in the query.

X	Y		
		Y	X
		Z	X
		Z_1	X
	X	Z_2	

Figure 14.6 Tableau for conjunctive query b_2.

Example 14.14: The tableau of Figure 14.6 represents the query b_2 of Example 14.1 (Section 14.1), which is

$$b_2: \quad \texttt{fp(X,Y)} \texttt{ :- e(Y,X) \& e(Z,X) \& e(Z}_1\texttt{,X) \& fp(X,Z}_2\texttt{).}$$

The first two columns represent the arguments of fp and the last two represent the arguments of e.[12]

---

[12] In truth, the occurrence of fp in the head of the conjunctive query or, equivalently, in the summary of the tableau, has nothing to do with the occurrence of fp as a subgoal

The rows of this tableau are minimized by a containment mapping that sends Z and Z_1 to Y and is the identity on other variables; this mapping eliminates the second and third rows. Note that we cannot map Z_2 to one of the anonymous symbols in the second column of the first three rows, because to do so, we would have to map X to the anonymous symbol in the first column of the same row. However, X, being a distinguished variable, cannot be mapped to anything but itself, or else the summary is destroyed. $\square$

Although we got the right answer in Example 14.14 when we tried to minimize the rows of the tableau in Figure 14.6, we should be aware that tableaux support minimization under the assumption of weak equivalence. That is, the tacit assumption was made that the relation for fp in the body and the relation for e were the projection of a single relation. In Example 14.14, we were not able to send a row that came from fp into one that came from e, or vice-versa, because of the presence of distinguished variable X in the rows. However, there are situations where minimization under weak equivalence gives us the wrong answer.

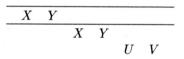

Figure 14.7 Tableau for conjunctive query (14.5).

Example 14.15: Consider the conjunctive query

$$p(X,Y) \; :- \; q(X,Y) \; \& \; s(U,V).$$ (14.5)

which says that p is q, unless s is empty, in which case the relation for p is the empty set. The tableau for this query is shown in Figure 14.7; the columns correspond to the two arguments of p, then those of q, and finally those of s. We can eliminate the last row by mapping U and V to the anonymous variables in the last two columns of the first row. Of course, the anonymous variables in the first two columns of the last row are mapped to the anonymous variables in the same columns of the first row, and the anonymous variables in the middle columns of the last row go to X and Y.

However, the conclusion is incorrect; the "equivalent" tableau,

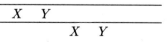

___

or row. We could place the symbols of the summary, in order, in any columns, and the effect would be the same.

represents the conjunctive query

p(X,Y) :- q(X,Y).

which is not equivalent to (14.5) in the case that the relation for s is empty and q's is not. Note that under the assumption of a universal relation, it would not be possible for q's relation to be empty while s's was not. However, we made no assumption of a universal relation for conjunctive queries, so we would not normally permit the elimination of subgoal $s(U, V)$ in (14.5). $\square$

Tagged Tableaux

To adapt the tableau notation to handle conjunctive queries, we need only *tag* each row with the relation or predicate from which it came. Then we forbid a containment mapping that turns a row into a row with a different tag. We leave it as an exercise that this modification recaptures our notion of "equivalence" from Section 14.1, which we can call *strong equivalence* to distinguish it from weak.

Example 14.16: The tableau of Example 14.15, with tags at the right ends of the rows, is

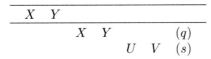

Now, no containment mapping can send either row to the other, since the tags are different. Thus we conclude that (14.5) is an already minimized conjunctive query. $\square$

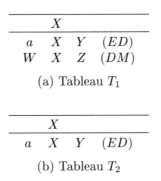

(a) Tableau T_1

(b) Tableau T_2

Figure 14.8 Tagged tableaux.

Example 14.17: In Figure 14.8 we have added tags to the tableaux of Figure 14.3; call these tableaux T_1 and T_2. The identity containment mapping still serves to send T_2 to T_1, because the tag (ED) is preserved. Thus, $T_1 \subseteq T_2$. However, no containment mapping can send T_1 to T_2, because the second row of T_1, with tag (DM), cannot map to the row of T_2, which has a different tag. We thus conclude again that T_1 and T_2 are not equivalent if ED and DM are allowed to be arbitrary relations, including relations with dangling tuples. $\square$

14.4 OPTIMIZING UNIONS OF CONJUNCTIVE QUERIES

In Section 14.1 we saw that there is a simple rule for minimizing subgoals in a conjunctive query; each subgoal that can be eliminated is eliminated by a single other subgoal, to which the first is mapped by a containment mapping. In particular, it is not possible for two or more subgoals to "team up" and together do the job of another subgoal, or for $n - 1$ subgoals to do the work of n. A similar phenomenon occurs when we consider unions of conjunctive queries, such as the (infinite) union $a_0 \cup a_1 \cup \cdots$ representing the result of the recursive "funny paths" rules, discussed in Example 14.1. That is, if a term (conjunctive query) in the union is redundant, then there is one other term in which it is contained. It is not possible that the result of one term is contained in the union of two or more terms, unless that term is in fact contained in one term of the union.

Example 14.18: Consider the three conjunctive queries

Q_1:   fp(X,Y) :- e(X,Y) & e(Y,Z).
Q_2:   fp(X,Y) :- e(X,W) & e(W,Y).
Q_3:   fp(X,Y) :- e(X,Y) & e(X,U) & e(U,Y).

Here, we have defined a new notion of "funny paths"; Q_1 says there is a funny path from X to Y if there is an edge from X to Y, and some edge out of Y. Q_2 says a path of length two is a funny path, and Q_3 says there is a funny path from X to Y if there is both an edge and a path of length two.

If we apply the containment test of Theorem 14.1, we find that $Q_3 \subseteq Q_2$, but no other relationships hold. The containment mapping from Q_2 to Q_3 sends X and Y to themselves, and sends W to U. Thus, the same notion of "funny paths" is defined by rules Q_1 and Q_2 alone; Q_3 is redundant. As Q_1 and Q_2 are minimized conjunctive queries, that is, none of their subgoals is redundant, they together are the unique (up to renaming of variables) minimal way to express these "funny paths" as a collection of Horn clauses. $\square$

We shall now prove the theorem that gives us a containment test for unions of conjunctive queries. Let $\mathcal{Q} = Q_1 \cup Q_2 \cup \cdots$ and $\mathcal{R} = R_1 \cup R_2 \cup \cdots$ be two (possibly infinite) unions of conjunctive queries, all of which have a common head predicate. We say $\mathcal{Q} \subseteq \mathcal{R}$ if for any EDB, the relation that is the union of the relations returned by the Q_i's is a subset of the relation formed from the union of the relations returned by the R_i's. We say $Q \equiv R$ if $Q \subseteq R$ and $R \subseteq Q$.

It is useful to speak of a *containment* from Q to R, whenever $Q \subseteq R$. Formally, a containment α is a map from the conjunctive queries in

$$Q = Q_1 \cup Q_2 \cup \cdots$$

to those in $R = R_1 \cup R_2 \cup \cdots$, such that if $\alpha(Q_i) = R_j$, then $Q_i \subseteq R_j$.[13] Note that the containment goes from the union with the smaller relation to the one with the larger relation, unlike a containment mapping, which goes from the larger to the smaller.

Theorem 14.4: Let $Q = Q_1 \cup Q_2 \cup \cdots$ and $R = R_1 \cup R_2 \cup \cdots$. Then $Q \subseteq R$ if and only if there is a containment from Q to R.

Proof: The proof follows the techniques introduced in Theorem 14.1.

If: Suppose that for each Q_i in Q, there is some R_j in R for which $Q_i \subseteq R_j$. Every tuple μ in the relation for Q is in the relation for some Q_i. Thus, μ is in the relation for the associated R_j, and therefore μ is in the relation for R. Hence, $Q \subseteq R$.

Only If: Suppose Q_i is contained in none of the R's. Convert the variables of Q_i to constants; each variable becomes a constant that appears nowhere else in Q_i. Now create an EDB consisting of exactly the subgoals of Q_i, with these constants substituted for the variables. The same substitution turns the head of Q_i into a tuple μ.

Given that $Q \subseteq R$, we know that μ is in the relation produced by R from this EDB. Then there is some particular R_j whose relation contains μ. As in Theorem 14.1, it is easy to argue that R_j can produce μ only if there is a symbol mapping from the variables of R_j to the EDB tuples; this mapping also serves as a containment mapping from R_j to Q_i. Thus, $Q_i \subseteq R_j$, contrary to our assumption that Q_i was contained in none of the R's. □

Example 14.19: Consider the expansion of the "funny paths" recursion of Example 14.1 into conjunctive queries $a_0, a_1, \ldots$, where the first two terms are

$$a_0: \quad \texttt{fp(X,Y) :- e(X,Y).}$$
$$a_1: \quad \texttt{fp(X,Y) :- e(Y,X) \& e(X,Z}_0\texttt{).}$$

and the general term is

$$a_i: \quad \texttt{fp(X,Y) :- e(Y,X) \& e(Z}_0\texttt{,X) \&}$$
$$\texttt{e(Z}_1\texttt{,X) \& e(Z}_2\texttt{,X) \& } \cdots \texttt{ \& e(Z}_{i-2}\texttt{,X) \& e(X,Z}_{i-1}\texttt{).}$$

Here, we have replaced Z by Z_0 to fit the pattern created by the other Z's.

---

[13] Containment between conjunctive queries Q_i and R_j is the ordinary notion of containment introduced in Section 14.1.

Let $\mathcal{Q} = a_0 \cup a_1$, and let $\mathcal{R}$ be the infinite union $a_0 \cup a_1 \cup \cdots$. For all $i \geq 2$, we can show $a_i \subseteq a_1$ if we use the containment mapping that sends X and Y to themselves and Z_0 to Z_{i-1}. It follows that $\mathcal{R} \subseteq \mathcal{Q}$, since we just argued that α, defined by $\alpha(a_0) = a_0$ and $\alpha(a_i) = a_1$ for all $i \geq 1$, is a containment from $\mathcal{R}$ to $\mathcal{Q}$. It is trivial that $\mathcal{Q} \subseteq \mathcal{R}$, so we conclude $\mathcal{Q} \equiv \mathcal{R}$. That is, the infinite recursion of Example 14.1 is equivalent to the union of the two conjunctive queries a_0 and a_1. $\square$

Minimization of Unions of Conjunctive Queries

In analogy with Corollary 14.1, we might hope that for each union of conjunctive queries there is an essentially unique subset of the union that is its minimal equivalent. Unfortunately, infinite sets often behave in strange ways, and that need not be the case. Exercise 14.7 gives an example of an infinite union where there is no minimal equivalent at all. However, for finite unions, we can prove the following corollary to Theorem 14.4.

Corollary 14.4: Given any finite union of conjunctive queries,

$$\mathcal{Q} = \mathcal{Q}_1 \cup \mathcal{Q}_2 \cup \cdots$$

we can find a subset $\mathcal{R}$ of $\mathcal{Q}$, such that

1. $\mathcal{R} \equiv \mathcal{Q}$,
2. For no proper subset $\mathcal{R}'$ of $\mathcal{R}$ is $\mathcal{R}' \equiv \mathcal{Q}$, and
3. If $\mathcal{Q}_m$ is any equivalent to $\mathcal{Q}$, then there is a containment from $\mathcal{Q}_m$ to $\mathcal{R}$, but none from $\mathcal{Q}_m$ to any proper subset $\mathcal{R}'$ of $\mathcal{R}$.

Proof: $\mathcal{R}$ consists of all and only those Q_i for which

a) There is no Q_j for which Q_i is properly contained in Q_j, that is, $Q_i \subseteq Q_j$, but not $Q_j \subseteq Q_i$. We shall use $Q_i \subset Q_j$ to denote proper containment.
b) There is no Q_j equivalent to Q_i such that $j < i$.

First we must prove that (1) holds. $\mathcal{R} \subseteq \mathcal{Q}$ follows because each Q_i in $\mathcal{R}$ is also in $\mathcal{Q}$. Now, we must demonstrate $\mathcal{Q} \subseteq \mathcal{R}$. If Q_i is in $\mathcal{Q}$, then either Q_i is in $\mathcal{R}$, or Q_i was eliminated by rule (a) or (b). If by (a), then there is some Q_j such that $Q_i \subset Q_j$. If by (b), then there is a $Q_j \equiv Q_i$ such that $j < i$. If Q_j is in $\mathcal{R}$, we are done for Q_i; we have found a member of $\mathcal{R}$ in which Q_i is contained. However, Q_j may itself be eliminated by (a) or (b).

If we repeat this argument as many times as necessary, we obtain a sequence $Q_{i_1} \subseteq Q_{i_2} \subseteq Q_{i_3} \subseteq \cdots$ where $i_1 = i$ and $i_2 = j$. As long as this sequence is not infinite, we eventually come to some Q_k that remains in $\mathcal{R}$ and that contains Q_i. We claim that as long as there are only a finite number of conjunctive queries in $\mathcal{Q}$, this sequence cannot be infinite. In proof, suppose that some query repeats in the sequence, say $Q_{i_m} = Q_{i_n}$, where $m < n$. Then

$$Q_{i_m} \equiv Q_{i_{m+1}} \equiv \cdots \equiv Q_{i_n}$$

because Q_{i_m} cannot be contained properly in Q_{i_n}, which is itself. It follows that each of these queries was eliminated by rule (b). But then we have

$$i_m > i_{m+1} > \cdots > i_n = i_m$$

a contradiction.

Now let us show (2). Suppose that $\mathcal{R}' \equiv \mathcal{R}$, but $\mathcal{R}'$ is a proper subset of $\mathcal{R}$. Let Q_i be in $\mathcal{R} - \mathcal{R}'$. Then there is some Q_j in $\mathcal{R}'$ such that $Q_i \subseteq Q_j$. If $Q_i \subset Q_j$, then Q_i would be eliminated by (a), and would not be in $\mathcal{R}$. If $Q_i \equiv Q_j$, then one of Q_i and Q_j would have been eliminated from $\mathcal{R}$ by (b). Thus, $\mathcal{R}'$ cannot exist.

Finally, we show (3). If $\mathcal{Q}_m \equiv \mathcal{Q}$, then, as $\mathcal{Q} \equiv \mathcal{R}$, we have $\mathcal{Q}_m \equiv \mathcal{R}$; thus there is a containment from $\mathcal{Q}_m$ to $\mathcal{R}$. Suppose there is a containment from $\mathcal{Q}_m$ to some $\mathcal{R}'$, a proper subset of $\mathcal{R}$. There is a containment from $\mathcal{Q}$ to $\mathcal{Q}_m$, since $\mathcal{Q} \equiv \mathcal{Q}_m$. It follows that there is a containment from $\mathcal{Q}$ to $\mathcal{R}'$, contradicting (2). $\square$

We conclude the section with two more examples where it is possible to determine a minimal equivalent for an infinite union of conjunctive queries.

Example 14.20: Consider our usual ancestor rules,

```
r₁:   anc(X,Y) :- par(X,Y).
r₂:   anc(X,Y) :- par(X,Z₀) & anc(Z₀,Y).
```

We chose Z_0 as the existentially quantified variable in the body of r_2, in order to conform with the pattern that develops as we expand these rules.

Let us follow the procedure outlined in Example 14.1, where we substitute the bodies of both r_1 and r_2 for the recursive subgoal in r_2. The ith time we substitute r_2, we use Z_i in place of Z_0 to avoid conflicts among variable names. We obtain an infinite sequence of conjunctive queries $Q_0, Q_1, \ldots$, where Q_i is the result of using r_2 i times and then r_1. The sequence begins

```
Q₀:   anc(X,Y) :- par(X,Y).
Q₁:   anc(X,Y) :- par(X,Z₀) & par(Z₀,Y).
```

and the general term is

```
Qᵢ:   anc(X,Y) :- par(X,Z₀) & par(Z₀,Z₁) & ···
              par(Zᵢ₋₂,Zᵢ₋₁) & par(Zᵢ₋₁,Y).
```

That is, Q_i is the $(i+1)$st-generation relationship.

We claim that for no $i \neq j$ is $Q_i \subseteq Q_j$, so the union $\mathcal{Q} = Q_0 \cup Q_1 \cup \cdots$ is its own minimal equivalent. In particular, unlike Example 14.1, where we found that the infinite recursion was equivalent to the union of two conjunctive queries, here we find that the recursion is real; it is not equivalent to any finite number of conjunctive queries.

Now, we need to show that for no distinct i and j is $Q_i \subseteq Q_j$. First, suppose

$i > j$. If we look at Q_i and Q_j we note that the distinguished variables[14] X and Y must map to themselves under any containment mapping h from Q_j to Q_i; otherwise, the head of Q_j would not be transformed to the head of Q_i. Given that $h(X) = X$, the subgoal $par(X, Z_0)$ in Q_j can only be transformed to the same subgoal in Q_i, because no other subgoal of Q_i has X as its first argument. It follows that $h(Z_0) = Z_0$. Similarly, $par(Z_0, Z_1)$ in Q_j must map to the same subgoal in Q_i, because only one subgoal has Z_0 as its first argument.

It follows that h must be the identity on all of the variables X, Y, $Z_1, \ldots, Z_{j-1}$ of Q_j. However, as $i > j$, the subgoal $par(Z_{j-1}, Y)$ cannot map to any subgoal of Q_i, since in Q_i, the only subgoal with Z_{j-1} as first argument has Z_j as second argument, and Y, being distinguished, cannot map to Z_j.

The case where $i < j$ is handled similarly. We again see that h must be the identity on all variables of Q_j. Then, $par(Z_{j-1}, Y)$ cannot map to any subgoal, because the only subgoal of Q_i with Y as the second argument has Z_{i-1} as the first argument, and $h(Z_{j-1}) = Z_{j-1} \neq Z_{i-1}$, as $i \neq j$. $\square$

Example 14.21: In previous examples, we have found that the minimal equivalent for an infinite union of conjunctive queries was finite (Example 14.19) or the entire union (Example 14.20). There are examples where the minimal equivalent is infinite, but a proper subset of the given union. As a trivial example, let $\mathcal{Q}$ be the union

$$Q_1 \cup Q_1' \cup Q_2 \cup Q_2' \cup \cdots$$

where the Q's are the conjunctive queries from Example 14.20, and Q_i' is a copy of Q_i, with variables renamed. Then there are an infinite number of minimal equivalents to $\mathcal{Q}$, each consists of one of Q_1 and Q_1', one of Q_2 and Q_2', and so on. Note that all of these minimal subsets are essentially the same; they differ only in the variables used in their member queries. $\square$

14.5 CONTAINMENT OF CONJUNCTIVE QUERIES IN LOGICAL RECURSIONS

In this section we shall explore another generalization of the basic conjunctive query questions. Suppose we have a conjunctive query Q defining a predicate p and we have a logic program (collection of rules) $\mathcal{P}$ that also defines a predicate p. We would like to know whether, for every EDB, the relation produced by Q is a subset of the relation for p that is produced by $\mathcal{P}$ (a condition we write as $Q \subseteq \mathcal{P}$). Chapter 15 contains a number of instances where this question is significant.

We may recall from Examples 14.1 and 14.20 that it is possible to expand

---

[14] We find it useful to call variables appearing in the head of a conjunctive query "distinguished" and others "nondistinguished." This classification is exactly what we would get if we converted a conjunctive query to a tableau.

logical rules into an infinite sequence of conjunctive queries. In those examples we considered only linear rules with a single IDB predicate. However, the same idea works for any logic program. We construct a collection of conjunctive queries, starting with the rules themselves and repeatedly substituting the body of some rule for some IDB subgoal of some conjunctive query in the set. Among the conjunctive queries generated, some will have predicate p in the head and will have only EDB subgoals; normally there will be an infinite number of these. It is left as an exercise to show that the union of the relations produced by these conjunctive queries is the same, for any EDB, as the relation for p defined by applying bottom-up evaluation to the logic program and this EDB. (See Exercise 14.20 for a precise statement of the expansion algorithm.)

Suppose that the logic program $\mathcal{P}$ produces the equivalent set of conjunctive queries $P_1, P_2, \ldots$ for the predicate p. The question of whether Q is contained in the union of these conjunctive queries is a special case of Theorem 14.4, where the first union consists of a single conjunctive query. We could thus, in principle, decide whether $Q \subseteq \mathcal{P}$ by testing $Q \subseteq P_1$, $Q \subseteq P_2, \ldots$. However, that test is not guaranteed to terminate; if there are an infinite number of P's, and Q is contained in none of them, we don't know when to stop.

Fortunately, there is a direct approach that is guaranteed to decide whether $Q \subseteq \mathcal{P}$, as long as the rules of $\mathcal{P}$ are datalog or, more generally, are rules for which bottom-up evaluation converges after a finite time with any finite EDB; the technique is a natural generalization of Theorem 14.1. Treat the subgoals of Q as if they were the only EDB facts. With this database, apply naive or semi-naive evaluation to $\mathcal{P}$. If the p-fact that is the head of Q is inferred, then $Q \subseteq \mathcal{P}$ holds, as we shall prove. If this fact is not derived, then we have an example of a fact that Q derives and $\mathcal{P}$ does not, demonstrating that $Q \subseteq \mathcal{P}$ is false. The idea is formalized in the following algorithm and theorem.

Algorithm 14.2: Testing Whether a Conjunctive Query is Contained in the Relation Defined by a Logic Program.

INPUT: A conjunctive query Q, which we write as

$$H \text{ :- } G_1 \text{ \& } \cdots \text{ \& } G_k.$$

and a logic program $\mathcal{P}$. We assume that $\mathcal{P}$ has a finite least fixed point for any finite EDB; that is, bottom-up evaluation converges after a finite time, given any finite database.

OUTPUT: A decision whether $Q \subseteq \mathcal{P}$.

METHOD: We begin by selecting a mapping τ that assigns to every variable X of Q a unique constant $\tau(X)$. We extend τ to atoms in the obvious way. Then construct the EDB consisting of the k facts $\tau(G_1), \ldots, \tau(G_k)$. That is, if G_i is the atom $q(t_1, \ldots, t_m)$, then the tuple $\big(\tau(t_1), \ldots, \tau(t_m)\big)$ is in the EDB relation for predicate q.

With this database, evaluate $\mathcal{P}$, using one of the bottom-up methods. By our assumption regarding $\mathcal{P}$, this evaluation will finish after a finite time. If $\tau(H)$ is in the IDB relation constructed for p, the predicate of the head H, then answer "yes"; else answer "no." □

Example 14.22: Let $\mathcal{P}$ consist of the two rules

r_1: p(X,Y) :- e(X,Z) & e(Z,Y).
r_2: p(X,Y) :- p(X,Z) & p(Z,Y).

If e represents edges in a graph, then p represents even-length paths. Suppose Q is the conjunctive query

Q: p(X,Y) :- e(X,U) & e(U,V) & e(V,Y).

that is, paths of length three.

Let us turn the variables of Q into constants by the mapping $\tau(X) = 1$, $\tau(Y) = 2$, $\tau(U) = 3$, and $\tau(V) = 4$. Then the EDB formed from the subgoals of Q has the tuples $(1, 3)$, $(3, 4)$, and $(4, 2)$ in the relation for e. Mapping τ applied to the head of Q is $(1, 2)$, so this is the tuple we hope to find in the relation for p, when we apply rules r_1 and r_2 to this EDB. Unfortunately, on round 1, rule r_1 gives us tuples $p(1, 4)$ and $p(3, 2)$, but nothing else. On the next round, these tuples do not satisfy the body of r_2, and of course r_1 cannot produce anything new, so we have converged without inferring $p(1, 2)$. Thus, $\mathcal{P}$ does not produce everything that Q produces on every database; in particular, we have exhibited a database where Q produces a p-fact based on a path of length three, and $\mathcal{P}$ cannot produce this fact.

Now, consider the same logic program with the conjunctive query

Q': p(X,Y) :- e(X,U) & e(U,V) & e(V,W) & e(W,Y).

Let τ map X, Y, U, V, and W to $1, \ldots, 5$, respectively. Then the EDB consists of the tuples $(1, 3)$, $(3, 4)$, $(4, 5)$, and $(5, 2)$ for e, and we again hope to derive the head of Q', which is $p(1, 2)$. Now, r_1 gives us $p(1, 4)$, $p(3, 5)$, and $p(4, 2)$ on the first round of bottom-up evaluation, and on the second round, r_2 combines $p(1, 4)$ with $p(4, 2)$ to infer $p(1, 2)$. Thus, we conclude the intuitively obvious result that $\mathcal{P}$ produces everything that Q produces, independent of what database is chosen; that is, $\mathcal{P}$ produces all the paths of length four. □

Theorem 14.5: Algorithm 14.2 correctly determines whether $Q \subseteq \mathcal{P}$.

Proof: If Algorithm 14.2 says "no," then the example database it has constructed serves as a counterexample. That is, the tuple $\tau(H)$ is in the relation produced by Q for the given database, but has been found not to be in the relation for p produced by $\mathcal{P}$.

Now suppose $\tau(H)$ is inferred from $\mathcal{P}$ and the constructed database. Intuitively, there is some proof of $\tau(H)$, and this proof yields a particular conjunctive query among those in the expansion of $\mathcal{P}$ that contains Q. More formally, we know $\tau(H)$ has a proof tree, as discussed at the beginning of Section 12.3. In this tree, the leaves are facts from the constructed EDB, and at each interior node, the fact at that node and the facts at its children form the head and body, respectively, of a substituted instance of one of $\mathcal{P}$'s rules. Let this tree be T.

Let D be any database, on which we shall evaluate Q and $\mathcal{P}$. Let ρ be a substitution for the variables of Q that turns each subgoal into a tuple in the appropriate relation of D. Now, replace each constant a appearing in the tree T by $\rho(\tau^{-1}(a))$. That is, interpret a as the variable of Q to which it corresponds, and make the substitution ρ on that variable. We claim that the new tree, T', is a proof tree for $\mathcal{P}$ and the database D. First, at each interior node of T' there is a substituted rule instance. That is, suppose T has $\psi(r)$ at node N, where r is a rule of $\mathcal{P}$, and ψ is some substitution. Then at N in T' we have $\rho(\tau^{-1}(\psi(r)))$, another substitution on r. If N is a leaf of T with label $\tau(G_i)$, where G_i is a subgoal of Q, then in T' the label at N is $\rho(\tau^{-1}(\tau(G_i)))$, which is $\rho(G_i)$. Since $\rho(G_i)$ must be a tuple of D, we conclude that T' is a proof tree.

The root of T is $\tau(H)$, so the root of T' is $\rho(\tau^{-1}(\tau(H)))$, or $\rho(H)$. But $\rho(H)$ is the tuple that Q produces from database D and the arbitrary substitution ρ. Thus, every tuple Q produces from D has a proof tree in $\mathcal{P}$, using database D. We conclude that $Q \subseteq \mathcal{P}$ whenever Algorithm 14.2 says "yes." $\square$

Example 14.23: Let us reconsider the logic program $\mathcal{P}$ of Example 14.22,

$$r_1: \quad \text{p(X,Y)} \text{ :- } \text{e(X,Z)} \text{ \& } \text{e(Z,Y)}.$$
$$r_2: \quad \text{p(X,Y)} \text{ :- } \text{p(X,Z)} \text{ \& } \text{p(Z,Y)}.$$

and the conjunctive query

$$Q': \quad \text{p(X,Y)} \text{ :- } \text{e(X,U)} \text{ \& } \text{e(U,V)} \text{ \& } \text{e(V,W)} \text{ \& } \text{e(W,Y)}.$$

In that example, we created a database from Q by making the substitution $\tau(X) = 1$ and so on, to produce the relation $E = \{13, 34, 45, 52\}$ for predicate e. We then discovered a proof for $p(1,2)$ whose tree is that shown in Figure 14.9. Note, for example, that the root of Figure 14.9 and its two children form an instance of r_2, where we have substituted 1, 2, and 4 for X, Y, and Z, respectively.

If we look at the leaves in Figure 14.9, and we apply τ^{-1} to replace the constants by their corresponding variables, we see that this tree represents a particular expansion of $\mathcal{P}$ that yields the conjunctive query Q itself. It should thus be no surprise that Q is contained in $\mathcal{P}$. For example, suppose we have the database D that gives e the relation $\{ab, bc, cd, da\}$. Then Q lets us derive $p(a, a)$ by the substitution $\rho(X) = \rho(Y) = a$, $\rho(U) = b$, $\rho(V) = c$, and $\rho(W) = d$. If we substitute $\rho(\tau^{-1}(i))$ for each integer i in Figure 14.9, we get the tree of Figure 14.10. Evidently, this tree proves $p(a, a)$ from the database D and shows how $\mathcal{P}$ would infer $p(a, a)$ bottom-up from D. $\square$

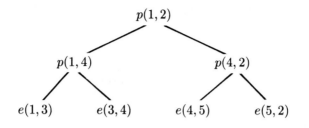

Figure 14.9 Proof tree for $p(1,2)$.

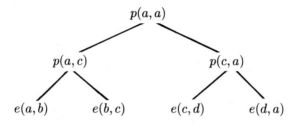

Figure 14.10 Proof tree for $p(a,a)$.

EXERCISES

14.1: Find all equivalences and containments among the four conjunctive queries of Figure 14.11. Note that c is a constant in Q_4.

$$
\begin{aligned}
&Q_1: \quad \text{p(X,Y)} \; :- \; \text{q(X,A)} \; \& \; \text{q(A,B)} \; \& \; \text{q(B,Y)}. \\
&Q_2: \quad \text{p(X,Y)} \; :- \; \text{q(X,A)} \; \& \; \text{q(A,B)} \; \& \; \text{q(B,C)} \; \& \; \text{q(C,Y)}. \\
&Q_3: \quad \text{p(X,Y)} \; :- \; \text{q(X,A)} \; \& \; \text{q(B,C)} \; \& \; \text{q(D,Y)} \; \& \\
&\qquad\qquad\qquad\qquad\quad \text{q(X,B)} \; \& \; \text{q(A,C)} \; \& \; \text{q(C,Y)}. \\
&Q_4: \quad \text{p(X,Y)} \; :- \; \text{q(X,A)} \; \& \; \text{q(A,c)} \; \& \; \text{q(c,B)} \; \& \; \text{q(B,Y)}.
\end{aligned}
$$

Figure 14.11 Conjunctive queries for Exercise 14.1.

14.2: For the conjunctive queries of Figure 14.11:
   a) Minimize each.
   b) Minimize the union $Q_1 \cup Q_2 \cup Q_3 \cup Q_4$.
   c) Convert each to a tableau.

14.3: For the tagged tableau of Figure 14.12:

    a)   Minimize it under weak equivalence.

    b)   Minimize it under strong equivalence.

    c)   Convert it to a conjunctive query.

    d)   Give an equivalent expression of relational algebra.

A	B	C	D
S			
S	V		(p)
T	V	W	(q)
U	V	X	(q)
Y	Z	X	(q)

Figure 14.12 Tableau for Exercise 14.3.

14.4: Determine whether each of the conjunctive queries

```
p(X,Y) :- e(X,A) & e(A,Y) & e(X,B) &
              e(B,Y) & X<A & B<Y.
p(X,Y) :- e(X,Z) & e(Z,Y) & X<Z & Z<Y.
```

is contained in the other. If not, give a counterexample.

14.5: Find all consequences of the inequalities $A \leq B$, $B \leq C$, $B \leq D$, $C \leq E$, $D \leq E$, $E \leq F$, and $C \neq D$. You need not list $X \leq Y$ and $X \neq Y$ when $X < Y$ holds.

14.6: Construct a tableau for the algebraic expression

$$\left(\pi_{AC}(AB \bowtie BC)\right) \bowtie \left(\pi_{CD}(CB \bowtie BD)\right)$$

14.7: Consider the infinite union of conjunctive queries $Q_1 \cup Q_2 \cup \cdots$, where Q_k is

$$p(X) :\text{-} e(X, Z_1) \ \& \ e(Z_1, Z_2) \ \& \ \cdots \ e(Z_{k-1}Z_k) \ \& \ e(Z_k, X).$$

Note that Q_k represents (not necessarily simple) cycles of length $k + 1$ in a graph whose arcs are represented by e. Find all containments among the Q's. Show that there is no minimal equivalent union of conjunctive queries.

14.8: Expand the rules of Example 14.22 (even-length paths) into an infinite set of conjunctive queries. What is the minimal equivalent union of conjunctive queries?

* 14.9: Consider the logic program $\mathcal{P}$ consisting of the rules

```
p(X,Y,Z) :- q(X,Y,Z).
p(X,Y,Z) :- p(A,A,A) & p(A,X,Y) &
            s(X) & s(Y) & s(Z) & s(A).
```

and the conjunctive query

```
Q:  p(X,Y,Z) :- q(B,B,B) & q(B,A,A) & q(A,X,Y) &
            s(X) & s(Y) & s(Z) & s(A) & s(B).
```

a)   Show that $Q \subseteq \mathcal{P}$.
b)   Give a particular conjunctive query in the expansion of $\mathcal{P}$ that contains Q.

X	Y
X	Z
Z	Y

(a) For Q_1

X	Y
X	A
B	Y

(b) For Q_2

Figure 14.13 Tableaux for Exercise 14.10.

14.10: Suppose we have a conjunctive query Q whose head and all subgoals have predicate p. We can write Q as a tableau in which the columns correspond to the arguments of p. For example, the two conjunctive queries

```
Q₁:  p(X,Y) :- p(X,Z) & p(Z,Y).
Q₂:  p(X,Y) :- p(X,A) & p(B,Y).
```

are equivalent to the tableaux of Figure 14.13(a) and (b), respectively. We can regard a tableau T for such a conjunctive query Q as if it were a tuple-generating dependency.[15] To obtain the dependency DEP(Q), simply move the summary to the bottom and treat it as the conclusion.

a)   Find DEP(Q_1) and DEP(Q_2), where Q_1 and Q_2 are the conjunctive queries given above. Informally, what do these dependencies say?
* b)   Let Q and R be arbitrary conjunctive queries satisfying the constraint of this exercise (only one predicate). Prove that if $Q \subseteq R$, then DEP(R) logically implies DEP(Q).
** c)   Is the converse of (b) true; that is, if DEP(R) implies DEP(Q), does it follow that $Q \subseteq R$?

---

[15] See Section 7.11 of Volume I.

** 14.11: Show that the minimal equivalent for a conjunctive query is unique up to renaming of variables and reordering of subgoals. Likewise, the minimal equivalent union of conjunctive queries for a finite union of conjunctive queries is unique up to renaming of variables, reordering subgoals within conjunctive queries, and reordering queries within the union.

* 14.12: Provide the missing details for Case (2) of Lemma 14.1.

* 14.13: Show that the algorithm at the end of Section 14.2 for finding S^+ works and takes $O(n^3)$ time. That is, prove it is sufficient in step (3) to apply axiom A8 to only the original $\neq$ and $<$ facts, and not to the inferred $\neq$ facts.

* 14.14: Consider the conjunctive queries

$$Q_1: \quad \text{p(A,B)} \ \text{:- q(A,C) \& r(C,B)}.$$
$$Q_2: \quad \text{p(A,B)} \ \text{:- q(B,D) \& r(D,A)}.$$

Does the symbol mapping $\tau(B) = A$, $\tau(D) = C$, and $\tau(A) = B$ demonstrate that $Q_1 \subseteq Q_2$? Why or why not?

14.15: Complete the proof of Theorem 14.3.

14.16: Prove Corollary 14.3.

14.17: Give algorithms to convert from conjunctive queries to tagged tableaux, and vice versa.

** 14.18: If $\mathcal{Q}$ and $\mathcal{P}$ are unions of conjunctive queries, $\mathcal{Q} - \mathcal{P}$ applied to a database returns all those tuples produced by $\mathcal{Q}$ but not by $\mathcal{P}$. Show that

$$\mathcal{Q}_1 - \mathcal{P}_1 \subseteq \mathcal{Q}_2 - \mathcal{P}_2$$

if and only if $\mathcal{Q}_1 \subseteq \mathcal{Q}_2$ and $\mathcal{P}_2 \subseteq \mathcal{P}_1$.

** 14.19: Suppose we are given a set of functional dependencies F. If Q_1 and Q_2 are conjunctive queries, we say that $Q_1 \subseteq_F Q_2$ if on every database that satisfies F, Q_1 produces a subset of the tuples that Q_2 produces.

    a)   Give an example of Q_1, Q_2, and F such that $Q_1 \subseteq_F Q_2$ holds, but not $Q_1 \subseteq Q_2$.

    b)   Give an algorithm to test whether $Q_1 \subseteq_F Q_2$. You may assume all subgoals of Q_1 and Q_2 are ordinary subgoals (no arithmetic).

** 14.20: In Figure 14.14 we see an algorithm to expand a given set of rules into an infinite set of conjunctive queries S. Prove that for an IDB predicate q, the union of the set of conjunctive queries in S that have q for the head predicate and have only EDB subgoals in the body produces, for any database, exactly what the logic program produces for predicate q with that database.

```
S := given set of rules;
repeat forever
    for each previously unconsidered conjunctive
        query Q in S do
        for each IDB subgoal p(t₁,...,tₖ) in the
            body of Q do
            for each rule r for p do begin
                rename variables of r so there are none
                in common with Q;
                unify the head of r with p(t₁,...,tₖ)
                to get MGU τ;
                add to S the conjunctive query formed from
                τ(Q) by replacing τ(p(t₁,...,tₖ)) by τ
                applied to the body of r
    end
```

Figure 14.14 Expanding a recursion into conjunctive queries.

* 14.21: Show it is $\mathcal{NP}$-complete to determine

    a)   Whether one conjunctive query is contained in another.

    b)   Whether a conjunctive query has a minimal set of subgoals.

BIBLIOGRAPHIC NOTES

Conjunctive queries, their containment, and equivalence were first studied by Chandra and Merlin [1977]. The treatment of conjunctive queries with arithmetic inequalities in Section 14.2 is from Klug [1988], which was written in 1982 and published posthumously.

Tableaux and weak equivalence, from Section 14.3, were considered by Aho, Sagiv, and Ullman [1979a,b], and the extension of Section 14.4 to unions of conjunctive queries is from Sagiv and Yannakakis [1981].

The technique of Section 14.5 for testing containment of a conjunctive query in a logic program appears in Ramakrishnan, Sagiv, Ullman, and Vardi [1988]. Maher [1986] and Sagiv [1987] discuss equivalence and containment of logic programs; Algorithm 14.2 is implicit in the latter paper and also in Cosmadakis and Kanellakis [1986].

Notes on Exercises

Exercise 14.10, on the relationship between logic programs and dependencies, is discussed in Sagiv [1987].

A solution to Exercise 14.18, the containment test for differences of unions of conjunctive queries, is found in Sagiv and Yannakakis [1981].

Aho, Sagiv, and Ullman [1979a,b] offers a solution to Exercise 14.19 on containments in the presence of functional dependencies. Johnson and Klug [1983b] extend the result to handle both functional and inclusion dependencies.

Exercise 14.21, the $\mathcal{NP}$-completeness results for the basic questions about conjunctive queries, is from Chandra and Merlin [1977]. Aho, Sagiv, and Ullman [1979a,b] and Johnson and Klug [1983a] discuss special cases that have polynomial time algorithms to decide containment.

CHAPTER 15

Optimization
of
Linear Recursions

There are certain common situations where the magic rules developed in Chapter 13 are not as efficient as possible. Most important are certain cases where the recursion is *linear*; that is, there is at most one subgoal of any rule that is mutually recursive with the head. In this chapter we shall consider these classes of linear recursions. Although the restrictions we place on rules in these sections seem severe, in practice the great majority of recursions are linear recursions, and of these, the great majority meet one or another of the constraints we consider, and thus can be evaluated by these methods.

In Section 15.1, we consider "right-linear" recursions, where the recursive subgoal most naturally is placed at the right end of the body, that is, last. The next section, considers "left-linear" recursions, where the recursive subgoal is naturally placed at the left end, or first in the list of subgoals. The algorithms for left- and right-linear recursions are provably as good or better than the magic-sets approach, for the classes of rules to which they apply. Moreover, they share an important feature not found in the magic-set rules: the arity of the recursive predicate is smaller in the transformed rules than in the original rules.

In Section 15.3, we introduce the notion of commutativity of linear rules, and we show how to test commutativity using the containment test for conjunctive queries given in Section 14.1. In particular, left-linear and right-linear rules commute, and we exploit this observation in Section 15.4. Section 15.5 discusses a class of rules called "counting-linear," that are neither left- nor right-linear, yet allow some reduction in the arity of recursive predicates.

In the next sections, we explore transitive closures of graphs as a recursion mechanism. In essence, left- and right-linear recursions are transitive closures, and in Section 15.6 we see that any linear recursion can be expressed as a transitive closure, provided we are willing to accept an underlying graph whose number of nodes greatly exceeds the size of the database. Then, in Section 15.7, we consider the "closed semiring" structure for path problems that generalizes transitive closure, yet allows algorithms similar to transitive closure to be used for their solution. Finally, in Section 15.8, we consider how to convert certain nonlinear recursions into linear recursions.

15.1 RIGHT-LINEAR RECURSIONS

Let us motivate the definition and treatment of right-linear rules with an example where a binary (arity two) recursive predicate can be replaced by a unary (arity one) recursive predicate.

Example 15.1: Consider the ancestor rules that served as a running example in Sections 12.5 through 12.7,

r_1:   anc(X,Y) :- par(X,Y).
r_2:   anc(X,Y) :- par(X,Z) & anc(Z,Y).

If we apply Algorithm 13.1 to these rules with query $anc(x_0, Y)$, and we then simplify as discussed in Section 13.4, we wind up with the rules of Figure 15.1.

m_anc(x_0).
m_anc(Z) :- $sup_{2.1}$(X,Z).

$sup_{2.1}$(X,Z) :- m_anc(X) & par(X,Z).

anc(X,Y) :- m_anc(X) & par(X,Y).
anc(X,Y) :- $sup_{2.1}$(X,Z) & anc(Z,Y).

Figure 15.1 Magic rules for ancestors.

Intuitively, $m\_anc(X)$ is true whenever X is a (not necessarily proper) ancestor of x_0; $sup_{2.1}(X, Z)$ is true whenever Z is a parent of X and X is an ancestor of x_0, and $anc(X, Y)$ is true whenever Y is a proper ancestor of X, and X is an ancestor of x_0. The reader may check by a simple induction on the number of rounds of semi-naive evaluation, that these are exactly the facts deduced for the rules of Figure 15.1.

However, something is wrong. To begin, m_anc itself produces almost the set we are looking for. We want the (proper) ancestors of x_0, and m_anc gives us these plus x_0 himself. Predicate anc produces facts that are in some sense relevant, but not all of them are needed. Specifically, suppose we have a *par* relation with n tuples, and an index on the first argument of *par* lets us retrieve those *par* tuples with a given first component, in time proportional to the number of tuples retrieved. Then we can answer the query "who are

x_0's ancestors" by searching the graph whose arcs are the parent pairs, starting from x_0. This algorithm takes $O(n)$ time on a graph of n edges.[1]

However, suppose that the relation for *par* consists of a line of parents,

$$par(x_0, x_1),\ par(x_1, x_2),\ldots, par(x_{n-1}, x_n)$$

Then the magic rules of Figure 15.1 derive the $\Omega(n^2)$ facts $anc(x_i, x_j)$, for $0 \le i < j \le n$, and thus must take $\Omega(n^2)$ time.[2] $\Box$

Definition of Right-Linear Rules

If we examine the rule/goal tree for the ancestor rules, whose upper levels were shown in 12.18, we can observe what makes these rules special. All root-to-leaf paths in the tree consist of some number of applications of r_2, the recursive rule, followed by one application of r_1, the basis rule. When *anc* is called with the *bf* adornment, the recursive call to *anc* also has that adornment, and moreover, the variable in the free argument position of the recursive call is the same variable that appears in the free argument of the head (that variable is Y in r_2, or W in the tree of 12.18). Thus, any values for that variable found by the basis rule are propagated up as many levels as there are, until they reach the root. Figure 15.2 suggests the way bindings are passed down a path in the rule/goal tree and how answers are returned from the bottom, unchanged.

There is another factor that we find essential: the initial binding for the bound argument at the root must be a single value x_0. This condition lets us determine the values for the free argument of *anc* without concern for the matching bound argument. We know that when any value y_0 for the second argument of *anc* reaches the root, it will be paired with x_0 to make a tuple (x_0, y_0). If we had started with more than one value in the binding set for Z_0 at the root of 12.18, then we would have to propagate ancestor tuples, rather than the ancestors themselves, up the tree, in order to keep track of who was an ancestor of whom. In that case, the magic-sets approach would be about as efficient as possible.[3]

We may generalize the ancestor example to a class of rules for which the same evaluation technique works. These rules involve one IDB predicate p. The tuples in m_p, the magic predicate for p, are used with the basis rule or rules

---

[1] See Aho, Hopcroft, and Ullman [1983] for details of graph-searching algorithms. For example, we could use either a depth-first or a breadth first search here.

[2] Prolog programmers will observe that the usual implementation of Prolog takes only $O(n)$ time on these rules. The reason is that the way Prolog handles variables allows a form of "tail-recursion optimization," where the last subgoal of a rule effectively substitutes for the head of the rule, in this example. As a result, the facts $anc(x_i, x_j)$ are proved only implicitly unless $i = 1$. The technique proposed in this section may be viewed as another implementation of tail-recursion optimization.

[3] However, if Z_0 were bound to a small set of values, we could explore individually from each, and possibly obtain the answer faster than the magic-sets algorithm would.

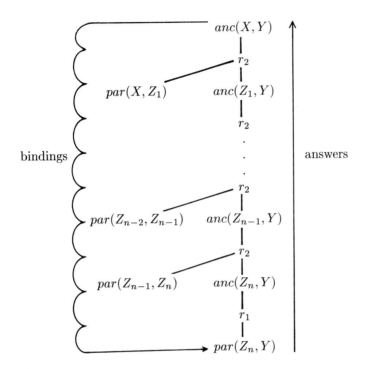

Figure 15.2 A path in rule/goal tree for right-linear recursion.

(the nonrecursive rules defining p), to obtain answer tuples. If the conditions listed below are met, these answer tuples will be all and only the tuples that, when coupled with the constants in the query, are answers to the query itself.

The advantage to evaluating the query this way is that the recursively defined predicate, m_p, has fewer arguments than the original recursive predicate, p. Thus, the evaluation of m_p can be much faster than the evaluation of p itself, as we observed for the ancestor rules.

Suppose we are given a collection of rules with a single IDB predicate, p, and a query goal p^α. We say these rules are *right-linear* (with respect to the adornment α) if

1. All of the rules are either *basis rules* (they have no occurrence of p among the subgoals), or they are *recursive rules*, with a single occurrence of p among the subgoals.

2. If we start with the head adornment p^α and order the subgoals so that the p-subgoal is listed last, then the adornment on the p subgoal is α.

3. For each recursive rule, each argument of p that α says is free has the same

variable in both the head and the recursive subgoal, and each of these variables appears in only these two positions.

Note condition (2) implies that the variables appearing in the free arguments of p^{α} appear in no subgoal but p, while those that appear in the bound arguments of the p-subgoal also appear either in a bound position of the head or in another subgoal. It is easy to test whether condition (2) is met, since the condition that the adornment on p, when it appears last, is α, does not depend on the order of the other subgoals. However, we may wish to consider the order of the other subgoals carefully; for example, we would like to avoid an all-free adornment if possible, since that requires the lookup of an entire EDB relation.

Example 15.2: Consider the rules

r_1:   p(U,V,W,X) :- q(X,W,V,U).
r_2:   p(A,B,C,D) :- s(A,E,F) & t(B,F) & p(E,A,C,D).

and suppose the query is an instance of adorned goal p^{bbff}. If we construct the portion of the rule/goal graph starting with p^{bbff}, and we order the subgoals of r_2 as listed above, we find that when we get to the p-subgoal, E and A are bound, while C and D are free. Thus, the recursive subgoal has the same adornment as the head, which meets condition (2). We also observe that the variables in the third and fourth positions, both in the head of r_2 and in the p-subgoal of r_2, are the same — C in the third position and D in the fourth. Since these are the free positions according to adornment $bbff$, condition (3) is met. Evidently condition (1) is met, since r_1 is a basis rule and r_2 is a recursive rule with a single occurrence of p. Thus, the example rules are right-linear, with respect to the query adornment $bbff$.

If the query adornment were $bfff$ instead, then the same rules would not be right-linear. One reason is that condition (2) would be violated, since the p-subgoal would still have adornment $bbff$ when it appears last. Another reason is that the head and recursive subgoal would not share variables in all free positions, as condition (3) requires.

Suppose we kept r_1 as it is, but replaced r_2 by a similar rule with C and D switched in the p-subgoal; that is,

r_3:   p(A,B,C,D) :- s(A,E,F) & t(B,F) & p(E,A,D,C).

Then, condition (3) would be violated, assuming the query goal has adornment $bbff$. The reason is that the third argument holds C in the head of r_3 and holds D in the p-subgoal. However, we could expand the p-subgoal by applying the algorithm of Figure 13.12. That step does not get rid of p, since p appears as a subgoal of one of its own rules. However, it does "straighten out" the permuted variables C and D. The resulting rules are

r_1:   p(U,V,W,X) :- q(X,W,V,U).
r_4:   p(A,B,C,D) :- s(A,E,F) & t(B,F) & q(C,D,A,E).
r_5:   p(A,B,C,D) :- s(A,E,F) & t(B,F) &
                               s(E,G,H) & t(A,H) & p(G,E,C,D).

Now, all conditions for right-linearity are met for binding pattern $bbff$. Of course, the answer to a query of the form p^{bbff} will be the same, whether rules r_1 and r_2 are used, or $\{r_1, r_4, r_5\}$ is used. $\square$

Evaluating Right-Linear Logic Programs

We shall now give a formal algorithm for the evaluation of right-linear rules. The modified rules generated by this algorithm are at least as efficient as the magic-set rules, and in many cases, they are more efficient, because the arity of the recursive predicate is reduced.

Algorithm 15.1: Efficient Evaluation of Right-Linear Rules.

INPUT: A collection of rules with IDB predicate p and a query goal p^α, such that the rules are right-linear with respect to adornment α.

OUTPUT: A modified set of rules that produce the answer to the query. The recursive predicate of these rules has arity equal to the number of bound arguments that p has in the query goal.

METHOD: Let us assume for convenience that the arguments of p that are bound according to adornment α precede the arguments that are free. We begin by generating the rules for the magic predicate m_p; the idea is essentially that of Algorithm 13.1, but we can produce rules for m_p without consideration of supplementary predicates, because of the simple form of right-linear rules. Let

$$p(t_1, \ldots, t_n, X_1, \ldots, X_m) :- G_1 \& \cdots \& G_k \&$$
$$p(s_1, \ldots, s_n, X_1, \ldots, X_m).$$

be a recursive rule, with the subgoals listed in the desired order. We assume that the first n arguments of p are bound and the last m are free.[4] Then we have the magic rule

$$m\_p(s_1, \ldots, s_n) :- m\_p(t_1, \ldots, t_n) \& G_1 \& \cdots \& G_k.$$

To this set of rules, we add the basis rule for the magic set,

$$m\_p(x_1, \ldots, x_n).$$

where $x_1, \ldots, x_n$ are the bound values in the query goal.

---

[4] Note that we do not require the rules to be datalog; the first n arguments of p in the recursive rules can hold arbitrary terms. However, the right-linear condition (3) does require the free arguments to hold variables. In the basis rules, none of the arguments are required to be single variables.

Now we create rules for the *answer predicate*, a_p, which is the set of tuples that appear in the free arguments of p. The rules for a_p come from the basis rules, since it is the values from the basis that are propagated all of the way up the rule/goal tree to become answers. Thus, for each basis rule

$$p(t_1, \ldots, t_n, s_1, \ldots, s_m) :\text{-} G_1 \& \cdots \& G_k.$$

we construct the rule

$$a\_p(s_1, \ldots, s_m) :\text{-} m\_p(t_1, \ldots, t_n) \& G_1 \& \cdots \& G_k.$$

Finally, the answer to the query can be constructed from a_p by

$$p(x_1, \ldots, x_n, Y_1, \ldots, Y_m) :\text{-} a\_p(Y_1, \ldots, Y_m).$$

The set of rules described above form the output of the algorithm. $\square$

Example 15.3: The ancestor rules of Example 15.1 with query goal $anc(x_0, Y)$ are transformed to those shown in Figure 15.3. Rule (2) in Figure 15.3 comes from the recursive rule for ancestors, r_2, while rule (3) in that figure is from the basis rule, r_1. Rule (4) converts the answers into the desired form: ancestor pairs whose first component is x_0. Note that these rules evaluate ancestors in the intuitive way; we search the *par* relation from x_0 to obtain all ancestors of x_0. Rule (4) is not even necessary if we are only looking for the set of ancestors, rather than ancestor pairs.

(1)   m_anc(x_0).
(2)   m_anc(Z) :- m_anc(X) & par(X,Z).
(3)   a_anc(Y) :- m_anc(X) & par(X,Y).
(4)   anc(x_0,Y) :- a_anc(Y).

Figure 15.3 Transformed rules for ancestors.

For a more complex example, consider rules r_1, r_4, and r_5, developed in Example 15.2, and suppose the query is $p(x_1, x_2, W, X)$. Here, r_1 and r_4 are basis rules, and r_5 is the lone recursive rule. The transformed rules are shown in Figure 15.4. $\square$

Theorem 15.1: The transformed right-linear rules from Algorithm 15.1 produce the same answer as the original rules.

Proof: The justification was given informally in connection with the ancestor rules, but generalizes to any set of right-linear rules. When we consider the rule/goal tree with the query goal as root, we observe that along every path, the free arguments of the IDB predicate p hold the same variables at every step. Further, the binding tuples for the bound arguments of p that appear somewhere

```
m_p(x₁,x₂).
m_p(G,E)  :- m_p(A,B) & s(A,E,F) &
                 t(B,F) & s(E,G,H) & t(A,H).

a_p(W,X)  :- m_p(U,V) & q(X,W,V,U).
a_p(C,D)  :- m_p(A,B) & s(A,E,F) & t(B,F) & q(C,D,A,E).

p(x₁,x₂,Y,Z)  :- a_p(Y,Z).
```

Figure 15.4 Transformed rules from Example 15.2.

in the tree are exactly those in the relation defined for m_p, as simple inductions on the length of a path and on the number of applications of the rules for m_p will show. Thus, the tuples in m_p are exactly those that get passed to the basis rules, and the answers produced by these rules are propagated unchanged, up the tree, to become the answers to the query. $\square$

Efficiency of the Transformed Right-Linear Rules

It is easy to show that the rules generated by Algorithm 15.1 are no worse than the magic rules produced by Algorithm 13.1. On the other hand, Example 15.1 showed that the rules of Algorithm 15.1 could be significantly more efficient than the magic rules, $O(n)$ compared with $O(n^2)$ in that case.

To see why Algorithm 15.1 produces rules that are never worse than the magic rules, note that the rules produced for m_p are the same as the magic rules for m_p, after we simplify the rules to eliminate the supplementary predicates. The transformation of Figure 13.12, which justifies that simplification, was observed never to degrade the efficiency of the rules, provided we preserved the left-to-right join order of subgoals that was forced by the way Algorithm 13.1 generates its rules.

Next, note that the rules for a_p generated by Algorithm 15.1 are simpler than rules generated by Algorithm 13.1; they are essentially the Group IV rules generated for p from the basis rules, with m_p substituted for the zeroth supplementary predicates, and with the bound arguments of p omitted from the head. Thus, these rules are also evaluated at no more cost than is incurred for the corresponding rules of Group IV, during semi-naive evaluation of the magic rules. Finally, the rule that defines p in terms of a_p can be implemented by attaching the query constants to each a_p tuple as we generate that tuple. We conclude that the rules of Algorithm 15.1 are never more expensive than the magic rules, and frequently the former are much less expensive to evaluate.

15.2 LEFT-LINEAR RECURSIONS

There is a "trick" dual to that discussed in the previous section; this trick allows us to recognize another common case where the rule/goal tree has a useful, special property.

Example 15.4: We can illustrate this case best by considering the ancestor rules from Example 15.1, but with a query goal $anc(X, y_0)$, which has the fb binding pattern. These rules, recall, are

r_1: `anc(X,Y) :- par(X,Y).`
r_2: `anc(X,Y) :- par(X,Z) & anc(Z,Y).`

Suppose we order the subgoals of r_2 in the reverse order, with $anc(Z, Y)$ first, that is,

r_2: `anc(X,Y) :- anc(Z,Y) & par(X,Z).`

If we do so, we make the following observations.

1. The fb adornment on anc appears not only in the head, but also in the subgoal of r_2.
2. The bound argument in the head of r_2 and in the anc subgoal of r_2 share the same variable, Y.

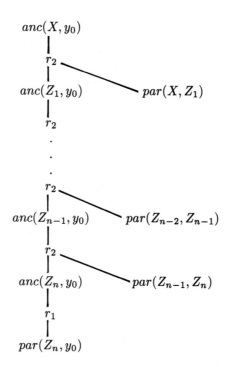

Figure 15.5 Typical path in rule/goal tree for ancestor rules.

As a consequence of (1) and (2), y_0 is the only value that ever becomes a binding for the second argument of anc, in any subgoal of the rule/goal tree. Equivalently, the magic predicate m_anc gets the singleton relation $\{y_0\}$ as its value. If we look at a typical path in the rule/goal tree, say that shown in Figure 15.5, where we apply r_2 n times and then apply r_1, we see that each path causes us to find the children of y_0 (these are the bindings for Z_n in Figure 15.5). Then, we apply the recursive rule r_2 once, to get the grandchildren of y_0 (as the bindings for Z_{n-1} in Figure 15.5), and so on. The bindings for X returned by this path would be the nth-level descendants of y_0.[5]

If we consider what happens along other paths of the rule/goal tree, where n has a different value, we observe that the calculation at the ith level from the bottom is the same along every path that has at least i levels; the ith-generation descendants of y_0 are computed. We can consolidate this computation if we "borrow" the result of the path with n occurrences of r_2, to do all but the highest-level step of the path with $n + 1$ occurrences of r_2. That is, we can rewrite the rules and the given query as

```
a_anc(X)  :- par(X,y_0).
a_anc(X)  :- a_anc(Z) & par(X,Z).
anc(X,y_0)  :- a_anc(X).
```

In these rules, a_anc, the "answer" predicate for anc, accumulates all descendants of y_0, at any level. We know that each such descendant will be returned as an answer along the path of the rule/goal tree in which r_2 is used as many times as the recursive rule for a_anc is applied. □

Left-Linear Logic Programs

We can generalize the principle embodied in Example 15.4, by defining "left-linear" rules, with respect to an adornment α. The essential requirements are that the adornment of the IDB predicate remains α if we order the subgoals so the IDB predicate appears first, and that the bound arguments share the same variables in the head and subgoal. Formally, a collection of rules with a single IDB predicate p is *left-linear* with respect to an adornment α for p if

1. All of the rules are either basis rules (no occurrence of p among the subgoals) or recursive rules with a single subgoal having predicate p.
2. For each recursive rule, when we list the p-subgoal first, the adornment on that subgoal is α.
3. For each recursive rule, each argument that α says is bound has the same variable in both the head and the recursive subgoal, and no variable appears in two different bound arguments of the recursive predicate.

---

[5] It is useful to think of X as Z_0, to follow the pattern suggested by Figure 15.5.

We now give an algorithm for transforming left-linear rules into a new set of rules whose recursive predicate has a smaller arity than the original recursive predicate. We expect the new rules to be evaluable more efficiently than the original, because of the predicate with smaller arity is likely to produce fewer tuples. Specifically, we can show that the new rules constructed have no worse performance than the magic rules produced by Algorithm 13.1 on the same input rules and query.

Algorithm 15.2: Evaluation of Left-Linear Rules.

INPUT: A set of rules involving IDB predicate p and a query goal p^α, such that the rules are left-linear with respect to α.

OUTPUT: A revised set of rules that produce the answer to the query. The arity of the recursive predicate in these rules equals the number of free arguments in the adornment α.

METHOD: We assume for convenience that all bound arguments of α precede all free arguments. Also, let $x_1, \ldots, x_n$ be the bound arguments appearing in the query goal. Then a typical recursive rule can be written

$$p(X_1, \ldots, X_n, t_1, \ldots, t_m) \text{ :- } p(X_1, \ldots, X_n, s_1, \ldots, s_m) \ \& $$
$$G_1 \ \& \ \cdots \ \& \ G_k.$$

We know that the only possible binding for X_i is x_i, for $i = 1, 2, \ldots, n$, if this rule is to contribute to the query's answer. Thus, from this rule we may produce a rule for the "answer" predicate a_p; this rule is formed from the original by substituting x_i for X_i, for $1 \le i \le n$, and then removing the first n arguments of p, which can be understood to be $x_1, \ldots, x_n$. Let σ be the substitution that replaces each X_i by x_i and leaves other symbols unchanged. The rule for a_p is then

$$a\_p\big(\sigma(t_1), \ldots, \sigma(t_m)\big) \text{ :- } a\_p\big(\sigma(s_1), \ldots, \sigma(s_m)\big) \ \& \ \sigma(G_1) \ \& \ \cdots \ \& \ \sigma(G_k).$$

For each basis rule

$$p(t_1, \ldots, t_n, s_1, \ldots, s_m) \text{ :- } G_1 \ \& \ \cdots \ \& \ G_k.$$

unify $q(t_1, \ldots, t_n)$ with $q(x_1, \ldots, x_n)$ to obtain the MGU τ.[6] Extend τ by letting it be the identity on symbols other than those appearing in the t's. Then produce the "answer" rule

$$a\_p\big(\tau(s_1), \ldots, \tau(s_m)\big) \text{ :- } \tau(G_1) \ \& \ \cdots \ \& \ \tau(G_k).$$

Finally, we translate a_p to p by attaching the query constants,

---

[6] Symbol q has no significance here. We use it to force the terms $t_1, \ldots, t_n$ to be unified with the query constants $x_1, \ldots, x_n$, because Algorithm 12.5, the unification algorithm, requires a single pair of expressions as input. Also note that unification is impossible if t_i is a nontrivial term, unless x_i is also a term with function symbols, rather than a single constant.

$$p(x_1, \ldots, x_n, Y_1, \ldots, Y_m) :\text{-} a\_p(Y_1, \ldots, Y_m).$$

The collection of rules described above forms the output of the algorithm. $\square$

Example 15.5: Let us consider the rules $\{r_1, r_4, r_5\}$ from Example 15.2, along with the query goal $p(Y, Z, x_1, x_2)$. These rules are repeated here with the recursive subgoal in r_5 listed first, and with the third and fourth arguments of p moved to the front, to conform with our assumptions in Algorithm 15.2.

r_1: p(W,X,U,V) :- q(X,W,V,U).
r_4: p(C,D,A,B) :- s(A,E,F) & t(B,F) & q(C,D,A,E).
r_5: p(C,D,A,B) :- p(C,D,G,E) & s(A,E,F) & t(B,F) &
                       s(E,G,H) & t(A,H).

These rules are easily seen to be left-linear with respect to the adornment $bbff$. Note that this adornment corresponds to the query goal, since that goal becomes $p(x_1, x_2, Y, Z)$ after permutation of the arguments of p.

From r_5 we get the recursive rule for a_p,

a_p(A,B) :- a_p(G,E) & s(A,E,F) &
              t(B,F) & s(E,G,H) & t(A,H).

For the basis rule r_1 we need to unify $q(W, X)$ with $q(x_1, x_2)$, which gives us the MGU $\tau(W) = x_1$ and $\tau(X) = x_2$; τ is the identity on all other variables. Thus, one basis rule for a_p is

a_p(U,V) :- q(x_2,x_1,V,U).

The MGU ρ for the second basis rule, r_4, is defined by $\rho(C) = x_1$ and $\rho(D) = x_2$. The second basis rule in our constructed logic program is therefore

a_p(A,B) :- s(A,E,F) & t(B,F) & q(x_1,x_2,A,E).

Finally, the rule

p(x_1,x_2,Y,Z) :- a_p(Y,Z).

completes the transformation. $\square$

Analysis of the Left-Linear Transformation

We claim that the transformation of Algorithm 15.2 is both correct and efficient, in the sense that it never does worse than the magic-sets transformation. The correctness is a generalization of the informal argument about the ancestor rules given in the introduction to this section. That is, we consider each path from the root to a leaf in the rule/goal tree, and we observe that the only binding ever passed down the tree is the binding of the query, $x_1, \ldots, x_n$. The results passed up along this path are obtained by unifying the query constants with the head of the basis rule, to get an initial set of answers, in a manner mirrored by the way basis rules are transformed in Algorithm 15.2. These answers are then operated upon some number of times as they pass up the tree; each recursive rule encountered bottom-up along the path applies one operation. These operations are easily seen to be reflected by the transformed recursive rules.

To see why the rules generated by Algorithm 15.2 can be no less efficient than the magic rules for the same problem, observe again that the magic predicate m_p will have only the tuple $(x_1, \ldots, x_n)$. The rules generated by Algorithm 15.2 are thus obtainable from the Group IV rules of Algorithm 13.1 by the following steps.

1. Perform the simplifications outlined in Section 13.4, to eliminate the supplementary predicates.
2. Substitute $x_1, \ldots, x_n$ for the variables appearing in the arguments of m_p.
3. Eliminate the first n arguments of p, since they are forced to have values $x_1, \ldots, x_n$.
4. Change the name of the predicate p to a_p.

It follows that bottom-up evaluation of the rules for a_p require no more work than evaluation of the Group IV rules generated by Algorithm 13.1, and they may require less. The only other rule, that converting a_p-tuples into p-tuples, is basically a copying of answer tuples. Its cost can be avoided if we attach the constants to all a_p-tuples as we generate them, and then call these p-tuples at the end. Thus, at the worst, the rules from Algorithm 15.2 are as expensive to evaluate as the magic rules.

15.3 COMMUTATIVITY OF RULES

We now make a technical digression to explore the issue of when two linear rules commute. The reason will become clear after the next section, where we consider logic programs with both left- and right-linear rules. Suppose we have two linear rules r_1 and r_2 with a common recursive predicate p. Informally, $r_1 r_2 \subseteq r_2 r_1$ means that whenever we have a proof tree with a use of r_1 immediately above a use of r_2, as suggested by Figure 15.6(a), we can replace it by the use of r_2 above r_1, as suggested by Figure 15.6(b). Of course, each of the uses of r_1 and r_2 are instances of these rules after appropriate substitutions, and we shall consider carefully the matter of how we rewrite the rules when going from Figure 15.6(a) to Figure 15.6(b).

Another way to look at Figure 15.6 is that whenever we have a use of r_1 above r_2 in a rule/goal tree, we can find another path in the same tree that produces the same answers, but the uses of r_1 and r_2 are reversed in the latter path. Thus, we can ignore all paths in the tree except those where all uses of r_2 are above the uses of r_2. That condition gives us evaluation opportunities not present in arbitrary rule/goal trees. Equivalently, from the viewpoint of proof trees, by applying the transformation suggested by Figure 15.6 until it can no longer be applied, we conclude that it suffices to consider proof trees in which

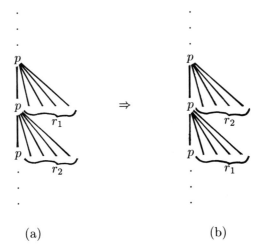

(a)   (b)

Figure 15.6 Reordering uses of rules.

all uses of r_1 are below those of r_2.

In order to make our intuition precise, we need a formal definition of "commutativity." Of course, the condition $r_1 r_2 \subseteq r_2 r_1$ does not say that r_1 and r_2 can be used in any order, as would be expected if the rules truly "commuted." However, in most cases we shall consider, when we have $r_1 r_2 \subseteq r_2 r_1$, we also have $r_2 r_1 \subseteq r_1 r_2$, and thus r_1 and r_2 really can be used in arbitrary order; for example, we could move all r_1's ahead of all r_2's or vice versa.

Let

$$r_1: H :\text{-} P \,\&\, G_1 \,\&\, \cdots \,\&\, G_n.$$
$$r_2: I :\text{-} Q \,\&\, J_1 \,\&\, \cdots \,\&\, J_m.$$

be two linear rules for predicate p, where P and Q are the recursive subgoals. Assume that r_1 and r_2 have no variables in common. Let τ be the MGU of P and I, and let C_{12} denote the conjunctive query

$$C_{12}: \tau(H) :\text{-} \tau(Q) \,\&\, \tau(J_1) \,\&\, \cdots \,\&\, \tau(J_m) \,\&\, \tau(G_1) \,\&\, \cdots \,\&\, \tau(G_n).$$

That is, we substitute the body of r_2 for the recursive subgoal P, by the algorithm suggested in Figure 13.12. Similarly, let σ be the MGU of Q and H, and let C_{21} denote the conjunctive query

$$C_{21}: \sigma(I) :\text{-} \sigma(P) \,\&\, \sigma(G_1) \,\&\, \cdots \,\&\, \sigma(G_n) \,\&\, \sigma(J_1) \,\&\, \cdots \,\&\, \sigma(J_m).$$

Then we formally define the condition $r_1 r_2 \subseteq r_2 r_1$ to hold exactly when the containment of conjunctive queries $C_{12} \subseteq C_{21}$ holds.

Example 15.6: Consider the rules

$$r_1: \quad \text{p(X,Y)} \;:\text{-}\; \text{p(Z,Y)} \;\&\; \text{a(X,Z)}.$$
$$r_2: \quad \text{p(U,V)} \;:\text{-}\; \text{p(U,W)} \;\&\; \text{b(W,V)}.$$

For the conjunctive query C_{12} we unify the head $p(U, V)$ with subgoal $p(Z, Y)$. A suitable MGU is that which substitutes Z for U and Y for V, leaving the other variables intact. The resulting conjunctive query is

$$C_{12}: \quad \text{p(X,Y)} \;:\text{-}\; \text{p(Z,W)} \;\&\; \text{b(W,Y)} \;\&\; \text{a(X,Z)}.$$

Similarly, we can unify the head $p(X, Y)$ with the subgoal $p(U, W)$ and establish the MGU that substitutes U for X and W for Y. That gives us the conjunctive query

$$C_{21}: \quad \text{p(U,V)} \;:\text{-}\; \text{p(Z,W)} \;\&\; \text{a(U,Z)} \;\&\; \text{b(W,V)}.$$

It is easy to check that $C_{12} \subseteq C_{21}$, using the containment mapping that sends U to X, V to Y, and other variables to themselves. Hence, $r_1 r_2 \subseteq r_2 r_1$. Incidentally, it is also true that $C_{21} \subseteq C_{12}$, so we also have the "commutativity" law $r_2 r_1 \subseteq r_1 r_2$. In this case, r_1 and r_2 really do commute. $\square$

Significance of Commutativity

By definition, it is easy to test the condition $r_1 r_2 \subseteq r_2 r_1$, since we need only to test containment for conjunctive queries. However, what is not immediately obvious is what this condition says about logic programs. We need to show that when $r_1 r_2 \subseteq r_2 r_1$ holds, we can, if fact, assume all r_2's are above all r_1's. There are at least two ways we can make that notion formal.

1. Given any logic program including rules r_1 and r_2, and given any database D, each deducible fact is the root of a proof tree in which no node representing a use of r_1 has a child that represents a use of r_2.

2. Under the same conditions as (1), we can omit all of the paths in a rule/goal tree that have a rule node for r_1 that is the grandparent of (next rule node above) some rule node for r_2.

These are closely related ideas, and we shall prove (1), leaving (2) for an exercise. Suppose the two rules in question are

$$r_1: H \text{ :- } P \;\&\; G_1 \;\&\; \cdots \;\&\; G_n.$$
$$r_2: I \text{ :- } Q \;\&\; J_1 \;\&\; \cdots \;\&\; J_m.$$

where P and Q are the recursive subgoals. Also suppose we have a piece of a proof tree with a use of r_1 above r_2, as suggested by Figure 15.7(a). There, τ is a substitution for the variables of r_1, and σ is a substitution for the variables of r_2; both replace variables by ground terms only, since there are no variables in a proof tree.

It is important to note that $\tau(P) = \sigma(I)$, because both must be the same ground atom for the proof tree to be valid. Suppose without loss of generality

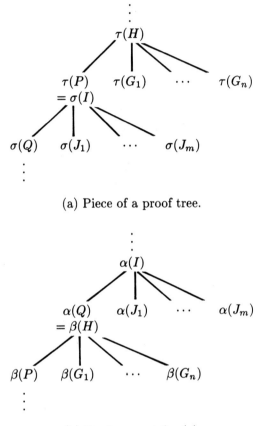

(a) Piece of a proof tree.

(b) Replacement for (a).

Figure 15.7 Moving r_2 above r_1.

that r_1 and r_2 have no symbols in common, and let ρ be the MGU of P and I. Let ω be the mapping that agrees with τ and σ wherever either is defined; since they are never defined on the same symbol, ω exists. Since ρ is the most general unifier, it follows that ω can be expressed as the composition of some mapping applied after ρ. That is, $\omega = \omega_1\rho$ for some mapping ω_1. As usual, we assume ρ is the identity on symbols not appearing in P or I.

Now, let γ be the MGU of Q and H. By definition of $r_1r_2 \subseteq r_2r_1$, we know there is a containment mapping ψ from

$$C_{21}\colon \gamma(I) \coloneq \gamma(P) \ \& \ \gamma(G_1) \ \& \ \cdots \ \& \ \gamma(G_n) \ \& \ \gamma(J_1) \ \& \ \cdots \ \& \ \gamma(J_m).$$

to

$$C_{12}: \rho(H) \text{ :- } \rho(Q) \text{ \& } \rho(J_1) \text{ \& } \cdots \text{ \& } \rho(J_m) \text{ \& } \rho(G_1) \text{ \& } \cdots \text{ \& } \rho(G_n).$$

We need to show that for some substitutions α and β, we can convert the tree of Figure 15.7(a) into the tree of Figure 15.7(b), where all of the external nodes are the same in both trees. That is, $\alpha(I) = \tau(H)$, $\alpha(J_i) = \sigma(J_i)$ for $i = 1, 2, \ldots, m$, $\beta(G_i) = \tau(G_i)$, for $i = 1, 2, \ldots, n$, and $\beta(P) = \sigma(Q)$.

We select $\alpha = \beta = \omega_1 \psi \gamma$. Then

$$\alpha(I) = \omega_1 \psi \gamma(I) = \omega_1 \rho(H) = \tau(H)$$

The justifications for the three equalities, in order, are

1. Definition of α.
2. Containment mapping ψ maps the head of C_{21}, which is $\gamma(I)$, to the head of C_{12}, which is $\rho(H)$.
3. $\tau = \omega_1 \rho$.

Similarly, we can prove each of the required identities for the external nodes of the trees shown in Figure 15.7.

$$\alpha(J_i) = \omega_1 \psi \gamma(J_i) = \omega_1 \rho(J_i) = \sigma(J_i)$$
$$\beta(G_i) = \omega_1 \psi \gamma(G_i) = \omega_1 \rho(G_i) = \tau(G_i)$$
$$\beta(P) = \omega_1 \psi \gamma(P) = \omega_1 \rho(Q) = \tau(Q)$$

We have thus proved the following theorem.

Theorem 15.2: If $r_1 r_2 \subseteq r_2 r_1$, then for every proof tree T there is another proof tree T' that has the same ground atoms at the root and leaves and has no occurrence of a use of r_1 immediately above a use of r_2.

Proof: By the foregoing reasoning, every occurrence of the piece of tree shown in Figure 15.7(a) can be replaced by that shown in Figure 15.7(b). Evidently, the number of nodes does not change by this transformation. We need to show that the transformation cannot be applied indefinitely. Define the following figure of merit F: the sum of the depths of the interior nodes that have a use of r_2. The replacement of Figure 15.7(a) by Figure 15.7(b) decreases F by one. As the initial value of F is finite, eventually we must reach a tree in which the transformation is not possible. At that point, we have the proof tree claimed by the theorem. $\square$

Example 15.7: Let us consider the rules of Example 15.6, along with a suitable basis rule,

```
r1:   p(X,Y)  :- p(Z,Y) & a(X,Z).
r2:   p(U,V)  :- p(U,W) & b(W,V).
r3:   p(S,T)  :- c(S,T).
```

Suppose the EDB facts are $a(1, 2)$, $c(2, 3)$, $b(3, 4)$, and $b(4, 5)$. Then in Figure 15.8(a) we see a proof tree for $p(1, 5)$, with a use of r_1 above two uses of r_2.

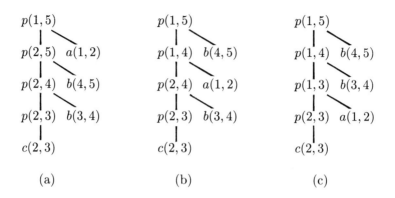

Figure 15.8 Moving r_2 above r_1.

In Figure 15.8(b) we see the affect of applying the transformation of Theorem 15.2 to the top three p-nodes in Figure 15.8(a). Notice that we create a node with an IDB fact $p(1,4)$ that was not present in Figure 15.8(a); it is a fact that has a proof, of course, as we can see from Figure 15.8(b). Finally, in Figure 15.8(c) we have applied the transformation of Theorem 15.2 to the bottom three p-nodes in Figure 15.8(b). This tree has no occurrence of r_1 with a use of r_2 below. $\square$

A Syntactic Condition for Commutativity

In the next section, we shall need a large family of pairs of rules that commute. To prove commutativity in an infinite number of cases, we need to have some broad sufficient conditions for commutativity; the next theorem develops such a condition. First, we fix our attention on a pair of rules of the form

$$r_1:\ p(X_1,\ldots,X_n) :\text{-} p(Y_1,\ldots,Y_n)\ \&\ G_1\ \&\ \cdots\ \&\ G_k. \tag{15.1}$$
$$r_2:\ p(X_1,\ldots,X_n) :\text{-} p(Z_1,\ldots,Z_n)\ \&\ J_1\ \&\ \cdots\ \&\ J_m.$$

We assume the rules are safe datalog, and that the distinguished variables (the X's) are all distinct; that is, the heads are rectified. Distinguished variable X_i is said to have *home position* i.

Theorem 15.3: Let r_1 and r_2, in the form (15.1), satisfy the following additional conditions.

a) If $Y_i \neq X_i$, then X_i does not appear among the subgoals $J_1,\ldots,J_m$.
b) If $Z_i \neq X_i$, then X_i does not appear among $G_1,\ldots,G_k$.
c) If $Y_i = X_j$, for some $j \neq i$, then $Z_i = X_i$, and $Z_j = X_j$.
d) If $Z_i = X_j$, for some $j \neq i$, then $Y_i = X_i$ and $Y_j = X_j$.[7]

---

[7] Notice that each of conditions (a) through (d) says that if an argument of the recursive

Then $r_1 r_2 \subseteq r_2 r_1$ and $r_2 r_1 \subseteq r_1 r_2$.

Proof: We shall prove $r_1 r_2 \subseteq r_2 r_1$. First, let us assume that r_1 and r_2 have identical heads, as in (15.1), but that they share no variables other than the distinguished variables $X_1, \ldots, X_n$. Define the two substitutions

$$\tau(X_i) = Y_i$$
$$\sigma(X_i) = Z_i$$

Both τ and σ are the identity on nondistinguished variables. Then the containment mappings for testing $r_1 r_2 \subseteq r_2 r_1$ are

$$C_{12}: \; p(X_1, \ldots, X_n) :\!\!- p\big(\tau(Z_1), \ldots, \tau(Z_n)\big) \; \&$$
$$\tau(J_1) \; \& \; \cdots \; \& \; \tau(J_m) \; \& \; G_1 \; \& \; \cdots \; \& \; G_k.$$
$$C_{21}: \; p(X_1, \ldots, X_n) :\!\!- p\big(\sigma(Y_1), \ldots, \sigma(Y_n)\big) \; \&$$
$$J_1 \; \& \; \cdots \; \& \; J_m \; \& \; \sigma(G_1) \; \& \; \cdots \; \& \; \sigma(G_k).$$

We shall show that the identity mapping is a containment mapping from C_{21} to C_{12}.[8] Evidently, the identity maps the head to the head. Let us show that the p-subgoal of C_{21} is mapped to the p-subgoal of C_{12}; that is, we must show $\sigma(Y_i) = \tau(Z_i)$ for all i.

Case 1: $Y_i = X_i$. Then $\sigma(Y_i) = \sigma(X_i) = Z_i$, by definition of σ. We must therefore show $\tau(Z_i) = Z_i$. There are three subcases.

1. $Z_i = X_i$. Then $\tau(Z_i) = \tau(X_i) = Y_i$, by definition of τ. But we assumed $Y_i = X_i$, so $\tau(Z_i) = X_i$. As we also assume $Z_i = X_i$ in this subcase, we have $\tau(Z_i) = Z_i$.

2. Z_i is a nondistinguished variable. Then $\tau(Z_i) = Z_i$, because τ is the identity except on the X's.

3. $Z_i = X_j$, for some $j \neq i$. Then by (d), $Y_j = X_j$. Thus, $\tau(Z_i) = \tau(X_j) = Y_j = X_j = Z_i$.

We thus conclude $\sigma(Y_i) = \tau(Z_i)$ in Case 1.

Case 2: Y_i is nondistinguished. To begin, we claim Z_i must be X_i in this case. Suppose not. Then X_i must appear somewhere else in the body of r_2, because rules are assumed safe. However, (a) says that X_i cannot appear in the EDB subgoals, and (d) says that if $Z_l = X_i$ for some $l \neq i$, then $Y_i = X_i$, contradicting our assumption that Y_i is nondistinguished. We therefore conclude $Z_i = X_i$.

We know $\sigma(Y_i) = Y_i$, since σ is the identity on nondistinguished variables. We also have $\tau(Z_i) = \tau(X_i) = Y_i$, by definition of τ and the fact that $Z_i = X_i$. Thus, $\sigma(Y_i) = \tau(Z_i)$ in this case also.

---

subgoal of one rule satisfies a condition, then there is a constraint placed on the other rule.

[8] It is also a containment mapping in the other direction, incidentally.

Case 3: $Y_i = X_j$, for some $j \neq i$. Then $\sigma(Y_i) = \sigma(X_j) = Z_j$. By (c), we know $Z_i = X_i$ and $Z_j = X_j$. Hence, $\tau(Z_i) = \tau(X_i) = Y_i = X_j = Z_j$. We conclude $\sigma(Y_i) = \tau(Z_i)$ in all cases.

Next, we must show that each subgoal $\sigma(G_j)$ in C_{21} maps under the identity containment mapping to a subgoal of C_{12}, namely G_j. The only reason that might not be the case is if a distinguished variable X_i appears in G_j, because σ is the identity on all nondistinguished variables. However, if X_i appears in G_j, then by condition (b), $Z_i = X_i$. Then, by the definition of σ, $\sigma(X_i) = Z_i = X_i$, so σ is the identity on X_i.

The last part, that each J_j maps to $\tau(J_j)$ is proved similarly, and we leave it as an exercise for the reader. $\square$

Example 15.8: Consider the rules of the two previous examples, which we rewrite in the form (15.1) as

r_1: p(X,Y) :- p(Z,Y) & a(X,Z).
r_2: p(X,Y) :- p(X,W) & b(W,Y).

Evidently, the rules are safe datalog. In r_1, the nondistinguished variable Z appears in the first argument of the recursive subgoal. To satisfy condition (a) of Theorem 15.3, we must check that the variable in the first argument in the recursive subgoal of r_2 does not appear in the EDB subgoals of r_2. The variable in question is X, and we indeed can verify that X does not appear in the b-subgoal. To satisfy condition (b), we must also verify that Y, the symbol opposite the nondistinguished variable W in the second argument of the recursive subgoal, is missing from the EDB subgoals of r_1. Again, we see that is the case. For (c) and (d), we look for a distinguished variable appearing outside its home position in a recursive subgoal. Finding none, we conclude that (c) and (d) are satisfied vacuously. Thus, r_1 and r_2 commute. $\square$

15.4 COMBINED LEFT- AND RIGHT-LINEAR RECURSIONS

There are certain linear recursions where some of the recursive rules must be treated as right-linear, and other rules for the same predicate must be treated as left-linear. The two modes mesh nicely, if we are careful. Let us begin with an example to illustrate the technique.

r_1:   p(X,Y,Z) :- q(X,Y,Z).
r_2:   p(X,Y,Z) :- a(X,A) & p(A,Y,Z).
r_3:   p(X,Y,Z) :- b(Y,B) & p(X,B,Z).
r_4:   p(X,Y,Z) :- c(Z,C) & p(X,Y,C).

Figure 15.9 Rules for Example 15.9.

Example 15.9: Consider the rules of Figure 15.9, with a query of the form $p(x_0, Y, Z)$. The adornment for p is thus bff, and this pattern must be preserved in the p-subgoals of rules r_2, r_3, and r_4, if we are to apply the techniques of Sections 15.1 and 15.2. The subgoals of rule r_2 can remain in the order written, since then the first argument of p, holding variable A, will be bound. However, for rules r_3 and r_4, we must place the p-subgoal first, rewriting these rules as

r_3: `p(X,Y,Z) :- p(X,B,Z) & b(Y,B).`
r_4: `p(X,Y,Z) :- p(X,Y,C) & c(Z,C).`

Thus, r_1 is a basis rule, and r_2 is a right-linear rule, while r_3 and r_4 are left-linear rules.

Of these rules, only r_2 produces new bindings for the first argument of p; it does so by "applying" the EDB predicate a to an old binding. That is, the magic set m_p contains the set of values reachable from x_0 in a graph whose arcs are the pairs in the relation for a. Then, the basis, rule r_1, gives us a set of (y, z) pairs for each of the x's in the magic set m_p. Finally, these pairs can yield new pairs, when we apply either r_3, to change the y-value, or r_4, to change the z-value. All of the resulting pairs are answers to the original query. The transformed rules suggested by these observations are shown in Figure 15.10. They involve both a magic predicate m_p, to hold the legitimate values of the first argument of p, and an "answer" predicate a_p, to hold answer pairs for the second and third arguments of p. □

```
m_p(x0).
m_p(A) :- m_p(X) & a(X,A).

a_p(Y,Z) :- m_p(X) & q(X,Y,Z).
a_p(Y,Z) :- a_p(B,Z) & b(Y,B).
a_p(Y,Z) :- a_p(Y,C) & c(Z,C).

p(x0,Y,Z) :- a_p(Y,Z).
```

Figure 15.10 Transformed rules for Example 15.9.

One may be puzzled, in Example 15.9, by our assertion that we could first apply the right-linear rule r_2, then the basis rule r_1, and finally the left-linear rules r_3 and r_4. Do we not have to consider sequences in which rules r_2, r_3, and r_4 are mixed? It turns out that we do not, because there is a simple condition under which a left-linear rule and a right-linear rule commute.

Strict Left- and Right-Linearity

In order to be sure that a left- and a right-linear rule commute, we shall combine the conditions of left- and right-linearity with the conditions needed for Theorem 15.3. There are other cases in which left- and right-linear rules commute, and to be sure, we can always apply the conjunctive-query test of Theorem 15.2. However, as we shall see, the conditions of Theorem 15.3 and the linearity conditions "fit" well. We say a rule is *strictly right linear* with respect to adornment α if

1. It is a safe datalog rule.
2. It is right linear with respect to α.

A rule is *strictly left linear* with respect to adornment α if

1. It is a safe datalog rule.
2. It is left linear with respect to α.
3. A variable that appears in a bound argument of the head (and therefore in its home position in the recursive subgoal) appears nowhere else in the rule.[9]

Example 15.10: Consider the rules of Example 15.9 with respect to the adornment bff. We argued in that example that r_2 is right-linear, while r_3 and r_4 are left-linear. It is easy to check that all rules are safe datalog. The last thing to check is that the variables appearing in the bound positions of the recursive subgoals of the left-linear rules appear nowhere else. For both r_3 and r_4, X is the variable in the lone bound position of the recursive subgoal, and it appears neither in $b(Y, B)$ of r_3, in $c(Z, C)$ of r_4, nor in the second argument of a head or recursive subgoal. $\square$

Lemma 15.1: For any given adornment α, a strictly left-linear rule and a strictly right-linear rule commute.

Proof: Assume without loss of generality that the heads of both rules are $p(X_1, \ldots, X_n)$. Let the recursive subgoal of the left-linear rule be $p(Y_1, \ldots, Y_n)$ and that of the right-linear rule be $p(Z_1, \ldots, Z_n)$. Suppose for convenience that the adornment α binds the first m arguments of p and leaves the last $n - m$ arguments free. We have only to show that the rules in question satisfy conditions (a) through (d) of Theorem 15.3.

For (a), suppose that $Y_i \neq X_i$. Then $i > m$, because Y_i would be X_i if i were a bound position in a left-linear rule. It follows that $Z_i = X_i$, because i is one of the free arguments of p. The right-linearity property guarantees that Z_i appears nowhere else in the right-linear rule, other than position i of the head. Thus, (a) of Theorem 15.3 is satisfied.

---

[9] Note that the analog of condition (3) is not needed in the strictly-right-linear case. For right-linear rules, if a variable appears in a free position of the recursive subgoal, it cannot appear in an EDB subgoal, for then it would be bound when the recursive subgoal is listed last. It cannot appear in a bound position of the head or the recursive subgoal, or else it would be bound in its home position in the recursive subgoal.

To verify (c), suppose $Y_i = X_j$, for some $j \neq i$. Then again we conclude $i > m$ and $Z_i = X_i$. It is not possible that $j \leq m$, for then positions i and j in the recursive subgoal of the left-linear rule would share a variable, X_j, and we could not have one argument bound and the other free, as would be required by left-linearity if $j \leq m < i$. We conclude that $j > m$, and so $Z_j = X_j$ by right linearity. Similarly, we know from $i > m$ that $Z_i = X_i$. Thus, we conclude (c).

For (b), suppose $Z_i \neq X_i$. Then $i \leq m$, and $Y_i = X_i$, by the right-linearity definition. Now, condition (3) of the strict left-linearity definition guarantees that Y_i does not appear elsewhere, except in position i of the head. Thus, condition (b) of Theorem 15.3 is met.

Finally, we must check (d). If $Z_i = X_j$ for $j \neq i$, then $i \leq m$, as for (b). Also, $j \leq m$, or else we have $Z_i = Z_j = X_j$, and violate right-linearity, which requires that Z_i be bound if $i \leq m$ but requires that Z_j is free if $j > m$. Since i and j are both m or less, we know that $Y_i = X_i$ and $Y_j = X_j$, by left-linearity. We conclude (d). $\square$

Efficient Evaluation of Mixed-Linear Rules

We can now use the commutativity lemma to justify an evaluation algorithm where we first apply the right-linear rules and then the left-linear rules. The applications of these two groups of rules resemble the techniques of Sections 15.1 and 15.2, respectively. In effect, we evaluate a collection of mixed strictly left- and right-linear rules by taking two transitive closures. The first transitive closure handles the right-linear rules and the second handles the left-linear rules. Lemma 15.1 provides the justification for factoring the problem in this way.

Algorithm 15.3: Efficient Evaluation of Left- and Right-Linear Rules.

INPUT: A set of rules involving IDB predicate p and a query goal p^α, such that each of the rules is either a basis (nonrecursive) rule, strictly right-linear, or strictly left-linear with respect to α.

OUTPUT: A revised set of rules that produce the answer to the query. These rules have two recursive predicates, m_p of arity equal to the number of arguments of p made bound by α, and a_p of arity equal to the number of arguments made free by α.

METHOD: Again, assume for convenience that the bound arguments of p precede the free arguments. Also, let $x_1, \ldots, x_n$ be the constants appearing in those arguments of the query goal.

1. For each right-linear rule

$$p(A_1, \ldots, A_n, X_1, \ldots, X_m) :\!\text{-}\ G_1 \ \& \ \cdots \ \& \ G_k \ \&$$
$$p(B_1, \ldots, B_n, X_1, \ldots, X_m).$$

generate the rule

$$m\_p(B_1, \ldots, B_n) :- m\_p(A_1, \ldots, A_n) \ \& \ G_1 \ \& \ \cdots \ \& \ G_k.$$

2. To this set of rules, add the basis rule for the magic set,

$$m\_p(x_1, \ldots, x_n).$$

3. For each basis rule,

$$p(t_1, \ldots, t_n, s_1, \ldots, s_m) :- G_1 \ \& \ \cdots \ \& \ G_k.$$

generate a rule to initialize the calculation of a_p,

$$a\_p(s_1, \ldots, s_m) :- m\_p(t_1, \ldots, t_n) \ \& \ G_1 \ \& \ \cdots \ \& \ G_k.$$

4. For each left-linear rule,

$$p(X_1, \ldots, X_n, A_1, \ldots, A_m) :- p(X_1, \ldots, X_n, B_1, \ldots, B_m) \ \& \\ G_1 \ \& \ \cdots \ \& \ G_k.$$

generate a recursive rule for a_p,

$$a\_p(A_1, \ldots, A_m) :- a\_p(B_1, \ldots, B_m) \ \& \ G_1 \ \& \ \cdots \ \& \ G_k.$$

5. Generate the rule that translates a_p to p,

$$p(x_1, \ldots, x_n, Y_1, \ldots, Y_m) :- a\_p(Y_1, \ldots, Y_m).$$

The collection of rules so generated is the output of the algorithm. $\square$

Example 15.11: The construction of Example 15.9, where we produced the rules of Figure 15.10 from those of Figure 15.9, is an example of Algorithm 15.3. The first rule for m_p in Figure 15.10 comes from the query goal, and the second comes from the right-linear rule r_2. The three rules for a_p come from the basis (rule r_1), and the two left-linear rules (r_3 and r_4), respectively. The last rule in Figure 15.10 converts a_p to p. $\square$

Theorem 15.4: The rules generated by Algorithm 15.3

a) Produce the same answer to the query as the input rules.

b) Are, to within a constant factor, no less efficient than the magic rules constructed from the input rules.

Proof: (a) The heart of the proof is Lemma 15.1, which, with Theorems 15.2 and 15.3, says that the answer to the query is equivalent to the set of answers produced along those rule paths in which the right-linear rules precede the left-linear rules. Let us call such a rule path *normalized*, and let the *middle* of such a path be the goal node that is a descendant of all right-linear rule nodes and an ancestor of all left-linear rule nodes, as suggested in Figure 15.11. We also refer to the last p-goal node on the path, the one just before the basis rule node, as the *bottom*.

Then a simple induction on the number of steps in a bottom-up evaluation

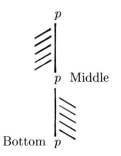

p

p Middle

Bottom p

Figure 15.11 Normalized rule path.

shows that a tuple is placed in m_p if and only if it is in the binding relation for some goal node that is the middle of a normalized path. The left-linear rules do not change the bindings, so the relation for m_p consists of exactly the tuples that reach the binding relation for some bottom goal node.

The rules initializing a_p place in its relation exactly the free components (those components made free in the unique binding pattern for p) of those tuples that are returned as answers by bottom nodes of some normalized rule path. Moreover, notice that the set of tuples returned by a bottom node depends only on the sequence of right-linear rules on the path and on the basis rule used; it does not depend on the left-linear rules.

Finally, the recursive rules for a_p cause it to produce the free components of each tuple that is obtained by starting with some tuple returned by a bottom node, and propagating it upward through some sequence of left-linear rules. Since the tuples returned by bottom nodes are independent of the left-linear rules in the rule path, we know that each tuple returned by any bottom node is returned by the bottom node of some normalized rule path with any desired sequence of left-linear rules. Thus, the set of free components of tuples returned by the middle node of some normalized rule path is exactly the relation for a_p. Since the right-linear rules propagate the free components upward without change, a_p also has all and only the free components of tuples returned by the root. The rule that translates a_p into p attaches the query constants to those answers, yielding exactly what the normalized rule paths produce.

(b) The argument for efficiency was given, in its essential points, in Sections 15.1 and 15.2. That is, the rules for m_p are simplifications of Group I rules with the supplementary predicates substituted out. The rules for a_p are Group IV rules with the supplementary predicates substituted out, and the rule converting a_p to p is easily seen not to cost extra running time, provided we carry the query constants along as we evaluate a_p. $\Box$

15.5 A COUNTING TECHNIQUE FOR LINEAR RULES

There are certain rules that are linear, in the sense that they have only one recursive subgoal, yet for a particular query goal, they fall into neither the left-linear nor right-linear class.

Example 15.12: Perhaps the simplest example is the "same-generation" rules,

$$r_1: \quad \texttt{sg(X,X)} \ :- \ \texttt{person(X).}$$
$$r_2: \quad \texttt{sg(X,Y)} \ :- \ \texttt{par(X,Xp)} \ \& \ \texttt{sg(Xp,Yp)} \ \& \ \texttt{par(Y,Yp).}$$

with the query goal sg^{bf}. These rules cannot be left- or right-linear with respect to adornment bf, because the recursive subgoal, $sg(Xp, Yp)$ does not share any variables with the head, $sg(X, Y)$, of r_2.

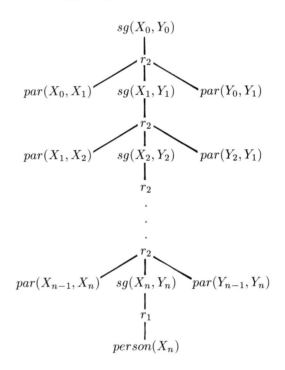

Figure 15.12 Typical rule/goal tree path for same-generation rules.

However, we can make the bf adornment propagate from the head to the recursive subgoal of r_2 if (and only if) we order the subgoals as shown above, that is, with sg in the middle. With this ordering, a typical path in the rule/goal tree for a query $sg(a, Y_0)$ is as shown in Figure 15.12. That is, we apply rule r_2 some number of times, say n, followed by one application of the basis rule r_1.

If X_0 at the root is bound to $\{a\}$, the effect of the path in Figure 15.12 is to bind X_n to the set S of nth-generation ancestors of individual a. Then, Y_n is bound to the subset of those individuals that are members of the relation for *person*. Finally, the trailing *par* subgoals bind Y_0 to the set of nth-generation descendants of the individuals in S. The answer to the query is the union, over all n, of the result of performing the above steps.

We can make the calculation more efficient if we combine the work associated with different values of n as best we can. In particular, having computed the $(n-1)$st-generation of ancestors of a, we can use that set to compute the nth-generation by one more use of the *par* EDB relation. Then, having found the subset of the nth generation that is in *person*, and having used *par* to find their parents, we have, in effect, a set of $(n-1)$-generation ancestors of a that have already met the acceptance test of the *person* relation. These can be combined with the individuals found by the path of length $n-1$ to be $(n-1)$st-generation ancestors of a, and together, they can be brought back $n-1$ generations, accumulating the results of shorter rule/goal tree paths as we go.

```
(1)     u_sg(a,0).
(2)     u_sg(Xp,I) :- par(X,Xp) & u_sg(X,I-1).
(3)     d_sg(X,I) :- u_sg(X,I) & person(X).
(4)     d_sg(Y,I-1) :- par(Y,Yp) & d_sg(Yp,I).
(5)     sg(a,Y) :- d_sg(Y,0).
```

Figure 15.13 Counting rules for same-generation problem.

The effect of counting up the generations and then back down can be expressed, informally, by the rules of Figure 15.13. There, we introduce two additional predicates, u_sg to count "up" the genealogy, and d_sg to count down. Each has a second argument, which counts how many generations above the individual a the individual mentioned in the first argument is. Formally, an argument $I-1$ in rules (2) and (4) of Figure 15.13 makes no sense. However, we can handle integer arithmetic by using a function symbol, such as *succ* for "successor" as in Example 12.2. That is, we should think of rule (2) as

```
u_sg(Xp,succ(J)) :- par(X,Xp) & u_sg(X,J).
```

and rule (4) as

```
d_sg(Y,J) :- par(Y,Yp) & d_sg(Yp,succ(J)).
```

Then, we can evaluate the rules of Figure 15.13 bottom-up. The relation for u_sg will consist of all those pairs (X, I) such that X is an Ith-generation ancestor of a, and d_sg will contain all those pairs (Y, I) such that for some K there is an individual that is

1. A person,
2. A Kth-generation ancestor of a, and
3. A $(K - I)$th-generation ancestor of Y.

Thus, Y is a cousin of a if and only if $(Y, 0)$ is in the relation for d_sg. $\square$

The Need for Acyclicity

There is a sense in which Example 15.12 does not tell the full story. We converted the original same-generation rules into a group of seemingly simpler rules that yield the same answer to the query. Moreover, as with the rest of the techniques discussed in this chapter, the constructed rules are amenable to bottom-up processing, yet do not explore "irrelevant" portions of the database. However, the arithmetic involved in the rules of Figure 15.13 takes us out of the datalog class of rules, and we do not know that the minimal model of these rules is finite, even though the database is finite. In particular, if there were cycles in the *par* relation, then we could get facts of the form $u\_sg(X, I)$ for an infinite number of different values of I.

Of course the answer to the query must be finite, even if the minimal model of the rules in Figure 15.13 is infinite, but the way to stop the iteration performed by semi-naive evaluation of these rules is not easy to see. We can, however, guarantee that the minimal model is finite, and therefore that semi-naive evaluation will converge, if the *par* relation is acyclic and finite. For then, there must be a limit on the number of generations back that we must explore from individual a, and therefore, u_sg will contain no pairs (X, I) for I above this limit.

Counting-Linear Rules

We now see roughly what the limits of the technique suggested by Example 15.12 are. First, we cannot handle more than one recursive rule conveniently, because then, instead of being able to count the number of applications of the one recursive rule with an integer-valued argument, we would have to record the exact sequence of rules applied going "up," so that the matching pieces of the same rules could be applied going "down." It is possible to do so; instead of one *succ* function symbol, we use one function symbol for each rule. However, it does mean that we need to consider a number of paths in the rule/goal tree that is exponential in the number of "generations" found in the database, rather than considering only a linear number. Generally, the cost of that exponential search exceeds what would be obtained by some other method, such as magic-sets.[10]

---

[10] If we have several recursive rules, but they commute, we can avoid the exponential

Our second requirement is acyclicity of the "up" computation. Again, it is not fatal if we don't have this condition, but there is usually some better way to solve the problem if we do not.

Third, we must be able to compute the "up" and "down" portions of the recursive rule in isolation. Thus, we shall require no sharing of variables between portions of the rule involved in the "up" calculation and portions involved in the "down" calculation. This condition will be made precise below.

We shall define a logic program to be *counting-linear* with respect to a given adornment α if the following conditions are satisfied.

1. There is a single IDB predicate, p.

2. There is exactly one rule that has a p-subgoal. This rule, which we call the *recursive rule*, has exactly one such subgoal.

3. It is possible to order the subgoals of the recursive rule so that the p-subgoal has adornment α. Let the subgoals that precede the p-subgoal be called the *up subgoals* and those that follow be called the *down subgoals*.

4. Define the *up arguments* to be those that appear either in an up subgoal, or in the bound arguments (according to α) of the head or of the recursive subgoal. Similarly define the *down arguments* to be the arguments in the down subgoals, and in the free arguments of the head and recursive subgoal. Then no variable may appear in both an up argument and in a down argument.

For example, the same-generation rules meet all of these conditions if we pick the order with sg in the middle of r_2, as was done in Example 15.12. The up arguments are those where X or Xp appear, and the down arguments are those holding Y or Yp. Note that the conditions above do not address the condition of acyclicity, which is best enforced when we write down the modified rules for counting-linear logic programs. We show how to do so in the next algorithm.

Algorithm 15.4: The Counting Algorithm for Single Linear, Recursive Rules.

INPUT: A set of rules involving IDB predicate p, and a query goal p^α, such that the rules are counting-linear with respect to α.

OUTPUT: A revised set of rules that produce the answer to the query. These rules have two recursive predicates, whose arities are one greater than the number of bound arguments and the number of free arguments, respectively, in adornment α.

---

growth in the number of rule/goal tree paths that must be considered.

METHOD: As in the past, let us assume that the bound arguments of p precede the free arguments, and let $x_1, \ldots, x_n$ be the constants appearing the in bound arguments of the query goal. Let the recursive rule be

$$p(s_1, \ldots, s_n, t_1, \ldots, t_m) \text{ :- } G_1 \ \& \ \cdots \ \& \ G_k \ \& \\ p(u_1, \ldots, u_n, v_1, \ldots, v_m) \ \& \ H_1 \ \& \ \cdots \ \& \ H_l.$$

Here, $s_1, \ldots, s_n$ and $u_1, \ldots, u_n$ are terms appearing in the bound arguments of p, in the head and recursive subgoal, respectively, and the t's and v's similarly occupy the free positions. The G's are the up subgoals and the H's are the down subgoals.

We generate rules as follows.

1. For the "up" predicate u_p, generate the basis rule

    $$u\_p(x_1, \ldots, x_n, 0).$$

2. Generate the recursive rule for u_p,

    $$u\_p(u_1, \ldots, u_n, I) \text{ :- } G_1 \ \& \ \cdots \ \& \ G_k \ \& \ u\_p(s_1, \ldots, s_n, I - 1).$$

3. For each basis (nonrecursive) rule

    $$p(w_1, \ldots, w_{n+m}) \text{ :- } J_1 \ \& \ \cdots \ \& \ J_j.$$

    generate the initializing rule for the "down" predicate d_p,

    $$d\_p(w_{n+1}, \ldots, w_{n+m}, I) \text{ :- } u\_p(w_1, \ldots, w_n, I) \ \& \ J_1 \ \& \ \cdots \ \& \ J_j.$$

4. Generate the recursive rule for d_p,

    $$d\_p(t_1, \ldots, t_m, I - 1) \text{ :- } d\_p(v_1, \ldots, v_m, I) \ \& \ H_1 \ \& \ \cdots \ \& \ H_l.$$

5. Produce the answer with the rule

    $$p(x_1, \ldots, x_n, Y_1, \ldots, Y_m) \text{ :- } d\_p(Y_1, \ldots, Y_m, 0).$$

The output of the algorithm is the collection of rules generated thereby. $\square$

Example 15.13: Rules (1) through (5) of Figure 15.13 are generated by the steps (1) through (5), respectively, in Algorithm 15.4. $\square$

Theorem 15.5: Algorithm 15.4 produces a logic program that answers the input query.

Proof: We leave this result as an exercise for the reader, generalizing the arguments given in Example 15.12, in connection with the same-generation rules. $\square$

Convergence for Counting-Linear Rules

Notice that there is no requirement that the input rules for Algorithm 15.4 be datalog. Thus, the original rules may not converge after a finite amount of time. However, even if they do have a finite minimal model, the new rules, generated by Algorithm 15.4, may not have a finite minimal model and therefore may not converge when we perform semi-naive evaluation on them. The condition that corresponds to acyclicity of the *par* relation in Example 15.12 is the following.

1. The minimal model for the rules must be finite, given a finite EDB.
2. Let D be the (finite) set of values that can appear in bound arguments of p in the minimal model.
3. Draw a graph whose nodes are the n-tuples chosen from D. Let there be an arc from $(y_1, \ldots, y_n)$ to $(z_1, \ldots, z_n)$ if there is a substitution of values for the variables in the recursive rule for u_p [item (2) in Algorithm 15.4] that makes the recursive subgoal become $u\_p(y_1, \ldots, y_n, i-1)$ and the head become $u\_p(z_1, \ldots, z_n, i)$, for some i.
4. Then this graph must be acyclic.

Example 15.14: In Example 15.12, the rule for u_p (which is u_sg in that example) is

```
u_sg(Xp,I) :- par(X,Xp) & u_sg(X,I-1).
```

The finite domain D is contained in the set of values appearing in the *par* relation, and the graph has an arc from X to Xp exactly when $par(X, Xp)$ is true. Thus, condition (4) above is equivalent to acyclicity of the *par* relation in this example. □

We shall also leave to the reader a proof that the conditions above are sufficient for the rules generated by Algorithm 15.4 to converge.

Efficiency of the Rules Generated by the Counting Method

First, let us observe that, should the recursive rule be left-linear or right-linear, then the rules generated by Algorithm 15.4 are never as efficient as those generated by Algorithms 15.2 or 15.1, respectively. However, if the recursive rule does not fall into either of these classes, then the only significant comparison is with the magic-sets algorithm. Here the comparison is less clear. It turns out that which method is better can depend on the data in the database. We give two examples to illustrate the point.

Example 15.15: Let us consider the same-generation rules again and compare the counting rules of Figure 15.13 with the simplified magic rules of Figure 13.15. For an example where counting is better, consider the *par* relation represented by Figure 15.14, where lines run from a child below to a parent above. That is, the *par* relation consists of the tuples $par(a, b_i)$ and $par(b_i, c)$, for $i = 1, 2, \ldots, n$. We also assume that *person* contains all of the individuals appearing in Figure 15.14, so the *person* relation can be ignored.

For equity in the comparison of the two methods, we make the uniform assumption that we can give a value for either argument of *par* and find all of the matching tuples in time proportional to the number of tuples retrieved. We also assume it is possible to test whether $person(X)$ is true for any individual X in $O(1)$ time.

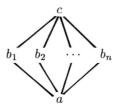

Figure 15.14 Example where counting is better.

Given the query $sg(a, Y)$, the counting rules of Figure 15.13 deduce the facts $u\_sg(a, 0)$, $u\_sg(b_i, 1)$ for $1 \le i \le n$, and $u\_sg(c, 2)$. It takes $O(n)$ time to make these inferences. That is, in $O(n)$ time we query par about child a, getting back answers $b_1, \ldots, b_n$. Then, for each of these b's we query par to find their lone parent c, again taking $O(n)$ time.

Similarly, we can infer the basis d_sg facts, which are $d\_sg(a, 0)$, $d\_sg(b_i, 1)$, for $1 \le i \le n$, and $d\_sg(c, 2)$. That step takes $O(n)$ time to query the $person$ relation. Now, when we compute d_sg recursively, we rediscover $d\_sg(b_i, 1)$ from $d\_sg(c, 2)$ in $O(n)$ time, since that is the cost of interrogating the par relation for children of c. Likewise, finding the children of the b's takes time $O(n)$, since they each have only one child, a. These discoveries only repeat the known fact $d\_sg(a, 0)$. Thus, the sole answer to the query, $sg(a, a)$, is discovered in $O(n)$ time by the counting rules.

In comparison, the magic rules of Figure 13.15 must infer all of the facts $sg(b_i, b_j)$, for $1 \le i, j \le n$. These discoveries cannot be done in less than $\Omega(n^2)$ time. We conclude that counting is significantly better than magic-sets on the data of Figure 15.14. $\Box$

Example 15.16: On the other hand, consider the same rules, but with the data of Figure 15.15. There, the par relation consists of the facts $par(a_{i-1}, a_i)$, for $i = 1, 2, \ldots, n$ and the facts $par(a_0, a_j)$ for $j = 2, 3, \ldots, n$. We also assume that $person$ includes all of the individuals mentioned in Figure 15.15.

Notice that a_j is a kth-generation ancestor of a_0 for all $1 \le k \le j$. Thus the counting method infers all of the facts $u\_sg(a_j, k)$ for $1 \le k \le j \le n$, that is, $\Omega(n^2)$ facts. Hence, the running time of the counting method on the data of Figure 15.15 must be $\Omega(n^2)$.

However, when we apply the magic-sets algorithm to the data of Figure 15.15, we find that in one round we infer all of the facts $sup_{2.1}(a_0, a_i)$, for $i = 1, 2, \ldots, n$ using rule (4) of Figure 13.15. Then on the next two rounds we infer $m\_sg(a_i)$ and $sup_{2.1}(a_{i-1}, a_i)$, for $i = 1, 2, \ldots, n$, using rules (1) and (4)

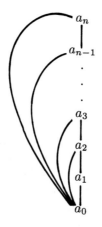

Figure 15.15 Example where magic-sets is better than counting.

of Figure 13.15. That is, all individuals are in the relation for m_sg, and all of the *par* facts are in the relation for $sup_{2.1}$. These inferences take $O(n)$ time.

By the third round, we can also use rule (6) of Figure 13.15 to infer the facts $sg(a_i, a_i)$, for $i = 0, 1, \ldots, n$; again, only $O(n)$ work is needed to discover these facts. Then, in one more round, we find that $sg(a_0, a_i)$ and $sg(a_i, a_0)$, for $i = 1, 2, \ldots, n-1$. As each individual has at most two children, these inferences too take $O(n)$ time. There are no more inferences to be made, as we now have the entire sg relation for this data. Thus, we conclude that magic-sets takes $O(n)$ time on this example, compared with $\Omega(n^2)$ for counting. $\square$

15.6 TRANSITIVE CLOSURE

The *transitive closure* of a directed graph G is the set of pairs of nodes (N, M) such that there is a path of length 1 or more from N to M. Calculation of the transitive closure is a fundamental problem, and algorithms for computing the transitive closure give us solutions to many other natural problems as well, as we shall see in the next section. In this volume, we have met the transitive closure in the guise of parents and ancestors. That is, we may think of a graph whose nodes are individuals, with an arc $N \rightarrow M$ if and only if M is a parent of N. Then the transitive closure of this graph is the ancestor relation; that is, there is a path from N to M if and only if M is an ancestor of N.

In general, the transitive closure t of a graph whose arcs are represented by the predicate a can be expressed by linear logical rules,

$$
\begin{aligned}
&\texttt{t(X,Y) :- a(X,Y).} \\
&\texttt{t(X,Y) :- a(X,Z) \& t(Z,Y).}
\end{aligned}
\tag{15.2}
$$

or

```
t(X,Y) :- a(X,Y).
t(X,Y) :- t(X,Z) & a(Z,Y).
```
(15.3)

We can even use an equivalent nonlinear logic program,

```
t(X,Y) :- a(X,Y).
t(X,Y) :- t(X,Z) & t(Z,Y).
```
(15.4)

We shall leave it to the reader to check that all three recursive definitions of paths are correct. Program (15.2) says that a path is either a single arc or an arc followed by a path; (15.3) says a path is either a single arc or a path followed by an arc, and (15.4) says a path is either an arc or the concatenation of two paths.

A Graph Representation of Linear Logic Programs

It turns out that any linear logic program can be converted to a transitive closure if we are willing to tolerate a sufficiently large set of nodes in the underlying graph. Suppose we have a linear logic program $\mathcal{P}$ and a database of relations for the EDB predicates of $\mathcal{P}$. We construct a domain D consisting of all ground terms that can appear as arguments of IDB facts. If $\mathcal{P}$ is a datalog program, and the database is finite, then D is the finite set of all components of all tuples in the database, plus all constants appearing in the rules of $\mathcal{P}$. If there are function symbols in $\mathcal{P}$, then D may be infinite, even though the database is finite, since we generally must include all ground terms built from the constants in the database and in the rules, to which are applied the function symbols appearing in $\mathcal{P}$.

Then, from $\mathcal{P}$ we construct a graph G as follows. The nodes of G correspond to the atoms $p(t_1, \ldots, t_k)$, where p is a k-ary IDB predicate symbol of $\mathcal{P}$, and $t_1, \ldots, t_k$ are values in D. There is an arc from node $p(t_1, \ldots, t_k)$ to node $q(s_1, \ldots, s_m)$ whenever there is a rule of the form

$$q(u_1, \ldots, u_m) :\text{-} p(v_1, \ldots, v_k) \& E_1 \& \cdots \& E_n.$$

such that some substitution of ground terms for the variables makes each of the EDB subgoals E_i into a database fact, makes $q(u_1, \ldots, u_m)$ become $q(s_1, \ldots, s_m)$, and makes $p(v_1, \ldots, v_k)$ become $p(t_1, \ldots, t_k)$. Of course the IDB subgoal p need not appear first in the rule; it could have any position.

If D is finite, this graph is finite, although when the database has size n, the graph could have a number of nodes equal to $O(n^k)$, where k is the largest arity of any IDB predicate of $\mathcal{P}$. Moreover, the number of arcs could be the square of that number. If D is infinite, then the graph is infinite, which presents considerable problems, but is not necessarily fatal; for example, there may be only a finite number of nodes accessible from any given node, thus allowing queries with all arguments bound to be answered.[11]

Example 15.17: Consider the same-generation rules,

```
sg(X,X).
sg(X,Y) :- par(X,Xp) & par(Y,Yp) & sg(Xp,Yp).
```

and let the EDB consist of the facts $par(1,2)$, $par(1,3)$, $par(2,4)$, and $par(3,4)$. The nonsafety of the first rule turns out to be unimportant, since in the graph we construct, X will be restricted to values 1 through 4 anyway.

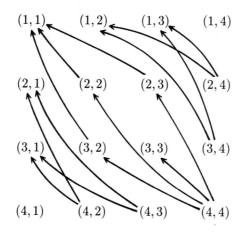

Figure 15.16 Graph constructed from same-generation rules.

The nodes of the graph are the 16 pairs (i,j), where $1 \le i, j \le 4$. To find the arcs into (i,j), we find each parent k of i and each parent l of j and draw an arc $(k,l) \to (i,j)$. The resulting graph is shown in Figure 15.16. □

There are several kinds of questions we can answer by taking the transitive closure of a graph, or a portion of the transitive closure. Most simple is a query with all bound arguments, for instance, "is 1 a cousin of 2?" in the database of Example 15.17. We trace backward from the node $(1,2)$ to find all those nodes that reach it; in Example 15.17 that would be $(1,2)$, $(2,4)$, and $(3,4)$. Note that here, all of the relevant paths are of length one or less, but in general, they could be long. We then ask of each of these nodes whether they are implied by the basis rules. In Example 15.17, that is the same as asking if any are of the form (i,i). As none are, we conclude that 1 is not a cousin of 2.

---

[11] When there are function symbols, we are generally limited in the sorts of queries we can answer anyway; see, for instance, the discussion of the "goodList" rules in Example 12.34.

Next simplest is a query in which some arguments are bound and the others free. We can trace backward from each of the nodes that match the bound arguments, and see which reach nodes implied by the basis. For example, given the query "who are 2's cousins?" referring to the database of Example 15.17, we trace backward from each of nodes $(2,1)$, $(2,2)$, $(2,3)$, and $(2,4)$, to find which of these are reached from nodes implied by the basis, that is, from nodes of the form (i,i). Of these, $(2,2)$ is reached from itself and from $(4,4)$, while $(2,3)$ is reached from $(4,4)$; the other two nodes are not reached from a basis node. We conclude that 2's cousins are 2 and 3.

Finally, we may be given a query with all free arguments. In this case, there is nothing better than to compute the whole transitive closure.[12] We first find all of the nodes implied by the basis rules, and then determine which nodes are reachable from these; the reachable set is the answer to the query. For instance, in Example 15.17, the nodes implied by the basis are those on the main diagonal, (i,i). These reach only themselves and the nodes $(2,3)$ and $(3,2)$. Thus, the six pairs

$$\{(1,1),\ (2,2),\ (3,3),\ (4,4),\ (2,3),\ (3,2)\}$$

are the entire sg relation.

Methods for Computing Transitive Closure

There are a number of algorithms that compute transitive closures efficiently, and many are adaptable to a model of computation in which we assume that retrieval of arcs, given the node at either end, takes time proportional to one plus the number of arcs retrieved. That model is valid if we assume there are indices on both attributes of the relation that stores the arcs. However, it ignores the additional efficiency that can be had if we arrange that the arcs are clustered according to the node at one end.[13]

Many algorithms, such as Warshall's,[14] require lookups from both ends of arcs; that is, sometimes we ask the query $a(n, X)$ and sometimes the query $a(X, n)$, for particular node n. There is no structure that allows clustering according to two different attributes, although partial match structures, as discussed in Sections 6.12 through 6.14 of Volume I, can provide some efficiency for lookups on several different attributes. Also, for Warshall's algorithm in particular, the lookups from one end predominate, so clustering on one end of

---

[12] Computation of the full transitive closure also may be preferred if some of the arguments are bound by the query, but the binding is unable to restrict search to a small fraction of the graph.

[13] See Section 6.7 (Volume I) and Section 11.2 for a discussion of clustering.

[14] See Aho, Hopcroft, and Ullman [1974, 1983] for a discussion of Warshall's algorithm, depth-first search, and other algorithms for graph searching and transitive closure. The next section contains a generalization of Warshall's algorithm.

the arcs is adequate to attain close to the optimum efficiency.

Another important approach, depth-first search, allows us to find the nodes reachable from a given node in time proportional to the number of arcs that must be traversed, and only requires that lookups be made to find the arcs out of (never into) a given node. Thus, clustering arcs according to their tails and using an index on tails seems effective. The major problem that can occur is that depth-first search often follows long paths, keeping many nodes "open"; that is, having explored some, but not all, of the arcs out of the nodes along the path. If there are too many open nodes, we cannot keep all their arcs in main memory, and must read the arcs for the same node more than once.

Left- and Right-Linear Rules as Transitive Closures

If we review Sections 15.1 and 15.2, we see that the reduction in arity afforded by Algorithms 15.1 and 15.2 makes the transitive closure interpretation of rules more palatable than it is in general. In the right-linear case, the nodes of the graph for the rules constructed by Algorithm 15.1 correspond to possible tuples of values for the bound arguments of the given predicate. Thus, the set of nodes is much smaller than for the original rules, provided at least one argument of the query is free. Further, the constructed rules can be evaluated by searching from the node corresponding to the constants in the query; we do not even have to construct or look at inaccessible portions of the graph. Once we have the reachable nodes, we have only to determine which yield answers through the basis rules.

A similar search, this time through nodes representing "answers," which are tuples of values for the free arguments of the original rules, occurs for a left-linear logic program. Again, the size of the graph is reduced, and we need not look at inaccessible portions. As in the right-linear case, once we have computed the nodes reachable from the query, we are essentially done. Thus, in a significant sense, all left-linear and all right-linear logic programs are instances of transitive closure on a graph of appropriate size.

15.7 CLOSED SEMIRINGS AND GENERALIZED TRANSITIVE CLOSURE

In Example 13.3 we considered the following rules,

> r_1:   p(X,Y,D) :- a(X,Y,D).
> r_2:   p(X,Y,D) :- p(X,Z,E) & p(Z,Y,F) & D=E+F.

EDB predicate $a(X, Y, D)$ is interpreted as saying there is an arc from node X to node Y of length D, and $p(X, Y, D)$ is then interpreted as asserting there is a path from X to Y of length D. This computation is a generalized transitive closure, where we not only want to know about the existence of paths; we need to know how long they are.

However, often we do not want to know about the lengths of all paths from X to Y, but only some aggregate quantity such as the length of the shortest path or the length of the longest path. That is, after constructing the IDB relation P for p, we want to group the tuples of P by the first two components, and for each a and b compute the minimum value of D such that (a, b, D) is a tuple of P.

This aggregation is not expressible by logical rules; that is, we cannot write rules such that only the tuples (a, b, d) for which d is the minimum-length path from a to b will appear in the relation P. The situation is not unlike what we encountered in Chapter 4 (Volume I) when we talked about relational query languages. In Sections 4.3, 4.4, and 4.6 we saw that aggregate operators like min and sum, a "group by" operator, and other dictions were added on top of the basic query language, which is equivalent to relational calculus (that is, to nonrecursive datalog with stratified negation). We also saw in Section 4.4, when we discussed the ALL. and UN. operators of Query-by-Example, that duplicate-elimination is sometimes an issue when we take aggregations. The next example explores this issue in the context of recursive logical rules.

Example 15.18: The "parts explosion" problem can be expressed as follows. We are given an EDB predicate $partOf(X, Y, N)$ meaning that part X directly uses N of part Y in its assembly. Some parts are made of constituent parts that are not themselves atomic, but are composed of constituents, which may themselves be constructed from other parts, and so on. We assume that there are no cycles, since a part cannot be a constituent of itself, even indirectly. However, the number of levels of assembly can be large. We may therefore wish to define a predicate $uses(X, Y, N)$ that says the assembly of an X uses N copies of Y, either directly or indirectly. The rules defining $uses$ might be

```
uses(X,Y,N)  :- partOf(X,Y,N).
uses(X,Y,N)  :- partOf(X,Z,L) & uses(Z,Y,M) & M=L*N.
```

These rules do not quite give us what we want. Intuitively, we can think of a graph whose arcs are the first two arguments of $partOf$; that is, there is an arc from X to Y with weight N if $partOf(X, Y, N)$ is true. Then, for each distinct path from a to b, we shall find tuple $uses(a, b, c)$, where c is the product of the weights along the path. If we want the actual number of b's used in the assembly of one a, we must sum the c's in all tuples of the form $uses(a, b, c)$.

However, when we perform the sum, we must be careful not to eliminate duplicates first. That is, suppose an a consists of two b's and two c's, while a b has two d's and a c also has two d's. Then the EDB consists of the following $partOf$ tuples:

$$\{(a, b, 2), \ (a, c, 2), \ (b, d, 2), \ (c, d, 2)\}$$

The only $uses$ tuple with first components a and d is $(a, d, 4)$. But we should not therefore conclude that there are four d's in an a. In truth there are eight, because there are two "paths" from a to d — one through b and one through c — and each accounts for four d's.

Our conclusion is that if we compute the number of copies of one part found in another part by computing the *uses* relation and then grouping by the first two components and summing over the third, then we must do the grouping and summing before eliminating duplicates. That puts a strain on the value-oriented view of logic, since we do not formally have any way to distinguish between two different "facts" $uses(a, d, 4)$, for example. In the logical view, either $uses(a, d, 4)$ is true or it isn't; it cannot be true twice. We need to take an "object-oriented" view of facts,[15] where each tuple has its own object-identity. Only then can we distinguish among several occurrences of the same fact in the relation for an IDB predicate. □

As we shall see, there is another approach to computing aggregate functions such as these. In the method to be discussed next, we compute the aggregate function directly, without ever instantiating the IDB relations, such as *uses*, to which we apply an aggregation.

Closed Semirings

We have now examined three problems in which we performed a transitive-closure-like calculation on graphs that had "weights" associated with the arcs.

1. Transitive closure itself.
2. Shortest path.
3. Parts explosion.

In each case, we had an operator that combined weights along paths, to get a weight for the entire path, and an operator that combined the weights of all paths between two nodes, to get a value associated with that pair of nodes.

1. For transitive closure, we can imagine there is an arc from any node a to any node b; the weight is 1 if the arc is present in the graph and 0 if not. To combine the weights along a path, use the logical AND. That is, a path exists only if all arcs along that path exist. To combine paths, use logical OR. Thus, there is a path from a to b if and only if one of the possible paths from a to b has weight 1; that is, it really exists.

2. For shortest paths, weights on arcs are distances, and we may think of a missing arc as having infinite distance. To combine weights along a path, we sum the weights of the arcs on the path, and to combine paths between two nodes, we take the minimum of the weights of the paths.

---

[15] See Sections 1.5 and 2.7 of Volume I.

3. For parts explosion, the weight of an arc $a \to b$ is the number of b's that are immediate constituents of an a, that is, the number n such that

$$partOf(a, b, n)$$

is true. If no b's are immediate constituents of an a, take the weight of arc $a \to b$ to be 0. We combine weights along a path by taking the product, and we combine paths between two nodes by taking the sum of their weights.

These examples and others can be abstracted to an algebraic structure for which we offer algorithms that work for all instances of the structure. In this structure, called a *closed semiring*, there are two operators, an *additive operator*, which we denote $\oplus$, and a *multiplicative operator*, denoted $\otimes$. There are two special constants, **0** and **1**, which are the additive and multiplicative identities. Each closed semiring has a *domain* of values, which includes **0** and **1**, upon which $\oplus$ and $\otimes$ are defined. The algebraic laws followed by a closed semiring are these.

1. $\oplus$ is infinitely commutative and associative. That is, we can add a finite or infinite set of values in any order we choose, and the result will be the same. As special cases, we get the usual commutative law, $x \oplus y = y \oplus x$, and associative law $x \oplus (y \oplus z) = (x \oplus y) \oplus z$, and we also get some equalities that do not follow from a finite number of applications of the usual laws, such as

$$x_1 \oplus x_2 \oplus x_3 \oplus x_4 \oplus \cdots = (x_1 \oplus x_3 \oplus \cdots) \oplus (x_2 \oplus x_4 \oplus \cdots)$$

2. $\otimes$ is at least finitely associative; $x \otimes (y \otimes z) = (x \otimes y) \otimes z$. Note that $\otimes$ is not required to be commutative, although it is in the examples cited above.

3. The identity elements behave as identities; that is, $\mathbf{0} \oplus x = x$ and

$$\mathbf{1} \otimes x = x \otimes \mathbf{1} = x$$

Also, **0** is a "multiplicative annihilator," so $\mathbf{0} \otimes x = x \otimes \mathbf{0} = \mathbf{0}$.[16]

4. $\otimes$ is infinitely distributive over $\oplus$. That is,

$$x \otimes (y_1 \oplus y_2 \oplus \cdots) = (x \otimes y_1) \oplus (x \otimes y_2) \oplus \cdots$$

and $(y_1 \oplus y_2 \oplus \cdots) \otimes x = (y_1 \otimes x) \oplus (y_2 \otimes x) \oplus \cdots$. This law includes the usual finite distributivity as a special case.

The abstraction is given meaning when we have a graph in which each arc has an associated element, or *weight*, from the domain of a closed semiring. Missing arcs are deemed to have weight **0**. The *weight of a path* is the product ($\otimes$) of the weights along the arcs of that path, in order. That is, a path

$$a_0 \to a_1 \to \cdots \to a_n$$

---

[16] Note we may assume $\mathbf{0} \oplus x = x \oplus \mathbf{0}$ by (1), but we must state that $\mathbf{1} \otimes x = x \otimes \mathbf{1}$ and $\mathbf{0} \otimes x = x \otimes \mathbf{0}$.

with weight w_i on the arc $a_{i-1} \rightarrow a_i$ has weight $w_1 \otimes w_2 \otimes \cdots \otimes w_n$. Convention- ally, a path of length zero (no arcs) has weight $\mathbf{1}$. We shall call a path *proper* if it is not of length zero, and in general, we shall consider only proper paths in our computations.

We can then associate a single element of the closed semiring with each pair of nodes (a, b). This *value* for (a, b) is the sum $(\oplus)$ over all proper paths from a to b, of the weight of the path. If there are no paths from a to b, then this sum is $\mathbf{0}$. The number of paths may be infinite, but infinite sums make sense and the sum may take place in any order because of the infinite commutativity and associativity of $\oplus$.

Example 15.19: For transitive closure, we use the Boolean closed semiring, whose only elements are 0 (false) and 1 (true). $\oplus$ is $\vee$ (logical OR) and $\otimes$ is $\wedge$ (logical AND). $\mathbf{0}$ is 0, and $\mathbf{1}$ is 1. The sum of a finite or infinite number of elements is 1 if any element is 1 and 0 otherwise. Thus, condition (1) for a closed semiring is satisfied. Condition (2) says that $\wedge$ is associative, which we can easily check. The laws for the identities in (3) are likewise obvious: $1 \wedge x = x \wedge 1 = x$, $0 \vee x = x$, and $0 \wedge x = x \wedge 0 = 0$. Finally, infinite distributivity says that $x \wedge (y_1 \vee y_2 \vee \cdots) = (x \wedge y_1) \vee (x \wedge y_2) \vee \cdots$. If $x = 0$, both sums are 0, and if $x = 1$, both sums are either 1 (if some $y_i = 1$) or 0 (if all of the y's are 0). A similar check covers the case where the multiplication by x is on the right.

We associate value 1 with any arc that exists and 0 with an arc not present in the graph. Then the weight of a sequence of nodes is 1 if and only if all of the arcs along that sequence are present, that is, the sequence is a path in the graph; otherwise the weight is 0. The value associated with pair of nodes (a, b) is 1 if there is any proper path from a to b, and 0 if not. Thus, the values associated with pairs of nodes gives us the transitive closure. $\square$

Example 15.20: For the shortest-path problem, we use the real numbers as the domain of our closed semiring. Let $\otimes$ be addition and $\oplus$ be min. For $\mathbf{1}$ we have 0 and for $\mathbf{0}$ we must chose ∞, for we want the laws $0 + x = x + 0 = x$ (that is, $\mathbf{1} \otimes x = x \otimes \mathbf{1} = x$) and $\min(\infty, x) = x$ (that is, $\mathbf{0} \oplus x = x$). Also,

$$\infty + x = x + \infty = \infty$$

(that is, $\mathbf{0} \otimes x = x \otimes \mathbf{0} = \mathbf{0}$).

We must be careful about infinite "sums," since the minimum of an in- finite set of reals might be a limit, and not a member of the set itself. For example, $\min(.1, .01, .001, \ldots) = 0$. With that point in mind, the associative, commutative, and distributive laws are easy to verify.

Now, let us associate a weight with each arc of a graph. Missing arcs get weight $\mathbf{0}$, which is ∞. Then the weight of a path is the arithmetic sum of the weights along that path. Thus, a path is given a weight equal to what we normally think of as its length, and a sequence of nodes that does not form a path (because one or more arcs are missing) gets "length" ∞. The value associated with pair of nodes (a, b) is the minimum, over all proper paths from a to b, of the length of that path.

If $a = b$, then there is always the path of length zero, whose weight is **1**, that is, the real number 0 in this example. That may or may not be the minimum-weight path from a to itself, since we have not ruled out negative-weight arcs. In fact, if there is a negative-weight cycle in the graph, many or all of the values associated with node pairs may be $-\infty$. Often, it is desirable to include the path of length zero from a node to itself in our calculations, but in the algorithm to be given in this section, that would not be done automatically. It would be necessary to set the value for (a, a) to the minimum of 0 and the value computed by that algorithm, which considers only the proper paths from a to a in its calculation. $\square$

Example 15.21: Finally, let us take up the parts-explosion problem. The domain for the closed semiring will be the nonnegative integers and ∞. $\otimes$ is ordinary product and $\oplus$ is ordinary sum. The identities are **1** $= 1$ and **0** $= 0$, as we would expect. The laws of a closed semiring are easy to verify, once we understand that the sum of an infinite number of positive integers is ∞.

We create a graph with an arc from a to b weighted with the number of times part b is an immediate constituent of part a (as represented by the *partOf* predicate in Example 15.18); 0 is the appropriate weight if b is not an immediate constituent of a. The weight of a path from a to b is the number of b's that are in an a because of the constituents represented by this particular path; that is, the weight of the path is the product of the weights of the arcs along the path. The value for the pair (a, b) is the sum, over all distinct paths, of the weight of that path. If the graph has cycles, this sum might be infinite and would not make sense. However, the parts-explosion problem would normally be solved only for acyclic graphs, in which case the value of (a, b) is the number of b's needed to make one a. $\square$

An Algorithm for Taking Generalized Transitive Closures

There are many algorithms that have been used for taking transitive closures or their generalization to path computations on closed semirings. We shall here give only one approach, which is appropriate for the case where the entire transitive closure is wanted, rather than "reachability" information, such as the value associated with a single pair of nodes or with all pairs (a, b) for a given a. The idea behind this algorithm is originally due to Kleene [1956], who used it to convert finite automata to regular expressions. Essentially the same "trick" appears in algorithms known as Warshall's algorithm for transitive closure and Floyd's or Hu's algorithm for shortest paths.

Algorithm 15.5: Kleene's Algorithm for Generalized Transitive Closure.

INPUT: A directed graph G, each of whose arcs has a weight chosen from some closed semiring with operators $\oplus$, $\otimes$ and identities $\mathbf{0}$ and $\mathbf{1}$.

OUTPUT: For each pair of nodes (a, b), the sum $(\oplus)$ over all proper paths from a to b, of the product $(\otimes)$ of the weights of the arcs along those paths, in order.

METHOD: Let us assume the nodes are named by the integers $1, 2, \ldots, n$. A path $i_1 \to i_2 \to \cdots \to i_k$, for $k \geq 2$, is an m-path if it does not go through any node higher than m. That is, $i_2, \ldots, i_{k-1}$ are each m or less. Note that the endpoints i_1 and i_k can be greater than m on an m-path. Also, the 0-paths are the arcs, and the n-paths are all of the proper paths, since no nodes are numbered above n.

We shall compute, by induction on m, the sum, over all m-paths from i to j, of the weights of those paths; we call this sum v_{ij}^m. When we reach $m = n$, we have the desired values for all i and j. For the basis, let $v_{ij}^0 = w_{ij}$, where w_{ij} is the weight of the arc $i \to j$ ($\mathbf{0}$ if the arc doesn't exist). This initialization reflects the fact that the only 0-paths are those that follow a single arc.

> **for** $m := 1$ **to** n **do**
>   **for** $i := 1$ **to** n **do**
>   **for** $j := 1$ **to** n **do**
> $v_{ij}^m := v_{ij}^{m-1} \oplus \left(v_{im}^{m-1} \otimes \left(v_{mm}^{m-1} \right)^* \otimes v_{mj}^{m-1} \right)$

Figure 15.17 Inductive calculation of v_{ij}^n.

For the induction, we need to define the *Kleene closure* (star) operator, which is

$$x^* = \mathbf{1} \oplus x \oplus (x \otimes x) \oplus (x \otimes x \otimes x) \oplus \cdots$$

We may use the convention that x^i is the product $(\otimes)$ of x with itself i times. Then $x^0 = \mathbf{1}$, conventionally, and we can write

$$x^* = \bigoplus_{i \geq 0} x^i$$

The inductive computation of the v_{ij}^m's is given in Figure 15.17. Intuitively, when we consider node m as the "pivot," we compute v_{ij}^m by considering two kinds of m-paths. Some do not go through m at all; these are included in the sum v_{ij}^{m-1}. Others go through m one or more times. v_{im}^{m-1} gives the sum for all $(m-1)$-paths that get us from i to m the first time. The value $(v_{mm}^{m-1})^*$ accounts for all paths that go from m to m, zero or more times (that is, including the zero-length path), without going through nodes higher than m. Finally, v_{mj}^{m-1}

accounts for all ways to get from m to j without going through m or a node higher than m. These sets of paths are suggested in Figure 15.18.

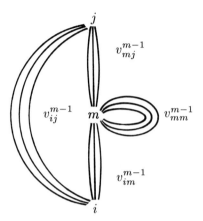

Figure 15.18 The set of m-paths.

We should note that every m-path is counted exactly once by this reckoning. Either it does not go through m, and is therefore covered by v_{ij}^{m-1}, or it goes through m p times for some $p \geq 1$. In that case, the path is covered by the product of

1. v_{im}^{m-1},
2. The term $(v_{mm}^{m-1})^{p-1}$ in the sum represented by $(v_{mm}^{m-1})^*$, and
3. v_{mj}^{m-1}.

Note particularly, that a path going through m exactly once is covered by the **1** term in the sum that $(v_{mm}^{m-1})^*$ represents. $\square$

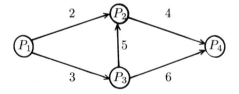

Figure 15.19 Example of parts explosion.

Example 15.22: Consider the instance of the parts-explosion problem represented by Figure 15.19. In what follows, we shall identify part P_i with the integer i. Algorithm 15.5 begins by initializing the values v_{ij}^0. All are 0 except for the five that correspond to the arcs of Figure 15.19; for example, v_{34}^0 is initialized to 6. As the graph is acyclic, all but the six families of values represented by Figure 15.20 remain 0 as m increases from 0 to 4. In particular, note that for any i and m,

$$(v_{ii}^m)^* = 1 + 0 + 0^2 + 0^3 + \cdots = 1$$

For $m = 1$, we find there are no changes to the values, since for no i and j is there a path that goes into and out of node 1 in Figure 15.19. For example,

$$v_{32}^1 = v_{32}^0 + \left(v_{31}^0 \times (v_{11}^0)^* \times v_{12}^0\right) = 5 + (0 \times 1 \times 2) = 5$$

However, when we consider $m = 2$, there are some new paths that get included, namely the paths $1 \rightarrow 2 \rightarrow 4$ and $3 \rightarrow 2 \rightarrow 4$. For example,

$$v_{34}^2 = v_{34}^1 + \left(v_{32}^1 \times (v_{22}^1)^* \times v_{24}^1\right) = 6 + (5 \times 1 \times 4) = 26$$

When m reaches 3, we get to include the paths $1 \rightarrow 3 \rightarrow 2$, $1 \rightarrow 3 \rightarrow 2 \rightarrow 4$, and $1 \rightarrow 3 \rightarrow 4$. For example,

$$v_{14}^3 = v_{14}^2 + \left(v_{13}^2 \times (v_{33}^2)^* \times v_{34}^2\right) = 8 + (3 \times 1 \times 26) = 86$$

Notice that the value 26 for v_{34}^2 represents both the paths $3 \rightarrow 4$ and $3 \rightarrow 2 \rightarrow 4$. Thus, v_{14}^3 represents all three paths from 1 to 4, namely $1 \rightarrow 2 \rightarrow 4$ (weight 8), $1 \rightarrow 3 \rightarrow 4$ (weight 18), and $1 \rightarrow 3 \rightarrow 2 \rightarrow 4$ (weight 60).

At the last step, we consider $m = 4$. However, there are no paths of nonzero weight into and out of 4, so no changes occur; that is, $v_{ij}^4 = v_{ij}^3$ for all i and j. The calculations are summarized in Figure 15.20. $\square$

	v_{12}^m	v_{13}^m	v_{14}^m	v_{24}^m	v_{32}^m	v_{34}^m
$m = 0$:	2	3	0	4	5	6
$m = 1$:	2	3	0	4	5	6
$m = 2$:	2	3	8	4	5	26
$m = 3$:	17	3	86	4	5	26
$m = 4$:	17	3	86	4	5	26

Figure 15.20 Parts-explosion calculation by Kleene's algorithm.

Theorem 15.6: Algorithm 15.5 correctly computes the sum ($\oplus$) over all proper paths from i to j, of the weights of those paths.

Proof: The proof is a simple induction on m that after m iterations of the outer loop of Figure 15.17, v_{ij}^m is the sum of the weights of all m-paths from i to j. The reasoning was given in the algorithm itself and was illustrated by Figure 15.18. That is, the m-paths from i to j are the paths

1. $i \stackrel{m-1}{\Longrightarrow} j$,
2. $i \stackrel{m-1}{\Longrightarrow} m \stackrel{m-1}{\Longrightarrow} j$,
3. $i \stackrel{m-1}{\Longrightarrow} m \stackrel{m-1}{\Longrightarrow} m \stackrel{m-1}{\Longrightarrow} j$,
4. $i \stackrel{m-1}{\Longrightarrow} m \stackrel{m-1}{\Longrightarrow} m \stackrel{m-1}{\Longrightarrow} m \stackrel{m-1}{\Longrightarrow} j$,

and so on, where $\stackrel{m-1}{\Longrightarrow}$ represents an $(m-1)$-path. Each of these classes of paths is disjoint from the others, and together they cover all m-paths from i to j. The formula for v_{ij}^m used in Algorithm 15.5, with the star operation expanded, is

$$v_{ij}^{m-1} \oplus v_{im}^{m-1} \otimes \left(1 \oplus v_{mm}^{m-1} \oplus \left(v_{mm}^{m-1} \otimes v_{mm}^{m-1}\right) \oplus \cdots\right) \otimes v_{mj}^{m-1}$$

The paths of group (1) are covered by v_{ij}^{m-1}, and those of group (2) are covered by v_{im}^{m-1} and v_{mj}^{m-1} with the first term, 1, of the expansion of the star. Group (3) is represented by the same but with the second term, v_{mm}^{m-1}, in place of 1, while group (4) uses the third term, $v_{mm}^{m-1} \otimes v_{mm}^{m-1}$, and so on.

We conclude that v_{ij}^m is the sum of the weights of the m-paths from i to j. Since the n-paths are all paths, and the v_{ij}^n's are the output of the algorithm, we have proved its correctness. $\square$

Efficiency of Kleene's Algorithm

Suppose we count as one unit of time each of the operations $\oplus$, $\otimes$, and $*$ in Figure 15.17. Then it is not hard to see that Algorithm 15.5 takes time $O(n^3)$ on a graph of n nodes. However, there is no guarantee that these three basic closed-semiring operations can be computed in constant time. In our three examples, $\oplus$ and $\otimes$ were chosen from the logical operations $\wedge$ and $\vee$, and the arithmetic operations $+$, $\times$, and min. Thus, at least in these examples, our unit time assumption is realistic for $\oplus$ and $\otimes$.

However, $*$, being shorthand for an infinite sum, might not be computable at all, let alone computable in constant time. In our three examples, it is not hard to compute. For transitive closure, x^* is $1 \vee x \vee (x \wedge x) \vee \cdots$, which is always 1. For shortest paths, x^* is $\min(0, x, x + x, \ldots)$, which is either 0, if $x \geq 0$, or $-\infty$, if $x < 0$. Finally, for parts explosion, $x^* = 1 + x + x^2 + \cdots$, which is 1 if $x = 0$ and ∞ if $x > 0$. The sum is not defined if $x < 0$, but fortunately, we never expect to apply the parts-explosion computation to examples with negative weights ("part a occurs -2 times in part b"). In fact, since we normally expect the graph to be acyclic, we should only apply $*$ to the value 0, in which case the factors $(v_{mm}^{m-1})^*$ in Figure 15.17 are always 1 and can be dropped from the formula.

None of these observations guarantee that in the application of Algorithm 15.5 to an arbitrary closed semiring, we shall not have problems applying $\oplus$, $\otimes$, or $*$ in unit time. Thus, while the examples discussed in this section, and many others, have $O(n^3)$ time implementations of Kleene's algorithm, the reader should be aware of potential problems. One must check that the infinite sum represented by x^* can be computed from x easily, and also that the representation of values in the domain of the closed semiring allows a reasonably efficient implementation of $\oplus$ and $\otimes$.

15.8 MAKING NONLINEAR RULES LINEAR

We have seen in this chapter that there are several algorithms that make processing of large classes of linear rules quite efficient. Even the processing of arbitrary linear logic programs is conceptually simpler than handling nonlinear logic, because, for example, there is essentially one path in a rule/goal tree. Thus, it would be nice if we had a way to convert nonlinear rules to linear ones. Unfortunately, there is no method guaranteed to convert arbitrary datalog programs to equivalent linear datalog programs, even for very simple classes, such as two rules, one of which is a basis rule and one of which is a recursive rule with two occurrences of the IDB predicate.

Example 15.23: Consider the rules

```
on(X) :- input(X).                              (15.5)
on(X) :- on(Y) & on(Z) & and(Y,Z,X).
```

These rules directly represent a problem called *path systems*. We shall not discuss path systems here; rather, the data for these rules may be thought of as a collection of AND-gates, OR-gates, and wires; the variables represent wires. EDB relation *input(X)* says that wire X is "on" (set to 1). EDB relation *and(Y, Z, X)* says that there is an AND-gate with inputs Y and Z and output X; that is, $X = Y \wedge Z$. The OR-gates are hidden in the fact that there can be several *and* tuples with the same third component. If we want an OR-gate whose inputs are wires a and b, we select a name, say c, for the output of this OR-gate, and we place in *and* the tuples aac and bbc. We can also find that certain wires represent complex functions of inputs, which involve both AND and OR. For example, if we have the tuples abe and cde in the relation for *and*, then the wire e has value $(a \wedge b) \vee (c \wedge d)$.

It is believed that rules (15.5) are not equivalent to any linear datalog rules, because of some theorems in complexity theory that are beyond the scope of this book.[17] Briefly, given EDB relations *input* and *and*, finding whether *on(X)*

---

[17] It is, however, possible to give linear, nondatalog rules computing the same relation *on* as (15.5).

is true for a given X is a $\mathcal{P}$-complete problem (not to be confused with $\mathcal{NP}$-complete problems). If (15.5) were equivalent to a linear datalog program, then some very unlikely things would be true. For example, every problem that could be solved deterministically in polynomial time could be solved on a parallel computer with a number of processors that is polynomial in the input size and with an amount of time that is sublinear in the input size.

However, if the reader is unfamiliar with these concepts, it is of no matter. A short time spent trying to find equivalent linear datalog rules for (15.5) should convince the skeptical that we cannot find linear datalog equivalents for all nonlinear datalog programs. □

Therefore, in this section we shall explore a technique for converting nonlinear programs into equivalent linear ones. It is successful in common cases such as the nonlinear version of transitive closure (15.4) that we saw in Section 15.6. We remarked there that (15.4) is equivalent to both the "right-linear" form (15.2) and the "left-linear" form (15.3).[18] In this section we shall develop a test that verifies these equivalences. We focus only on the question of whether a nonlinear logic program is equivalent to a right-linear logic program; the equivalence to a left-linear logic program can be treated in a symmetric manner.

The result we shall obtain applies to the simplest possible nonlinear recursion, although it can be generalized in several ways discussed in the exercises. In this section, we shall assume we are given a logic program $\mathcal{P}_N$ of the form

$$r_1\colon p(X_1,\ldots,X_n) \colon\!\!- p_0(X_1,\ldots,X_n).$$
$$r_2\colon p(X_1,\ldots,X_n) \colon\!\!- p(Y_1,\ldots,Y_n)\ \&\ p(Z_1,\ldots,Z_n)\ \&\qquad\qquad (\mathcal{P}_N)$$
$$G_1\ \&\ \cdots\ \&\ G_k.$$

where p_0 is an EDB predicate, and the subgoals $G_1,\ldots,G_k$ are EDB subgoals with arbitrary predicates. We want to know whether $\mathcal{P}_N$ is equivalent to the logic program $\mathcal{P}_L$,

$$r_1\colon p(X_1,\ldots,X_n) \colon\!\!- p_0(X_1,\ldots,X_n).$$
$$r_2'\colon p(X_1,\ldots,X_n) \colon\!\!- p_0(Y_1,\ldots,Y_n)\ \&\ p(Z_1,\ldots,Z_n)\ \&\qquad\qquad (\mathcal{P}_L)$$
$$G_1\ \&\ \cdots\ \&\ G_k.$$

Note that the only difference between $\mathcal{P}_N$ and $\mathcal{P}_L$ is that in the latter, the first p-subgoal's predicate has been changed to p_0.

One might think that $\mathcal{P}_L$ puts a severe restriction on the form of the linear logic program equivalent to $\mathcal{P}_N$; for example, it excludes programs with several

---

[18] The reader should beware that we shall use the terms "left-linear" and "right-linear" with a meaning somewhat different from that used in Sections 15.1 and 15.2. True, with respect to the adornment bf (15.2) is right-linear and (15.3) is left-linear. However, in this section, "left-linear" will refer only to the fact that the recursive subgoal is first (leftmost) and "right-linear" similarly signifies that the recursive subgoal is last (rightmost).

recursive linear rules or several basis rules, and rules in which the subgoals $G_1, \ldots, G_k$ appear several times or don't appear at all. There is a powerful theory of linearization, of which we shall only scratch the surface here, which indicates that examples of linear programs of the form $\mathcal{P}_N$ that are linearizable, but not equivalent either to $\mathcal{P}_L$ or to the symmetric pair of rules where the second p-subgoal in r_2 is replaced by p_0, will be encountered rarely in practice.

Example 15.24: Let us take up an example of rules of the form $\mathcal{P}_N$ that are linearizable and explore by example the ideas involved behind a test that is sufficient (although not known to be necessary) to tell that $\mathcal{P}_N \equiv \mathcal{P}_L$. The rules we have in mind, which are only slightly more complex than the nonlinear transitive closure rules (15.4), are the "red/blue path" rules of Exercise 13.1,

$r_1:$ path(X,Y) :- red(X,Y).
$r_2:$ path(X,Y) :- path(X,U) & blue(U,V) & path(V,Y).

The fact that the *blue* subgoal appears between the two *path* subgoals is irrelevant; these rules are clearly of the form $\mathcal{P}_N$. Recall these rules can be thought of as defining $path(X, Y)$ to be true if there is a path from X to Y of alternating red and blue arcs, beginning and ending with a red arc. It thus should be no surprise that these rules are equivalent to their $\mathcal{P}_L$ form, in which we replace the first occurrence of *path* by *red*, that is,

$r_1:$ path(X,Y) :- red(X,Y).
$r_2':$ path(X,Y) :- red(X,U) & blue(U,V) & path(V,Y).

Let us now offer a formal proof of that claim. The idea is to show how any proof tree using r_1 and r_2 can be transformed into a right-linear proof tree, of the form shown in Figure 15.21(a). A tree of that form can be converted to one using rules r_1 and r_2', as in Figure 15.21(b), by combining all but the rightmost *red* leaf with its *path* parent. It will then follow that for every proof tree using r_1 and r_2, there is a tree that has the same fact at the root and uses r_1 and r_2'.

Let us recall Section 15.3, where we dealt with the question of whether two rules (also called r_1 and r_2) commuted. We expressed the most general condition that we wanted to avoid, in that case a use of r_1 above a use of r_2, as a conjunctive query, by substituting the body of r_2 into the recursive subgoal of r_1, after the appropriate renaming of variables and unification. We then tested whether that conjunctive query was contained in another conjunctive query that represents "setting things right"; in that case, the use of r_2 was moved above the use of r_1. We saw in the proof of Theorem 15.2 that the containment between these conjunctive queries was sufficient to transform arbitrary proof trees into trees that proved the same fact, but had all uses of r_2 above the uses of r_1.

For the question of transforming arbitrary proof trees to right-linear proof trees, the bad situation is shown in Figure 15.22(a), where we see what happens

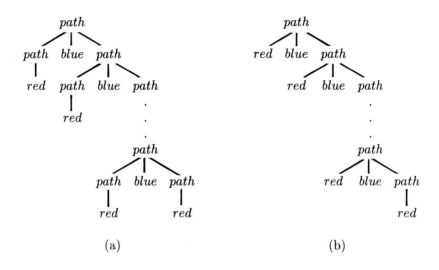

Figure 15.21 Right-linear trees.

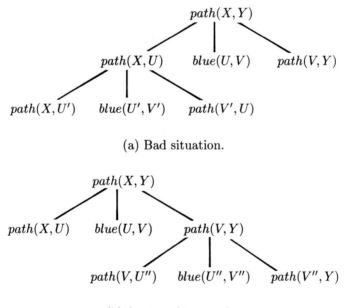

Figure 15.22 Tree transformation for red/blue path rules.

when we expand a fact $path(X, Y)$ by the recursive rule and then expand the left occurrence of $path$ again by the recursive rule. Notice that if we remove all occurrences of this pattern from a proof tree, then we shall have a right-linear tree. Also note that we here follow the same procedure as in Section 15.3 to expand the rules. That is, we imagine another copy of r_2 with primed variables. We then unify the head, $path(X', Y')$, with the first recursive subgoal of r_2, that is $p(X, U)$, to get the substitution that replaces X' by X, Y' by U, and leaves U' and V' alone. The resulting body forms the bottom three subgoals in Figure 15.22(a).

Figure 15.22(b) shows the desired replacement for Figure 15.22(a), where we have expanded the right occurrence of $path$. We could, in principle, have expanded $path(X, Y)$ by replacing the right occurrence of $path$ any number of times, from zero upwards. However, in this and many other cases, the correct choice is two expansions.[19] In order to show that Figure 15.22(b) is a proper replacement for Figure 15.22(a), we look at the conjunctive queries formed from the roots and leaves of these two trees. These are

Q_a: path(X,Y) :- path(X,U') & blue(U',V') & path(V',U) &
                       blue(U,V) & path(V,Y).
Q_b: path(X,Y) :- path(X,U) & blue(U,V) & path(V,U'') &
                       blue(U'',V'') & path(V'',Y).

for Figure 15.22(a) and Figure 15.22(b), respectively. It is easy to check that $Q_a \subseteq Q_b$. The needed containment mapping τ sends distinguished variables X and Y to themselves, of course, and sends U to U', V to V', U'' to U, and V'' to V.

However, a containment mapping from Q_b to Q_a is not enough to guarantee that arbitrary proof trees can be converted to right-linear ones. It is also important to notice that τ sends each of the $path$ subgoals of Q_b to a different one of the $path$ subgoals of Q_a. We can then look, in an arbitrary proof tree, for occurrences of a "bad" node, which is a $path$ node that is expanded by r_2, and whose first $path$ child is also expanded by r_2, as suggested in Figure 15.23(a). If we match Figure 15.22(a) to the explicitly shown portion of Figure 15.23(a), by making an appropriate substitution of ground terms for variables, then the containment $Q_a \subseteq Q_b$ tells us that we may replace Figure 15.23(a) by Figure 15.23(b); the argument is analogous to that used in Theorem 15.2.

It is important to observe that the number of nodes in the trees of Figure 15.23 are the same. It is somewhat tricky to prove that there is an order in which we can apply the transformation of Figure 15.22 to bad nodes so that we eventually reach a right-linear tree. The intuitive idea is that we continue to work on the topmost explicitly-shown $path$ node in Figure 15.23 (which may not be the root of the entire tree), until at some point, the tree T_1 is a single

---

[19] Exercise 15.31 explores some examples where different numbers of expansions are needed.

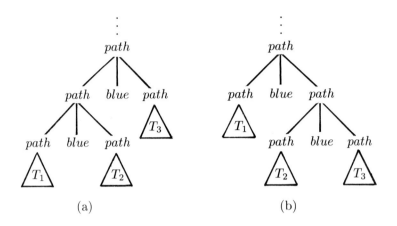

Figure 15.23 Transformation preserving subtrees.

use of the basis rule r_1. At that point, the topmost node is no longer bad, and we can work on its right subtree. Since the number of nodes is preserved by the transformation, we know that this subtree is smaller than the tree we were working on, so the process eventually converges and removes all bad nodes. At that point, we have converted an arbitrary proof tree into a right-linear tree and proven the equivalence between sets of rules $\{r_1, r_2\}$ and $\{r_1, r_2'\}$. Notice that if, for example, τ had mapped two of the *path* subgoals of Q_b to the subgoal $path(V, Y)$ in Q_a, then Figure 15.23(b) would have two occurrences of T_3. If that subtree were large, Figure 15.23(b) could have more nodes than Figure 15.23(a), and the conversion process might never converge. $\square$

To generalize Example 15.24, we shall construct the conjunctive query Q, analogous to Q_a in Example 15.24, that represents the structure we must remove if we are to convert arbitrary proof trees to right-linear trees. We then search for a containing conjunctive query that comes from a right-linear tree, analogous to Q_b. We cannot be sure that the containing tree has the form of Figure 15.22(b), and we cannot be sure that the containment mapping maps the recursive subgoals in such a way that we can prove the conversion to right-linear form converges. However, one simple test we can make is to see whether the conjunctive query Q is contained in the logic program $\mathcal{P}_L$, using the test of Algorithm 14.2. Strictly speaking, we must modify Q so its IDB subgoals have predicate p_0 instead of p. Then, if we find $Q \subseteq \mathcal{P}_L$ is false, we have a counterexample to the condition $\mathcal{P}_N \equiv \mathcal{P}_L$. There is a specific database, formed by turning the subgoals of Q into ground atoms, such that $\mathcal{P}_N$ generates the head of Q and $\mathcal{P}_L$ does not.

A Sufficient Condition for $\mathcal{P}_N \equiv \mathcal{P}_L$

Unfortunately, if we find $Q \subseteq \mathcal{P}_L$, we cannot be sure that $\mathcal{P}_N \equiv \mathcal{P}_L$, because the containment mapping might not guarantee we can convert arbitrary proof trees into right-linear ones by applying a finite sequence of transformations. In many cases, we can guarantee that such a transformation exists. For example, we know $\mathcal{P}_N \equiv \mathcal{P}_L$ if the EDB subgoals of r_2 all have predicates that are distinct from each other and from p_0. However, in the general case, we need a restriction on the containment mapping, if we are to be sure a suitable transformation exists. This restriction is that the containment mapping must not map any leaf but the rightmost in the containing tree to the rightmost leaf in the contained tree. For example, only $path(V'', Y)$ could map to $path(V, Y)$ in Figure 15.22.

We can test for this condition as follows. First, we create the conjunctive query Q that represents the expansion of the first p-subgoal of r_2. The steps are analogous to the process whereby we created Q_{12} in Section 15.3.

1. Make another copy of r_2, call it $\hat{r}_2$, with variables distinct from those of r_2.

2. Unify the head of $\hat{r}_2$ with the first p-subgoal of r_2, and let τ be the MGU.

3. Let Q be $\tau(r_2)$ with τ, applied to the body of $\hat{r}_2$, in place of the first p-subgoal of $\tau(r_2)$.

4. Replace the predicate of the first two p-subgoals in Q by a and the last of the three occurrences by b. Here, a and b are assumed to be new predicate symbols, not appearing in r_2.

Example 15.25: The conjunctive query Q_a in Example 15.24 was constructed by steps (1) to (3). We made a copy $\hat{r}_2$ of r_2 by putting primes on all of the variables. Then, when we unified the head, $path(X', Y')$, of $\hat{r}_2$ with the subgoal $path(X, U)$ in r_2, we obtained the substitution τ that is the identity on all variables except $\tau(X') = X$ and $\tau(Y') = U$. In step (4), we must replace the p's by a's and b, and

```
path(X,Y) :- a(X,U') & blue(U',V') & a(V',U) &
             blue(U,V) & b(V,Y).
```

is the result. $\square$

Now, we construct a logic program $\mathcal{P}$ whose expansion is the infinite set of conjunctive queries that represent right-linear trees in which only the rightmost subgoal can map to the last subgoal of Q. The fact that we renamed the predicates in Q allows us to enforce this condition. $\mathcal{P}$ generates only a's recursively, and at the final step, has the option of generating either an a or a b. Since containment mappings must respect the predicate names in subgoals, only the last of the subgoals generated by $\mathcal{P}$ can map to the subgoal in the conjunctive query Q that represents the rightmost leaf in its tree. The logic program $\mathcal{P}$ formed from $\mathcal{P}_N$ is

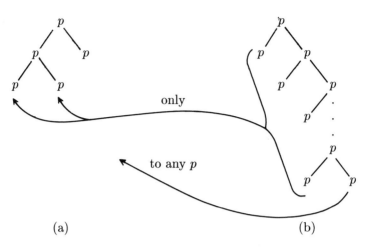

only

to any p

(a)   (b)

Figure 15.24 Restricted containment mapping.

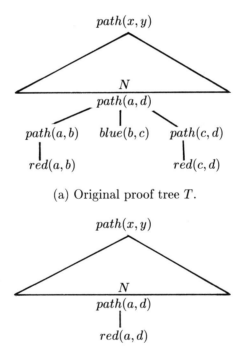

(a) Original proof tree T.

(b) Proof tree T' with "cooked" database fact.

Figure 15.25 Reducing the size of a proof tree.

$$p(X_1, \ldots, X_n) :- a(Y_1, \ldots, Y_n) \; \& \; p(Z_1, \ldots, Z_n) \; \& \\ G_1 \; \& \; \cdots \; \& \; G_k.$$
$$p(X_1, \ldots, X_n) :- a(X_1, \ldots, X_n).$$
$$p(X_1, \ldots, X_n) :- b(X_1, \ldots, X_n).$$

Example 15.26: For the rules of Example 15.24, $\mathcal{P}$ is

```
(1)      path(X,Y)  :- a(X,U) & blue(U,V) & path(V,Y).
(2)      path(X,Y)  :- a(X,Y).
(3)      path(X,Y)  :- b(X,Y).
```

To apply the test for $Q \subseteq \mathcal{P}$ of Algorithm 14.2, let us convert Q to ground atoms by replacing X, U', V', U, V, and Y by 1 though 6, respectively. Then the database consists of the facts

$$\begin{array}{ccc} a(1,2) & blue(2,3) & b(5,6) \\ a(3,4) & blue(4,5) & \end{array}$$

We must derive the head of Q, which is $path(1,6)$. Rule (3) gives us $path(5,6)$. One application of (1) gives $path(3,6)$ and a second gives $path(1,6)$, as desired. Thus, $Q \subseteq \mathcal{P}$. As we shall see in the next theorem, that containment is sufficient to show the nonlinear rules of Example 15.24 are equivalent to their right-linear version. $\Box$

Theorem 15.7: If the containment $Q \subseteq \mathcal{P}$ holds, then $\mathcal{P}_N \equiv \mathcal{P}_L$.

Proof: To begin, if $Q \subseteq \mathcal{P}$, we know there is some tree generated by $\mathcal{P}$ whose leaves have a containment mapping to the leaves of the tree corresponding to Q. Moreover, this containment mapping obeys the restriction suggested in Figure 15.24, that only the rightmost p-leaf of the containing tree (b) can map to the rightmost p-leaf of the contained tree, (a). In that figure, we show none of the EDB subgoals, concentrating on how the p-leaves correspond.

We shall show by induction on the number of interior nodes of a proof tree in the logic program $\mathcal{P}_N$, that there is an equivalent right-linear proof tree. By "equivalent," we mean that the leaves are chosen from the same database of EDB facts, and the roots are the same p-fact. The basis, one interior node, is trivial, since that tree itself is right-linear.

For the induction, suppose we have a tree T with $m > 1$ interior nodes, and assume that any tree with fewer than m interior nodes has an equivalent right-linear proof tree. Since $m > 1$, we can find in T some interior node N that is expanded by r_2, but both of its p-children are expanded by basis rule r_1. Figure 15.25(a) suggests this situation for the red/blue rules of Example 15.24.

To allow the inductive hypothesis to apply, we shrink the size of T by pretending that the fact at N comes directly from the EDB. That is, we take the database D on which T is based and add to it a p_0-fact corresponding to the p-fact at N, to get a new database D'. We may then remove two interior nodes

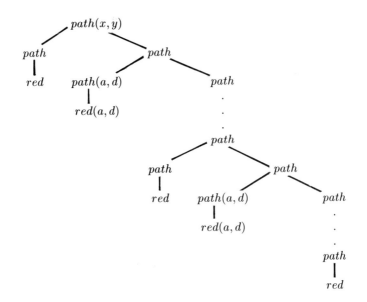

Figure 15.26 Right-linear tree S in database D'.

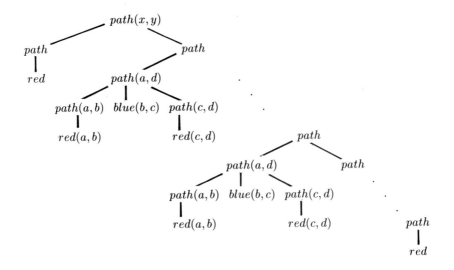

Figure 15.27 Nonlinear tree S' that uses database $D..$

from T to get a smaller proof tree T'. This process is suggested by example in Figure 15.25(b).

By the inductive hypothesis, T' is equivalent to some right-linear proof tree S with leaves chosen from the database D'. This tree is suggested by Figure 15.26, where we have shown two explicit uses of the "cooked" database fact $red(a, d)$. Next, we restore the database D by replacing the uses of the "cooked" EDB fact by uses of the recursive rule r_2 followed, by two uses of r_1 and the EDB facts from D, as appeared at node N in the original tree T. The result is a tree S'. This process is suggested for the tree of Figure 15.26 in Figure 15.27.

S' is not a right-linear tree, but the instances of nonlinearity are simple. They are each a copy of node N in tree T and its descendants, hanging off of an occurrence of p that is the first of the p-subgoals of its parent. Note that a use of the "cooked" EDB fact at the rightmost leaf of S does not cause a violation of right-linearity. We remove each of the occurrences of nonlinearity by working up the tree and applying the transformation of Figure 15.24, in which we replace instances of left-linearity, as shown in the left side of Figure 15.28, by right-linear structures, as on the right of Figure 15.28.

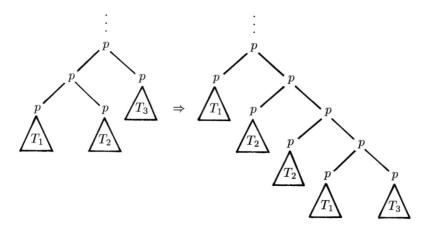

Figure 15.28 Restoring right-linearity.

Note that the trees T_1 and T_2 in Figure 15.28 are each single p_0-leaves. Also, the constraints on the containment mapping implied by Figure 15.24 guarantees that only T_1 and T_2 may appear on the right of Figure 15.28, except in the position where we have shown T_3. That position may also hold T_1 or T_2, which is a degenerate case in which the (possibly large) tree T_3 does not appear at all in the constructed proof tree.

If we apply the transformation of Figure 15.28 to S' bottom-up, we may assume that tree T_3 is right-linear. As T_1 and T_2 are leaves, it then follows that the replacing tree is right linear, whether or not the rightmost subtree is T_3 or one of the leaves represented by T_1 and T_2. Thus, S' is eventually converted to a right-linear proof tree for the logic program $\mathcal{P}_N$. The final step, where we convert this proof tree to a proof tree in the logic program $\mathcal{P}_L$, was suggested by Figure 15.21. That is, we combine the occurrences of $p(X_1, \ldots, X_n)$ that are leftmost children of their parent and have a child $p_0(X_1, \ldots, X_n)$, into a leaf $p_0(X_1, \ldots, X_n)$. We have now shown that every proof tree in $\mathcal{P}_N$ has an equivalent proof tree in $\mathcal{P}_L$, so $\mathcal{P}_N \equiv \mathcal{P}_L$. $\square$

EXERCISES

15.1: Determine for which adornments each of the following recursions are right- or left-linear. Apply Algorithm 15.1 or Algorithm 15.2, as appropriate, to transform the rules in cases where these algorithms apply.

a)   The rules of Example 15.2.

b)   The rules

```
out(D,B)  :- gen(D,B).
out(D,B)  :- out(D,C) & succ(C,B) & clear(D,B).
```

These rules represent a simplified form of "data flow analysis," as discussed in Section 16.1.

c)   The rules

```
q(W,X,Y,Z)  :- par(W,Y) & par(X,Z).
q(W,X,Y,Z)  :- q(W,X,U,V) & par(U,Y) & par(V,Z).
```

These rules represent the "same-generation" rules converted to a transitive closure as discussed in Section 15.6.

d)   The rules

```
sum(X,0,X)  :- int(X).
sum(X,succ(Y),succ(Z))  :- sum(X,Y,Z).
```

15.2: In Example 15.1 we made a claim about what facts are placed in the relations for m_anc and $sup_{2.1}$. Prove this claim.

15.3: Prove that the left- and right-linear transformations of Sections 15.1 and 15.2 preserve safety of rules.

15.4: Generalize the left- and right-linear transformations to linear rules that have several predicates. Also generalize to allow variables that are shared by the head and recursive subgoal, appear in the same set of arguments of each, but do not appear in the same order.

15.5: Consider the rules

$$r_1: \quad p(W,X,Y,Z) \quad :- \quad q(W,X,Y,Z).$$
$$r_2: \quad p(W,X,Y,Z) \quad :- \quad p(U,V,Y,Z) \ \& \ a(U,W) \ \& \ b(V,X).$$
$$r_3: \quad p(W,X,Y,Z) \quad :- \quad p(W,X,U,V) \ \& \ c(U,Y) \ \& \ d(V,Z).$$

a) Show that r_2 and r_3 commute.

b) For what adornments do rules r_1 and r_2 satisfy the conditions for the counting-linear transformation of Section 15.5?

c) Use Algorithm 15.4 (the counting-linear transformation) to transform $\{r_1, r_2\}$ with respect to the adornments found in (b).

** d) Generalize the counting-linear transformation to the case where there are several recursive rules that are commutative, and apply it to these rules with adornment $bfbf$. On the assumption that a and c have acyclic EDB relations, your constructed rules should be evaluable in time that is polynomial in the size of the database.

e) For what adornments are r_2 and/or r_3 strictly left-linear? For what adornments are they strictly right-linear?

15.6: The rules

$$r_1: p(X_1, \ldots, X_n) :- p(X_2, \ldots, X_n, X_1).$$
$$r_2: p(X_1, \ldots, X_n) :- p(X_n, \ldots, X_1).$$

do not obey the condition $r_1 r_2 \subseteq r_2 r_1$.

a) Verify that claim.

* b) Show that they satisfy the condition $r_1 r_2 \subseteq r_2 r_1^{n-1}$; that is, r_1 above r_2 can be replaced in proof trees by r_2 above $n-1$ uses of r_1.

** c) Is the condition of (b) sufficient that we need only consider proof trees (for rules r_1, r_2, and a basis rule for p) that have r_2 above r_1?

** 15.7: Is it possible for the left-linear transformation (Algorithm 15.2) ever to produce rules that are much better (that is, more than a constant factor faster) in running time than the magic-set rules of Algorithm 13.1, when semi-naive evaluation is applied to both?

** 15.8: In Section 15.3 we handled left- and right-linear rules by showing that we need only to consider paths in a rule/goal tree in which the right-linear rules precede the left-linear rules. Is is also true that we could consider only the paths in which the left-linear rules precede the right-linear rules?

* 15.9: Show that if $r_1 r_2 \subseteq r_2 r_1$ for linear rules r_1 and r_2, then for any database and any set of rules including r_1 and r_2, the paths in a rule/goal tree that have no r_1-node a grandparent of (next rule node above) an r_2-node generate all of the answers to the query generated by any path.

15.10: Give a test for whether the containment $r_1 r_2 \subseteq r_2 r_1^*$ holds, where r_1 and r_2 are linear rules. *Hint*: Use the technique of Section 14.5.

5.11: Show that in Theorem 15.3, the identity mapping sends conjunct J_j to conjunct $\tau(J_j)$.

5.12: For the rules of Figure 15.9, show that r_2 is right-linear if the first argument of p is bound in the query; otherwise r_2 is left-linear. Similarly, show r_3 is right-linear if the second argument of p is bound and left-linear if it is free, and r_4 is right- or left-linear if the third argument of p is bound or free, respectively.

5.13: Consider the rules

```
p(X,Y,Z) :- a(X,Y) & a(Y,Z).
p(X,Y,Z) :- p(X,Y,W) & a(W,Z).
p(X,Y,Z) :- p(W,Y,Z) & a(X,W).
```

Apply Algorithm 15.3 (mixed-linear transformation) to these rules with the query goal $p(x_0, Y, Z)$.

5.14: Show that the same-generation rules of Example 15.12 are right-linear with the adornment bb. Apply the right-linear transformation of Algorithm 15.1 to these rules. Are they left-linear with respect to the adornment ff?

5.15: Generalize the counting-linear method to handle overlap between the up predicates and variables and the down predicates and variables. What is the arity of the recursive predicates in the constructed rules?

5.16: Prove Theorem 15.5, the correctness of the counting linear transformation of Algorithm 15.4.

5.17: Prove the convergence of the rules generated by Algorithm 15.4 whenever the conditions prior to Example 15.14 (acyclicity of a certain graph) are met.

5.18: Suppose we have the rule

```
p(X,Y) :- p(U,V) & a(X,U,V) & b(Y).
```

and the EDB facts are $a(1,2,3)$, $a(2,1,4)$, $a(3,1,3)$, $b(3)$ and $b(4)$.

a) Draw the graph whose nodes are pairs of integers 1 through 4, and whose arcs $(c,d) \rightarrow (e,f)$ represent the fact that $p(e,f)$ is inferred from the EDB and $p(c,d)$.

b) Compute the transitive closure of that graph.

c) Suppose we have a basis rule for p that tells us $p(1,3)$ is true. What other p-facts are inferred?

5.19: Show that (15.2), (15.3), and (15.4) are each correct definitions of the transitive closure.

* 15.20: In Figures 15.14 and 15.15 we saw two families of databases of size $O(n)$ that can be interpreted as graphs. Suppose that arcs are stored in blocks of B arcs, clustered according to tails, that is, the lower nodes for each of the arcs in Figures 15.14 and 15.15. Also suppose that only M blocks may be held in main memory at once. If we do a depth-first search, how large, as a function of B and M, may n be before we start "thrashing"; that is, we are forced to read the same block into main memory twice

a)   Starting from node a in Figure 15.14.

b)   Starting from node a_0 in Figure 15.15.

* 15.21: Suppose we perform Kleene's algorithm on a machine that can hold M blocks in main memory and can store B of the values v_{ij}^m on one block. How large can n, the database size, get if we are to avoid thrashing (storing and then rereading a block) or recomputation of values, on the graphs (databases) of

a)   Figure 15.14.

b)   Figure 15.15.

15.22: Suppose we convert the same-generation rules to a transitive closure, as in Example 15.17. How many nodes and arcs are there, as a function of the size of the *par* relation, if that relation is represented by the data of

a)   Figure 15.14.

b)   Figure 15.15.

15.23: In Section 15.7 we discussed an IDB predicate $p(X, Y, D)$ that represents the fact that there is a path from X to Y of length D. Write an SQL query that, when applied to the relation P for p, gives the shortest path between each pair of nodes X and Y.

15.24: We also discussed in Section 15.7 the IDB predicate $uses(X, Y, N)$. A tuple (a, b, i) in the relation for *uses* means that there are i copies of part b in part a, due to one particular "path" from part a to part b (see Example 15.18). Write an SQL query that gives us the total number of copies of each part B in each part A.

* 15.25: Suppose we use the following, nonlinear rules to express "parts explosion."

```
uses(X,Y,N) :- partOf(X,Y,N).
uses(X,Y,N) :- uses(X,Z,L) & uses(Z,Y,M) & N=L*M.
```

Do these rules correctly compute the parts explosion values? What is their result on the data of Figure 15.19?

15.26: Apply Kleene's algorithm to the graph of Figure 15.19 using the closed semiring in which $\oplus = \min$ and $\otimes = +$.

5.27: Show that if graphs are restricted to be acyclic, then the factor $(v_{mm}^{m-1})^*$ in the formula of Figure 15.17 (Kleene's algorithm) can be deleted; that is, the inner loop can be replaced by

$$v_{ij}^m := v_{ij}^{m-1} \oplus \left(v_{im}^{m-1} \otimes v_{mj}^{m-1} \right)$$

and the algorithm will still be correct.

5.28: Suppose we have a closed semiring with domain S of "scalars," with operations $\oplus$ and $\otimes$, and with identities $\mathbf{0}$ and $\mathbf{1}$. We can create another closed semiring whose domain is n by n matrices of scalars. The operation $\oplus_m$ is matrix addition, that is, $(M \oplus_m N)[i, j] = M[i, j] \oplus N[i, j]$. Operation $\otimes_m$ is matrix multiplication,

$$(M \otimes_m N)[i, j] = \bigoplus_{k=1}^{n} M[i, k] \otimes N[k, j]$$

The additive identity $\mathbf{0}_m$ is a matrix of all $\mathbf{0}$'s, and the multiplicative identity $\mathbf{1}_m$ has $\mathbf{1}$'s along the main diagonal and $\mathbf{0}$'s elsewhere. Verify that matrices of scalars form a closed semiring when the operations and identity elements are defined this way.

5.29: Suppose we start with a closed semiring S of scalars as in Exercise 15.28, and build another closed semiring whose elements are polynomials in one variable, x, and whose coefficients are chosen from S. Let $\oplus_p$ and $\otimes_p$ be polynomial addition and multiplication, with $\otimes$ used for multiplication of coefficients and powers of x,[20] and $\oplus$ used for addition of terms of the form $a \otimes x^i$.

   a)   What are suitable values for $\mathbf{0}_p$ and $\mathbf{1}_p$, the identities for polynomials?
   b)   Show that with your choice from (a), the polynomials over S form a closed semiring.
   c)   Suppose we run Kleene's algorithm on a graph of n nodes with weights from the closed semiring of polynomials over S. Assuming that $\oplus$ and $\otimes$ require unit time, how long does Kleene's algorithm take? *Hint:* In principle, we cannot take the infinite sum

$$\mathbf{1}_p + f(x) + f^2(x) + f^3(x) + \cdots$$

   that is needed to compute the star operation. However, we may represent this sum by $\mathbf{1}_p/\left(\mathbf{1}_p - f(x)\right)$, and then perform our calculation with rational functions.

---

[20] Note that x^i means $x \otimes x \otimes \cdots \otimes x$ (i times). Also, as $\otimes$ is not necessarily commutative, we must assume that all multiplication by coefficients occurs on the left. That is, $(a \otimes x^i) \otimes_p (b \otimes x^j) = (a \otimes b) \otimes x^{i+j}$. Another way to look at polynomials is that x is irrelevant, polynomials are lists of coefficients, and $\otimes_p$ is convolution.

* 15.30: Find linear, nondatalog rules that produce the same answer as the rules (15.5) in Example 15.23. *Hint*: You may use several different predicates in your rules.

15.31: Test the following nonlinear rules for equivalence to their linear form in which the first recursive subgoal is replaced by the basis predicate.

a) The rules

```
p(X,Y,Z) :- a(X,Y,Z).
p(X,Y,Z) :- p(X,A,B) & p(C,D,Y) & b(C,Z).
```

b) The rules of Exercise 14.9.

In each case, what is the containing tree analogous to Figure 15.24(b)?

15.32: Generalize the techniques of Section 15.8 to test equivalence between the nonlinear rules and a linear form in which the second recursive subgoal is replaced by the basis predicate.

* 15.33: Generalize the techniques of Section 15.8 to allow

a) More than two recursive subgoals.

b) Several recursive rules for the same predicate.

BIBLIOGRAPHIC NOTES

References for this section are covered under the following subtopics.

Left- and Right-Linear Recursions

Aho and Ullman [1979b] was an early attempt to reduce the arity of recursive relations; The theory was advanced significantly by Beeri, Kanellakis, Bancilhon, and Ramakrishnan [1987], which characterizes a large class of recursions that can be made monadic (IDB predicates have a single-argument).

Chang [1981] gave an algorithm for evaluating a class of recursions that behave like transitive closures. Naughton [1987] greatly generalized the class of covered logic programs, and this theme was expanded by Han and Henschen [1987] and Youn, Henschen, and Han [1988].

Mixed-Linear Recursions

The commutativity technique of Section 15.3 is from Ramakrishnan, Sagiv, Ullman, and Vardi [1988].

Naughton [1988b] introduced "separable" recursions, which is a large class including mixed left- and right-linear rules. Independently, Han [1988] offers a somewhat smaller class along the same lines. Naughton, Ramakrishnan, Sagiv, and Ullman [1988] generalize these classes by use of the commutativity theorem, as in Section 15.4.

Counting Algorithms

A general algorithm for datalog evaluation that turns out to be important only for linear rules was given by Henschen and Naqvi [1984]. It is similar, but not identical to, the counting technique discussed in Section 15.5.

Counting algorithms were proposed by Bancilhon, Maier, Sagiv, and Ullman [1986] and Sacca and Zaniolo [1986, 1987b]; the latter has significantly more generality than the technique presented here.

Marchetti-Spaccamela, Pelaggi, and Sacca [1987] evaluate counting algorithms, along with several other techniques. Haddad and Naughton [1988] extend counting methods to situations where there is no acyclicity property to limit the count.

Transitive Closure

Evaluation of algorithms for performing transitive closure with a database-oriented model of computation appears in Ioannidis [1986b], Agrawal and Jagadish [1987], Lu, Mikkilineni, and Richardson [1987], and Valduriez and Koshafian [1988]. Biskup and Steifeling [1988] survey the subject.

The observation that all linear recursions can be expressed as a transitive closure, as long as you are willing to deal with a graph that is much larger than the database, was made by Jagadish, Agrawal, and Ness [1987].

Closed-Semiring Techniques

The closed semiring axioms and their use as a generalized transitive closure is from Aho, Hopcroft, and Ullman [1974]. Lehmann [1977] independently gave a similar algebra. As was mentioned, the particular algorithm given in Section 15.7 dates back to Kleene [1956].

Tarjan [1981] discussed algorithms for transitive closure in closed semirings, including single-source problems (reachability from a single node). The lattice-theoretic formulation of data-flow analysis also involves algorithms relevant to generalized transitive closure; see Aho, Sethi, and Ullman [1986].

In the context of knowledge-base systems, Rosenthal, Heiler, Dayal, and Manola [1986] and Cruz and Norvell [1988] consider some classes of closed-semiring computations. Ioannidis and Ramakrishnan [1988] look at depth-first-search as a technique for single-source problems on closed semirings and evaluate their technique along with several others.

Nonlinear-to-Linear Transformations

Zhang and Yu [1987] and Ioannidis and Wong [1988] give sufficient conditions for the equivalence of the nonlinear and linear pairs of programs $\mathcal{P}_N \equiv \mathcal{P}_L$ discussed in Section 15.8. The more general condition discussed there is from Ramakrishnan, Sagiv, Ullman, and Vardi [1988].

Zhang, Yu, and Troy [1988] give a condition that is both necessary and sufficient for $\mathcal{P}_N \equiv \mathcal{P}_L$ in the case that the recursive rule has a single EDB subgoal. This result is extended to the case of many EDB subgoals with distinct predicates by Saraiya [1988]. The key idea in both these proofs is that there is a limit on the depth of containing trees that we must consider.

Afrati and Cosmadakis [1988] give some datalog examples that are inherently nonlinear.

Boundedness

Sometimes a recursion is equivalent to a finite union of conjunctive queries, as was seen in Example 14.1. Such recursions are called *bounded*. Minker and Nicolas [1981] gave a sufficient condition for boundedness.

Independently, Ioannidis [1986a] and Naughton [1986b] gave considerably more general conditions, and Naughton and Sagiv [1987] generalizes all these classes.

The undecidability of boundedness for datalog recursions was shown by Gaifman, Mairson, Sagiv, and Vardi [1987]. Vardi [1988b] shows that boundedness is decidable for binary, linear datalog programs. Also, Cosmadakis, Gaifman, Kanellakis, and Vardi [1988] show that for monadic recursions, boundedness is decidable.

Other Issues

Several related topics worth considering have not been covered in this section. For example, Ioannidis and Wong [1987b] offer an algebraic approach to describing algorithms that evaluate linear recursions. Naughton [1986a] shows how some recursions may be simplified by having some subgoals removed from their recursive rules.

CHAPTER 16

Some
Experimental
Knowledge-Base
Systems

Recall from Section 1.6 (Volume I) that we regard a knowledge-base system as a programming system that

1. Has a declarative language, that is, logic in one of its many possible forms, serving as both a host language and as a query language, and

2. Supports the principal capabilities of a database system, that is, efficient access to massive amounts of data, sharing of data, concurrent access to data, and resiliency in the face of failures.

In the late 1980's, there are no commercial systems of this nature, but there are a number of experiments in progress that are headed in that direction. In this chapter, we shall look at three of these projects and see how the theory developed in Chapters 11 through 15 is being applied.

We begin with a study of the author's own NAIL! project at Stanford. Then we consider the LDL project at MCC. Both these systems use many of the optimization techniques discussed in previous chapters, in order to evaluate logical rules efficiently. Finally, we examine the Postgres system, under development at Berkeley. This system is an attempt to extend INGRES, a database system whose query language QUEL was discussed in Section 4.3 of Volume I, to a system with many of the capabilities of a knowledge system, as well as many of the characteristics of an object-base system.

The reader should be warned that the systems described in this chapter are each under development as this book is written. As time goes on, the systems may evolve, and they should not be assumed to match exactly their descriptions here. We have chosen to cover aspects of the systems that are likely to be of interest in the long term.

16.1 APPLICATIONS OF KNOWLEDGE-BASE SYSTEMS

In Section 1.6 (Volume I) we gave some examples of application areas for which knowledge-base systems are expected to be useful. In general, such application areas deal with massive amounts of data and need a query facility more powerful than that of typical query languages such as SQL. Recall from Section 3.7 (Volume I) that such database languages have essentially the power of nonrecursive logical rules with negation permitted in subgoals, but do not have the power of recursive application of rules. Thus, applications require a knowledge-base system if they have a recursive or nested structure that needs to be queried. General classes of applications of this type include

1. Design databases, where objects are composed hierarchically. An important example is a VLSI CAD (Computer Aided Design) database, where chips are designed as cells, cells are composed of subcells, and so on, down to some finite level that depends on the particular design. Expansion of a design, so we can see or process the entire represented object, is a recursively-defined operation, and cannot be done in the query language of a typical database system.[1]

2. Computer Aided Software Engineering (CASE) databases, where programs are represented, typically, as recursive structures such as parse trees. Other aspects of program representation are graphlike, and require searching through graphs of arbitrary size, another operation that cannot be done in a typical query language. An example of such a graph is the flow graph used in data-flow analysis of a program. Another example is a graph of dependencies, indicating how changes to one piece of code affect other pieces of code, documentation, and so on.

3. Pattern recognition databases, where raw data, perhaps bits, are grouped into progressively more complex structures. An example is a database for representing photographs, such as pictures of terrain. We might want to group bits into lines and curves, then group lines and curves into simple patterns, collections of similar patterns into regions, and so on. A similar pattern-recognition problem involves strings of proteins that make up a gene. In many cases, it is useful to describe structures grammatically, that is, according to a recursive definition, and again, queries asking for recursively defined patterns cannot be handled by a typical database query language.

We shall next give two specific examples of the sorts of problems alluded

---

[1] Of course, as discussed in Section 1.3 of Volume I, anything can be done in a combination of the query languages and the host language. But then database system facilities, such as built-in index structures or support for concurrency, cannot be used for the entire computation.

to above; these problems fall within the capabilities of the systems described in this chapter.

Example 16.1: One of our first examples, in Section 1.6, discussed a database for artwork, which could, for example, be part of a CAD database. There, we had an EDB relation $set(I, X, Y)$ that means cell I has point (X, Y) set (i.e., that point, or "pixel," has value 1). Another EDB relation $contains(I, J, X, Y)$ says that cell I contains a copy of cell J, with J's origin at point (X, Y) in I's coordinate system. We then defined an IDB relation $on(I, X, Y)$ to mean that in cell I, considering all its subcells, their subcells, and so on, the pixel (X, Y) is set. The rules defining *on* are

```
on(I,X,Y) :- set(I,X,Y).
on(I,X,Y) :- contains(I,J,U,V) & on(J,W,Z) &
             X=U+W & Y=V+Z.
```

The last two subgoals are not of the form we have generally permitted, since they involve not only a built-in comparison predicate, but the addition operation. However, we saw in Example 13.3 how to handle such a subgoal: regard it as an EDB subgoal $sum(U, W, X)$, meaning that the third argument is the sum of the first two. Then, require that the first two arguments are bound when we access the "relation" for predicate *sum*.

These rules are neither right-linear, left-linear, nor counting-linear for any adornment of *on*, except fff (i.e., expand all of the cells); in the latter case, the rules are trivially left-linear, since there are no bound arguments. However, a magic-sets transformation helps for the typical query, $on(i_0, X, Y)$, that is, "expand cell i_0." The reader can work the details as an exercise, but the essential idea is that after a magic-sets transformation, the magic predicate $m\_on(J)$ computes all those cells J that are direct or indirect constituents of i_0. We then look up that portion of the *set* relation needed to find, for each of those cells, the pixels with value 1. Finally, we recursively translate those points into the coordinate systems of parent cells, until eventually, everything is translated into the coordinate system of i_0. □

Example 16.2: An important operation in an optimizing compiler is *data-flow analysis*, where a program is divided into *basic blocks* (segments of code that can only be entered at the top and exited at the bottom), and information about program variables is propagated among blocks. A simple example is *use-def chaining*, where it is desired to know, for some use U of a variable X (U might be A := X+Y, for example), at what statements X could last have been defined when program control reaches U. Thus, if it is discovered that X could only have been defined previously at an assignment or assignments of the form X := 2, then we know X has the value 2 at U, and we can replace U by the simpler assignment A := Y+2. Figure 16.1 illustrates the requirements for a definition D of variable X to reach a use U of X.

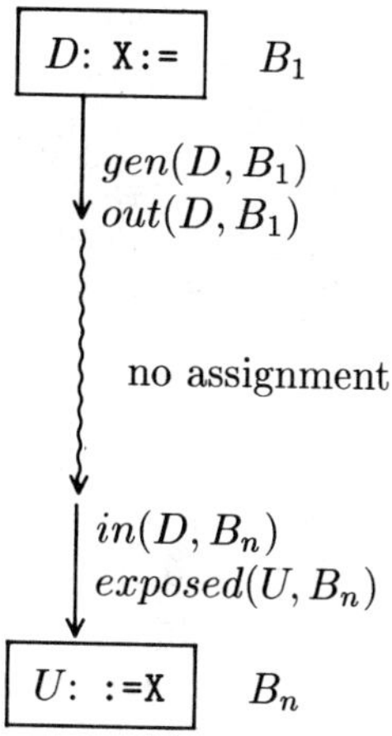

$$D: \texttt{X:=} \quad B_1$$

$gen(D, B_1)$
$out(D, B_1)$

no assignment to X

$in(D, B_n)$
$exposed(U, B_n)$

$$U: \texttt{:=X} \quad B_n$$

Figure 16.1 Path allowing definition D to reach use U.

We need to know that D is "gen'd" by block B_1, meaning that D appears in that block, and after D there is no statement in B_1 that assigns a new value to the same variable that D assigns. When D is "gen'd" by B_1, we also say that D comes "out" of B_1.

```
r₁:   clear(D,B) :- dvar(D,X) & ¬kill(X,B).

r₂:   out(D,B) :- gen(D,B).
r₃:   out(D,B) :- in(D,B) & clear(D,B).

r₄:   in(D,B) :- out(D,C) & succ(C,B).

r₅:   reach(D,U) :- in(D,B) & exposed(U,B) &
                    dvar(D,X) & uvar(U,X).
```

Figure 16.2 Rules for reaching definitions.

Then, we need to find a path through the blocks, such that D is not "killed," meaning that there is no assignment to X in any block of the path. If that path reaches block B_n we say that D comes "in" to block B_n. If, in addition, B_n has within it, use U of X, and that use is "exposed," meaning that prior to U in block B_n, there is no definition of X, then we say that D reaches U. Figure 16.2 shows rules that express the notion of a definition "reaching" a use. The EDB predicates are

1. $gen(D, B)$, meaning that definition D is generated by block B.
2. $exposed(U, B)$, meaning that use U is exposed in block B.
3. $kill(X, B)$, meaning that block B "kills" definitions with variable X, that is, B has a definition of X within it.
4. $dvar(D, X)$, meaning that definition D defines variable X.
5. $uvar(U, X)$, meaning that use U is a use of variable X.
6. $succ(C, B)$, meaning that block B is a successor of block C.

The IDB predicates are

7. $in(D, B)$, meaning definition D comes into block B.
8. $out(D, B)$, meaning definition D comes out of block B.
9. $clear(D, B)$, meaning that the variable defined by definition D is not killed by block B.
10. $reach(D, U)$, meaning that definition D reaches use U.

The reader may note the unsafe use of negation in r_1, where variable B appears only in the head and in the negated subgoal, and thus is not limited to a finite set. In practice, there is no problem, since we can treat $\neg kill$ as if it were an EDB predicate, often called $trans$, where $trans(X, B)$ means that block B "transmits," that is, does not kill, variable X. Since it generally requires less space to store $kill$, we can instead store an additional EDB relation $block(B)$, listing the blocks, and simply add the subgoal $block(B)$ to r_1, as

```
clear(D,B) :- dvar(D,X) & block(B) & ¬kill(X,B).
```

In this manner, we avoid trying to infer $clear(D, B)$ for nonexistent blocks.

We can understand the recursion more easily if we combine the two mutually recursive rules, r_3 and r_4, into one rule. We do so by substituting the body of r_4 for the subgoal $in(D, B)$, to create a new rule, which we shall call r_6. (Technically, we need to unify the head of r_4 with that subgoal, but here the MGU is the identity function.)

```
r₂:  out(D,B) :- gen(D,B).
r₆:  out(D,B) :- out(D,C) & succ(C,B) & clear(D,B).
```

We can now eliminate r_3, although we need r_4, which now is nonrecursive, so we can compute the in relation and use it in r_5.[2]

If the query goal is out^{bf}, that is, given a definition D, which blocks does D come out of, then this recursion is left-linear. That is, r_2 and r_6 are best solved by exploring the graph defined by the $succ$ EDB relation, starting at the block containing D, but not following a successor arc to any block that kills the variable of D.

Unfortunately, we are more likely to ask a query of the form out^{fb}, that is, given a block B, find all of the definitions that come out of B. Now, r_6 is neither

---

[2] We could eliminate r_4 by substituting for $in(D, B)$ in r_5.

right- nor left-linear. In particular, it is not right-linear because the variable D, shared by the free argument of the head and recursive subgoal, is also found in another subgoal, $clear(D, B)$.[3] We can still use a magic-sets transformation to speed up the evaluation of out^{fb}. The effect of this transformation is to restrict our computation to those blocks that can reach B in the flow graph. Unfortunately, that set is frequently a large portion of the flow graph. $\square$

16.2 THE NAIL! SYSTEM

NAIL! (Not *Another* Implementation of Logic!) is an experimental knowledge-base system being developed by the author and his students at Stanford University. The primary goal of the project is to study optimization of logical queries. As a result, the architecture, shown in Figure 16.3, makes use of an SQL database system to handle the "standard" features of a DBMS, such as index maintenance. Undoubtedly, that is not the proper way to handle database access, and a more closely integrated database system would be necessary in a commercial system.

NAIL! Source Code

Logical rules are written in the notation presented in this book, but with the keyword **not** in place of ¬. Rules must be safe, and negation must be stratified; that is, no recursion involving negation is permitted (see Section 3.6 of Volume I for details). A source program is compiled into internal tables, involving some modification of rules, which will not be covered here. Most importantly, predicates are partitioned into *strongly connected components* (SCC's). An SCC is either

1. A single, nonrecursive predicate (either IDB or EDB), or
2. A minimal set of mutually recursive predicates.

Example 16.3: The logic program of Figure 16.2 is essentially NAIL! source code, although r_1 would have to be rewritten, in one of the ways suggested in Example 16.2, to avoid the unsafe use of negation, for instance, as

```
clear(D,B) :- dvar(D,X) & block(B) & not kill(X,B).
```

Each of the IDB and EDB predicates except *in* and *out* are in their own SCC. We place *in* and *out* in one SCC because they are mutually recursive. $\square$

Once the rules are compiled, the system is ready to accept queries. A query is a predicate with some of its arguments constant and others variable. The answer to the query is the set of tuples for that predicate matching the constants. For each query, the system selects an evaluation strategy, which is a

---

[3] Recall that there is no corresponding requirement for (nonstrict) left-linearity, which is why r_6 with adornment bf is left-linear.

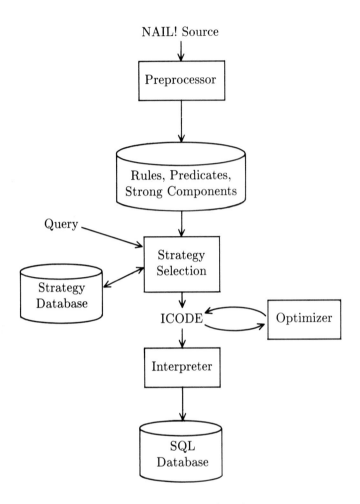

Figure 16.3 The NAIL! architecture.

choice of algorithms for evaluating a collection of adorned goals; this collection
includes the query goal and others determined by the system to be necessary
for the evaluation of the query, in a manner to be described next.

Strategy Selection

The SCC is the unit for which a decision is made regarding how a piece of
logic is to be handled. The strategy-selection component of the NAIL! system
is designed to take an adorned goal p^α and choose a strategy for evaluating
the relevant part of the relation for p, given a relation containing the binding

tuples for whatever arguments α indicates are bound. To do so, we may need to call upon the strategy-selection algorithm to solve certain lower-level problems, which are represented by adorned goals q^β, where q is a predicate in an SCC on which the SCC of p depends. That is, the rules for predicates in the SCC of p normally have subgoals whose predicates are outside the SCC of p. Those predicates must be "lower-level" than p, since if they in turn depended on p, they would be mutually recursive with p and thus belong to the same SCC as p.

Given adorned goal p^α, the strategy-selection algorithm begins by constructing a rule/goal graph for the SCC of p.[4] All predicates not in the SCC of p are treated as if they were EDB subgoals. If we are successful in constructing a rule/goal graph, we examine all of the *external* adorned goals, which are those whose predicates are outside the SCC of p. Each must have a strategy selected for it by another application of the strategy selection algorithm. Since external goals are at a lower level than p, we must eventually reach a point where we have only EDB adorned goals and built-in arithmetic goals to handle. These either succeed trivially or they fail trivially; for example we can evaluate $=^{bf}$ (given a set $\{a_1, \ldots, a_n\}$ of constants as a binding, return the set of pairs $\{(a_1, a_1), \ldots, (a_n, a_n)\}$) but we cannot evaluate $<^{bf}$, because an infinite set of pairs is called for.

Example 16.4: In Figure 16.4 we see one of the possible rule/goal graphs that might be constructed for the adorned goal in^{bb}. There are actually several different graphs that might be constructed, because NAIL! selects subgoal order by the heuristic:

1. Pick the remaining subgoal with the largest number of bound arguments.
2. Break ties by picking the subgoal with the fewest free arguments.
3. If a tie remains, break it arbitrarily.

In this case, there are several points where ties must be broken arbitrarily. For example, in r_4, starting with in^{bb}, we get bindings for both variables B and D that appear in the head. Thus, both subgoals, $out(D, C)$ and $succ(C, B)$, have one bound argument and one free argument. We have chosen to list out^{bf} first, followed by $succ^{bb}$, but we could just have well listed $succ^{fb}$ followed by out^{bb}. Depending on the data, one or the other order could lead to more efficient evaluation than the other.

Assuming NAIL! has constructed the rule/goal graph of Figure 16.4, we observe the following. The adorned goal in^{bb} has caused the consideration of

---

[4] Actually, the rule/goal graph is the default way to process an SCC, but provision is made for other approaches to be inserted. Moreover, the rule/goal graph construction algorithm is frequently modified to require certain adornments. For example, if we were trying to use the left-linear strategy for evaluating p^α, we would insist that all occurrences of p in the rule/goal graph have adornment α; if not, the attempt to use the left-linear method fails, and we try another method for the same SCC.

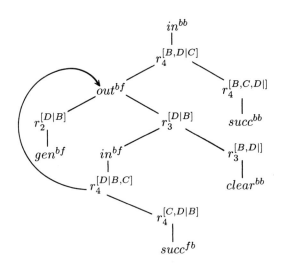

Figure 16.4 Rule/goal graph for data-flow analysis example.

"internal" adorned goals in^{bf} and out^{bf}; it has also caused us to need solutions for the external adorned goals gen^{bf}, $succ^{bb}$, $succ^{fb}$, and $clear^{bb}$. Since these are all EDB goals, there is no reason to expect that any of them fail. As a result, in^{bb} succeeds. That information may be essential to allow an adorned goal of a higher SCC, for example, $reach^{fb}$, to succeed.[5]

Now, let us suppose that for some reason, gen^{bf} failed.[6] That would tell us the rule/goal graph of Figure 16.4 is not acceptable. We might be able to find another rule/goal graph for in^{bb}, one that avoids subgoal gen^{bf}. For example, we could order the *out* subgoal of r_4 second instead of first, as we did in Figure 16.4. If we find an acceptable rule/goal graph, then in^{bb} succeeds; otherwise, in^{bb} fails. The failure of this adorned goal may cause the failure of rule/goal graphs for which it is an external goal, and a rippling effect may result in failure of many adorned goals. □

Capture Rules

The decisions regarding what strategy to use, to satisfy a given adorned goal, are made by *capture rules*. Each capture rule corresponds informally to an

---

[5] That would be the case if the rule/goal graph constructed for $reach^{fb}$ ordered its subgoals with $in(D, B)$ last, a possibility, given the arbitrary tie-breaking rule.

[6] Imagine, contrary to fact, that *gen* is an IDB predicate. An IDB predicate could fail, for example, if it had a rule with a built-in subgoal like $X < Y$, which can produce an infinite relation if X and Y are not bound. It could also fail if there were a recursion involving function symbols in a free argument.

idea for evaluating logical rules, such as "left-linear recursion," "magic sets," or "look up an EDB relation in the database." A capture rule consists of two pieces of code.

1. A *test* algorithm decides whether a particular idea is applicable to the adorned goal at hand. The test can construct a rule/goal graph, perhaps one constrained by the needs of the informal idea, as is the case for left- or right-linear recursions, where the recursive subgoal must appear in a particular position with a particular adornment.

2. An *execution* algorithm. If later called upon to do so, this algorithm generates intermediate code (ICODE) to compute the tuples matching the goal, given a relation of bindings for the bound arguments of that goal.

The choice of capture rule for a given adorned goal p^α is a two-stage process. First, we decide the *class* to which the SCC of p belongs. The set of classes is easily adjustable within the NAIL! system, but each SCC must fall into exactly one class. The initial set of classes is

1. EDB predicate.
2. Built-in (arithmetic comparison) predicate.
3. Nonrecursive, datalog predicate.
4. Nonrecursive, nondatalog predicate, that is, a nonrecursive predicate one or more of whose rules have function symbols.
5. Linear, recursive datalog.
6. Linear, recursive, nondatalog.
7. Nonlinear, recursive datalog.
8. Nonlinear, recursive, nondatalog.

For each class, we list one or more capture rules. The test portions of these rules are tried in turn, until one succeeds. For example, the linear-recursive datalog class might have, in order, capture rules for the strategies

i) Left-linear.
ii) Right-linear.
iii) Left-and-right-linear.
iv) Counting-linear.
v) Magic sets.

However, certain conditions, not apparent from the rule/goal graph, are necessary for some of these methods to apply. Methods (*i*) to (*iii*) require that the binding set be a singleton. Thus, they can only be applied safely to the initial query goal and some other special cases; in general we cannot tell at query-processing time which intermediate binding relations will be singletons. Method (*iv*) requires that certain predicates have acyclic relations. To provide the additional declarations needed to make such decisions, the NAIL! source has a built-in predicate *extraHelp*, that allows us to transmit such clues to the strategy-selection algorithm.[7]

The Strategy Database

When NAIL! discovers a strategy for a given adorned goal, it stores its decision in the *strategy database*. Then, the next time we encounter the same adorned goal, even with a different binding relation, we do not have to reconsider the various capture rules and rule/goal graphs; rather, we look up the proper strategy in the database.

What we actually store for a successful "capture" of p^α is

1. The external adorned goals and, if used, the rule/goal graph for the SCC of p^α.
2. The capture rule that was successful.

Since we succeeded in "capturing" p^α, we know that we also succeeded with all of the external adorned goals for this SCC. Thus, we know that the successful strategies for each of the external goals will also be stored in the strategy database, and they can be looked up when we generate intermediate code for these SCC's.

To avoid repeated aimless search, we also store negative facts, stating that we found no capture rule capable of handling a certain adorned goal p^α. Before attempting to capture any p^β we shall look in the strategy database, and if β is *no more bound* than α, that is, α has b wherever β has b, we shall conclude without further search that p^β cannot be captured. The rationale is that a bound argument should not make it harder to answer a query. At the very worst, we could use a method where we pretend the bound argument is free, and then, at the last step, perform a selection on that argument.

Note that we cannot do the mirror-image simplification with discovered strategies. If we find that p^{fb}, say, can be captured by some strategy, then we expect that p^{bb} can also be captured. However, there may be a simpler, more efficient strategy that works for p^{bb} but not for p^{fb}. If we omitted doing a full strategy search for p^{bb}, just because we found a strategy for p^{fb} in the strategy database, then we would miss this more efficient strategy. However, should we not find a better strategy for p^{bb}, then we shall enter the same strategy as for p^{fb} into the database, thus inhibiting repeated search for a better strategy that does not exist.

The NAIL! Intermediate Code

As indicated in Figure 16.3, the result of a successful strategy for answering

---

[7] However, singleton bindings are passed by an s adornment, which acts like a b adornment in most cases, but tells a capture rule that it may expect the binding to be a singleton.

a query is a program in a language called ICODE. This language consists of statements for each of the relational algebra operations, select, project, product, union, difference, and various forms of join. All but union and difference can also be performed by ICODE statements in the form of Prolog rules. However, unlike a Prolog statement, a rule in ICODE has an operational, rather than declarative meaning; when we reach such a statement, the relation of the head is evaluated in terms of the relations for the body, and the new relation is stored in the database.

To permit sequencing of statements, ICODE has many of the usual control-flow features: labels and goto's, conditional branches, call and return. ICODE variables may be treated as arrays or stacks of relations; push and pop are provided, as well as arbitrary indexing into an array.

ICODE statements that are Prolog rules allow function symbols and integer arithmetic operators. As a result, there is the possibility that constructed relations have values that are not elementary, as the relational model assumes, but are complex terms. Since all data is actually stored in an SQL database, complex terms must be described by tuples of relations. NAIL! uses a single relation called CONS, in which are stored, roughly, the nodes of the parse tree for the complex terms. For example, to store the term $f(a, b, g(c))$, there would be one tuple representing f and its first argument, a. A second tuple would represent the next two arguments of f, that is, b and $g(c)$. The structure of the subterm $g(c)$ would be represented by a third tuple, which contained the symbol g and the first argument c.

```
m_anc(joe).
m_anc(Z)  :- m_anc(X) & par(X,Z).

a_anc(Y)  :- m_anc(X) & par(X,Y).

anc(joe,Y) :- a_anc(Y).
```

Figure 16.5 Right-linear transformation on ancestor rules.

Example 16.5: We shall illustrate the flavor of ICODE by a simple example. If we take our usual right-linear rules for ancestors,

```
r₁:   anc(X,Y) :- par(X,Y).
r₂:   anc(X,Y) :- par(X,Z) & anc(Z,Y).
```

with the query goal $anc(joe, Y)$, NAIL! would use the right-linear transformation to evaluate the query. That is, NAIL! would act as if the rules were as shown in Figure 16.5. These rules, in turn, would be transformed into the ICODE program of Figure 16.6.

```
(1)          relation(par(child,parent));
(2)          initial(dma,(joe));
(3)          makeEmpty(ma);
(4)      label(beginLoop)
(5)          union(ma,dma,ma);
(6)          ndma(Z) :- dma(X), par(X,Z);
(7)          diff(ndma,ma,dma);
(8)          ifNotEmpty(beginLoop,dma);
(9)          aa(Y) :- ma(X), par(X,Y);
(10)         anc(joe,Y) :- aa(Y);
```

Figure 16.6 ICODE for evaluation of ancestor rules.

The ICODE variables ma and aa correspond to the predicates m_anc and a_anc, respectively. Variable dma, or "delta magic ancestors," is the set of tuples added to m_anc in the most recent round. Finally, ndma, or "new delta magic ancestors," is a temporary used to help compute dma.

Statement (1) of Figure 16.6 declares relation *par* to be a permanent relation in the database, with attributes named *child* and *parent*. Other relations, not so declared, are created as needed and then dropped from the database before the ICODE program ends.

Statement (2) initializes dma to $\{joe\}$, and statement (3) initializes ma to be empty. At statement (5), the beginning of the loop, the current dma, or new tuples for ma, are inserted into ma; for example, at the first round, ma is set equal to $\{joe\}$. In general, $union(A, B, C)$ means $C := A \cup B$.

Statement (6) computes ndma to be equal to the set of parents of individuals currently in dma; these are all of the individuals we might not have met on previous rounds, but who now become reachable because one of their children was discovered, and therefore was put in dma, on the previous round. At line (7), we throw out all those individuals that have, in fact, been reached before, and the remainder, the individuals never seen before, become the new value of dma. In general, $diff(A, B, C)$ means $C := A - B$.

Statement (8) causes a jump back to the beginning of the loop if dma is not empty, that is, if we have more individuals to consider. When we have found the complete magic set, consisting of Joe and his ancestors, we reach statements (9) and (10), which implement the last two rules of Figure 16.5, to compute the answer. □

16.3 THE LANGUAGE LDL

The LDL (Logic Data Language) system and language are under development at MCC, in Austin, Texas. The overall structure and aims of the system are similar to those of NAIL!, but LDL is far more ambitious, being a complete DBMS as well as a logic processor. The source language, also called LDL, is similar to the notation for rules used in this book, but with a left arrow for "if," comma for logical AND, and $\sim$ for negation. Function symbols in rules are permitted, and negation is required to be stratified, as in NAIL!.

Example 16.6: The rule for *clear* from Figure 16.2 would appear as

```
clear(D,B)  ←  dvar(D,X),  ~ kill(X,B).
```

in LDL. □

Rules are translated to an internal form called a *predicate connection graph*, which is similar to a rule/goal graph, but without the adornments to indicate bound and free arguments. After an extensive query-optimization process, to be discussed in the next section, rules are translated to an intermediate code called FAD. This language, like the NAIL! ICODE, is essentially relational algebra augmented with the capability to handle function symbols and flow of control.

Set Operations in LDL

LDL permits variables and arguments to take sets as values. If a variable X in the head of a rule is surrounded by triangular brackets, then the argument where $<X>$ appears takes, as its own value, the set of values assumed by X as the variables of the rule range over all their possible values that make the body true.[8]

Like negation, uses of the set-grouping operator $<X>$ must be stratified. That is, if $<X>$ appears as an argument of predicate p in the head of a rule, and variable X itself appears in a subgoal of that rule with predicate q, then q must not depend on p, either directly or indirectly.

Example 16.7: In the data-flow analysis problem of Example 16.2, it would make sense to think of sets of definitions associated with each block. For example, we might give $in(D, B)$ the meaning that D is the set of definitions that reach the beginning of block B. Thus, there would be, in the relation for in, only one tuple for each block B. In comparison, the rules of Figure 16.2 required that in's relation have one tuple with second component B for each definition that reaches B. Similarly, we could treat $clear(D, B)$ as meaning that D is the set of definitions whose variable is not redefined in block B, and we could regard $out(D, B)$ as saying that D is the set of definitions reaching the end of block B. Thus, we could rewrite r_1 of Figure 16.2 as

```
r₁:  clear(<D>,B)  ←  dvar(D,X),  ~ kill(X,B).
```

---

[8] This set grouping operator was encountered in Section 4.4 (Volume I), when we discussed the "ALL." operator of Query-by-Example.

Here, we assume that the EDB relations *dvar* and *kill* have not changed the data types of their arguments.

The meaning of the new r_1 is that for each B, we accumulate in $<D>$, the first argument of *clear*, the set of values that D assumes in variable assignments that make the body true. That is, every time we find a definition d whose variable X is not killed by this particular block B, we add d to the set that becomes the value of the first component of a *clear* tuple with second component B.

If the EDB relation *gen* is stored as in Example 16.2., that is, its relation is the set of pairs (D, B) such that definition D is generated by block B, then we could replace r_2 by

r_2:   out(<D>,B) ← gen(D,B).

However, if EDB relation *gen* were stored as tuples whose second component was a block, and whose first component was the set of definitions generated by that block, we could write r_2 as in Example 16.2,

r_2:   out(D,B) ← gen(D,B).

but now, the first arguments of both *out* and *gen* would be set-valued.

We could write r_3 as

r_3:   in(D,B) ← out(E,C), clear(F,B), inter(E,F,D).

where *inter* is a predicate that says its third argument is the intersection of its first two. This predicate is not built into LDL, and we shall discuss how to express it in the next example.

We might be tempted to write r_4 as

r_4:   in(D,B) ← out(D,C), succ(C,B).

and expect that the first arguments of *in* and *out* could be interpreted as sets. However, this rule would place in the relation for *in* a tuple (D, B), whenever B was a block and D was the set of definitions coming out of some predecessor of B. That is not what we want; we want one tuple for each B, to be the union of the sets of definitions coming out of B's predecessors. We shall see shortly the correct way to express this operation. □

Built-in Set Operations

There are several built-in operators that help us talk about sets. These are

1.   Curly braces, $\{\cdots\}$, which are used to denote specific sets. For example, $\{\}$ denotes the empty set, and $\{X\}$ denotes a singleton set whose lone member becomes the value of X. If we write $\{X, Y\}$, we can match any singleton or doubleton set; in the former case, X and Y are both instantiated to the lone member of the set.

2. A built-in predicate $union(A, B, C)$, which is made true if and only if the set C is the union of sets A and B.

3. A built-in predicate $member(X, S)$, which is made true if and only if X is a member of set S.

4. A built-in function symbol $scons(X, S)$, whose value is $S \cup \{X\}$, provided X is not a member of S. If X is already in S, $scons(X, S)$ is not defined.

Example 16.8: A useful predicate to have is $disjoint(S, T)$, which is true if and only if $S \cap T = \emptyset$; that is, S and T are disjoint sets. The following rules define $disjoint$ by induction on the size of its first argument.

```
disjoint({},S).
disjoint(scons(X,T),S) :- ~ member(X,S), disjoint(T,S).
```

The first rule says that the empty set is disjoint from any set S. The second rule asserts that if $U = T \cup \{X\}$, X is not a member of S, and T is disjoint from S, then U is also disjoint from S. Note that U is the value of $scons(X, T)$ in the second rule above.

We can apply rules such as these bottom-up to make inferences, much as we do for rules without set-valued variables. For example, the first rule lets us assert that the sets $\emptyset$ and $\{a, b\}$ are disjoint, by substituting the latter set for S. The second rule lets us assert $disjoint(\{c\}, \{a, b\})$, by substituting $\{a, b\}$ for S, c for X, and $\emptyset$ for T. It then allows us to assert $disjoint(\{c, d\}, \{a, b\})$, if we substitute $\{a, b\}$ for S, d for X, and $\{c\}$ for T.

We can use the $disjoint$ predicate to define the intersection predicate used in Example 16.7. The idea is to express intersection inductively on the number of elements in the intersection.

```
inter(S,T,{}) :- disjoint(S,T).
inter(scons(X,S),scons(X,T),scons(X,U)) :- inter(S,T,U).
```

Here, the first rule says that the intersection of disjoint sets is empty. The second says that we can compute the intersection of nondisjoint sets by finding some common member X, deleting it from both, taking the taking the intersection of the remainders, and inserting X into the result. □

Example 16.9: Now let us see how to write the rule r_4 from Example 16.2, which says that the set of definitions coming into a block is the union of definitions coming out of its predecessors. Here, we assume we want the interpretation of $out(D, B)$ to be that D is the set of definitions coming out of block B, and the interpretation of in is analogous.

First, we accumulate the sets of definitions coming out of the predecessors of each block into one set whose members are themselves sets of definitions. The rule that does this job is

```
outSets(<D>,B) ← out(D,C), succ(C,B).
```

Now, we need a predicate $unionOver(S, T)$, whose first argument is a set of sets, say $S = \{S_1, \ldots, S_n\}$, and whose second argument is the union of all the members of S; that is, $T = S_1 \cup \cdots \cup S_n$. This predicate can be defined by induction on the number of members of S, as

```
unionOver({},{}).
unionOver(scons(S,S1),T) ← unionOver(S1,T1),
                             union(S,T1,T).
```

The first rule says that the union over an empty set of sets is empty. The second rule asserts that if S is one of the sets in the first argument of $unionOver$, we can delete it to leave the set of sets $S1$, take the union over $S1$, say $T1$, then take the union of $T1$ with S.

Now, we can convert the set of sets of definitions that is the first argument of $outSets$ to the union over this collection of sets, which is the set of definitions coming into a given block. The rule

```
in(D,B) ← outSets(Ds,B), unionOver(Ds,D).
```

serves. □

Updates as Subgoals

LDL expresses updates to EDB relations with a syntax that is quite similar to that used for expressing queries. A + preceding a subgoal, say $+p(X_1, \ldots, X_n)$, means that every assignment to $X_1, \ldots, X_n$ that

1. Makes all subgoals true, and
2. Makes the head consistent with whatever bindings appear in a "call" to the head predicate,

causes the tuple $(X_1, \ldots, X_n)$ to be inserted into the EDB relation for p. Of course, each of the arguments $X_1, \ldots, X_n$ must be bound, either because it is a constant, it appears in a previous subgoal, or it is bound in the call to the head. Similarly, $-$ preceding a subgoal causes the resulting tuple or tuples to be deleted from the corresponding relation.

Example 16.10: Let us consider the rules from Example 16.1 for defining cells, which we reproduce here in the LDL style,

```
on(I,X,Y) ← set(I,X,Y).
on(I,X,Y) ← contains(I,J,U,V), on(J,W,Z), X=U+W, Y=V+Z.
```

We can write a "procedure" that adds a copy of cell J at position (X, Y) in cell I with the rule

```
addCell(I,J,X,Y) ← + contains(I,J,X,Y).
```

We can call $addCell$ only if all arguments are bound, because otherwise one or more arguments of the subgoal $contains(I, J, X, Y)$ will be unbound when that subgoal is reached. Thus, if we execute the "query" $addCell(47, 23, 10, 20)$, the tuple $(47, 23, 10, 20)$ is inserted into the EDB relation for *contains*, and a copy of cell 23 becomes a part of cell 47, with the origin of 23 at the point $(10, 20)$ in the coordinate system of 47.

For a more complicated example, suppose we want to shift a cell I right by distance D. We can write the rules shown in Figure 16.7. The first rule breaks the job into two parts: moving the explicitly defined points and moving the cells whose copies appear in I. The second rule handles the points. We need to have I and D bound in the call. X and Y are bound by the subgoal $set(I, X, Y)$, and $X1$ is bound by the subgoal $X1 = X + D$. The effect of the second rule is that every point that is set in the cell I can be the value for the coordinates (X, Y), and all such points are deleted from the relation for *set*. Then, all corresponding points, with D added to the X-coordinate, are inserted into the *set* relation, effectively moving all points of I right by D units. A similar operation is caused by the last rule, but for the *contains* relation. $\square$

```
shift(I,D) ← shiftPoints(I,D), shiftSubcells(I,D).

shiftPoints(I,D) ← set(I,X,Y), X1=X+D,
                   - set(I,X,Y), + set(I,X1,Y).

shiftSubcells(I,D) ← contains(I,J,X,Y), X1=X+D,
                     - contains(I,J,X,Y),
                     + contains(I,J,X1,Y).
```

Figure 16.7 Shift cell I right by D units.

16.4 THE LDL QUERY OPTIMIZER

The architecture of the LDL query optimizer differs substantially from that of NAIL!, although the net effect is frequently the same. In response to a query, with some bound and some free arguments, LDL determines the binding patterns for all predicates needed to answer the query. Unlike NAIL!, LDL does not reorder subgoals at this point, but LDL does consider carefully the order in which it joins relations corresponding to the subgoals, when it later performs semi-naive evaluation of the rules.

Once the binding patterns are known, rules are rewritten for the purposes of this one query. The transformations used are

1. Magic sets.
2. Special transformations for rules that are left- or right-linear, as discussed in Chapter 15.

3. A "counting" transformation for linear rules, similar to that discussed in Section 15.5.

4. A transformation that makes projections be done as soon as feasible, in much the way the left- and right-linear transformations perform selections as early as possible; we shall discuss this technique shortly.

When more than one technique is applicable, the left- and/or right-linear transformations are preferred over all, and counting is preferred to magic sets. After applying whatever transformations are possible, the resulting rules are evaluated by the semi-naive (bottom-up) technique.

The Projection-Pushing Transformation

Let us now discuss transformation (4) above, a rule-rewriting technique whereby components of a predicate that will eventually be projected out are removed as early in the bottom-up query evaluation as possible. The basic idea is that many (although not all) such opportunities are detectable by distinguishing *existential* arguments from those that are not. Intuitively, an existential argument is one where we need to know that there is some value it can take, according to the current EDB, but we don't care which value. There are two primary sources of existential arguments.

1. We can be given a query in which an argument is explicitly marked as existential. For example, we could interpret the query $p(a, X, \_)$ to mean that we want the set of X's for which there exists some Y such that (a, X, Y) is in the relation for p.

2. If an argument in the body of a rule has a variable that appears nowhere else in the rule, then that argument is existential in the rule. For example, in the rule

    ```
    husband(X) :- male(X) & married(X,Y).
    ```

    the second argument of *married* is existential. If *married* were an IDB predicate, then we could treat the heads of rules for *married* as if the query were $married(a, \_)$.

We can propagate existential arguments through a set of rules, even recursive ones, much as we propagated bound and free arguments through rules by constructing a rule/goal graph. We use two new adornment symbols, e (existential) and n (not existential). Adornments propagate by the following two rules.

i) If a goal node has adornment α, then the head of each rule for that goal has adornment α.

ii) An argument of a subgoal has an e adornment if either

    a) It has a variable that elsewhere appears only in the head, and the adornment for its lone position in the head is e, or

b)   It has a variable that appears nowhere else in the rule.

Otherwise, its adornment symbol is n.

Example 16.11: Suppose we start with a query $in(\_, b)$, referring to the rules of Figure 16.2. This query asks if there are there any definitions that enter block b. For simplicity, we shall assume that *clear* is an EDB predicate. The relevant rules are thus

```
r₂:   out(D,B) :- gen(D,B).
r₃:   out(D,B) :- in(D,B) & clear(D,B).
r₄:   in(D,B) :- out(D,C) & succ(C,B).
```

We may construct a "rule/goal graph" for the e and n adornments as shown in Figure 16.8. As the order of subgoals is irrelevant for our purposes, we have omitted specifying an order, and instead show each subgoal as a child of its rule node.

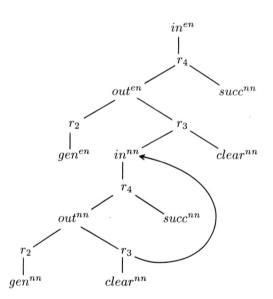

Figure 16.8 Propagating existential arguments.

We start out with the first argument of *in* existential. The existentiality propagates, in r_4, to the first argument of *out*, since *in* and *out* share variable D, but that variable appears nowhere else. However, in r_3, neither argument of *in* is existential, because the variables D and B each appear twice in the body. Observe it is insufficient to find a definition d_1 such that $in(d_1, b)$ is true, and also find a definition d_2 such that $clear(d_2, b)$ is true. These two facts do not let us conclude, with rule r_3, that there is some d for which $out(d, b)$ is true; the reason is that d_1 and d_2 might be different. Thus, our temptation to adorn both subgoals with the *en* adornment, when the head of r_3 is adorned *en*, must be resisted. $\square$

Example 16.12: Consider the ancestor rules

```
r₁:   anc(X,Y) :- par(X,Y).
r₂:   anc(X,Y) :- par(X,Z) & anc(Z,Y).
```

with the query goal $anc(a, \_)$, that is, does a have any ancestors? The "rule/goal graph" for this situation is shown in Figure 16.9.

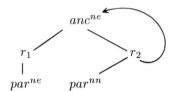

Figure 16.9 Existential arguments for ancestor query.

Since we need only *anc* with the *ne* adornment, we may rewrite the rules to replace *anc* by a one-argument predicate, corresponding to the first argument of *anc*. These rules are

```
r₃:   has_anc(X) :- par(X,Y).
r₄:   has_anc(X) :- par(X,Z) & has_anc(Z).
```

Treated as conjunctive queries, $r_4 \subseteq r_3$. Thus, the entire recursion boils down to the basis rule r_3. Intuitively, that is correct, because a has an ancestor if and only if a has a parent, which is what r_3 answers. $\square$

Join Ordering in LDL

Now, we shall discuss how LDL's query processor handles nonrecursive queries. These techniques are used not only where the query involves no recursion at all, but also for performing a round of semi-naive evaluation of recursive queries, where new IDB tuples are computed in terms of EDB relations and the previous values of the (incremental) IDB tuples.

The first step is to create and simplify a *processing graph*, whose nodes correspond to rules and goals, but with no adornments and with no order of subgoals implied. The simplifications are of two types.

1. A rule node for a rule with only one subgoal is identified with the goal node for that subgoal.

2. A goal node whose predicate has only one rule is identified with the rule node for that rule.

The effect is essentially that of the rule substitutions discussed in Section 13.4.

The result of these simplifications is to make rule bodies as long as possible. Since the evaluation of a rule body involves joining relations for each of its subgoals (with the exception of those with built-in arithmetic predicates), an order for the subgoals, that is, a join order for the relations involved, must be selected. LDL uses a heuristic that involves a certain amount of exhaustive search. It is claimed to be exact on acyclic hypergraphs,[9] although there is the tacit assumption that for a given root, each acyclic hypergraph has a unique parse tree, which is not true, in general. Further, there are a number of assumptions needed to claim optimality, even for acyclic hypergraphs. Nevertheless, the technique seems to be an excellent compromise between exhaustive search and more naive heuristics, as are used in NAIL!.

Join Selectivity

In Section 11.4 we estimated the size of the join $R(A, B) \bowtie S(B, C)$ as the size of R, times the size of S, divided by the size of the domain of attribute B. If R and S correspond to subgoals of a datalog rule, the corresponding estimate for the size of the join is the product of the relation sizes divided by the product of the domains for each of the variables that are arguments of both R and S. The domain of a variable can frequently be treated as the largest of the domains of the arguments in which that variable appears, as was justified in Section 11.4.

We may express the estimate of the join size as the product of the sizes of the relations being joined, times a parameter of the join, called the *selectivity*. By what we just said, a reasonable estimate of the selectivity is 1 divided by the product of the domain sizes for the common attributes or variables.

The key "trick" that makes an exhaustive algorithm possible, given a parse tree of an acyclic hypergraph, is that we may associate the selectivity of a join with one of the relations involved in the join. Suppose we fix a parse tree, and we join all of the relations in some top-down order, starting at the root. We take the selectivity of a relation to be the selectivity of the one join of which it is an operand; this join has another operand that is the join of one or more relations, including its parent in the tree. The selectivity of the root is taken conventionally to be 1.

Example 16.13: Consider the simple acyclic hypergraph of Figure 16.10(a), and two of its parse trees, shown in Figure 16.10(b, c). In Figure 16.10(b), the join must start with DE, which could be joined to either CD or EF first. Eventually, CD is included in the join, at some time after DE is included and

---

[9] Section 12.5 defines acyclic hypergraphs.

before its child BC is included. Thus, the join involving CD as an operand is either $CD \bowtie DE$ or $CD \bowtie (DE \bowtie EF)$. In either case, the common attribute of the join is D, so the selectivity of the join is the inverse of the domain size for D.

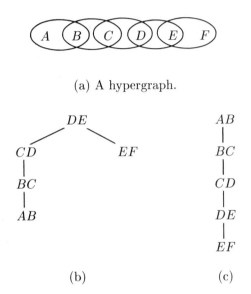

(a) A hypergraph.

(b)   (c)

Figure 16.10 A hypergraph and two of its parse trees.

Similarly, if the parse tree of Figure 16.10(c) is used, CD must be an operand of the join $CD \bowtie (BC \bowtie AB)$. Here, C is the common attribute, and the selectivity is the inverse of the domain size of C. Thus, for the parse tree of Figure 16.10(b), we may give CD the selectivity 1 divided by the domain size of D, while for Figure 16.10(c), we may use 1 over the domain size of C as the selectivity of CD. □

We can generalize Example 16.13 as follows. In an acyclic hypergraph, when relation (hyperedge) E is removed by ear removal, say in favor of hyperedge F, some of the attributes of E are in F and some are not. F becomes the parent of E in the parse tree, and we know that, if we join the hyperedges in some top-down order, then when E is an operand of a join, say $E \bowtie R$, then every attribute of $E \cap F$ will be an attribute of R, and none of the attributes of $E - F$ will be attributes of R. The reason is that R must include all of the attributes of F, but it cannot include any of the attributes of $E - F$, because these appear only in E and in hyperedges that are descendants of E in the parse tree. The latter hyperedges could not be included in R because we are joining in a top-down fashion. Hence, the selectivity of E is the inverse of the product of the domain sizes for the attributes in $E \cap F$.

Ranking Terms in a Join

Let us now assume that we have fixed a parse tree for the join of relations $R_1, \ldots, R_n$, which form an acyclic hypergraph. More precisely, these relations correspond to subgoals of a rule, and the hypergraph whose nodes are the variables of the rule and whose hyperedges are the sets of variables appearing in one subgoal, is an acyclic hypergraph. By the foregoing analysis, we concluded that, given a parse tree, we can associate with each relation R_i a selectivity s_i. If we let n_i be the number of tuples in R_i, then in any of the possible top-down orders of joins according to the given parse tree, if R_i is joined with a relation of size N, then a fair estimate of the size of the result is $n_i s_i N$.

We also need an estimate of the cost of taking this join. LDL uses several different methods, but assumes that for each of these, the cost can be estimated by $g(n_i)N$, where g is a function associated with the join method used. If we look at the table in Figure 11.6, we see that most frequently the dominant term in a join is proportional to the product of the sizes. Specifically, $g(n_i) = n_i s_i$, which is the size of R_i divided by the size of the common domain in the join, matches many of the dominant terms. For sort-join and index-creation join there are terms of order $n \log n$, where n is the size of one of the relations. We can approximate this situation by using $g(n_i) = O(\log n_i)$, although technically, this choice gives a cost of $N \log n_i$, which is neither $N \log N$ or $n_i \log n_i$. However, if N and n_i are not too disparate in size, the estimate $g(n_i) = \log n_i$ is reasonable.

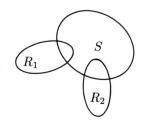

Figure 16.11 A choice of ears.

Thus, let us make the simplifying assumption that the cost of joining R_i with any relation of size N is $g(n_i)N$ for some, unspecified function g. We can then consider the situation depicted in Figure 16.11, where there are two ears, corresponding to relations R_1 and R_2, and a remaining set of hyperedges, S, during some phase of the ear reduction and parse-tree construction. When joining according to some top-down order of the parse tree, we could make R_1 the last joined and R_2 the next-to-last, or we could make R_2 last and R_1 penultimate. We could, possibly, use other orders as well, but let us focus on these two possibilities.

Suppose that the join of the relations represented by S has size N, and the optimal cost of these joins is C. If we join R_1 after R_2, the total cost is

$$C + g(n_2)N + g(n_1)s_2n_2N \tag{16.1}$$

That is, $g(n_2)N$ is the assumed cost of joining R_2 with S. The size of that join is, by hypothesis, s_2n_2N, so the last term of (16.1) is the cost of joining R_1 with $R_2 \bowtie S$. Similarly, the cost of making R_2 last is

$$C + g(n_1)N + g(n_2)s_1n_1N \tag{16.2}$$

Under what circumstances is (16.1) less than (16.2)? Equivalently, when do we prefer to have R_1 follow R_2 in the join order? Some simple algebra on (16.1) and (16.2) tells us we prefer R_1 to follow R_2 if and only if

$$\frac{s_2n_2 - 1}{g(n_2)} < \frac{s_1n_1 - 1}{g(n_1)} \tag{16.3}$$

If we define $\text{RANK}(R_i)$ to be $(s_in_i - 1)/g(n_i)$, then (16.3) says that we prefer to have R_1 follow R_2 in the join order exactly when $\text{RANK}(R_1) > \text{RANK}(R_2)$. Note that the rank of a relation can be either positive or negative.

Since R_1 and R_2 could be arbitrary relations, constrained only by the condition that either could precede the other (that is, in the parse tree, neither is an ancestor of the other), we can use the ranks of nodes to find an optimal join order for a parse tree by the algorithm of Figure 16.12. The essence is that we repeatedly pick the leaf with greatest rank and delete it from the parse tree. The nodes are listed in the reverse of the order in which they are selected. The algorithm takes $O(n \log n)$ time on an n-node tree, if the proper data structure, for example, a priority queue, is used.

The LDL optimizer, given a rule with an acyclic hypergraph of n subgoals, forms one parse tree with each possible root. It optimizes the order according to each of these trees. Recall that different trees assign different selectivities to different relations, and different trees imply different constraints on the relative order of relations; for both these reasons, different parse trees can give different optimal orders. The best of all these orders is chosen. The actual algorithm used does some sharing of the calculations for different parse trees, resulting in an algorithm that runs in time $O(n^2)$ for an n-subgoal rule.

Handling Cyclic Joins

If the hypergraph for the join of $R_1, \ldots, R_n$ is cyclic, we cannot use the technique described above directly. In essence, LDL converts a cyclic hypergraph

```
function order(T:  tree):  list of nodes;
begin
     find the leaf R_i of T with greatest rank;
        /* R_i will wind up last in the current tree T */
     let T' be T with R_i deleted;
     L := order(T');
     return(L, R_i)
end

     /* main program follows */
let T_0 be the parse tree in question;
compute the ranks of all nodes, according to T_0;
order(T_0)
```

Figure 16.12 Ordering the nodes of a parse tree.

into an acyclic one by splitting nodes to remove the intersections between hyperedges, until the hypergraph becomes acyclic. The above method for acyclic hypergraphs is then applied, but different versions of the same original node are treated as the same attribute when taking joins. To select which nonempty intersections to eliminate, LDL uses the heuristic "weakest selectivity first"; that is, it favors retaining joins whose selectivity factor is small, and will therefore tend to reduce the size of the resulting join.

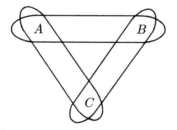

Figure 16.13 Cyclic hypergraph.

Example 16.14: Consider the cyclic hypergraph of Figure 16.13. We can make the hypergraph acyclic by eliminating any of the three intersections. For example, we could split A, the intersection of AB and AC, to create the hypergraph of Figure 16.14. This hypergraph is already acyclic, so no further splitting is necessary.

   Symmetrically, we could have chosen to split B or C instead. Which one LDL chooses depends on which join has the largest selectivity factor. That is, the node we split is the one that LDL estimates has the smallest domain size.

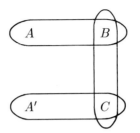

Figure 16.14 Acyclic hypergraph after splitting.

Supposing that to be A, the optimizer then works on the acyclic hypergraph of Figure 16.14, considering parse trees with AB as root, with BC as root, and with $A'C$ as root. Suppose, for example, that its optimal order turns out to be $AB \bowtie (A'C \bowtie BC)$. The actual join taken recognizes that A and A' are really the same attribute, and the true computation is $AB \bowtie (AC \bowtie BC)$. $\square$

16.5 THE LANGUAGE POSTQUEL

The POSTGRES project at Berkeley is a successor to the INGRES project (see Section 4.4 of Volume I). Its aim is to develop a knowledge-base system by simple and natural extensions to the INGRES database system. In this section, we shall discuss its query language, POSTQUEL, which is to a large degree an extension of QUEL, the INGRES query language. The next section discusses some of the implementation details that make use of database system technology in unexpected ways, to support queries involving logical rules.

Basic POSTQUEL Syntax

The simplest query form in POSTQUEL is a combination of the QUEL retrieve-statement (see Section 4.4) and the SQL select-statement (See Section 4.6). We may write

```
retrieve (<list of attributes>)
from t₁ in R₁,...,tₙ in Rₙ
    where <conditions>
```

to cause the tuple variables t_i to range over their respective relations. Each time the conditions in the where-clause are met, the tuple formed from the list of attributes in the retrieve-clause is added to the result relation. As in QUEL, attributes are denoted $t_i.A$, where A is one of the attributes of relation R_i, over which t_i ranges. The conditions of the where-clause involve comparisons among attributes and constants, and Boolean combinations of comparisons. The meaning of the POSTQUEL retrieve-statement above is the same as that of the QUEL retrieve-statement

```
range of t₁ is R₁
      ...
range of tₙ is Rₙ
retrieve (<list of attributes>)
    where <conditions>
```

or the SQL select-statement

```
SELECT <list of attributes>
FROM R₁ t₁,...,Rₙ tₙ
WHERE <conditions>
```

As in QUEL, we can store the result of a query into relation R by using the retrieve-clause

```
retrieve into R (<list of attributes>)
```

Statement Iteration

In order to support recursion, POSTQUEL allows us to specify that a retrieval is to be repeated until a fixed point is reached, that is, until at one repetition, no changes are made to the relation into which tuples are being retrieved. This iteration is indicated by using the keyword `retrieve*` in place of `retrieve`. Any datalog rule can be expressed as a single POSTQUEL statement without iteration; this result is an easy exercise. Thus, a single retrieve*-statement can simulate the application of any one recursive datalog rule.

Example 16.15: Let us again consider the computation of reaching definitions according to the rules

```
out(D,B) :- gen(D,B).
out(D,B) :- in(D,B) & clear(D,B).
in(D,B) :- out(D,C) & succ(C,B).
```

We revert to the original interpretation of these rules, where D stands for a single definition, rather than the set-oriented interpretation of Section 16.3. Here, *gen*, *succ*, and *clear* are EDB predicates with relations

```
GEN(DEF, BLOCK)
SUCC(FROM, TO)
CLEAR(DEF, BLOCK)
```

respectively.

The first rule, the basis, can be simulated by a retrieve-statement without repetition, as in the first two lines of Figure 16.15. However, the last two rules, which are mutually recursive, must be combined into one. The simplest approach is to substitute for the *in* subgoal in the second rule, so *in* disappears altogether, leaving the recursive rule

```
out(D,B) :- out(D,C) & succ(C,B) & clear(D,B).          (16.4)
```

The retrieve∗-statement in Figure 16.15 applies (16.4) until OUT stabilizes. To understand this retrieve∗-statement, notice that the tuple variables o, s, and c represent typical tuples in the relations for the three subgoals of (16.4). The first condition in the where-clause says that the first components of the tuples in OUT and CLEAR must be the same; that condition is equivalent to the constraint implied by the use of the same variable, D, in both positions of (16.4). Similarly, the second and third conditions of the where-clause correspond to the two places where B occurs and the two places where C occurs, respectively.

```
retrieve into OUT(g.DEF,g.BLOCK)
from g in GEN

retrieve* into OUT(o.DEF,s.TO)
from o in OUT, s in SUCC, c in CLEAR
    where o.DEF = c.DEF and
          s.TO = c.BLOCK and
          o.BLOCK = s.FROM
```

Figure 16.15 Computing reaching definitions.

The retrieve∗-statement of Figure 16.15 is executed by repeatedly evaluating the result, using the current value of the OUT relation, and checking if any new tuples are generated. If so, they are inserted into OUT, and the evaluation is repeated. If there are no new tuples, then the least fixed point of the rule (16.4) has been found, and execution halts. □

Attribute Types in POSTQUEL

The type system of POSTQUEL includes the usual integers, reals, and fixed-length character strings. Arrays, with arbitrary numbers of dimensions and lengths along these dimensions are also permitted; for example, a variable-length character string is a one-dimensional array whose elements are single characters.

However, the most significant departure from conventional practice is that POSTQUEL allows procedural values. An attribute of type postquel has a value that is a sequence of POSTQUEL statements. An attempt to obtain the value of a component of type postquel causes the statements to be executed, and the set of tuples returned becomes the value of the component.[10] Thus, components of tuples may, in effect, be relations themselves.

---

[10] The POSTGRES architecture calls for such statements to be executed spontaneously, using "spare cycles" of the machine(s) on which the system is running. Thus, fortuitously,

Even more powerful is an attribute of type procedure. The value of such an attribute is a procedure written in a general-purpose language, such as C. The reader should note that attributes of type postquel or type procedure can have a different piece of code for each tuple. However, doing so makes it virtually impossible to do the query optimization that is essential for all but the most trivial queries. A more restrictive, but still very useful scheme is to use a single piece of code with a parameter as the value of the attribute. Then a postquel attribute might be able to participate significantly in query optimization, although it is still unlikely that an attribute of type procedure could do so.

Using Postquel Attributes to Simulate Objects

One important use of attributes of type postquel is to simulate an object-oriented structure in the data model of POSTQUEL, which is relational and therefore value-oriented. The general idea is that objects of one class T_1 may appear to be parts of objects of class T_2 if, in T_2, there is a postquel attribute whose value is code to get the appropriate tuple or tuples from the relation that represents objects of class T_1. Object-identity is supported, since modification to an object O of class T_1 automatically changes its appearance in any objects of class T_2 that reference O.

Example 16.16: Let us consider the object-oriented scheme design of Figure 5.22, in Section 5.6 (Volume I), which covered the OPAL language. Part of that scheme involved items, item-quantity pairs, and orders. An item is a pair consisting of a name and an item number; this class is elementary, and its objects look like ordinary tuples of a relation. An item-quantity pair is an object with two components. The first is an object of class item, and the second is an integer, the quantity. An order is a set of item-quantity pairs, together with an order number.

The relation corresponding to items is declared in a conventional manner, involving none of the powerful types of POSTQUEL. We can write

```
create ITEMS(NAME=char[20], NUMBER=integer)
```

to declare a relation ITEMS of the desired type.

We can define the relation

IQPAIRS(ID, ITEM, QUANT)

by the POSTQUEL statement

---

the desired value may already be stored and need not be computed when accessed. This mode of operation requires invalidation of values as soon as something on which they depend changes, using a technique discussed in Section 16.6. Whether technology will eventually justify this reliance on "spare cycles" and on a place to store data that may never be needed remains to be seen.

```
create IQPAIRS(ID=integer, ITEM=postquel, QUANT=integer)
```

The intent is that ID is a unique identifier for pairs; we'll need this identifier to handle orders conveniently.[11] QUANT, evidently, is the quantity portion of the pair. The value of the ITEM attribute is POSTQUEL code. In principle, any sequence of statements could appear there in each of the tuples of relation IQPAIRS. In practice, we want to place in each tuple code that returns one particular tuple of the ITEMS relation. Supposing that NAME is a key for ITEMS, we could put in each IQPAIRS tuple code like the following, which would be used for tuples in which the item is Brie.

```
retrieve (i.NAME, i.NUMBER)
from i in ITEMS
    where i.NAME = "Brie"
```

The value of the ITEM component of the tuple where this code appeared would be the pair (Brie, 47), say, if the item number for Brie were 47. However, neither Brie nor 47 appears physically in the component, and if, say, we changed the item number of Brie to 48, then the next time we referenced that IQPAIRS tuple, the value of the item number would be 48, not 47. Moreover, every other IQPAIRS tuple whose item was Brie would have the same change made automatically, provided those tuples also had code that referred to the Brie ITEMS tuple.

Incidentally, we could refer to components of the ITEM component by a cascaded dot notation. For example, if q were a tuple variable ranging over IQPAIRS, then q.ITEM.NUMBER refers to the NUMBER component of the pair referred to in the ITEM component of the tuple in IQPAIRS.

Now, let us define a relation ORDERS(O#, INCLUDES) by

```
create ORDERS(O#=integer, INCLUDES=postquel)
```

The intent is that INCLUDES is the set of item-quantity pairs comprising the order. We can place in the INCLUDES component of the tuple for order i a statement that retrieves the relevant item-quantity pairs, using the ID attribute of IQPAIRS, which is a key for this relation. A possible statement for an order whose item-quantity pairs have ID's 3, 35, and 104 is

```
retrieve (q.ITEM, q.QUANT)
from q in IQPAIRS
    where q.ID=3 or q.ID=35 or q.ID=104
```

Then, for example, if we wanted to know the items on order number 46, we could refer to any member of this set as o.INCLUDES.ITEM.NAME, if o were

---

[11] A better scheme would store item-quantity pairs in the relation for orders, rather than using a separate relation for these pairs. However, the approach we use here illustrates how unique identifiers, along with procedures as values, help support object identity.

a tuple variable ranging over ORDERS. □

Single Procedures for Attributes

It is greatly to our advantage if we use one procedure for all tuples of a relation. It makes optimization more feasible if procedures are, in effect, part of the scheme rather than part of the data. Even neglecting optimization, it is feasible to compile one procedure, while compiling thousands of similar procedures stored in the database is less realistic. Finally, storing one procedure called from many tuples saves space, compared with storing one procedure per tuple.

POSTQUEL offers the capability to store a procedure for an entire column of a relation. We shall not go into the mechanism in detail, but the procedure is declared for some attribute A, and in each tuple, the component for A is a call to that procedure, with the appropriate arguments.

Example 16.17: For the ITEM field of IQPAIRS tuples in Example 16.16, we could have a single procedure named *getItem*.

```
retrieve (i.NAME, i.NUMBER)
from i in ITEMS
     where i.NAME = $1
```

Here, $1 is a formal parameter. In the ITEM component of an IQPAIRS tuple representing Brie, we would have a call to *getItem*("Brie"). □

Recursive Queries from Stored Procedures

Another important use of procedures as data is to implement recursion without having to iterate a query. The technique is best illustrated with an example.

Example 16.18: Let us again attempt to represent the artwork database of Example 16.1. Recall that the rules defining when a cell I has point (X, Y) on (set equal to 1) are

```
on(I,X,Y) :- set(I,X,Y).
on(I,X,Y) :- contains(I,J,U,V) & on(J,W,Z) & X=U+W & Y=V+Z.
```

In POSTQUEL, we can represent the situation by a relation

ON(CELL, PIXEL)

whose first component is a cell number, of type integer, and whose second component is of type postquel. The idea is that the code for PIXEL in the tuple for cell I will produce a relation of pairs (X, Y), consisting of all points in cell I that are on, either because they are set directly, or because they appear in a subcell of I.

The code for PIXEL does not have to expand cell I completely. Rather, it consults the relation

CONTAINS(CELL, SUBCELL, X, Y)

that gives the immediate subcells of cell I and the (X, Y) coordinates of their origins in the coordinate system of I. The PIXEL code simply consults ON for the points found (directly or indirectly) in each such cell J, and translates those points to the coordinates of I. Figure 16.16 shows the code for the procedure *pixel*. The ON tuple for each cell I has a call to $pixel(I)$ in its PIXEL component. A call to $pixel(I)$ causes the constituents of I to be fully expanded, and these constituents are then translated to the coordinate system of I, to form the full expansion of I. Notice that, while the code itself is not recursive, the call to $pixel(I)$ causes calls to $pixel(J)$ for each subcell J of I; these call *pixel* for the subcells of each J, and so on.

```
(1)  retrieve (X=s.X, Y=s.Y)
(2)  from s in SET
(3)      where s.CELL = $1

(4)  retrieve (X=o.PIXEL.X+c.X, Y=o.PIXEL.Y+c.Y)
(5)  from o in ON, c in CONTAINS
(6)      where c.CELL = $1 and c.SUBCELL = o.CELL
```

Figure 16.16 The procedure *pixel*.

To understand Figure 16.16, note that we use a relation SET(CELL, X, Y) to store the relation for the *set* predicate. The relation for PIXEL is intended to have two components, X and Y, and the retrievals in lines (1) and (4) give those names to the components retrieved. Lines (1)–(3) simply examine the SET relation for all points that pertain to the given cell, which is denoted by formal parameter $1.

Lines (5) and (6) establish a relationship between a tuple o in ON and a tuple c in CONTAINS. The goal is to find the subcells of cell $1, so in line (6) we have the condition that c.CELL = $1. We also need to consult the ON relation for each subcell of $1; hence the condition that c.SUBCELL = o.CELL in line (6). That condition makes o refer to the ON tuple for a typical subcell J of $1. In line (4), the term o.PIXEL.X refers to the X-component of a typical tuple in the PIXEL relation for J, while c.X refers to the X-offset for this copy of cell J in the coordinate system of $1. Their sum is the proper X-coordinate for the image of J's point in cell $1. Similarly, the Y-component of line (4) does the same calculation for the same point in the PIXEL relation, but using the corresponding Y-coordinates.

Suppose we refer to the PIXEL field of a particular cell, say by printing the PIXEL value for cell 10. The *pixel* procedure causes relation ON to be examined recursively for each of the subcells of cell 10, then their subcells, and so on, until all of the points in cell 10 that are on get printed. ☐

Triggers

There are a number of situations where we would like a change in one relation to cause another change, to the same or a different relation. In terms of logical rules, we might like to apply certain rules continuously, making the appropriate change to the head relation whenever one of the relations in the body changed. More generally, the rule might call for either insertion into or deletion from some relation, each time a change to the body occurred, as is the case with the update rules discussed in Section 16.3, in connection with LDL.

POSTQUEL expresses a *trigger* by the keyword **always**, preceding a command such as retrieve, insert, or delete. A statement with this keyword is deemed to operate continuously. As soon as a change to one of the relations that are input to the statement occurs, execution of the statement is "triggered," and the system performs whatever action is implied by the statement.

Example 16.19: Suppose we want to keep a stored copy of the *reach* predicate discussed in Example 16.2, concerning reaching definitions. The rule describing this computation is

```
reach(D,U) :- in(D,B) & exposed(U,B) &
              dvar(D,X) & uvar(U,X).
```

We may suppose that there are five relations involved,

IN(DEF, BLOCK)	EXPOSED(DEF, BLOCK)
DVAR(DEF, VAR)	UVAR(USE, VAR)
REACH(DEF, USE)	

The way to translate a single rule into POSTQUEL was illustrated in Example 16.15. The same technique can be applied here, to obtain the query in Figure 16.17. The only nuance is the keyword **always**, which causes the statement to be executed whenever any of the four relations IN, EXPOSED, DVAR, or UVAR changes. ☐

```
always retrieve into REACH (i.DEF, e.USE)
from i in IN, e in EXPOSED, d in DVAR, u in UVAR
   where i.DEF = d.DEF and
         i.BLOCK = e.BLOCK and
         e.USE = u.USE and
         d.VAR = u.VAR
```

Figure 16.17 Trigger for computation of the REACH relation.

The reader should observe the difference between the style of computation for which triggers are useful and the style in which procedures as values are useful. With triggers, the defined relation, such as REACH in Example 16.19, is kept up-to-date at all times; that is, it is effectively an EDB relation. We could, alternatively, have given the REACH relation an attribute of type postquel, which would hold code similar to that given in Figure 16.17. In that case, the relation, or the portion of it relevant to a given query, would only be constructed as needed.[12] Thus, REACH would behave as if it were an IDB relation.

Evaluation on Demand

Another capability of POSTQUEL is demand evaluation of certain attributes, which are defined by statements and not actually stored in the relation. One use of this feature is to support object identity, since the attributes so defined become, in effect, virtual fields.[13] Another use is to define a field by a list of rules, sometimes contradictory. Rules have priorities from 0 to 15, and in case of conflict the highest-priority rule takes precedence.

The form of such rules is

```
replace demand R (A = <value>)
    where <conditions>
```

If called upon to evaluate attribute A of relation R, we find the highest-priority rule for A and R whose conditions are met; note these conditions may involve other attributes besides A. That rule causes its <value> to become the value of $R.A$.

To denote attributes in conditions, we use terms $R.A$, where R is a relation and A one of its attributes. This convention is somewhat at variance from the usual QUEL or POSTQUEL style of having a tuple variable t range over R and referring to an attribute as $t.A$.

Example 16.20: Let us return to the IQPAIRS relation of Example 16.17. Another approach to supporting items as objects is to define the relation

IQPAIRS(INAME, I#, QUANT)

and define the I# field by a single rule that copies the NUMBER field of the ITEMS relation, for the appropriate item. To do so, we would declare the following rule.

```
replace demand IQPAIRS (I# = ITEMS.NUMBER)            (16.5)
    where ITEMS.NAME = IQPAIRS.INAME
```

The effect of (16.5) is to find that tuple of the ITEMS relation whose NAME

---

[12] Although POSTGRES would sometimes evaluate and store such relations spontaneously, as we mentioned earlier.

[13] As in the hierarchical model discussed in Section 2.6 of Volume I.

field equals the INAME field of the tuple in IQPAIRS whose I# field is currently being evaluated; the NUMBER field of that ITEMS tuple becomes the I# field of the IQPAIRS tuple. Note that relation names substitute for tuple variables ranging over those relations here.

We could also modify the rule (16.5) with higher-priority exceptions. For example, suppose that we wanted the item number of Brie in the IQPAIRS relation to be 48, independent of its value in the ITEMS relation. Then we could add a rule

```
replace demand IQPAIRS (I# = 48)                          (16.6)
    where IQPAIRS.INAME = "Brie"
```

If (16.6) were given priority over (16.5), then the desired effect would be achieved. If (16.5) has priority over (16.6), then (16.6) would be invisible, provided that ITEMS had a tuple with NAME equal to "Brie." □

16.6 IMPLEMENTATION OF POSTQUEL EXTENSIONS

An important insight used in the architecture of the POSTGRES system is that the locking mechanisms needed to support concurrency can be extended naturally to support the new operations that appear in POSTQUEL.[14] There are three primitive operations that we need to support.

1. *Triggering.* An attempt to write a value for a data item may cause the execution of one or more POSTQUEL statements; these statements would have an "always" in them. For instance, in Example 16.19, we would want to trigger the statement of Figure 16.17 whenever there was an attempt to write one of the relations IN, EXPOSED, DVAR, or UVAR.

2. *Demand evaluation.* An attempt to read an attribute defined by replace-demand-statements causes the execution of one of these statements. For instance, in Example 16.20, we would want to execute (16.5) or (16.6) whenever there was an attempt to read the I# attribute of some tuple of IQPAIRS. Note that writing a value for such an attribute makes no sense, and is illegal; if we want to change values of such an attribute, we need to write additional rules.

3. *Invalidation.* We alluded in Section 16.5 to the fact that POSTGRES can evaluate spontaneously attributes of type postquel or procedure. Moreover, once evaluated, these values are not discarded unless they become invalid. Whenever an item *I* changes, any other items that depend for their evaluation on *I* become invalid; items that depend on an invalid item themselves become invalid, and so on. Any item known to be invalid may not have its current value read in the future. If the concurrency control mechanism is

---

[14] The reader should, if necessary, review Chapter 9 of Volume I, especially Section 9.5 on lock modes.

designed properly, a transaction reading an item I that should be invalid, yet has not been rendered so because the chain of invalidations has not reached I, can be allowed to complete; it will appear that this transaction was executed before the transaction that invalidated I, in the equivalent serial order.

New Lock Modes

Each of these problems can be solved by the creation of a new lock mode. Recall from Chapter 9 that each "item" in the database can be locked, and locking is essential if transactions are not to interact in ways that damage the integrity of the database. In conventional database systems, read (R) and write (W) locks are generally sufficient, and they interact according to the simple lock compatibility matrix of Figure 16.18. This matrix enforces the rule that a transaction requesting a read-lock on an item A can be granted that lock (Y for "yes") if there are only read-locks on A held by other transactions but cannot be granted the lock (N for "no") if another transaction holds a write-lock on A. The request for a write-lock cannot be granted if any other locks are held on the same item. Of course, locks can always be granted if no locks at all are held on the item.

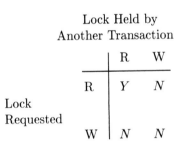

Figure 16.18 Lock compatibility matrix for read and write.

In POSTGRES, there are three additional lock modes.

1. The T, or *trigger*, lock is placed on an item A whenever a change to A requires some action to be triggered. That is, if A is used in the evaluation of some statement with the `always` keyword, then whenever an attempt to write A is made, the write operation is permitted, but a list of procedures associated with A is executed.

2. To handle replace-demand-statements, a D, or *demand* lock is used. An attempt to read an item A on which a D lock has been placed causes the evaluation of the item before the read is allowed to be done.

3. To handle the problem of invalidation of stored results, we can place an I, or *invalidate* lock on an item A. Then, any attempt to write A is allowed to proceed, but each item on a list of items associated with A is invalidated, and, recursively, the invalidated items are treated as if they had been written, so the invalidation proceeds recursively to invalidate items on the lists of the invalidated items.

	R	W	T	D	I
R	Y	N	Y	(b)	Y
W	N	N	(a)	N	(c)
T	Y	N	Y	Y	Y
D	N	N	(a)	Y	(c)
I	Y	N	Y	Y	Y

Figure 16.19 Lock compatibility matrix for T, D, and I locks.

The lock compatibility matrix for these three new lock modes, along with R and W locks, is shown in Figure 16.19. We should understand that there are several different kinds of locks that are compatible, and a single item could be locked by various transactions in, say, R, T, D, and I modes at the same time. A lock of type T can be granted on an item A if and only if for every type S of lock currently held on A, the entry in the row for T and the column for S has something other than an N. If the entry is other than Y, one of three special actions, (a), (b), and (c), described below, must be performed. The explanations for these entries are given row-by-row, as follows.

Read-Locks: If we request a read lock on an item A, we can proceed unless A is write-locked, for reasons discussed in Chapter 9. No problem exists if there are I or T locks on A; those only have an effect when the value of A changes. However, if there is a D lock on A, then the value of A is determined by some replace-demand-statement, which must be run. The value (b) in the (R, D) entry of Figure 16.19 represents this action of awakening the definition procedure for A, followed by granting of the read-lock.

Write-Locks: The second row, for write-locks, indicates that we cannot write a new value of a read-locked or write-locked item, as discussed in Chapter 9. We cannot write a demand-locked item under any circumstances, because such items are fields whose definition is given by a procedure, and there is no way we can store a physical value in such an item. If there is a trigger-lock on item A, we can write A, but we must then awaken all of the commands with "always" in them that depend on the value of A. These commands must be reexecuted after the new value is written. This action is represented by the (a) value in the (W, T) entry of Figure 16.19. Similarly, attempting to write an item A with invalidate-locks set causes the invalidation procedure to commence for all items whose value becomes invalid when the value of A changes; that is the meaning of the (c) entry in Figure 16.19.

Trigger-Locks: Now, suppose we try to obtain a trigger lock on item A; that is, we define an "always" procedure that depends on the value of A. We can do so at any time, as long as there is no write-lock on A. If there is, the value of A is in the process of changing, and if we also placed a T lock on A at this time, it would be unclear whether the change should or should not trigger the procedure. These observations explain the third row of Figure 16.19.

Demand-Locks: In the fourth row we see the effects of taking a demand-lock on an item A. This action changes the value of A, since apparently we have modified the rules defining A. Thus, the fourth row, for demand-locks, mirrors the row for write-locks, except that there is no reason not to allow a demand-lock just because another is already held; the new demand-lock just represents a change in the rules for evaluating A.

Invalidate-Locks: Finally, the fifth row, for invalidate-locks, looks just like the row for trigger-locks, for the same reasons.

Implementation Issues for POSTQUEL Locks

In an ordinary lock system, with read- and write-locks, there is no reason for the lock table to be resilient, that is, to survive a crash. The reason is that the recovery mechanism will have to determine what transactions committed (completed), and redo them if necessary, in a serial fashion. Locks held by uncommitted transactions are removed and the transactions are treated as if they had never occurred. The database system then restarts after the crash with nothing locked, so there is no reason to remember what locks were held before the crash.

However, the T, D, and I locks held on items form part of the data in the database. Just because a crash occurs does not mean that statements like replace-demand or always-statements are no longer valid. Thus, POSTGRES stores locks with the values of the items themselves, rather than storing locks in a main-memory lock table, which lists only the items on which locks are currently held. When a transaction commits, any T, D, or I locks it has set on items are entered into the journal and forced into stable storage (secondary memory), just as values written by the transaction must be.

EXERCISES

16.1: Modify the artwork rules of Example 16.1 to allow the following enhancements.

   a)   Rotation of a cell. That is, suppose there is a relation

   $$rotate(I, J, Theta)$$

   that defines cell I to be a copy of cell J, rotated $Theta$ degrees counter-clockwise.

   b)   Scaling of a cell. Let $scale(I, J, R)$ be a relation that defines cell I to be a copy of cell J, but with all distances to the origin multiplied by R.

* 16.2: Suppose cell 1 is a picture of a man watching a blank television screen, which is square, 100 pixels on a side, with center at $(300, 200)$. Suppose that cell 1 itself is a square 400 pixels on a side, with lower left corner at the origin. Using the extended rules you develop in Exercise 16.1, write a definition of cell 2, which is a picture of a man watching a picture of himself watching a picture of himself, ...

16.3: Perform a magic-sets transformation on the artwork rules of Example 16.1, with query goal on^{bff}.

* 16.4: Express the predicate $kill$ in Example 16.2 in terms of the predicates gen, $uvar$, and $dvar$. *Hint*: It is not a problem if a definition "kills" itself, because that definition will either be "gen'd" by its own block or is killed by another definition of the same variable in the same block.

* 16.5: Express the reaching-definitions problem of Example 16.2 as a generalized transitive closure (see Section 15.7) on the graph whose nodes are the blocks and whose arcs are given by the $succ$ relation. The problem is to find a closed semiring such that we can assign weights to the arcs based on the contents of the EDB relations, and such that the value associated with the pair of blocks (B_0, B), where B_0 is the start node of the flow graph, tells us the set of definitions that reach block B. *Hint*: The values should be mappings from sets of definitions to sets of definitions, such that when the mapping is applied to the empty set, you get the set of reaching definitions.

16.6: The NAIL! subgoal-ordering heuristic (see Example 16.4) allows several different orders for the subgoals of rule r_5 in Figure 16.2. Give each permitted order, assuming the binding pattern for the head is (a) bb (b) bf (c) fb (d) ff.

```
a(0,s(0)).
a(s(X),s(Y)) :- a(X,Y).

p(X,Y) :- a(X,Y).
p(X,Y) :- a(X,Z) & p(Z,Y).
```

Figure 16.20 Rules for Exercise 16.7.

16.7: Consider the rules of Figure 16.20. If we regard s as a successor function, then a becomes the arcs of the infinite graph with nodes $0, 1, \ldots$ and arcs $0 \rightarrow 1 \rightarrow 2 \rightarrow \cdots$. Further, the predicate p represents the paths in this graph.

    a)   Suppose that our available capture rules allow us to capture a^α only when the binding pattern α is sufficient to guarantee that only a finite number of a-tuples match a given binding. For what values of α can we capture a^α?

    b)   Under the assumptions of (a), for what values of adornment β can we capture p^β?

16.8: Translate one round of naive evaluation of the data-flow rules of Figure 16.2 into the NAIL! ICODE.

16.9: Express the following predicates using rules and the set primitives of the LDL language.

    a) $contains(S, T)$, which is true if and only if set S is a subset (not necessarily proper) of set T.

    * b) $power(S, P)$, which is true if and only if P is the power set of S; that is, the members of P are all of the subsets of S.

16.10: Recall the Beer-Drinkers' Database from Exercise 11.20, which consists of the following relations.

       FREQUENTS(DRINKER, BAR)
       SERVES(BAR, BEER)
       LIKES(DRINKER, BEER)

Write LDL rules to define the following predicates. Avoid using negation in (b) and (c).

    a) $canDrink(D, Bs)$, meaning that Bs is the set of beers that are served by one or more bars frequented by drinker D.

    * b) $veryHappy(D)$ if drinker D likes at least one beer served in every bar he frequents.

    * c) $ecstatic(D)$ if drinker D likes every beer served in every bar he frequents.

* 16.11: Given the usual parenthood relation *par*, write an LDL program that defines predicate $anc(X, Ys)$, meaning that Ys is the set of ancestors of individual X.

16.12: Write an update rule for the relation $set(I, X, Y)$ of Example 16.1 that forces each cell to be convex. That is, pixel (X, Y) must be set if both the pixels above and below it, $(X, Y + 1)$ and $(X, Y - 1)$, are set, or if the pixels to the left and right, $(X - 1, Y)$ and $(X + 1, Y)$, are set.

* 16.13: Show how to express each insertion and deletion in the Query-by-Example language (Section 4.4 of Volume I) as LDL update rules.

16.14: What are the existential arguments if we have a query $anc(\_, a)$, applied to the usual ancestor rules, as in Example 16.12?

16.15: Suppose we have a hypergraph with hyperedges

$$\{AB,\ BCD,\ BEF,\ FGH,\ HJ,\ GHI\}$$

a) For which hyperedges is there more than one parse tree with that hyperedge as root? What is the total number of parse trees?

b) For each hyperedge, select one parse tree with that hyperedge as root. Assume that the domain sizes for attributes $A,\ B, \ldots, J$ are $10, 20, \ldots, 100$, respectively. Find an optimal join order for each parse tree.

c) Find the overall optimum join order.

d) Repeat (b) and (c) with the addition of hyperedge AI to the hypergraph.

16.16: Show how to express any datalog rule as a retrieve-statement of POST-QUEL. Show how to express any recursion with a single datalog basis rule and a single datalog recursive rule as a retrieve*-statement.

16.17: For the Beer-Drinkers' Database mentioned in Exercise 16.10, show how to set up the following as POSTQUEL relations and rules.

a) A relation DRINKERS(NAME, BARS, BEERS), such that BARS is the set of bars frequented by the drinker named NAME, and BEERS is the set of beers he likes. This information should not be stored explicitly; rather arrange that when queried, the current information from the FREQUENTS and LIKES relations is obtained by execution of POSTQUEL statements.

b) Drinker Charles Chugamug likes every beer served at any bar. Thus, if the SERVES relation is changed to add a new beer, the fact that Chugamug likes that beer must be entered immediately into the LIKES relation. If no bar serves a beer any more, Chugamug still likes it.

c) The BEER attribute of the LIKES relation is to be evaluated on demand, according to high- and low-priority rules. The high-priority rules reflect the usual LIKES information, that is, the specific beers that each drinker likes. The low priority rules say that a drinker likes any beer served at a bar he frequents. What answer do we get when we try to find what beers a given drinker likes?

6.18: Set up a POSTQUEL relation SG(PERSON, COUSIN), where COUSIN is of type postquel and evaluates to the set of cousins at the same generation for the person mentioned in the first component. You may assume there is a relation PAR(CHILD, PARENT) available.

BIBLIOGRAPHIC NOTES

Zaniolo [1987] is a compendium of articles about various experiments in knowledge-base system implementation.

NAIL!

The basic architecture comes from Ullman [1985]. Morris, Ullman, and Van Gelder [1986] and Morris et al. [1987] describe the system implementation.

Morris [1988] describes the strategy-selection algorithm, and Ullman and Vardi [1988] shows that this problem is inherently intractable.

LDL

Naqvi and Tsur [1988] is a book about the system, and Zaniolo [1988] and Chimenti et al. [1987] survey aspects of the system.

Two papers describing the implementation of sets in the language are Tsur and Zaniolo [1986] and Beeri, Naqvi, Ramakrishnan, Shmueli, and Tsur [1987]. Naqvi and Krishnamurthy [1988] describes the update features of the language. Information about the intermediate language FAD can be found in Danforth, Khoshafian, and Valduriez [1988].

The optimization of subgoal ordering for joins, discussed in Section 16.4, is covered by Krishnamurthy, Boral, and Zaniolo [1986]. Ramakrishnan, Beeri, and Krishnamurthy [1988] describe the optimization used for existential variables.

POSTGRES

Design of the system is discussed in Stonebraker [1986], and Stonebraker and Rowe [1986a,b]. An initial manual for POSTQUEL is available as Wensel [1988].

Other Systems

There are a number of similar projects we have not covered in this chapter. IBM's Starburst system, mentioned in the references of Chapter 11, has many of the characteristics of a knowledge-base system, for example.

NU-Prolog, being developed at the University of Melbourne, is an implementation of Prolog that has acquired many of the characteristics of a database system. The system is surveyed in Ramamohanarao et al. [1987]. The storage structure, superimposed coding (see Knuth [1973]), is described by Thom, Ramamohanarao, and Naish [1986] and Ramamohanarao and Shepherd [1986].

The PROBE system of CCA is described in Dayal and Smith [1986]. Rosenthal, Heiler, Dayal, and Manola [1986] talks about the form of recursion, which is essentially the generalized transitive closure scheme of Section 15.7, used by the system.

Syllog is a system developed at IBM by Walker [1986]. It implements a structured natural language, which it interprets as logical rules.

CHAPTER 17

The Universal Relation

as a

User Interface

A "universal relation" is an imaginary relation that represents all of the data in the database. A query language that lets us refer to the universal relation, rather than to the actual database scheme, can be much simpler than typical relational query languages, because we need to mention only attributes, rather than attribute-relation pairs. As an especially important example, a natural-language interface to a database is designed for use by people who understand little or nothing of the scheme. All natural-language interfaces effectively refer to the universal relation, and queries about the universal relation must be translated by the system into queries about the existing scheme.

Interpreting queries over a universal relation is an admittedly difficult task. Yet it is one that must be performed if we are to have natural language interfaces or, indeed, any interface less formal than those described in Chapters 4, 5, and 16. After an introduction and some motivation in Section 17.1, we introduce the "window function" concept in Section 17.2. Window functions let us differentiate the various approaches to interpreting queries over universal relations. In Section 17.3 we briefly mention the strategy of the universal-relation system Q, which requires the user to make all decisions. Sections 17.4 and 17.5 discuss the "representative instance," a universal relation with nulls, and a query-interpretation algorithm that uses this notion of a universal relation. Sections 17.6, 17.7, and 17.8 introduce "object structures," and give query-interpretation algorithms based on this view of the universal relation.

17.1 THE UNIVERSAL RELATION CONCEPT

Let us imagine that the data of an entire database were kept in a single relation, called a *universal relation*, whose scheme consists of all attributes appearing in any of the relation schemes of the database. We assume that attributes representing the same thing in different relation schemes are given the same name, and attributes representing different things are given different names.

For an example of a universal relation, Example 7.15 (Volume I) discussed the decomposition of a database scheme $CTHRSG$, the six attributes standing for courses, teachers, hours, rooms, students, and grades, respectively. Figure 7.7 gave an example of a hypothetical relation over this scheme, which we repeat here as Figure 17.1. We would never really wish to store the data in this way, because of the various anomalies and redundancy that are present. However, we are not proposing that the data be stored as in Figure 17.1, only that the user be allowed to perceive the data as if it were stored that way. The advantage is that the user is thus spared memorizing details concerning which attributes are grouped with which to form relation schemes.

C	T	H	R	S	G
CS101	Deadwood	M9	222	Weenie	B+
CS101	Deadwood	W9	333	Weenie	B+
CS101	Deadwood	F9	222	Weenie	B+
CS101	Deadwood	M9	222	Grind	C
CS101	Deadwood	W9	333	Grind	C
CS101	Deadwood	F9	222	Grind	C

Figure 17.1 A sample relation for scheme $CTHRSG$.

In order that the universal relation make sense as a conceptual tool, we sometimes must use null values to pad out (imaginary) tuples, and thereby avoid the problems associated in Section 7.1 with unnormalized relations. For example, we could use nulls in the S and G components of the $CTHRSG$ universal relation to record information about courses before students registered. We shall discuss nulls in more detail in Section 17.4, but for the moment, the reader should be reminded that, since the universal relation is imaginary rather than stored physically, we have the flexibility necessary to handle anomalies by using nulls. If we were to store unnormalized relations in reality, we might use too much space storing tuples with nulls, and handling updates in the presence of possible null values could be too time consuming.

In a sense, we propose going one step further than the relational model generally attempts to do, by removing from the user not only concern about the physical organization of the data, but about some of the logical organization as well. The penalty we pay is that the DBMS must work harder to interpret queries and updates on the database, than it would if the user had to specify the query in terms of the conceptual database itself. The penalty is not a great one, however, and it is analogous to the additional work of optimization that is contributed by any relational DBMS to relieve the user of specifying his query in terms even lower than relations, as one would using systems based on nonrelational data models.

A Simple Query Language for Universal Relations

In order to make the capabilities and problems associated with the universal relation concept more concrete, let us introduce the language of System/U, an experimental system for supporting a universal relation data view developed by the author at Stanford.[1] Its query language is similar to QUEL (Section 4.3 of Volume I), with two simplifications.

1. Since all tuple variables range over the universal relation, there is no need for declarations of tuple variables.

2. Since most queries in ordinary QUEL that require two or more tuple variables involve joins, and joins — at least natural joins — are hidden by the universal relation view of data, it is rare that a query to System/U requires more than one tuple variable. Thus we make the assumption that there is an "invisible" tuple variable, called *blank*, and let an attribute A appearing alone stand for *blank.A*.

Example 17.1: Consider the $CTHRSG$ universal relation mentioned above. If we want to know in which rooms Prof. Deadwood teaches, we write

          retrieve (R)   (17.1)
              where T = "Deadwood"

The reader should compare the simplicity of this query with the standard QUEL query to do the same thing. Assuming the actual database scheme is $\{CT, CHR, CSG\}$, the QUEL query is

          range of t is CT
          range of s is CHR
          retrieve (s.R)
              where t.T = "Deadwood" and t.C = s.C

Some queries to System/U do require one or more nonblank tuple variables. For example, if we want to know all of the courses that meet in the same room as CS101, we could write

          retrieve (C)   (17.2)
              where R = t.R and t.C = "CS101"

The terms R and C stand for *blank.R* and *blank.C*, and are thereby differentiated from $t.R$ and $t.C$. In effect, tuple variable t represents CS101, and *blank* represents some course that meets in the same room as CS101.

---

[1] The name was originated by H. Korth as a way of embarrassing the author. The "U" stands for "universal," and nothing else.

Query (17.1) is implemented in System/U by taking the natural join of CT and CHR, selecting for $T =$ "Deadwood", and then projecting onto R. However, the user does not have to know this fact. If, for example, there were a THR relation in the database scheme, the query would instead be answered by taking the selection and projection on this relation alone.[2]

Query (17.2) would be answered by taking an equijoin on $R = R$ of two copies of the CHR relation, then selecting for the first C component equal to CS101, and finally projecting onto the second C component. That is, we would compute

$$\pi_4\big(\sigma_{\$1=\mathrm{CS}101}(CHR \underset{\$3=\$3}{\bowtie} CHR)\big)$$

How System/U, or any system that supports universal relations, decides on these responses to queries is the major subject of this chapter. $\square$

Motivation Behind the Universal Relation Viewpoint

We have seen that a universal relation interface saves us some typing when we enter queries. However, that would hardly be sufficient reason for implementing such an interface. The real motivation is that a universal relation interface allows queries to be posed by people who understand nothing of the structure of the relations. It is far more natural to pose queries in terms of entity sets like "courses," without having to know whether the C attribute appears in a relation with scheme CT, CHR, CS, CSG, or any subset of these, than it is to pose queries in terms of the particular relation schemes stored in the database. The extreme example of this phenomenon is a natural-language interface, where users speak in the terms most familiar to them, certainly not in terms of the database scheme, and the system is required to infer what the user is talking about, in terms that refer to the actual database scheme.

While the need for a universal-relation model of some sort in natural-language systems is indisputable, the universal-relation concept has been subject to a startling array of attacks in print. Often, these objections are of the form that certain queries cannot be expressed in a universal system. In fact, as we shall see, a language like that of System/U, or any of the other languages designed for a universal-relation interface, allows the expression of any query

---

[2] One may wonder how the user can know what answer to expect, since the knowledge of whether there is a THR relation, or CT and CHR relations, or all three, is hidden, and the answer produced from the THR relation need not be the same as that produced from the join of CT and CHR. Generally, the desired response is the simplest possible expression. That is, don't take a join if a single relation scheme contains the attributes needed; this is the response chosen by System/U. However, in the case that the user is aware of the particular relation schemes used in the database, and a circuitous connection among certain attributes is wanted, one can express any QUEL query in System/U's language, by using as many tuple variables as needed.

that can be written in relational algebra; thus, they have the same power as typical relational query languages.

Of far more concern are objections based on the fact that the translation from a query about the universal relation into a query about a particular scheme appears to be "black magic," and there is no reason to believe that the intuition of the user matches that of the system or its designer. For example, what happens if the user of a universal-relation interface to our $CTHRSG$ database thinks that "grades" refer to the grades of wallpaper in the classrooms? Indeed, there is nothing we can do if there is a significant mismatch between the world view of the user and that of the person who designed the database scheme and its attribute names. We can only point out that there is a great variety of techniques for interpreting queries over a universal relation, and careful design, including attention to the naming of attributes, can often minimize misinterpretations. However, the real counterargument is that "there ain't nothing better." If we are to use natural-language interfaces or any interface more abstract than a typical relational language, we have no choice but to solve the problem of implementing a universal-relation as best we can.

17.2 WINDOW FUNCTIONS

The naive vision of a universal relation presented in the previous section, where there is one relation over all of the attributes, is adequate only in simple cases, such as the $CTHRSG$ database discussed in Example 17.1. A more general viewpoint is that answering a query is a two-stage process.

1. Determine the set of attributes X mentioned in the query, and compute, using some algorithm built into the system, the *window* for X, denoted $[X]$. The window is a relation with scheme X, but all we know about its connection to the actual database scheme is that it is some function, called the *window function*, of the database. The window function depends upon X but not upon the query itself (except for the fact that the query mentions the attributes in set X and no others).

2. The query is evaluated as if it applied to the relation $[X]$.

Example 17.2: Let us reconsider the query (17.1) from Example 17.1, which is

```
retrieve (R)
    where T = "Deadwood"
```

As before, suppose the database scheme is $\{CT, CHR, CSG\}$. The window function used by System/U, in simple cases such as this, is to take $[X]$ to be the natural join of the minimal set of relations whose scheme includes all of the attributes in set X,[3] projected onto X. Here, $X = RT$, so the minimal join is

---

[3] Naturally, there is no guarantee that a unique minimal join exists when queries are more

$CT \bowtie CHR$, and

$$[X] = \pi_{RT}(CT \bowtie CHR)$$

In the second stage, we apply the query to $[X]$; that is, we compute $\pi_R\big(\sigma_{T=\text{"Deadwood"}}([X])\big)$, which is

$$\pi_R\left(\sigma_{T=\text{"Deadwood"}}\big(\pi_{RT}(CT \bowtie CHR)\big)\right)$$

Note that the projection onto RT is algebraically superfluous, and it would be combined with the projection onto R, by an ordinary query optimizer like Algorithm 11.2. $\square$

Queries Over Multiple Copies of the Universal Relation

When a query involves several tuple variables, it is really a query over several copies of the universal relation, one copy for each tuple variable. We must generalize the window-function approach to determine the set of attributes for each tuple variable and then compute the window for each of these sets. That is, if a query mentions tuple variables $t_1, \ldots, t_n$, including the "blank," and X_i is the set of attributes A such that $t_i.A$ appears in the query, then we suppose that the range of the tuple variable t_i is the relation $[X_i]$.

Example 17.3: Let us consider the query (17.2) from Example 17.1,

```
retrieve (C)
    where R = t.R and t.C = "CS101"
```

There are two tuple variables, *blank* and t. We see t associated with C and R in terms $t.C$ and $t.R$. Thus, the set of attributes for t is CR, and we regard t as ranging over the relation $[CR]$, whatever that may be. Likewise, *blank* is associated with C and R, because those are the attributes that appear without any tuple variable at all. Thus, *blank* also ranges over $[CR]$. Naturally, there are examples when the windows for the different tuple variables are different.

With our usual assumption about the underlying database scheme,

$$\{CT,\ CHR,\ CSG\}$$

System/U choses $[CR] = \pi_{CR}(CHR)$, since the one relation CHR covers both attributes C and R. We thus treat the query as if it were the QUEL query

```
range of blank is [CR]
range of t is [CR]
retrieve (C)
    where blank.R = t.R and t.C = "CS101"
```

The algebraic expression

---

complex. We shall discuss the details of the System/U algorithm in Section 17.8.

$$\pi_1 \Big(\sigma_{\$2=\$4 \wedge \$3=\text{``CS101''}} \big(\pi_{CR}(CHR) \times \pi_{CR}(CHR) \big) \Big)$$

reflects the meaning of this QUEL query and is algebraically equivalent to the simpler expression for the query given in Example 17.1. $\square$

17.3 A SIMPLE WINDOW FUNCTION

Perhaps the simplest strategy for defining window functions is that of the Q universal-relation system implemented at Bell Laboratories by Brian Kernighan. Here, the user constructs a *rel file*, which is a list of relational expressions. In principle, these expressions can be arbitrary, although in practice, they are usually joins of relations in the database. Each expression must define a relation over some set of attributes.

Given a query, expressed in an AWK-like language (see Aho, Kernighan, and Weinberger [1988]), over the hypothetical universal relation, Q determines the set of attributes X involved in the query. It then examines the rel file for the first expression whose attribute set is a (not necessarily proper) superset of X. The projection of this expression onto X is the window $[X]_Q$,[4] and the query is applied to this relation. If there is no expression in the rel file whose attributes include X, then $[X]_Q$ is taken to be the projection onto X of the join of all the relations.

Example 17.4: For the $CTHRSG$ database with relations CT, CHR, and CSG, we might choose the list of expressions

1. CT.
2. CHR.
3. CSG.
4. $CT \bowtie CHR$.
5. $CT \bowtie CSG$.
6. $CHR \bowtie CSG$.
7. $CT \bowtie CHR \bowtie CSG$.

The last is superfluous, since the join of all three would be taken as a default anyway.

In response to the query (17.1), involving attributes R and T, the search of the rel file would reach item (4), the first whose scheme includes both R and T. We would then take $[RT]_Q = \pi_{RT}(CT \bowtie CHR)$, and the query would be answered by the same expression,

$$\pi_R \Big(\sigma_{T=\text{``Deadwood''}} \big(\pi_{RT}(CT \bowtie CHR) \big) \Big)$$

---

[4] We use $[\cdots]_Q$ for the window function used by the Q system.

as in Example 17.2. As we mentioned before, the projection onto RT is superfluous, and Q would not actually perform this projection. Rather, the query would be applied directly to $CT \bowtie CHR$. $\square$

Query (17.2), which involves two copies of the universal relation would be difficult to express in Q. We would have to establish a universal relation that was, in effect, the cross product of two copies of the relation $CTHRSG$, with two different attributes for C, two for T, and so on, each with distinct names. We could then express (17.2) as a query over this universal relation.

Q offers the advantage that the database scheme designer can select the exact window he wants for every set of attributes X. He must list the expressions of the rel file in such an order that the desired expression for X uses exactly the set of attributes X (projection from a larger set of attributes may be part of the expression, if necessary), and it precedes the expression for any superset of X. For example, if we wanted a query on the $CTHRSG$ database that mentioned only attribute C to be answered by consulting the CHR relation, we could list $\pi_C(CHR)$ in the rel file, prior to any other expression involving C. That expression would then be selected as $[C]_Q$.

17.4 THE REPRESENTATIVE INSTANCE AS A UNIVERSAL RELATION

The more complex is the database scheme, the less sense it makes to imagine that there is a universal relation whose tuples extend over all of the attributes. For example, we mentioned in Section 17.1 how, in our $CTHRSG$ database, we might wish to imagine that a universal relation exists, even if there are no students yet registered. The solution proposed was to pad out $CTHR$ tuples with nulls in the S and G components. A more extreme example is seen if we consider what happens should the database also include attributes A and D, representing alumni and their donations. Even after students have registered and been given grades, it makes no sense to think of tuples over all eight attributes; we would expect at most tuples over $CTHRSG$, with nulls in AD, or tuples over AD with nulls in $CTHRSG$.

It is natural to expect that if R is a relation scheme, then the window $[R]$ will contain at least the tuples of relation R. Thus, we may regard any relation over all the attributes as a candidate universal relation, provided it has at least the relation for R in the components of its tuples that correspond to the attributes of R. Under reasonable assumptions, there is essentially a unique minimal candidate universal relation. We can formalize this notion of a minimal candidate through the concepts of "weak instances," which are the candidate universal relations mentioned above, and "representative instances," which are minimal candidates. We require a series of definitions.

Total Projections

To get at the notion of a weak instance, let us regard a universal relation as a set of tuples with (possible) null values, and define the *total projection* of a universal relation u onto set of attributes X to be[5]

$$\{\mu[X] \mid \mu \text{ is in } u \text{ and } \mu \text{ has no nulls in the components for } X\}$$

We denote the total projection by $\pi\!\downarrow_X(u)$.

Example 17.5: Let the universal set of attributes be $ABCD$, and let the universal relation be $u = \{abc\perp_1, \ e\perp_2 fg\}$. Then $\pi\!\downarrow_{AB}(u) = \{ab\}$, $\pi\!\downarrow_{AC}(u) = \{ac, \ ef\}$, and $\pi\!\downarrow_{BD}(u) = \emptyset$. $\square$

Weak Instances

Given a database with relation schemes $R_1, \ldots, R_n$ and relations $r_1, \ldots, r_n$, a *weak instance* for this database is any relation u over all of the attributes, such that for each i, $\pi\!\downarrow_{R_i}(u) \supseteq r_i$. That is, u's total projection onto each relation scheme includes at least those tuples the relation for that scheme has.

Generally, we are not interested in just any weak instance for a database. Rather, there are dependencies that hold in the various relations, and these must also apply to the weak instance. We say that u is a *weak instance with respect to set of dependencies* $\mathcal{D}$ if u is a weak instance in the sense above, and u satisfies all the dependencies in $\mathcal{D}$. Note that dependencies apply to nulls, as well as to nonnull symbols.

Example 17.6: Let our database scheme consist of relation schemes AB, BC, and AC, with relations $\{ab\}$, $\{bc_1\}$, and $\{ac_2\}$, respectively. If there are no dependencies, the universal relation of Figure 17.2(a) serves as a weak instance. In fact, its total projection onto each relation scheme consists of exactly the tuple in the corresponding relation.

However, suppose we are given the dependencies $\mathcal{D} = \{A \rightarrow C, \ B \rightarrow C\}$. Then the functional dependency $A \rightarrow C$ tells us that in Figure 17.2(a), $\perp_1$ must be the same as c_2. Thus, our candidate weak instance becomes that shown in Figure 17.2(b). Now, we can apply the functional dependency $B \rightarrow C$ to infer that $c_1 = c_2$. However, while it makes sense to equate nulls to other values, we cannot equate the concrete values c_1 and c_2.

We conclude that there is no weak instance with respect to $\mathcal{D}$ for this database. In proof, any such database must surely contain the three tuples of Figure 17.2(a), perhaps with nulls replaced by concrete values; otherwise, one of its total projections is missing a tuple that has to be there. However, we just argued that any universal relation containing these three tuples must violate one of the dependencies of $\mathcal{D}$. $\square$

---

[5] Recall that $\mu[X]$ means the components of tuple μ for the attributes in set X.

A	B	C
a	b	$\perp_1$
$\perp_2$	b	c_1
a	$\perp_3$	c_2

(a)

A	B	C
a	b	c_2
$\perp_2$	b	c_1
a	$\perp_3$	c_2

(b)

Figure 17.2 Creating a weak instance.

Independent Schemes

It is desirable that the problem illustrated in Example 17.6 not occur. We would like to know that, whenever we have relations satisfying the given dependencies $\mathcal{D}$, as do the relations in that example, there is at least one weak instance for those relations. A relation scheme is called *independent* if, whenever the relations satisfy $\mathcal{D}$, there is a weak instance with respect to $\mathcal{D}$.

In the next section, we shall consider "unique" schemes. These are guaranteed not only to be independent, but to have a simple way of computing window functions.

Tuple Subsumption

Weak instances represent all of the data in the database, but they can represent much more; for example, a weak instance can have tuples using symbols that do not appear anywhere in the database. To avoid this irrelevancy, we shall define a "representative instance" for a database, with respect to a set of dependencies $\mathcal{D}$, to be a weak instance that contains only the facts found in all weak instances. To make the notion of a representative instance precise, we need to talk about "subsumption" of tuples.

Tuple μ *subsumes* tuple ν if there is a symbol mapping h that is the identity on all nonnull symbols, and such that $h(\nu) = \mu$. We shall call h a *subsumption mapping*. Note that subsumption mappings go from the less specific tuple (one with more nulls) to the more specific tuple. More generally, we say that a set of tuples S subsumes set of tuples T if there is a subsumption mapping h that maps each tuple of T to a tuple of S. For example, $\{ab\perp_1, \perp_2bc, a\perp_3c\}$ subsumes $\{a\perp_1\perp_2, \perp_3bc\}$, but does not subsume $\{a\perp_1\perp_2, \perp_1\perp_3c\}$, because there is no consistent way to map the two occurrences of $\perp_1$, while also mapping a and c

to themselves.

Representative Instances

A *representative instance* for a given database and set of dependencies $\mathcal{D}$ is a weak instance w such that every weak instance for the same database and dependencies subsumes w. If the scheme is not independent with respect to $\mathcal{D}$, then there are no weak instances (at least for some databases), and therefore no representative instances. However, if the scheme is independent, then at least one representative instance exists.

Note that by definition, all representative instances for a database and dependencies must subsume each other. It is thus easy to show that the total projection of any representative instance, onto a given set of attributes, is the same. Thus, if we take the window function to be the total projection of a representative instance, it does not matter which representative instance we choose.

The following algorithm, which generalizes the construction given in Example 17.6, shows how to construct one representative instance, for a broad class of dependencies. Often, the representative instance constructed by this algorithm is not "smallest," in the sense that it contains tuples that are subsumed by others. Nevertheless, the relation computed by this algorithm is usually referred to as "the" representative instance. We discuss cleansing the representative instance of subsumed tuples after giving the algorithm.

Algorithm 17.1: Construction of the Representative Instance.

INPUT: A database scheme consisting of relation schemes $R_1, \ldots, R_n$, relations $r_1, \ldots, r_n$ for these schemes, respectively, and a set of full tuple- and equality-generating dependencies $\mathcal{D}$.[6]

OUTPUT: The representative instance for the relations with respect to $\mathcal{D}$, or an indication that none exists.

METHOD: We begin by constructing a candidate universal relation like that of Figure 17.2(a) by taking each tuple of the database relations and padding it with nulls that appear nowhere else, to make a tuple over the full set of attributes $A_1, \ldots, A_m$. Formally, for each tuple μ in some r_i, we construct ν over the scheme $A_1 \cdots A_m$ by

1. If A_j is an attribute of relation scheme R_i, then $\nu[A_j] = \mu[A_j]$.
2. If A_j is not an attribute of R_i, then $\nu[A_j]$ is a null symbol that appears nowhere else.

Now we "chase" the candidate universal relation.[7] That is, we apply the de-

---

[6] Recall from Section 7.11 (Volume I) that these include all functional dependencies and multivalued dependencies as special cases.

[7] The chase is another concept for which the reader should consult Section 7.11.

pendencies in $\mathcal{D}$ to infer new tuples (if they are tuple-generating dependencies) or to infer the equality of symbols (if they are equality-generating dependencies), until no changes are possible. If we wish to equate a null to a nonnull symbol, we replace the null by the nonnull. To equate two nulls, we replace one by the other; it does not matter which. In all cases, "replace a symbol" means that all occurrences of the symbol are replaced. If we are ever forced to equate two distinct nonnull symbols, then we conclude that there is no representative instance. In this case, it must be that the database scheme is not independent with respect to $\mathcal{D}$.

As we chase, eventually one of two things will happen. Either we try to equate two distinct nonnull symbols, in which case no representative instance exists, or we reach a relation where no new tuples can be added and no more equalities can be established. The reason we must converge eventually is that full tuple-generating or equality-generating dependencies never create new symbols. Thus, we cannot indefinitely add new tuples or equate symbols; a formal proof appears in Theorem 7.12 (Volume I). The resulting relation is the output of the algorithm. $\square$

Optionally, we may perform subsumption of tuples, to simplify the representative instance without changing its total projections. If the dependencies of $\mathcal{D}$ are all equality-generating dependencies, such as functional dependencies, then it suffices to look for tuples ν that are subsumed by another tuple μ, and delete ν. Note that deleting a tuple can never violate an equality-generating dependency. The reader may show as an exercise that if we delete subsumed tuples, in any order, until no longer possible, we reach a unique relation that is a representative instance, and has as few tuples as any other representative instance for the same database and dependencies.

When there are tuple-generating dependencies involved, the process is combinatorially explosive, and we must look for any subset of the constructed relation that subsumes the entire relation and satisfies the dependencies. The reader should remember that simplification by subsumption is optional, because total projections cannot be affected by deleting subsumed tuples.

It is in general convenient to perform subsumption as we chase, but we must be careful not to get caught in a cycle where we generate new tuples and then subsume them. We also must be careful not to delete prematurely a tuple that is subsumed, but has a null that appears more than once. Such a tuple may participate in a dependency, and the subsuming tuple may not be able to substitute.

Example 17.7: Let us see how the universal relation of Figure 17.1 is derived from the facts that it apparently represents,

1.   Deadwood teaches CS101.
2.   CS101 meets Monday 9AM in room 222.

3. CS101 meets Wednesday 9AM in room 333.
4. CS101 meets Friday 9AM in room 222.
5. Weenie is taking CS101 and getting a B+.
6. Grind is taking CS101 and getting C.

The universal relation in question turns out to be the representative instance constructed by Algorithm 17.1, with subsumption of tuples performed where possible. In the following construction, we shall perform subsumption as early as we can, but the reader should remember that there are situations where subsumption must be deferred until we are finished with the chase.

To begin, we take the six facts above, and pad them with nulls to form the candidate universal relation, as shown in Figure 17.3(a). In Examples 7.15 and 7.18 we found that the following five functional dependencies and one multivalued dependency reasonably can be expected to hold in this database, and that they imply all of the other dependencies that are plausible,

$$C \rightarrow T \qquad CS \rightarrow G \qquad TH \rightarrow R$$
$$RH \rightarrow C \qquad SH \rightarrow R \qquad C \twoheadrightarrow HR$$

To begin the chase, we can apply $C \rightarrow T$ to infer that all of the nulls in the column for T must be Deadwood. Then, we can apply the multivalued dependency $C \twoheadrightarrow HR$ to add a seventh tuple with the HR components of tuple (2) and the $CTSG$ components of tuple (5). The universal relation now looks like Figure 17.3(b).

Now, we see that tuple (7) subsumes (1), (2), and (5), because each of the latter agree with (7) except in positions where (7) has a concrete value and the other tuple has a null. Thus, we simplify by eliminating (1), (2), and (5), as shown in Figure 17.3(c). Similarly, we can apply $C \twoheadrightarrow HR$ followed by subsumption, to tuples (3) and (7) and obtain a tuple that combines the facts for Wednesday with the facts for Weenie; then we do the same with tuples (4) and (7) to combine the Friday facts and the Weenie facts. The universal relation now looks like Figure 17.3(d).

As the last sequence of steps, we can apply $C \twoheadrightarrow HR$ to tuple (6), once with each of (7), (8), and (9), to get tuples in which the Grind facts appear with the Monday, Wednesday, and Friday facts. These new tuples all subsume (6), and the result is the universal relation that we first saw in Figure 17.1. In this example, we have completely eliminated the nulls. However, there is no guarantee that we can always do so. Tuples with nulls in the universal relation still participate in the windows of those sets of attributes where they have no nulls. $\square$

Theorem 17.1: Algorithm 17.1 computes a representative instance.

Proof: First, we show that the algorithm produces a weak instance, if it succeeds. The initial relation is clearly a weak instance, since it is constructed from all tuples of all relations of the database; however, this weak instance

	C	T	H	R	S	G
1)	CS101	Deadwood	$\perp_1$	$\perp_2$	$\perp_3$	$\perp_4$
2)	CS101	$\perp_5$	M9	222	$\perp_6$	$\perp_7$
3)	CS101	$\perp_8$	W9	333	$\perp_9$	$\perp_{10}$
4)	CS101	$\perp_{11}$	F9	222	$\perp_{12}$	$\perp_{13}$
5)	CS101	$\perp_{14}$	$\perp_{15}$	$\perp_{16}$	Weenie	B+
6)	CS101	$\perp_{17}$	$\perp_{18}$	$\perp_{19}$	Grind	C

(a)

	C	T	H	R	S	G
1)	CS101	Deadwood	$\perp_1$	$\perp_2$	$\perp_3$	$\perp_4$
2)	CS101	Deadwood	M9	222	$\perp_6$	$\perp_7$
3)	CS101	Deadwood	W9	333	$\perp_9$	$\perp_{10}$
4)	CS101	Deadwood	F9	222	$\perp_{12}$	$\perp_{13}$
5)	CS101	Deadwood	$\perp_{15}$	$\perp_{16}$	Weenie	B+
6)	CS101	Deadwood	$\perp_{18}$	$\perp_{19}$	Grind	C
7)	CS101	Deadwood	M9	222	Weenie	B+

(b)

	C	T	H	R	S	G
3)	CS101	Deadwood	W9	333	$\perp_9$	$\perp_{10}$
4)	CS101	Deadwood	F9	222	$\perp_{12}$	$\perp_{13}$
6)	CS101	Deadwood	$\perp_{18}$	$\perp_{19}$	Grind	C
7)	CS101	Deadwood	M9	222	Weenie	B+

(c)

	C	T	H	R	S	G
6)	CS101	Deadwood	$\perp_{18}$	$\perp_{19}$	Grind	C
7)	CS101	Deadwood	M9	222	Weenie	B+
8)	CS101	Deadwood	W9	333	Weenie	B+
9)	CS101	Deadwood	F9	222	Weenie	B+

(d)

Figure 17.3 Constructing a representative instance.

probably does not satisfy the dependencies. Application of a tuple- or equality-generating dependency does not remove any tuple from any total projection, since we always replace nulls by nonnull symbols. Thus, at each stage of the chase, the current universal relation is a weak instance, and hence so is u, the relation that is output of the algorithm.

Now, we must show that u is a representative instance, that is, any weak instance w satisfying $\mathcal{D}$ subsumes u, and to do so, we follow the argument of Example 17.6. That is, we show by induction on the number of steps of the chase performed during Algorithm 17.1, that w subsumes the current weak instance. Let u_i be the weak instance constructed by Algorithm 17.1 after i chase steps.

The basis, that w subsumes u_0 is simple. The initially constructed weak instance, u_0, contains only tuples μ that are database tuples padded with nulls that appear nowhere else. Any weak instance w must have a tuple ν that agrees with μ on its nonnull symbols, so we may define subsumption mapping h to have $h(\mu) = \nu$. As the nulls of μ appear nowhere else, h is defined consistently when we consider all tuples μ in u_0.

For the induction, suppose h is a subsumption mapping from u_i to w, and the next chase step applies a tuple-generating dependency with hypothesis rows H and conclusion row c. Then there is some symbol mapping τ such that $\tau(H)$ is some subset v of u_i, and $\tau(c)$ is a tuple μ not in u_i. Thus, $u_{i+1} = u_i \cup \{\mu\}$. Now, $h\big(\tau(H)\big)$ is $h(v)$, a subset of w. Since w satisfies $\mathcal{D}$, it must be that $h\big(\tau(c)\big)$, which is $h(\mu)$, is in w. Thus, h is also a subsumption mapping from u_{i+1} to w. We leave the remaining part, where u_{i+1} is constructed by an equality-generating dependency, as an exercise. In this part, we may find that the subsumption mapping h must be changed, and we must consider the possibility that we reach a contradiction, and no representative instance exists. $\square$

The Representative Instance Window Function

If we take the representative instance as our vision of the universal relation, then the correct window function to use is the total projection of the representative instance onto the set of attributes in question, that is, $[X] = \pi\!\downarrow_X(u)$, where u is the representative instance constructed from the given database and dependencies by Algorithm 17.1. We call this particular window function $[X]_{RI}$, if we need to distinguish it from other possible window functions.

We are now faced with the problem of computing $[X]_{RI}$, given the database. Algorithm 17.1 provides a solution in principle, but the idea of physically constructing the representative instance is not very appealing. What we really want, for each X, is an expression of relational algebra that maps the database to $[X]_{RI}$. For some relation schemes with some dependencies, that is not possible; rather, one can prove that no such expression exists. In other cases, the expressions exist and we can find them easily. For example, if a scheme is independent with respect to a collection of functional dependencies, then we can find such algebraic expressions. We shall consider an important special case of this class of schemes in the next section.

17.5 UNIQUE SCHEMES

We shall now give a condition on a database scheme and its dependencies that offers us a simple way to compute the representative-instance window function for such schemes. The definition is a technical one, but we shall see its intuitive meaning in the example that follows. We say a database scheme $\{R_1, \ldots, R_n\}$ is *unique* with respect to a set of dependencies F if

1. All of the dependencies in F are functional dependencies, and what is more, they are *key dependencies*, meaning that we can partition F into $F_1, \ldots, F_n$, such that each dependency $X \to Y$ in F_i has $XY = R_i$. That is, the dependency asserts X is a key for R_i.

2. The following holds for each $i = 1, 2, \ldots, n$. Let $G = F - F_i$, that is, all the dependencies except for the key dependencies of R_i. Then for no $X \to Y$ in F_i and for no $j \neq i$ does R_j^+ include both all the attributes of X and one or more attributes of Y, when the closure of set of attributes R_j is taken with respect to the dependencies of G only.[8]

Example 17.8: Consider the scheme $\{AB, BC, CD, AD\}$ with the key dependencies $F = \{A \to B,\ B \to C,\ C \to D,\ A \to D\}$. This scheme does not obey the uniqueness condition. In proof, let R_i in condition (2) above be AD, so $F_i = \{A \to D\}$. Let R_j be AB. Then

$$G = F - \{A \to D\} = \{A \to B,\ B \to C,\ C \to D\}$$

Thus, $R_j^+ = ABCD$. Since $ABCD$ includes both the left side of $A \to D$ and an attribute on the right side, we conclude this scheme is not unique.

We can see the importance of the uniqueness property by noting what can happen as we compute the representative instance when a scheme is not unique. Suppose that the relations for AB, BC, and CD are $\{ab\}$, $\{bc\}$, and $\{cd\}$, respectively, while the relation for AD is empty. In Figure 17.4(a) we see the initial universal relation for this database constructed by Algorithm 17.1, and in Figure 17.4(b) we see the result of chasing it with the given functional dependencies. The total projection of Figure 17.4(b) onto AD is $\{ad\}$. That is, even though the relation AD is empty, the scheme and functional dependencies imply some tuples in $[AD]_{RI}$. In addition to making little sense, the presence of such tuples can make the scheme not be independent; that is, the relation for AD could have been $\{ad_1\}$, which would force the universal relation to violate the functional dependency $A \to D$, even though none of the database relations violated that dependency. $\square$

---

[8] Recall that U^+, the closure of a set of attributes U with respect to G, is the set of attributes A such that $U \to A$ follows logically from G. See Section 7.3 of Volume I for details and an algorithm to compute U^+.

A	B	C	D
a	b	$\perp_1$	$\perp_2$
$\perp_3$	b	c	$\perp_4$
$\perp_5$	$\perp_6$	c	d

(a) Initial universal relation

A	B	C	D
a	b	c	d
$\perp_3$	b	c	d
$\perp_5$	$\perp_6$	c	d

(b) Representative instance.

Figure 17.4 Constructing a representative instance for Example 17.8.

Extension Joins

Suppose we are given a database scheme $\{R_1, \ldots, R_n\}$ and a set of key dependencies F. Let s be a relation over set of attributes S, and let R_i be one of the relation schemes. We say $S \bowtie R_i$ is an *extension join* if $S \cap R_i$ is a key for R_i. We also call a sequence of relation schemes $R_{i_1}, \ldots, R_{i_k}$ an *extension-join sequence* if for each $j > 1$, $(R_{i_1} \cup \cdots \cup R_{i_{j-1}}) \bowtie R_{i_j}$ is an extension join.

Example 17.9: Let our database scheme be $\{AB, AC, BCD, DE\}$ with key dependencies $\{A \rightarrow B, \ A \rightarrow C, \ BC \rightarrow D, \ D \rightarrow E\}$. The sequence

$$AB, \ AC, \ BCD, \ DE$$

is an extension-join sequence. The first join in the sequence is $AB \bowtie BC$, and the intersection of the schemes, which is B, is a key for BC. The second join is $ABC \bowtie BCD$, and the intersection, BC, is a key for BCD. Finally, the last join is $ABCD \bowtie DE$, and again the intersection, D, is a key for DE. $\square$

One useful property of an extension join sequence is that the sizes of the results of the successive joins form a nonincreasing sequence. That is, the presence of the functional dependency each time we join S with R_i tells us that each tuple of S can be "extended" with at most one tuple of R_i. The following theorem describes the importance of extension joins for computing the windows defined by representative instances. We omit the proof, which can be found in Sagiv [1983].

Theorem 17.2: Suppose we are given a unique scheme with respect to some set of key dependencies F. Then

1.   The scheme is independent with respect to F, so the representative instance for any database exists.

2. For every database, the total projection of the representative instance onto some set of attributes X equals the union of the relations formed from extension-join sequences that include all of the attributes of X. $\square$

Moreover, we can eliminate some extension-join sequences from the union, because they are subsumed by others. We say an extension-join sequence $S_1, \ldots, S_k$ is *subsumed* by another extension-join sequence $T_1, \ldots, T_m$ if for every $i = 1, 2, \ldots m$, T_i is one of the S_j's. That is, a set of relations subsumes any of its supersets. We can eliminate from the union of Theorem 17.2 any extension-join sequence that is subsumed by another member of the union. The reason is that whenever $X \subseteq R$, we have $\pi\downarrow_X(R) \supseteq \pi\downarrow_X(R \bowtie S)$ for any S. That is, once we have all of the attributes of X in the scheme of a join, joining with additional relations can only knock tuples out of the total projection onto X (if they are dangling with respect to the join $R \bowtie S$); joining can never add any tuples. As a consequence, we really only need the smallest extension-join sequences that include all of the attributes of X, if we want $[X]_{RI}$.

In fact, we can show that at the worst, we need in the union of Theorem 17.2 one extension join sequence that begins with any particular relation. We mentioned that the sizes of relations never increase as we perform the joins of an extension-join sequence. Thus, the number of tuples we must construct to find $[X]_{RI}$ for unique schemes is no greater than the product of the size of the database (sum of the number of tuples in each relation) times the number of relations. If we use indices to facilitate the joins, the time to compute $[X]_{RI}$ is bounded above by roughly this quantity.

That would still not be acceptable in most situations, although if the query calls for the entire window, there is little else we could do, whether or not a universal-relation system is used. Typical queries will call for selections that greatly restrict the set of tuples from the window that we want. If so, a query optimizer can push the selections into the extension joins. Then, we never materialize the entire window, thus achieving the same performance·as a standard DBMS with the same query optimizer.

Example 17.10: Let us reconsider the scheme of Example 17.9. The following are all of the extension-join sequences:

AB	AC	BCD
DE	$AB \bowtie AC$	$AC \bowtie AB$
$BCD \bowtie DE$	$AB \bowtie AC \bowtie BCD$	$AC \bowtie AB \bowtie BCD$
	$AB \bowtie AC \bowtie BCD \bowtie DE$	$AC \bowtie AB \bowtie BCD \bowtie DE$

If we desire $[BC]_{RI}$ there are two sequences, BCD and $AB \bowtie AC$, that together subsume all of the other sequences that contain both attributes B and C. Thus, $[BC]_{RI} = \pi_{BC}(BCD) \cup \pi_{BC}(AB \bowtie AC)$.

For $[AE]_{RI}$, only the last two sequences include both A and E. Either subsumes the other. Thus, $[AE]_{RI} = \pi_{AE}(AB \bowtie AC \bowtie BCD \bowtie DE)$. $\square$

17.6 THE OBJECT STRUCTURE OF UNIVERSAL RELATIONS

Suppose we were to write a domain-relational-calculus expression to describe the tuples that belong in some universal relation. We would find that in writing the expression, we had to invent certain predicates. These predicates would involve subsets of the attributes, and those subsets indicate our intuitive notion of the fundamental relationships in the database. The following example illustrates this point.

Example 17.11: The contents of the universal $CTHRSG$ relation could be described as

$$\{CTHRSG \mid T \text{ teaches course } C, \text{ and}$$
$$\text{course } C \text{ meets in room } R \text{ at hour } H, \text{ and} \qquad (17.3)$$
$$\text{student } S \text{ is getting grade } G \text{ in course } C\}$$

In (17.3) we see that there are three fundamental relationships dictating the structure of the universal relation. One is the relationship between C and T, that is, between courses and teachers, which we termed "teaches" above. A second is among C, R, and H, which we expressed as "meets in $\cdots$ at." The third is between C, S, and G, and is expressed by "getting $\cdots$ in."

It is important to note how our expression of the universal relation in the form (17.3) reflects our understanding of how attributes relate. For example, since we said that one fundamental relationship involved all three attributes course, hour, and room, it is implied that we cannot express this relationship by factoring it into two. In contrast, if we had said "C meets in room R and C is held at hour H," then we would be presenting a different view of the world, one in which each course meets in the same room all of the time. However, as is apparent from Figure 17.1, we believe that courses can meet in different rooms at different hours. Let us emphasize that there is no way to determine which viewpoint is correct; we should simply be aware that there is an opportunity to reflect different assumptions about the "real world" by phrasing the set-former defining the universal relation in different ways.

The description of the universal relation by a set former makes sense even when the fundamental relationships are not all connected. For example, we could add components A and D, representing alumni and donations, and add the clause "and A gives donation D" to (17.3). Then, tuples of the universal relation would each be a $CTHRSG$ fact paired with an unrelated AD fact, in all possible ways.[9] □

---

[9] It is useful to compare this view of the universal relation with that provided by the representative instance. In the latter approach, $CTHRSG$ tuples were padded with nulls in the AD components, and vice-versa. Here, we can get nonempty windows like $[CA]$, where each course would be paired with each alumnus, while with the representative instance approach, $[CA]_{RI}$ would be empty. Since we should not be asking such queries, it matters little which we choose.

The fundamental relationships in the set-former description of a universal relation have traditionally been called *objects*, and we shall adopt this term here. However, the reader should be aware that there is no relationship between this notion of "object" and the objects "of object-oriented" database systems.

Example 17.11 can be generalized by saying that the current value of the universal relation is to be expressed as

$$\{A_1 \cdots A_n \mid p_1(O_1) \wedge \cdots \wedge p_k(O_k)\} \tag{17.4}$$

In (17.4), the p_i's are predicates about sets of attributes O_i; the O_i's are what we called *objects* above. $A_1, \ldots, A_n$ are all of the attributes, and each argument of a predicate p_i is one of these attributes that is a member of O_i. For example, in (17.3), O_1 would be CT, and $p_1(C, T)$ is "teaches." O_2 is CHR, and $p_2(C, H, R)$ is "meets in $\cdots$ at." Finally, O_3 is CSG, and $p_3(C, S, G)$ is "getting $\cdots$ in."

In general, we must assume that no predicate can be broken into the conjunction of two predicates; that is, we cannot write $p(O) = q(O') \wedge r(O'')$, where O' and O'' are both proper subsets of O. We shall also assume, for reasons that will become clear when we talk about interpreting queries, that each object is a (possibly proper) subset of a relation scheme.

Database Scheme Design with Objects

Often, we can write down the objects directly, without thinking of a domain-calculus expression such as (17.3). For example, to develop an object structure directly from an entity/relationship diagram, we may do the following.

1. Start by listing all attributes of all entity sets. When we do so, we must be careful not to confuse attributes of two entity sets by giving them the same name. Rather, distinct attributes must always be given distinct names.

2. Select the key for each entity set. For each nonkey attribute A of that entity set, there is an object consisting of A and the attribute(s) of the key.

3. For each relationship, there is an object that includes the key attribute(s) of each of the connected entity sets. The exception is when an entity set participates more than once in the relationship. In that case, another copy of the key attribute(s) for the entity set must be made, with distinct names. Also, create new copies of the nonkey attributes for the entity set, and relate them to the new key attributes, as in (2).

Example 17.12: The following is an example of the exception in (3) above. Suppose we have the entity/relationship diagram for parenthood; it appeared in Figure 2.1(b) of Volume I, and is reproduced here as Figure 17.5(a), with an additional attribute AGE for PERSONS. The entity set PERSONS, with key attribute NAME, participates twice in the relationship PARENT_OF. We make two copies of NAME — call them PARENT and CHILD, and two copies of AGE, called CH_AGE and PAR_AGE. The relationship PARENT_OF is represented by the CHILD–PARENT object, and each of these attributes forms an object with its corresponding AGE attribute, according to rule (2). The resulting object structure is shown in Figure 17.5(b). □

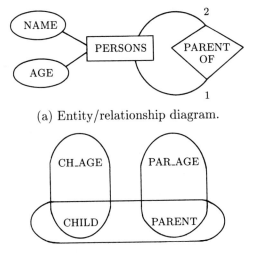

(a) Entity/relationship diagram.

(b) Object structure.

Figure 17.5 Splitting attributes.

Example 17.13: For a more substantial design, let us convert the YVCB database of Figure 2.2 to an object structure. For simplicity, we shall eliminate some of the attributes, namely, department numbers, item numbers, dates for orders, quantities of items, and customer balances. We are left with the following eleven attributes.

1. E (Employee name).
2. S (Salary of an employee).
3. D (Department name).
4. M (Manager of a department).
5. I (Item name).
6. P (Price of an item charged by a particular supplier).
7. Su (Supplier name).
8. Sa (Address of a supplier).
9. $O\#$ (Order number).
10. C (Customer name).
11. Ca (Address of a customer).

Notice that we use different attributes for names of employees, departments, customers, and suppliers. We also distinguish between addresses for customers and suppliers.

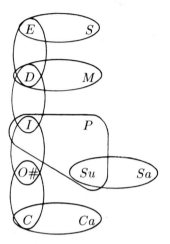

Figure 17.6 Object structure for YVCB database.

The object structure of these attributes is shown in Figure 17.6. For example, the object ES represents the fundamental connection between an employee and his salary attribute. The ED object represents the relationship WORKS_IN between employees and departments The object $SuIP$, which is the only one here with more than two attributes, represents the ternary relationship SUP-PLIES of Figure 2.2, among suppliers, items, and prices. □

Join-Dependency Characterization of Universal Relations

There is a straightforward and important relationship between join dependencies and database structures defined by objects. Recall from Section 7.11 (Volume I) that a join dependency is a kind of tuple-generating dependency that says the join of several relations is lossless. Formally, the join dependency $\bowtie(R_1, \ldots, R_k)$ holds for a relation scheme R if for every relation r over R, the join of the projections of r onto the R_i's equals r itself; that is,

$$r = \pi_{R_1}(r) \bowtie \cdots \bowtie \pi_{R_k}(r)$$

The following theorem tells us when a relation can be expressed as a set former like (17.4).

Theorem 17.3: A relation is constructible by Equation (17.4) from some values of the p_i's if and only if it satisfies the join dependency on the objects, that is, the join dependency $\bowtie(O_1, \ldots, O_k)$.

Proof: *If:* Suppose r satisfies the join dependency $\bowtie(O_1, \ldots, O_k)$. Let us define $r_i = \pi_{O_i}(r)$. If p_i is chosen to be true for exactly the tuples in r_i, then the relation defined by (17.4) is $r_1 \bowtie \cdots \bowtie r_k$, which we shall call s. Since r satisfies the join dependency, and $r_i = \pi_{O_i}(r)$, we know that $r = s$. Thus, r is expressible as a universal relation satisfying (17.4).

Only if: Conversely, suppose r is constructed by (17.4) from some predicates $p_1(O_1), \ldots, p_k(O_k)$ Then $r_i = \pi_{O_i}(r)$ must be a subset of those tuples for which p_i is true. It follows that $r_1 \bowtie \cdots \bowtie r_k$ is a subset of r. But it cannot be a proper subset, by Lemma 7.5(a). Thus r satisfies $\bowtie(O_1, \ldots, O_k)$. $\square$

Starting only with the assumption that the universal relation could be defined by predicates about the various attributes, we have proven, in Theorem 17.3, a surprising condition that appears to place a lot of structure on the universal relation. Of course, in the worst case, there could be but a single predicate over all of the attributes, in which case Theorem 17.3 says nothing. A key assumption, which is generally true in practice, is that real-world databases do not have a trivial structure. Rather, there are many small objects, so Theorem 17.3 generally places significant structure on typical databases.

Theorem 17.3 also enables us to deduce many multivalued dependencies that hold in the universal relation — the multivalued dependencies that follow logically from the join dependency on the objects. In fact, it appears that almost every full multivalued dependency holding in reality either follows from this join dependency or follows from a given functional dependency trivially by axiom A7 (Section 7.9), which says that $X \to Y$ implies $X \twoheadrightarrow Y$.

As seen from Examples 17.12 and 17.13, we can represent an object structure by a hypergraph in which the nodes are attributes and the hyperedges are the objects. By Theorem 17.3, we can represent the join dependency on the objects by the same hypergraph. The next theorem shows how to deduce multivalued dependencies from a join dependency by inspecting its hypergraph.

Theorem 17.4: Let $X_1, \ldots, X_k$ be a set of objects, and Y any subset of

$$X_1 \cup \cdots \cup X_k$$

Then $Y \twoheadrightarrow Z$ follows logically from join dependency $j = \bowtie(X_1, \ldots, X_k)$, where Z is disjoint from Y, if and only if Z is the union of one or more of the connected components of the hypergraph of j when the nodes in Y are deleted.

Proof: We shall use the chase algorithm of Section 7.11 to verify that the multivalued dependency $Y \twoheadrightarrow Z$ follows from j. In the chase test, we must begin with rows

Y	Z	$U - YZ$
$a_1 \cdots a_m$	$a_{m+1} \cdots a_p$	$b_{p+1} \cdots b_n$
$a_1 \cdots a_m$	$b_{m+1} \cdots b_p$	$a_{p+1} \cdots a_n$

where U is the complete set of attributes, and we must try to deduce $a_1 \cdots a_n$.

Recall that j can be represented as a generalized dependency in which there is one hypothesis row for each X_i, and we may suppose that row has distinguished symbol a_l in the lth column if the lth attribute is in X_i, and a symbol appearing nowhere else otherwise. The conclusion row is $a_1 \cdots a_n$. We use this generalized dependency to produce the desired row from the hypothesis rows for $Y \twoheadrightarrow Z$ above in one step. To do so, we use the symbol mapping that is the identity on the a_i's and maps symbols appearing only once as needed. We can thus map the row for any X_i that is a subset of YZ to the first hypothesis row. If X_i is not a subset of YZ, then since Z is a union of connected components when Y is removed, it must be that X_i is disjoint from Z, and we can therefore map its row to the second of the hypothesis rows for $Y \twoheadrightarrow Z$.

We have thus proved that all of the multivalued dependencies in which the left side is Y and the right side is the union of some of the connected components of the hypergraph of j, with Y removed, follow logically from j. The converse portion of Theorem 17.4, that no multivalued dependency follows logically from j unless it is one of these, or it follows logically from one of these, is true, but we leave it as an exercise for the reader. $\square$

Example 17.14: We may interpret Figure 17.6 as the hypergraph for the join dependency

$$\bowtie(ES,\ ED,\ DM,\ DI,\ SuIP,\ SuSa,\ O\#I,\ O\#C,\ CaC)$$

If we delete I, the hypergraph splits into three parts: $ESDM$, $SuSaP$, and $O\#CaC$. Thus, the multivalued dependencies $I \twoheadrightarrow ESDM$, $I \twoheadrightarrow SuSaP$, and $I \twoheadrightarrow O\#CaC$ hold. It happens that the multivalued dependency $I \twoheadrightarrow D$ also holds, but not because of the join dependency. Rather, it holds because $I \to D$ may be assumed; that is, the entity/relationship diagram of Figure 2.2 made the relationship CARRIES be many-to-one from ITEMS to DEPTS. Thus, the dependency basis for I is

$$I \twoheadrightarrow D\ |\ ESM\ |\ SuSaP\ |\ O\#CaC$$

As another example, suppose we delete both I and C from Figure 17.6. Then $O\#$ becomes a connected component by itself, and we conclude the multivalued dependency $IC \twoheadrightarrow O\#$. Intuitively, this dependency says that, given an item and a customer, there is an associated set of orders — the orders the customer placed that include the item. $\square$

17.7 A WINDOW FUNCTION USING OBJECTS

There is a simple window function using objects that makes sense when the object-structure hypergraph is acyclic, as is the YVCB hypergraph of Figure 17.6, for example. In the next section, we shall discuss the System/U query interpretation algorithm, which generalizes the simple algorithm and often gives a more appropriate interpretation of queries when the object structure is a cyclic hypergraph.

Our window function is based on the assumption that a query must be applied to a relation constructed from the actual relations in the database by a lossless join.[10] The motivation for this assumption, as discussed at the beginning of Section 7.4, is that if we view relations in the database, say AB and BC, as representing an ABC relation, but the join of AB and BC is not lossless, then some relations r and s over AB and BC, respectively, will be the projection of two or more different relations over ABC. In that case, it is not clear that our database represents a specific relation over ABC at all, so trying to answer queries about an ABC relation may lead to ambiguities that cannot be resolved.

Fortunately, we always know one way to get a lossless join that involves any set of attributes; the join of all objects must be lossless by Theorem 17.3. However, that join often is not the simplest or most efficient lossless join to take. Thus, we shall use the weak equivalence test developed in Section 14.3 to find a minimal weakly equivalent join. We are justified in using $\equiv_w$ rather than ordinary, or "strong," equivalence, in minimizing joins, because we assumed the query was about a universal relation, and weak equivalence is tailored to finding equivalent expressions exactly under the condition that all relations are assumed to be the projection of a universal relation.

The effect of this minimization is that objects not required to connect the attributes involved in the query are eliminated from the join. Because the relations of the actual database may contain dangling tuples, this minimization under weak equivalence may change the value computed, which seems to say that we should not use $\equiv_w$. However, as we argued in Section 14.3, we feel this change in value is for the better. That is, we do not wish to eliminate tuples from the answer if they are dangling only because of objects outside the portion of the hypergraph that connects attributes in the query.[11]

Example 17.15: Suppose we ask of the YVCB database of Figure 17.6 the query

```
retrieve (C)
    where I = "Brie"
```

---

[10] Note that the extension-join method for computing windows, discussed in Section 17.5, also produces only lossless joins; that is, every extension join is lossless by Theorem 7.5.

[11] Our decision to optimize under weak equivalence is one point that distinguishes a universal relation system from an ordinary relational database system with a view that is the join of all objects. In the latter arrangement, since ordinary relational database systems must optimize using strong equivalence, the terms of the join that represent objects not on paths between the attributes of the query could not be eliminated, for fear of a dangling tuple changing the value of the computed expression. Thus answering queries about this "universal view" would often be too time consuming to be feasible.

That is, print the names of the customers who ordered Brie. Using the above approach, we interpret this query as a request to take the join of the nine objects of Figure 17.6, select for $I =$ "Brie", and project onto C. This query has the tableau shown in Figure 17.7.

	E	S	D	M	I	P	Su	Sa	O#	C	Ca
										c	
1)	e	s									
2)	e		d								
3)			d	m							
4)			d		"Brie"						
5)					"Brie"	p	u				
6)							u	a			
7)					"Brie"				o		
8)									o	c	
9)										c	b

Figure 17.7 Tableau for query on YVCB universal relation.

Let us minimize this tableau under weak equivalence. To do so, we must find a containment mapping that sends all of the rows to as few rows as possible. Recall that we can regard a containment mapping either as a mapping on symbols that sends each row to a row and the summary to the summary, or as a mapping on rows that sends each symbol to only one symbol, and sends distinguished symbols to themselves. Also, the composition of containment mappings is a containment mapping, so we can eliminate rows in stages, rather than all at once, if we choose.

In the tableau of Figure 17.7, we may start by mapping row (1) to row (2). That is, we send symbol s to the anonymous symbol in the S column of row 2; e is mapped to e, and the anonymous symbols in row (1) are mapped to the corresponding anonymous symbols in row (2). Thus, row (1) is eliminated from the tableau, or put another way, the tableau of Figure 17.7 is weakly equivalent to itself with row (1) deleted.

Now, with only one occurrence of e remaining, in row (2), we can map row (2) to row (4), by sending e to the anonymous symbol in the E column of row (4). We can also map row (3) to row (4). The resulting tableau has only rows (4) through (9) of Figure 17.7.

In this tableau, there is only one occurrence of d, so row (4) maps to row (5); that is, row (4) has also been eliminated. Now, we map both rows (5) and (6), simultaneously, to (7). The symbol u is mapped to the anonymous

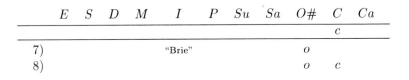

E	S	D	M	I	P	Su	Sa	O#	C	Ca
									c	
7)				"Brie"				o		
8)								o	c	

Figure 17.8 Minimized tableau.

symbol in the Su column, while a is mapped to the anonymous symbol in the Sa column. We are now down to rows (7), (8), and (9).

Finally, we can map row (9) to row (8), leaving the tableau of Figure 17.8. We cannot eliminate row (7), because the constant "Brie" cannot map to another symbol, and we cannot eliminate row (8), because the distinguished variable c cannot map to another symbol. Thus, our example query is answered as if it were

$$\pi_C\big(\sigma_{I=\text{"Brie"}}(O\#I \bowtie O\#C)\big) \qquad (17.5)$$

If objects $O\#I$ and $O\#C$ are relations of the database, (17.5) is the answer to the query. That is to say, the window constructed by this query-interpretation strategy is $[IC]_{Obj} = \pi_{IC}(O\#I \bowtie O\#C)$.[12] Recall that all objects are assumed to be subsets of relation schemes. If one or both of the objects $O\#I$ and $O\#C$ are nontrivial subsets of relation schemes, we would insert the appropriate projection into the window function, to turn the relation into an object. $\square$

Example 17.16: Let us take another example, one where there is more than one tuple variable. Consider the database consisting of ES and EM objects, where the attributes E, M, and S stand for employee, manager, and salary, respectively. A traditional query is to ask for the employees that make more than their managers, which can be expressed in the System/U query language as

```
retrieve (E)
    where M=t.E and S>t.S
```

That is, the blank tuple variable stands for the employee, and the tuple variable t for the manager. The condition $S > t.S$ says that the salary in the tuple for the employee is larger than the salary in the tuple for the manager, and the condition $M = t.E$ says that the employee represented by t is the manager of the employee represented by the blank tuple variable.

To represent the relationships between the two tuple variables, we take the Cartesian product of two copies of the universal relation, one corresponding to the blank, and the other to t. We shall distinguish the two copies by using

---

[12] We shall use $[\cdots]_{Obj}$ to distinguish the window function described in this section and generalized in the next section.

subscript 1 for the first and subscript 2 for the second. The reader should understand that the symbols E_1 and E_2 stand for the same attribute, E; the subscript serves only to distinguish different components of relations when both components have claim to the name E.

We obtain the first copy of the universal relation, which we denote $E_1 S_1 M_1$, by joining the two objects, which we also distinguish by subscript 1. We obtain the second copy similarly. Thus, the selection and projection of the query will be applied to the expression

$$(E_1 S_1 \bowtie E_1 M_1) \times (E_2 S_2 \bowtie E_2 M_2)$$

For the first selection condition, $M = t.E$, remember that an M standing alone, without a tuple variable, is associated with the blank tuple variable, that is, with subscript 1 above, and $t.E$ is associated with subscript 2. Thus the condition $M = t.E$ is expressed $M_1 = E_2$. Similarly, the second condition, $S > t.S$, is expressed $S_1 > S_2$. The projection onto E is really onto E_1, so we may write the expression for the complete query as

$$\pi_{E_1} \left(\sigma_{M_1=E_2 \wedge S_1>S_2} \left((E_1 S_1 \bowtie E_1 M_1) \times (E_2 S_2 \bowtie E_2 M_2) \right) \right)$$

The tableau for this query is shown in Figure 17.9. The selection condition $M_1 = E_2$ has been expressed by using the same symbol, m_1, to represent both the attributes M_1 and E_2 in the rows corresponding to objects with one of these attributes. The other selection condition, $S_1 > S_2$, is listed under the tableau as an additional condition that must be satisfied.

	E_1	S_1	M_1	E_2	S_2	M_2
	e_1					
1)	e_1	s_1				
2)	e_1		m_1			
3)				m_1	s_2	
4)				m_1		m_2

$$s_1 > s_2$$

Figure 17.9 Find the employees that earn more than their managers.

Not much can be done to reduce Figure 17.9. We can map row (4) to row (3) by using a containment mapping that sends m_1 to itself, and every other symbol in row (4) to the corresponding symbol in row (3). Since no symbol but m_1 in row (4) appears anywhere else, we have a legal containment mapping.

However, we cannot map row (1) anywhere, because that would involve mapping s_1 to one of the symbols represented by anonymous variables in column S_1. Since no anonymous symbol is involved in an inequality, we would never be able to deduce $h(s_1) > h(s_2)$, if h were the containment mapping.[13] Similarly, we cannot map row (2) anywhere, since we could not provide a single symbol that would be $h(m_1)$. Likewise, row (3) cannot map to another and still let us have $h(s_1) > h(s_2)$, since $h(s_2)$ would have to be an anonymous variable.

Thus, the minimum tableau weakly equivalent to Figure 17.9 consists of the first three rows. These rows evidently come from objects ES, EM, and ES, respectively. On the assumption that the objects are the relations, the optimized expression can be written as

$$\pi_1\big(\sigma_{\$1=\$3\wedge\$4=\$5\wedge\$2>\$6}(ES \times EM \times ES)\big)$$

The condition $\$1 = \$3$ enforces the fact that the two occurrences of e_1 in Figure 17.9 represent the same individual. Condition $\$4 = \$5$ comes from the fact that m_1 is used in both columns M_1 and E_2, and $\$2 > \$6$ comes from $s_1 > s_2$. □

The Query Interpretation Algorithm

The two examples above embody most of the ideas of the general case. One detail that has not come up concerns the relationship between rows of the optimized tableau and relations. Call a symbol *essential* if either it is distinguished, is a constant, appears in an arithmetic comparison associated with the tableau, or appears more than once in the rows of the tableau. For example, in Figure 17.9, all of the symbols given explicit names, except for m_2, are essential, and none of the symbols represented by blanks are essential, of course.

To represent the object corresponding to a given row of the tableau, we shall take the union of all relations whose schemes include all of the columns with essential symbols in that row. There must always be at least one such relation, because we made the assumption that each object was a subset of some relation. However, there could be more than one relation covering a given row. For instance, if for the database of Example 17.16 we simply asked to retrieve the employees, we would get the tableau

E	S	M
e		
e		

Both relations ES and EM cover the row e, so we take the union of the projections of these relations onto E. That is, we interpret the query as asking for all entries in the employee columns of the relations that have employee as an attribute. If there were no dangling tuples permitted, then either relation would do, but to play safe, we shall retrieve all employees for which either a salary or manager, or both, is listed.

We are now ready to describe an algorithm for query interpretation in a

---

[13] See Section 14.2 for how we deal with arithmetic inequalities when reducing conjunctive queries; the principle is the same when dealing with tableaux.

universal relation system. This approach is a simple version of the System/U algorithm, and it often fails in cases where there is a cyclic hypergraph for an object structure. Also notice that, while we describe the algorithm as going directly from a query to an expression over the database, implicitly we compute the window for each tuple variable; it is the projection of the join of the objects that remain after minimization under weak equivalence.

Algorithm 17.2: Object-Based Interpretation for Queries Over a Universal Relation.

INPUT: A query in the System/U query language, along with the relation schemes and objects of the database.

OUTPUT: An algebraic expression that represents our interpretation of the query.

METHOD: We construct the expression of relational algebra as follows. Note that the resulting expression is not necessarily optimized, and we should later apply to it an algorithm for optimizing under strong (not weak) equivalence, as we would for any query in relational algebra or another relational language.

1. Let the tuple variables used by the query be $t_1, \ldots, t_k$. By convention, we always take t_1 to be the blank tuple variable. Identify the subscript i with tuple variable t_i. Begin by writing the expression $U_1 \times \cdots \times U_k$, where U_i is the copy of the universal relation associated with tuple variable t_i.

2. Replace each U_i in the above expression by the natural join of all objects. We distinguish the attributes in the join for U_i by subscripting each attribute with i.

3. In the query, replace each occurrence of attribute A alone by A_1 (recall that t_1 is taken to be the blank tuple variable, and A_1 stands for the attribute called A in the copy of the universal relation associated with t_1). Replace each occurrence of $t_i.A$ by A_i. Complete the algebraic expression for the query by applying, to the result of (2), selection by the formula in the where-clause of the query (which is modified as above, by translating A to A_1 and $t_i.A$ to A_i), and then projecting onto the list of attributes (also modified as above) found in the retrieve-clause.

4. Construct the tableau for the expression from (3), and optimize it under weak equivalence.

5. Build an algebraic expression for the result of (4) by taking the product

    $$T_1 \times \cdots \times T_m$$

    where each T_i is the union of all relations whose schemes include all of the columns with essential symbols in the ith row, projected onto those columns. Then apply the selections needed to enforce the equality of components in the product that correspond to identical symbols in the tableau.

Also apply selections to reflect the constraints associated with the tableau, again using the obvious correspondence from the symbols of the tableau to components in the product. □

Examples 17.15 and 17.16 serve to illustrate the process described above.

17.8 MAXIMAL OBJECTS AND QUERIES ABOUT CYCLIC DATABASES

In this section, we consider how to modify Algorithm 17.2 when the object structure is cyclic. It may not be obvious that cycles cause problems, but we shall see an example shortly (Example 17.18). Intuitively, the problem is that when cycles exist in the object structure, there may be several different connections between attributes A and B. Algorithm 17.2 produces for the window $[AB]_{Obj}$ the intersection of the joins of the objects along each of these connections. However, it is frequently more appropriate to take the union of these joins. That is, if we ask for the B's that are connected to a given A, we usually, want those that are connected in one of the several possible ways, rather than only those that are connected in all possible ways.

To handle cyclic structures, we must back off a bit from our goal of letting the user mention any set of attributes in his query without restriction. We back off as little as possible, by allowing each tuple variable of a query, including the blank tuple variable, to range only over a set of objects that have some "strong" connection.

There are several degrees of "strength" that we might try to enforce in these connections among sets of objects. For example, David Maier's PIQUE system allows the user to define arbitrary subsets of the objects, called *associations*, over which tuple variables are allowed to range. Here, we shall describe the System/U approach to automatic selection of associations, which are called *maximal objects*.[14]

We build maximal objects, starting from single objects, in a way that enables us to prove at each step that we have a lossless join. Further, the losslessness of the join must follow from the given functional dependencies and the join dependency on the objects. This condition about losslessness of joins is the degree of binding "strength" we require, so that a set of objects may be the range of a tuple variable.

The motivation for requiring a lossless join has been discussed before; it is necessary for the objects of the database to represent a unique relation over the full set of attributes. Notice we not only require the set of objects in a maximal object to have a lossless join, but we require the subsets of objects from which the maximal object is built to have a lossless join as well. This condition guarantees that when we apply tableau optimization to a query about the join

---

[14] System System/U also allows the user to select the maximal objects if desired.

over the objects in a maximal object, the subset of objects that results will also have a lossless join.

Algorithm 17.3: Construction of Maximal Objects.

INPUT: A collection of objects and functional dependencies on the attributes of those objects.

OUTPUT: The collection of maximal objects for the input structure.

METHOD: We begin by constructing for any object O the largest set of objects containing O such that we can adjoin each object in turn with a lossless join that follows either from

1. Theorem 7.5 and a functional dependency, or
2. Theorem 7.11 and a multivalued dependency. Further, this multivalued dependency, since none are given directly, must be one of those that follow from Theorem 17.4 and the given join dependency.

In what follows, we use $\text{ATTR}(\mathcal{M})$ to stand for the set of attributes that is the union of all objects in set of objects $\mathcal{M}$. The steps in Figure 17.10 construct $\mathcal{M}$ from object O.

```
M := {O};
while changes to M occur do
    for each object P such that either
        (P ∩ ATTR(M)) → P,
        (P ∩ ATTR(M)) → ATTR(M), or
        P − ATTR(M) is disconnected from ATTR(M) − P
    when P ∩ ATTR(M) is deleted from the hypergraph do
        M := M ∪ {P}
```

Figure 17.10 Constructing the maximal object from an object O.

Having constructed a set of objects by expanding each object, we may find that some sets of objects are subsets of others. Drop from consideration all that are proper subsets of others. The remaining sets of objects are the maximal objects. □

Example 17.17: Figure 17.11 shows the object structure of a hypothetical bank database, where customers are related to branches by being the owner of an account or the holder of a loan. Both accounts and loans can be shared by several customers, but each loan and each account is at a single branch. The attributes are Br (branch), Ac (account number), Ba (balance of an account), L (loan number), Am (amount of a loan), C (customer), and Ad (customer's address). The objects are shown as hyperedges, and arrows indicate functional dependencies. For example, $AcBa$ is an object, and $Ac \to Ba$ is a functional dependency.

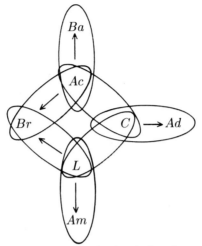

Figure 17.11 The bank database.

The maximal objects are built from the AcC and CL objects. Starting from AcC, we can use the functional dependency rule to add $AcBa$, $BrAc$, and AdC. Similarly, starting from CL we can add LAm, LBr, and AdC. Starting with any other object gives us a subset of one of these. Thus, there are two maximal objects, $\mathcal{M}$, with $\text{ATTR}(\mathcal{M}) = \{Br, Ac, Ba, C, Ad\}$, and $\mathcal{N}$, with $\text{ATTR}(\mathcal{N}) = \{Br, L, Am, C, Ad\}$. $\square$

An important fact about maximal objects is that they do not affect acyclic databases in any way, because there is only one maximal object, the complete set of objects. There is an easy proof by induction on the number of objects in the database. For the basis, if there is only one object, Algorithm 17.3 clearly produces only one maximal object.

Suppose the result is true for sets of up to $n - 1$ objects, and suppose we have an acyclic database with n objects. Let P be the first ear removed by the GYO reduction process of Section 11.12. Then the inductive hypothesis applies to the remaining $n - 1$ objects, and we know that starting with one of them produces a set $\mathcal{M}$ consisting of all $n - 1$ objects. But since P is an ear, we know that removal of $P \cap \text{ATTR}(\mathcal{M})$ will disconnect $P - \text{ATTR}(\mathcal{M})$ from the rest of the hypergraph, since every attribute in $P - \text{ATTR}(\mathcal{M})$ appears in no other object. Thus we can adjoin P to $\mathcal{M}$ by Algorithm 17.3. We have thus proved the following theorem.

Theorem 17.5: Every acyclic hypergraph has only one maximal object — the set of all objects. $\square$

Interpreting Queries in the Presence of Maximal Objects

Having constructed the maximal objects for a database, we shall use them to interpret queries as follows. Each tuple variable t in a query, including the blank, is assumed to refer to each of the maximal objects $\mathcal{M}$ that *covers t*, in the sense that every attribute A such that $t.A$ appears in the retrieve-clause or where-clause of the query is in ATTR($\mathcal{M}$). We consider all connections among attributes that stay within one maximal object to be equally valid, so we allow t to assume as a value any tuple in the join of the objects in any of the maximal objects that covers t.

There follows an algorithm to interpret queries in this manner. It is essentially the strategy followed by System/U.

Algorithm 17.4: Interpretation of Queries Using Maximal Objects.

INPUT: A query in the System/U query language, along with the relation schemes, objects, and maximal objects of the database.

OUTPUT: An algebraic expression that represents our interpretation of the query.

METHOD: Do each of the following steps.

1. As in step (1) of Algorithm 17.2, let the tuple variables of the query be $t_1, \ldots, t_k$, with t_1 the blank tuple variable. Begin with the Cartesian product of k copies of the universal relation, the expression $U_1 \times \cdots \times U_k$, where subscript i is identified with tuple variable t_i, for $i = 1, 2, \ldots, k$.

2. For each i let S_i be the set of maximal objects that covers t_i. Replace each U_i by the union of the maximal objects in S_i. Then distribute the Cartesian product over the unions, so the expression becomes a union of products of maximal objects. For example, if $k = 2$, $S_1 = \{\mathcal{M}_1, \mathcal{M}_2\}$, and $S_2 = \{\mathcal{M}_2, \mathcal{M}_3\}$, then the expression $(\mathcal{M}_1 \cup \mathcal{M}_2) \times (\mathcal{M}_2 \cup \mathcal{M}_3)$ is converted to

$$(\mathcal{M}_1 \times \mathcal{M}_2) \cup (\mathcal{M}_1 \times \mathcal{M}_3) \cup (\mathcal{M}_2 \times \mathcal{M}_2) \cup (\mathcal{M}_2 \times \mathcal{M}_3)$$

3. Replace each maximal object in the expression from (2) by the natural join of all objects in that maximal object. As in Algorithm 17.2, we shall subscript occurrences of an attribute A by the copy of the universal relation to which it corresponds. Note that each term of the union is the product of k maximal objects, with the ith maximal object corresponding to the ith copy of the universal relation.

4. As in Algorithm 17.2, rephrase the query by replacing each occurrence of A by A_1 and $t_i.A$ by A_i. Apply to each term of the union from (3) the selection expressed in the where-clause and the projection onto the attributes of the retrieve-clause.

5. Construct the tableau for each term of the union from (4). Optimize it under the weak equivalence criterion.

6. Determine, using the test for containment of conjunctive queries, whether the mapping defined by one tableau in the list from (5) is a subset of the mapping defined by another. Eliminate any tableau that is a proper subset of another, and eliminate all but one of a set of tableaux that are equivalent.

7. Build an expression from each of the tableaux that remain after (6), by the method of step (5) of Algorithm 17.2. The output is the union of these expressions. $\Box$

Example 17.18: Let us consider the following query about the banking database of Example 17.17.

> retrieve (C)   (17.6)
>   where Br=t.Br and t.C="Jones"

That is, print all of the customers who bank at a branch that Jones banks at. If we used Algorithm 17.2 to interpret this query, reduction of the tableau would not be able to eliminate the cycle consisting of the objects $BrAc$, AcC, CL, and BrL. Thus, the answer to the query would be based on the assumption that the connection between branches and customers is the join of all four of these objects; that is, the customer is required to have both a loan and an account at the branch. The answer to the query would be the set of customers with both loans and accounts at some branch at which Jones has both a loan and an account. We claim it is more intuitive that the connection between customers and branches should be that the customer has either a loan or an account at the branch, not necessarily both. To see how the maximal-object structure gives us the preferred interpretation, observe Figure 17.12, which repeats Figure 17.11, but shows the two maximal objects, $\mathcal{M}$ and $\mathcal{N}$, as dashed regions.

As there are two tuple variables, *blank* and t, in the query (17.6), we create two copies of the universal relation, $U_1 \times U_2$. We then observe that the set of attributes associated with each tuple variable is $\{Br, C\}$, and these attributes are members of both maximal objects. Thus, both maximal objects cover both tuple variables, and U_1 and U_2 are each replaced by the union of $\mathcal{M}$ and $\mathcal{N}$. When we distribute the product over the unions, we get the expression

$$(\mathcal{M}_1 \times \mathcal{M}_2) \cup (\mathcal{M}_1 \times \mathcal{N}_2) \cup (\mathcal{N}_1 \times \mathcal{M}_2) \cup (\mathcal{N}_1 \times \mathcal{N}_2)$$

The subscripts 1 and 2 indicate the copy of the universal relation to which each of the maximal objects pertain. Now we must replace $\mathcal{M}_1$ by

$$Br_1Ac_1 \bowtie Ac_1Ba_1 \bowtie C_1Ac_1 \bowtie C_1Ad_1$$

and $\mathcal{M}_2$ by a similar join involving attributes subscripted with 2. Also, $\mathcal{N}_1$ and $\mathcal{N}_2$ are replaced by joins of the objects in the maximal object $\mathcal{N}$, with all

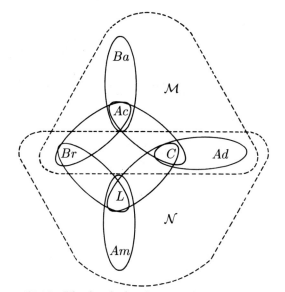

Figure 17.12 The bank database and its maximal objects.

Br_1	Ac_1	Ba_1	C_1	Ad_1	Br_2	L_2	Am_2	C_2	Ad_2
			c						
br	ac								
	ac	ba							
	ac		c						
			c	ad					
					br	l			
						l	am		
						l		"Jones"	
								"Jones"	ad'

Figure 17.13 Tableau for $\mathcal{M}_1 \times \mathcal{N}_2$.

attributes subscripted 1 or 2 as appropriate.

Now we are ready to form the tableaux for the terms. We show only one, for $\mathcal{M}_1 \times \mathcal{N}_2$, in Figure 17.13. Notice that we have used one symbol, br, for the branches of both Jones and the hypothetical customer c, because they are equated by a constraint. Similarly, we use "Jones" in the tableau, rather than a symbol equated to "Jones" by a constraint.

It happens that there are no containment relationships among the four tableaux, so each is optimized by itself. The result of optimizing Figure 17.13 is shown in Figure 17.14. We can see that this expression gives us those customers

c that have an account at a branch at which Jones has a loan. It is implemented most efficiently by finding the loans that Jones has, then the branches of those loans, the accounts at those branches, and the customers owning those accounts. Any of the relevant optimization algorithms from Chapter 11 would find this evaluation sequence. $\square$

Br_1	Ac_1	Ba_1	C_1	Ad_1	Br_2	L_2	Am_2	C_2	Ad_2
			c						
br	ac								
	ac		c						
					br	l			
						l		"Jones"	

Figure 17.14 Result of optimizing Figure 17.13.

The System/U Data Definition Language

In order that the system may make the response to queries indicated by Algorithm 17.4, it must be given a variety of kinds of information. Without going into notational details, let us simply list the kinds of information that the data definition language of System/U lets us provide.

1. The attributes and their data types.

2. The relation schemes and the names of relations.

3. The objects. Each object is defined to be a projection of one of the relations, and renaming of attributes is allowed. Thus, for example, we could have a relation PM, giving persons and their mothers. There could be an object PM, but also an object MG, or mother-grandmother, with attributes M and G of the object corresponding to P and M, respectively, in the relation. Thus, we could have a universal relation PMG supported by the single PM relation.

4. Any functional dependencies that hold.

In addition, after calculating the maximal objects from the given functional dependencies and the objects, the maximal objects are printed and the database designer is asked if they are satisfactory. By an interactive process, the designer can delete any of the maximal objects or create new ones.

Example 17.19: In the bank database, we might suppose that the functional dependency $L \to Br$ did not hold; that is, groups of branches could get together to make one loan. If that is the case, then $\mathcal{N}$ is no longer a maximal object. It is replaced by $\mathcal{P}$ and $\mathcal{Q}$, with $\text{ATTR}(\mathcal{P}) = \{Br, L, Am\}$ and $\text{ATTR}(\mathcal{Q}) =$

$\{L, Am, C, Ad\}$. This change has the effect that if we ask for the branches at which Jones does business, we get only those at which he has an account; there is no longer a connection between branches and customers through loans.

We might believe that there really is such a connection. If so, we are in effect saying that each person sharing loan 12345 is related to each branch making loan 12345, which is a reasonable way to view things. Formally, we are asserting the embedded multivalued dependency $L \twoheadrightarrow Br \mid C$ for the universal relation.

We can simulate the effect of this embedded multivalued dependency by deleting the maximal objects $\mathcal{P}$ and $\mathcal{Q}$ and replacing them by the maximal object $\mathcal{N}$. Then the database will continue to respond as before, when we assumed the functional dependency $L \rightarrow Br$. $\square$

EXERCISES

17.1: Let us refer to the YVCB database as described by objects in Figure 17.6 (Section 17.6). Express the following queries in the System/U language.

a)   Find the items ordered by Zack Zebra.

b)   Find the managers of all departments that sell items supplied by Ajax.

c)   Find the salaries of all employees in departments that sell items ordered by Zack Zebra.

d)   Find all customers who ordered items also ordered by Zack Zebra.

* e)   Find all customers whose address is the same as the address of some supplier of an item the customer ordered.

17.2: Suppose that the functional dependencies of the YVCB database in Figure 17.6 are $E \rightarrow S$, $E \rightarrow D$, $D \rightarrow M$, $M \rightarrow D$, $SuI \rightarrow P$, $Su \rightarrow Sa$, $O\# \rightarrow C$, and $C \rightarrow Ca$. Interpret each of the queries from Exercise 17.1 according to the representative-instance window function of Section 17.4.

* 17.3: Is the YVCB scheme, with the functional dependencies of Exercise 17.2, a unique scheme? Prove your answer.

17.4: Interpret each of the queries of Exercise 17.1 according to Algorithm 17.2 (Section 17.7).

17.5: Suppose we merge the attributes Sa and Ca in the YVCB database of Figure 17.6; that is, we use one attribute for both customer and supplier addresses. What are the maximal objects for the revised scheme, assuming the functional dependencies of Exercise 17.2?

17.6: Interpret each of the queries of Exercise 17.1, according to Algorithm 17.4 (Section 17.8), applied to the scheme of Exercise 17.5.

17.7: In Exercise 11.20 we met the Beer Drinkers' Database.

    a)   Express this database scheme as an object structure, as in Section 17.6.

    b)   What are the maximal objects for this scheme?

* 17.8: Express the queries of Exercise 11.20 in the System/U language.

17.9: Interpret each of your queries from Exercise 17.8 according to Algorithm 17.4.

17.10: Suppose we have attributes E (Employee), C (City), and W (Warehouse), with relations EC, meaning the employee lives in the city, and WC, meaning the warehouse is located in the city. Assume the universal relation EWC has objects EC and WC, and that functional dependencies $E \to C$ and $W \to C$ hold.

    a)   Express the query "find all employees who live in a city with one or more warehouses" in the System/U language. *Hint*: You need more than one tuple variable. In order to make the tuples variables range over the proper sets of objects, we can use a condition of the where-clause like $t.A = t.A$ to force tuple variable t to include attribute A in its range.[15]

    b)   Show that the interpretation of your query from (a) is correct under the representative-instance window function $[\cdots]_{RI}$.

    c)   Show that the interpretation of your query is also correct if the object-based window function $[\cdots]_{Obj}$ is used.

17.11: Modify the YVCB object structure of Figure 17.6 to include the omitted attributes, which are department numbers, item numbers, order dates, quantities of items, and customer balances.

* 17.12: For the library database of Example 11.15

    a)   Give a suitable set of objects and the functional dependencies that can be expected to hold among attributes.

    b)   Express the query of Figure 11.7 in the System/U language.

    c)   Interpret your query from (b), applied to your scheme from (a), according to the representative-instance window function.

    d)   Repeat (c) for the object-based window function.

    e)   Do your answers for (c) and (d) agree with the query of Figure 11.7?

---

[15] Actually, System/U allows a conjunct in the where-clause to be just $t.A$ for this purpose.

17.13: Convert to relational algebra the following queries about the bank database of Example 17.17 (Section 17.8), assuming interpretation of queries is by Algorithm 17.4.

a)
```
retrieve (Br)
    where C="Jones"
```

b)
```
retrieve (L)
    where Ac=12345
```

* c)
```
retrieve (Ac, Ba)
    where Ad=t.Ad and t.Am>1000
```

* 17.14: Find a suitable rel file for the bank database so that the system Q (see Section 17.3) will interpret queries in the same way as Algorithm 17.4 would. You may assume that each of the seven objects are also relations.

17.15: Suppose we used the "universal join" window function, where $[X]_{UJ}$ is the projection onto set of attributes X of all objects in the database scheme, regardless of X. How would the interpretation of the queries of Exercise 17.1 differ, under $[\cdots]_{UJ}$, compared with their interpretation under $[\cdots]_{Obj}$?

17.16: Consider the database scheme with relations AB, AC, and BC, and functional dependencies $A \to B$ and $B \to C$. Suppose the relation for AB is $\{a_1b_1\}$, for AC it is $\{a_1c_1, a_2c_2\}$, and for BC it is $\{b_1c_1\}$.

a)   Find the representative instance for this database.

b)   Find a weak instance, other than the representative instance, for this database.

<* 17.17: For which of the following sets of dependencies is the database scheme $\{AB, AC, BC\}$ independent?

a)   No dependencies.

b) $A \to B$ and $B \to C$.

c) $A \to C$ and $B \to C$.

d) $A \to BC$.

* 17.18: Complete the proof of Theorem 17.1 by showing that if weak instance u_{i+1} is constructed from u_i using an equality-generating dependency, then any weak instance that subsumes u_i also subsumes u_{i+1}. Also show that if the chase produces a contradiction, where two nonnull symbols are equated, then the scheme is not independent.

7.19: Suppose a scheme has only equality-generating dependencies. Construct a representative instance u from a given database by Algorithm 17.1, and then, until no longer possible, find some pair of tuples μ and ν in u such that μ subsumes ν, and delete ν. Show that the resulting relation is a representative instance, and that it is unique, independent of the order in which subsumed tuples are deleted.

7.20: Prove that any two representative instances for the same database and dependencies subsume each other, and that they have the same total projections onto any given set of attributes.

7.21: Consider the scheme $\{AB, \ AC\}$ with functional dependencies $A \rightarrow C$ and $B \rightarrow C$. Let the database have relation $\{a_1 c_1\}$ for AC, and for AB the relation

$$\{a_1 b_1, \ a_2 b_1, \ a_2 b_2, \ a_3 b_2, \ldots, a_n b_n, \ a_{n+1} b_n\}$$

  a)   Find the representative instance for this database and scheme.

  ** b)   Show that there is no expression of relational algebra that computes the representative instance from (arbitrary) relations AB and AC for this scheme.

7.22: The sequence $AB \bowtie BC \bowtie CD \bowtie DE$ might be an extension-join sequence. What functional dependencies are required, and what functional dependencies are forbidden, if the sequence is an extension-join sequence?

7.23: Prove Theorem 17.2, that (a) unique schemes are independent, and (b) $[X]_{RI}$ equals the union of the projections onto X, of all extension joins containing set of attributes X.

7.24: Show that the sizes of the relations in an extension-join sequence is nonincreasing.

7.25: Show that the relations of a unique scheme are in Boyce-Codd Normal Form, not only with respect to their key dependencies (which is obvious), but with respect to all functional dependencies in the scheme.

7.26: Prove the converse of Theorem 17.4, that $Y \twoheadrightarrow Z$ does not follow from join dependency j unless Z is the union of connected components of the hypergraph for j, when set of nodes Y is deleted.

7.27: In Example 17.15 (Section 17.7), we constructed expression (17.5) to translate a certain query on the assumption that objects $O\#I$ and $O\#C$ were database relations. Modify the expression (17.5) if the relations are those originally given in Figure 2.8 (Volume I); in particular, the relevant relations are $O\#IQ$ and $O\#DC$, where Q and D stand for quantity and date, respectively.

17.28: In Figure 17.13 (Section 17.8) we constructed one of the four tableaux needed for Example 17.18.

    a)   Construct the other three tableaux.

    b)   Optimize them under weak equivalence.

    c)   Show there are no containment relationships among the four tableaux.

* 17.29: Show how to simulate every QUEL retrieve-statement by a System/U query.

BIBLIOGRAPHIC NOTES

Vardi [1988a] surveys development of the universal relation idea, and Maier, Rozenshtein, and Warren [1986] surveys the various window functions that have been proposed in the literature. The notion of a window function and the two-stage approach to answering universal-relation queries are from Maier, Ullman, and Vardi [1984].

Implementations

The system Q, described in Section 17.3, is the unpublished work of Brian Kernighan. System/U is described in Korth et al. [1984].

PIQUE is from Maier [1983], and its "association-object" data model is found in Stein and Maier [1985]. Kuck and Sagiv [1982] describes a system, AURICAL, based on the representative-instance window function.

Other implementations of a universal relation are described in Addis [1982], Biskup and Brüggemann [1983], and Semmel [1988].

Early History

The universal-relation concept has evolved over time. Bernstein [1976] can be said to have originated the idea, in the sense that he studied database scheme design from the point of view that there was a universal set of attributes, from which the database schemes were built. In another direction, Carlson and Kaplan [1976] examined the question of how one would select a connection among attributes automatically.

The first notion of interpretation of queries over a universal relation was the taking of a lossless join that included the attributes of the query (Aho, Beeri, and Ullman [1977]). Schenk and Pinkert [1977] and Kambayashi [1978] suggested algorithms for finding minimal lossless joins.

Chang [1980] and Osborn [1979] proposed taking the union of certain joins to answer queries involving attributes connected by more than one path. The latter proposed a criterion similar to extension-joins, which were the idea of Honeyman [1980].

However, these early works were limited by the tacit assumption that the universal relation really contained tuples over all the attributes, with nulls forbidden. For example, Honeyman, Ladner, and Yannakakis [1980] shows that it is $\mathcal{NP}$-complete to tell whether a given database is the projection of a universal relation in this sense. Thus, the later development of the field involved the modification of the universal-relation concept to allow more flexibility regarding the extent of tuples.

The Representative Instance

The idea of a weak instance is from Honeyman [1982], who used it to define when a database as a whole satisfies a functional dependency. It also appears independently in Vassiliou [1980]. Mendelzon [1984] uses the collection of weak instances to characterize the information content of a database scheme.

Based on early versions of these works, Sagiv [1981, 1983] and Yannakakis [1981] saw the representative instance as a more appropriate definition of the universal relation to which queries should be applied.

Sagiv [1983] also pioneered the consideration of scheme independence. A characterization of independent schemes with functional dependencies was given by Graham and Yannakakis [1984].

Atzeni and DeBernardis [1987] discuss weak instances in which nulls are given an intuitive meaning of "inapplicable," rather than the conventional "unknown value."

Computing the Representative-Instance Window Function

Further exploration of the representative-instance concept required finding classes of database schemes for which the representative-instance window function could be computed efficiently. Yannakakis [1981] shows we can do so when the only dependency is the join of all relations in the scheme.

Sagiv [1983] defines unique schemes (Section 17.5) and proves Theorem 17.2, that these schemes are independent and can be computed efficiently by the union of projections of extension joins. This result was extended to allow functional dependencies that are not key dependencies (as required for unique schemes) by Maier, Rozenshtein, and Warren [1986] and Chan [1984], independently. Complexity issues are discussed by Atzeni and Chan [1985].

Maier, Ullman, and Vardi [1984] offers a characterization of when $[X]_{RI}$ can be computed by an expression of relational algebra, applied to the relations of the database, although the characterization is not effective. A solution to Exercise 17.21(b) appears there. Sagiv [1985b] proves that, for schemes with only tuple-generating dependencies, such an algebraic expression exists if and only if the dependencies are equivalent to one join dependency.

Yannakakis [1986] shows that all unions of tableau mappings on the representative instance have equivalent algebraic expressions on the database, although in the worst case, these expressions are exponentially larger than the original tableau mappings.

The Object-Based Window Function

The proposal to use an acyclic join dependency as a model for the structure of the universal relation is from Fagin, Mendelzon, and Ullman [1982]; Theorem 17.3 on the relationship between objects and join dependencies, and Theorem 17.4, on the relationship between multivalued dependencies and join dependencies, are from there. Sciore [1981] attempts to justify the assumption of acyclic schemes. Lien [1982] studied a stronger form of acyclicity, called "acyclic Bachman diagrams," and proved a weaker version of Theorem 17.4 independently.

The treatment of cyclic database schemes of Section 17.8 is based on Maier and Ullman [1983a]; it is also described in Korth et al. [1984].

Many references on acyclic schemes appear in the bibliographic notes of Chapter 11. In addition, we should note Sciore [1981] and Biskup, Brüggemann, Schnetgöte, and Kramer [1986], who relate acyclic schemes to assumptions about the universal relation.

The War Over the Universal Relation

Possibly based on a misunderstanding of how the early concepts described above led to more realistic theories such as representative-instance and object-based definitions, there appeared in Kent [1981] and Atzeni and Parker [1982] a collection of arguments against the universal-relation as a data model. Ullman [1982a] is a rebuttal to these claims. A debate on the subject appears in Kent [1983] and Ullman [1983].

A second round of argument followed the article Vardi [1988a], which is a simple survey of universal-relation technology. This article was answered by Codd [1988], who advanced many of the same arguments as the original opponents. For example, the claim is made that there is no way to handle the query of Exercise 17.10 in a universal-relation context. A rebuttal by Vardi to Codd's claims is included in Codd [1988].

BIBLIOGRAPHY FOR VOLUMES I AND II

Abiteboul, S. and S. Grumbach [1987]. "COL: a language for complex objects based on recursive rules," unpublished memorandum, INRIA, Le Chesnay, France.

Abiteboul, S. and R. Hull [1987]. "IFO: a formal semantic data model," *Proc. Third ACM Symp. on Principles of Database Systems*, pp. 119–132.

Abiteboul, S. and V. Vianu [1988]. "Procedural and declarative database update languages," *Proc. Seventh ACM Symp. on Principles of Database Systems*, pp. 240–250.

Addis, T. R. [1982]. "A relation-based language interpreter for a content-addressable file store," *ACM Trans. on Database Systems* **7**:2, pp. 125–163.

Afrati, F., C. H. Papadimitriou, G. Papageorgiou, A. Roussou, Y. Sagiv, and J. D. Ullman [1986]. "Convergence of sideways query evaluation," *Proc. Fifth ACM Symp. on Principles of Database Systems*, pp. 24–30.

Aghili, H. and D. G. Severance [1982]. "A practical guide to the design of differential files for recovery of on-line databases," *ACM Trans. on Database Systems* **7**:4, pp. 540–565.

Agrawal, R., M. J. Carey, and M. Linvy [1985]. "Models for studying concurrency control performance: alternatives and implications," *ACM SIGMOD Intl. Conf. on Management of Data*, pp. 108–121.

Agrawal, R. and D. J. DeWitt [1985]. "Integrated concurrency control and recovery mechanisms: design and performance evaluation," *ACM Trans. on Database Systems* **10**:4, pp. 529–564.

Agrawal, R. and H. V. Jagadish [1987]. "Direct algorithms for computing the transitive closure of database relations," *Proc. Intl. Conf. on Very Large Data Bases*, pp. 255–266.

Aho, A. V., C. Beeri, and J. D. Ullman [1979]. "The theory of joins in relational databases," *ACM Trans. on Database Systems* **4**:3, pp. 297–314. Corrigendum: *ACM Trans. on Database Systems* **8**:2, pp. 287.

Aho, A. V., J. E. Hopcroft, and J. D. Ullman [1974]. *The Design and Analysis of Computer Algorithms*, Addison-Wesley, Reading Mass.

Aho, A. V., J. E. Hopcroft, and J. D. Ullman [1983]. *Data Structures and Algorithms*, Addison-Wesley, Reading Mass.

Aho, A. V., B. W. Kernighan, and P. J. Weinberger [1979]. "Awk—a pattern scanning and processing language," *Software Practice and Experience* **9**, pp. 267–279.

Aho, A. V., B. W. Kernighan, and P. J. Weinberger [1988]. *The AWK programming Language*, Addison-Wesley, Reading Mass.

Aho. A. V., R. Sethi, and J. D. Ullman [1986]. *Compilers: Principles, Techniques, and Tools*, Addison-Wesley, Reading Mass.

Aho, A. V., Y. Sagiv, and J. D. Ullman [1979a]. "Equivalence of relational expressions," *SIAM J. Computing* **8**:2, pp. 218–246.

Aho, A. V., Y. Sagiv, and J. D. Ullman [1979b]. "Efficient optimization of a class of relational expressions," *ACM Trans. on Database Systems* **4**:4, pp. 435–454.

Aho, A. V. and J. D. Ullman [1979a]. "Optimal partial match retrieval when fields are independently specified," *ACM Trans. on Database Systems* **4**:2, pp. 168–179.

Aho, A. V. and J. D. Ullman [1979b]. "Universality of data retrieval languages," *Proc. Sixth ACM Symp. on Principles of Programming Languages*, pp. 110–120.

ANSI [1975]. "Study group on data base management systems: interim report," *FDT* **7**:2, ACM, New York.

Apers, P. M. G., A. R. Hevner, and S. B. Yao [1983]. "Optimizing algorithms for distributed queries," *IEEE Trans. on Software Engineering* **SE9**:1, pp. 57–68.

Apt, K. R. [1987]. "Introduction to logic programming," TR–87–35, Dept. of CS, Univ. of Texas, Austin. To appear in *Handbook of Theoretical Computer Science* (J. Van Leeuwen, ed.), North Holland, Amsterdam.

Apt, K. R., H. Blair, and A. Walker [1985]. "Towards a theory of declarative knowledge," unpublished memorandum, IBM, Yorktown Hts., N. Y. Appears in Minker [1988], pp. 89–148.

Apt, K. R. and J.-M. Pugin [1987]. "Maintenance of stratified databases viewed as a belief revision system," *Proc. Sixth ACM Symp. on Principles of Database Systems*, pp. 136–145.

Apt, K. R. and M. H. Van Emden [1982]. "Contributions to the theory of logic programming," *J. ACM* **29**:3, pp. 841–862.

Armstrong, W. W. [1974]. "Dependency structures of data base relationships," *Proc. 1974 IFIP Congress*, pp. 580–583, North Holland, Amsterdam.

Arora, A. K. and C. R. Carlson [1978]. "The information preserving properties of certain relational database transformations," *Proc. Intl. Conf. on Very Large Data Bases*, pp. 352–359.

Astrahan, M. M. and D. D. Chamberlin [1975]. "Implementation of a structured English query language," *Comm. ACM* **18**:10, pp. 580–587.

Astrahan, M. M., et al. [1976]. "System R: a relational approach to data management," *ACM Trans. on Database Systems* **1**:2, pp. 97–137.

Astrahan, M. M., et al. [1979]. "System R: a relational database management system," *Computer* **12**:5, pp. 43–48.

Astrahan, M. M., M. Schkolnick, and W. Kim [1980]. "Performance of the system R access path selection mechanism," *Information Processing* **80**, pp. 487–491.

Atzeni, P. and E. P. F. Chan [1985]. "Efficient query answering in the representative instance approach," *Proc. Fourth ACM Symp. on Principles of Database Systems*, pp. 181–188.

Atzeni, P. and M. C. DeBernardis [1987]. "A new basis for the weak instance model," *Proc. Sixth ACM Symp. on Principles of Database Systems*, pp. 79–86.

Atzeni, P. and D. S. Parker [1982]. "Assumptions in relational database theory," *Proc. First ACM Symp. on Principles of Database Systems*, pp. 1–9.

Bachman, C. W. [1969]. "Data structure diagrams," *Data Base* **1**:2, pp. 4–10.

Badal, D. S. [1980]. "The analysis of the effects of concurrency control on distributed database system performance," *Proc. Intl. Conf. on Very Large Data Bases*, pp. 376–383.

Balbin, I., K. Meenakshi, and K. Ramamohanarao [1988]. "An efficient labelling algorithm for magic set computation on stratified databases," TR 88/1, Dept. of Computer Science, Univ. of Melbourne.

Balbin, I., G. S. Port, and K. Ramamohanarao [1987]. "Magic set computation for stratified databases," TR 87/3, Dept. of Computer Science, Univ. of Melbourne.

Balbin, I. and K. Ramamohanarao [1986]. "A differential approach to query optimization in recursive deductive databases," TR–86/7, Dept. of Computer Science, Univ. of Melbourne.

Bancilhon, F. [1986]. "A logic-programming/object-oriented cocktail," *SIGMOD Record*, **15**:3, pp. 11–21.

Bancilhon, F. [1986]. "Naive evaluation of recursively defined functions," in Brodie and Mylopoulos [1986], pp. 165–178.

Bancilhon, F. and S. Khoshafian [1986]. "A calculus for complex objects," *Proc. Fifth ACM Symp. on Principles of Database Systems*, pp. 53–59.

Bancilhon, F., D. Maier, Y. Sagiv, and J. D. Ullman [1986]. "Magic sets and other strange ways to implement logic programs," *Proc. Fifth ACM Symp. on Principles of Database Systems*, pp. 1–15.

Bancilhon, F. and R. Ramakrishnan [1986]. "An amateur's introduction to recursive query-processing strategies," *ACM SIGMOD Intl. Conf. on Management of Data*, pp. 16–52.

Baroody, J. A. Jr. and D. J. DeWitt [1981]. "An object-oriented approach to database system implementation," *ACM Trans. on Database Systems* **6**:4, pp. 576–601.

Batory, D. S. [1988]. "Concepts for a database system synthesizer," *Proc. Seventh ACM Symp. on Principles of Database Systems*, pp. 184–192.

Batory, D. S., T. Y. Leung, and T. E. Wise [1988]. "Implementation concepts for an extensible data model and data language," *ACM Trans. on Database Systems* **13**:3, pp. 231–262.

Bayer, R. [1985]. "Query evaluation and recursion in deductive database systems," unpublished memorandum, Technical Univ. of Munich.

Bayer, R., K. Elhardt, H. Heller, and A Reiser [1980]. "Distributed concurrency control in database systems," *Proc. Intl. Conf. on Very Large Data Bases*, pp. 275–284.

Bayer, R. and E. M. McCreight [1972]. "Organization and maintenance of large ordered indices," *Acta Informatica* **1**:3, pp. 173–189.

Bayer, R. and M. Schkolnick [1977]. "Concurrency of operating on B-trees," *Acta Informatica* **9**:1, pp. 1–21.

Beck, L. L. [1978]. "On minimal sets of operations for relational data sublanguages," TR–CS–7802, Southern Methodist Univ., Dallas, Tex.

Beech, D. [1987]. "Groundwork for an object database model," in *Research Directions in Object-Oriented Programming* (B. Shriver and P. Wegner, eds.), MIT Press.

Beeri, C. [1980]. "On the membership problem for functional and multivalued dependencies," *ACM Trans. on Database Systems* 5:3, pp. 241–259.

Beeri, C. and P. A. Bernstein [1979]. "Computational problems related to the design of normal form relation schemes," *ACM Trans. on Database Systems* 4:1, pp. 30–59.

Beeri, C., P. A. Bernstein, and N. Goodman [1978]. "A sophisticate's introduction to database normalization theory," *Proc. Intl. Conf. on Very Large Data Bases*, pp. 113–124.

Beeri, C., P. A. Bernstein, N. Goodman, M. Y. Lai, and D. E. Shasha [1983]. "A concurrency control theory for nested transactions," *Proc. Second ACM Symp. on Principles of Database Systems*, pp. 45–62.

Beeri, C., R. Fagin, and J. H. Howard [1977]. "A complete axiomatization for functional and multivalued dependencies," *ACM SIGMOD Intl. Conf. on Management of Data*, pp. 47–61.

Beeri, C., R. Fagin, D. Maier, and J. D. Ullman [1983]. "On the desirability of acyclic database schemes," *J. ACM* 30:3, pp. 479–513.

Beeri, C. and P. Honeyman [1981]. "Preserving functional dependencies," *SIAM J. Computing* 10:3, pp. 647–656.

Beeri, C, P. C. Kanellakis, F. Bancilhon, and R. Ramakrishnan [1987]. "Bounds on the propagation of selection into logic programs," *Proc. Sixth ACM Symp. on Principles of Database Systems*, pp. 214–226.

Beeri, C., A. O. Mendelzon, Y. Sagiv, and J. D. Ullman [1981]. "Equivalence of relational database schemes," *SIAM J. Computing* 10:2, pp. 352–370.

Beeri, C., S. A. Naqvi, R. Ramakrishnan, O. Shmueli, and S. Tsur [1987]. "Sets and negation in a logic database language (LDL1)," *Proc. Sixth ACM Symp. on Principles of Database Systems*, pp. 21–37.

Beeri, C. and R. Ramakrishnan [1987]. "On the power of magic," *Proc. Sixth ACM Symp. on Principles of Database Systems*, pp. 269–283.

Beeri, C. and M. Y. Vardi [1981]. "The implication problem for data dependencies," *Automata, Languages and Programming* (S. Even and O. Kariv, eds.), pp. 73–85, Springer-Verlag, New York.

Beeri, C. and M. Y. Vardi [1984a]. "Formal systems for tuple- and equality-generating dependencies," *SIAM J. Computing* **13**:1, pp. 76–98.

Beeri, C. and M. Y. Vardi [1984b]. "A proof procedure for data dependencies," *J. ACM* **31**:4, pp. 718–741.

Bentley, J. L. [1975]. "Multidimensional binary search trees used for associative searching," *Comm. ACM* **18**:9, pp. 507–517.

Bentley, J. L. and J. H. Friedman [1979]. "Data structures for range searching," *Computing Surveys* **11**:4, pp. 397–410.

Bentley, J. L. and D. Stanat [1975]. "Analysis of range searches in quad trees," *Information Processing Letters* **3**:6, pp. 170–173.

Bernstein, P. A. [1976]. "Synthesizing third normal form relations from functional dependencies," *ACM Trans. on Database Systems* **1**:4, pp. 277–298.

Bernstein, P. A. and D. W. Chiu [1981]. "Using semijoins to solve relational queries," *J. ACM* **28**:1, pp. 25–40.

Bernstein, P. A. and N. Goodman [1980a]. "What does Boyce-Codd normal form do?" *Proc. Intl. Conf. on Very Large Data Bases*, pp. 245–259.

Bernstein, P. A. and N. Goodman [1980b]. "Timestamp-based algorithms for concurrency control in distributed database systems," *Proc. Intl. Conf. on Very Large Data Bases*, pp. 285–300.

Bernstein, P. A. and N. Goodman [1981a]. "The power of natural semijoins," *SIAM J. Computing* **10**:4, pp. 751–771.

Bernstein, P. A. and N. Goodman [1981b]. "Concurrency control in distributed database systems," *Computing Surveys* **13**:2, pp. 185–221.

Bernstein, P. A. and N. Goodman [1983]. "Multiversion concurrency control—theory and algorithms," *ACM Trans. on Database Systems* **8**:4, pp. 463–483.

Bernstein, P. A. and N. Goodman [1984]. "An algorithm for concurrency control and recovery in replicated, distributed databases," *ACM Trans. on Database Systems* **9**:4, pp. 596–615.

Bernstein, P. A., N. Goodman, and V. Hadzilacos [1983]. "Recovery algorithms for database systems," *Proc. 1983 IFIP Congress*, pp. 799–807, North Holland, Amsterdam.

Bernstein, P. A., N. Goodman, J. B. Rothnie Jr., and C. H. Papadimitriou [1978]. "Analysis of serializability of SDD-1: a system of distributed databases (the fully redundant case)," *IEEE Trans. on Software Engineering* **SE4**:3, pp. 154–168.

Bernstein, P. A, N. Goodman, E. Wong, C. L. Reeve, and J. B. Rothnie, Jr. [1981]. "Query processing in a system for distributed databases (SDD-1)," *ACM Trans. on Database Systems* **6**:4, pp. 602–625.

Bernstein, P. A., V. Hadzilacos, and N. Goodman [1987]. *Concurrency Control and Recovery in Database Systems* Addison-Wesley, Reading Mass.

Bernstein, P. A. and D. W. Shipman [1980]. "The correctness of concurrency control mechanisms in a system for distributed databases (SDD-1)," *ACM Trans. on Database Systems* **5**:1, pp. 52–68.

Bernstein, P. A., D. W. Shipman, and J. B. Rothnie, Jr. [1980]. "Concurrency control in a system for distributed databases (SDD-1)," *ACM Trans. on Database Systems* **5**:1, pp. 18–51.

Bidiot, N. and R. Hull [1986]. "Positivism vs. minimalism in deductive databases," *Proc. Fifth ACM Symp. on Principles of Database Systems*, pp. 123–132.

Biliris, A. [1987]. "Operation specific locking in B-trees," *Proc. Sixth ACM Symp. on Principles of Database Systems*, pp. 159–169.

Biskup, J. [1980]. "Inferences of multivalued dependencies in fixed and undetermined universes." *Theoretical Computer Science* **10**:1, pp. 93–106.

Biskup, J. and H. H. Brüggemann [1983]. "Universal relations views: a pragmatic approach," *Proc. Intl. Conf. on Very Large Data Bases*, pp. 172–185.

Biskup, J., H. H. Brüggemann, L. Schnetgöte, and M Kramer [1986]. "One flavor assumption and γ-acyclicity for universal relation views," *Proc. Fifth ACM Symp. on Principles of Database Systems*, pp. 148–159.

Biskup, J., U. Dayal, and P. A. Bernstein [1979]. "Synthesizing independent database schemas," *ACM SIGMOD Intl. Conf. on Management of Data*, pp. 143–152.

Biskup, J. and H. Steifeling [1988]. "Transitive closure algorithms for very large databases," unpublished memorandum, Hochschule Hildesheim, Hildesheim, W. Germany.

Bitton, D., H. Boral, D. J. DeWitt, and W. K. Wilkinson [1983]. "Parallel algorithms for the execution of relational database operations," *ACM Trans. on Database Systems* **8**:3, pp. 324–354.

Blasgen, M. W., et al. [1981]. "System R: an architectural overview," *IBM Systems J.* **20**:1, pp. 41–62.

Bocca, J. [1986]. "EDUCE: a marriage of convenience: Prolog and a Relational Database," *Symp. on Logic Programming*, pp. 36–45, IEEE, New York.

Bolour, A. [1979]. "Optimality properties of multiple key hashing functions," *J. ACM* **26**:2, pp. 196–210.

Bosak, R., R. F. Clippinger, C. Dobbs, R. Goldfinger, R. B. Jasper, W. Keating, G. Kendrick, and J. E. Sammet [1962]. "An information algebra," *Comm. ACM* **5**:4, pp. 190–204.

Boyce, R. F., D. D. Chamberlin, W. F. King, and M. M. Hammer [1975]. "Specifying queries as relational expressions: the SQUARE data sublanguage," *Comm. ACM* **18**:11, pp. 621–628.

Brodie, M. L. [1984]. "On the development of data models," in Brodie, Mylopoulos, and Schmidt [1984], pp. 19–48.

Brodie, M. L. and J. Mylopoulos [1986]. *On Knowledge Base Management Systems*, Springer-Verlag, New York.

Brodie, M. L., J. Mylopoulos, and J. W. Schmidt [1984]. *On Conceptual Modeling*, Springer-Verlag, New York.

Brown, M. R., K. Kolling, and E. A. Taft [1984]. "The Alpine file system," CSL–84–4, Xerox, Palo Alto.

Buckley, G. N. and A. Silberschatz [1985]. "Beyond two-phase locking," *J. ACM* **32**:2, pp. 314–326.

Burkhard, W. A. [1976]. "Hashing and trie algorithms for partial match retrieval," *ACM Trans. on Database Systems* **1**:2, pp. 175–187.

Burkhard, W. A., M. L. Fredman, and D. J. Kleitman [1981]. "Inherent complexity trade-offs for range query problems," *Theoretical Computer Science* **16**:3, pp. 279–290.

Cardenas, A. F. [1979]. *Data Base Management Systems*, Allyn and Bacon, Boston, Mass.

Carey, M. J. [1983]. "Granularity hierarchies in concurrency control," *Proc. Second ACM Symp. on Principles of Database Systems*, pp. 156–165.

Carey, M. J., D. J. DeWitt, D. Frank, G. Graefe, J. E. Richardson, E. J. Shekita, and M. Muralikrishna [1986]. "The architecture of the EXODUS extensible DBMS," *Proc. Intl. Workshop on Object-Oriented Database Systems*, Asilomar, CA., Sept., 1986.

Carlson, C. R. and R. S. Kaplan [1976]. "A generalized access path model and its application to a relational database system," *ACM SIGMOD Intl. Conf. on Management of Data*, pp. 143–156.

Casanova, M. A., R. Fagin, and C. H. Papadimitriou [1984]. "Inclusion dependencies and their interaction with functional dependencies," *J. Computer and System Sciences* **28**:1, pp. 29–59.

Ceri, S., G. Gottlob, and G. Wiederhold [1987]. "Interfacing relational databases and Prolog efficiently," in Kerschberg [1987], pp. 207–223.

Ceri, S. and G. Pelagatti [1980]. "Correctness of execution strategies of read-only transactions in distributed database systems," Rept. 80–16, Inst. di Elettrotechnica, Politecnico di Milano.

Ceri, S. and G. Pelagatti [1984]. *Distributed Databases: Principles and Systems*, McGraw-Hill, New York.

Chakravarthy, U. S. and J. Minker [1986]. "Multiple query processing in deductive databases using query graphs," *Proc. Intl. Conf. on Very Large Data Bases*, pp. 384–391.

Chamberlin, D. D., et al. [1976]. "SEQUEL 2: a unified approach to data definition, manipulation, and control," *IBM J. Research and Development* **20**:6, pp. 560–575.

Chamberlin, D. D., et al. [1981a]. "Support for repetitive transactions and ad-hoc queries in System R," *ACM Trans. on Database Systems* **6**:1, pp. 70–94.

Chamberlin, D. D., et al. [1981b]. "A history and evaluation of System R," *Comm. ACM* **24**:10, pp. 632–646.

Chandra, A. [1988]. "Theory of database queries," *Proc. Seventh ACM Symp. on Principles of Database Systems*, pp. 1–9.

Chandra, A. K. and D. Harel [1980]. "Computable queries for relational database systems," *J. Computer and System Sciences* **21**:2, pp. 156–178.

Chandra, A. K. and D. Harel [1982]. "Structure and complexity of relational queries," *J. Computer and System Sciences* **25**:1, pp. 99–128.

Chandra, A. K. and D. Harel [1985]. "Horn clause queries and generalizations," *J. Logic Programming* **4**:1, pp. 1–15.

Chandra, A. K., H. R. Lewis, and J. A. Makowsky [1981]. "Embedded implicational dependencies and their inference problem," *Proc. Thirteenth Annual ACM Symp. on the Theory of Computing*, pp. 342–354.

Chandra, A. K. and P. M. Merlin [1977]. "Optimal implementation of conjunctive queries in relational databases," *Proc. Ninth Annual ACM Symp. on the Theory of Computing*, pp. 77–90.

Chandy, K. M., J. C. Browne, C. W. Dissly, and W. R. Uhrig [1975]. "Analytic models for rollback and recovery strategies in database systems," *IEEE Trans. on Software Engineering* **SE-1**:1, pp. 100–110.

Chan, E. P. F. [1984]. "Optimal computation of total projections with unions of chase join expressions," *ACM SIGMOD Intl. Conf. on Management of Data*, pp. 149–163.

Chang, C. L. [1980]. "Finding missing joins for incomplete queries in relational databases," RJ2145, IBM, San Jose, Calif.

Chang, C. L. [1981]. "On the evaluation of queries containing derived relations in relational databases," in Gallaire, Minker, and Nicolas [1981], pp. 235–260.

Chen, P. P. [1976]. "The entity-relationship model: toward a unified view of data," *ACM Trans. on Database Systems* **1**:1, pp. 9–36.

Childs, D. L. [1968]. "Feasibility of a set-theoretical data structure—a general structure based on a reconstituted definition of relation," *Proc. 1968 IFIP Congress*, pp. 162–172, North Holland, Amsterdam.

Chimenti, D., T. O'Hare, R. Krishnamurthy, S. A. Naqvi, S. Tsur, C. West, and C. Zaniolo [1987]. "An overview of the LDL system," in Zaniolo [1987], pp. 52–62.

Chiu, D.-M., P. A. Bernstein, and Y.-C. Ho [1981]. "Optimizing chain queries in a distributed database system," TR–01–81, Harvard Univ. Cambridge, Mass.

Cincom [1978]. *OS TOTAL Reference Manual*, Cincom Systems, Cincinnati, Ohio.

Clark, K. L. [1978]. "Negation as failure," in Gallaire and Minker [1978], pp. 293–322.

Clocksin, W. F. and C. S. Mellish [1981]. *Programming in Prolog*, Springer-Verlag, New York.

CODASYL [1971]. *CODASYL Data Base Task Group April 71 Report*, ACM, New York.

CODASYL [1978]. *COBOL J. Development*, Materiel Data Management Center, Quebec, Que. Earlier editions appeared in 1973 and 1968.

Codd, E. F. [1970]. "A relational model for large shared data banks," *Comm. ACM* **13**:6, pp. 377–387.

Codd, E. F. [1972a]. "Further normalization of the data base relational model," in *Data Base Systems* (R. Rustin, ed.) Prentice-Hall, Englewood Cliffs, New Jersey.pp. 33–64.

Codd, E. F. [1972b]. "Relational completeness of data base sublanguages," *ibid.* pp. 65–98.

Codd, E. F. [1975]. "Understanding relations," *FDT* **7**:3–4, pp. 23-28, ACM, New York.

Codd, E. F. [1979]. "Extending the data base relational model to capture more meaning," *ACM Trans. on Database Systems* **4**:4, pp. 397–434.

Codd, E. F. [1988]. "'Universal' relation fails to replace relational model," *IEEE Software*, June, 1988. Also see reply by M. Y. Vardi.

Comer, D. [1978]. "The difficulty of optimum index selection," *ACM Trans. on Database Systems* **3**:4, pp. 440–445.

Comer, D. [1979]. "The ubiquitous B-tree," *Computing Surveys* **11**:2, pp. 121–138.

Cooper, E. C. [1980]. "On the expressive power of query languages for relational databases," TR–14–80, Aiken Computation Lab., Harvard Univ.

Cosmadakis, S. S. and F. Afrati [1988]. "Expressiveness of restricted recursive queries," unpublished memorandum, IBM T. J. Watson Research Center, Yorktown Hts., N. Y.

Cosmadakis, S. S., H. Gaifman, P. C. Kanellakis, and M. Y. Vardi [1988]. "Decidable optimization problems for database logic programs," *Proc. Twentieth Annual ACM Symp. on the Theory of Computing*, pp. 477–490.

Cosmadakis, S. S. and P. C. Kanellakis [1986]. "Parallel evaluation of recursive rule queries," *Proc. Fifth ACM Symp. on Principles of Database Systems*, pp. 280–293..

Cruz, I. F. and T. S. Norvell [1988]. "Aggregative closure: an extension of transitive closure," unpublished memorandum, Dept. of CS, Univ. of Toronto, to appear in Fifth IEEE Conf. on Database Engineering.

Culik, K. II, Th. Ottmann, and D. Wood [1981]. "Dense multiway trees," *ACM Trans. on Database Systems* **6**:3, pp. 486–512.

Cullinane [1978]. *IDMS DML Programmer's Reference Guide*, Cullinane Corp., Wellesley, Mass.

Danforth, S., S. Khoshafian, and P. Valduriez [1988]. "FAD—A database programming language," unpublished memorandum, MCC, Austin, Tex.

Daniels, D., P. G. Selinger, L. M. Haas, B. G. Lindsay, C. Mohan, A. Walker, and P. F. Wilms [1982]. "An introduction to distributed query compilation in R*," RJ–3497, IBM, Almaden.

Date, C. J. [1986]. *An Introduction to Database Systems*, two volumes, Addison-Wesley, Reading Mass.

D'Atri, A. and M. Moscarini [1986]. "Recognition algorithms and design methodologies for acyclic database schemes," in Kanellakis [1986], pp. 43–68.

Davidson, S. B. [1984]. "Optimism and consistency in partitioned distributed database systems," *ACM Trans. on Database Systems* **9**:3, pp. 456–482.

Dayal, U. and P. A. Bernstein [1978]. "The updatability of relational views," *Proc. Intl. Conf. on Very Large Data Bases*, pp. 368–377.

Dayal, U. and P. A. Bernstein [1982]. "On the correct translation of update operations on relational views," *ACM Trans. on Database Systems* **7**:3, pp. 381–416.

Dayal, U. and J. M. Smith [1986]. "PROBE: a knowledge-oriented database management system," in Brodie and Mylopoulos [1986], pp. 227–258.

Debray, S. K. and D. S. Warren [1986]. "Automatic mode inference for Prolog programs," *Symp. on Logic Programming*, pp. 78–88, IEEE, New York.

Delobel, C. [1978]. "Normalization and hierarchical dependencies in the relational data model," *ACM Trans. on Database Systems* **3**:3, pp. 201–222. See also, "Contributions theoretiques a la conception d'un systeme d'informations," doctoral dissertation, Univ. of Grenoble, Oct., 1973.

Delobel, C. and R. C. Casey [1972]. "Decomposition of a database and the theory of boolean switching functions," *IBM J. Res. Devel.* **17**:5, pp. 370–386.

DeWitt, D. J. and R. Gerber [1985]. "Multiprocessor hash-based join algorithms," *Proc. Intl. Conf. on Very Large Data Bases*, pp. 151–164.

Dietrich, S. W. [1987]. "Extension tables: memo relations in logic programming," *Proc. Symposium on Logic Programming*, pp. 264–272, IEEE Computer Society.

Dietrich, S. W. and D. S. Warren [1985]. "Dynamic programming strategies for the evaluation of recursive queries," TR 85/31, Dept. of CS, SUNY Stony Brook.

DiPaola, R. A. [1969]. "The recursive unsolvability of the decision problem for a class of definite formulas," *J. ACM* **16**:2, pp. 324–327.

Dwork, C. and D. Skeen [1983]. "The inherent cost of nonblocking commitment," *Proc. Second ACM Symp. on Principles of Distributed Computing*, pp. 1–11.

Eager, D. and K. Sevcik [1983]. "Achieving robustness in distributed database systems," *ACM Trans. on Database Systems* **8**:3, pp. 354–381.

Earley, J. [1970]. "An efficient context-free parsing algorithm," *Comm. ACM* **13**:2, pp. 94–102.

El Abbadi, A., and S. Toueg [1986]. "Availability in partitioned, replicated databases," *Proc. Fifth ACM Symp. on Principles of Database Systems*, pp. 240–251.

Ellis, C. S. [1980]. "Concurrent search and insertion in 2-3 trees," *Acta Informatica* **14**:1, pp. 63–86.

Ellis, C. S. [1987]. "Concurrency in linear hashing," *ACM Trans. on Database Systems* **12**:2, pp. 195–217.

El Masri, R. and G. Wiederhold [1979]. "Data model integration using the structural model," *ACM SIGMOD Intl. Conf. on Management of Data*, pp. 191–202.

Epstein, R., M. Stonebraker, and E. Wong [1979]. "Distributed query processing in a relational database system," *ACM SIGMOD Intl. Conf. on Management of Data*, pp. 169–180.

Eswaran, K. P., J. N. Gray, R. A. Lorie, and I. L. Traiger [1976]. "The notions of consistency and predicate locks in a database system," *Comm. ACM* **19**:11, pp. 624–633.

Fagin, R. [1977]. "Multivalued dependencies and a new normal form for relational databases," *ACM Trans. on Database Systems* **2**:3, pp. 262–278.

Fagin, R. [1978]. "On an authorization mechanism," *ACM Trans. on Database Systems* **3**:3, pp. 310–319.

Fagin, R. [1981]. "A normal form for relational databases that is based on domains and keys," *ACM Trans. on Database Systems* **6**:3, pp. 387–415.

Fagin, R. [1982]. "Horn clauses and database dependencies," *J. ACM* **29**:4, pp. 952–983.

Fagin, R. [1983]. "Degrees of acyclicity for hypergraphs and relational database schemes," *J. ACM* **30**:3, pp. 514–550.

Fagin, R., A. O. Mendelzon, and J. D. Ullman [1982]. "A simplified universal relation assumption and its properties," *ACM Trans. on Database Systems* **7**:3, pp. 343–360.

Fagin, R., J. Nievergelt, N. Pippenger, and H. R. Strong [1979]. "Extendible hashing—a fast access method for dynamic files," *ACM Trans. on Database Systems* **4**:3, pp. 315–344.

Fagin, R. and M. Y. Vardi [1986]. "The theory of data dependencies—a survey," in *Mathematics of Information Processing* (M. Anshel and W. Gewirtz, eds.), *Symposia in Applied Mathematics* **34**, pp. 19–72.

Fekete, A., N. Lynch, M. Merritt, and W. Weihl [1987]. "Nested transactions and read/write locking," *Proc. Sixth ACM Symp. on Principles of Database Systems*, pp. 97–111.

Fernandez, E. B., R. C. Summers, and C. Wood [1980]. *Database Security and Integrity*, Addison-Wesley, Reading Mass.

Fillat, A. I. and L. A. Kraning [1970]. "Generalized organization of large databases: a set theoretic approach to relations," MIT MAC TR–70, June, 1970.

Finkel, R. A. and J. L. Bentley [1974]. "Quad trees, a data structure for retrieval on composite keys," *Acta Informatica* **4**:1, pp. 1–9.

Fischer, P. C. and D.-M. Tsou [1983]. "Whether a set of multivalued dependencies implies a join dependency is $\mathcal{NP}$-hard," *SIAM J. Computing* **12**:2, pp. 259–266.

Fischer, P. C. and D. Van Gucht [1984]. "Weak multivalued dependencies," *Proc. Third ACM Symp. on Principles of Database Systems*, pp. 266–274.

Fishman, D. H., et al. [1986]. "Iris: an object-oriented DBMS," STL–86–15, Hewlett-Packard, Palo Alto.

Fong, A. C. and J. D. Ullman [1976]. "Induction variables in very high-level languages," *Proc. Third ACM Symp. on Principles of Programming Languages*, pp. 104–112.

Franaszek, P. and J. T. Robinson [1985]. "Limitations on concurrency in transaction processing," *ACM Trans. on Database Systems* **10**:1, pp. 1–28.

Fredman, M. F. [1981]. "A lower bound on the complexity of orthogonal range queries," *J. ACM* **28**:4, pp. 696–705.

Freytag, J. C. [1987]. "A rule-based view of query optimization," *ACM SIGMOD Intl. Conf. on Management of Data*, pp. 173–180.

Frost, R. [1986]. *Introduction to Knowledge Base Systems*, MacMillan, New York.

Furtado, A. L. [1978]. "Formal aspects of the relational model," *Information systems* **3**:2, pp. 131–140.

Gaifman, H., H. Mairson, Y. Sagiv, and M. Y. Vardi [1987]. "Undecidable optimization problems for database logic programs," *Proc. Second ACM Symp. on Logic in Computer Science*, Ithaca, NY.

Galil, Z. [1982]. "An almost linear time algorithm for computing a dependency basis in a relational database," *J. ACM* **29**:1, pp. 96–102.

Gallaire, H. and J. Minker [1978]. *Logic and Databases*, Plenum Press, New York.

Gallaire, H., J. Minker, and J.-M. Nicolas [1981]. *Advances in Database Theory*, Vol. I, Plenum Press, New York.

Gallaire, H., J. Minker, and J.-M. Nicolas [1983]. *Advances in Database Theory*, Vol. II, Plenum Press, New York.

Gallaire, H., J. Minker, and J.-M. Nicolas [1984]. "Logic and databases: a deductive approach," *Computing Surveys* **16**:1, pp. 154–185.

Gangopadhyay, D. [1987]. "On uniform implementation of optimizations for recursive queries," unpublished memorandum, IBM, Hawthorne, NY.

Garcia-Molina, H. [1979]. "Performance comparison of update algorithms for distributed databases," Part I: Tech. Note 143, Part II: Tech. Note 146, Digital Systems Lab., Stanford Univ.

Garcia-Molina, H. [1982]. "Elections in a distributed computing system," *IEEE Trans. on Computers* **C-31**:1, pp. 48–59.

Garcia-Molina, H. and J. Kent [1985]. "An experimental evaluation of crash recovery algorithms," *Proc. Fourth ACM Symp. on Principles of Database Systems*, pp. 113–121.

Gardarin, G. and C. de Maindreville [1986]. "Evaluation of database recursive logic programs as recurrent function series," *ACM SIGMOD Intl. Conf. on Management of Data*, pp. 177–186.

Garey, M. R. and D. S. Johnson [1979]. *Computers and Intractability: A Guide to the Theory of NP-Completeness*, Freeman, San Francisco.

Gelenbe, E. and D. Derochette [1978]. "Performance of rollback recovery systems under intermittent failures," *Comm. ACM* **21**:6, pp. 493–499.

Gelfond, M. and V. Lifschitz [1988]. "The stable model semantics for logic programming," unpublished memorandum, Dept. of CS, Stanford Univ.

Gelfond, M., H. Przymusinska, and T. C. Przymusinski [1986]. "The extended closed world assumption and its relationship to parallel circumscription," *Proc. Fifth ACM Symp. on Principles of Database Systems*, pp. 133–139.

Genesereth, M. R. [1983]. "MRS: a metalevel representation system," HPP–83–28, Knowledge Systems Laboratory, Stanford Univ.

Genesereth, M. R. and N. J. Nilsson [1988]. *Logical Foundations of Artificial Intelligence*, Morgan-Kaufmann, Los Altos.

Ginsberg, M. [1988]. *Nonmonotonic Reasoning*, Morgan-Kaufmann, Los Altos.

Ginsburg, S. and S. M. Zaiddan [1982]. "Properties of functional dependency families," *J. ACM* **29**:3, pp. 678–698.

Goldberg, A. and D. Robson [1980]. *Smalltalk-80: The Language and Its Implementation*, Addison-Wesley, Reading Mass.

Gonzalez-Rubio, R., J. Rohmer, and A. Bradier [1987]. "An overview of DDC: a delta driven computer," DSG/CRG/87007, Bull, Louveciennes, France.

Goodman, J. R. [1981]. "An investigation of multiprocessor structures and algorithms for database management," UCB/ERL M81/33, Dept. of EECS, UC Berkeley.

Goodman, L. A. [1970]. "The multivariate analysis of qualitative data: interactions among multiple classifications," *J. Amer. Stat. Assn.* **65**, pp. 226–256.

Goodman, N. and O. Shmueli [1982]. "Tree queries: a simple class of relational queries," *ACM Trans. on Database Systems* **7**:4, pp. 653–677.

Goodman, N. and O. Shmueli [1983]. "Syntactic characterization of tree database schemas," *J. ACM* **30**:4, pp. 767–786.

Gotlieb, C. C. and F. W. Tompa [1973]. "Choosing a storage schema," *Acta Informatica* **3**:3, pp. 297–319.

Gotlieb, L. R. [1975]. "Computing joins of relations," *ACM SIGMOD Intl. Conf. on Management of Data*, pp. 55–63.

Gottlob, G. [1987]. "Computing covers for embedded functional dependencies," *Proc. Sixth ACM Symp. on Principles of Database Systems*, pp. 58–69.

Gouda, M. G. and U. Dayal [1981]. "Optimal semijoin schedules for query processing in local distributed database systems," *ACM SIGMOD Intl. Conf. on Management of Data*, pp. 164–181.

Graefe, G. and D. J. DeWitt [1987]. "The EXODUS optimizer generator," *ACM SIGMOD Intl. Conf. on Management of Data*, pp. 160–172.

Graham. M. H. [1979]. "On the universal relation," technical report, Univ. of Toronto, Toronto, Ont., Canada.

Graham, M. H., A. O. Mendelzon, and M. Y. Vardi [1986]. "Notions of dependency satisfaction," *J. ACM* **33**:1, pp. 105–129.

Graham, M. H. and M. Yannakakis [1984]. "Independent database schemas," *J. Computer and System Sciences* **28**:1, pp. 121–141.

Grahne, G. and K.-J. Raiha [1986]. "Characterizations for acyclic database schemes," in Kanellakis [1986], pp. 19–42.

Gray, J. N. [1978]. "Notes on database operating systems," in *Operating Systems: an Advanced Course* (R. Bayer, R. M. Graham, and G. Seegmuller, eds.), Springer-Verlag, New York.

Gray, J. N., et al. [1981]. "The recovery manager of the system R database manager," *Computing Surveys* **13**:2, pp. 223–242.

Gray, J. N., R. A. Lorie, and G. R. Putzolo [1975]. "Granularity of locks in a shared database," *Proc. Intl. Conf. on Very Large Data Bases*, pp. 428–451.

Gray, J. N. and F. Putzolo [1987]. "The 5 minute rule for trading memory for disc accesses and the 10 byte rule for trading memory for CPU time," *ACM SIGMOD Intl. Conf. on Management of Data*, pp. 395–398.

Gray, J. N., G. R. Putzolo, and I. L. Traiger [1976]. "Granularity of locks and degrees of consistency in a shared data base," in *Modeling in Data Base Management Systems* (G. M. Nijssen, ed.), North Holland, Amsterdam.

Greenblatt, D. and J. Waxman [1978]. "A study of three database query languages," in Shneiderman [1978], pp. 77–98.

Griffiths, P. P., M. M. Astrahan, D. D. Chamberlin, R. A. Lorie, and T. G. Price [1979]. "Access path selection in a relational database management system," *ACM SIGMOD Intl. Conf. on Management of Data*, pp. 23–34.

Griffiths, P. P. and B. W. Wade [1976]. "An authorization mechanism for a relational database system," *ACM Trans. on Database Systems* **1**:3, pp. 242–255.

Gudes, E. and S. Tsur [1980]. "Experiments with B-tree reorganization," *ACM SIGMOD Intl. Conf. on Management of Data*, pp. 200–206.

Gurevich, Y. and H. R. Lewis [1982]. "The inference problem for template dependencies," *Proc. First ACM Symp. on Principles of Database Systems*, pp. 221–229.

Haas, L. M. et al. [1988]. "An extensible processor for an extended relational query language," RJ–6182, IBM Almaden.

Haberman, S. J. [1970]. "The general log-linear model," Ph. D. Thesis, Dept. of Statistics, Univ. of Chicago.

Haddad, R. W. and J. F. Naughton [1988]. "Counting methods for cyclic relations," *Proc. Seventh ACM Symp. on Principles of Database Systems*, pp. 333–340.

Hadzilacos, T. and C. H. Papadimitriou [1985]. "Some algorithmic aspects of multiversion concurrency control," *Proc. Fourth ACM Symp. on Principles of Database Systems*, pp. 96–104.

Hadzilacos, T. and M. Yannakakis [1986]. "Deleting completed transactions," *Proc. Fifth ACM Symp. on Principles of Database Systems*, pp. 43–46.

Hadzilacos, V. [1982]. "An algorithm for minimizing roll back cost," *Proc. First ACM Symp. on Principles of Database Systems*, pp. 93–97.

Hadzilacos, V. [1987]. "A knowledge-theoretic analysis of atomic commitment protocols," *Proc. Sixth ACM Symp. on Principles of Database Systems*, pp. 129–134.

Haerder, T. and A. Reuter [1983]. "Principles of transaction oriented database recovery—a taxonomy," *Computing Surveys* 15:4, pp. 287–317.

Hagihara, K., M. Ito, K. Taniguchi, and T. Kasami [1979]. "Decision problems for multivalued dependencies in relational databases," *SIAM J. Computing* 8:2, pp. 247–264.

Hall, P. A. V. [1976]. "Optimization of a single relational expression in a relational database," *IBM J. Research and Development* 20:3, pp. 244–257.

Hammer, M. and D. McLeod [1981]. "Database description with SDM: a semantic database model," *ACM Trans. on Database Systems* 6:3, pp. 351–386.

Hammer, M. and D. Shipman [1980]. "Reliability mechanisms for SDD-1: a system for distributed databases," *ACM Trans. on Database Systems* 5:4, pp. 431–466.

Han, J. [1988]. "Selection of processing strategies for different recursive queries," *Proc. Third Intl. Conf. on Data and Knowledge Bases*, Jerusalem, Israel.

Han, J. and L. J. Henschen [1987]. "Handling redundancy in the processing of recursive database queries," *ACM SIGMOD Intl. Conf. on Management of Data*, pp. 73–81.

Harel, D. [1986]. "Logic and databases: a critique," *SIGACT News* **18**:1, pp. 68–74.

Heath, I. J. [1971]. "Unacceptable file operations in a relational data base," *ACM SIGFIDET Workshop on Data Description, Access, and Control*, pp. 19–33.

Heiler, S. and A. Rosenthal [1985]. "G-WHIZ: a visual interface for the functional model with recursion," *Proc. Intl. Conf. on Very Large Data Bases*, pp. 209–218.

Held, G. and M. Stonebraker [1978]. "B-trees reexamined," *Comm. ACM* **21**:2, pp. 139–143.

Henschen, L. J. and S. A. Naqvi [1984]. "On compiling queries in first-order databases," *J. ACM* **31**:1, pp. 47–85.

Hill, R. [1974]. "LUSH resolution and its completeness," DCL Memo 78, School(!) of Artificial Intelligence, Univ. of Edinburgh.

Holt, R. C. [1972]. "Some deadlock properties in computer systems," *Computing Surveys* **4**:3, pp. 179–196.

Honeyman, P. [1980]. "Extension joins," *Proc. Intl. Conf. on Very Large Data Bases*, pp. 239–244.

Honeyman, P. [1982]. "Testing satisfaction of functional dependencies," *J. ACM* **29**:3, pp. 668–677.

Honeyman, P., R. E. Ladner, and M. Yannakakis [1980]. "Testing the universal instance assumption," *Information Processing Letters* **10**:1, pp. 14–19.

Hull, R. and R. King [1987]. "Semantic database modeling: survey, applications, and research issues," CRI–87–20, Computer Research Inst., USC.

Hull, R. and J. Su [1988]. "On the expressive power of database queries with intermediate types," *Proc. Seventh ACM Symp. on Principles of Database Systems*, pp. 39–51.

Hull, R. and C. K. Yap [1984]. "The format model, a theory of database organization," *J. ACM* **31**:3, pp. 518–537.

Hunt, H. B. III and D. J. Rosenkrantz [1979]. "The complexity of testing predicate locks," *ACM SIGMOD Intl. Conf. on Management of Data*, pp. 127–133.

Ibaraki, T. and T. Kameda [1984]. "On the optimal nesting order for computing N-relational joins," *ACM Trans. on Database Systems* 9:3, pp. 482–502.

IBM [1978a]. *Query-by Example Terminal Users Guide*, SH20–2078-0, IBM, White Plains, N. Y.

IBM [1978b]. IMS/VS publications, especially GH20–1260 (*General Information*), SH20–9025 (*System/Application Design Guide*), SH20–9026 (*Application Programming Reference Manual*), and SH20–9027 (*Systems Programming Reference Manual*), IBM, White Plains, N. Y.

IBM [1984]. "SQL/data system application programming for VM/system product," SH24–5068–0, IBM, White Plains, N. Y.

IBM [1985a]. "SQL/RT database programmer's guide," IBM, White Plains, NY.

IBM [1985b]. "Easy SQL/RT user's guide," IBM, White Plains, NY.

Imielinski, T. [1986]. "Query processing in deductive database systems with incomplete information," *ACM SIGMOD Intl. Conf. on Management of Data*, pp. 268–280.

Imielinski, T. and W. Lipski Jr. [1984]. "Incomplete information in relational databases," *J. ACM* 31:4, pp. 761–791.

Imielinski, T. and S. A. Naqvi [1988]. "Explicit control of logic programs through rule algebra," *Proc. Seventh ACM Symp. on Principles of Database Systems*, pp. 103–116.

Immerman, N. [1982]. "Relational queries computable in polynomial time," *Proc. Fourteenth Annual ACM Symp. on the Theory of Computing*, pp. 147–152. Also in *Information and Control* 68:1, pp. 86–104.

Ioannidis, Y. E, [1986a]. "Processing recursion in database systems," UCB/ERL M86/69, Dept. of EECS, Univ. of Calif., Berkeley.

Ioannidis, Y. E. [1986b]. "On the computation of the transitive closure of relational operators," *Proc. Intl. Conf. on Very Large Data Bases*, pp. 403–411.

Ioannidis, Y. E., J. Chen, M. A. Friedman, and M. M. Tsangaris [1988]. "BERMUDA—an architectural perspective on interfacing Prolog to a database machine," *Proc. Second Intl. Conf. on Expert Database Systems* (L. Kerschberg, ed.), pp. 91–105.

Ioannidis, Y. E. and R. Ramakrishnan [1988]. "Efficient transitive closure algorithms," TR–765, Dept. of CS, Univ. of Wisconsin.

Ioannidis, Y. E. and E. Wong [1987a]. "Query optimization by simulated annealing," *ACM SIGMOD Intl. Conf. on Management of Data*, pp. 9–22.

Ioannidis, Y. E. and E. Wong [1987b]. "An algebraic approach to recursive inference," in Kerschberg [1987], pp. 295–309.

Ioannidis, Y. E. and E. Wong [1988]. "Transforming nonlinear recursion to linear recursion," *Proc. Second Intl. Conf. on Expert Database Systems* (L. Kerschberg, ed.), pp. 187–207.

Jaeschke, G. and H.-J. Scheck [1982]. "Remarks on the algebra of non first normal form relations," *Proc. First ACM Symp. on Principles of Database Systems*, pp. 124–138.

Jagadish, H. V., R. Agrawal, and L. Ness [1987]. "A study of transitive closure as a recursion mechanism," *ACM SIGMOD Intl. Conf. on Management of Data*, pp. 331–344.

Jarke, M., J. Clifford, and Y. Vassiliou [1984]. "An optimizing Prolog front end to a relational query system," *ACM SIGMOD Intl. Conf. on Management of Data*, pp. 296–306.

Jarke, M. and J. Koch [1984]. "Query optimization in database systems," *Computing Surveys* **16**:2, pp. 111–152.

Johnson, D. S. and A. Klug [1983a]. "Optimizing conjunctive queries that contain untyped variables," *SIAM J. Computing* **12**:4, pp. 616–640.

Johnson, D. S. and A. Klug [1983b]. "Testing containment of conjunctive queries under functional and inclusion dependencies," *J. Computer and System Sciences* **28**:1, pp. 167–189.

Jou, J. H. and P. C. Fischer [1983]. "The complexity of recognizing 3NF relation schemes," *Information Processing Letters* **14**:4, pp. 187–190.

Kambayashi, Y. [1978]. "An efficient algorithm for processing multi-relation queries in relational databases," ER78–01, Dept. of Information Science, Kyoto Univ., Kyoto, Japan.

Kambayashi, Y. [1981]. *Database a Bibliography*, Computer Science Press, Rockville, Md.

Kanellakis, P. [1986]. *Advances in Computing Research* **3**, JAI Press, London.

Kanellakis, P. C., S. S. Cosmadakis, and M. Y. Vardi [1983]. "Unary inclusion dependencies have polynomial time inference problems," *Proc. Fifteenth Annual ACM Symp. on the Theory of Computing*, pp. 264–277.

Kanellakis, P. C. and C. H. Papadimitriou [1981]. "The complexity of distributed concurrency control," *Proc. Twenty-Second Annual IEEE Symp. on Foundations of Computer Science*, pp. 185–197.

Kanellakis, P. C. and C. H. Papadimitriou [1984]. "Is distributed locking harder?," *J. Computer and System Sciences* **28**:1, pp. 103–120.

Kedem, Z. and A. Silberschatz [1979]. "Controlling concurrency using locking protocols." *Proc. Twentieth Annual IEEE Symp. on Foundations of Computer Science*, pp. 274–285.

Kedem, Z. and A. Silberschatz [1980]. "Non-two phase locking protocols with shared and exclusive locks," *Proc. Intl. Conf. on Very Large Data Bases*, pp. 309–320.

Keller, A. [1985]. "Algorithms for translating view updates into database updates for views involving selections, projections, and joins," *Proc. Fourth ACM Symp. on Principles of Database Systems*, pp. 154–163.

Kellogg, C., A. O'Hare, and L. Travis [1986]. "Optimizing the rule-data interface in a KMS," *Proc. Intl. Conf. on Very Large Data Bases*, pp. 42–51.

Kemp, D. B. and R. W. Topor [1988]. "Completeness of a top-down query evaluation procedure for stratified databases," *Proc. Fifth Intl. Symp. on Logic Programming*, pp. 178–194.

Kent, W. [1979]. "Limitations of record-based information models," *ACM Trans. on Database Systems* **4**:1, pp. 107–131.

Kent, W. [1981]. "Consequences of assuming a universal relation," *ACM Trans. on Database Systems* **6**:4, pp. 539–556.

Kent, W. [1983]. "The universal relation revisited," *ACM Trans. on Database Systems* **8**:4, pp. 644–648.

Kerschberg, L. (ed.) [1987]. *Expert Database Systems*, Benjamin-Cummings, Menlo Park, CA.

Kerschberg, L., A. Klug, and D. C. Tsichritzis [1977]. "A taxonomy of data models," in *Systems for Large Data Bases* (Lockemann and Neuhold, eds.), North Holland, Amsterdam, pp. 43–64.

Khoshafian, S. N. and G. P. Copeland [1986]. "Object identity," *OOPSLA '86 Proceedings*, ACM, New York, pp. 406–416.

Kifer, M. and E. L. Lozinskii [1985]. "A framework for an efficient implementation of deductive databases," unpublished memorandum, SUNY, Stony Brook, NY.

Kifer, M., R. Ramakrishnan, and A. Silberschatz [1988]. "An axiomatic approach to deciding query safety in deductive databases," *Proc. Seventh ACM Symp. on Principles of Database Systems*, pp. 52–60.

Kim, W. [1979]. "Relational database systems," *Computing Surveys* **11**:3, pp. 185–210.

Kim, W. [1981]. "On optimizing an SQL-like nested query," RJ3063, IBM, San Jose, Calif.

Kleene, S. C. [1956]. "Representation of events in nerve nets and finite automata," in *Automata Studies* (C. E. Shannon and J. McCarthy, eds.), Princeton Univ. Press, pp. 3–40.

Klug, A. [1981]. "Equivalence of relational algebra and relational calculus query languages having aggregate functions," *J. ACM* **29**:3, pp. 699–717.

Klug, A. [1988]. "On conjunctive queries containing inequalities," *J. ACM* **35**:1, pp. 146–160.

Knuth, D. E. [1968]. *The Art of Computer Programming*, Vol. 1, *Fundamental Algorithms*, Addison-Wesley, Reading Mass.

Knuth, D. E. [1973]. *The Art of Computer Programming*, Vol. 3, *Sorting and Searching*, Addison-Wesley, Reading Mass.

Kolaitis, P. G. [1987]. "The expressive power of stratified programs," unpublished memorandum, Dept. of CS, Stanford Univ.

Koliatis, P. G. and C. H. Papadimitriou [1988]. "Why not negation by fixpoint?," *Proc. Seventh ACM Symp. on Principles of Database Systems*, pp. 231–239.

Korth, H. F. [1983]. "Locking primitives in a database system," *J. ACM* **30**:1, pp. 55–79.

Korth, H. F., G. M. Kuper, J. Feigenbaum, J. D. Ullman, and A. Van Gelder [1984]. "System/U: a database system based on the universal relation assumption," *ACM Trans. on Database Systems* **9**:3, pp. 331–347.

Korth, H. F. and A. Silberschatz [1986]. *Database System Concepts*, McGraw-Hill, New York.

Kowalski, R. A. [1974]. "Predicate logic as a programming language," *Proc. 1974 IFIP Congress*, pp. 569–574, North Holland, Amsterdam.

Kowalski, R. A. [1975]. "A proof procedure using connection graphs," *J. ACM* **22**:4, pp. 572–595.

Kowalski, R. A. [1988]. "The early years of logic programming," *Comm. ACM* **31**:1, pp. 38–43.

Kowalski, R. A. and D. Kuehner [1971]. "Linear resolution with selection function," *Artificial Intelligence* **2**, pp. 227–260.

Krishnamurthy, R., H. Boral, and C. Zaniolo [1986]. "Optimization of nonrecursive queries," *Proc. Intl. Conf. on Very Large Data Bases*, pp. 128–137.

Krishnamurthy, R., R. Ramakrishnan, and O. Shmueli [1988]. "A framework for testing safety and effective computability of extended datalog," *ACM SIGMOD Intl. Conf. on Management of Data*, pp. 154–163.

Kuck, S. M. and Y. Sagiv [1982]. "A universal relation database system implemented via the network model," *Proc. First ACM Symp. on Principles of Database Systems*, pp. 147–157.

Kuhns, J. L. [1967]. "Answering questions by computer; a logical study," RM-5428-PR, Rand Corp., Santa Monica, Calif.

Kung, H.-T. and C. H. Papadimitriou [1979]. "An optimality theory of concurrency control for databases," *ACM SIGMOD Intl. Conf. on Management of Data*, pp. 116–126.

Kung, H.-T. and J. T. Robinson [1981]. "On optimistic concurrency control," *ACM Trans. on Database Systems* **6**:2, pp. 213–226.

Kunifuji, S. and H. Yokuta [1982]. "PROLOG and relational databases for fifth-generation computer systems," TR002, ICOT, Tokyo.

Kuper, G. M. [1987]. "Logic programming with sets," *Proc. Sixth ACM Symp. on Principles of Database Systems*, pp. 11–20.

Kuper, G. M. [1988]. "On the expressive power of logic programming with sets," *Proc. Seventh ACM Symp. on Principles of Database Systems*, pp. 10–15.

Kuper, G. M. and M. Y. Vardi [1984]. "A new approach to database logic," *Proc. Third ACM Symp. on Principles of Database Systems*, pp. 86–96.

Kuper, G. M. and M. Y. Vardi [1985]. "On the expressive power of the logical data model," *ACM SIGMOD Intl. Conf. on Management of Data*, pp. 180–189.

Lacroix, M. and A. Pirotte [1976]. "Generalized joins," *SIGMOD Record* **8**:3, pp. 14–15.

Lamport, L. [1978]. "Time, clocks, and the ordering of events in a distributed system," *Comm. ACM* **21**:7, pp. 558–565.

Lampson, B. and H. Sturgis [1976]. "Crash recovery in a distributed data storage system," unpublished memorandum, Xerox PARC, Palo Alto, CA.

Larson, P. [1978]. "Dynamic hashing," *BIT* **18**:2, pp. 184–201.

Larson, P. [1982]. "Performance analysis of linear hashing with partial expansions," *ACM Trans. on Database Systems* **7**:4, pp. 565–587.

Laver, K., A. O. Mendelzon, and M. H. Graham [1983]. "Functional dependencies on cyclic database schemes," *ACM SIGMOD Intl. Conf. on Management of Data*, pp. 79–91.

Lee, M. K., J. C. Freytag, and G. M. Lohman [1988]. "Implementing an optimizer for functional rules in a query optimizer," RJ 6125, IBM Almaden Research Center, San Jose, CA.

Lehmann, D. J. [1977]. Algebraic structures for transitive closure," *Theoretical Computer Science* **4**:1, pp. 59–76.

Lehman, P. L. and S. B. Yao [1981]. "Efficient locking for concurrent operations on B-trees," *ACM Trans. on Database Systems* **6**:4, pp. 650–670.

Levien, R. E. [1969]. "Relational data file: experience with a system for propositional data storage and inference execution," RM–5947–PR, Rand Corp., Santa Monica, Calif.

Levien, R. E. and M. E. Maron [1967]. "A computer system for inference execution and data retrieval," *Comm. ACM* **10**:9, pp. 715–721.

Le, V. T. [1985]. "General failure of logic programs," *J. Logic Programming* **2**:2, pp. 157–165.

Lien, Y. E. [1979]. "Multivalued dependencies with null values in relational databases," *Proc. Intl. Conf. on Very Large Data Bases*, pp. 61–66.

Lien, Y. E. [1982]. "On the equivalence of database models," *J. ACM* **29**:2, pp. 333–362.

Lifschitz, V. [1985]. "Closed world databases and circumscription," *Artificial Intelligence* **28**:1, pp. 229–235.

Lifschitz, V. [1988]. "On the declarative semantics of logic programs," in Minker [1988].

Ling, T. W., F. W. Tompa, and T. Kameda [1981]. "An improved third normal form for relational databases," *ACM Trans. on Database Systems* **6**:2, pp. 329–346.

Lipski, W. Jr. [1981]. "On databases with incomplete information," *J. ACM* **28**:1, pp. 41–70.

Lipski, W. Jr. and C. H. Papadimitriou [1981]. "A fast algorithm for testing for safety and deadlocks in locked transaction systems," *J. Algorithms* **2**:2, pp. 211–226.

Litwin, W. [1980]. "Linear hashing: a new tool for file and table addressing," *Proc. Intl. Conf. on Very Large Data Bases*, pp. 212–223.

Litwin, W. [1984]. "MALPHA, A Multidatabase manipulation language," *Proc. IEEEDEC*, April, 1984.

Liu, L. and A. Demers [1980]. "An algorithm for testing lossless joins in relational databases," *Information Processing Letters* **11**:1, pp. 73–76.

Lloyd, J. W. [1984]. *Foundations of Logic Programming*, Springer-Verlag, New York.

Lohman, G. M. [1988]. "Grammar-like functional rules for representing query optimization alternatives," *ACM SIGMOD Intl. Conf. on Management of Data*, pp. 18–27.

Lohman, G. M., C. Mohan, L. M. Haas, B. G. Lindsay, P. G. Selinger, P. F. Wilms, and D. Daniels [1984]. "Query processing in R*," RJ–4272, IBM, Almaden.

Lorie, R. A. [1977]. "Physical integrity in a large segmented database," *ACM Trans. on Database Systems* **2**:1, pp. 91–104.

Lozinskii, E. L. [1985]. "Evaluating queries in a deductive database by generating," *Proc. Ninth IJCAI*, pp. 173–177.

Lucchesi, C. L. and S. L. Osborn [1978]. "Candidate keys for relations." *J. Computer and System Sciences* **17**:2, pp. 270–279.

Lueker, G. S. [1978]. "A data structure for orthogonal range queries," *Proc. Nineteenth Annual IEEE Symp. on Foundations of Computer Science*, pp. 28–33.

Lu, H., K. Mikkilineni, and J. P. Richardson [1987]. "Design and evaluation of algorithms to compute the transitive closure of a database relation," *Proc. Third IEEE Conf. on Data Engineering*, pp. 112–119.

Lum, V. and H. Ling [1970]. "Multi-attribute retrieval with combined indices," *Comm. ACM* **13**:11, pp. 660–665.

Mackert, L. F. and G. M. Lohman [1986]. "R* optimizer validation and performance evaluation for local queries," *ACM SIGMOD Intl. Conf. on Management of Data*, pp. 84–95.

Maher, M. J. [1986]. "Equivalences of logic programs," *Proc. Third Intl. Symp. on Logic Programming*, pp. 410–424, Springer-Verlag, New York.

Maier, D. [1980]. "Minimum covers in the relational database model," *J. ACM* **27**:4, pp. 664–674.

Maier, D. [1983]. *The Theory of Relational Databases*, Computer Science Press, Rockville, Md.

Maier, D. [1986]. "A logic for objects," TR CS/E–86–012, Oregon Graduate Center, Beaverton, Ore.

Maier, D., A. O. Mendelzon, F. Sadri, and J. D. Ullman [1980]. "Adequacy of decompositions in relational databases," *J. Computer and System Sciences* **21**:3, pp. 368–379.

Maier, D., A. O. Mendelzon, and Y. Sagiv [1979]. "Testing implications of data dependencies," *ACM Trans. on Database Systems* **4**:4, pp. 455–469.

Maier, D., D. Rozenshtein, and D. S. Warren [1986]. "Window Functions," in Kanellakis [1986], pp. 213–246.

Maier, D., Y. Sagiv, and M. Yannakakis [1981]. "On the complexity of testing implications of functional and join dependencies," *J. ACM* **28**:4, pp. 680–695.

Maier, D., J. Stein, A. Otis, and A. Purdy [1986]. "Development of an object-oriented DBMS," *OOPSLA '86 Proceedings*, ACM, New York, pp. 472–482.

Maier, D. and J. D. Ullman [1983a]. "Maximal objects and the semantics of universal relation databases," *ACM Trans. on Database Systems* **8**:1, pp. 1–14.

Maier, D. and J. D. Ullman [1983b]. "Fragments of Relations," *Proc. ACM Symp. on Management of Data*.

Maier, D., J. D. Ullman, and M. Y. Vardi [1984]. "On the foundations of the universal relation model," *ACM Trans. on Database Systems* **9**:2, pp. 283–308.

Maier, D. and D. S. Warren [1988]. *Computing with Logic: Logic Programming with Prolog*, Benjamin Cummings, Menlo Park, CA.

Malvestuto, F. M. [1986]. "Modelling large bases of categorical data with acyclic schemes," *First Intl. Conf. on Database Theory*, Rome, Italy.

Manber, U. and R. E. Ladner [1984]. "Concurrency control in a dynamic search structure," *ACM Trans. on Database Systems* **9**:3, pp. 439–455.

Manna, Z. and R. Waldinger [1985]. *The Logical Basis for Computer Programming*, Addison-Wesley, Reading Mass.

Marchetti-Spaccamela, A., A. Pelaggi, and D. Sacca [1987]. "Worst-case complexity analysis of methods for logic query optimization," *Proc. Sixth ACM Symp. on Principles of Database Systems*, pp. 294–301.

Maurer, W. D. and T. G. Lewis [1975]. "Hash table methods," *Computing Surveys* **7**:1, pp. 5–20.

McCarthy, J. [1980]. "Circumscription—a form of nonmonotonic reasoning," *Artificial Intelligence* **13**:1, pp. 27–39.

McKay, D. and S. Shapiro [1981]. "Using active connection graphs for reasoning with recursive rules," *Proc. Seventh IJCAI*, pp. 368–374.

McLean, G. [1981]. "Comments on SDD-1 concurrency control mechanisms," *ACM Trans. on Database Systems* **6**:2, pp. 347–350.

Menasce, D. A. and R. R. Muntz [1979]. "Locking and deadlock detection in distributed data bases," *IEEE Trans. on Software Engineering* **SE-5**:3, pp. 195–202.

Menasce, D. A., G. J. Popek, and R. R. Muntz [1980]. "A locking protocol for resource coordination in distributed databases," *ACM Trans. on Database Systems* **5**:2, pp. 103–138.

Mendelzon, A. O. [1979]. "On axiomatizing multivalued dependencies in relational databases," *J. ACM* **26**:1, pp. 37–44.

Mendelzon, A. O. [1984]. "Database states and their tableaux," *ACM Trans. on Database Systems* **9**:2, pp. 264–282.

Mendelzon, A. O. [1985]. "Functional dependencies in logic programs," *Proc. Intl. Conf. on Very Large Data Bases*, pp. 324–330.

Mendelzon, A. O. and D. Maier [1979]. "Generalized mutual dependencies and the decomposition of database relations," *Proc. Intl. Conf. on Very Large Data Bases*, pp. 75–82.

Minker, J. [1978]. "Search strategy and selection function for an inferential relational system," *ACM Trans. on Database Systems* **3**:1, pp. 1–31.

Minker, J. [1982]. "On indefinite databases and the closed world assumption," *Proc. Sixth Conf. on Automated Deduction* (D. Loveland, ed.), Springer-Verlag, New York.

Minker, J. [1987]. "Perspectives in deductive databases," CS–TR–1799, Dept. of CS, Univ. of Maryland.

Minker, J. [1988]. *Foundations of Deductive Databases and Logic Programming*, Morgan-Kaufmann, Los Altos.

Minker, J. and J.-M. Nicolas [1981]. "On recursive axioms in relational databases," *Information Systems* **8**:1, pp. 1–13.

Minoura, T. [1980]. "Resilient extended true-copy token algorithm for distributed database systems," Ph. D. Thesis, Dept. of EE, Stanford Univ., Stanford, Calif.

Minsky, N. H. and D. Rozenshtein [1987]. "Law-based approach to object-oriented programming," *Proc. 1987 OOPSLA Conf.*

Mitchell, J. C. [1983]. "Inference rules for functional and inclusion dependencies," *Proc. Second ACM Symp. on Principles of Database Systems*, pp. 58–69.

Moffat, D. S. and P. M. D. Gray [1986]. "Interfacing Prolog to a persistent data store," *Proc. Third Intl. Conf. on Logic Programming*, pp. 577–584.

Mohan, C., B. G. Lindsay, and R. Obermarck [1986]. "Transaction management in the R* Distributed database management system," *ACM Trans. on Database Systems* **11**:4, pp. 378–396.

Morris, K. [1988]. "An algorithm for ordering subgoals in NAIL!," *Proc. Seventh ACM Symp. on Principles of Database Systems*, pp. 82–88.

Morris, K., J. F. Naughton, Y. Saraiya, J. D. Ullman, and A. Van Gelder [1987]. "YAWN! (yet another window on NAIL!)," in Zaniolo [1987], pp. 28–43.

Morris, K., J. D. Ullman, and A. Van Gelder [1986]. "Design overview of the NAIL! system," *Proc. Third Intl. Conf. on Logic Programming*, pp. 554–568.

Morris, R. [1968]. "Scatter storage techniques," *Comm. ACM* **11**:1, pp. 38–43.

MRI [1978]. *System 2000 Reference manual*, MRI Systems Corp., Austin, Tex.

Naish, L. [1986]. "Negation and control in Prolog," Lecture Notes in Computer Science **238**, Springer-Verlag, New York.

Napheys, B. and D. Herkimer [1988]. "A look at loosely-coupled Prolog/database systems," *Proc. Second Intl. Conf. on Expert Database Systems* (L. Kerschberg, ed.), pp. 107–115.

Naqvi, S. A. [1986]. "Negation in knowledge base management systems," in Brodie and Mylopoulos [1986], pp. 125–146.

Naqvi, S. A. and R. Krishnamurthy [1988]. "Database updates in logic programming," *Proc. Seventh ACM Symp. on Principles of Database Systems*, pp. 251–262.

Naqvi, S. A. and S. Tsur [1988]. *A Logic Language for Data and Knowledge Bases*, Computer Science Press, Rockville, Md.

Natarajan, K. S. [1987]. "Optimizing backtrack search for all solutions to conjunctive queries," *Tenth IJCAI*, pp. 955–958.

Naughton, J. F. [1986a]. "Redundancy in function-free recursive rules," *Symp. on Logic Programming*, pp. 236–245, IEEE, New York.

Naughton, J. F. [1986b]. "Data independent recursion in deductive databases," *Proc. Fifth ACM Symp. on Principles of Database Systems*, pp. 267–279.

Naughton, J. F. [1987]. "One sided recursions," *Proc. Sixth ACM Symp. on Principles of Database Systems*, pp. 340–348.

Naughton, J. F. [1988a]. "Benchmarking multi-rule recursion evaluation strategies," CS–TR–141–88, Dept. of CS, Princeton Univ.

Naughton, J. F. [1988b]. "Compiling separable recursions," *ACM SIGMOD Intl. Conf. on Management of Data*, pp. 312–319.

Naughton, J. F., R. Ramakrishnan, Y. Sagiv, and J. D. Ullman [1988]. "Efficient evaluation of left-linear and right-linear rules," unpublished memorandum, Dept. of CS, Stanford Univ.

Naughton, J. F. and Y. Sagiv [1987]. "A decidable class of bounded recursions," *Proc. Sixth ACM Symp. on Principles of Database Systems*, pp. 227–236.

Neiman, V. S. [1986]. "Deduction search with single consideration of subgoals," *Dokl. Akad. Nauk SSSR* **286**:5, pp. 251–254.

Nicolas, J. M. [1978]. "Mutual dependencies and some results on undecomposable relations," *Proc. Intl. Conf. on Very Large Data Bases*, pp. 360–367.

Obermarck, R. [1982]. "Distributed deadlock detection algorithm," *ACM Trans. on Database Systems* **7**:2, pp. 187–208.

Olle, T. W. [1978]. *The Codasyl Approach to Data Base Management*, John Wiley and Sons, New York.

Orenstein, J. A. and T. H. Merrett [1984]. "A class of data structures for associative searching," *Proc. Fourth ACM Symp. on Principles of Database Systems*, pp. 181–190.

Osborn, S. L. [1977]. "Normal forms for relational databases," Ph. D. Thesis, Univ. of Waterloo.

Osborn, S. L. [1979a]. "Testing for existence of a covering Boyce-Codd normal form," *Information Processing Letters* **8**:1, pp. 11–14.

Osborn, S. L. [1979b]. "Towards a universal relation interface," *Proc. Intl. Conf. on Very Large Data Bases*, pp. 52–60.

Ozsoyoglu, G. and H. Wang [1987]. "On set comparison operators, safety, and QBE," unpublished memorandum, Dept. of CSE, Case Western Reserve Univ., Cleveland, Ohio.

Ozsoyoglu, M. Z. and L.-Y. Yuan [1985]. "A normal form for nested relations," *Proc. Fourth ACM Symp. on Principles of Database Systems*, pp. 251–260.

Paige, R. and J. T. Schwartz [1977]. "Reduction in strength of high level operations," *Proc. Fourth ACM Symp. on Principles of Programming Languages*, pp. 58–71.

Palermo, F. P. [1974]. "A database search problem," *Information Systems COINS IV* (J. T. Tou, ed.), Plenum Press, N. Y.

Papadimitriou, C. H. [1979]. "The serializability of concurrent database updates," *J. ACM* **26**:4, pp. 631–653.

Papadimitriou, C. H. [1983]. "Concurrency control by locking," *J. ACM* **12**:2, pp. 215–226.

Papadimitriou, C. H. [1986]. *The Theory of Database Concurrency Control*, Computer Science Press, Rockville, Md.

Papadimitriou, C. H., P. A. Bernstein, and J. B. Rothnie Jr. [1977]. "Computational problems related to database concurrency control," *Proc. Conf. on Theoretical Computer Science*, Univ. of Waterloo, Waterloo, Ont.

Papadimitriou, C. H. and P. C. Kanellakis [1984]. "On concurrency control by multiple versions," *ACM Trans. on Database Systems* **9**:1, pp. 89–99.

Paredaens, J. and D. Jannsens [1981]. "Decompositions of relations: a comprehensive approach," in Gallaire, Minker, and Nicolas [1980].

Paredaens, J. and D. Van Gucht [1988]. "Possibilities and limitations of using flat operators in nested algebra expressions," *Proc. Seventh ACM Symp. on Principles of Database Systems*, pp. 29–38.

Pecherer, R. M. [1975]. "Efficient evaluation of expressions in a relational algebra," *Proc. ACM Pacific Conf.*, pp. 44–49.

Peleg, D. [1987]. "Time-optimal leader election in general networks," unpublished memorandum, Dept. of CS, Stanford Univ.

Pereira, F. C. N. and D. H. D. Warren [1983]. "Parsing as deduction," *Proc. Twenty-first Annl. Meeting of the Assn. for Computational Linguistics*, pp. 137–144.

Perl, Y., A. Itai, and H. Avni [1978]. "Interpolation search—a log log n search," *Comm. ACM* **21**:7, pp. 550–553.

Pirotte, A. [1978]. "High level data base query languages," in Gallaire and Minker [1978], pp. 409–436.

Porter, H. H. III [1986]. "Earley deduction," TR CS/E-86-002, Oregon Grad. Center, Beaverton, OR.

Port, G. S., I. Balbin, K. Meenakshi, and K. Ramamohanarao [1988]. "Magic sets made simple," TR 88/20, Dept. of CS, Univ. of Melbourne.

Przymusinski, T. C. [1986]. "An algorithm to compute circumscription," unpublished memorandum, Dept. of Math. Sci., Univ. of Texas, El Paso.

Przymusinski, T. C. [1988]. "On the declarative semantics of stratified deductive databases and logic programs," in Minker [1988].

Ramakrishnan, R. [1988]. "Magic templates: a spellbinding approach to logic programs," *Proc. Fifth Intl. Symp. on Logic Programming*, pp. 140–159.

Ramakrishnan, R., F. Bancilhon, and A. Silberschatz [1987]. "Safety of recursive Horn clauses with infinite relations," *Proc. Sixth ACM Symp. on Principles of Database Systems*, pp. 328–339.

Ramakrishnan, R., C. Beeri, and R. Krishnamurthy [1988]. "Optimizing existential datalog queries," *Proc. Seventh ACM Symp. on Principles of Database Systems*, pp. 89–102.

Ramakrishnan, R., Y. Sagiv, J. D. Ullman, and M. Y. Vardi [1988]. "Proof-tree transformation theorems and their applications," unpublished memorandum, Dept. of CS, Stanford Univ., to appear in 1989 *PODS*.

Ramamohanarao, K. and J. Sheperd [1986]. "A superimposed codeword indexing scheme for very large Prolog databases," *Proc. Third Intl. Conf. on Logic Programming*, pp. 84–98.

Ramamohanarao, K., J. Shepherd, I. Balbin, G. Port, L. Naish, J. Thom, J. Zobel, and P. Dart [1987]. "The NU-Prolog deductive database system," in Zaniolo [1987], pp. 10–19.

Ramarao, K. V. S. [1985]. "On the complexity of commit protocols," *Proc. Fourth ACM Symp. on Principles of Database Systems*, pp. 235–244.

Reed, D. P. [1978]. "Naming and synchronization in a decentralized computer system," Ph. D. thesis, Dept. of EECS, MIT, Cambridge, Mass. Adiba, M. [1980]. "Derived relations: a unified mechanism for views, snapshots, and distributed data," RJ2881, IBM, San Jose, Calif.

Reis, D. R. and M. Stonebraker [1977]. "Effects of locking granularity in a database management system," *ACM Trans. on Database Systems* **2**:3, pp. 233–246.

Reis, D. R. and M. Stonebraker [1979]. "Locking granularity revisited," *ACM Trans. on Database Systems* **4**:2, pp. 210–227.

Reiter, R. [1978]. "On closed world databases," in Gallaire and Minker [1978], pp. 55–76.

Reiter, R. [1980]. "Equality and domain closure in first-order databases," *J. ACM* **27**:2, pp. 235–249.

Reiter, R. [1984]. "Towards a logical reconstruction of relational database theory," in Brodie, Mylopoulos, and Schmidt [1984], pp. 191–233.

Reiter, R. [1986]. "A sound and sometimes complete query evaluation algorithm for relational databases with null values," *J. ACM* **33**:2, pp. 349–370.

Reuter, A. [1984]. "Performance analysis of recovery techniques," *ACM Trans. on Database Systems* **9**:4, pp. 526–559.

Rissanen, J. [1977]. "Independent components of relations," *ACM Trans. on Database Systems* **2**:4, pp. 317–325.

Rissanen, J. [1979]. "Theory of joins for relational databases—a tutorial survey," *Proc. Seventh Symp. on Mathematical Foundations of C. S.*, Lecture notes in CS, **64**, Springer–Verlag, pp. 537–551.

Rivest, R. L. [1976]. "Partial match retrieval algorithms," *SIAM J. Computing* **5**:1, pp. 19–50.

Robinson, J. A. [1965]. "A machine oriented logic based on the resolution principle," *J. ACM* **12**:1, pp. 23–41.

Robinson, J. T. [1981]. "The K-D-B tree; a search structure for large, multidimensional dynamic indices," *ACM SIGMOD Intl. Conf. on Management of Data*, pp. 10–18.

Robinson, J. T. [1986]. "Order preserving linear hashing using dynamic key statistics," *Proc. Fifth ACM Symp. on Principles of Database Systems*, pp. 91–99.

Rohmer, J., R. Lescoeur, and J. M. Kerisit [1986]. "The Alexander method—a technique for the processing of recursive axioms in deductive databases," *New Generation Computing*, **4**:3, pp. 273–286.

Rosenberg, A. L. and L. Snyder [1981]. "Time- and space-optimality in B-trees," *ACM Trans. on Database Systems* **6**:1, pp. 174–193.

Rosenkrantz, D. J., R. E. Stearns, and P. M. Lewis II [1978]. "System level concurrency control for distributed data base systems," *ACM Trans. on Database Systems* **3**:2, pp. 178–198.

Rosenthal, A., S. Heiler, U. Dayal, and F. Manola [1986]. "Traversal recursion, a practical approach to supporting recursive applications," *ACM SIGMOD Intl. Conf. on Management of Data*, pp. 166–176.

Ross, K. A. and R. W. Topor [1987]. "Inferring negative information in deductive database systems," TR 87/1, Dept. of CS, Univ. of Melbourne.

Ross, K. A., A. Van Gelder, and J. S. Schlipf [1988]. "Unfounded sets and well-founded semantics for general logic programs," *Proc. Seventh ACM Symp. on Principles of Database Systems*, pp. 221–230.

Roth, M., H. F. Korth, and A Silberschatz [1984]. "Theory of non-first-normal-form relational databases," TR–84–36, Dept. of CS, Univ. of Texas, Austin.

Rothnie, J. B. Jr., et al. [1980]. "Introduction to a system for distributed databases (SDD-1)," *ACM Trans. on Database Systems* **5**:1, pp. 1–17.

Rothnie, J. B. Jr. and N. Goodman [1977]. "A survey of research and development in distributed database management," *Proc. Intl. Conf. on Very Large Data Bases*, pp. 48–62.

Rothnie, J. B. Jr. and T. Lozano [1974]. "Attribute based file organization in a paged memory environment," *Comm. ACM* **17**:2, pp. 63–69.

Rustin, R. (ed.) [1974]. *Proc. ACM/SIGMOD Conf. on Data Models: Data-Structure-Set vs. Relational*, ACM, New York.

Sacca, D., F. Manfredi, and A. Mecchia [1984]. "Properties of database schemata with functional dependencies," *Proc. Third ACM Symp. on Principles of Database Systems*, pp. 19–28.

Sacca, D. and C. Zaniolo [1986]. "On the implementation of a simple class of logic queries for databases," *Proc. Fifth ACM Symp. on Principles of Database Systems*, pp. 16–23.

Sacca, D. and C. Zaniolo [1987a]. "Implementation of recursive queries for a data language based on pure Horn logic," *Proc. Fourth Intl. Conf. on Logic Programming*, pp. 104–135, MIT Press,Cambridge.

Sacca, D. and C. Zaniolo [1987b]. "Magic counting methods," *ACM SIGMOD Intl. Conf. on Management of Data*, pp. 49–59.

Sacca, D. and C. Zaniolo [1988]. "Differential fixpoint methods and Stratification of logic programs," *Proc. Third Intl. Conf. on Data and Knowledge Bases*, Jerusalem, Israel.

Sacco, G. M. and M. Schkolnick [1986]. "Buffer management in relational database systems," *ACM Trans. on Database Systems* **11**:4, pp. 473–498.

Sadri, F. and J. D. Ullman [1981]. "Template dependencies: a large class of dependencies in relational databases and their complete axiomatization," *J. ACM* **29**:2, pp. 363–372.

Sagiv, Y. [1981]. "Can we use the universal instance assumption without using nulls?", *ACM SIGMOD Intl. Conf. on Management of Data*, pp. 108–120.

Sagiv, Y. [1983]. "A characterization of globally consistent databases and their correct access paths," *ACM Trans. on Database Systems* **8**:2, pp. 266–286.

Sagiv, Y. [1985a]. "Concurrent operations on B-trees with overtaking," *Proc. Fourth ACM Symp. on Principles of Database Systems*, pp. 28–37.

Sagiv, Y. [1985b]. "On computing the restricted projection of the representative instance," *Proc. Fourth ACM Symp. on Principles of Database Systems*, pp. 173–180.

Sagiv, Y. [1987]. "Optimizing datalog programs," *Proc. Sixth ACM Symp. on Principles of Database Systems*, pp. 349–362. Also in Minker [1988], pp. 659–698.

Sagiv, Y., C. Delobel, D. S. Parker, and R. Fagin [1981]. "An equivalence between relational database dependencies and a fragment of propositional logic," *J. ACM* **28**:3, pp. 435–453.

Sagiv, Y. and O. Shmueli [1986]. "On finite FD-acyclicity," *Proc. Fifth ACM Symp. on Principles of Database Systems*, pp. 173–182.

Sagiv, Y. and S. Walecka [1982]. "Subset dependencies and a completeness result for a subclass of embedded multivalued dependencies," *J. ACM* **29**:1, pp. 103–117.

Sagiv, Y. and M. Yannakakis [1981]. "Equivalence among relational expressions with the union and difference operators," *J. ACM* **27**:4, pp. 633–655.

Samet, H. [1984]. "The quad tree and related hierarchical data structures," *Computing Surveys* **16**:2, pp. 187–260.

Saraiya, Y. [1988]. "Linearising nonlinear recursions in linear time," unpublished manuscript, Dept. of CS, Stanford Univ., to appear in 1989 *PODS*.

Schenk, K. L. and J. R. Pinkert [1977]. "An algorithm for servicing multirelational queries," *ACM SIGMOD Intl. Conf. on Management of Data*, pp. 10–19.

Scheuermann, P. and M. Ouksel [1982]. "Multidimensional B-trees for associative searching in database systems," *Information Systems* **7**:2, pp. 123–137.

Schkolnick, M. and P. Sorenson [1981]. "The effects of denormalization on database performance," RJ3082, IBM, San Jose, Calif.

Schkolnick, M. and P. Tiberio [1985]. "Estimating the cost of updates in a relational database system," *ACM Trans. on Database Systems* **10**:2, pp. 163–179.

Schmid, H. A. and J. R. Swenson [1976]. "On the semantics of the relational model," *ACM SIGMOD Intl. Conf. on Management of Data*, pp. 9–36.

Schwarz, P. M., W. Chang, J. C. Freytag, G. M. Lohman, J. McPherson, C. Mohan, and H. Pirahesh [1986]. "Extensibility in the Starburst database system," *Proc. Intl. Workshop on Object-Oriented Database Systems*, Asilomar, CA., Sept., 1986.

Sciore, E. [1979]. "Improving semantic specification in the database relational model," *ACM SIGMOD Intl. Conf. on Management of Data*, pp. 170–178.

Sciore, E. [1981]. "Real-world MVD's," *ACM SIGMOD Intl. Conf. on Management of Data*, pp. 121–132.

Sciore, E. [1982]. "A complete axiomatization of full join dependencies," *J. ACM* **29**:2, pp. 373–393.

Sciore, E. [1986]. "Comparing the universal instance and relational data models," in Kanellakis [1986], pp. 139–162.

Sciore, E. and D. S. Warren [1986]. "Towards an integrated database-Prolog system," *Proc. First Intl. Conf. on Expert Database Systems*, pp. 801–815, Benjamin-Cummings, Menlo Park CA.

Segall, A. and O. Wolfson [1987]. "Transaction commitment at minimal communication cost," *Proc. Sixth ACM Symp. on Principles of Database Systems*, pp. 112–118.

Seki, H. [1988]. "On the power of continuation passing, Part I: an analysis of recursive query processing methods," unpublished manuscript, ICOT, Tokyo.

Seki, H. and H. Itoh [1988]. "A query evaluation method for stratified programs under the extended CWA," *Proc. Fifth Intl. Symp. on Logic Programming*, pp. 195–211.

Selinger, P. G. and M. Adiba [1980]. "Access path selection in distributed database management systems," RJ2883, IBM, San Jose, Calif.

Sellis, T. K. [1986]. "Global query optimization," *ACM SIGMOD Intl. Conf. on Management of Data*, pp. 191–205.

Semmel, R. D. [1988]. "Experience in using MUMPS for AI applications," *MUG Quarterly* **18**:1, pp. 1–6.

Servio Logic [1986]. "Programming in OPAL," Servio Logic Development Corp., Beaverton, Oregon.

Shapiro, L. D. [1986]. "Join processing in database systems with large main memories," *ACM Trans. on Database Systems* **11**:3, pp. 239–264.

Shepherdson, J. C. [1984]. "Negation as failure: a comparison of Clark's completed data base and Reiter's closed world assumption," *J. Logic Programming* **1**:1, pp. 51–79.

Shepherdson, J. C. [1988]. "Negation in logic programming," in Minker [1988], pp. 19–88.

Shipman, D. W. [1981]. "The functional data model and the data language DAPLEX," *ACM Trans. on Database Systems* **6**:1, pp. 140–173.

Shmueli, O. [1987]. "Decidability and expressiveness aspects of logic queries," *Proc. Sixth ACM Symp. on Principles of Database Systems*, pp. 237–249.

Shmueli, O. and S. A. Naqvi [1987]. "Set grouping and layering in Horn clause programs," *Proc. Fourth Intl. Conf. on Logic Programming*, pp. 152–177.

Shneiderman, B. (ed.) [1978]. *Database: Improving Usability and responsiveness*, Academic Press, New York.

Sibley, E. (ed.) [1976]. *Computer Surveys* **8**:1, March, 1976.

Sickel, S. [1976]. "A search technique for clause interconnectivity graphs," *IEEE Trans. on Computers* **C-25**:8, pp. 823–834.

Silberschatz, A. and Z. Kedem [1980]. "Consistency in hierarchical database systems," *J. ACM* **27**:1, pp. 72–80.

Skeen, D. [1981]. "Nonblocking commit protocols," *ACM SIGMOD Intl. Conf. on Management of Data*, pp. 133–142.

Skeen, D., F. Cristian, and A. El Abbadi [1985]. "An efficient fault-tolerant algorithm for replicated data management," *Proc. Fourth ACM Symp. on Principles of Database Systems*, pp. 215–229.

Skeen, D. and M. Stonebraker [1981]. "A formal model of crash recovery in a distributed system," *Proc. Fifth Berkeley Workshop on Distributed Data Management and Computer Networks*, pp. 129–142.

Skeen, D. and D. D. Wright [1984]. "Increasing availability in partitioned database systems," *Proc. Fourth ACM Symp. on Principles of Database Systems*, pp. 290–299.

Smith, D. E. [1985]. "Controlling inference," Ph. D. thesis, Dept. of CS, Stanford Univ.

Smith, D. E. and M. R. Genesereth [1985]. "Ordering conjunctive queries," *Artificial Intelligence* **26**, pp. 171–215.

Smith, J. M. and P. Y. Chang [1975]. "Optimizing the performance of a relational algebra database interface," *Comm. ACM* **18**:10, pp. 568–579.

Smith, J. M. and D. C. P. Smith [1977]. "Database abstractions: aggregation and generalization," *ACM Trans. on Database Systems* **2**:2, pp. 105–133.

Snyder, L. [1978]. "On B-trees reexamined," *Comm. ACM* **21**:7, pp. 594.

Software AG [1978]. *ADABAS Introduction*, Software AG of North America, Reston, Va.

Soisalon-Soininen, E. and D. Wood [1982]. "An optimal algorithm for testing safety and detecting deadlocks," *Proc. First ACM Symp. on Principles of Database Systems*, pp. 108–116.

Stearns, R. E., P. M. Lewis II, and D. J. Rosenkrantz [1976]. "Concurrency control for database systems," *Proc. Seventeenth Annual IEEE Symp. on Foundations of Computer Science*, pp. 19–32.

Stein, J. and D. Maier [1985]. "Relaxing the universal scheme assumption," *Proc. Fourth ACM Symp. on Principles of Database Systems*, pp. 76–84.

Stonebraker, M. [1975]. "Implementation of integrity constraints and views by query modification," *ACM SIGMOD Intl. Conf. on Management of Data*, pp. 65–78.

Stonebraker, M. [1979]. "Concurrency control and consistency of multiple copies in distributed INGRES," *IEEE Trans. on Software Engineering* **SE-5**:3, pp. 188–194.

Stonebraker, M. [1980]. "Retrospection on a database system," *ACM Trans. on Database Systems* **5**:2, pp. 225–240.

Stonebraker, M. [1986]. "Triggers and inference in database systems," in Brodie and Mylopoulos [1986], pp. 297–314.

Stonebraker, M. and L. A. Rowe [1977]. "Observations on data manipulation languages and their embedding in general purpose programming languages," TR UCB/ERL M77–53, Univ. of California, Berkeley, July, 1977.

Stonebraker, M. and L. A. Rowe [1986a]. "The design of Postgres," *ACM SIGMOD Intl. Conf. on Management of Data*, pp. 340–355.

Stonebraker, M. and L. A. Rowe [1986b]. "The Postgres papers," UCB/ERL M86/85, Dept. of EECS, Univ. of Calif., Berkeley

Stonebraker, M. and P. Rubinstein [1976]. "The INGRES protection system," *Proc. ACM National Conf.*, pp. 80–84.

Stonebraker, M. and E. Wong [1974]. "Access control in a relational database management system by query modification," *Proc. ACM National Conf.*, pp. 180–187.

Stonebraker, M., E. Wong, P. Kreps, and G. Held [1976]. "The design and implementation of INGRES," *ACM Trans. on Database Systems* **1**:3, pp. 189–222.

Swami, A. and A. Gupta [1988]. "Optimizing large join queries," *ACM SIGMOD Intl. Conf. on Management of Data*, pp. 8–17.

Tamaki, H. and T. Sato [1986]. "OLD resolution with tabulation," *Proc. Third Intl. Conf. on Logic Programming*, pp. 84–98, Springer-Verlag, New York.

Tanaka, K., Y. Kambayashi, and S. Yajima [1979]. "Properties of embedded multivalued dependencies in relational databases," *J. IECE of Japan* **62**:8, pp. 536–543.

Tanimoto, S. L. [1987]. *The Elements of Artificial Intelligence*, Computer Science Press, Rockville, Md.

Tarjan, R. E. [1981]. "A unified approach to path problems," *J. ACM* **28**:3, pp. 577–593..

Tarjan, R. E. and M. Yannakakis [1984]. "Simple linear-time algorithms to test chordality of graphs, test acyclicity of hypergraphs, and selectively reduce acyclic hypergraphs," *SIAM J. Computing* **13**:3, pp. 566–579.

Tarski, A. [1955]. "A lattice theoretical fixpoint theorem and its applications," *Pacific J. Math.* **5**:2, pp. 285–309.

Tay, Y. C., N. Goodman, and R. Suri [1985]. "Locking performance in centralized databases," *ACM Trans. on Database Systems* **10**:4, pp. 415–462.

Tay, Y. C., R. Suri, and N. Goodman [1985]. "A mean value performance model for locking in databases: the no-waiting case," *J. ACM* **32**:3, pp. 618–651.

Thomas, R. H. [1975]. "A solution to the update problem for multiple copy databases which use distributed control," Rept. 3340, Bolt Beranek, and Newman, Cambridge, Mass.

Thomas, R. H. [1979]. "A majority consensus approach to concurrency control," *ACM Trans. on Database Systems* **4**:2, pp. 180–219.

Thom, J. A., K. Ramamohanarao, and L. Naish [1986]. "A superjoin algorithm for deductive databases," in Minker [1988], pp. 519–544.

Todd, S. J. P. [1976]. "The Peterlee relational test vehicle—a system overview," *IBM Systems J.* **15**:4, pp. 285–308.

Traiger, I. L., J. N. Gray, C. A. Galtieri, and B. G. Lindsay [1982]. "Transactions and consistency in distributed database systems," *ACM Trans. on Database Systems* **7**:3, pp. 323–342.

Treitel, R. and M. R. Genesereth [1987]. "Choosing directions for rules," *J. Automated Reasoning* **3**:4, pp. 395–431.

Treitel, R. and D. E. Smith [1988]. "Effects of inference direction on the optimal ordering of a rule's premises," unpublished memorandum, Intellicorp, Mountain View, CA.

Tsichritzis, D. C. and A. Klug (eds.) [1978]. *The ANSI/X3/SPARC Framework*, AFIPS Press, Montvale, N. J.

Tsichritzis, D. C. and F. H. Lochovsky [1982]. *Data Models*, Prentice-Hall, Englewood Cliffs, New Jersey.

Tsou, D.-M. and P. C. Fischer [1982]. "Decomposition of a relation scheme into Boyce-Codd normal form," *SIGACT News* **14**:3, pp. 23–29. Also appears in *Proc. 1980 ACM Conf.*

Tsur, S. and C. Zaniolo [1986]. "LDL: a logic-based data-language," *Proc. Intl. Conf. on Very Large Data Bases*, pp. 33–41.

Ullman, J. D. [1982a]. "The U. R. strikes back," *Proc. First ACM Symp. on Principles of Database Systems*, pp. 10–22.

Ullman, J. D. [1982b]. *Principles of Database Systems*, Computer Science Press, Rockville, Md.

Ullman, J. D. [1983]. "On Kent's 'consequences of assuming a universal relation'," *ACM Trans. on Database Systems* **8**:4, pp. 637–643.

Ullman, J. D. [1984]. "Flux, sorting, and supercomputer organization for AI applications," *J. Parallel and Distributed Computing* **1**:2, pp. 131–151.

Ullman, J. D. [1985]. "Implementation of logical query languages for databases," *ACM Trans. on Database Systems* **10**:3, pp. 289–321.

Ullman, J. D. [1987]. "Database theory—past and future," *Proc. Sixth ACM Symp. on Principles of Database Systems*, pp. 1–10.

Ullman, J. D. [1988]. "Bottom-up beats top-down for datalog," unpublished manuscript, Dept. of CS, Stanford Univ., to appear in 1989 *PODS*.

Ullman, J. D. and A. Van Gelder [1988]. "Testing applicability of top-down capture rules," *J. ACM* **35**:2, pp. 345–373.

Ullman, J. D. and M. Y. Vardi [1988]. "The complexity of ordering subgoals," *Proc. Seventh ACM Symp. on Principles of Database Systems*, pp. 74–81.

Valduriez, P. [1987]. "Join indices," *ACM Trans. on Database Systems* **12**:2, pp. 218–246.

Valduriez, P. and H. Boral [1987]. "Evaluation of recursive queries using join indices," in Kerschberg [1987], pp. 271–293.

Valduriez, P. and S. Koshafian [1988]. "Transitive closure of transitively closed relations," *Proc. Second Intl. Conf. on Expert Database Systems* (L. Kerschberg, ed.), pp. 177–185.

Van Emden, M. H. and R. A. Kowalski [1976]. "The semantics of predicate logic as a programming language," *J. ACM* **23**:4, pp. 733–742.

Van Gelder, A. [1986a]. "Negation as failure using tight derivations for general logic programs," *Proc. Symp. on Logic Programming*, IEEE, pp. 127–139. Also in Minker [1988], pp. 149–176.

Van Gelder, A. [1986b]. "A message-passing framework for logical query evaluation," *ACM SIGMOD Intl. Conf. on Management of Data*, pp. 155–165.

Van Gelder, A. [1988]. "Expressive power of the well-founded semantics for logic programs with negation," unpublished memorandum, Dept. of ICS, Univ. of California, Santa Cruz.

Van Gelder, A. and R. W. Topor [1987]. "Safety and correct translation of relational calculus formulas," *Proc. Sixth ACM Symp. on Principles of Database Systems*, pp. 313–327.

Van Gucht, D. and P. C. Fischer [1986]. "Some classes of multilevel relational structures," *Proc. Fifth ACM Symp. on Principles of Database Systems*, pp. 60–69. Also in *J. Computer and System Sciences* **36**:1 (1988), pp. 77–105.

Vardi, M. Y. [1982]. "Complexity of relational queries," *Proc. Fourteenth Annual ACM Symp. on the Theory of Computing*, pp. 137–145.

Vardi, M. Y. [1983]. "Inferring multivalued dependencies from functional and join dependencies," *Acta Informatica* **19**:2, pp. 305–324.

Vardi, M. Y. [1984]. "The implication and finite implication problems for typed template dependencies," *J. Computer and System Sciences* **28**:1, pp. 3–28.

Vardi, M. Y. [1985]. "Querying logical databases," *Proc. Fourth ACM Symp. on Principles of Database Systems*, pp. 57–65.

Vardi, M. Y. [1986]. "On the integrity of databases with incomplete information," *Proc. Fifth ACM Symp. on Principles of Database Systems*, pp. 252–266.

Vardi, M. Y. [1988a]. "The universal-relation data model for logical independence," *IEEE Software*, pp. 80–85, March, 1988.

Vardi, M. Y. [1988b]. "Decidability and undecidability results for boundedness of linear recursive queries," *Proc. Seventh ACM Symp. on Principles of Database Systems*, pp. 341–351.

Vardi, M. Y. [1988c]. "Fundamentals of dependency theory," in *Trends in Theoretical Computer Science* (E. Borger, ed.), pp. 171–224, Computer Science Press, Rockville, Md.

Vassiliou, Y. [1979]. "Null values in database management—a denotational semantics approach," *ACM SIGMOD Intl. Conf. on Management of Data*, pp. 162–169.

Vassiliou, Y. [1980]. "Functional dependencies and incomplete information," *Proc. Intl. Conf. on Very Large Data Bases*, pp. 260–269.

Vielle, L. [1987]. "Recursive axioms in deductive databases: the query/subquery approach," in Kerschberg [1987], pp. 253–268.

Vielle, L. [1988]. "From QSQ towards QoSaQ: global optimization of recursive queries," *Proc. Second Intl. Conf. on Expert Database Systems*.

Walker, A. [1986]. "Syllog: an approach to Prolog for nonprogrammers," in *Logic Programming and its Applications* (M. van Canaghem and D. H. D. Warren, eds.), Ablex.

Warren, D. H. D. [1981]. "Efficient processing of interactive relational database queries expressed in Prolog," *Proc. Intl. Conf. on Very Large Data Bases*, pp. 272–282.

Weikum, G. [1986]. "A theoretical foundation of multi-level concurrency control," *Proc. Fifth ACM Symp. on Principles of Database Systems*, pp. 31–42.

Wensel, S. [1988]. "The Postgres reference manual," UCB/ERL M88/20, Dept. of EECS, Univ. of Calif., Berkeley.

Wiederhold, G. [1983]. *Database Design*, McGraw-Hill, New York.

Wiederhold, G. [1986]. "Views, objects, and databases," *Computer*, Dec., 1986.

Wiederhold, G. [1987]. *File Organization for Database Design*, McGraw-Hill, New York.

Wiederhold, G. and R. El Masri [1980]. "The structural model for database design," *Proc. Intl. Conf. on the Entity-Relationship Approach to System Analysis and Design* (P. P. Chen, ed.), North Holland, Amsterdam.

Willard, D. E. [1978a]. "New data structures for orthogonal range queries," TR–22–78, Aiken Computation Lab., Harvard Univ.

Willard, D. E. [1978b]. "Predicate-oriented database search algorithms," TR–20–78, Aiken Computation Lab., Harvard Univ.

Willard, D. E. and G. S. Lueker [1985]. "Adding range restriction capability to dynamic data structures," *J. ACM* **32**:3, pp. 597–617.

Wolfson, O. [1987]. "The overhead of locking (and commit) protocols in distributed databases," *ACM Trans. on Database Systems* **12**:3, pp. 453–471.

Wolfson, O. and M. Yannakakis [1985]. "Deadlock-freedom (and safety) of transactions in a distributed database," *Proc. Fourth ACM Symp. on Principles of Database Systems*, pp. 105–112.

Wong, E. and K. Youssefi [1976]. "Decomposition—a strategy for query processing," *ACM Trans. on Database Systems* **1**:3, pp. 223–241.

Yannakakis, M. [1981]. "Algorithms for acyclic database schemes," *Proc. Intl. Conf. on Very Large Data Bases*, pp. 82–94.

Yannakakis, M. [1982a]. "A theory of safe locking policies in database systems," *J. ACM* **29**:3, pp. 718–740.

Yannakakis, M. [1982b]. "Freedom from deadlock of safe locking policies," *SIAM J. Computing* **11**:2, pp. 391–408.

Yannakakis, M. [1984]. "Serializability by locking," *J. ACM* **31**:2, pp. 227–245.

Yannakakis, M. [1986]. "Querying weak instances," in Kanellakis [1986], pp. 185–212.

Yannakakis, M. and C. H. Papadimitriou [1980]. "Algebraic dependencies," *J. Computer and System Sciences* **25**:1, pp. 2–41.

Yannakakis, M. and C. H. Papadimitriou [1985]. "The complexity of reliable concurrency control," *Proc. Fourth ACM Symp. on Principles of Database Systems*, pp. 230–234.

Yannakakis, M., C. H. Papadimitriou, and H.-T. Kung [1979]. "Locking policies: safety and freedom from deadlock," *Proc. Twentieth Annual IEEE Symp. on Foundations of Computer Science*, pp. 283–287.

Yao, A. C., and F. F. Yao [1976]. "The complexity of searching a random ordered table," *Proc. Seventeenth Annual IEEE Symp. on Foundations of Computer Science*, pp. 173–177.

Yao, S. B. [1979]. "Optimization of query evaluation algorithms," *ACM Trans. on Database Systems* **4**:2, pp. 133–155.

Youn, C., L. J. Henschen, and J. Han [1988a]. "One-directional recursive formulas," *Proc. Third Intl. Conf. on Data and Knowledge Bases*, Jerusalem, Israel.

Youn, C., L. J. Henschen, and J. Han [1988b]. "Classification of recursive formulas in deductive databases," *ACM SIGMOD Intl. Conf. on Management of Data*, pp. 320–328.

Yu, C. T. and M. Z. Ozsoyoglu [1979]. "An algorithm for tree-query membership of a distributed query," *Proc. IEEE COMPSAC*, pp. 306–312.

Zaniolo, C. [1976]. "Analysis and design of relational schemata for database systems," doctoral dissertation, UCLA, July, 1976.

Zaniolo, C. [1984]. "Database relations with null values," *J. Computer and System Sciences* **28**:1, pp. 142–166.

Zaniolo, C. [1985]. "The representation and deductive retrieval of complex objects," *Proc. Intl. Conf. on Very Large Data Bases*, pp. 458–469.

Zaniolo, C. [1986]. "Safety and compilation of nonrecursive Horn clauses," *Proc. First Intl. Conf. on Expert Database Systems*, pp. 167–178, Benjamin-Cummings, Menlo Park, CA.

Zaniolo, C. [1987]. (ed.) *Data Engineering* **10**:4.

Zaniolo, C. [1988]. "Design and implementation of a logic based language for data intensive applications," *Proc. Fifth Intl. Symp. on Logic Programming*, pp. 1666–1687.

Zaniolo, C. and M. A. Melkanoff [1981]. "On the design of relational database schemata," *ACM Trans. on Database Systems* **6**:1, pp. 1–47.

Zhang, W. and C. T. Yu [1987]. "A necessary condition for a doubly recursive rule to be equivalent to a linear recursive rule," *ACM SIGMOD Intl. Conf. on Management of Data*, pp. 345–356.

Zhang, W., C. T. Yu, and D. Troy [1988]. "A necessary and sufficient condition to linearize doubly recursive programs in logic databases," unpublished memorandum, Dept. of EECS, Univ. of Illinois at Chicago.

Zloof, M. M. [1975]. "Query-by-Example: operations on the transitive closure," IBM RC 5526, Yorktown Hts., N. Y.

Zloof, M. M. [1977]. "Query-by-Example: a data base language," *IBM Systems J.* **16**:4, pp. 324–343.

Zloof, M. M. [1978]. "Security and integrity within the Query-by-Example data base management language," IBM RC 6982, Yorktown Hts., N. Y.

Zook, W., K. Youssefi, N. Whyte, P. Rubinstein, P. Kreps, G. Held, J. Ford, R. Berman, and E. Allman [1977]. *INGRES Reference Manual*, Dept. of EECS, Univ. of California, Berkeley.

INDEX FOR VOLUMES I AND II

A

Abiteboul, S. 95, 824
Abort, of transaction 469, 476, 508, 512, 517, 520, 530, 557, 579–581
Abstract data type 22, 43, 95
See also Class, Data abstraction, Encapsulation
Access control 2
See also Security
Active transaction 509
Acyclic graph 835, 944, 947, 962–963
Acyclic hypergraph 633–634, 698–699, 704, 707, 709, 711–713, 729, 732–733, 1003–1006, 1058, 1069
See also Cyclic hypergraph
Acyclic polygraph 495
ADABAS 292
Addis, T. R. 1067
Additive operator 956, 959
Address 301
Address calculation search
See Interpolation search
Adiba, M. 731
Adornment 795–796, 800, 988, 1000–1001
See also Binding pattern, Forbidden adorned goal, Interesting adorned goal, Permissible adornment
Afrati, F. 822, 981
Aggregation 95, 145, 171, 175, 194–195, 203–204, 216–219, 954
Aggregation by groups
See Group-by
Aggressive protocol 511–512, 515–516, 540

Aghili, H. 542
Agrawal, R. 542, 586, 980
Aho, A. V. 65, 95, 239, 362, 374–375, 421, 441, 445, 654, 871, 915–916, 919, 952, 979–980, 1032, 1067
Algebraic dependency 444
Algebraic simplification 637–638, 662–673
Allman, E. 238
Alpha-acyclicity
See Acyclic hypergraph
Alpine 587
Annihilator 956
Anomaly
See Deletion anomaly, Insertion anomaly, Update anomaly
ANSI/SPARC 29
Answer predicate 923, 926–927, 939–940
Answer relation 770, 776, 789–791, 843
Apers, P. M. G. 731
Append statement 191
Application program 14–15
Apt, K. R. 171, 173, 822–823
Archiving 523–524
Argument 101
Arithmetic comparison 885–892, 1054
See also Built-in predicate
Arity 44, 101
Armstrong, W. W. 384, 441
Armstrong's axioms 384–387, 414, 441
Arora, A. K. 442
Assignment 175, 177, 191–192, 272
Association 1056, 1067
Associative law 62–63, 664, 956
Astrahan, M. M. 238, 731
Atom 24

Atomic formula 24, 101, 146, 735
Atomicity 468–469, 542, 545–546
ATOV 747–749, 777
Attribute 3, 25, 35, 37, 44, 226, 273, 634, 1045
   See also Prime attribute
Attribute renaming 179, 192, 217
Atzeni, P. 1068–1069
Augmentation 384, 414–415
AURICAL 1067
Authorization table 17, 460
Automatic insertion 258
Average
   See Aggregation
Avni, H. 375
AWK 239, 1032
Axioms 384, 414–415, 443–445, 886
   See also Armstrong's axioms, Inference, of dependencies

B

Bachman, C. W. 94
Bachman diagram 94, 1069
Backtracking 756–758, 766, 774–775, 788
Backup
   See Archiving
Backward-chaining 755
   See also Top-down logic evaluation
Badal, D. S. 586
Balbin, I. 172, 822, 876, 1025
Bancilhon, F. 95, 171–172, 822–823, 875–876, 979–980
Baroody, J. A. Jr. 30
Basic block 984
Basis rule 920, 922–923, 926–927, 940, 946
Batory, D. S. 733
Bayer, R. 172, 375, 541, 585, 822
BCNF
   See Boyce-Codd normal form
Beck, L. L. 95
Beech, D. 95

Beeri, C. 172, 416, 418, 421, 441–445, 542, 732, 822, 824, 875, 979, 1024, 1067
Bentley, J. L. 375
Berman, R. 238
Bernstein, P. A. 31, 239, 441–442, 445, 540–542, 585–586, 731–732, 1067
Bidiot, N. 172
Biliris, A. 541
Binary search 313–314
Binary search tree 362
Binding pattern 734, 805–806
   See also Adornment, Unique binding pattern
Binding relation 770, 776, 778–782, 790–791, 843, 919
   See also Magic predicate
Biskup, J. 442–443, 980, 1067, 1069
Bitton, D. 733
Blair, H. 173, 823
Blank tuple variable 1028
Blasgen, M. W. 238
Block 296, 518, 635
   See also Basic block
Block access 296, 635, 641–642
Block directory
   See Directory
Blocking, of transactions 559–560, 564–573
Bocca, J. 30, 823
Body, of a rule 102, 107–111, 852–854
Bolour, A. 375
Boral, H. 731, 733, 1024
Bosak, R. 94
Bottom-up logic evaluation 734, 754, 758–760, 773, 793–794, 838–841, 860, 871–872
   See also Naive evaluation, Seminaive evaluation
Bound argument
   See Binding relation
Bound variable 145–147
   See also Supplementary relation
Bounded recursion 981
Bound-is-easier assumption 809–810, 992

Boyce, R. F. 238
Boyce-Codd normal form 401–409, 420, 438, 440, 442–443, 445, 1066
Bradier, A. 172, 822
Breadth-first search 789
Broadcast 582
Brodie, M. L. 30, 94
Brown, M. R. 587
Browne, J. C. 542
Bruggemann, H. H. 1067, 1069
B-tree 321–328, 331, 351–352, 357, 375, 502, 541, 637
Bucket 306–307, 659
Buckley, G. N. 541
Buffer 296, 733
Built-in predicate 101–102, 107, 735, 805, 833–834, 889–892, 989, 991
Burkhard, W. A. 375

C

C 227–234
CAD database 19, 354, 983–984
CALC location mode 344–347
CALC-key 250–252, 259
Candidate key 48, 383
Capture rule 990–992
Cardenas, A. F. 292–293
Carey, M. J. 541, 586, 733
Carlson, C. R. 442, 1067
Cartesian product
See Product
Casanova, M. A. 444
Cascade, of selections and projections 664–665, 667–669
Cascading rollback 510–511, 529–531
CASE database 983
See also Software engineering database
Casey, R. C. 441
Central node locking 553–554, 579
Ceri, S. 585, 731, 823
Chain mode 346
Chain query 732
Chakravarthy, U. S. 732
Chamberlin, D. D. 238, 731

Chan, E. P. F. 1068
Chandra, A. K. 95, 171–172, 444, 822–823, 915–916
Chandy, K. M. 542
Chang, C. L. 979, 1067
Chang, P. Y. 731
Chang, W. 733
Chase 430–434, 444, 1036–1037
Checkpoint 522–524
Chen, J. 823
Chen, P. P. 94
Childs, D. L. 94
Chimenti, D. 1024
Chiu, D. W. 732
Choice (operator) 717, 720
Cincom 292
Circumscription 173
Clark, K. L. 172–173
Class 85, 271–272, 275
See also Abstract data type
Clause 102
See also Horn clause, Rule
Clifford, J. 30
Clippinger, R. F. 94
Clock 573–574
Clocksin, W. F. 30
Closed semiring 918, 955–963, 978, 980
Closed world assumption 161–164, 172–173
Closure
See Kleene closure
Closure, of a set of attributes 386, 388–389, 400, 445, 1041
Closure, of a set of dependencies 383, 388–390, 399, 418
Cluster (of nodes) 717–718
Clustering index 636–637, 641–642, 658–659, 952–953
Clustering of records 335–337, 367–368
COBOL 240, 246
CODASYL 29, 94, 292
CODASYL DBTG 240
CODASYL DDL 240–246, 344–346, 352, 457
CODASYL DML 4–5, 246–262

Codd, E. F. 43, 94–95, 171–172, 174, 238, 441–442, 1069

Code optimization
    See Query optimization

Combined record 79

Comer, D. 375

Commit point 509, 556

Commitment, of transactions 509, 511, 520, 530, 557–573, 586, 1020

Common subexpression 667

Communication area 229

Communication cost
    See Transmission cost

Commutative law 62–63, 664–667, 956

Commutativity, of rules 929–936, 938–939, 975

Compacted tree 717–718

Complementation 128, 137, 143, 202, 415

Complete language 145, 174–175, 179, 192–193, 206–207, 221–223

Complete tree 366

Completed transaction 509

Completeness 385, 415–416, 445, 887–889

Complex object 22, 82, 95, 824

Complex selection 140

Component 44

Computational meaning of rules 99–100

Conceptual database 8–9, 11, 29
    See also Logical data independence, Physical data independence

Conclusion row 424

Concurrency control 6, 17, 446, 467–542, 546–557, 573–575, 585
    See also Transaction management

Concurrent access table 17

Condition box 205–206

Condition hyperedge 677

Conflict-serializability 493–500

Conjunctive query 877–916, 930–931
    See also Containment, of conjunctive queries, Tableau

Connection hypergraph 677–692

CONS 993

Conservative protocol 511–515, 533, 540

Consistent state 519

Constraint table 453, 455–456

Containment mapping 881–883, 889–890

Containment (mapping between unions of conjunctive queries) 904

Containment, of conjunctive queries 877–883, 889–891, 913–914, 930, 965–967

Containment, of unions of conjunctive queries 903–905, 907–911, 914, 968–974, 1060

Convergence 119

Cooper, E. C. 95

Coordinator 557, 570–571

Copeland, G. P. 30

Cosmadakis, S. S. 444–445, 915, 981

Count
    See Aggregation

Counting-linear recursion 917, 942–949, 980, 991, 1000

Crash recovery
    See Resiliency

Cristian, F. 586

Cruz, I. F. 980

Culik, K. II 375

Cullinane 292

Currency pointer 246–249

Current of record type 247–249, 251

Current of run-unit 247–250, 256–257, 260–261, 264

Current of set type 247–249, 259

Current parent 264, 268–269

Cursor 231

CWA
    See Closed world assumption

Cyclic hypergraph 698, 709–710, 1006–1008, 1056–1063, 1069
    See also Acyclic hypergraph

Cylinder 17

D

DAG
    See DAG protocol, Directed acyclic graph

DAG protocol 537, 541
Danforth, S. 1024
Dangling reference 298, 320
Dangling tuple 50–53, 394, 701–702, 892–893, 1050
Daniels, D. 731
Dart, P. 1025
Data abstraction
    See Encapsulation
Data curator 464
Data definition language 8, 12–13, 207–210, 223–227, 240–246, 262–265, 271–278, 1062–1063
Data dependency
    See Dependency
Data independence 11–12
Data item 241
Data manipulation language
    See Query language, Subscheme data manipulation language
Data model 2–3, 8, 32–34, 96
    See also Association, Datalog, Entity-relationship model, Hierarchical model, Network model, Object model, Object structure, Relational model
Database 2
Database administrator 16
Database catalog 225–227
Database integration 9, 29
Database key 250–251, 345
Database management system 1–7
Database manager 16–17
Database record 74–76, 266, 333, 347
Database scheme 45, 376
Data-flow analysis 980, 984–987
Datalog 26, 32, 100–106, 139, 427, 825, 871–872, 874, 963, 991, 1009
Datalog equation 115–121
Date, C. J. 31, 94, 293
D'Atri, A. 732
Davidson, S. B. 586
Dayal, U. 30, 239, 442, 731–732, 980, 1025
DBMS
    See Database management system

DBTG DDL
    See CODASYL DDL
DBTG DML
    See CODASYL DML
DBTG set 240–244
    See also Link, Singular set
DDL
    See Data definition language
Deadlock 473–474, 476, 508, 513–515, 542, 557, 576–581, 586
DeBernardis, M. C. 1068
Debray, S. K. 823
Declarative language 21, 24, 175, 177
Decomposition 412, 442
    See also Dependency preservation, Lossless join
Decomposition join 676
Decomposition, of a relation scheme 392
Decomposition rule 386, 416–417
Deductive database 171
Default segment 462
Degree
    See Arity
Delayed evaluation 177–178
Delete statement 190, 262, 270
Deleted bit 298, 304
Deletion 190, 204, 220, 260–262, 270–271, 284–285, 305–306, 309, 317, 320, 322, 325–329, 338, 449–451, 453, 458, 998–999
Deletion anomaly 378
Delobel, C. 441, 443
Demand evaluation 1016–1017
Demand-lock 1018–1020
Demers, A. 441
DeMorgan's laws 140
Dense index 328–331, 336, 339, 341–342, 347
Dependency 376–377
    See also Algebraic dependency, Equality-generating dependency, Functional dependency, Generalized dependency, Implicational dependency, Inclusion dependency, Join dependency, Key dependency, Multivalued dependency, Subset

dependency, Tuple-generating dependency

Dependency basis 417–419, 443

Dependency graph 103–104, 106

Dependency preservation 398–401, 403–404, 408–412, 442

Depth, of a transaction 483

Depth-first search 953, 980

Derivative 172, 447, 449–452, 465, 752

Derochette, D. 542

DeWitt, D. J. 30, 542, 733

Dictionary order
See Lexicographic order

Dietrich, S. W. 876

Difference 55–57, 178, 189–190, 634, 666, 668–669, 914–916, 993

DiPaola, R. A. 172

Direct location mode 345

Directed acyclic graph 537

Directory 303

Dirty data 509–510

Disjoint sets 997

Disk 17–18, 296–297, 468

Dissly, C. W. 542

Distinguished attribute 713

Distinguished node 685

Distinguished symbol 1054

Distinguished variable 893

Distributed system 543–587, 692–702

Distributive law 956

DL/I 262, 264, 266–271

DML
See Data manipulation language

Dobbs, C. 94

Domain 43, 208, 950, 956

Domain closure assumption 162

Domain relational calculus 148–156, 195–196

Domain size 443–444, 648–649, 1003, 1005

Domain variable 196

Domain-independent formula 151–152, 172

Down predicate 946

Down subgoal/argument 945

DRC
See Domain relational calculus

Dull tuple 874

Duplicates 201, 203–204, 216, 954–955

Dwork, C. 586

E

Eager, D. 586

Ear, of a hypergraph 698

Ear removal 698, 711–712
See also GYO reduction

Earley deduction 876

Earley J. 876

EDB
See Extensional database

Edge
See Hyperedge

El Abbadi, A. 586

El Masri, R. 29, 95

Election, of a coordinator 570–571, 586

Elhardt, K. 585

Ellis, C. S. 541–542

Embedded dependency 426–428, 439

Embedded multivalued dependency 422–423, 443

Empty relation 93

Empty tuple 93

Encapsulation 22
See also Data abstraction

Encryption 456

Entity 34

Entity set 33–34, 37, 45–46, 48, 67, 380, 1045

Entity-relationship diagram 37–38, 40, 45–49, 67, 73, 87

Entity-relationship model 33–42, 65

Epstein, R. 587

Equality index 286–287

Equality-generating dependency 424, 430, 432–433, 440, 1036–1037, 1039, 1066

Equijoin 59, 72

Equivalence, of conjunctive queries 881, 892

Equivalence, of decompositions 442

Equivalence, of expressions 663
Equivalence, of schedules 478, 487, 493, 498
Equivalence, of sets of dependencies 389–390
Equivalence, of unions of conjunctive queries 904
Essential symbol 1054
Eswaran, K. P. 540–541
EVAL 115, 122, 742
EVAL-RULE 109
Event 842–843, 871
Exclusive lock
    See Write-lock
Execute-immediate statement 229
Execution algorithm 991
Existence constraint 51, 258, 451–452
    See also Inclusion dependency
Existential quantifier 25, 102–103, 146–147, 215
EXODUS 733
Expansion, of logic programs 878–880, 907–911, 914–915
Expert system shell 24
Extension
    See Instance, of a database, ISBL extension
Extension join 1042–1043, 1066–1068
Extensional database 10–11, 100–101, 171, 735, 806
ExtraHelp 991–992

F

FAD 995, 1024
Fagin, R. 375, 416, 441, 443–445, 466, 732, 1069
Fail 757
Failure
    See Media failure, Network failure, Node failure, System failure
Fatal error 476, 479
Feasibility, of rule/goal graphs 806–817
Feigenbaum, J. 1067, 1069
Fekete, A. 542
Fernandez, E. B. 466

Field 66, 82, 242–243, 295
    See also Data item, Virtual field
Field name 2–3
Fifth-generation project 1
File 295
File manager 17–18
File system 2
Filliat, A. I. 94
Final transaction 494
Find statement 249–257
Finkel, R. A. 375
First normal form 95, 402
Fischer, P. C. 95, 442–443, 445
Fishman, D. H. 30
Fixed point 116, 171, 1009
    See also Least fixed point, Minimal fixed point
Floyd's algorithm 958
Focus 793
Fong, A. C. 172
Forbidden adorned goal 811
Ford, J. 238
Forest 72
Format, for a block 301–303, 337–338
Format, for a record 295, 298–301
Formula 145–148
Forward-chaining 754
    See also Bottom-up logic evaluation
Forwarding address 320
Fourth normal form 420–422, 443
Fragment 545
Fragment, of a relation 692–694
Franaszek, P. 540
Frank, D. 733
Fredman, M. L. 375
Free variable 145–147
Freytag, J. C. 733
Friedman, J. H. 375
Friedman, M. A. 823
Frost, R. 30
Full dependency 426–427, 432
Full reducer 703–707, 710–711, 728, 732
Function symbol 24–25, 96, 100, 734, 736, 773, 848–852, 993, 995

Functional dependency 376–412, 414–416, 422, 424, 436, 440–443, 445, 453, 465, 914, 916, 1041
Furtado, A. L. 95

G

Gaifman, H. 981
Galil, Z. 443
Gallaire, H. 171, 822
Galtieri, A. 585
Gangopadhyay, D. 876
Garcia-Molina, H. 542, 554, 585–586
Garey, M. R. 440
Gelenbe, E. 542
Gelfond, M. 172–173
Gemstone 30, 271, 293, 462
    See also OPAL
Generalization 95
Generalized closed world assumption 164, 173
Generalized dependency 423–434, 440, 443–444
Generalized magic sets 860–872, 874–875
Generalized projection 167
Generalized supplementary magic sets 875
Genesereth, M. R. 30, 732, 822, 876
GENESIS 733
Gerber, R. 733
Get statement 249, 264, 266–269
Ginsberg, M. 172, 823
Ginsburg, S. 442
Global clock 573–574, 585
Global consistency 728–729
    See also Full reducer
Global item 545–546
Global transaction 546
Goal node 767, 857
Goldberg, A. 293
Goldfinger, R. 94
Gonzalez-Rubio, R. 172, 822
Goodman, J. R. 733
Goodman, L. A. 732

Goodman, N. 31, 441, 540–542, 585–586, 732
Gotlieb, C. C. 374
Gotlieb, L. R. 731
Gottlob, G. 442, 823
Gouda, M. G. 732
Graefe, G. 733
Graham, M. H. 443, 732, 1068
    See also GYO-reduction
Granularity 469–470, 540–541
Graph
    See Acyclic graph, Dependency graph, Directed acyclic graph, Hypergraph, Polygraph, Predicate connection graph, Processing graph, Rule/goal graph, Serialization graph, Transitive closure, Waits-for graph
Graphics database 19–20, 354
Gray, J. N. 540–542, 585–586, 733
Gray, P. M. D. 30, 823
Greenblatt, D. 238
Griffiths, P. P. 466, 731
    See also Selinger, P. G.
Ground atom 162, 736
    See also Nonground atom
Ground term 736
Group 461
Group-by 195, 217–219
Grumbach, S. 95
Guard condition 694–696
Gudes, E. 375
Gupta, A. 732
Gurevich, Y. 444
GYO-reduction 698–699, 706–707

H

Haas, L. M. 731, 733
Haberman, S. J. 732
Haddad, R. W. 980
Hadzilacos, T. 541–542
Hadzilacos, V. 31, 540, 542, 565, 585–586
Haerder, T. 542
Hagihara, K. 443

Hall, P. A. V. 731
Hammer, M. M. 95, 238, 586
Han, J. 979
Harel, D. 95, 171–172, 822
Hash function 306–307
Hash table 3, 347
Hashing 306–310, 328, 331, 351, 357, 375, 659, 733
  See also Partitioned hashing
Head, of a rule 102, 735
  See also Rectified rule
Heap 304–306, 351
Heath, I. J. 441
Heiler, S. 95, 980, 1025
Held, G. 238, 375
Heller, H. 585
Henschen, L. J. 979–980
Herkimer, D. 823
Hevner, A. R. 731
Hierarchical model 28, 72–82, 94, 346–350, 457, 502, 736
  See also IMS
Hill, R. 822
HISAM 347–349
Holt, R. C. 542
Home position 934
Homogeneous relation 874
Honeyman, P. J. 442–443, 1067–1068
Hopcroft, J. E. 65, 362, 374, 654, 919, 952, 980
Horizontal fragment 693
Horn clause 25, 47–128, 163, 448, 736, 773
Host language 14–16, 18–21, 28–30, 227–234, 246
Howard, J. H. 416, 441, 443, 445
Hull, R. 95, 172, 824
Hunt, H. B. III 541
Hu's algorithm 958
Hyperedge 677
Hypergraph 633, 676–679, 1048–1049, 1066
  See also Acyclic hypergraph, Connection hypergraph, Cyclic hypergraph, Object structure
Hypothesis row 424

I

Ibaraki, T. 731
IBM 238, 293, 466
ICODE 991–994
IDB
  See Intensional database
Idempotence 521
Identification
  See User identification
Identity 956
Identity index 287
IDMS 292
Image size 637, 641
  See also Domain size
Imielinski, T. 94, 824
Immerman, N. 173
Implicational dependency 444
IMS 262–271, 293, 347–350, 457
Inclusion dependency 423, 444
  See also Existence constraint, Unary inclusion dependency
Incremental evaluation
  See Semi-naive evaluation
Incremental relation 125
Increment-lock 491–492
Independence, of relational algebra operators 93
Independent components 442
Independent scheme 442, 1035, 1037, 1042, 1065–1066, 1068
Index 3, 13, 65, 208, 223–224, 227, 250, 285–288, 312, 321, 352, 636, 806, 842
  See also Clustering index, Dense index, Isam, Nonclustering index, Primary index, Secondary index, Sparse index
Indexed sequential access method
  See Isam
Index-join 656–662, 1005
Inference, of dependencies 382–392, 416–420, 430–434, 440–441, 445
Infinite relation 104–105, 149
Inflationary semantics 823–824

Ingres 185, 351, 466, 587, 673, 982, 1008
    See also QUEL
Initial transaction 494
Initialization rule 830, 858
Input cost (for joins and products) 644–647, 651–662, 709
Insert statement 260, 269–270
Insertion 14, 191, 204–205, 219–220, 258, 260, 269–270, 280–281, 305, 308–309, 316–317, 320, 322–325, 329, 338–339, 363–364, 449–451, 453, 458, 998–999
Insertion anomaly 377
Instance, of a class 272
Instance, of a database 10
Instance, of a pattern 332
Instance variable 275, 295
Integrity 7, 446–456, 466
Integrity constraint 102, 379, 398, 447–448
Intension
    See Scheme
Intensional database 11, 100–101, 171, 735
Interesting adorned goal 811–812, 821
Intermediate code
    See FAD, ICODE
Interpolation search 314–315, 375
Interpretation 97–98
Intersection 57–58, 62, 168, 178, 997
Invalidate-lock 1017, 1019–1020
Ioannidis, Y. E. 823, 876, 980–981
IRIS 30
Isa hierarchy 35–37, 40, 67
    See also Type hierarchy
Isam 310–321, 331, 347, 351, 357, 636
ISBL 177–185, 238, 457
ISBL extension 184–185
Itai, A. 375
Item 469, 502, 545–546
Ito, M. 443
Itoh, H. 876

J

Jaeschke, G. 95
Jagadish, H. V. 980
Jannsens, D. 444
Jarke, M. 30, 733
Jasper, R. B. 94
Johnson, D. S. 440, 916
Join 64–65, 176–178, 239, 450, 464–465, 470, 634, 638, 647–664, 668–669, 673–676, 708, 719–722, 731, 757, 759–760, 777, 825, 864–868, 877, 895–896, 993, 1003–1008
    See also Extension join, Natural join, Select-project-join query, Semijoin, θ-join, Unification join, Universal join
Join dependency 425–426, 440, 444–445, 1047–1049, 1066, 1068–1069
Jou, J. H. 443
Journal
    See Log

K

Kambayashi, Y. 31, 443, 1067
Kameda, T. 442, 731
Kanellakis, P. C. 444–445, 541, 585, 915, 979, 981
Kaplan, R. S. 1067
Kasami, T. 443
KBMS
    See Knowledge-base management system
k-d-tree 361–368, 375
Keating, W. 94
Kedem, Z. 503, 541
Keller, A. 239
Kellogg, C. 30
Kemp, D. B. 876
Kendrick, G. 94
Kent, J. 542
Kent, W. 238, 1069
Kerisit, J. M. 875
Kernighan, B. W. 239, 1032, 1067
Kerschberg, L. 94

Key 35–36, 47–50, 205, 208, 294, 297–298, 304, 308, 311, 323, 381, 383, 402, 440, 443–445, 452–453, 470, 1045

See also Database key

Key dependency 1041

Khoshafian, S. N. 30, 95, 980, 1024

Kifer, M. 823, 876

Kim, W. 238, 731

King, R. 95

King, W. F. 238

Kleene closure 959, 962

Kleene, S. C. 980

Kleene's algorithm 958–963

Kleitman, D. J. 375

Klug, A. 29, 94, 171, 915–916

Knowledge system 23–24, 30, 32

Knowledge-base management system 1, 24, 28–29, 982–987

See also Knowledge system, LDL, NAIL!, NU-Prolog, POSTGRES, Starburst

Knuth, D. E. 307, 374–375, 654, 1025

Koch, J. 733

k-of-n locking 550, 554, 577, 582, 585

Kolaitis, P. G. 824

Kolling, K. 587

Korth, H. F. 31, 95, 540, 1028, 1067, 1069

Kowalski, R. A. 30, 171, 822–823

Kramer, M. 1069

Kranning, L. A. 94

Kreps, P. 238

Krishnamurthy, R. 1024

Kuck, S. M. 1067

Kuehner, D. 822

Kuhns, J. L. 94, 171

Kung, H.-T. 540–541

Kunifuji, S. 30

Kuper, G. M. 95, 171–172, 824, 1067, 1069

L

Lacroix, M. 94

Ladner, R. E. 542, 1068

Lai, M. Y. 542

Lamport, L. 585

Lampson, B. 586

Larson, P. 375

Laver, K. 732

LDL 30, 824, 982, 994–1008, 1024

Le, V. T. 172

Least fixed point 117, 119, 122–123, 126–129, 131, 742–743, 753–754, 773, 793–794

See also Minimal fixed point

Lee, M. K. 733

Left-linear recursion 917, 924–929, 936–941, 953, 979, 986–987, 991, 999–1000

Leftmost child 349–350

Leftmost record 266–267

Lehman, P. L. 541

Lehmann, D. J. 980

Lescouer, R. 875

Leung, T. Y. 733

Level number 242

Levels of abstraction 7, 10, 29

Levien, R. E. 94, 171

Lewis, H. R. 444

Lewis, P. M. II 540, 586

Lewis, T. G. 375

Lexicographic order 311

Lien ,Y. E. 443, 1069

Lifschitz, V. 172–173

Limited variable 105, 153, 158

Lindsay, B. G. 585, 587, 731

Linear recursion 917–981, 991

Ling, H. 375

Ling, T. W. 442

Link 66–67, 71, 73, 78, 240, 342–343, 543

See also Many-one relationship

Linvy, M. 586

Lipski, W. Jr. 94, 542

Literal 102, 146

Litwin, W. 29, 375

Liu, L. 441

Livelock 472–473, 513–514

Lloyd, J. W. 171, 822

Local consistency 728–729

Local item 545–546

Local transaction 546

Local-area network 543

Location mode 344–346

Lochovsky, F. H. 94, 292–293

Lock 17–18, 270, 467–472, 477–479, 502,
    505, 512, 540, 546–554, 575
    See also Demand-lock, Increment-
    lock, Invalidate-lock, Read-lock,
    Trigger-lock, Warning lock, Write-
    lock

Lock compatability matrix 490, 507–
    508, 1018–1019

Lock manager 469–471

Lock mode 490–492, 537, 540, 1018

Lock point 485, 524, 556

Lock table 470, 529

Log 510, 516–524, 529–531, 542, 563–
    564

Logic 20–21, 23–27, 96–173, 734–824
    See also Relational calculus

Logic programming 24, 95, 102
    See also Prolog

Logical data independence 12

Logical item
    See Global item

Logical record 66, 241, 295

Logical record format 66

Logical record type 66, 73, 241

Logical relation 692–693, 697

Logical rule
    See Rule

Lohman, G. M. 731, 733

Lookup 305, 308, 313–314, 316, 319,
    323, 328–329, 335–337, 359–360,
    362–366

Lorie, R. A. 540–542, 731

Lossless join 393–398, 403–408, 411–
    412, 419–420, 440–442, 444, 882,
    1050, 1056, 1067

Lozano, T. 375

Lozinskii, E. L. 876

LR-parsing 871

Lu, H. 980

Lucchesi, C. L. 445

Lueker, G. S. 375

Lum, V. 375

LUSH resolution
    See SLD-resolution

Lynch, N. 542

M

Mackert, L. F. 731

Magic predicate 827–835, 854–855, 861–
    863, 920, 922, 926, 939–940
    See also Binding relation

Magic rule 830

Magic sets 734, 774, 782, 825–876, 918–
    919, 924, 929, 940–941, 947–949,
    987, 991, 999–1000

Maher, M. J. 915

Maier, D. 30, 293, 432, 441–445, 732,
    875, 980, 1056, 1067–1069

Main file 312

Main memory
    See Volatile storage

Mairson, H. 981

Majority locking 548–550, 554

Makowsky, J. A. 444

Malvestuto, F. M. 732

Manber, U. 542

Mandatory retention 258

Manfredi, F. 732

Manna, Z. 171

Manola, F. 980, 1025

Manual deletion 260–261

Manual insertion 258, 260

Many-many relationship 33, 39–40, 48,
    72, 78–79

Many-one relationship 39, 49, 65, 380
    See also Link

Mapping
    See Containment, Containment
    mapping, Set-of-mappings (repre-
    sentation of relations), Subsump-
    tion mapping, Symbol mapping,
    Tableau

Marchetti-Spaccamela, A. 980
Maron, M. E. 94, 171
Matrix 978
Maurer, W. D. 375
Max
    See Aggregation
Maximal object 1056–1063
McCarthy, J. 173
McCreight, E. M. 375
McKay, D. 876
McLean, G. 586
McLeod, D. 95
McPherson, J. 733
Mecchia, A. 732
Media failure 508, 516, 523–524
Meenakshi, K. 876
Melkanoff, M. A. 443
Mellish, C. S. 30
Member 241, 251, 997
Memoing 876
    See also Magic sets
Menasce, D. A. 586
Mendelzon, A. O. 432, 442–444, 732, 823, 1068–1069
Merge-sort
    See Multiway merge-sort
Merlin, P. M. 915–916
Merritt, M. 542
Method 85, 272–274
MGU
    See Most general unifier
Mikkilineni, K. 980
Min
    See Aggregation
Minimagic 854–857, 875
Minimal cover 390–392, 409–411, 436–437, 445
Minimal fixed point 116–117, 131–132, 138–139
    See also Least fixed point
Minimal model 98–99, 114–116
Minimization, of conjunctive queries 883–885, 891, 914
Minimization, of tableaux 900, 1050–1052, 1060

Minimization, of unions of conjunctive queries 905–907, 912
Minker, J. 171, 173, 731–732, 822, 981
Minoura, T. 585–586
Minsky, N. H. 30, 95
Mitchell, J. C. 444
Model 97–100, 171
    See also Fixed point, Minimal model, Perfect model
Modification
    See Update
Modify statement 261
Moffat, D. S. 30, 823
Mohan, C. 587, 731, 733
Monotonicity 119, 121–124, 144–145, 171, 449
Morris, K. 30, 823, 1024
Morris, R. 375
Moscarini, M. 732
Most general unifier 760–762, 773
MRI 293
MRS 876
Multilist 343–344, 354
Multiple copies 544–554, 586
Multiplicative operator 956, 959
Multirelation 731
Multivalued dependency 377, 413–424, 440, 442–443, 465, 1048–1049, 1069
Multiversion concurrency control 531–534
Multiway join
    See Three-way join
Multiway merge-sort 654–656
Muntz, R. R. 586
Muralikrishna, M. 733
Mylopoulos, J. 30, 94

N

NAIL! 30, 982, 987–995, 1024
Naish, L. 172, 1025
Naive evaluation 119, 126, 741–742, 751–752, 819, 822, 841
Napheys, B. 823
Naqvi, S. A. 172, 824, 980, 1024

Natural join 59–60, 62, 72, 122
    See also Join
Natural language 1026, 1030
Naughton, J. F. 30, 979–981, 1024
Navigation 3–4, 21, 64, 71–72, 86–87, 249, 281–282, 346
Negation by failure 172–173
Negation, in rules 97, 99, 128–139, 145, 172, 986
    See also Stratified negation
Negation, logical 139–141
Negative literal 102
Neiman, V. S. 876
Ness, L. 980
Nested record structure 330, 332–339, 342, 346, 352
Nested transaction 542
Network 66, 73–74, 77, 543–545
Network failure 559, 582
Network model 28, 65–72, 94, 292, 342–346, 457
    See also CODASYL, CODASYL DDL, CODASYL DML
Nicolas, J.-M. 171, 444, 822, 981
Nievergelt, J. 375
Nilsson, N. J. 30, 822
Node 543
Node failure 544, 565
Nonclustering index 636–637, 641–643
Nondistinguished variable 893
Nonfatal error 475–476, 478–479
Non-first-normal-form relation 95
Nonground atom 825, 861–872
Nonlinear recursion 963–974, 980–981
Nonprime attribute 402
Nonrecursive predicate 103–104, 106–115, 139, 141, 144
Normal form 401
    See also Boyce-Codd normal form, First normal form, Fourth normal form, Second normal form, Third normal form
Normalization 76, 246, 442–444, 1027
Norvell, T. S. 980
$\mathcal{NP}$-completeness 440, 443, 445, 501, 710, 885, 915–916, 1068

Null value 51–53, 94, 1026–1027, 1034, 1068
NU-Prolog 823, 1025

O

Obermarck, R. 586–587
Object 272, 295, 1011–1013
Object identity 22–23, 28–29, 33, 43, 66, 82, 95, 955, 1011
Object model 82–87, 94–95, 171, 245–246
Object structure 1026, 1044–1063, 1069
Object-base 1
Object-oriented database system
    See OO-DBMS
Occurrence, of a variable 146
Offset 298, 320
O'Hare, A. 30
O'Hare, T. 1024
Olle, T. W. 292
One-one relationship 38–39, 48
OO-DBMS 20–23, 28–30, 85–86, 240–293
    See also Complex object, Data abstraction, Object identity, Object-base
OPAL 87, 271–288, 293, 462–464, 466
Operational meaning of rules
    See Computational meaning of rules
Optimistic concurrency control 531, 533–534
Optimization
    See Query optimization
Optional retention 258
Ordering, of joins 1002–1003
Ordering, of subgoals 795, 805–817, 990
Ordinary predicate 101, 107
Osborn, S. L. 442–443, 445, 1067
Otis, A. 30, 293
Ottmann, Th. 375
Ouskel, M. 375
Output cost (for joins and products) 644–645, 647–651, 709, 730
Owner 68, 76, 241, 251, 259, 461

Ozsoyoglu, G. 172
Ozsoyoglu, M. Z. 95, 732
    See also GYO-reduction

P

Packed relation 635, 640
Page
    See Block
Page manager 518–519
Page table 518
Paging strategy 518
Paige, R. 172
Palermo, F. P. 731
Papadimitriou, C. H. 444, 540–542, 585–586, 822, 824
Papageorgiou, G. 822
Parameter 273–274
Paredaens, J. 444, 824
Parent 263
Parker, D. S. 443, 1069
Parse tree, for an acyclic hypergraph 711–712, 1003–1006
Partial-match query 356–357, 359–361, 364–366, 373, 375, 870
Participant 557
Partition, of networks 544–545
Partitioned hashing 358–361, 373
Parts explosion 954–955, 958
Password 456
Pattern 332
Pattern matching 201, 213
Pattern recognition 983
$\mathcal{P}$-completeness 963–964
Pecherer, R. M. 731
Pelagatti, G. 585, 731
Pelaggi, A. 980
Peleg, D. 586
Pereira, F. C. N. 876
Perfect model 138–139, 170, 173, 773
Perl, Y. 375
Permissible adornment 806–807, 809
Persistent data 2
Phantom deadlock 579–581
Physical data independence 11–12, 54
Physical database 7, 11, 29, 294–375

Physical item
    See Local item
Physical relation 693, 697
Physical scheme 13
Pinkert, J. R. 1067
Pinned record 298, 318–319, 322, 329, 331, 338–339, 351
Pippenger, N. 375
PIQUE 1056, 1067
Pirahesh, H. 733
Pirotte, A. 94
Pixel 19, 27
PL/I 184
Pointer 76, 246, 263, 281, 295, 297, 320, 348–350
    See also Virtual record type
Pointer array mode 346
Polygraph 495–499, 540
Polynomial 978
Popek, G. J. 586
Port, G. S. 876, 1025
Porter, H. H. III 876
Positive literal 102
POSTGRES 30, 982, 1008, 1017, 1024
POSTQUEL 1008–1020, 1024
Precedence, of operators 147
Precompiler 228
Predicate connection graph 995
Predicate lock 541
Predicate splitting 799–800, 803, 847
Predicate symbol 24, 100, 735
Preorder threads 349–350
Preorder traversal 263, 333–334, 347, 352
Prepare statement 230
Preservation of dependencies
    See Dependency preservation
Price, T. G. 731
Primary copy locking 550–554, 585
Primary index 294, 304, 339, 347
Primary key 48, 51, 383
Primary site locking 550–551, 554, 585
Prime attribute 402
Principal functor 746
Priority, of rules 1016
Priority queue 1006

Privacy lock 458
Privilege 461, 463–464
PROBE 30, 1025
Procedure, as value 1010–1015
Processing graph 1002
Product 43, 56–57, 122, 179, 449, 634,
    643–647, 663–665, 667–669, 895,
    993
    See also Select-project-join query
Production system 24
Projection 56–57, 122, 177–178, 449,
    634, 664–669, 720, 748, 895, 993,
    1000–1002
    See also Generalized projection,
    Select-project-join query, Total
    projection
Projection, of dependencies 398–399,
    405, 421, 439, 442, 445
Project-join mapping 393–394
Prolog 24–25, 30, 54, 99–100, 172, 755,
    757, 766, 774–775, 823, 919, 993
    See also SLD-resolution
Proof 97, 118, 129, 161–162, 171
Proof tree 754, 910–911, 929–934, 965–
    968, 970–974
Proper path 957
Propositional calculus 443
Protocol 476–477
    See also Aggressive protocol, Con-
    servative protocol, Multiversion
    concurrency control, Redo proto-
    col, Strict protocol, Three-phase
    commit, Tree protocol, Two-phase
    commit, Two-phase locking, Undo
    protocol, Wait-die, Warning proto-
    col, Wound-wait
PRTV 177
    See also ISBL
Przymusinska, H. 173
Przymusinski, T. C. 173
Pseudotransitivity rule 385–386, 417
Pugin, J.-M. 173
Purdy, A. 30, 293
Putzolo, F. 733
Putzolo, G. R. 540–541

Q

Q 1032–1033, 1067
QBE
    See Query-by-Example
QRGT 783–794, 806, 825–826, 838–841,
    843–852, 870–871
QUEL 185–195, 201, 238, 458, 662–663,
    673, 982, 1008–1009, 1028
    See also Wong-Youssefi algorithm
Query 148, 157
    See also Lookup, Partial-match
    query, Range query
Query language 4–5, 13–16, 18–21, 28–
    30, 54, 447–448, 458
    See also CODASYL DML, Dat-
    alog, DL/I, ISBL, LDL, NAIL!,
    OPAL, POSTQUEL, QUEL, Que-
    ry-by-Example, Relational alge-
    bra, Relational calculus, SQL, Sys-
    tem/U
Query optimization 16, 21, 33, 54, 65,
    171, 176–177, 633–733, 1027–1028,
    1055
Query-by-Example 195–210, 238, 425,
    452–460, 465–466, 663, 893–894,
    954
Queue-based rule/goal tree expansion
    See QRGT
Quotient 58, 62

R

Ramakrishnan, R. 171–172, 822–824,
    875–876, 915, 979–980, 1024
Ramamohanarao, K. 172, 822, 876,
    1025
Ramarao, K. V. S. 586
Range query 356–357, 359, 361, 365–
    367, 375
Range statement 185
Read-lock 470, 486–487, 490–493, 1018–
    1020
Read-set 493
Read-time 526, 574–575
Read-token 551

Receiver 272

Record 241, 263, 295
See also Logical record, Variable-length record

Record format
See Format, for a record, Logical record format

Record structure 2–3

Record type 241–243, 252, 274–276
See also Logical record type

RECORDOF 83

Record-oriented system
See Value-oriented system

Recovery 516–524, 529, 563–564, 569–573, 575–576, 586
See also Cascading rollback

Rectified rule 111–112, 934

Rectified subgoal 801–803, 822, 844, 860

Recursion 18–19, 26–27, 1009
See also Bounded recursion, Counting-linear recursion, Left-linear recursion, Linear recursion, Nonlinear recursion, Right-linear recursion, Separable recursion, Tail-recursion optimization

Recursive predicate 103–104, 115–128, 991

Recursive rule 920, 926, 945

Redo protocol 519–521, 542

Reduced relation 703

Reduction in strength 172

Redundancy 33, 76, 244–246, 377–379, 403

Reed, D. P. 541

Reeve, C. L. 586

Reflexivity 384, 414–415

Reis, D. R. 540

Reiser, A. 585

Reiter, R. 171, 173

Rel file 1032

Relation 3, 22, 25, 43–45, 351–354, 634–635, 663, 735

Relation for a predicate 112–115

Relation for a rule 107

Relation hyperedge 677

Relation scheme 44, 146, 376, 634

Relational algebra 53–65, 72, 93–94, 106, 109–110, 128, 139–145, 149–150, 154–155, 158–159, 161, 175–177, 212, 448–449, 634, 746, 993, 995, 1068

Relational calculus 23, 53, 145–148, 171–172, 175–177
See also Domain relational calculus, Tuple relational calculus

Relational expression 663

Relational model 28–29, 32, 43–65, 71, 94, 100–101, 376–445

Relational read/write file 185

Relationship 36–37, 46, 67, 1045
See also Many-many relationship, Many-one relationship, One-one relationship

Relationship set 36

Relevant variable 776

Remove statement 260

Renaming of attributes
See Attribute renaming

Repeating group 332

Replace statement 270–271

Representative instance 1026, 1033–1043, 1066–1068

Resiliency 2, 508, 510, 516–524, 529–531, 542, 544–545, 1020

Resolution 734, 773, 822
See also SLD-resolution, Unification

Restart, of transactions 533–535

Result relation
See Answer relation

Retention class 258

Retrieve statement 185–186, 1009

Reuter, A. 542

Richardson, J. E. 733

Richardson, J. P. 980

Rieter, R. 94

Right sibling 349–350

Right-linear proof tree 965

Right-linear recursion 917–924, 936–941, 953, 979, 986–987, 991, 999–1000

Rights 456

Rissanen, J. 441–442, 444
Rivest, R. L. 375
Robinson, J. A. 822
Robinson, J. T. 375, 540–541
Robson, D. 293
Rohmer, J. 172, 822, 875
Root 263
Rosenberg, A. L. 375
Rosenkrantz, D. J. 540–541, 586
Rosenthal, A. 95, 980, 1025
Ross, K. A. 172, 824
Roth, M. 95
Rothnie, J. B. Jr. 375, 540–541, 585–586
Roussou, A. 822
Row, of tableau 893
Rowe, L. A. 30, 1024
Rozenshtein, D. 30, 95, 1067–1068
Rubinstein, P. 238, 466
Rule 25, 96–100, 102, 735
    See also Horn clause, Rectified rule, Safe rule
Rule adornment 795–796
Rule node 767, 857–858
Rule/goal graph 734, 795–817, 823, 857–859, 989–990
Rule/goal tree 766–773, 919, 926, 928–929, 931, 942–943
    See also QRGT
Run-unit 247
Rustin, R. 94

                        S

Sacca, D. 732, 822, 980
Sacco, G. M. 733
Sadri, F. 443–444
Safe formula 149, 151–161, 172, 188–189
Safe rule 104–106, 136–139, 143, 161, 736, 802, 818, 823, 864, 874, 934, 986–987
Sagiv, Y. 429, 432, 442–444, 541, 732, 822, 875, 915–916, 979–981, 1067–1068
Samet, H. 375
Sammet, J. E. 94

Saraiya, Y. 30, 981, 1024
SAT 436
Satisfaction, of a dependency 382, 428–429, 443
Sato, T. 876
SCC
    See Strongly connected component
Scheck, H.-J. 95
Schedule 474
Scheduler 476, 512
Scheme 10–11
    See also Conceptual database, Database scheme, Logical record format, Relation scheme
Schenk, K. L. 1067
Scheuermann, P. 375
Schkolnick, M. 375, 442, 541, 731, 733
Schlipf, J. S. 824
Schmid, H. A. 95
Schmidt, J. W. 94
Schnetgote, L. 1069
Schwartz, J. T. 172
Schwarz, P. M. 733
Sciore, E. 30, 95, 444, 823, 1069
Scons 997
SDD-1 541, 586
Search key 346
    See also Secondary index
Second normal form 402, 437
Secondary index 294, 339–342, 351–352, 375
Secondary storage 296
    See also Stable storage
Security 6–7, 17, 446, 456–464, 466
Seek time 17–18
Segall, A. 586
Segment 462
Seki, H. 875–876
Select statement 210–212
Selection 56–57, 122, 177–178, 282–283, 294, 449, 634, 638–643, 665–669, 720, 748, 895–896, 993
    See also Simple selection
Selection-on-a-product join 651–652, 661–662
Selectivity, of a join 1003–1005

Select-project-join expression 177
Select-project-join query 732, 895–897
    See also Semijoin program, Wong-Youssefi algorithm, Yannakakis' algorithm
Self 274
Selinger, P. G. 731
    See also Griffiths, P. P.
Sellis, T. K. 733
Semantic data model 95
    See also Object model
Semijoin 60–62, 93, 634, 674, 681, 683, 700–704, 732, 772
Semijoin program 702
    See also Full reducer
Semi-naive evaluation 124–128, 172, 742, 752–753, 819, 822, 825, 841–852, 870–871, 993–994, 1000
Semi-pinned record 304
Semiring
    See Closed semiring
Semmel, R. D. 1067
Separable recursion 979
SEQUEL
    See SQL
Serial schedule 468, 474–475
Serializable schedule 474–476, 480–485, 487–490, 493–501, 503–504, 506–507, 524–529, 540, 546, 555
Serialization graph 480–481, 487–489, 491
Servio Logic 293, 466
Set 200–201, 213–216, 241, 274, 276, 824, 995–998
    See also DBTG set
Set grouping 995–996
Set mode 346
Set occurrence 241, 251–256, 260–261
Set selection 258–260
Sethi, R. 871, 980
SETOF 82
Set-of-lists (representation of relations) 43–44, 55, 62, 100
Set-of-mappings (representation of relations) 44–45, 55
Sevcik, K. 586

Severance, D. G. 542
Shadow paging 542
Shapiro, L. D. 731
Shapiro, S. 876
Shared lock
    See Read-lock
Shasha, D. E. 542
Shekita, E. J. 733
Shepherd, J. 1025
Shepherdson, J. C. 173, 824
Shipman, D. W. 95, 586
Shmueli, O. 172, 732, 824
Shortest paths 954–955, 957–958
Sibley, E. 94
Sickel, S. 823
Sideways information passing 770, 772, 776–778, 782–783
Sideways information passing strategy 820, 822–823
Silberschatz, A. 31, 95, 172, 503, 541, 823
Simple selection 140, 207
Simulated annealing 876
Singleton set 215
Singular set 254–255
SIPS
    See Sideways information passing strategy
Site
    See Node
Skeen, D. 586
Skeleton 196
SLD-resolution 734, 822, 841
    See also Prolog
Small relation 683
Smalltalk 271, 293
Smith, D. C. P. 95
Smith, D. E. 732, 876
Smith, J. M. 30, 95, 731, 1025
Snyder, L. 375
Software AG 292
Software engineering database 19
Soisalon-Soininen, E. 542
Sorenson, P. 442
Sorted file
    See B-tree, Isam

Sorting 311
Sort-join 652–656, 661–662, 1005
Soundness 385, 415–416, 445, 886–887
Source, for a virtual field 245
Sparse index 312, 328
Splitting, of nodes 1006
SQL 6–7, 13–14, 210–234, 238, 457, 460–462, 466, 639, 663, 987, 993, 1009
SQUARE 238
Stable storage 516, 523
Stack 993
Stanat, D. 375
Starburst 733, 1024
Statistical database 467
Stearns, R. E. 540, 586
Steifeling, H. 980
Stein, J. 30, 293, 1067
Stonebraker, M. 30, 238, 375, 466, 540, 585–587, 1024
Store statement 258
Strategy database 992
Stratification 133–135, 995
Stratified negation 132–139, 172–173, 822–823, 876, 987, 995
Strict protocol 511–512, 530–531, 540, 556–557
Strictly left/right linear rule 937–941
Strong, H. R. 375
Strongly connected component 987
Sturgis, H. 586
Su, J. 824
Subclass 275
Subgoal 102, 735
Subgoal rectification
    See Rectified subgoal
Subquery 214
Subscheme 11
    See also View
Subscheme data definition language 8–9, 13
Subscheme data manipulation language 9
Subset dependency 429
Substitution, for subgoals 852–853, 986
Subsumption mapping 1035

Subsumption, of extension-join sequences 1043
Subsumption, of nonground atoms 869–870
Subsumption, of tuples 1035–1037, 1066
Subtransaction 546
    See also Coordinator, Participant
Subtype
    See Type hierarchy
Sum
    See Aggregation
Summary 893
Summers, R. C. 466
Superimposed coding 1025
Superkey 383
Supplementary predicate 827–835, 854–855, 857, 862–863
Supplementary relation 770, 776, 778–783, 789–791, 843
Suri, R. 540
Swami, A. 732
Swenson, J. R. 95
Syllog 1025
Symbol mapping 428, 881
    See also Containment mapping, Subsumption mapping
System failure 508, 516–523
System R 210, 238, 351–354, 542, 638–643, 731
System R* 587, 717–725, 731
System 2000 293
System/U 1028–1030, 1056, 1062–1063, 1067

T

Table directory 207
Tableau 893–903, 913, 915, 1068
    See also Conjunctive query, Minimization, of tableaux, Weak equivalence/containment of conjunctive queries
Taft, E. A. 587
Tagged tableau 902–903
Tail-recursion optimization 919
Tamaki, H. 876

Tanaka, K. 443
Taniguchi, K. 443
Tanimoto, S. L. 822
Tarjan, R. E. 732, 980
Tarski, A. 171
Tay, Y. C. 540
Template 246–247, 249, 264
Term 736
Term matching 745–747, 770–771, 869
Test algorithm 991
θ-join 59, 62, 122
Third normal form 402–403, 409–412,
    437, 439, 442–443
Thom, J. 1025
Thomas, R. H. 585
Three-phase commit 564–573, 586
Three-way join 673–676
Tiberio, P. 733
Timeout 560, 563, 566, 577
Timestamp 468, 524–535, 541, 573–576,
    579–581, 586
Timestamp table 529
Todd, S. J. P. 238
Tompa, F. W. 374, 442
Top-down logic evaluation 734, 753–
    760, 766–794, 822–823, 826, 841,
    871
    See also Resolution
Topological sort 484
Topor, R. W. 172, 876
TOTAL 292
Total projection 1034, 1043
Toueg, S. 586
Traiger, I. L. 540–541, 585
Transaction 468, 546
    See also Nested transaction
Transaction management 2, 5–6
    See also Concurrency control
Transitive closure 26, 92–93, 117, 145,
    175, 917–918, 939, 949–953, 955,
    957–963, 980
    See also Closed semiring
Transitivity 384, 414–416
Transmission cost 692–693, 700–702,
    710, 716–725
Travis, L. 30

TRC
    See Tuple relational calculus
Tree 73, 77, 263, 502–507
    See also B-tree, Compacted tree,
    Database record, Hierarchical mo-
    del, k-d-tree, Proof tree, Rule/goal
    tree
Tree protocol 502–504, 540
Tree query 732
    See also Acyclic hypergraph
Treitel, R. 876
Trigger 452–453, 1015–1018
Trigger-lock 1018–1020
Trivial dependency 384
Troy, D. 981
Tsangaris, M. M. 823
Tsichritzis, D. C. 29, 94, 292–293
Tsou, D.-M. 442, 445
Tsur, S. 30, 172, 375, 824, 1024
Tuple 3, 22, 43, 295, 634, 663, 735
    See also Nonground atom
Tuple identifier 352, 697
Tuple relational calculus 156–161, 174,
    185, 212
Tuple variable 156, 185–186, 200, 212–
    213, 1028
Tuple-generating dependency 424, 427,
    430–431, 433, 440, 444, 913, 1036–
    1037, 1039, 1068
Two-index-join 658–659, 661–662
Two-phase commit 560–564, 586
Two-phase locking 468, 478, 484–486,
    489–490, 500, 511–512, 524–526,
    540, 555–557
Type A/B event 843
Type hierarchy 30, 82, 85–86, 95, 272,
    276, 278
    See also Isa hierarchy
Type union 85
Typed dependency 425
Typeless dependency 425, 427

U

Uhrig, W. R. 542

Ullman, J. D. 30, 65, 95, 172, 362, 374–375, 421, 441–445, 732–733, 822–823, 875–876, 915–916, 979–980, 1024, 1067–1069

Unary inclusion dependency 440–441, 445

Undecidability 444

Undo protocol 542

Unification 760–766, 825, 865–866, 870

Unification join 866, 872, 874

Unifier

See Most general unifier

Union 55, 57, 122, 178, 189, 191, 449, 634, 665–669, 721, 993, 997

Union, of conjunctive queries 903–911

Union rule 385–386, 416–417

Unique binding pattern 795, 799–805, 827, 844, 848–849, 873

Unique scheme 1035, 1041–1043, 1066, 1068

Unique symbol 426, 428, 430

Universal join 1065

Universal quantifier 102–103, 147, 215

Universal relation 893–894, 1026–1069

Universe, secret of 632

UNIX 239, 460

Unlock 477, 486, 502, 505

Unpinned record 298, 304, 315, 322, 329–330

Unsafe rule

See Safe rule

Up predicate 946

Up subgoal/argument 945

Update 14, 205, 221, 261, 270–271, 279, 305–306, 309, 316, 320, 323, 328–329, 453, 458, 733, 998–999, 1027

Update anomaly 377

Use-def chaining 984

Used/unused bit 299

Useless transaction 495

User identification 456

User profile 462

User working area 246–247

V

Valduriez, P. 731, 980, 1024

Value-oriented system 23, 28–29, 33, 43, 285

See also Logic, Relational model

Van Emden, M. H. 171, 822

Van Gelder, A. 30, 172–173, 822–824, 876, 1024, 1067, 1069

Van Gucht, D. 95, 824

Vardi, M. Y. 94–95, 171, 441–445, 823, 915, 979–981, 1024, 1067–1069

Variable-length record 299–304, 306, 337

Vassiliou, Y. 30, 94, 1068

Vertical fragment 693

Via set (location mode) 345–347, 352, 635

Vianu, V. 824

Vielle, L. 876

View 6–7, 9–10, 29, 178–179, 208–210, 224–226, 239–240, 246, 457, 461, 878, 880, 1050

See also Logical data independence, Subscheme

View-serializability 493, 500–501

Violation, of a dependency 382

Virtual field 76, 244–245, 378

Virtual record type 76–82, 245, 263, 378

VLSI database

See CAD database

Volatile storage 516

Voting 557

VTOA 747, 750–751, 777–778, 863–864

W

Wade, B. W. 466

Wait-die 580–581, 586

Waits-for graph 474, 542, 577–581

Waldinger, R. 171

Walecka, S. 429

Walker, A. 30, 173, 731, 823, 1025

Wang, H. 172

Warning lock 505, 507–508

Warning protocol 504–507, 536–537, 541

Warren, D. H. D. 30, 823, 876

Warren, D. S. 30, 823, 876, 1067–1068

Warshall's algorithm 952–953, 958

Waxman, J. 238

Weak equivalence/containment of conjunctive queries 877, 880, 899, 915, 1050

See also Tableau

Weak instance 1033–1034, 1036, 1065, 1068

Weight 956–957

Weihl, W. 542

Weikum, G. 542

Weinberger, P. J. 239, 1032

Wensel, S. 1024

West, C. 1024

Whyte, N. 238

Wiederhold, G. 29–31, 95, 293, 374, 823

Wilkinson, W. K. 733

Willard, D. E. 375

Wilms, P. F. 731

Window function 1026, 1030–1033, 1040, 1043, 1049–1052, 1059–1062, 1065, 1067

Wise, T. E. 733

Wolfson, O. 586

Wong, E. 238, 466, 586–587, 732, 876, 981

Wong-Youssefi algorithm 673, 679–692, 699–700

Wood, C. 466

Wood, D. 375, 542

Workspace 246, 264, 468

Wound-wait 580–581, 586

Wright, D. D. 586

Write-lock 470, 486–487, 490–493, 1018–1020

Write-locks-all 547–552, 554, 556

Write-set 493

Write-time 526, 574–575

Write-token 551

Y

Yajima, S. 443

Yannakakis' algorithm 707–717

Yannakakis, M. 442, 444, 501, 540–542, 586, 732, 915–916, 1068

Yao, A. C. 375

Yao, F. F. 375

Yao, S. B. 541, 731–732

Yap, C. K. 95

Yokuta, H. 30

Youn, C. 979

Youssefi, K. 238, 732

See also Wong-Youssefi algorithm

Yu, C. T. 732, 980–981

See also GYO-reduction

Yuan, L.-Y. 95

Yuppie Valley Culinary Boutique 40–42

YVCB

See Yuppie Valley Culinary Boutique

Z

Zaiddan, S. M. 442

Zaniolo, C. 30, 94–95, 172, 443, 822–823, 980, 1024

Zhang, W. 980–981

Zloof, M. M. 238, 466

Zobel, J. 1025

Zook, W. 238